KNOWLEDGE CAPITALISM

In his newest book, Stehr builds on his classic book *Knowledge Societies* (1994) to expand the concept toward one of knowledge capitalism for a now much-changed era. It is not only because of the onset of the Covid-19 pandemic that we are living in a new epoch; it is the idea that modern societies increasingly constitute comprehensive knowledge societies under intensive capitalism, whereby the legal encoding of knowledge through national and international law is the lever that enables the transformation of the knowledge society into knowledge capitalism. The Trade Related Aspects of Intellectual Property Rights agreement, negotiated between 1986 and 1994 as part of the World Trade Organization, is the backbone of the modern society and marks a clear historical demarcation, and although knowledge capitalism is primarily an economic development, the digital giants who are in the driver's seat have significant effects on the social structure and culture of modern society.

Nico Stehr is Karl Mannheim Professor of Cultural Studies Emeritus at the Zeppelin University, Friedrichshafen, Germany. He is a fellow of the Royal Society (Canada). He is one of the authors of the Hartwell Paper on climate policy. His recent books include *The Power of Scientific Knowledge* (with Reiner Grundmann, 2012); *Is Liberty a Daughter of Knowledge?* (2016); *Understanding Inequality: Social Costs and Benefits* (with Amanda Machin, 2016); *Knowledge: Is Knowledge Power?* (with Marion Adolf, Routledge, 2017); *Society & Climate* (with Amanda Machin, 2019); *Money: A Social Theory of Modernity* (with Dustin Voss, Routledge, 2020).

"Much writing and talking about 'knowledge society', I have to admit, has struck me as shallow and fashionable. In contrast, Nico Stehr's renewed treatment of the topic has convinced me of the analytical potential of the concept. This is so due to the author's compelling investigation of the sociological features of knowledge capitalism: knowledge, although intangible and reproduced with marginal costs of almost zero, is being transformed, thanks to political arrangements such as patent law, into something tradeable and profitable. Yet the radical expansion of options for strategic agency that follows from the centrality of knowledge production seems to make the future of knowledge capitalism highly contingent—virtually unknowable."

—**Claus Offe**, Humboldt University Emeritus

"Why is a complex society also a more fragile one? Should we always expand our action and knowledge? These questions and many others form the gist of what a modern society is. This book is a major contribution both to the question of what characterizes a modern society and how sociology should approach knowledge capitalism."

—**Eva Illouz**, Directrice, École des hautes études en sciences sociales (EHESS)

"Nico Stehr argues persuasively that the 'knowledge society' created by science and technology has been captured by 'knowledge monopoly capitalism'. Digital giants, entrenched by intellectual property rights, use their control of electronic communication to shape social behaviour for private gain. The appropriation of a free good by the platforms in turn encounters resistance and generates alternatives. Stehr's formidable book brings into focus the permanent tensions at the heart of modernity."

—**Lord Skidelsky**, Professor Emeritus of Political Economy, University of Warwick

"*Knowledge Capitalism* provides a brilliant analysis of the ways in which intellectual monopolies are shaping the world economy, causing increasing inequality and secular stagnation. Stehr's book gives us very useful tools for formulating political strategies which can improve our life in this last stage of capitalism. The knowledge about knowledge offered in this book should become an important reference for university courses dealing with the structure of contemporary societies."

—**Ugo Pagano**, Professor of Economics, University of Siena

KNOWLEDGE CAPITALISM

Nico Stehr

Routledge
Taylor & Francis Group
NEW YORK AND LONDON

Cover image: © Shutterstock

First published 2022
by Routledge
605 Third Avenue, New York, NY 10158

and by Routledge
4 Park Square, Milton Park, Abingdon, Oxon, OX14 4RN

Routledge is an imprint of the Taylor & Francis Group, an informa business

Library of Congress Cataloging-in-Publication Data
Names: Stehr, Nico, author.
Title: Knowledge capitalism/Nico Stehr.
Description: New York, NY: Routledge, 2022. | Includes bibliographical references and index.
Identifiers: LCCN 2021061287 | ISBN 9781032282909 (pbk) | ISBN 9781032282916 (hbk) | ISBN 9781003296157 (ebk)
Subjects: LCSH: Capitalism. | Information society.
Classification: LCC HB501. S8977 2022 | DDC 330.12/2—dc23/eng/20220114
LC record available at https://lccn.loc.gov/2021061287

ISBN: 978-1-032-28291-6 (hbk)
ISBN: 978-1-032-28290-9 (pbk)
ISBN: 978-1-003-29615-7 (ebk)

DOI: 10.4324/9781003296157

Typeset in Bembo
by Apex CoVantage, LLC

CONTENTS

DETAILED TABLE OF CONTENTS

PREFACE

> Our age gives the impression of being an interim state; the old ways of thinking, the old cultures are still partly with us, the new not yet secure and habitual and thus lacking in decisiveness and consistency. It looks as though everything is becoming chaotic, the old becoming lost to us, the new proving useless and growing even feebler.
>
> —Friedrich Nietzsche ([1878] 1986:117–118)

It sounds like a cliché and is indeed a truism: it is not only since and because of the onset of the corona pandemic that we are living in a new epoch. As far as I can see, the most valuable diagnosis of the new epoch comes from the field of sociology. It is the idea that modern societies increasingly constitute *comprehensive knowledge societies*. Specifically, modern knowledge societies are transformed into the Gestalt of *knowledge capitalism*.[1] The legal encoding of knowledge through national and international law is the lever that enables the transformation of the knowledge society into knowledge capitalism. It is the TRIPS agreement (Trade Related Aspects of Intellectual Property Rights), negotiated between 1986 and April 15, 1994 as part of the WTO (World Trade Organization), that is the backbone of the modern, legal encircling of knowledge. Knowledge capitalism marks a clear historical demarcation. Although knowledge capitalism is primarily an economic development, the warranted suspicion is that the new digital giants who are in the driver's seat in knowledge capitalism have significant effects on the social structure and culture of modern society: Facebook for example reaches one-third of humankind.[2] Big technology companies have a decisive impact on how we live.[3]

The emergence of the knowledge society—a late offspring of the Age of Enlightenment and the successor of industrial society—was first diagnosed about three decades ago. Could it be that the idea has already become obsolete—or that we need to assess the prospects of our societies in a radically different way? Is it even possible to imagine a viable future society, especially in light of the pressing societal problems of the day, other than in terms of a broad-based knowledge society? The reason perhaps is that the once upbeat and favorable interpretation of the knowledge-based economy as a key driver of future economic prosperity, well-paying jobs, and the maintenance of democracy, so prevalent in the policy discourse in many countries and political parties in the 1990s, has given way to a much more sober analysis of the cultural, political, economic, and ecological prospects of modern society? *Knowledge societies have not stood still* or managed to transcend the essential contingency of social relations; the knowledge economy in particular develops and spreads. As the knowledge economy spreads, it makes labor and the "practice of production more closely resemble the workings of the imagination" (Unger, 2019:286). That production looks increasingly like the production of knowledge is new.

This much more sober analysis is mainly based on a number of controversial developments and expectations:

(1) The extent to which the developmental path of modern society is self-destructive. This applies, in particular, to the long-standing failure to take account of society's footprint on the natural environment, especially in view of humanity's climatic and biodiverse living conditions;
(2) the fear that another human "achievement" in terms of automation and artificial intelligence could fundamentally alter the world of work and employment in the new century;
(3) the incalculable impact of the current and possible future pandemics on the architecture of society;
(4) the ongoing expansion and strengthening, over the past three decades, of the agency of many modern individuals and, as its corollary, the curtailing of the agency of the once-powerful major social institutions of state, business, church, labor unions, and science to control the world they co-created, including the fragility of the digital infrastructure;
(5) the sweeping expansion and critical role of the globally sanctioned legal encoding of knowledge since the mid-1990s, resulting in a legally sanctioned knowledge monopoly capitalism, which has the additional effect of fueling societal inequality formation and sharpening the crisis of democracy; the strengthening of intellectual property systems is not only important for "new" industries such as microelectronics and biotechnology, but also for mature industries such as petroleum and steel;
(6) the fact that industrial society's "historical mission" of overcoming widespread existential poverty and need has in the rich nations been accomplished since about the mid-1980s—one of sociology's successful, serious social diagnoses.

In short, we face massive, thorny, and highly consequential issues that strongly suggest the need to reconsider and further develop the theory of modern society as a knowledge society.

But it is not only the world of labor, or climate change, or the disenchantment and enclosure of knowledge that are fraught with uncertainty and risks. The once-dominant magic triangle of capitalism, democracy, and science/technology appears to be in crisis and in retreat, or is at least subject to ongoing significant changes, with each of its elements changing in its own way both internally and in its relation to each other. The financial crisis, terrorism, the revolts of the disenfranchised strata, populism, the dawning of new authoritarianism, the fear of an uncontainable pandemic, the era of post-truth, the ascent of China, the increase in social inequality, the escalating civil wars, the asymmetric corporate power, and, last but not least, the dangerous environmental repercussions of human conduct—they all signify the by-now startling *fragility* or, what others may call the alarming instability of modern society and its major social institutions, as well as the newly experienced *fragility* of nature. In light of these new societal contingencies, what has the concept of modern society as a knowledge society to offer? Can it still be a constructive alternative to competing theoretical perspectives? The novel psychological, social, political, and economic developments listed earlier obviously call for a further evaluation of the concept in order to advance and extend our understanding of modern societies as knowledge societies.

But, on the other hand, has the concept of modern knowledge societies really been successfully challenged in the social science discourse of recent years? Among the more lenient criticisms of the idea of modern society as a knowledge society and modern economy as knowledge-based are observations such as "the knowledge-economy is turning out to be a bit disappointing" (Scott, 2005:297) or, already somewhat more critical, "the knowledge society is what advanced capitalism looks like to intellectuals, once they have been assimilated into its mode of production" (Fuller, 2005:82) and "the knowledge society depicts a Western bias in its onward march across the world" (SinghaRoy, 2014:42). Can we really imagine living in a society that is founded on and sustained and driven by knowledge? What is more, the transition to such a society is "fraught with hazards" (Portella, 2003:5), and "in effect, the term 'knowledge society' has become the delusory mask which hides the ever-widening gaps of an unjust world" (Dyer, 2012:341). A more substantial criticism is offered by Sebastian Haunss (2013:75), who observes that my account of the knowledge society, while accurate in principle, fails to "identify a mechanism (or a set of mechanisms) that would be responsible for the growing centrality of knowledge". The answer is that of Max Weber and, as already emphasized in 1994, the relentless accumulation that characterizes the capitalist economic form. But a major puzzle and challenge in the study of the growth of modern economies has been to account for the continual growth in output exceeding what can be explained by the observed growth of capital and worker-hours.

Accumulation in knowledge societies and economic prosperity increasingly rests, in a general sense, on *knowledge* and its useful application (Kuznets, 1966; Teece, 1981:82; Stehr, 2002).

The dominant resource of advanced capitalism is *intangible* assets (knowledge) and an intangible-intensive production. "Intangible assets" refers to the financial contours of commodities. Intangible assets are a pecuniary term, a business concept, not a technological one. As Thorstein Veblen (1908:111) explained more than a century ago:

> The tangibility of tangible assets is a matter of the materiality of the items of wealth of which they are made up, while they are assets to the amount of their value. . . . They are capital in the measure of the income which they may yield to their owner. . . . [The] intangibility [of the intangibles] is a matter of the immateriality of the items of wealth—object of ownership—of which they are made up.

Compared to the tangible-intensive production of *industrial society*, the marginal cost of the production of intangibles—as scalable assets—in *knowledge societies*, i.e., software, standards, organization know-how, platforms, and texts, approaches zero. Returns on tangible capital, given their physical nature and the diseconomies of scale, tend to be finite. Returns on intangible assets are almost infinite. Infinite returns to scale annul the iron law of diminishing marginal returns that governed industrial society. Corporate reliance and strategy in knowledge societies is therefore largely directed toward the generation and purchase of *Intellectual Property Rights* (IPRs—patents, copyrights, trademarks, brands, digital platforms). IPRs, in turn, are political creatures. Reversing the economic law of diminishing returns has a profound impact on society:

My general response to these rather ambivalent but important points of criticism is that a further *refinement and development* of my theory of modern society as a knowledge society and the knowledge economy is called for. Hence, the explication of the transformation of knowledge societies into knowledge capitalism becomes a core objective of my study. Capitalism—contrary to Rifkin (2014)—is not vanishing, but transformed.

I will try to demonstrate that the negative appraisal and disparagement of the idea of the knowledge society is unwarranted; also, it should be made clearer than in the 1994 account why knowledge is becoming an ever more significant resource. It is perhaps worth stating right at the outset that in a *post-pandemic world*, the *practical* importance of knowledge societies will have increased measurably.

In the context of a brief foreword, I mainly propose to offer a rough sketch of what has happened elsewhere to the idea of the knowledge society in the last three decades since the 1990s. Undoubtedly, a lot has happened. Both within and beyond the science community, the progress made by the concept of modern knowledge societies is best captured by Robert K. Merton's ([1949] 1968:27–28,

35–37) appropriate metaphor of "obliteration by incorporation";[4] by now, defining the modern economy as "knowledge-based" is a commonplace.

Unlike the vague criticism of the theory of the knowledge society voiced in the social sciences, the idea has met with widespread resonance in society at large; the UNESCO, for example, has published a *Knowledge Societies Policy Handbook* (2015). The knowledge society theory has met with resonance in a wide variety of disciplines and research fields in the humanities and the social sciences, such as education, geography, economics, history, political science, linguistics, policy studies, and communication studies. Thus, the motto of the 2012 annual convention of the *American Association for the Advancement of Science* (AAAS), a prominent scientific organization, in Vancouver, British Columbia, Canada, was "Flattening the World: Building a Global Knowledge Society". Institutions, in particular universities, have been examined from a knowledge society perspective (Frank and Meyer, 2020). Furthermore, the idea of the knowledge society has become an asset in political struggles, serving as a core political strategy in political parties and national and international political organizations, e.g., the UNESCO (2005). Nation-states have realigned their educational systems with what they perceive to be the needs of the knowledge economy. Nevertheless, one should be careful not to ascribe too much causal power to one's own ideas.

Even if we do not agree with Friedrich Nietzsche's image of modern societies as somehow essentially chaotic and applicable to the present age, we do agree with him on one fundamental observation, namely that societies at any given time contain distinctive beliefs and layers and patterns of social conduct and social structures from various epochs. Given the speed of social change that is characteristic of modern societies, the likelihood of finding this kind of "contamination" has considerably increased. In a more formal vein, observing the presence of social "facts" that date back to other epochs means referring to the "simultaneity of the non-simultaneous" of social phenomena. At the same time, it is about overcoming entrenched dichotomies: culture versus economy or nature and society.

Unsurprisingly, an almost inexhaustible list of micro and macro social relations attests to the simultaneity of the non-simultaneous as an elementary feature of modern societies; cases in point are the simultaneous presence of multiple generations at any given time in the history of societies, the juxtaposition of industrial and post-industrial economic formations, or the coexistence of distinct cultures in science, for example. As Paul Feyerabend ([1994] 2019) observed with respect to this essential heterogeneity in science:

> [M]any scientists have lived and are still living with ambiguity and contradiction. They could not possibly live in any other way. New problems need new approaches. But new approaches do not fall like manna from the heaven of creativity. Old ideas continue to be used; they are slowly twisted around until some orderly minds perceive an entirely new structure.

In my analysis of modern knowledge societies, I will as a matter of course invoke and analyze many other examples, if only to avoid the fallacy of thinking about societies only in terms of clear-cut dichotomies which are reflected and cemented in social life and to counter the idea that they are highly unitary social phenomena.

I propose to advance my project of analyzing modern societies as knowledge societies that are transformed into knowledge capitalism in a number of steps. First, a discussion, in the tradition of the history of ideas, of major theories of society; this is following by a comprehensive account of our knowledge about knowledge made necessary last but not least because economists who now widely acknowledge the core economic role of the resource knowledge have little to say about knowledge. In economic relations, monopolies of knowledge can become a significant danger. The third chapter addresses the emergence of knowledge capitalism, including its competing perspectives in social science theory. The next chapter attends to the politics of knowledge societies and policy challenges that follow from its development. The conclusion of the study addresses selected issues that remain and remain open.

The result, however, will not be a study in future forecasting. I cannot predict the future.[5] Nor are the social sciences, whose record in this respect has been, and still is, and is bound to continue to be poor.[6] But the examination of knowledge capitalism is not altogether silent about the future. It is fruitful, as I will try to show that the identification of mayor social changes "that have already taken happened, irrevocably, and that will have predictable effects in the next decade or two. . . . It is possible, in other words, to identify and prepare for the future *that has already happened*" (Drucker, 1997:20). At the same time, the future is open, and perhaps even more so than in past epochs, and this is last but not least due to the fact that social action is increasingly knowledge-based. In order to understand the "future", we must try to understand the present.

What is new

My examination and theory of knowledge capitalism draws on my monograph *Knowledge Societies* (1994). Given the time that has elapsed since the early 1990s and the progress that has been made in empirical and theoretical work in the social sciences, as well as the social, political, and economic changes that we have encountered (and are experiencing), my analysis of modern knowledge societies has been considerably broadened, while maintaining and complementing the considerations that I believe have proven their value.

Finally, I close the preface with a brief comparison of the 1994 edition and the new 2022 edition of this monograph in order to give a clearer idea of what was not included, what was revised, and what is new. All chapters listed for both the 2021 and the 1994 edition have been substantially revised and enlarged as compared to 1994. Here's an overview in tabular form:

2022	1994/2021
Preface (new)	-----
Chapter 1: Theories of society (mostly new)	Chapter 2 (from 10 pages to 47 pages)
Chapter 2: Knowledge about knowledge (mostly new)	Chapter 5 (from 28 pages to 105 pages)
Chapter 3: From knowledge societies to knowledge capitalism (mostly new)	Chapter 1 (12 pages to 90 pages)
Chapter 4: The politics of knowledge capitalism (new)	-----
Conclusions (new)	-----
Not included	Chapter 6: Now Stehr, 2002
Not included	Chapter 7: Now Stehr and Grundman, 2011

Notes

1. The initial use of the term of "knowledge capitalism" occurs, as far as I can see, in a monograph by Alan Burton-Jones (1999:224, 2003) that carries the title "Knowledge Capitalism: Business, Work and Learning in the New Economy". However, the concept knowledge capitalism is never explained and appears to have been used more or less accidentally. The emphasis in his book is on the role of knowledge and appropriate skills in the economy; for example. "the current era is best described as an era of 'global knowledge capitalism', in which the need to move physical resources around the world is becoming less important and the need to move knowledge more important."
2. Sheera Frenkel and Cecilia Kang (2021:300) in their analysis and critique of the domination of Facebook conclude: "Throughout Facebook's *seventeen-year history*, the social network's massive gains have repeatedly come at the expense of consumer privacy and safety and the integrity of democratic systems" (my emphasis).
3. The big tech companies in question are a *novel* phenomenon: The companies, e.g., Facebook (Meta), reached the trillion-dollar status on the stock exchange within less than two decades of its existence. On June 28, 2021, Facebook became the fastest company to reach a one-trillion market value, just 17 years after its founding and only nine years after it went public.
4. It should be noted that Johann Gottfried Herder (1794: Preface, 4) in the introduction to his *Ideas on the Philosophy of the History of the History of Mankind* (1784–91) expresses a similar view with regard to the fate of his *Also a Philosophy of History for the Education of Mankind* (1774): "I had noticed that some of the ideas in my little work, without also mentioning me, had passed into other books and had been applied to an extent that I had not thought of." In other words, the very idea is self-exemplifying, as Robert Merton would have noted.
5. Although, as Randell Collins ([1981] 2019:388) aptly notes, it is an intellectually stimulating task that cannot always be avoided.
6. See the excellent study by Elke Seefried (2015) on the failed attempt to establish futurology in Germany.

ACKNOWLEDGMENTS

Acknowledgments 2021

This publication has benefited from a research stay at GESIS—Leibniz Institute for the Social Sciences (Cologne, Germany)—and was financially supported by GESIS as well as by fellowships at the International Research Center for Cultural Studies (Vienna, Austria) and the Potsdam Institute for Advanced Sustainability Studies (Potsdam, Germany).

I am grateful to a large number of critical readers of my manuscript, or parts of it, for many constructive comments as well as to individuals who kindly assisted me in gaining access to materials that were relevant to my analysis of knowledge societies. These are, in alphabetic order: Karl Acham, David Altheide, Dean Baker, Hella Beister, Johannes Berger, Fred Block, Peter Burke, Andrea Cerroni, Stewart Clegg, Michael Dauderstädt, Steve Fuller, Bruno Frey, Ronald Glassman, Bruno Grauzelli, Reiner Grundmann, Marian Grodzki, Anil Gupta, Dieter Haselbach, Horst Helle, Bruno Hopp, Ben Johnson, Klaus Lichtblau, Jason Mast, Christoph Lau, Scott McNall, Volker Meja, Richard Münch, Claus Offe, Karl-Dieter Opp, Holger Pausch, Dick Pels, Linda Phillips, Martin Schulte, Harris Shekeris, Alan Sica, Hermann Strasser, Steve Vallas, Ugo Pagano, Alexander Ruser, Stephen Park Turner, Luk van Langenhove, Dustin Voss, Rafał Wierzchosławski. The usual disclaimer applies.

However, my special thanks and indebtedness are to Marion Adolf. My thanks not only are with reference to the current manuscript, although Marian has commented and edited the entire manuscript on *Knowledge Capitalism* in German and English, but for an intense collaboration over many years, going back to his efficient assistance while I held the Paul Lazarsfeld Chair at the University of Vienna during the academic year 2002–2003. Subsequently, I was able to persuade him in a Viennese café to relocate to Zeppelin University on Lake Constance. This in turn led for many years to a very productive collaboration and intellectual exchanges resulting in many publications in many languages. In many respects, our joint research—and teaching—is as far as I can see exemplary for the promise of the division of intellectual labor in the science community.

Acknowledgments 1994

It is with great pleasure that I recall the many contributions of friends, colleagues, and institutions to the first edition of my attempt to understand modern society as a knowledge society. My gratitude has not diminished over time; on the contrary, I often only now recognize the real value of having been fortunate enough to share so many challenging ideas.

Some formulations used in the text are idiosyncratic adaptations and extensions of ideas found in an essay first written in collaboration with Gernot Böhme and published as a contribution to our collection: Gernot Böhme and Nico Stehr (eds.), *The Knowledge Society*. Dordrecht: D. Reidel 1986. I am grateful to Gernot Böhme for his kind permission to do so. I am indebted to the generous support and excellent working conditions of the University of Alberta over the course of a number of years while working on this study. I am also grateful to the Rockefeller Foundation for an intellectually challenging stay at the Rockefeller Study Center in Bellagio, Italy. Central parts of this study were completed while in residence at the Center. Work on this project was facilitated by research funds from the Social Sciences and Humanities Research Council in Ottawa, Canada.

I am grateful for critical and encouraging comments on different chapters and aspects of this study by Paul Bernard, Zygmunt Bauman, David Bloor, Gernot Böhme, S.N. Eisenstadt, Richard V. Ericson, Eliot Freidson, Karol J. Krotki, Donald N. Levine, Robert K. Merton, Raymond Morrow and Hermann Strasser. It is perhaps needless to say that they do not necessarily always agree with the thrust of my formulations and the underlying interpretations of contemporary social reality. I am grateful to Dennis Bray and Guy C. Germain for the search for and acquisition of materials that were often very difficult to locate and assemble.

1

THEORIES OF SOCIETY

The following chapter deals, in a broad sweep, with social scientific theories of modern society. Our understanding of theories of modern society whose origin coincide with the emergence of social science in the Age of Enlightenment is best served by highlighting their basic assumption or intellectual interests. The very concept of society (Grundmann und Stehr, 2009), now an essential cognitive tool of social science, for the most part can be traced to the philosophers of the Scottish and French Enlightenment. In contrast to common language use, the emerging professional sociological discourse drew sharp distinctions, such as society versus church, society versus state, society versus community. However, once externalized, it reconceptualized these excluded elements as subsystems or gave them a place in the institutional structure of society. The choice of the terms system and institution is significant: the heirs of structural functionalism usually prefer system terminology; "institution" is the catchword of institutionalist theories.

My description of the nature of theories of society begins with a depiction of what I call the logic of the orthodox perspective. In total, four essential principles of the orthodox logic that continue to cast their shadows onto contemporary theorizing are listed and examined. This discussion is followed by stressing that societies are always in motion. The nature and the motor of the ongoing transition of societies is analyzed as the extension and enlargement of social relations as well as processes that point both forward into the future and backwards into the past. The final parts of the chapter address modern theories of society with an emphasis on the theories of society that dominated the discussion of the last half of the 20th century, the industrial and the so-called post-industrial society.[1] Some thoughts on the transition to knowledge societies complete the discussion.

DOI: 10.4324/9781003296157-1

The theory of theories of society

Does social theory create new realities, or does theory systematize new realities? Have our theories of society changed significantly in the course of their development? And why, if so, has our understanding of society changed? What attributes have characterized the theories of society since the French Revolution? Which intra-societal processes, their connections, and evolution are among the central characteristics of societies, for example, social institutions, social inequality, division of labor? Are modern societies always or can modern societies always be democratic societies? Why do theories of society fail? Is societal reality or the criticism of their critics responsible?[2] If theories of society are replaced, do they disappear completely and forever, or only partially, at any time, ready to be brought back to life? Is it the adherents of a theory of society who determine their life expectancy?

First of all, it should be noted that theories of society, at least since the 18th century, have increasingly lost the character of utopian designs. Gradually and hesitantly, modern theories of society reflect the changed social reality, or rather, they increasingly refrain from creating images of society whose desirability is used to measure social reality. But even this statement is not absolute. Utopian theories of society continue to exist, albeit perhaps only marginally, if one considers the number of their adherents who are pressing for their realization. But even theories of society apparently born from the middle of the social sciences are interpreted as blueprints of politics, or the urge of new social realities being drafted into the center of the theories of society should not be underestimated.

In any case, contingent social transformations are increasingly becoming a characteristic aspect of modern theories of society, which are therefore much more ambivalent and open and do not require ambitious prognoses even when compared to older theories from Comte to Marx and even Durkheim. However, a more systematic exposition of some of the salient theoretical attributes of classical discourse on modern society and how its assumptions may be transcended is still lacking. I will attempt to provide a first sketch of a perspective more in tune with contemporary social, economic, and political realities.

Daniel Bell's (1973) theory of post-industrial society was not only widely read, but also extensively commented upon, a work known by more people than who had actually read *The Coming of Post-Industrial Society* during the heroic days of sociology in the last third of the 20th century and often even interpreted as a blueprint for the politics of the day, even though the post-industrial society concept is not at all political. It is worthwhile to revisit his theory and his predictions in a new context. I will reflect on Bell's theory and his predictions in greater detail, also in light of their intellectual context, especially since this theory is one of the few works in which the critic cannot immediately think of the remark: " 'Post' is the code word for perplexity that gets caught in the fashionable" (Beck, 1986:12).[3]

Bell's (1973:373) theory of post-industrial society exemplifies the more recent, modern systemic features of theories of society, perhaps not in every detail but to a significant degree. Part of the ambiguity of Bell's theory of post-industrial society is linked, no doubt, to the fact that he has written and explicated its central features for more than a decade between the mid-sixties and the mid-seventies. It is unavoidable that my effort—in the spirit of symmetry—is by no means immune either, that this theoretical effort resonates with, and appeals to some degree at least, to the political issues of the day. The theory of the post-industrial society was in turn—in the analyses of many social theorists of the beginning 21st century—overtaken or replaced by the so-called "information age/revolution". To what extent the information age—often conceived only as a result of technical changes—should be better understood as the age of the knowledge society is one of the questions to which an answer should be found here.

Contemporary social theories are much more bound to the present and abstain from both extensive historical reflection and discussions of what might be termed utopias. Classical discourse, in contrast, was much less present-bound and took for granted that it was simultaneously concerned with history and with designs for the future. The restriction of contemporary social theory has a number of causes, chief among them being an increasingly rigid division of intellectual labor in social science. Also, the widespread credence of methodological prescriptions proclaim that "positive" discourse is best served through a "proper" delimitation of theoretical reasoning to assure a "genuine" disciplinary issue.

My brief discussion of the genealogy of theories of modern societies begins with a few remarks on the emergence of modern societies, in particular the logic of the orthodox perspective of modern communities. Among the traditional assumptions are four characteristics related to the space of modern society, the functional differentiation of the social fabric, the dominant culture, and the conviction that societies change according to a certain evolutionary logic. After a brief comment on the permanence with which societies are in transition, I analyze modernization as a question of the extension and expansion of social and intellectual action. Modernization is, one can also put it this way, an increase in complexity. Sociology is part of this increase in complexity and must be self-exemplifying. I then describe in greater detail modern society as an industrial society and the perspective of the so-called post-industrial society. The theory of knowledge society and knowledge capitalism must therefore be more complex than classical theories of industrial society and more multifaceted than the theory of post-industrial society. Novel concepts and relations are essential tools toward a more complex analysis of the expansion of social conduct.

The concept of society remains an essential idea of social science discourse in spite of recent challenges by the concept and process of globalization, often understood to be the largely separate (split from the rest of society) globalization of the economic system (e.g., Touraine, [2010] 2014:96). Even as the frontiers of the nation-state, as the traditional boundaries of society became less central in recent decades, the concept of society was elevated and converted to now—in some theoretical perspectives at least—world *society*. Examples of this theoretical development are theories of modernity or world system analysis, feminist or critical post-colonial theories.

The logic of the orthodox perspective

Our theoretical understanding of modern society in terms of what might be called the master paradigms and master concepts of the social sciences, which by now effectively shape and even govern everyday perspectives of social reality, continue to be intellectual descendants of 19th-century thought, or derivatives of classical discourse on society. There are dominant spatial as well as processual and substantive references. The prevalent spatial referent of most modern theories of society is the nation-state whose sovereignty as we all know happens to be under increasing threat while the master movement is social differentiation and its inevitable accompaniment of the growing rationalization of social relations.[4] Taken together, the sum total of the orthodox assumptions deals inadequately with the authentic *variety* of paramount worlds in the midst of what then is claimed to be a world dominated by increasingly uniform process and culture, for example, enforced by a relentless globalization process, leading to the global age, as Ulrich Beck ([2002] 2005) maintained, for example.

I will first critically outline the logic of the orthodox perspective and then attempt to offer an alternative theoretical perspective of long-term social development that is both non-teleological and non-evolutionary.

Despite the cognitive diversity and nuances of contemporary social science discourse, a fact which finally has become an important part of the self-consciousness of sociologists, economists, anthropologists, and historians, it is perhaps somewhat surprising to conclude that there are dominant intellectual orthodoxies and the appearance of "premature closure" among reigning theories of society including common blind spots. These attributes then transcend otherwise firmly entrenched strategic and substantive disagreements among social scientists about what problems need what attention, namely urgent researchable issues, proper theoretical strategies, fruitful methods, and interpretation of findings variously generated. In spite of vigorous cognitive dissent, there are a few common as well as core thematic features of theories of contemporary society, mostly derivative of classical discourse, which inform much of the theoretical and empirical work in social science today. Until recently, the various theories of modern society were united by a common blind spot, the failure to attend to the *carbonization* of the atmosphere as the result of the industrialization. Progress toward *decarbonization* has been dismal.

Among the important commonalties of contemporary social scientific theories of society are (1), the tendency to fix boundaries of societal systems as identical with those of nation-states; as a result, for most perspectives, "causality" is intrasocietial; (2), the conviction that the key to the distinctiveness of modern society is primarily related to the persistent functional differentiation of societal subsystems and greater specialization of social institutions; (3), the widespread confidence that traditional or irrational beliefs are transcended by rational knowledge resulting in a greater rationalization of social activities. The function of course is liberating society. Zygmunt Bauman (2000:3) explains, "the first sacreds to be profaned were traditional loyalties, customary rights and obligations which bound hands and feet, hindered moves and cramped the enterprise."

These expectations coming from the social sciences, as I will document, are disappointed again and again by the fact that not inconsiderable parts of the population in modern societies adhere to so-called "conspiracy theories" or fundamentally question scientific findings that are shared by a large number of scientists in modern societies; or even more elementary, that people arrange/explain their mundane everyday life (but also extraordinary events) based on traditional ideas and, far from being liberated, find themselves trapped with the confines of cages of the new order (such as social classes). Finally, (4), there is the virtual certainty that societal formations of one historical stage or type ultimately are replaced by entirely different, new social arrangements. In the final analysis, the last assumption about the course of society over time is one wedded strongly to the notion of progress.

Taken together, the premises of the orthodox logic of theories of societies that dominated social science discourse for a considerable period of time carried with it a distinct *politics* that claimed to have grasped the complete knowledge of the future. It is no accident therefore that Daniel Bell's (1973) subtitle of his *The Coming of Post-Industrial Society* is "A Venture in Social Forecasting". Although Francis Fukuyama (1999/2000:130) praises Daniel Bell for the accuracy of his forecasting, theories of society could just as well function as self-fulfilling prophecies. It is not unusual that political parties, corporations, cities, or international organizations take a theory of society as guide for their future. The theory of modern society as knowledge societies is no exception to this rule.

I will critically examine each of the premises of the orthodox logic of classical theories society in greater detail: The unit of (macro-)- social scientific analysis tends to be society in the sense of the *nation-state*. Society, for all intents and purposes, becomes indistinguishable from the nation-state.[5] Social transformations primarily occur as the result of mechanisms that are part of and built into the structure of a given society. The conflation of modern society with the nation-state is a legacy of the 19th-century origins of social science discourse. Obviously, there may have been and perhaps still are some good intellectual and practical-political reasons for the identification of the boundaries of the social system with those of the nation-state.[6] For example, the formation of social science discourse to some extent coincides with the constitution of the identity of the modern nation-state and violent struggles among nation-states. Yet, it is quite inadequate to retain the restrictive framework of the territorial state today. The major institutions of modern society, the market economy, large cities, the state, higher education, sport, tourism, religion, science, technical artifacts, everyday life, and also the ecology of a society are all profoundly affected by a progressive "globalization" or transnationalism of human affairs or by circumstances in which "disembodied institutions, linking local practices with globalised social relations, organize major aspects of day-to-day-life" (Giddens, 1990c:79). However, state-based territorial power and power plays have not disappeared but continue to be relevant attributes of geopolitics.

The complex networks along many axes that have developed are a revolutionary social development in the recent history of mankind. The course of human history was almost always marked by information and knowledge, which geographically speaking included at most a daily foot march and social integration based on face-to-face interaction. There are undoubtedly exceptions today that represent the principle of the simultaneity of the non-simultaneous but in most cases the (empirically) relevant boundaries of the social system and human consciousness are no longer those of national borders.

The eclipse of time and distance in economic activities, environmental changes that recognize no boundaries, the global connectedness of the electronic media, the internet, the progressive internationality of the scientific community, growing transnational cultural activities, and the dynamics of multinational corporate activity and political institutions all represent persuasive evidence for re-constituting the focus of social science discourse away from society and the nation-state toward groups of national societies, networks of transnational political and economic power and divisions not only within the world, but also the global society (Bauman, 1992; Giddens, 1990c; Beck and Malsow, 2014). In short, the spatial identity of major social processes, communication, economic activities, social mobility, and inequality are no longer aligned with national boundaries. The Covid-19 pandemic of 2020 and 2021 and its predecessors in turn clearly shows that this has not always been the case in the past.

But to question the adequacy of such an emphasis does not necessarily imply embracing uncritically the notion of "global society" or a global economic and cultural unity and uniformity of humanity. A boundless world is unrealistic. The assertion of a boundless world misses "the link between boundary setting and identity: whoever wants identity must have boundaries" (Kocka, 2010:37). Nor does a shift in the primary theoretical referent toward a transnational focus already imply a definitive response to the question of whether the project of modernity simply continues to unfold, though under new circumstances and at a new level, or alternatively signals the emergence of a new historical epoch. However, to deny that the sole and dominant focus has to be society is to acknowledge the existence of systemic relations and trends which both divide and unite, which reduce the range of the sovereignty, the power, and the autonomy of the nation-state in important respects (cf. Giddens, [1973] 1980:265), and which assure that local, regional, and national identities and social action are intermeshed with various cultural and economic forces which reside at a distance and transcend national boundaries. At issue are not absolute similarities in development, but relational convergences and the assimilation of strange worlds into local contexts. Concretely, the question is not whether interest rates are identical in all nation-states, but whether their differences and their movement relative to each other tends to converge and how economic actors cope or construct adjustments through local practices to fluctuations induced elsewhere. Social science discourse is recognizing these new realities, although it often remains entangled in perspectives that deny the need to re-assess the notion of society as a nation-state. Paradoxically, the dissolution of the nation-state also presses forces to the forefront that in the midst, perhaps because of its transformation, would appear to raise anew the plausibility and viability of local and regional identities. In other words, globalization cannot only mean processes that originate somewhere in the world and affect everyone in the same, almost submissive and passive fashion, but must also be seen as active responses, in specific communities, to developments that may not be controlled locally but that have local adaptive repercussions. Disembedding forces have to be combined, as Giddens (1990c:79–80) also stresses, with "reembedding" activities that result in the "reappropriation or recasting of disembedded social relations so as to pin them down (however partially and transitory), to local conditions of time and place."

In any case, part of the general critique of the classical assumption of the power-political dominance of the nation-state as the basic unit of social theory, the "age of methodological nationalism" (Beck and Maslow, 2014:8), is therefore that this equation is no longer valid for the epoch of the 20th century and beyond. At the same time, however, it also shows that the trend towards a "relentless" globalization is by no means unstoppable. Globalization creates its own limits and resistances, as will be analyzed later. Finally, this means that the nation-state has not (and will not in the future) completely vanished from the stage of world history. And thus, in this respect the thesis of the simultaneous of the non-simultaneous is confirmed, whose principal theoretical and methodological relevance will be described in a brief note, the normality of diversity, at the end of the chapter in which I stress the theoretical and methodological virtue of the idea simultaneous of the non-simultaneous.

The major mechanism of functional differentiation

The pivotal and apparently irreplaceable (socio-evolutionary) master mechanism or (desirable) trend which represents, at least in some instances, *both* the conditions for the possibility, that is, the motor for social change, as well as the primary outcome of social change in modern society, is the notion of functional *differentiation*. But in the majority of the theoretical accounts of functional differentiation, it serves as an *explanans* and not as an *explanandum*, leaving the question of the reasons for an apparently perpetual social differentiation unanswered (cf.

Schimank, 1985). Similarly, questions of agency and the agents of differentiation, if any, often remain obscured.

However, before I discuss the conception of functional differentiation in greater detail, it should be pointed out that there appears to be a close bond between the thesis about the centrality of functional differentiation and frequent spatial focus of theories of society on intrastate processes. The notion of functional differentiation appears to be closely coupled to the nation-state as a frame of reference since the kind of social differentiation that serves as the paradigm for the separation and demarcation among social institutions makes sense only within the framework of a territorial state with a closed population, although the boundaries more typically are described as those of a society (cf. Bogner, 1992:41).

The idea of functional differentiation generally is that modern social reality, as it replaces traditional forms of life, is subjected to progressive specialization and that clusters of social activity, in relation to each other, for example, in the organization of production, education and government, become more and more self-contained, self-centered, and self-propelled subsystems of society.[7]

Society potentially loses, assuming it ever possessed it, its center. An implied consequence of functional differentiation, therefore, is the absence of an integrating system that serves to check the perpetual or insatiable (as Marx observes it in the case of capital) realization of self-centered, that is, specialized goals, such as profit. The consensus in social science I have in mind primarily refers to the process of functional differentiation as such. It does not necessarily extend to the repercussions of functional differentiation, and it most definitely does not extend to the question of the reasons for differentiation (and its reproduction), assuming that the process is not from the beginning seen as one which is largely self-propelled and therefore virtually beyond the control of individuals and groups. Differentiation for some is a process set in motion as the result of population pressures and therefore of efforts to adapt in a more efficient manner via greater specialization to increased density. For others, it is the historical emergence of certain ideas and social groups which promote and assure the gradual transformation of society. Still other theorists see the main cause of differentiation as the product of contradictions between the forces and the relations of production or as the result of complicated networks of actors, groups, social movements, institutions, states, and civilizations. Also contentious is the assumption of a governing or constitutive mechanism of some sort within modern society, such as a shift from the preeminence of the substructure to the superstructure. Is such a supposition in accord with the assertion about functional differentiation? As a matter of fact, functional differentiation is seen by some to be totally incompatible with such possibilities (e.g., Luhmann, 1988:11). My interest, however, is less with the theoretical admissibility of trans-institutional mechanisms (disembeddedness), in modern society, and more with the possible "causes" for or effects of functional differentiation.[8] It centers more on the question of the nature and the importance of the logic or the master process of functional differentiation itself. An important issue therefore becomes, as Raymond Aron (1967:211) noted, is there "an antinomy between the fact of differentiation and the ideal of equality"?

Nineteenth-century observers of social and political developments in general and the emergent social sciences in Europe in particular dealt with very real changes in their respective societies. In addition, the discovery of traditional or undifferentiated "primitive" society at the same time provided a further substantiation and legitimation of the logic of specialization. Although the master concept of differentiation was not uncontested in the 19th century, it has assumed the unrivaled status of cognitive authority in social science, proclaiming that first, "increasing differentiation was the dominant, nearly inexorable logic of large-scale change; (and), second, that over the long run differentiation leads to advancement" (Tilly, 1984:44). Differentiation generally is thought to improve the functional capacity (efficacy) of emerging smaller social units. The problem of integrating or coordinating a much more differentiated social context is, in some ways, also "solved" by further differentiation, namely new organizations, positions, and roles. In the post–World War II era, these core assumptions crystallized into theories of modernization and development. Structural differentiation all too easily became identified with a certain Western developmental path and fell short of the requirements of analyzing the experience of societal change in non-Western societies (cf. Nettl and Robertson, 1968:49–57). But these perspectives now have been challenged by dependency theories and the world-system approach (cf. So, 1990).

But instead of emphasizing the logic of differentiation as the principal concept and key for the analysis of social change, it is perhaps more sensible and closer to the historical evidence to be skeptical toward theoretical notions that excessively simplify what are not necessarily extremely complex processes, but rather social transformations that are extremely variable and contingent. Such variability includes the possibility not merely of repeating history but also reversing it. Integration, homogenization, de-differentiation (cf. Nettl and Robertson, 1968:45–49), or concentration may—depending on the circumstances, for example, the resolve of individual and corporate actors—displace differentiation. In addition, if the transformations themselves are seen as contributing toward further variability, fragility, instability, contingency, and volatility, then justification for a directional master concept becomes even more dubious. I believe Charles Tilly (1984:48) is correct when he stresses:

> Not that differentiation is an unimportant feature of social processes. Many significant social processes do involve differentiation. But many social processes also involve dedifferentiation: Linguistic standardization, the development of mass communication, and the agglomeration of petty sovereignties into national states provide clear examples. Furthermore, differentiation matters little to other important social processes such as capital concentration and the diffusion of world religions. Indeed, we have no

> warrant for thinking of differentiation in itself as a coherent, general, law-like social process.

Moreover, most theories of society that operate with the assumption of the salience of functional differentiation have difficulties, it seems to me, coping with cultural and cognitive entities (including knowledge) in the schemes of their designs. Parsons' treatment of the cultural system as both at the apex of regulative hierarchies and as somehow situated in a no-man's-land is only one indication. Cultural and cognitive factors, especially their boundaries, are conflated with the limits of subsystems in society, underestimating the ease with which they travel, without too many impediments, across alleged check points. In other words, what is at times much more important is the failure of boundaries to do their job, the number of unobserved spots on the frontiers, and the speed with which borders are penetrated.

Paradoxically perhaps, the *general* point about the master concept of differentiation therefore is that no *single* process is always basic to social transformations. In addition, as Anthony Giddens (1990c:21) has stressed, the notion of functional differentiation is not well equipped to handle the phenomenon of "the bracketing of time and space by social systems". For Giddens, the image invoked by the idea of "disembedding", that is, of lifting out of "social relations from local contexts of interaction and their restructuring across indefinite spans of time-space", is better suited to capture social mechanisms designed to transcend boundaries between contexts. The specific modes or media of bracketing Giddens discusses are expert systems (that is, knowledge), and symbolic tokens (for example, money), designed to bridge time and space. I would agree with Giddens that these media of interchange undercut the differentiation and specialization of institutions and that the process of disembedding is important. Nonetheless, the bracketing of time and space *within* specialized institutions, for example, the economy as the result of new products, production methods, and modes of organizing production, or in the national political systems as the result of integration, is equally or perhaps more important. At the same time, money and especially knowledge have very different properties, and it is perhaps somewhat misleading to conflate their qualities and overemphasize the extent to which the "application" of knowledge can emancipate itself and oneself from local constraints.

The evolution of modern societies insofar as it occurs in response to enduring functional differentiation does result in the establishment of a social institution whose exclusive business is knowledge. Knowledge is a total social fact, present in all social institutions that have emerged in modern societies.

Whether functional differentiation as an iron attribute of at least industrial societies if not knowledge societies is about to disappear, at least in the sense of a ruling processes, is an intriguing issue. I cannot be as affirmative about the displacement of functional differentiation as is Ulrich Beck ([1985] 1992) in his account of the *transcendence* of industrial societies (with its low-skilled bias); for he is confident that there are good reasons for assuming that functional differentiation will no longer be an indispensable core attribute of societies-in-the-making. The emergent form of society will demonstrate that the *myth* of indispensability of functional differentiation is mistaken. On the one hand, industrial society will—without too much fanfare (as the result of a revolution or being voted out)—disappear from the world stage. On other hand, social movement skeptical toward science and technology and not wedded anymore to the idea of progress will assure that industrial societies are a matter of the past. As Beck ([1985] 1992:11) notes, "in the Kant-inspired question about the conditions for the possibility of modern societies, the historically conditioned contours, lines of conflict and functional principles of industrial capitalism were elevated to the necessities of modernity."[9] The answer to the question of the future of functional differentiation could also be answered like this: history goes on.

The production of wealth is one of the central and persistent features of industrial society, i.e., the interlocking of continuity and caesura in the development of modern societies, but in my view under a different mark, namely the symbolic economy. For Ulrich Beck (1986:17), on the other hand, development is rather characterized by a gain in power of "technical-economic 'progress'" including the massive production and perception of risks in the form of global threats. In addition, there are socio-structural and cultural continuities and discontinuities between the decaying industrial society and its successors; for example, in the nuclear family, the world of work and politics. In short, (skill-biased) knowledge societies emerge from the "logic" and success of the industrial society itself; "people are set free from the forms of life and self-evidence of the industrial social epoch of modernity" (Beck, [1986] 1992:14).[10]

Ejecting God and nature

Also associated with the social, political, and economic developments of the 19th century is a major cultural transformation, namely the loss of *traditional certainties, beliefs, and expectations*. In the initial accounts of the developments, the inescapable advance of science and technology play a central role in the transformation toward a more rational and bureaucratized society. Although most classical social theorists agree about the nature of the impact of science on social relations, not all social scientists shared based on these observations a pessimistic outlook when it comes to an evaluation of the impact of these changes on society.

A societal process that Max Weber ([1919] 1948:139) for example describes in his lecture "Science as a Profession" is "disenchantment of the world". However, it would be a mistake to blame "scientific progress" alone for this "process of intellectualization" or a detraditionalization of the culture (Giddens, [1999] 2002:47); science is part and parcel of and the driving force behind the disenchantment that began thousands of years ago. For example, religious interpretations "of the world and ethics of religions created by intellectuals and meant to be rational have been strongly exposed to the imperative of consistency" (Weber, 1948:324). In recent times, this change has continued and even intensified due to the possible *globalization* of life worlds worldwide, as for example Giddens ([1999] 2001:47) sums up, "as the influence of tradition and customs shrink world-wide level, the very basis of our self-identity—our sense of self—changes."

The theoretical premise of a changing cultural identity in modern societies, "derived" from the thesis of increasing functional differentiation, is only formally associated with certain *structural* changes. The scientific world view robs society of meaning. Every step forward by science and technology leads "to an ever more devastating senselessness" (Weber, [1920] 1948:357).[11] It remains unclear why traditional values should necessarily give way or pushed aside by "modern" ideas or for what reason modern ideas can fulfil the functions of traditional ideas. The logic of major social institutions, the economy, and politics, is seen to operate more and more based on a scientific world view, especially linked to efficiency thinking or means/ends linkages. Nonetheless, the issues to which traditional ideas mainly attended have not disappeared, be it such profound puzzles as life and death, extreme events, or sheer "luck". In any case, rationalization is the death of tradition. Is the only thing that remains as a moral institution in such a "purified" society, if this is necessary at all, the (additional) moralization of science and technology (see Habermas, 1968:104)? I will critically analyze this widespread, but nevertheless dubious, thesis in a later chapter of this study.

As Kurt Hübner ([1978] 1983:214), reflecting the widespread agreement among social scientists now and in prior decades, recently observed, "the way in which present-day human society, as an industrialized society, understands itself rests, to a very great extent, on genuine technological-scientific forms and ideas." Earlier generations of social scientists shared this conviction. Max Scheler ([1926] 1960:207), for example, asserts essentially the same fateful development, because of the three ideal types of knowledge (knowledge of salvation, cultural knowledge, and knowledge of domination) he identifies, only the last type of knowledge, the ability to control and produce effects, has ever more exclusively been cultivated for the purpose of "changing the world" in the Occident while knowledge of culture and knowledge of salvation have been successively relegated to the background (cf. also Scheler, [1925] 1958:43).[12]

For Parsons (1937:752), Weber's work culminates precisely in his "conception of a law of increasing rationality as a fundamental generalization about systems of action". This law constitutes the most fundamental generalization that emerges from Weber's work. Emile Durkheim's discussion, in *Elementary Forms of Religious Life*, of the conflict or reciprocal relations between science and religion also proceeds from the premise that science will displace religion, although Durkheim ([1912] 1965:477–480) is prepared to grant a continual though limited role to religious knowledge in modern society. Of course, not all sociological classics assign science such an uncontested function in the structure and culture of modern society. Vilfredo Pareto celebrates and justifies the societal function of illogicality (as a capacity for action), though he attempts to do so on the basis of strictly logical reasoning. In spite of such exceptions, an overwhelming majority of social scientists anticipate either with fear or in disillusionment an "age of science and technology" and an increasing rationalization of irrational forces. In the end, however, all sides of the debate on the social and cultural capacity of modern science and technology in 19th-century sociological discourse and contemporary theoretical perspectives share the naive faith in the intellectual ability of science and scientific institutions to (re)shape the attitudes and beliefs of the individual mind. In short, modern science "undermines our day-to-day customary beliefs by providing alternatives, more powerful explanations for natural and social phenomena" (Gellner, 1987:175).

The conviction about the almost unassailable, irrevocable societal power of science and technology continues to be a prominent premise in contemporary theories of society; perhaps it is fair to suggest that its strength has increasingly been driven by the practical accomplishments not only of natural science and technology but also social science fields, for example, the considerable power of economics and policies derived from economic theory. The impact of other disciplines is highlighted as well, manifest for example in an assertion advanced by Zygmunt Bauman (1987:123, 48), which he shares with Michel Foucault about a scientifically elaborated punishment and reward systems that give rise to a new technology of power and control and to engineers of human behavior and the potential of a "total reshaping of human behavioral patterns". Knowledge and power are allies administering the minds and bodies of the greatest number of citizens.[13]

The "troubling" persistence of traditional beliefs or even a "derationalization" process in some spheres of society give one good reason to doubt the general assertion about the universal efficacy of scientific knowledge and the incessant and irresistible drive toward greater rationalization of all realms of life. Modernization and rationalization may not necessarily converge. Thus, recognition of the mutual importance of rationalization and counter-rationalization processes and the persistence of traditional beliefs is required. A more balanced perspective would be cognizant of the limits of the power of scientific knowledge in modern society and would not commit the fallacy of an over-commitment to rationalization or tradition. It is hardly necessary to stress that under these conditions the fate of democracy expires in a dead end.

Steps to the future

The interest in and the search for more or less exact boundaries between stages of social, economic, political, and cultural development of societal formations also is a legacy of 19th-century thought. Teleological, evolutionary, dualistic, and linear approaches prevailed. But the asymmetric dichotomy that above all preoccupied all of these theoretical endeavors was the search for indicators which separated *modern* from *traditional* society. Classical 19th-century theories of society were persuaded that there are ways or that there even is a singular method in which different types of societies can be clearly distinguished from each other. Thus, the theoretical perspectives that were developed presumed to be operative at the level of society or the territorial state. The model of the Western society of course served as the exemplary path societal transformation was bound to follow. The most "advanced" or developed society shows to others the image of their unavoidable future. One therefore finds, superimposed on the continuum of historical change, a bipolar conception of progressive versus regressive social developments. In addition, "various forms of belief in monolithic inevitability fell in with the misleading analogy between societal development and the stages through which an individual organism must pass" (Riesman, 1953/1954:141). In general, however, the attempt of classical sociological discourse from Auguste Comte to Talcott Parsons to press societal transformations into an *iron* dichotomy of traditional and modern has been discredited by history itself. Societies that appeared and claimed for themselves to have reached a higher evolutionary stage reached back into barbarism; also, the alleged medieval curses of miracle, magic, superstition, mystery, and false authority are still very much alive. Civilization has not passed successively and successfully in stages from the theological, to the metaphysical and the positive. At the same time, the actual path of social, political, and economic development of different societies is less than one-dimensional. Nonetheless, the purposes and the language of social theory require ways of differentiating forms of societies and attention to the question of the kinds of developmental patterns that characterize societies (cf. Touraine, 1986:15–16).

As a matter of fact, the social sciences, depending on their knowledge-guiding interests and the boundaries of their subject matter, employ a great variety of points of empirical and normative reference indicating different stages of societal development. Within classical sociological discourse, the specific empirical referent or process introduced for the purpose of capturing the iron pattern of social development may, on the one hand, refer to a fundamental mechanism such as the notion of contradiction (cf. Eder, 1992), which consistently initiates basic social changes or, on the other hand, fundamental attributes of social life such as the dissolution of a certain form of social solidarity that spell and signal the end of the identity of a particular type of society and simultaneously transcend in its consequences any single, historically concrete society. Within the Marxian theory of society, contradictions between corporate actors are the moving force of history. Auguste Comte's or Emile Durkheim's differentiation of societies is based on distinctions in the nature of the moral, legal, intellectual, and political relations and therefore the basis of social solidarity that may prevail in different societies. But types of societies may also be differentiated on the basis of the ways in which human needs, understood as anthropological constants and therefore as needs that transcend specific concrete societies, are fulfilled. In general, however, it is evident that typologies of societies rest on certain fundamental anthropological considerations about the nature of society and human individuals. Ultimately, there are quite a few contenders claiming to have discovered the master key to social evolution. Finally, it is not uncommon that theories of society are convinced that the master process of social evolution is one which operates in an almost self-propelled fashion which cannot be arrested or altered in any fundamental sense. Once set in motion, social evolution is bound to run its predetermined and often-linear course.

It is much easier to express credible doubt and creative skepticism toward these received notions of 19th-century social thought and therefore to break down the often absolute, binary classificatory categories found in the work of Malthus and Spencer, Comte and Durkheim, Pareto and Veblen, or Saint-Simon and Marx, than it is to imagine and develop potential alternative, less rigid approaches. As briefly indicated, the understanding of the development of human societies *does* require theoretical models in social science that aim to comprehend long-term transformations of social structure and culture. However, such theories do not have to be built on 19th-century assumptions about either the direction of long-term social processes nor on what are essentially holistic notions about the inescapable systemic (collective) identity of social order. It is questionable whether societies, their institutions, and everyday life indeed derive from an overall, definitive character of an assemblage of social patterns that give definition to virtually all its parts and unity to their interrelations. It is prudent, I believe, to proceed without rigid preconceptions about evolutionary stages and types of society.

For illustrative purposes at least, I will attempt to make a case for viewing modernization as not conforming to such strict historical stages and schemes of society, but as a much more moderate and open, even reversible process, namely as movement toward an *enlargement of social action*. To cite but one example, for a couple of decades now, one is able to observe a much broader and persistent growth in the participation of individual investors in stock trading. That is, in contrast to classical or orthodox assumptions, I propose to conceptualize of embedded social change that focuses on "marginal" or incremental change and therefore social development that consists of "additions", both forward *and* backward in time, as a more appropriate image both for the kinds of societies described by classical social science discourse and even more so contemporary society. I propose to conceptualize the modernization process as a process of "extension". A simple case of extension might for instance refer to the multiple avenues that transcend hunting and gathering societies on their way to establishing farming societies or, to refer to a more modern case, the intellectual claim by Gary Becker (1995:5) that "the economic approach provides a valuable unified framework for understanding *all* human behavior." An enlargement of the substantive and methodological scope of economists' interest (see Coase, 1978) is important not only for the neoliberal economists of the Chicago School,[14] but also for Michel Foucault (e.g., 2008, 268–269) and other scholars.

Hannah Arendt's (1961:59) distinction between "acting into nature" based on modern science and technology and "making" nature might serve as a further example of broad-based enlargement of human action:

> It is important to be aware how decisively the technological world we live in, or perhaps begin to live in, differs from the mechanized world as it arose with the Industrial Revolution. This difference corresponds essentially to the difference between action and fabrication. Industrialization still consisted primarily of the mechanization of work processes, the improvement in the making of objects, and man's attitude to nature still remained that of *homo faber*, to whom nature gives the material out of which the human artifice is erected. The world we have come to live in, however, is much more determined by man acting into nature, creating natural processes and directing them into the human artifice and the realm of human affairs.

While acting into nature is historically new, making nature does not vanish. Another case in point at the macro-level would be the enormous growth of the modern communication system, for example, of the in many ways invisible internet system that first and foremost represents an enlargement of communication opportunities rather than a functional differentiation of communication. Or, even while it is true that the functions of cities vary widely and that cities have taken more and different functions in the course of history, one of the most salient changes that affects cities and towns around the world is their persistent and tremendous increase in size.[15] A final example of the extension of social action—on the macro-level—could refer to the ability of actors to *restrict* options of action of other actors, once taken for granted. Globalization represents sociopolitical change that diminishes the capability of the range of action of nation-states, as it enlarges the power of transnational corporations and international organizations such as the World Trade Organization (WTO) (cf. Beck, [2002] 2005:118–125). Global law restricts national law yet enhances the reach of legal rules across national boundaries.

Part and parcel of the modernization of modern society is the enlargement of discourse about the limits or the end of the extension of social action: "When will it be enough?" to vary the title of a monograph by Robert and Edward Skidelsky (2012). On the other hand, the enlargement of capacities to act, such as the growth of the economic pie could be—as is often asserted not only in political campaigns—a key in keeping actors contended with the social order. At the individual level, the extension of social action, for example, as an enlargement of available opportunities to take in information comes into conflict with or struggles against limits in the amount *attention* humans are able to mobilize. The internet amplifies such conflicts.[16] For Zygmunt Bauman (2000:29), characteristic of our form of modernity is precisely the gradual collapse of the early modern illusion that there "is an end to the road along which we proceed . . . a state of perfection to be reached tomorrow . . . some sort of good society", in short, a "perfect order". The contemporary discourse about the limits of enlargement differs sharply from these illusions about a limitless "improvement" of the *status quo*. Today, in the age of the Anthropocene, the discourse about the end of the extension of social action is preoccupied with the self-imposed end of civilization.

Social science discourse has lost much of its preoccupation with the search for evolutionary stages in the course of the social transformation of societies and the identification of distinctive societal formations. As a matter of fact, some observers, most notably Norbert Elias (1987b), even detected a more radical conversion and re-orientation in social science discourse, namely a shift away from describing history as structured toward a view of social change as essentially without any structure whatsoever or, as he diagnoses it, a "retreat of sociologists into the present". Despite Elias' observations that an abundance of contemporary empirical research in sociology is carried out without reference to theory or to long-term historical developments and his plea that the understanding of human society requires a comprehension of long-term processes as well as attention to certain universal properties found in all human societies, work in sociology and in the other social sciences which has a macro-orientation continues to involve, to some degree at least, attention to longer-term social transformations. The discussion about the end of industrial society is a prominent example.

Societies in transition

> If a topic is to be treated like today's society between yesterday and tomorrow, then the temptation is obvious to view today simply as a "transition", i.e., as a quantity that is not relevant in itself, but only through the relationship between yesterday and tomorrow.
>
> —René König ([1962] 1965:79)

At any point in the evolution (and "involution") of modern societies, these social formations are always societies in transition, that is, as societies between yesterday and tomorrow. Societies in repeated transition mode often change the conditions for social change. For this reason alone, it is a difficult undertaking for social scientists, as Ulrich Beck ([1986] 1992:12) rightly remarks, to track down new concepts that are already apparent today under the skin of the decay of the old order. That societies are in a permanent transition is not only a characteristic of the understanding of classical social theories, but is also an essential character of industrial, post-industrial, and knowledge societies. Movement and social change are fixed attributes of social realities. One cannot stop societies. The permanent exchange of society members alone is a guarantee that social action does not stand still. The transition from one form of society to another involves, as Samuel Huntington (1974:178) observes, "three major lines of cleavage: between rising and declaring social forces; between declining social forces; and between rising social forces".

The present is by no means irrelevant, given the fact that it will soon be overcome. However, the present suffers precisely from this temporary, deficient quality, and the effort to hold onto what is considered valuable and important. Avoiding the dreaded future can be the impetus for action in the present. A strong belief in retaining the present and hence avoiding a different future is frequently treated as a virtue. Such an attitude finds its most manifest and frequent reflection in holding onto and expressing a *zero-sum mentality*. Any addition or, as I will define it, any extension of social action, for example by extending the number of members of a community, is viewed with suspicion, as an economic or cultural threat. Additional members are perceived as a drain on available, allegedly static resources of a community and therefore a (proportional) loss to the established size of the collectivity. Political *populism*, in an age of accelerated extension of social action, is a response to an apprehended zero-sum mentality.

The phenomenon of generations is a good example of the "normality" of transition:

> The sociological phenomenon of generations is ultimately based on the biological rhythm of birth and death. . . . Were it not for the existence of social interaction between human beings—were there no definable social structure, no history based on a particular sort of continuity, the generation would not exist as a social location phenomenon; there would merely be birth, aging, and death. The sociological problem of generations therefore begins at that point where the sociological relevance of these biological factors is discovered. Starting with the elementary phenomenon itself, then, we must first of all try to understand the generation as a particular type of *social location*.
>
> (Mannheim, [1928] 19; emphasis added)

Social change is moving in different steps and at different speeds; the fact of inexorable movement becomes palpable simply by the fact that time is running out. Even if only time is passing, the members of society have the unmistakable feeling that something is changing. Aging can be such a feeling, while certain biographical stages of life provide the certainty of transition; stages of life (for example, from childhood to adolescence to adulthood) are obvious examples. The social process that determines the transition of societies is that of expansion and extension of social action, social values, conflicts, and interactions with the society's environment. Through the widespread process of social transition, the solution of the problem of continuity becomes one of the outstanding social necessities.

Modernization as extension and enlargement

> Modern societies, as contrasted with more traditional systems, continuously face the crucial problem of the ability of their central frameworks to "expand".
> —Shmuel Eisenstadt, 1973:4

Shmuel Eisenstadt's observation about an incessant and growing need to expand the central frameworks of modern society is mainly thought to originate from "demands" directed toward the center of society and issued by groups of its citizens;

> the number of demands has simply increased almost geometrically and is closely related to a broader access to resources and to a greater range of politically articulate groups and strata. . . . Around such demands and the center's responses to them emerge some of the major possibilities of conflict, cleavage, and crisis, that can undermine the respective regimes in modern societies.
>
> (Eisenstadt, 1973:4–5)

How does the expansion of political influence happen in the first place?

In this section, I will refer to an even more comprehensive and anthropologically constant pattern of social change—a change that is triggered by systemic, i.e., inter-societal and/or intra-societal conditions. This includes economic, political, scientific, technical, cultural, demographical, and ecological processes. These processes can, of course, have long-term consequences, such as demographic change due to mass migrations, just as they can be processes that trigger but short-term relevant change, such as a financial crisis or a natural disaster, and thus a return to the *status quo ante*. In such a case, social action manifests itself in a backward-looking development. I will define such ubiquitous changes, forward or backward, as triggered by and involving the *extension of social action*—manifesting the great malleability of human nature. There are, for example, in the course of human history, fewer and fewer hurdles and/or gatekeepers to control access to a participation in public conversation.

The enlargement of social action applies not only to structural changes of society, for example within the economic or political system, but also to matters of participation, orientation, dispersion in beliefs, convictions, motives, and of course knowledge. In a most general and unifying sense, the extension and enlargement of social action amounts to a process of building *societal complexity*. The evolution of complexity in turn enhances the fragility of society. But what is fragile about industrial society, its economy for example, linked to the iron law of marginal returns, is not what is fragile about knowledge society, for instance the relation to its environment or mounting social inequality. As has been the case in past societies, the enlargement of social action in knowledge societies does not occur in a linear fashion, but is fraught with persistent patterns of inequities and unevenness. For instance, access to large chunks of data, including instant data to monitor grocery deliveries or how many people are glued to "Squid Game", and their exploitation offer enlarged choices to tech-corporations, governments to meddle, and economists to observe the economy but leave citizens open to experimentation.

Motives from different epochs coexist, come into conflict, or tend to support each other. In knowledge societies, traditional motives, for example sacred convictions, exist alongside secular motives. In general, however, the *motive structure of knowledge societies* intensifies efforts in many spheres of everyday life to enlarge outcomes, for example, in terms of health, economic well-being, and collective accomplishments; thus, the motive structure of knowledge societies is dominated by multiple motives, old and new, egoistic and altruistic, competitive or indifferent, all empowered by the desire to enlarge desired benefits and inhibit risk and dangers of social action.

But instead of suggesting that the "modernization" process is driven by a kind of definitive and unavoidable master process such as functional differentiation, rationalization, or conflict and contradiction—which, moreover, is virtually unintentional as well as of fairly recent origin and therefore manifests itself almost exclusively in contemporary societies—I would like to contend that modernization essentially involves multiple and not necessarily unilinear processes of "extension" or "enlargement" and commences earlier in human history. The result of the successive expansion of social processes is the phenomenon of the *simultaneity of the non-simultaneous*. The "old" often and increasingly exists at the same time as the "new" in certain social contexts, for example the "coexistence" and the conflicts of different economic formations or cultural manifestations that in turn arose in diverse, distinguishable historical epochs as exemplified by the concept of cultural lag (Ogburn, [1922] 1950).

The agricultural economy will not disappear in a post-industrial society; it radically changes. Agriculture evolves from subsistence to hi-tech farming with but a very small proportion of society's labor force still employed in farming-related jobs. The agricultural sector develops, made possible by new techniques and technological advances, from a labor-intensive to a capital-intensive sector of the economy. However, the dependence on labor is by no means disappearing. The proportion of people employed in farming closely correlates with the wealth of nations. Today, the lower the proportion of farming-related jobs, the higher the society's wealth and vice versa. Both types of society currently exist side by side.

As Alain Touraine ([1984] 1988:104; also, Bell, 1976:47), for example, observes with respect to the historic transformation of the economic structures, "an industrial society does not give up the benefits acquired through commerce; a postindustrial society does not give up the organization of labor." By the same token, a post-industrial society "does not differ fundamentally from other stages of industrial society. It is simply (at present) the most advanced manifestation" (Touraine, [2010] 2014:17). In practical affairs, as Daniel Bell (1973:127) summarizes, "life is never as 'one-dimensional' as those who convert every tendency into an ontological absolute make it out to be. Traditional elements remain."

Expanding the field of social action

Extension is based and refers, on the one hand, to the enlargement, expansion, or "growth" of sentiments, social connections, widening of choices, knowledge, personal transactions or exchanges, and their progressive multiplication, their increasing density, and liberation from barriers—for example, those of time (e.g. life expectancy), economic misery (e.g. broad enhancement of economic wealth along with the emergence of the modern welfare state), and place (e.g. the environment), taken for granted in some ages—in the course of human history and, on the other hand, to the dissolution or retrenchment, but not always in the sense of elimination, of cultural practices and structural figurations that come into conflict with novel expectations and forms of conduct generated and supported by extension. The significant difference in the course of modernization is not so much the acceleration of change but "the enlargement of an individual's world that accompanies the advance of technology. There is a tremendous change in the scale of the number of persons one knows or knows of" (Bell, 1976:48). Individuals in modern societies were not restricted in their choices to what their father or mother was, which was basically a farmer or housewife in earlier societal formations. The extension of social action may be viewed as hardly noticeable, as creeping (generational, life expectancy extension), slow but persistent addition of capacities of action that enlarge risks, fragilities, and uncertainties, and, at the other extreme, are seen to proceed at an accelerated speed (war, revolution, natural disasters, pandemics, economic crises, major inventions). The expansion of social action possibilities includes not least the growing formations of solidary action, for example, the women's movement and in distribution efforts of surplus. Social problem-solving behavior (*social solution*) takes place on a collective (legal system) and not an individual level (cf. Saez, 2021).

Extension and enlargement of social conduct involves both intentional (purposive) action and non-intentional strategies and consequences (cf. Merton, 1936b). Life once meant social encounters virtually confined to familiar acquaintances; now everyday life for many means living with growing numbers of strangers daily. However, "the loss of insulating space" or eclipse of distance, for example,

> is not only the foreshortening of time and space in flying across continents, or in being in instant communication with any part of the globe by television or radio, it also is, as regards the *experienced* time of the person, an eclipse of social, esthetic and psychic distance as well.
>
> (Bell, 1973:314)

Extension of time and distance cannot be viewed as a simple linear or additive process whereby equal increments are added in equal installments to all existing aggregate structures and practices. Extension is a process embedded in local circumstances that produces an authentic variety of forms. Colonization not only transforms the colonies, but also those who colonize. Extension is a stratified process. As a matter of fact, stratification itself is not immune to extension. Gradients and patterns of social inequality today are both much steeper and much more varied than they have ever been. Increments of extension are unevenly distributed and do not necessarily promote greater equality.

Moreover, the speed of extension (and dissolution) is not constant or evenly distributed, nor are reversals in the density of social links impossible. The extension and expansion of cultural practices, production, trade, legal rules (for example, the stubborn enlargement of the copyright term and the extension of what can be subjected to patent law, especially in comparison to the law of intellectual property at the time it was discovered), media of exchange, communication, and social reproduction generally do not always follow the same pattern, especially patterns established in the past. What appears to be a contraction of social density or a decline in a certain attribute of social existence may in fact be a case of expansion. For example, the collapse of an empire actually constitutes a form of expansion in the conditions for identity formation, the basis of social inequality, the ethos of social conduct and acceptable beliefs, etc. The decline of infant mortality actually represents, at the individual level, an extension in life expectancy and, at the aggregate level, one of the bases for the population explosion. The decline in the use of manual labor constitutes an enlargement of physical power and productivity. At times, extension may only constitute an enlargement of cognitive *possibilities*, that is, of what is now imaginable conduct, for example, as the result of the production of new forms of art or access to new fiction. The separation of the private from the public spheres constitutes a form of extension and not merely obliteration of sanctioned forms of conduct. Criteria and units constitutive of social order may be enlarged. Ascriptive (naturalized) criteria such as birth, color, race, and religious or social class decline, but the dissolution is based on the emergence of more achievement-oriented standards and therefore an extension in the relevant criteria for an accumulation of status attributes but not necessarily the complete elimination of ascriptive features of social conduct. Of course, some forms of inequality may be marginalized in the process of expanding the basis of inequality. Emerging standards and criteria of inequality often even have a common hostility to past standards, but they rarely succeed in canceling these social constraints.

The process of extension generally also involves the absorption of novel connections into existing figurations and their transformation, representing yet another means of extension. Enlargement and extension, in contrast to the prevailing sense and direction of movement and time in most orthodox modernization theories, do not necessarily have to have occur in but one direction, namely "forward". On the contrary, extension can also involve enlargement directed "backwards" or toward our past, as contemporary archeologists and others for example begin to expand our understanding of the Maya civilization, as archives of totalitarian regimes are opened, or as modernist elites reactivate traditional values (e.g., Zghal, 1973), to bolster the legitimacy of their power. In the aftermath of the fall of the Berlin Wall, a world without borders was on the forefront of the political imagination in many countries. Only a few decades later, not only because of the pandemic, a return to a world full of borders is the new reality. Extension in one sphere may result in a concomitant enlargement in another; as some observers for instance are quick to note, any extension of knowledge may be accompanied by an enlargement of the area of asymmetric knowledge.

Since the extension of social connections or the enlargement of production and commodities accumulated has a rather close affinity to the notion of *growth*, also in the sense of a growth in knowledge or consumption patterns, it is important to stress that the concept of growth does not quite do justice to the dynamic under consideration or fully express the transformations which result from an expanded social, cognitive, or material density. With Norbert Elias ([1987] 1991:99–100), I would want to emphasize that enlargement and accumulation result in a change of the *level* of activity, consciousness, or standards, for example, the number of children typically born into a family signifying, among other things, the enhanced range and number of choices available to females.

The special advantage (or difficulty, as it may be), with the notion of a change in level is, as Elias also stresses, that new viewpoints, for instance, do not simply abolish perspectives from other levels of consciousness. In the course of the successive extension of human consciousness, it becomes a multi-layered consciousness enabling us to discover perspectives that rise above the horizon of past societies forming the foundation of new forms of self-consciousness. Enlargement and extension of the capacity to act also transforms the *kind* of consciousness that prevails in social relations; for example, as the capacity to act is enlarged, interest in and, as some might argue, an excessive concern with the conviction that the *status quo* has to be transgressed become prevalent as a motive force. The social sciences have been at the forefront of viewing more and more aspects of social life as subject to an enlargement of the range of human phenomena that are cultural rather than material. Race may have been defined as natural in the earlier intellectual history of the social science; but any effort to retain such a conception today will encounter vigorous opposition.

As a matter of fact, as the extension of social connections accelerates, the retrieval or number and the reliability of depositories of past standards of conduct and patterns of consciousness increases as well, reducing the probability that social structures which have undergone massive change and the cultural practices which appear to have been abandoned actually vanish without a trace. Memory expands as well. Protests mount, and stronger and stronger feelings of misgiving against extension appear. Opposition to the extension of social connections not only is fostered by the sense of conserving the status quo or even past conditions imagined to be less troubling, but also by the realization that extension does not always heal past and present plights and without fail offers a therapeutic solution to perceived existential dilemmas.

Space and time are widened and lengthened in both directions, that is, forward and backward, as the result of modernization through extension. The present does not constitute a complete break with the past.[17] Space once confined to the boundaries of a village has exploded to include, for some but certainly not for all, much of the globe. Time has accelerated and become more varied both "backwards" into historical realms as well as "forward".

Extension may be based on imitation, violence, curiosity, disintegration, conquest, a premium placed on novelty, multiplication of options, diffusion, a desire to achieve recognition, the attempt to overcome embeddedness in conventional relations, the basic need for physical reproduction, etc. The mere enumeration of multiple and often-interconnected ways in which extension may be set in motion and sustained already indicates that the process of extension may be quite deliberate or often driven by fortuitous circumstances.

The enlargement of social action is obviously linked to and explains individual participation in major social institutions or the lack thereof—for instance, the desire for political participation and the engagement with politics. The enlargement of social section and political participation are a subset of the much broader and deeper notion of the extension of social action. Nonetheless, political activity, characterized for example by the "Civic Voluntarism Model" (Verba et al., 1995:269–287) is a conceptual idea that captures elements of the ways in which social action extends into the political realm. Responding to the question why people fail to engage in politics, Sidney Verba and his colleagues list three factors: "because they can't; because they don't want to; or because nobody asks them" (Verba et al., 1995:269). Political participation takes resources, engagement, and recruitment whereby the resources that facilitate participation are most important component, followed by the variety of psychological dispositions; least significant is recruitment. There is somewhat of an elective affinity of the civic voluntarism model with the concept of the enlargement of social action, especially when it comes to the emphasis of *resources* as levers of social action. Resources that the model of political participation emphasizes are time, money, and civic skills; they can be found and are practiced in major societal institutions.

The broad range of attributes encompassing and spreading into all nooks and crannies of society that constitute the enlargement of social action are much broader in function and substance than the resources the model of civic voluntarism stresses. The enlargement of social action refers to capacities not as society-specific and recent as the resources time, money, and civic skills.

Extension is facilitated by expanding the media of exchange, but the enlargement of social action generally results in a decreasing degree of social integration. And knowledge societies, to use a metaphor Alain Touraine ([1984] 1988:109) employs, do not refer their actors back to "one central point but rather to separate centers of decision that form a mosaic rather than a pyramid".

In view of these considerations, therefore, it can be stated that the modernization process *commences* once social conduct no longer is a zero-sum game. Once the production of intellectual and material resources exceeds immediate needs and results in a surplus, modernization becomes a process of enlarging means and ends of conduct. Though initially modernization may have been limited to some spheres of social life, it subsequently is evident and manifests itself in every social institution.

Modern society as industrial society

Constitutive of *classical* sociological discourse and therefore of the concerted effort to reflect on the emergence of modern society out of the womb of "traditional" society is, in the work of Ferdinand Toennies, Karl Marx, Herbert Spencer, Emile Durkheim, Georg Simmel, Max Weber, and the perhaps last classical social theorist, Talcott Parsons (e.g., Bottomore, 1960; cf. Meja and Stehr, 1988), the strong conviction that the modern and traditional are worlds apart.[18] Industrialized societies no longer experience, as Alain Touraine (1977:112) describes it, "the traditional alliance between the gods and nature, yet are attracted by two opposing images of themselves that of natural society and that of rational society". The danger or miracle from today's point of view may be that new gods and nature are making their return into modern societies.

Identity, communality, conformity, consensus, and the like, but not inequality, power, or the division of labor, as basic social features of a disappearing form of life, give way to social differences in and conflicts about identities, structures, and opinions. Homogeneity is replaced by heterogeneity. The growing lack of uniformity is, one could also summarize, the operative principle and direction of social change. In many instances, the changes described are viewed as distinctively progressive forces or, at least, as the conditions for the possibility of a progressive transformation of society located in the not-too-distant future—despite evident but temporary tensions, struggles, and suffering. For many early social theorists, the exact nature of the emerging social order is not quite evident. The foundations of the society on the horizon are based on what are precarious and fragile but also transitory conditions. Once the process of "functional differentiation" is fully operational and well understood as the main theoretical principle governing theories of modern society, the notion of modernity is firmly installed and accepted.

It took a considerable period of time before sociological discourse began to sketch in firmer terms the contours of modern society. As a matter of fact, it is only after World War II that social theorists, based on the particulars of the historical experiences, especially the rapid and sustained economic expansion[19] and of course the exemplars of classical discourse, developed the outlines of theories of society which took contemporary social, political, and economic conditions as its core explanatory problematic.

Despite even more recent and extensive reflections about its demise as a promising ideal type for the analysis of modern society, the most important sociological reconstruction of contemporary society in the post-war era still is the notion of modern society as an *industrial society*. The theory of industrial society, moreover, is linked quite closely to the intellectual history of sociology itself because it is only with the emergence of "scientific" sociology at the turn of the 20th century that the term "industrial society" is employed with increasing frequency. Thus, as Ralf Dahrendorf ([1967] 1974:65), observed: "Sociology is, on the one hand, an offspring of industrial society; it appears and gains in significance in the course of industrialization." On the other hand, "industrial society itself is the favorite child of sociology; its concept can be understood as the product of modern social science."

The origins and contours of industrial society

Although the term "industrial society" goes back to the 19th century, its full recognition and wide application only occurred during the last few decades of that century:

> The political economists and social scientists of the 18th century did not have a name for the change taking place in front of their own eyes. In the 19th century sociologists polemically viewed their society mainly as a capitalist society, as a society of alienation, injustice, poverty and subjugation.
> (Dahrendorf, 1974:67)

It is evident, moreover, that the theory of industrial society continues to display the same primarily optimistic vision of classical sociological theory, for example in terms of the hopeful conviction and anticipation of a better world in which the gradients of social inequality, for instance, would be less pronounced.

The most well-known, ambitious, and detailed sociological exposition of the theory of industrial society may be found on the work of the French sociologist Raymond Aron. The core problematic of Aron's *18 Lectures on Industrial Society*, originally delivered as part of a trilogy of lectures on the comparative analysis of Soviet and Western societies at the Sorbonne, focused on the problem of accumulation not unlike the Marxian theory of capitalism. With this determination, Aron was decided that culture plays a subordinate, in each case a marginal role, within the framework of his social theory. Culture was not given an independent place in the industrialization of society. At best, culture was transcended by science and technology.[20] Aron substituted what he saw as the more general process than accumulation, namely, economic growth, and with it he took the language and premises of neo-classical economics on board, including an emphasis on the intentions of economic actors. Indeed, it was his ambition to produce a theory more general and less ideological than the Marxian perspective. More specifically, Raymond Aron ([19] 1967:41–42) asked:

> Given that we observe as a major fact in present-day societies, whether Western or Soviet, that science is being applied to industry and that this involves an increase in productivity and growth in the resources of the community and per head of the population, what are the consequences of this for social order?

The distinction between capitalist and communist industrial societies as well as a reference to the relations of production is secondary and based on ideological differences as well as differences in capital investment. The differentiation should lessen in time. All complex societies differentiate most basically along three axes: the economic, the social, and the political. In contrast to Daniel Bell's post-industrial society, the primary institution of industrial society is the political system. The benefits from industrialization or economic growth could mean a better life for everyone without necessarily eliminating all social conflicts. Social hierarchies remain and may even be hardened.

Inasmuch as the theory of modern society as an industrial society is the outcome of classical sociological discourse, it may be seen to represent the result of a complicated convergence of themes found in the writings of Weber, Durkheim, Spencer, and Comte, a convergence of classical sociological ideas in the sense in which Parsons, for example, postulated it for his theory of action in his *Structure of Social Action*.

More specifically, the theory of industrial society, as developed during the post-war era, can be traced to the intellectual traditions and developments associated with the work of Henri Saint-Simon and Auguste Comte. According to Saint-Simon and his disciples, the new society that originated with the French Revolution was characterized by a specific system of production, namely *industrialism*. For Comte, this type of society was destined to become universal. But Marxists have always been skeptical toward any theory of society proclaiming to formulate a theory of industrial civilization, since the notion of capitalism has a much more central theoretical function within Marxism. Marxist interpretation, therefore, attempts to formulate a theory of industrial society that makes the case for the existence of a single industrial civilization as an apologetic effort designed to hide the real nature of capitalism by talking about a societal formation incorporating both socialist and capitalist relations and conditions of production. The Marxian protest is of course a political one; speaking of industrial society implies the approval of the existing state of affairs as unobjectionable. Ralf Dahrendorf ([1957] 1959:40) agrees that capitalism "merely signifies one form of industrial society".

Whatever their objections may be, a political economy of industrial civilization certainly would represent a much broader and more powerful explanatory theory of society and more commanding policy perspective than either a theory of the historically specific form of socialist or capitalist society. Nonetheless, one cannot totally overlook the fact that the theory of industrial society evolved, in the minds of some, into a serious intellectual competitor and rival of Marxist theories of modern society (see Goldthorpe, 1971:265). Social theorists in the former socialist societies surely viewed the theory of industrial society as a rival theoretical (and political) program which that to be exposed for what is really was, namely an attempt to devise an apologetic perspective of capitalism under the guise of a social scientific analysis of modern society.[21]

Until recently, the conceptual attribute valued in Western societies was usually "industrial" and not "capitalist", while in socialist countries of the day the latter attribute was preferred over "totalitarian". This indicates, of course, that the notion of industrial society as well as capitalism became part of a polemical political discourse. The concept "industrial society" has a multiple career, by no means confined to the social sciences alone. But unless one is prepared to forgo completely the use of the concept in social science, one has to be cognizant of its varied and, at times, pejorative functions in different intellectual and political settings.

The transformation of industrial society

The theory of industrial society, as far as I can tell, does not anticipate or contemplate its own transcendence and therefore spend any intellectual time and effort on the possibility that it may give way to another type of society, as other social theorists, as we know, were quick to suggest just a few years later. Major changes underway in employment patterns or the kinds of work typically performed actually constitute evidence for the continuity of industrial society as the dominant modern social formation. For example, despite further shifts of employment toward the tertiary sector, the foundation of economic activities, *in terms of valued added*, remains agriculture and manufacturing (Aron, [1966] 1968:104).

In his autobiographical reflection about the origins and the nature of his influential conception of industrial society, Raymond Aron, however, reiterates his conviction that the idea of industrial society remains a valid theoretical model, though he does express doubt that the Soviet system as a distinctive political system is capable of surviving or, for that matter, will be able to generate economic wealth in step with capitalist societies. Aron underestimated the inefficiencies of the political organization for the economy. But Saint-Simon and Comte were correct when they foresaw the almost universal spread of industrialism. Aron (1990:277) affirms that the "Saint-Simonians saw clearly" while Marx "distorted their philosophy by substituting capital (or capitalism), for industrialism". But Aron (1990:277) also believes that what is now called post-industrial society "should be interpreted as an original phase in the application of science to production and more broadly to the very life of man".

One of the recent theoretical foci that has animated discussion among social scientists about the special qualities of developed societies is the characterization of contemporary societies as exemplars of "postmodern" societies. In the context of the assertion that we are in the midst of the transformation of modern society into a postmodern societal formation, one might for example ask whether, as Raymond Aron already asserts in the context of his conception of industrial society, that such a society is constituted as the result of a new phase in the application of science and technology, or whether the qualities of postmodernity, as might be suspected, primarily are seen as the outcome of symbolic and cultural changes in modern society. As I will try to show in the following section, the latter indeed appears to be the case for central contributions to discourse about postmodernity.

The design of post-industrial societies

Although the term "postmodern" was well into the new century, one of the favorite expression that professional observers invoked to symbolize and signal the boundary of an epoch as well as the transition to a new era, just 50 years ago, a very different term but one with a virtually identical message, rapidly gained ascendancy and had for a number of decades a lasting impact on social science and policy discourse, namely the observation that we are living in a *post-industrial society* and therefore also in an interstitial time whereby the terms postmodern and post-industrial are not too far apart even in the eyes of their proponents (see Lyotard, 1984). The postmodern diagnosis of modern society focuses primarily on a change in consciousness, while the post-industrial society is primarily concerned with economic change, the shift from manufacturing to services, from factories to offices, from the production of commodities to information processing, and from blue collar to white collar workers, the professional and the technical class.

In describing and discussing the design of post-industrial societies, I will primarily make reference to Daniel Bell's theoretical conception which is the most prominent among the theories of post-industrial society.[22] A number of observers consider the concept of the "information society"—which I will consider in more detail in Chapter 4—to be the twin concept of the concept of the post-industrial society. However, Bell's proposals for a theory of society, cognizant of the dramatic changes that bring about the demise of industrial society and signal the emergence of a type of society which retains some of the crucial features of its predecessor, for example, rapid economic expansion, and therefore is not a post-economic society, was, at the time, by no means the only theoretical perspective developed to stress the pending transformation of modern society into post-industrial society.[23] Perhaps most notable is the family resemblance between Bell's notion and the concurrent conception of a scientific-technological revolution (with a strong, conscious intellectual-political kinship to John D. Bernal's advocacy of the scientific planning of society in the 1930s in response to the decline of liberalism and the political successes of fascism)[24] explicated by

Radovan Richta and his research team which first appeared in 1967. Although Richta (e.g. 1977:27–29) strongly emphasizes the need to examine societal changes in advanced societies that have already taken place as the result of the application of science and technology, both theoretical approaches consciously describe *societal potentials* rather than merely actual conditions and thus already have a distinctive political orientation, that is, a criticism of the prevailing conditions or, at least, their position can easily be understood to incorporate such a critique of contemporary socio-political settings. Not surprisingly, Richta's (1977:29) position, on the surface at least, claims to be strongly linked to the Marxian notion of the forces and the relations of production which provides if only implicitly the solution to the theoretical task of understanding the scientific-technological revolution. Decisive is what now dominates and is characteristic for the economic forces production. Radovan Richta (1977:247) considers Helmut Schelsky's (1961) expression of the "scientific civilization" as a quite suitable description of the nature and the (complete) domination of science and technology and therefore of what now rules the (science-based) forces of production.

In his own analysis of the transition to post-industrial society, Daniel Bell (1973:105–112), favorably summarizes Radovan Richta's views concerning the crucial role of science and technology in production and the extent to which these developments force corrections upon accepted Marxist positions. I will also refer to Richta's ideas—which attempted to inspire to reform the Communist regimes from the inside and assist in catching up with the West—since they illustrate well the fact that the conception of a post-industrial society cannot be seen to represent an isolated (American), intellectual innovation. The theory of post-industrial (and what was, at the time, construed to be post-socialist), society[25] resonates with and refers to specific intellectual and historical developments in a number of societies. Daniel Bell and Radovan Richta endorse, with respect to this "new" level of societal development, Raymond Aron's views about the universality of industrial organization, and the core driver of science and technology independent of the political and cultural peculiarities of different states. A further, importance family resemblance—as well as a stark contrast to Aron's emphasis of the political—between Richta's theory of the scientific-technological revolution and Bell's theory of post-industrial society related to the role of government in economic affairs. The decision-making within the economic system will have increasingly technical character. The shift to science and technology enhances the role of government. Moreover, the "entire complex of prestige and status will be rooted in the intellectual and scientific communities" (Bell, 1973:345). There is then the error to assume as is the case for all technocratic reasoning, that certain political or economic decisions are unavoidable and that in the end humans become mere passive objects. Daniel Bell (1973:360) is aware of the pitfalls of technocratic reasoning when he emphasizes, "for as we have learned, no matter how technical social processes may be, the crucial turning points in a society occur in a political form. It is not the technocrat who ultimately holds power, but the politician."

The power of Daniel Bell's theory of post-industrial society, which is not really about *post*-industrial society, has many notable merits, and the challenging problems posed by his work should not obscure crucial difficulties associated with his theory. Although in subsequent pages I will stress the challenges posed by his approach, I also intend to refer to notable and attractive features of Bell's theory, for example, the lack of theoretical closure, its evolutionary elements, the indeterminateness and the deliberate openness of his conceptual apparatus, inviting constructive developments, which are a constitutive part of his perspective (cf. Bell, 1973:xxv; Brick, 1986). The theoretical construct of Bell's post-industrial society is not a theoretical approach opposed to capitalism or a reference to a form of society that follows capitalism.

Post-industrial attributes

One of the particular merits of his theory is, in my view, that he tries to engage with classical sociological discourse and its designs, on the one hand, and that he attempts to contrast quite explicitly, on the other hand, the period in history transformed and dominated by industrial society with that which appears to emerge, as the result of its peculiar modern economic dynamic, from its womb. At the same time, Bell's theory of post-industrial society is one of the most enduring as well as controversial theoretical designs and, at least in that important sense, successful theories of contemporary society.[26] Within the framework of his theory of post-industrial society, Daniel Bell (1976:47) sketches an opposite conception. For Bell, post-industrial society is future-oriented (planning, predicting), pre-industrial society is past-oriented, and industrial society is present-oriented.

The theory of post-industrial society[27] recognizes a particular central principle, viewed as a kind of dominant logic, which allows the observer to impose a specific conceptual order on vast societal developments of modern (Western) society. Bell describes his theory following the classification Aron advocated as concerned primarily with changes in the social framework of "society", that is, its *social structure* which analytically along with the *polity* and *culture* comprises society. The social structure of a society refers, more specifically, to its "economy, technology and the occupational system" (Bell, 1973:12), and the structure of social roles. Bell's theory of post-industrial society does grant a "central" role to "its political institutions, political processes, political rulers, or political values" (Huntington, 1974:164). It would follow that post-industrial society is not much of a political society. The kind of changes in the social structure Bell attempts to chart primarily are those induced by the "axial principle" of his theory of society, namely "the centrality of theoretical knowledge [that is, basic science] as the source of innovation and of policy formulation for the society" (Bell, 1973:14). Why theoretical knowledge, perhaps apart from the evolution of scientific knowledge in the course of the history of science, has moved to the center of society remains an open question, unless the precursors of theoretical knowledge as an exogenous motor of innovation have simply exhausted themselves.

The active moral core within each social order appears to be economizing. For all its scientific and technological sophistication, a post-industrial society lacks a higher moral purpose or transcendent ethos. For Daniel Bell (1979:164), the axial principle is likened to "director of social change" in and for post-industrial society. However, he does not claim, and in that sense the axial principle lacks deterministic centrality, that the changing social structure invariably produces corresponding transformations in the polity or the culture of society. But this cautionary methodological principle does not deter Bell from advancing a number of intriguing general assertions or projections about the nature of social life in post-industrial society.

For example,

> if the struggle between capitalist and worker, in the locus of the factory, was the hallmark of industrial society; the clash between the professional and the populace, in the organization and in the community, is the hallmark of conflict in post-industrial society.
>
> (Bell, 1972:167)

If I correctly interpret these remarks, the social scientist's well-established trend toward greater individualism in modern society[28] will be replaced, in post-industrial society, by a greater degree of communalism; that is, the dominant reference point for decisions are social units rather than individual actors. Public choice rather than individual demands become the mechanism for the allocation of goods (cf. Bell, 1972:166–167).[29] Nonetheless, Bell repeatedly endorses the virtues of what might be called theoretical ambivalence, of conditional conclusions and an explicit rejection of promises to be able to locate the master key to (an explanation of) social transitions in all sectors of modern society.[30]

However, these cautionary appeals that I believe are fully justified still introduce a peculiar tension into his analysis of the centrality of "theoretical knowledge" as the determining property of changing social structures in modern society. This is because one is confronted, on the one hand, with what is a much less rigorous, logically tight, and demanding form of "knowledge" about what, on the other hand, is represented as a rather concise, even scientistic exemplar of "theoretical knowledge" and its productive and almost surgical-like impact on social structural processes.

Compared to the theory of modern society as industrial or post-industrial society, we encounter a less widely discussed but much more diffuse concept, in the idea of late capitalism. Late capitalism presumably overlaps in parts of its development with post-industrial social relations. The origins of the idea of late capitalism can be traced to the work of Werner Sombart. Writing in the late years of the Weimar republic, it is part of his multi-volume discussion of modern capitalism. Sombart's primary interest in the development of the late capitalist economic system was the economic transformation of capitalism, while critical theory in the post-war period also employed the term "late capitalism" but mainly inquired about the political transformation of society in the face of changes in its economic system.

Late capitalism

The concept or even theory of society of late capitalism (*Spätkapitalismus*) we definitely inherit as we did the concept of *capitalism* from Werner Sombart. The term "late capitalism" did not originate alongside the post-war discussion of the theory of industrial or post-industrial society. Instead, Sombart's idea of late capitalism was first published 1927 in the third volume of his *Der Moderne Kapitalismus*. Sombart proposes a three-stage model of the development of capitalism. The third stage belongs to late capitalism. Capitalism presumably has reached that state as the last volume of *Modern Capitalism* appeared. The previous stages, pre-capitalist (feudal agriculture which lasted from the 13th to the middle of the 18th century) and full capitalist (which closed with the outbreak of World War I) although transformed would persist in late capitalism.[31] The period of late capitalism can best be described according to Sombart (1930:206–207) by referring to the changes of capitalism during its last decades. On the affirmative side, capitalism (industrialism) is spreading across the globe.

But in close affinity to the economic problems of the day, Sombart anticipate trends already visible in capitalism to persist during the epoch of late capitalism: a slowing of the pace technological inventions, slower productivity growth, mixed private-public undertakings, decline in motivational forces (all the entrepreneurial spirits—daring decision, intuitive judgments, instinctive grasp of the situation diminish), non-capitalist endeavors increase, lower international trade, concentration, oscillations of the economy increase, expansion and contraction of economic activity as a major driving force, more and more planning (the entrepreneur is gradually replaced by the authority of the state). "The entrepreneur is more and more disposed to build his business upon the foundation of systematized knowledge" (Sombart, 1930:207). The majority of Sombart's prognoses of the third phase of capitalism—as a declining system of capitalism—did not materialize.

The discussion of late capitalism was reborn after the war, at least among German sociologists, and revolves around the question what is the more appropriate term: industrial society or late capitalism? At the instigation of Theodor Adorno, the dichotomy was chosen as the theme of an annual meeting of the German Sociological Association in 1968. Presumably it was supposed to be at the center of inaugural lecture delivered by Theodor Adorno (1969 [2021]). The term "late capitalism" does appear in his lecture but once; the lecture does little to explicate the term. Adorno repeats Raymond Aron's perspective that industrial societies are defined by the regime of their forces of production—an observation that is still valid. The relations of production, on the other hand, determine capitalism as capitalism independent of the technical production regime: power over individuals continues to be exercised based of the social organization of the economy. But is not merely ownership of the forces of production that count in contemporary society. In addition, the administrative apparatus including the state regulation determine the nature of capitalism. The relations of production rule over the forces of production; "the relations of production have turned out to be less rigid than Marx had expected" (Adorno, 2021:233) And, as Adorno therefore stresses in 1972, the "capitalist system has been resilient enough to postpone the anticipated collapse indefinitely."

In 1973, a more comprehensive effort is made by Jürgen Habermas ([1973] 1976:33–60) to come to grips with the idea of late capitalism (also "state regulated" or "organized capitalism).[32] But Habermas' elaboration of the period of late capitalism also stressed decline, exhaustion, and the possible end of capitalism. "Liberal capitalism"—the state essentially operating as the "night watchman"—preceded the phase of late capitalism. Liberal capitalism was still characterized by a distinct public sphere before the state gained more and more influence over the relations of production. In his more recent work, Habermas does not refer to late or liberal capitalism anymore. Perhaps this is indicative of the theoretical value of the phrase "late capitalism" generally: given numerous definitions over quite a number of decades, the concept is merely the latest rehearsal of capitalism. As a matter of fact, Theodor Adorno (1969:17) is skeptical that the contemporary societal conditions permit the development of a coherent theory of society.

The surrender of agency as a characteristic of post-industrial society signals a degree of affinity with the notion of late capitalism and the role of government in its affairs.

Surrender of agency

In the post-industrial society, production and business *decisions* will be subject to or will be determined by other sectors in society. There is an element of a post-capitalist vision in Bell's theory of post-industrial society. The university has become the center of social dynamism as society remakes itself. More specifically, "the crucial decisions regarding the growth of the economy and its balance will come from government, but they will be based on the government's sponsorship of research and development, of cost-effectiveness and cost-benefit analysis." At the same time, it is important to note that decision-making, "because of the intricately linked nature of their consequences, will have an increasingly *technical character*" (Bell, 1973:344; emphasis added). The image of the centrality and independence of the role of science and technology in political decision-making, in this instance it seems, is somewhat tempered compared to the "end of ideology" debate of the Fifties and early Sixties (cf. Bell, 1960; Lipset, 1960),[33] where the idea that "political criteria decline in importance relative to more universalistic scientific criteria" (Lane, 1966:659; cf. also Vidich and Lyman, 1985:289–294) was a much more prominent expectation or projection about the state of politics in modern society.

The effort to restrict any built-in determinism is further underscored by Daniel Bell's (e.g., 1973:14) insistence that he merely refers to certain *tendencies* in social transformations which, in the end, may or may not work themselves out to their full logical potential. And as Bell (1987:1), obviously in a deliberately ambivalent fashion, has stressed, the three "levels of analysis" are not assumed to be "strongly linked, for society is not a 'system' wherein a set of changes in one sector has determinate consequences in all others. Yet they are interdependent in strong or loose fashion." We are expressly cautioned that

> there is no specific determinism between a "base" and a "superstructure"; on the contrary, the initiative in organizing a society these days comes largely from the political system. Just as various industrial societies—the United States, Great Britain, Nazi Germany, the Soviet Union, post-World-War II Japan—have distinctly different political and cultural configurations.
> (Bell, 1973:119)

And in that sense, Bell's conceptual scheme certainly constitutes a more open and flexible view of society than most competing contemporary theories of society, including neo-Marxist or structural-functionalist schemes. The openness in the degree of integration among sectors of society allows for a theoretical focus on incompatible, even contradictory, conflictual and divergent developments among these spheres of society. One of Bell's (1973:114), major theoretical preoccupations and contributions, then, is concerned with the tension and the "disjunction, in Western society, between the culture and the social structure, the one becoming increasingly anti-institutional and aninomian, the other oriented to functional rationality and meritocracy". This research interest culminates in the 1976 publication of Bell's analysis of *The Cultural Contradictions of Capitalism*. In the context of this study, Bell advances the argument that a *modernist, secular culture*, especially the hedonistic principles of unlimited self-fulfillment and enjoyment, increasingly contributes to the destruction of the moral prerequisites of a *rationalized society*; as a result, contradictions between the motivational principles which drive the economy and the administration of society embodied in the old values of the Protestant ethic and those of cultural activities afflict society. Capitalism loses, as Max Weber had anticipated, its original sacred legitimation.

The looseness of fit and multiple patterns of relationships among sectors of capitalist society signal the conditions for the possibility of a development of separate moral qualities or functions and therefore tensions between social and cultural modernity.[34] Bell (1973c:402), describes the distinct identities (or, different axial principles) of each social sphere and the contingent and antagonistic interrelations of spheres as follows:

> Culture embraces the areas of expressive symbolism (painting, poetry, fiction), which seek to explore these meanings in imaginative form; the codes of guidance for behavior which spell out the limits, prescriptive and prohibitive or moral conduct; and the character structures of individuals as they integrate these dimensions in their daily lives. But the themes of culture are the existential questions that face all human beings at all times in the consciousness of history--how one meets death, the nature of loyalty and obligation, the character of tragedy, the definition of heroism, the redemptiveness of love--and there is a principle of limited possibilities in the modes of response. The principle of culture is a ricorso, returning, not in its forms but in its concerns, to the same essential modalities that represent the finitude of human existence.
>
> The polity, which is the regulation of conflict under the constitutive principle of justice, involves the different forms of authority by which men seek to rule themselves: oligarchy and democracy, elite and mass, centralization and decentralization, rule and consent. The polity is *mimesis*, in which the forms are known and men choose those appropriate to their times.
>
> The social structure—the realm of the economy, technology and occupational system—is *epigenetic*. It is linear, cumulative and quantitative, for there are specific rules for the process of growth and differentiation.

The nature of the disjuncture of sectors of society, especially between social structure and culture, therefore reflects a sharp *gradient in the rationality* of activities in the sphere of social structure and culture. Such an assumption is quite common in sociological discourse and resonates quite well with many classical theories of society. However, one of the distinct "advances" of Bell's perspective is the absence of the assumption, still a central component of many classical theories, that the resolution of the disjuncture in rationalities is imminent and occurs with almost iron necessity in favor of the rationalization of those sectors of society which are still organized according to more traditional principles. Nonetheless, the remaining deficiency of this assumption constitutes one of the primary challenges posed by the theory of post-industrial society.

Post-industrial society is no longer organized around the coordination of individuals and machines for the production of commodities, but around knowledge.[35] It is a game between persons. Post-industrial society witnesses a shift from the commodity producing to the tertiary or service sector—jobs that do not involve making or harvesting things.[36] The extremely heterogeneous occupational structure of the service sector makes it sensible to divide the sector according to functions, as anthropologist David Graeber (2013: www.strike.coop.bullshit-jobs/) has suggested, for example: occupations that are genuinely useful and occupations that serve to give other people something to do (bullshit jobs)—with its rather heterogeneous occupations from the salesperson, the airline pilot, the physicians to the nuclear physicist and a corresponding decline in the preeminence of the occupations of the manufacturing sector of society. It is likely that many of the occupations nominally found in the service section actually reproduce industrial working conditions. One important contrast, therefore, is that a desirable standard of life in post-industrial society no longer is defined by the quantity of goods but by the quality of life as reflected in ready access to services and amenities such as health, education, leisure, and the arts (cf. Bell, 1972:166).

The occupational distribution shifts toward the "professional and technical class". By the end of the 20th century, this group, instead of the industrial worker, will be the largest occupational group (Bell, 1972:165). And the kind of work individuals increasingly perform requires theoretical knowledge. The chief "resource of the post-industrial society is its scientific personnel" (Bell, 1973:221). The importance of the "new class" of scientists, engineers, and professionals[37] also has the result that the normative center of society shifts toward the ethos of science (Bell, 1973:386; cf. also Whitehead, 1926; Lane, 1966; Gouldner, 1976). Daniel Bell's expectations and projections about changes in the employment sector were correct. Employment in manufacturing has declined in Western societies, and the share of the labor force working in the "service" sector now often approaches 80 percent. Within Bell's account of the structure of the post-industrial labor force, the definition of service sector employees is absent. What is perhaps more notable is the convergence of required skills and types of performance across sectors and the growth of jobs that demand but few skills.

But despite hints about a new normative centering in modern society, Bell's discussion of the possible basis for social solidarity and social integration of post-industrial society remains tentative and weak. It clearly is not among his central theoretical interests. By way of what Bell (1973:26; see also Holzner and Marx, 1979:31–32) optimistically describes as "new modes of technological forecasting", post-industrial societies may be able to plan and direct technological growth.[38]

Modern (Western) society creates for its benefit a new kind of "intellectual technology" in order to cope with the organized complexity of modern society, its varied forms of interdependence, and multiplication of interaction. Such an intellectual technology represents a response to this challenge, specifically, an attempt to replace intuitive judgments with algorithms (as problem-solving devices) (Bell, 1973:29). And, to the extent to which such a technology becomes "predominant in the management of organizations and enterprises, one can say that it is as central a feature of postindustrial society as machine technology is in industrial society" (Bell, 1979:167). In other words, the centrality of theoretical knowledge at least has a dual function. It is both the source of innovation and a foundation for policy formation in society. The extent to which and how intellectual technologies in the form of planning, for example, may also form the condition for the possibility of social solidarity and integration, however, is largely left aside by Bell as a topic of explicit consideration.[39] The significance of any "intellectual technology" is made all that more important in post-industrial society because Bell (1968:239) still anticipates, in addition to a general increase in the size of government, that we should expect the "increasing substitution of political for market decisions".

The axial structures of the emerging society are the university, research organizations, or institutions in which intellectuals work, and where "theoretical knowledge is codified and enriched" (Bell, 1973:26). Despite many persisting political and cultural differences among post-industrial societies, a common core of problems related largely to the management of the relations between science and public policy emerges in all of these societies (Bell, 1973:119; also, Dahrendorf, 1977:79–82).

Among the deficiencies and shortcomings of Bell's theory of post-industrial society is—aside from the mistaken assumption about the virtual disappearance of the economic importance of the industrial sector—the in-places tautological character of his line of reasoning, for example, the emphasis of the dominance of the service sector of the economy, which is both a definition of the post-industrial society and a forecast of its advent. Bell's theory has not surprisingly a distinctively American bias. But as Daniel Bell (1973:x) stresses, the post-industrial society involves

> primarily a change in the social structure, and its consequences will vary in societies with different political and cultural configurations. Yet as a social form it will be a major feature of the twenty-first century, in the social structures of the United States, Japan, the Soviet Union and Western Europe. The concept of the post-industrial society is on the level of abstraction. I take the United States as my singular unit of illustration, not only because it is the one, I know best, but because the processes of change are more advanced and visible here. It also allows me to deal with the particular, and gain the advantages of immediacy and recognition while retaining the context of sociological generalization.

The service sector in Bell's analysis clearly plays a central role but remains virtually unexplored in all its detail and heterogeneity, for example, in the extent to which high-productivity business services are inseparable from manufacturing (cf. Solow, 1987). The emphasis in Bell is in the anticipated *growth* of occupations in research, science, and technology. What is missing is an analysis of the social relations and interactions among members of the newly dominating grouping of occupations (cf. Coser, 1975:218) or the emerging set of skills that characterize service-centered work. The occupations Bell identified may well be a grouping-in-itself but apparently not for-itself.

A major critique of Bell's analysis of the emergence of post-industrial societies is therefore, aside from his misjudgment about the persistent importance of the value added by manufacturing sector for the economy,[40] the absence of a robust answer to the question of why the societal transition he describes is happening at all. His answers rests on mainly morphological reasoning: the

FIGURE 1.1

Source: Bureau of Economic Analysis

growth of the number of professional, technical, and kindred workers and their indispensability.

As I will explore in detail, Peter Drucker's unconventional analysis of the post-war growth of a more and more highly educated labor force that stresses *prior* political processes and demographic changes allows for the inference that the evolution of the post-industrial society is driven not by changes in the economic system but the evolution of the attributes of the supply of labor. A similar ambiguity if not contradiction may be observed with respect to Bell's analysis of the role of the political system and of corporations. Considerable power is attributed to corporations (Bell, 1973:270) only to expect that corporations will find themselves subordinated to politics and the community at large, for example, in the form of exercising social responsibility (cf. Tilton and Bell, 1973). Yet, the analysis of the politics of post-industrial society except for the politics of big science is a weak part of his theoretical perspective.

Although knowledge is an anthropological constant, as I will examine in much greater detail in the following chapter, the recognition within economic discourse that knowledge becomes in addition to the conventional forces of production, capital, land, and labor an additional, central, and novel force of production can within neo-classical economic discourse be traced to the work of Robert Solow in the 1950s. Solow posited a connection between knowledge and economic growth. Portions of economic growth in the United States (the residual) in the early 20th century that were not due to the deployment of labor or capital are ascribed by Solow to "technical change". Technical change broadly speaking were inputs that can be attributed to knowledge. Claiming that knowledge becomes a core force of production implies of course that such a shift has implication well beyond the economy. It follows that we are justified to inquire into modern societies as knowledge societies.

Transition to knowledge societies

What can we know and what do we know about knowledge societies? How will knowledge societies develop? The choice of the term *transition* to knowledge societies recognizes, as I have tried to explain, that the emergence of knowledge societies is not a revolutionary but an ongoing development in which the core attributes (in the plural) of society—for example, the economy—are changing and the gradual identity of a new society emerges more fully.

My basis assertion is that the *transition* to and the *prospects* of knowledge societies does not follow a *rigid* evolutionary path, for example, in the sense that modern societies as knowledge societies follow and follow only on a path from post-industrial or postmodern societies to knowledge societies. As far as I can see, the transition of modern societies into knowledge societies follows multiple patterns of transition. Always keeping in mind that the transition to knowledge societies does not take place abruptly nor does it involve the radical abolition of cultural and structural attributes of those societal formations it replaces, the common denominator among all these potentials (prospective) short-term and long-run societal paths is six-fold:

(1) It is a transition that completes the *reversal of the dominance* of the relations over the forces of production. The relations of production are the dominant field of activity including in the interaction of society with nature. The driving force of economic relations is symbolic capital (not only in the industrial one but in all sectors of the economy) and internationally mobile high-skilled workers. The system of knowledge acquires, in other words, a degree of autonomy from the structures of society.

(2) It represents an *extension of the motive structure* of social action from what often is described as a singular, homogeneous motive structure of a societal formation, for example, the profit motive or a supernatural purpose of life, to a multiplicity of motives that stand in competition with each other or even in harmony but are nevertheless distinct and can be identified as part of bouquet of motives among collectivities and individuals who pursue different motives under changed circumstances. The needs of individuals and their aspirations for a good life are not given and objective and homogeneous. The needs and avenues toward a good life vary considerably. Diversity is enabling.

(3) *Multiple forms of knowledge* are recognized as legitimate, as action-informing. The knowledge society is not the outcome of a shift in the structure of the scientific community. The multiplicity of knowledge claims that are invoked amount to a disenchantment in some sectors of society with scientific and technical knowledge. The diversity of knowledge that is mobilized, for example, in everyday life, limits the power of scientific and technical knowledge.
(4) The general acceleration of the *enlargement and restrictions of the capacity to act* among collectivities, small groups, and individuals has a range of consequences for society and its social institutions: new fields of political activity, for example, knowledge politics, migration politics, politics of highly skilled workers, migration and adaptation politics, technical devices and knowledge. Of particular significance in knowledge societies is the enhancement of the self-assertion of the individual supported, for example, by the judicial system. With the expansion of the capacity to act—compared to previous social formations—the fragility of society grows. Space for resistance is self-reinforcing, promoted by democratic techniques. On the other hand, the *legal encoding* of knowledge (for example, through patents and portfolios of patens can—as they exert practical effects—be worth a fortune) massively limits the ability to act.
(5) The struggle, contest, and crisis over environmental resources resulting from the enlargement of the engagement (or, a slow disengagement) of society with nature intensifies. Compared to earlier civilizational formations, in knowledge societies, the balance of the interaction switches in "favor" of human intervention. Society becomes the dominant element of the equation nature/society. Markets will increasingly be obligated to internalize the full costs of goods and services. There will be a decoupling of economic growth from energy demand. Fossil-fuel societies will be replaced. The fossil-fueled economy with its undesirable outcomes such as climate change will be superseded in knowledge societies. The dominant energy sources will be water, wind, and sun.
(6) The legal encoding of knowledge that leads to "knowledge monopoly capitalism" signifying the critical while enhanced role that the law plays in the architecture of the modern economy: "Law has been central to. . . [dominant] economic developments—not only providing the rules for new systems of extraction and upward redistribution, but also elaborating the ideas used to rationalize them" (Britton-Purdy et al., 2021:5).

The normality of diversity

The idea of the simultaneity of the non-simultaneous has been invoked in many discussions of modernity, especially by historians but less intensively by sociologists. The neglect of engaging with the issue constitutes a deficit in the sociological analysis of the nature and the history of social action and its transformation. The history of social relations, the development of ideas, and the transformation of social institutions including of course science, technology, and the economy have one attribute in common: it is their *layered* constitution.[41] More recently, the topic has been sharply criticized, voicing a preference for strict dichotomies, especially by advocates of postmodernism, social systems theory, and social anthropologists. But I would like to emphasize that the expression of the contemporaneity of the non-simultaneous is a kind of bracket that encloses my theoretical observations. For it allows me to conceive of social change both as non-synchronous and non-dichotomous, and thus as closer to the historical reality of social, economic, and cultural processes of change.

The ruling metaphors of the classical analysis of societal evolution but also political discourse of the day tend to embrace dichotomies: those who are vaccinated versus those who are not yet immunized or refuse to be vaccinated. The regression toward dichotomous and naturalized thought overreaches in asserting the "decoupling" from either side of the dichotomous divide, for example, for labor from politics, economics from culture, or nature from society. Historical processes are not automatically one-directional. In knowledge societies, as noted, the choices that can be made are significantly enlarged. Dichotomies tend to exaggerate differences and miss therefore how public and private goods, for example, often blend into each other.

The notion of ambiguity and the tolerance for ambiguous concepts, in practical terms, assist in avoiding confrontation, struggle, and crisis. Ambiguity is often built into salient concepts of everyday life, representing the essentially contested nature of the terms of everyday discourse, for example, responsibility, love, or incentives, and allow for smoother social interaction by operating as a kind of "oil" facilitating interaction in absence of "splendid" consensus. A simple concept of difference, in contrast, provokes and encourages polarization and divisions that conveniently hide communalities and convergencies as well as intermediate tones and shades of grey, for example, of cultural identities or ethnic groups. Instead, other more appropriate words and ideas come to mind: merging, transcending, cohabitation, ambivalence, coexistence, compartmentalization, non-synchronous, blending, absorption, contradiction, contemporality, and concomitance.

The twin-term of the simultaneity of the non-simultaneous expresses a fundamental feature of all social phenomena, the layered character of social phenomena putting in a compressed appearance at any given time in their existence. Our theoretical and methodological approaches should be cognizant of this layered character of social history as well as the relations that may have evolved between the layers of phenomena. The concept of simultaneity of the non-simultaneous in the analysis of the knowledge society calls for, just as Ulrich Beck ([1986] 1992:9) did for his theory of the risk society, "a delicate balancing between the contradictions of continuity and rupture within modernity".

Notes

1. The term "post-industrial" is first used, as far as I can see, by Arthur Penty as part of the title of a book published in London in 1917.
2. Theodor Adorno (1958:17) had in this respect a definite suspicion: "The irrationality of the present social structure prevents its rational development in theory."
3. This sentence cannot be found in the English rendering of Beck's ([1986] 1992) risk society.
4. Consistent with this characterization of the master concepts of sociological discourse, Jeffrey C. Alexander (1992a:179; also 1990b:11) underlines that "differentiation comes closer than any other contemporary conception to identifying the overall contours of civilizational change and the texture, immanent dangers, and real promises of modern life." However important the notion of differentiation may in fact be, it really cannot be severed from its cognitive twin, namely rationalization. And, differentiation theory, is seems, does not provide the theorist with any practical or predictive frame to forecast the course of societal development, for example, in the case of state socialist societies (see Alexander, 1990:13).
5. For a discussion of the traditional centrality of the nation-state and its sovereignty within political theory, especially theories and critiques of liberal democracy, see Held, 1991.
6. However, for a number of anthropologists, historians and archeologists' intra-societal frames are generally inadequate points of reference; as a result, their research and theorizing push the concept of a world-system back several thousand years (cf. Friedman, 1992:335–372).
7. Max Weber ([1920] 1978:571), describes the consequence of the differentiation and the gain in autonomy of different spheres of social action as the "construction of the specific nature of each special sphere existing in this world."
8. Cf. the general critique of the variety of theories of functional differentiation in Joas (1992:326–336), where he also formulates an alternative theory to functional differentiation that omits reference to transhistorical trends of social development and stresses instead the intentionality of social action, particularly the need to trace action, in order to make it comprehensible, to the intentionalities of specific actors.
9. My translation.
10. My translation.
11. As Weber ([1920] 1948:357) explains in more detail,

    > this devaluation results from the conflict between the rational realm and reality, between the rational ethic and the partly rational, and partly irrational values. With every construction of the specific nature of each special sphere existing in the world, this conflict has seemed to come to the fore ever more sharply and more insolubly . . . not only theoretical thought, disenchanting the world, led to this course, but also the very attempt of religious ethics practically and ethically to rationalize the world.

12. Max Weber's views about the vital omnipotence of modern science, quite similar to but better known than Scheler's, can be found in the "Zwischenbetrachtung" in his *Gesammelte Aufsätze zur Religionssoziologie* (Weber, [1920] 1978:564).
13. Perhaps but marginal voices in social science suspect that it is precisely the societal power of science as well as the relative autonomy of science and education that entices social scientists as well as ordinary citizens to embrace the idea that we are living in modern societies that are knowledge societies. Such a conception, the idea that knowledge and not power and capital commands amount to a widespread illusion among intellectuals about themselves and about their role in society (cf. Streckeisen, 2009).

14. The enlargement of the scope of the economists' interest of the Chicago School is exemplified by Richard Posner's (1977:3; my emphasis) definition of economics:

    > Economics, *the science of human choice* in a world in which resources are limited in relation to human wants, explores and tests the implications of the assumption that man is a rational maximizer of his ends in life, his satisfactions—what we shall call his "self-interest".

    Economics as a science of human (rational) decision behavior thus becomes the fundamental social science and coterminous with all of social science.
15. At the beginning of the 21st century, the majority of people are living in cities. Urbanization in its relation to economic development and knowledge creation follows fairly uniform processes across the world (cf. Bettencourt et al., 2007).
16. The trick is, as in advertising, how to gain and maintain attention.
17. Ulrich Beck and Martin Mulsow (2014:18–19) distinguish between "basic principles" and "basic institutions" that we may observe in processes of social change. Basic principles, i.e., cognitive-normative problems, change more slowly in the course of the social expansion of social action than institutions, for example the family, whose task it is to work through the problems. The discontinuity of social formations we owe to the changing institutions including a so-called *Nachmoderne* (not identical with postmodernism). The problems societies face represents the continuity, and the institutional adaptations the discontinuity of process of the extension of social action.
18. The same, implicit point of reference is evident from Jeffrey Alexander's (1992:187) description of what recommends Parsons' analytical apparatus more highly than Durkheim's theoretical treatment of modern society and what therefore constitutes theoretical progress in social science discourse:

    > Parsons is able to provide a much more intuitively compelling reconstruction of the modern world than Durkheim was able to provide himself. He can succeed in demonstrating what Durkheim merely suggested, namely, the extraordinary distance that has been traveled from band societies to the societies of the present day. In doing so, Parsons succeeds in legitimating the meaningful foundations of modern life.

19. The role and possible responsibility of Keynesian economic policy in the unprecedented economic expansion until the middle of the 1970s is discussed in Stehr, 1992.
20. A strong programmatic position in this respect may be found in Aron's (1967:164–165) observations about the displacement of "ideological" positions by scientific reasoning:

    > Beyond a certain stage in its development industrial society itself seems to me to widen the range of problems referable to scientific examination and calling for the skill of the social engineer. Even forms of ownership and methods of regulation, which were the subject of doctrinal or ideological controversies during the past century seem to . . . belong to the realm of technology.

21. The 1969 edition of the *Philosophische Wörterbuch* (see also Rose, 1971), published in the *German Democratic Republic*, refers, in the context of its entry "industrial society", explicitly to this difference and observes that the concept of industrial society is

    > a central notion of contemporary *bourgeoisie philosophy and sociology* and which is employed instead of the class-based concept of capitalist and socialist society as defined Marxism-Leninism. . . . The concept of industrial society is a notion of society void of its *social content*. It lacks reference to any of the essential social differences between capitalism and socialism and treats the decisive socio-structural issues of the societal formations of our age as a merely technical-organization problem.
    >
    > (Heyden, 1969: 520)

Since the theory of industrial society emphasizes, moreover, certain similarities in these societal formations, the author feels, convinced that socialism is the correct doctrine, literally put down (*diffamiert*), by the theory of industrial society. At most, the author of this entry concludes, "the concept of industrial society . . . is without scientific merit and does not lead to insights of any value but performs a purely apologetic function" (Hayden, 1969:520).

22. As far as the historical origin of the idea of the post-industrial society is concerned, Daniel Bell (1973:36) reports that many of his ideas that crystallized into his study of *The Coming of Post-Industrial Society* had their origin in a series of lectures at the Salzburg seminar in Austria in the summer of 1959. Other notable theories of the post-industrial society or "advanced industrial society" stem from Alain Touraine ([1969] 1971) and Norman Birnbaum's (1971) discussion of "late capitalism".
23. Daniel Bell is responsible for the contemporary meaning of the term post-industrial society and the prominence on the agenda of social science discourse of discussions about the possible demise of industrial society, but he did not coin the term. Bell began using the term, first in oral publication only, in 1959 (cf. also Bell, 1973:36–40). The concept may be found in earlier writings of social scientists, for example, in David Riesman's ([1958] 1964) analysis of leisure patterns in modern society and, much earlier, as Bell (1973:37n) also notes, in a now-forgotten work of Arthur Penty (e.g., 1917), who was concerned about the negative effects of industrialism in his book *Old World for New: A Study of the Post-Industrial State*. Similar considerations, in a way, affected Riesman's observations, since his concern with the increasing importance of leisure time in modern society was predicated on the belief that technological progress in the form of automating production would make work even less meaningful and challenging; hence, workers would try to seek and realize the meaning of life increasingly outside of work in leisure activities.
24. Bernals Ansichten und die seiner Kollegen nicht nur in England veranlassten Friedrich Hayek, mit seinem Traktat *The Road to Serfdom* als Anklage gegen die Tugend der Sozialplanung in die Diskussion zu einzutreten (vgl. Caldwell, 2020).
25. The collapse of state socialism is not, however, the result of a transformation of their economies by science and technology and therefore a consequence of a growing contradiction between economy, culture, and politics but is, contrary to the at least implicit expectations by Bell and Richta, the outcome of a vastly insufficient transformation of the productive systems in these states by modern science and technology. But the historical changes in Eastern Europe are not the reason for or the subject of this chapter.
26. Ezra Vogel (1980:9), as well as Feigenbaum and McCorduck (1983:22), refer for example to the tremendous reception and interest Bell's theory of post-industrial society found among Japanese engineers and intellectuals in the mid-Seventies. In addition, at this time, Bell's theory was quite influential in shaping Japanese science and technology policies.
27. This is an idea which from an epistemological point of view, as Bell (e.g., 1973:14) at times stresses, constitutes and acquires meaning as a *conceptual scheme* (or possibly as an ideal type), *only*. I am not sure what intentions Bell precisely attempts to pursue on the basis of what he obviously considers a restrictive principle, or what kind of criticism he may care to preempt by invoking the notion of an ideal type. Anyhow, the theorizing he in fact pursues has few formal resemblances to Weber's methodological notions.
28. It is a common assumption in social science theory that the ascent of "individualism" is a modern phenomenon, that individualization represents the highpoint of an evolutionary development and most certainly not a return to archaic social conditions. As Ulrich Beck (1986:123–124), for example, emphasizes "the interaction of a whole series of components results in the *individualization thrust* that detaches people from

traditional class ties and—for the sake of their material survival—makes them actors in their own labor market-mediated life course" (my emphasis; translated from the German edition). Some social anthropologists who have studied hunter-gatherer societies throughout the world are, persuaded based on their field studies that so-called "demand sharing societies" were highly individualistic, egalitarian and lacked coercive authority structures (Suzman, 2020:156–157). These conclusions are contested observations (cf. Buckner, 2017).

29. And as Daniel Bell (1973:481), stresses elsewhere,

> the political ethos of an emerging post-industrial society is communal. . . . It is sociologizing rather than economic . . . as the criteria of individual utility and profit maximization become subordinated to broader conceptions of social welfare and community interest.

30. In the context of his summary of Radovan Richta's conception of a scientific-technological revolution, Daniel Bell (1973:112) endorses an epistemological retreat from theory

> if by theory one means a model of social structure that specifies the determinate interaction of the crucial variables of a system, establishes empirical regularities that predict future states of relation, and provides an explanatory principle of its history and operation.

31. Werner Sombart's (1930:195–208) dating and definition of each of the three periods in his model of capitalism is most concise and informative in his entry "Capitalism" in the first edition of the *Encyclopedia of the Social Sciences*.
32. The English translation employs "advanced" rather than "late" capitalism; a considerable difference in the meaning the two terms, as far as I can see, tend to transport.
33. In a footnote in the post-industrial monograph, Bell (1973:34) corrects himself and suggests that a better title of the *End of Ideology* book should have been "The Waning of Utopia", which resonates with Lyotard's ([1979] 1984) report on the postmodern condition.
34. An affirmative stance toward the forces which sustain the social modernity of society and a denigration of the sources of cultural modernity characterize, according to Habermas ([1980] 1981:7–8, 1983b:78), all neoconservative diagnoses of contemporary society.
35. Of course, Daniel Bell (1976:48) recognizes that knowledge is an anthropological constant and social existence in human societies has always been dependent on knowledge. What assures that the function of knowledge in post-industrial societies is unique is due to the "accumulation and distribution of theoretical knowledge" which thereby "has come to the fore as a directive force of innovation and change".
36. Die äußerst heterogene Berufsstruktur des Dienstleistungssektor macht es sinnvoll, den Sektor nach Funktionen zu teilen, wie dies der Anthropologie David Graeber (2013: www.strike.coop.bullshit-jobs/) etwa vorgeschlagen hat: Berufe, die genuin nützlich sind und Berufe, die dazu dienen, anderen Personen etwas zu tun zu geben (*bullshit jobs*).
37. Radovan Richta's (1977:54) response to this kind of analysis is to argue that Bell's contentions about the rise of a "new class" is in essence designed to contend "with the Marxist findings concerning the crucial role of the working class in our epoch". Moreover, as the size of the scientific and technical class increases under capitalism, it will, in some ways at least, move closer to the working class and its interests and hence contribute to conditions that may lead to its own abolition. In short, the conditions of the scientific and technological revolution have not, at least according to Richta (1977:57–59), diminished the leading role of the working class.

38. Radovan Richta (1977:26) anticipates, perhaps even more optimistically than Daniel Bell, "a science-based control of social development, a science-based revolutionary reconstruction of society".
39. Fred Block and Larry Hirschhorn (1979:391) criticize Daniel Bell that he "examines these technologies of production and decision-making in a narrow frame—without asking how they reorganize people's experiences and commitments to work".
40. As the graphic next of the Federal Reserve Bank of St. Louis indicates, manufacturing's "share of real GDP [in the USA] has been fairly constant since the 1940s, ranging from 11.3 percent to 13.6 percent. It sat at 11.7 percent in 2015." It is possible that observers who have pointed to a decline in the economic significance of the manufacturing sector in recent decades have mistaken the nominal decline in the manufacturing's share of the GDP for decline of its contribution to the real GDP. The decline in manufacturing's share of nominal GDP is due to changes in prices and not due to a reduced role in the economy. Prices in manufacturing have grown at a slower pace than in the overall economy (see www.stlouisfed.org/on-the-economy/2017/april/us-manufacturing-really-declining). A further complication arises if one decomposes and/or rearranges the definition of the manufacturing sector; cf. Kakaomerlioglu and Carlsson (1999).
41. I owe the term "layered" as an essential element of social phenomena to Luk van Langenhove; it is another or, perhaps better, way of expressing the simultaneity of the non-simultaneous of social relations. Social facts always consist of layers from different eras.

2

KNOWLEDGE ABOUT KNOWLEDGE[1]

To talk about knowledge is to talk about people.

—Barry Barnes, 1988:179

My chapter on knowledge about knowledge in knowledge capitalism has a strong bias toward a sociological view of knowledge: knowledge as a social relation. We are dependent on other humans to gain knowledge. And there is a strong preference for the questions of the plural uses of knowledge. The issue of what constitutes human knowledge moves into the center of my inquiry. My response will be that knowledge in the broadest sense of the term is a *capacity to act* (capable of use)[2] rather than an object (or a subjective insight of our mind). Knowledge is a people's resource; and this applies whether the knowledge in question is a sophisticated mathematical theorem or the competence to prepare a tasty meal. However, moving knowledge into the center of my inquiry does not mean to foreground and to urgently ask the typical and in an era of post-truth undeniably important philosophical question "is knowledge true?", or what are, in general, the conditions for the possibility of knowledge, and, more specifically, for knowledge as justified true belief. The same reservation, in this context, applies to the so-called "production perspective" of knowledge, a perspective that continues to play a preeminent role in the social studies of science as well as in the multiple modalities of conflicts in which knowledge is the object of dispute.

As a matter of fact, such an analysis takes a back seat in the context at hand.[3] Any curiosity about the epistemological status of knowledge, how should we justify knowledge claims, is at best a secondary matter for my inquiry as are questions about the sources and the construction of knowledge. Or, as Foucault would have it, to make experiences such as madness, death, and crime into objects

DOI: 10.4324/9781003296157-2

of knowledge (*connaissance*). More significant for my purposes is the question, posed from various angles, what exactly is the importance of knowledge in social relations, how does its weight manifest itself, and how does knowledge—since there are other modes of discourse—differ most importantly from information? Is the content of a telephone directory knowledge or information? Observing the importance of knowledge in social relations implies also to look for the limits of its influence. For example, can one with justification speak of global knowledge, what ignorance is, how powerful knowledge really is, or is non-knowledge the Siamese twin of knowledge?

Knowing

Being human is knowledge.[4] Knowledge is being with others. Knowledge is ultimately connected to living entities. The philosophical, epistemological (science of science), or social aspect of the status of knowledge is important. But knowledge is more, much more. Knowledge about knowledge is a key to understanding humanity—hence my strong objection to Edward Shils' assertion (1982:7) that knowledge first immediately and necessarily raises the question of the validity and truthfulness of knowledge.[5] Knowledge is also much more comprehensive than the "recorded stock" (of knowledge), as Niklas Luhmann (1990:122) surmises. Science and technology are not identical with the human budget of knowledge (cf. Machlup, 1962:23).

In any case, knowledge is, to use a term coined by Marcel Mauss ([1925] 1990:3), a *total social fact*. Knowledge is more than the individual mental state. Knowledge is a social relation and hence embedded in individuals *and* society; that is, expressing knowledge as a total social fact brings into view the whole of society and its multiple social institutions. Knowledge as a total social fact accounts for example for its relative stability of knowledge compared to individual opinions. Societal knowledge accumulates over time, can be *transmitted* over generations, and easily exceeds the knowledge any individual can fit into his mind, learn, or generate over her lifetime. The definition of knowledge as a total social fact enables us to "better understand how knowledge becomes communicable, sharable, and, in some way, a common possession, not simply a personal state or belief. Doing so can also alert us to the ways in which knowledge is regulated, guarded, and controlled" (Wellmon, 2021:145). In other words, it is evident, especially within the context of arriving at a theory of modern society as a knowledge society, that it is worth knowing about what is known about knowledge.

Discourse of knowledge about knowledge moves knowledge beyond the fallacy of bifurcated terms of knowledge, for example, local and global knowledge, traditional/indigenous and modern knowledge, to the forefront with their explicit or implicit normative baggage (in terms of empathy and inferiority). Local knowledge is invariantly inferior to global knowledge (master vs. servant).

Indigenous knowledge is always backward/native when compared to contemporary knowledge (for a critical-constructive perspective of indigenous knowledge, see Sillitoe, 1998; Fletcher et al., 2021). As a discussion of the contemporaneity (simultaneity) of the non-contemporaneous (non-simultaneous) shows, convergences, mutual influences, and the like among knowledges, less so than binary separations, are a more realistic description of knowledge-in-action. The alleged divide between those who can access knowledge and those who cannot simply fails to recognize what I have indicated is human, namely to have knowledge.

Francis Bacon's motto *tantum possumus, quantum scimus* with its strong affinity to Bacon's better-known and famous motto, *scientia potentia est*, which is often wrongly translated as *knowledge is power*, reminds us for example of the important question whether our power is proportional to our knowledge. My discussion of knowledge as a sociological concept addresses precisely this general question of our knowledge about knowledge, as well as a variety of other attributes of our present-day knowledge about knowledge. Human society is knowledge-driven. Knowledge is a constitutive attribute of society. But such an elementary statement requires a fundamental understanding of the nature of knowledge and how it, if at all, gains or loses influence in society and is a guiding principle and resource for action (intellectual assets).

Toward a sociological concept of knowledge

> Humans in general are more interested to accomplish something rather than to know how it is done and achieving the former usually preceded insights about the latter.
>
> —Georg Simmel ([1890] 1989:115)

Knowledge does not exist, perhaps not even as a *Gedankenexperiment*, as an isolated "piece" of knowledge. Knowledge occurs in an aggregated collective condition.[6] It is not a flower in a bunch of flowers; it is the bunch of flowers and hence a *bundle of knowledge* or part of a system of statements, however small that bundle or system of statements may be in specific instances. This implies as well that knowledge is not an individual phenomenon in the sense of being an entity that carries but discrete attributes. Knowledge as an aggregated phenomenon has many authors, for example, inventors, experts who mediate between invention and use, peer-review filtering, councils, and so on.

For the purpose of some further explication of the concept of knowledge, one must distinguish between what is known, the content of knowledge, and knowing. Knowing is a relation to things and facts, but also to rules, laws, and programs. Some sort of participation is therefore constitutive for knowing: knowing things, rules, programs, facts is "appropriating" them in some sense, including them into our field of orientation and competence. The intellectual appropriation of things can be made independent or objective. That is, symbolic representation of the content of knowledge eliminates the necessity to get into direct contact with the things themselves. One is obviously able, in other words, to acquire knowledge from books (cf. also Collins, 1993). The social significance of language, writing, printing, data storage, etc. is that they represent knowledge symbolically or provide the possibility of objectified knowledge. Thus, most of what we today call knowledge and learning is not direct knowledge of facts, rules, and things, but objectified knowledge. Objectified knowledge is the highly differentiated stock of intellectually appropriated nature, and society which may also be seen to constitute the cultural resource of a society. Knowing is, then, *grosso modo* participation in the cultural resources of society. However, such participation is of course subject to stratification; life chances, lifestyle, and social influence of individuals depend on their access to the stock of knowledge at hand.

Nowadays, there is an enormous stock of objectified knowledge that mediates between humans and nature. Nature is or can hardly be experienced other than in the form of a human product or as part of human products; social relations are established with the help of a constantly growing network of administrative, legal, or technical systems. Material appropriation of nature means first of all the restructuring of nature and finally its gradual transformation into a human product. The new social structure that is imposed on it is basically objectified knowledge, or in other words, a realization of what we know: the laws of nature expanded by technology. The appropriation of society takes place in a similar way, through the process of rule production. As far as the production, distribution, and reproduction of knowledge is concerned, only a purely quantitative diagnosis can be made for contemporary society: the superstructure of society has become so immense that the majority of social actions are not production but reproduction, especially the reproduction of knowledge itself. The fact that reproduction is predominant is primarily due to the fact that a large part of scientific knowledge is at least treated as a form of "universal" knowledge.[7]

Knowledge, ideas, and information—to use quite deliberately very broad and ambivalent categories—are most peculiar entities with properties unlike those of commodities or secrets, for example. Unlike other resources (or production factors), their usage of knowledge (human capital) tends to grow (accumulate) rather than shrink. However, knowledge is not immune to ageing or depreciating. The *United Nations Economic Commission for Europe* (UNECE, 2016:37) even assumes a strict analogy of the ageing of all factors of production: "Like physical capital, human capital depreciated over time. . . [due to] the wear and tear of skills to aging." The difficulty with efforts to operationalize the assumption of an ageing knowledge is of course that the knowledge of individuals may command could actually increase over time with experience and learning relevant knowledge. The assumption of aging of knowledge is therefore arbitrary (cf. Yarrow, 2020:15).

If sold, knowledge enters other domains and yet remains within the domain of their producer/owner. From an economic perspective, knowledge is a *non-rival* good (i.e., easily shareable and not used up when used—and excluding other people from using it can be cost-intensive or even impossible, as in the case of scientific findings, published news items, or digitized music); knowledge as a non-rival asset raises of course the question, how to capture the benefits from one's discovery? In addition, and also from an economic view, the marginal cost of producing knowledge is compared to the production of physical capital small and typically relies on lower fixed cost. On the other hand, knowledge cannot simply be transferred like capital or land from generation to generation. Knowledge does not have zero-sum qualities. Knowledge is a public good. When revealed, knowledge does not lose its influence. However, knowledge as a non-rival good can be turned into a rival commodity. The development of patents for knowledge (as expression of capacities to act) and other intangible goods ensures that knowledge can be encircled. A tragedy of the knowledge commons is thereby limited if not precluded. Patenting physical goods, as an invention of the modern nation-state (North, 1981; Mokyr, 2009), results in restrictions to their use, but in comparison such limits are far less contestable than patenting knowledge. I will take up the issue of the role of encircling knowledge or of legally coding knowledge in the next chapter as one of the core issues within knowledge societies and the knowledge economy in particular.

While it has been understood for some time that the "creation" of knowledge is fraught with uncertainties, the conviction that its application is without risks and that its acquisition reduces uncertainty has only recently been debunked. While it is very reasonable and, in some sense, urgent to speak of the limits to growth in many spheres and resources of life, the same does not appear to hold for knowledge. Knowledge has virtually no limits to its growth.

Georg Simmel made the same observation, shortly after the end of World War I, although for him the lack of any real limits to the growth of knowledge (cultural products) above all signals a serious intellectual danger for individuals and society. It signals the danger of a "tragedy of culture" in which the growing cultural objectivations exceed the ability of the individual to absorb the plenitude of knowledge in any meaningful manner. Human products take on a life of their own while constraining human conduct. But as he stresses,

> everybody can contribute to the supply of objectified cultural contents without any consideration for other contributors. This supply may have a determined color during individual cultural epochs that is, from within there may be a qualitative but not likewise quantitative boundary. There is no reason why it should not be multiplied in the direction of the infinite, why not book should be added to book, work of art to work of art, or invention to invention. The form of objectivity as such possesses a boundless capacity for fulfillment.
>
> (Simmel, [1919] 1968:44)

For Simmel, the important and dangerous outcome is a broad discrepancy between the volume of cultural products and the ability of the individual to assign meaning to them.

Knowledge is often seen as a collective commodity par excellence; for example, the ethos of science demands that it is supposed to be made available to all, at least in principle (compare Merton, [1942] 1973). But is the "same" knowledge available to all? Is scientific knowledge when transformed into technology still subject to the same normative conventions?[8] What are the costs of the transmission of knowledge? Knowledge is virtually never, despite its reputation, uncontested. In science, its contestability is seen as one of its foremost virtues. In practical circumstances, the contested character of knowledge is often repressed and/or conflicts with the exigencies of social action.[9] The apparently unrestricted potential of its availability, which does not affect its meaning, makes it, in peculiar and unusual ways, resistant to private ownership (Simmel, [1907] 1978:438). Modern communication technologies ensure that access becomes easier, and may even subvert remaining proprietary restrictions, although concentration rather than dissemination is also possible and feared by some.[10] But one could just as easily surmise that the increased social importance of knowledge, and not so much its distinctiveness, may in fact undermine the exclusiveness of knowledge. Yet the opposite appears to be the case and therefore raises anew the question of the persisting basis for the power of knowledge.

Knowledge as a capacity to act

I would like to define knowledge as a *capacity for social action and as a model for reality*, as the possibility to set "something in motion",[11] for example, to solve a task or to be competent to prevent something from happening, for example, the onset of an illness[12] or how you see the world. My definition of knowledge resonates with the designation of human cognition by Arnold Gehlen. Gehlen (1940:52) emphasizes that cognition "is not there to be satisfied in theoretical acts".[13] On the contrary,

> human cognition essentially turns to the outside, it is to be defined almost as a phase of action, and we observe everywhere, on closer examination of its performance structure, that it is always the union of perceiving and acting activities that leads to a capability.[14]

However, we can also follow in the rather useful but narrower definition of knowledge (i.e., applicable to technical knowledge) of Heinrich Popitz ([1986] 2017:118), who defines the "*faculty of producing* . . . as a particular capacity, the human skill to modify intentionally the state of things. "Knowledge arises from the need to solve problems.

In this sense, knowledge is a universal human phenomenon, or an anthropological constant. Knowledge constitutes a central "cross-sectional area" of societal development. Knowledge creates, sustains, and changes existential conditions.[15] Human's endowed with knowledge have the capacity of self-transformation designing new existential settings, for example, "transforming human 'identity' from a 'given' into a 'task'" (cf. Bauman, 2001:144). "There is knowledge everywhere—and more than one can know" (Luhmann, 1990:147). That knowledge is everywhere, that is, that knowledge is system-indifferent cannot mean that all knowledge is everywhere. In all likelihood, at least that is how I would like to assume, one could already find a *division of knowledge* in the first human communities. From the elementary definition of knowledge as a capacity for action, however, it is immediately apparent that knowledge is a social phenomenon on which the characteristic of modernization described in the first chapter as extension and expansion can be exemplified in a particularly sustainable way. The growing productivity of economic processes, for example, is, as economists increasingly recognize, due to the extension or growth of knowledge.

That knowledge is a universal attribute of human society should not be mistaken to mean that the knowledge of the knowledge society, especially if understood as scientific knowledge, is universalistic in the sense that a "knowledge framework admits to no limits" (cf. Frank and Meyer, 2020:133–134). The assertion that knowledge literally imposes itself or realizes itself quite independently of any social context is a fallacy of misplaced concreteness.[16]

Scientific knowledge as a capacity to act

My definition of knowledge as a capacity to act does imply or aspire to offer a clear-cut way of differentiating between forms of knowledge, in particular, between scientific knowledge and traditional knowledge, modern science and everyday forms of knowledge, organized and unorganized knowledge and theory and practice. To recognize scientific knowledge as a particular, even as a privileged form of knowledge presents, in my case, at least a couple of difficulties.[17] Professional, popular, or craft knowledge cannot really be unambiguously separated from scientific knowledge, especially when it comes to the function such forms of knowledge are capable of performing. In such a way, at least the strength of the dichotomy is diminished. The additional issue is epistemological and is contentious from the point of view of a theory of science and the history of science (cf. Chartier, 2016); a transhistorical conception of science, for example, is doubtful. Keeping the issue of the distinction between scientific knowledge and other forms of knowledge open has the additional advantage that references to the influence of society on science and scientific knowledge are not *a priori* excluded.[18] Moreover, my definition of knowledge as a capacity to act does not imply *a priori* that the social control of knowledge is or can only be located within a specific social institution in modern society; for example, the state, as Poulantzas

(1978:61–62 as cited in Carnoy and Castells, 2001:9) confidently asserts: "It is the permanent monopolization of knowledge by the . . . State, by its apparatuses and its agents, which also determines the organizational functions and the directions of the State."

From the observation that there are multiple forms of knowledge and that the designation of different forms of knowledge as knowledge is justified, one important conclusion that can be drawn is that forms of knowledge can compete. The very fact that forms of knowledge compete with each other indicates that knowledge claims are interpreted as mutually exclusive traditions and do not simply stand side by side in a neutral manner. The competition and often unequal competitive conditions of the domain of knowledge already begin in a competition of talents; i.e., efforts by states and companies to recruit particularly qualified persons.[19]

Capacities

Knowledge refers to capacities (competences, capabilities). Knowledge creates, maintains, and changes existential conditions. Knowledge allows people to mobilize material and symbolic resources.[20] The temporal dimension of knowledge is therefore future-oriented. In the practical entanglement of knowledge and action, C.P. Snow's uncritically optimistic observation from the 1950s ([1959] 1964:11), for example, is therefore undoubtedly correct that scientists "have the future in their bones". Accordingly, discovering new dynamic capabilities for action is the function of knowledge production.

The ability to set something in motion or accomplish something can very well refer to the ability to achieve something symbolic—for example, formulating a hypothesis, finding a new metaphor for an established term, assessing "facts", classifying the literature on a topic, or defending a thesis against "new facts".[21] Knowledge allows us to say something or not to articulate it. For example, social statistics are not only mirrors of social reality; they problematize social reality by showing that it could be different, by suggesting and representing the capacity to act (cf. Canguilhem, 1978; Hunter, 1996:154).[22] In other words, the ability to act does not only refer to the possibility to accomplish something in the sense of a material-physical achievement—such as making a fire, driving a car, producing steel, selling a share, or defending oneself against an attacking person. Capacity to act also refers to intellectual abilities.[23]

In 1948, Claude Shannon published a small volume entitled *The Mathematical Theory of Communication*. In it, he explained how words, sound, and images could be converted into blips and sent electronically. While Shannon's mathematical and probabilistic communication model, the *bit* as the basis unit of information, has been surpassed by ever more complex models in communication theory, it might be argued that he foretold the digital revolution in communications. Knowledge as a symbolic "system" enables one to act on the world. Based on the same general definition of knowledge, a *software program* as a protocol for organizing "information" constitutes a form of knowledge. How to capture water power, how to smelt iron and craft tools, how to increase the output of heavy soils, how to structure a state and markets (cp. Goldstone, 2006:276–279) all constitute knowledge that made up the core of the emergence of modernizing societies.

Knowledge as an ability to act can also be understood as a thought experiment (*Gedankenexperiment*), similar to what Karl Marx ([1867] 1887:127) does in *Capital* when he describes work as an intellectual experiment of action:

> We pre-suppose labour in a form that stamps it as exclusively human. A spider conducts operations that resemble this of a weaver, and a bee puts to shame many an architect in the construction of her cells. But what distinguishes the worst architect from the best of bees is this, that the architect raises his structure in imagination before he erects it in reality. At the end of every labour-process, we get a result that already existed in the imagination of the labourer as its commencement.

Consequently, the realization of an intellectual experiment of action is a historical process "in which—objectively and subjectively—qualitative changes take place" (Lukács, 1981:33).

As far as I can see, *energy*, is another essential capacity for social action, that is also defined as the "ability to make a difference" (White, 1995). In the 19th and 20th centuries, fossil fuels were among the most important resources that made new forms of economic activity in particular and social action in general possible. As a result, the social institutions and organizations that controlled the production, distribution, and use of fossil fuels (which included not least the labor movement of this historical period) were among the most important centers of power in industrial society. At the present time, what Timothy Mitchell (2009) calls "carbon democracy" is increasingly becoming a thing of the past. Carbon democracy is being replaced by knowledge-based democracy. The societal rank of knowledge is displacing that of energy as a core capacity for action.

Rights, duties, and obligations are further capacities and possibilities for action that people attribute to each other and that are realized in social relationships in order to stabilize social conditions which are based, for example, on freedom and responsibility (cf. Rosanvallon, [2011] 2013:273–274). Among the conditions for the ability to make a difference is certainly in addition *language* (Koselleck, 1989:211) and, more generally, the totality of people's (objective) material and immaterial conditions of action.

Power is a capacity for action. In many definitions of power, for example, in the seminal definition of power advanced by Max Weber, as the chance that an individual in a social relationship can achieve his or her own will even against the resistance of others, power is however seen as the *ability to gain compliance* (see Barnes, 1988:180), using one among many possible means to enforce acquiescence.

And, what about *divine revelation*? Many people would insist that divine revelation represents knowledge.

Knowledge as a model for reality

Knowledge as an ability to act is a model *for reality*. Knowledge illuminates. Knowledge is emergence.[24] But knowledge is not only passive knowledge. Knowledge causes things to happen, also not necessarily on its own, as I will show, and enables making things. Knowledge as a first step to action is capable not only of changing reality,[25] but also of defending and maintaining it or organizing and legitimizing resistance to certain realities. Protecting knowledge from others is much more difficult than restricting their access to capital assets or weapons, for example (see Elias, 1984:252–253). I understand knowledge as a powerful "weapon" of weak social groups and movements that enables them to organize and mobilize counterforces against existing or planned social controls by large social institutions such as the state, companies, science, parties, etc. (see Stehr, 2014). Knowledge as *know-how* (see Zeleny, 1987; Ackoff, 1989; as implicit memory, non-declarative knowing, tacit knowledge (which is non-codified or non-codifiable) or the "unconscious", depending on the disciplinary respective)[26] as the ability to make a difference enriches human ability in many ways. Knowledge, but of course not only knowledge, changes society.

Furthermore, from the definition of knowledge as a capacity to act, it can be concluded that the "search" for knowledge, that the "function" of knowledge is not so much determined by the effort to achieve a "transformation of the unknown into the known" (Luhmann, 1990:148). In my view, it is more essential to maintain that the search for additional knowledge is based on the desire to expand the volume of *existing possibilities for action*, for instance, in the form of countervailing powers. The work on expanding the capacity to act is not only promoted by experts, analysts, advisors, and scientists, but also in everyday life by various cognitive "tools": for example, "use of theories, models, scenarios, evaluation criteria, decision strategies, experimental designs, and implicit experience in order to establish bits and pieces of orientation and certainty" (Krohn, 2002:8139). The tools for expanding possibilities for action can be seen to operate as capacities for action.

By defining knowledge as a *capacity* for action, we suspend, even if only temporarily for the sake of theoretical reflection, the analysis of the relationship between knowledge and social action. With this limitation in mind, we avoid attributing to knowledge an *immediate* performative efficiency (for example, in the sense of "knowledge equals or is the basis of control"),[27] privileging certain forms of knowledge, or disregarding the limits of the power of knowledge (Stehr, 1991; Martin, 2010). In other words, it remains open how knowledge is generated, whether there are different forms of knowledge, how it is socially distributed, how one or how we get from knowledge to action, and which structures may be conducive or obstructive in this process. However, as will be shown in more detail, despite the heuristic shortening of the concept of knowledge, for example by not taking into account the practices of gaining knowledge, the traditions of knowledge generated by us are related to our understanding of reality, the constitution of reality, and the modes of action that influence reality.

Knowledge is power

As I have already stated, my definition of the term "knowledge" is indebted to Francis Bacon's famous observation that *knowledge is power*,[28] a somewhat misleading translation of Bacon's Latin phrase: *scientia potentia est*. Bacon suggests that knowledge derives its utility from its capacity to set something in motion.[29] More specifically, Bacon asserts at the outset of his *Novum Organum* (I, Aph. 3) that "human knowledge and human power meet in one; for where the cause is not known the effect cannot be produced. Nature to be commanded must be obeyed; and that which in contemplation is the cause is in operation the rule."

The success of human action can be gauged from changes that have taken place in social and natural reality (Krohn, 1981, 1988:87–89), and knowledge acquires *distinction*, last but not least because of its apparent ability to transform reality. Knowledge is discovery. The added value of knowledge should be seen as a capacity to illuminate and to transform reality. Knowledge as an effective or productive model *for* reality, of course, requires knowledge *of* reality. My definition of knowledge as a capacity to act, as *enabling* knowledge, resonates with the conception of the term "know-how" by Daniel Sarewitz and Richard P. Nelson. Sarewitz and Nelson (2008:101) define know-how as knowledge, "some articulated and some tacit, that guides the actions of skilled agents who aim to achieve a particular practical objective."[30]

The theoretical conception of knowledge as a capacity to act opens up the space for the idea of (collective) *agency*, i.e., the self-determination of the actors in knowledge-determined social contexts (cf. Sen, 1985:203–204; Barth, 2002:3). The "ownership" of knowledge, and thus the power of disposal over knowledge, is usually not exclusive. But the prevailing legal doctrine demands precisely this exclusivity of the power of disposal as a primary characteristic of the institution of property. Formal law, as we know, knows owner and possessor; in particular, it knows individuals who should have but do not have. From the perspective of the legal system, property is indivisible. Nor does it matter what concrete tangible or intangible "things" are involved. The sociological significance of knowledge also lies primarily in the actual ability to have knowledge as a capacity to act. Knowledge gains distinction because of its ability to change reality.

Science is not merely, as once widely thought, the solution to the mysteries and miseries of the world; it is, rather, the becoming of a world. The idea that knowledge is a capacity for action that transforms, or even creates, reality is perhaps almost self-evident in the case of social science knowledge, but less persuasive in the case of the natural sciences. In the case of contemporary biology, however, one is prepared to acknowledge that biological knowledge extends to the fabrication of new living systems. Biology does not simply study nature. Biology transforms and produces novel natural realities. Biology and biotechnology are closely linked. As a result, (most of) the reality we confront in modern societies, and increasingly so, arises from and embodies knowledge. Thus, knowledge is not power (in the usual sense of the word), but at best it represents *potential power*. It is necessary, as a result, to distinguish between the possession of knowledge as a capacity to act and the ability to exercise or implement knowledge.

Not everybody knows everything; therefore, capacities to act are stratified, that is, not equally distributed throughout society; the social mechanisms of the distribution of knowledge therefore form a core subject matter of any sociological analysis of knowledge (cf. Schütz, 1964:121). But whether knowledge always flows to the powerful or if the powerful tend to be the stratum that most likely exploits the social control attributes of knowledge should not be determined *a priori*, but subject to theoretical and empirical analysis (see Stehr, 2016).

The notion of knowledge as a capacity for social action has the advantage, it seems to me, that it enables one to stress not merely one-sided but multifaceted consequences of knowledge for action.[31] The term "capacity for action" signals that knowledge may be left unused[32] or may be employed for irrational ends and leaves room, therefore, for a "dialectical" theory of the use of knowledge. The definition of knowledge as a capacity for action indicates strongly that the material realization and implementation of knowledge is dependent on, or embedded within, the context of specific social and intellectual conditions. Knowledge, as a capacity for action, does not signal that specific knowledge claims always convey or carry a kind of constant and fixed "value" enabling actors to translate and employ them for the identical purposes and for closely similar outcomes. Inasmuch as the realization of knowledge is dependent on the active elaboration of knowledge[33] as a capacity for action within specific social conditions, a first link between knowledge and social power becomes evident because the control of the relevant conditions requires social power; for example, the social conditions that allow for the transformation of knowledge into commercially valuable economic goods and services. The larger the scale of the transformative project, for example, the larger the need for social power in order to ensure control over conditions for the realization of knowledge as capacity for action (see also Radder, 1986).

Knowledge that matters

It is important to realize that knowledge, as an element of power relations, generates not merely coercive, distorting, and repressive consequences, as many traditional conceptions of power would imply, but has productive and enabling features as well. And a more developed theoretical notion of power requires the ability to incorporate both attributes of knowledge as a capacity for action. The use of a more differentiated concept of power, conscious of the constraining and enabling features of power, becomes all the more relevant the greater the actual amorphousness of power and the greater the malleability of social structures and conditions become for the realization of knowledge. Knowledge has many enabling features that allow individuals and groups to organize resistance, adaptation, avoidance, and generally opposition. Knowledge energizes. Such an emphasis becomes important not only because the degree and the effectiveness to which knowledge operates as a capacity for action increases but so does the dissemination and access to knowledge among strata that may have been cut off in the past. Since knowledge and access to knowledge is not evenly distributed, such a world is not a world without power and inequality.

Obviously, *scientific and technical knowledge* represent such "capacities for action" and maybe even quite a special capacity for action in modern society. However, this does not mean that scientific knowledge should be seen as a resource that lacks contestability, is not subject to interpretation, and can be reproduced at will.[34] The special importance of scientific and technical knowledge, in any modern society, derives not so much from the fact that it is at times treated as if it is essentially uncontested (or, objective), but that it constitutes, more than any other form of modern knowledge, an *incremental* capacity for social action or an *increase* in the ability of "how-to-do-it" which, moreover, may be "privately appropriated", if only temporarily. In economic settings, incremental knowledge has particular importance as a source of added value.

The strategic importance of incremental knowledge as an immediately productive force in economic contexts specifically may affect the ways in which production and the delivery of services is organized as well as the types of commodities and services that are produced. Thus, I agree with Giovanni Dosi (1984:88–89), who, in the field of industrial innovation, sums up the conditions for the possibility of technological innovation in market economies as best described and served by the dual conditions of technological opportunity *and* the private appropriability of the benefits of the innovative activities. The commitment of private firms to innovation is closely linked to their ability to temporarily appropriate the marginal additions to knowledge and therefore the economic advantages which may accrue from the control over such knowledge.

Generally, as I have noted, knowledge as a capacity for action enables one to set something into motion; at the same time, knowledge need not be perishable. In principle, a consumer or purchaser of knowledge may use it repeatedly at diminishing or even zero cost. Thus, what counts in the sense of gaining advantages in societal formations that primarily operate according to the logic of economic change (growth) and social transformation is access to and command of the *marginal additions to knowledge* and not the generally available stock of knowledge. Science and technology constantly *add* (in a non-pejorative sense) to the existing stock of knowledge and therefore the ability of individual and corporate actors to affect their circumstances of action. In this respect, that is in its ability and legitimacy to generate novel capacities of action, science is virtually without a competitor in modern society. Nonetheless, knowledge as a capacity for action cannot be reduced to scientific knowledge.[35]

More capacities for action

Other factors aside from knowledge constitute capacities for action and a basis for power because they are, in relation to the potential demand, scarce. Knowledge is not quite such a resource. John K. Galbraith (1967:67) claims, for example, that power "goes to the factor which is hardest to obtain or hardest to replace. . . . It adheres to the one that has greatest inelasticity of supply at the margin." Knowledge, as such, is not really a scarce commodity, though two features which can be a part of certain knowledge claims may well transform knowledge from a plentiful into a scarce phenomenon: (1) What is scarce and difficult to obtain is not access to any knowledge (perhaps even in the sense of random knowledge), but to *incremental knowledge*, that is, not merely to just another additional or "marginal unit" of knowledge but to a specific knowledge claim. Knowledge as such really is not scarce at all. But the greater the tempo with which knowledge ages or decays, the greater the potential influence of those who manufacture or augment knowledge, and correspondingly, of those who transmit such increments. (2) If sold, knowledge enters, as already indicated, the domain of others, yet remains within the domain of the producer, and can be spun off once again. This signals that the transfer of knowledge does not necessarily include the transfer of the cognitive ability to generate such knowledge, for example, the theoretical apparatus or the technological regime which yields such knowledge claims in the first place and on the basis of which it is calibrated and validated. Cognitive skills of this kind, therefore, are scarce. But they are not the only skills in demand since knowledge constantly has to be made available, interpreted, and linked to emerging local circumstances. This is the job performed by experts, counselors, and advisors.

The group of occupations designated here as counselors, advisers, and experts is needed to mediate between the complex distribution of changing knowledge and those who search for knowledge enabling to act because "ideas travel" as "baggage" of people whereas skills are embodied in people (cf. Collins, 1982). A chain of interpretations must come to an "end" in order to become relevant in practice and effective as a capacity of action. This function of ending reflection for the purpose of action is largely performed by experts in modern society. Knowledge does not move by itself and does not overcome obstacles by itself.

Whether scientific knowledge is particularly effective in practice, as most of its proponents would argue or hope for, is not at issue. The collective capacity to act, the extent to which our existential circumstances are socially constructed, has increased immeasurably in modern society. But one should not deduce from that, perhaps in an almost linear fashion, that the capacity to act of units of the collectivity, for example the individual, small groups, or even large entities such as nation-states has simultaneously been enlarged immeasurably. On the contrary, the potential to transform and construct at the collective or cumulative level goes in fact hand-in-hand with an increasing inability even of large social entities to affect their fate. That is, the capacity of the whole to make its history should not be misread to mean that this ability necessarily can be parlayed into planned, anticipated or even desired change. The fact that the human species makes its own evolution does not easily, if at all, translate into the ability of individual parts to do the same. Assuming the opposite constitutes a kind of "ecological fallacy".

Knowledge as a bundle of competencies or skills[36]

If one wants to acquire an idea of how knowledge as a "multifaceted" *resource and capacity of action* becomes implicated in social inequality, economic production, or governance (that is, how decision get made), it is necessary to specify on what basis knowledge may yield social advantages and disadvantages.

It seems to me that knowledge in this context has to be conceptualized as a *bundle of competencies or skills*, for example, in the sense of a particular agent's socially recognized capacity to speak and act legitimately (cf. Bourdieu, 1975:19), yielding different social benefits (or costs), for those who command and are able to mobilize its capacities in appropriate situations.[37] Economists would favor the term of *human capital* as a way of defining, as the OECD (2001) does, "the knowledge, skills, competencies and attributes embodied in individuals that facilitate the creation of personal, social and economic well-being". However, the bundle of competencies and skills specified here as crucial to knowledge societies are broader than the typically narrow indicators of research on human capital and are mobilized well beyond the boundaries of the economic system. The shortcuts taken by economists are indebted to the difficulties capturing empirically human capital as well as its more or less discrete attributes (cf. Liu and Fraumeni, 2020).[38]

The relation between material and cognitive factors of social inequality are reversed. Knowledge commands material well-being, its components and extension.[39] Digital technology has made an important contribution to this development and will continue to do so in the future; roughly speaking, digital technology is helping to establish a winner takes all income pattern in which means that the income share of the richest 1% increases while the average worker in rich countries has seen their income stagnate (Guellec and Paunov, 2017).

Even if knowledge is considered a mere means or basis of social inequality in modern society then at least it has to be conceptualized as a "meta-level" instrument capable of affecting the acquisition, protection and disposition of more traditional means of stratification. From a material point of view, but not only from such a perspective, knowledge should be seen as a resource insulating and protecting individuals and households from the immediate impact of the vagaries of the market and coercion. The choice and definition of knowledge as a "focal variable" of inequality also signals that its prerequisites and consequences in practice tend to be, for the time being, less definitive and consensual than alternative dimensions of inequality such as income, education, and occupation and tend to lead to less firmly established structures of inequality in industrial societies. Knowledge as a resource for generating and maintaining patterns of inequality is more tolerant of ambiguity, dissensus, unresolved disputes, and essentially contested patterns of inequalities.

My focus, therefore, is less on outcomes or the results of allocative processes (and the extent to which they are linked to what are almost ascriptive attributes of individuals), but rather on capacities to assert oneself or to achieve different desired ends in widely varying social contexts.[40] Within the context of economic activities, the greater the importance of intangible assets for competitive advantage, the greater the role of and rewards for the specific capacities of action of expert talent (that is, literati, numerati, and entrepreneurial managers, see Teece, 2011) listed later.

The question then is how such a viewpoint on knowledge either complements or differs from recent theoretical conceptions of social inequality which view inequality as a game of cognitive representations of social differences and as a struggle to dominate discourse and strategies about classifications of stratification. The concern of Pierre Bourdieu (1984), for example, is precisely such an analysis of social inequality as maps of cognitive representations. It is argued that classificatory contests in contemporary society have moved beyond a struggle for advantages which revolve around income. New types of conflicts emerge and center on struggles for certification, matters of taste and ethical superiority (cf. Eder, 1989). While such a perspective adds considerably to our understanding of the now multifaceted re-construction of categories of inequality, it can easily remain a (functionalist) view concerned *not* with the enabling (disabling) or constitutive features of inequality but merely with outcomes or products of classificatory struggles.

The focus on knowledge implies a focus on *the new bases for inequality*. What cognitive resources of action allow for the possibility of widely processing new types of classificatory struggles in the first place? And how broadly do these resources have to be socially distributed to make such an argument about inequality not merely restricted to an elite of societal members? More concretely, how does knowledge function as a resource in struggles for status or dominance in cognitive representations in society? And, importantly, how the extensive mobilization of knowledge contributes to more desirable forms of work that give more adequate expression to the humanity of human laboring (cf. Unger, 2019:277)?

As briefly indicated, in the context of focusing on social inequality formation and consciousness,[41] knowledge should be conceptualized as a bundle of social competencies that drive the process of forming and maintaining social prestige and status. Knowledge as a broad and heterogeneous bundle of competencies which has noticeable effects on the *process* of inequality formation, although the *outcomes* continue to involve hierarchies along traditional and not so traditional dimensions. Given this notion, knowledge is unlike earlier, much more singular mechanisms of social inequality. Unpacking the bundle of competencies can only mean to enumerate some of the important specific capacities knowledge confers that are mobilized depending on the demands of the specific contexts. The concrete distribution, the substitutive possibilities and multiple interdependencies among competencies result in a less and less "coherent" and transparent, at times at the surface even invisible, system of social inequality in knowledge societies. Social inequality becomes a heterogeneous and context dependent figuration.

Now I will list what I consider some of the most important social competencies which drive modern social inequality:

The *capacity to exploit discretion*: Since social rules and legal norms and regulations governing ordinary and extra-ordinary social conduct are never constituted and enforced in ways that do not provide for discretionary interpretation and execution or leeway for reconstruction, the competence to mobilize discretion refers to the capacity of individuals to gain comparative advantages, for example in the area of taxation, investment, schooling, income, etc.

The *facility to organize protection*: The capacity to put protective devices and measures in place is a matter of specialized competence which enables actors to mobilize access to differential knowledge in order to ensure for example that one's assets and entitlements are protected against structural or inordinate depreciation. The symbolic or material opportunity costs of being incapable of organizing protection can be considerable.

The *authority to speak* (cf. Bourdieu, 1975) is increasingly based on differential knowledge and immediately implies a parallel social division in opposition to those not authorized to speak. The authority to speak applies to many features and situations but also extends to the ability of a lay audience or a lay person to enter a discursive field of expertise as "speakers and confront the alleged truth of the discourse that justifies those practices" (Larson, 1990:37). By the same token, the inability to master knowledge becomes, independent of the modes of exclusions/inclusions always associated with differential education, increasingly interpreted as a sign of personal failure.

The *ability to mobilize defiance* constitutes another crucial component of the stratifying mode of knowledge. The ability to challenge the practices of experts, the state, or corporations becomes an important asset of knowledge as a capacity to form inequality. In the same sense, the ability to evade surveillance and obtain spaces of self-regulated autonomy acquires considerable significance and is based on the capacity to mobilize tools that often are seen as instruments exclusively enhancing scrutiny.

The *capacity of avoidance* and exclusion is a further stratifying trait which can be enlisted on the basis of different knowledge bases. I have in mind strategies which ensure that some of the risks of modern society tend to be distributed differentially, for example in the general areas of safety concerns, exposure to conflict or violence or incidents of health risks or environmental degradation or the ability to benefit emotionally and material from the capacity to co-operate. By the same token, the tremendous growth of the "informal economy" in most advanced societies, that is, of all kinds and forms of economic transactions uncontrolled by the state and the legal system, irrespective of their legality, should be seen among the socio-economic consequences of the rise of knowledge as a stratifying principle effecting the material basis of inequality.

More generally, the range of social competencies amount to stratified facilities to immediately *master one's life*, for example, one's health (life expectancy), financial well-being, personal life, aspirations, career or long-term security, or the ability to locate and gain assistance toward mastering these tasks, and are generalized effects of a differential command of relevant knowledge bases.[42] The ability to mobilize defiance, exploit discretion, develop strategies for coping, and organize protection are a significant part of such strategies and therefore the conviction that one somehow is in charge and not merely the object of fortuitous circumstances.

Science as an immediately productive force

Science and technology began as a marginal enterprise of amateurs in the seventeenth century; but modern science, especially after World War II, has received a large proportion of the public budget and constitutes a major source of investment for private capital. Individuals, trained as scientists or engineers, are a growing part of the labor force in modern society. The growth in the system of modern higher education is both the result and the motor of the increased importance of science and technology. Institutions which produce, distribute, or reproduce knowledge are now comparable in size to the industrial complex. Furthermore, it is now often emphasized that no area of social life will remain unaffected by the impact of natural science and technology although this does not mean, as will be discussed in some detail later, that scientific knowledge and technology will eradicate totally, as many theorists of the 19th and early 20th century expected, the "traditional" forms of knowing and conventional world views even in advanced society.

The changes in and for science take place in three steps. First, and up to the end of the 18th century, the scientific community had the function of enlightenment, that is, it was a producer of *meaning*. Second, in the following century science became a *productive* force. And, third, in this century science increasingly becomes an *immediate productive* or "performative" force.

In my view, the major change in the production of scientific knowledge, in turn providing one of the foundations of the possibility of a knowledge society, is the expansion in the social function of scientific knowledge and this expansion in functions served takes place without the elimination or a significant reduction of the earlier functions scientific knowledge has had in society.

Knowledge is a productive force inasmuch, as Karl Marx had observed, as it is frozen into machines.[43] However, inasmuch as science, during the 19th century, developed as a "pure" science, it is not a productive force. In the latter part of our century, science has evolved into an immediate productive force. Science also produces knowledge which, at least in the short run, serves no particular social or extra-scientific function. Science is perhaps the only institution in modern society that in the course of its development does not appear to lose some of its original purposes to other sectors of society, e.g., as the result of structural differentiation. On the contrary, science increasingly absorbs certain functions in society. In addition, it expands by generating new purposes or by taking them on. The institution of science therefore appears to be somewhat immune to the incessant forces of social differentiation and specialization.

Obviously, it is quite difficult to propose novel terms for each of these categories of knowledge produced by the scientific community. However, the following concepts might be a first approximation:

(1) *Meaningful knowledge*: The knowledge generated by most social science disciplines and the humanities is knowledge which in its primary social function affects mainly the (social), consciousness of members of society (*Deutungswissen* or *Orientierungswissen*, or *knowledge defined as cognitively stylized meaning* [Luhmann, 1990:138]).[44]
(2) *Productive knowledge*: Most of the traditional disciplines in the natural sciences generate productive knowledge (*Produktivwissen*), in that such knowledge can be converted into ways of directly appropriating natural phenomena.
(3) *Action knowledge*: The most recent form of knowledge, as an immediate productive force, may be considered to be action knowledge (*Handlungswissen* or practical knowledge), because such knowledge is already a direct form of social action. It is the immediate capacity for action, and this includes the capacity to generate more (new), knowledge.

Since science became a productive force in the 19th century, it has ceased to belong exclusively to the superstructure of society. The change from functioning as a producer or critic of world views to functioning as a productive force means, as indicated, that important aspects of science are now part of the material basis of society. Earlier science was not mature enough to be applied to problems of production while the material appropriation of nature in the sense of efficient control over boundary conditions or production of pure materials was not developed far enough to enable a realization of scientific results in dimensions relevant for production. In short, a change in the material and cognitive appropriation of nature in the 19th century turns science into a productive force and assists society to evolve into industrial society.

The material appropriation of nature aided by science means more specifically that nature as a whole is gradually transformed into a human product by superimposing a new structure, namely a social structure. The social structure in essence is objectified knowledge, that is, an explication and realization of what we know are the laws of nature extended by engineering design and construction. Nature scarcely is experienced otherwise than as a human product or within human products. Because the appropriation of nature is driven by science, scientific knowledge attains a preeminent position in society. Scientific knowledge as productive knowledge becomes the dominant type of knowledge.

In this century, science becomes an immediately productive force. "Immediacy" means that science now may, contrary to the relation between production and science in the 19th century, be relevant for production without being mediated by living, that is, corporeal labor. Hence one might be able to speak about the possible abolition of manual labor, especially of factory labor which requires strength and physical dexterity, and the exteriorization of human labor from production into that of the preparation and organization of production. Labor in the conventional sense of the term will become a kind of residual category and primarily knowledge-based. Science produces society directly. Most of the knowledge produced and employed in production no longer is embodied in machines. The effects of this are enormous. It crucially extends to diffusion patterns of technology, the decisions affecting the location of production, the interrelation between organizational structures and labor, patterns of conflict and co-operation, comparative advantages, and the mounting contingency of economic activity.[45]

Although Daniel Bell (1979a:167–168), makes reference to the need to conceive of a "knowledge theory of value" succeeding the obsolete labor theory of value because "knowledge and its applications replace labor as the source of 'added value' in the national product", his conception of the role of knowledge in the productive process ultimately reduces it to an "instrumental", dependent source of value or to a function in which knowledge itself is not as yet productive and capable of adding value independently. Bell (1979a:168), rather tersely stresses, "when knowledge becomes *involved* in some systematic form in the *applied transformation of resources* (through invention and design), then one can say that knowledge, not labor, is the source of value" (emphasis added). The role and the importance of scientific knowledge in production goes beyond the limits assigned to it by Bell.

The notion of the sciences as an immediate productive force is not easily understood, even if the thesis about the impending abandonment of traditional factors of labor and labor largely based on (practical, physical) experience is accepted. It may be objected that the work of the engineer must be "realized", that is, applied by the traditional labor of artisans or factory workers in producing machines for production. One has to ask: what does science actually produce as an immediately productive force?

Theorists of post-industrial society speak about the scientific penetration of labor and social practice. They hint at a process of analyzing, rationalizing, and generating data about labor and social practice. Realms of social life become subject to planning and control. Further, they expect a structural change of labor in the sense of a change in the composition of the working class. It can be observed that there is an increase of higher qualification, in particular, of the proportion of scientific-technical intelligence, a quantitative shift from the group of laborers employed within the sector of production to the sector of preparation, planning and regulation, and, of course, to services. Finally, the Radovan Richta group conceives of science as a productive force because the leading branches of industry, that is, chemical and electric industries, are to a large extent science based. The result is that the level of contemporary productive forces is largely determined by scientific-technological developments.

But why is science an immediately productive force and what is the product of science? The answer must be that science increasingly produces action knowledge, that is, data and theories, or better, data and programs.[46] Hence science can be called an immediately productive force only in cases where data and programs as such become components or even constitutive for society, a society in which the production of knowledge is immediate social production. Indeed, this is the case today. A considerable part of the total work within advanced societies already takes place on the metalevel; it is second level production. Production to a large extent is not metabolism with nature any longer, that is, material appropriation typical of industrial society. Part of production presupposes that nature already is materially appropriated; it consists in rearranging appropriated nature according to certain programs. The "laws" that govern the appropriation of appropriated nature, or secondary production are not the laws of nature but the rules of social constructs. At the level of social practice, we *potentially* meet an analogous situation. Some fields of the social sciences whose subject is society in the state of being appropriated are, for instance, operations research, cybernetics, theory of planning, decision theory, rational choice theory, etc. However, social sciences of this kind presuppose, in order to be successful and able to produce action knowledge as well, that society is bureaucratically conditioned and prepared for data processing. That this precondition in fact is lacking is one of the theses of this analysis, or paradoxically, the appropriation of society by the social sciences produces the opposite effect, namely, fragility rather than opportunities for planning and regulation. In other words, the social sciences are never as efficient as material productive forces as is a science that produces machines or living copper as labor.

But unlike labor under capitalism, the owners of the resource "knowledge" in a knowledge society acquire power and influence because owners of capital cannot, as was still the case for corporal labor, reduce its content in production through substitution of capital; at best, knowledge can be substituted through another knowledge. Notwithstanding the mechanization of brain work, there also always remains an irreducible amount of "personal knowledge", which can be converted into and valued as "intellectual" or "cultural" capital.

Knowledge as an individual/collective capacity for action

What distinguishes a knowledge society above all else from its historical predecessors is that it is a society which is to an unprecedented degree the product of its own action, or a society in which our secondary nature far outpaces and outgrows our primary nature.[47] Interventions by nature are, increasingly, the result of prior human interventions into nature. The balance of nature and society (cf. Stehr, 1978), or of facts beyond the control of humans and those subject to their control has shifted strikingly.[48] In the Richta Report (Richta, 1969:244), certain analogous observations may be found when the authors of the report for example underline that

> the scientific and technological revolution is essentially a part of the process of constituting the subjective factor, that is to say, the subjectivity of society, and then of man, who through its medium comes to master the processes by which the productive forces of human life are created. . . . These subjective factors discover that their own development offers radically new opportunities to intervene in the march of history.

Inasmuch as I attempt to stress the greater ability and range of social action as a constitutive feature of the knowledge society, I reject naturally the idea that such a society can be or is necessarily a "technocratic" enterprise, that is, a society which witnesses almost helplessly the inversion of technical means into social ends as sketched, for instance, by Helmut Schelsky (1961), and many others on the left and the right spectrum of the ideological divide in social science (cf. Marcuse, 1964; Freyer, 1958, 1960), as the "general law of scientific civilization" (see also Krämer, 1982).

Contemporary society has shifted more and more toward capacities which are socially constructed and allow society to operate on itself. More specifically, the material appropriation of nature means that nature in toto is gradually transformed into a human product by superimposing on nature new, socially constructed designs. This structure is objectified knowledge, namely, an explication and realization of what we know are the laws of natural processes extended by engineering design and construction. The same applies to social processes and social institutions. The horizon of human action and potential social action expands considerably in a knowledge society as already indicated; however, the process I have in mind is one which applies first and foremost at the *intermediate* level of action, that is, at the level of small groups, social movements, smaller corporations, and not necessarily at the so-called institutional level of social action referring for example to the state agencies, the political system, the economy, the educational system or even society and the nation-state. I am not suggesting, therefore, that such an extension in the range of social action is evenly distributed and extends necessarily, and does so invariably, to all individual actors in a knowledge society. The principle of stratified social action does not become inoperative. In a knowledge society many groups and individuals continue to face severe constraints on their range of social action. Nor does the concept advanced here mean that nature or natural facts have had to retreat totally, although these constraints will now be rooted in their restricted access to knowledge. On the contrary, and perhaps paradoxically, our increasing distance from nature may mean that nature can affirm itself catastrophically in knowledge societies.[49] I conceive of a knowledge society as a society in which science and technology has extensively heightened the capacities of society to act upon itself, its institutions, and its relation to the natural environment.

But the increase in possible courses of action, that is, in the ability of social organizations, for example, to adapt rapidly to changes (including the need to adapt to problems which represent unprecedented challenges and changes), and enlarge its range of conduct does not result merely from an increase in knowledge about society. The practical usefulness of natural science did not result only from more knowledge about processes "out there" in nature, at least not only and not most importantly. Natural scientific knowledge became useful only in technical contexts, that is, in contexts in which nature was already available materially. But the "veneer" of the socially constructed material culture is, in an important sense, quite thin; advanced technology and complex economic relations demand a sophisticated level of quality control and relatively stable social environments (cf. Ravetz, 1987). In an analogous sense, the growing usefulness of social science knowledge is dependent on a prior rationalization of societal contexts—which many argue is the case already in contemporary society. Societal contexts, individual and group capacities of action are increasingly transformed through the utilization of scientific knowledge. These are the processes which must be analyzed under the general heading of the scientization of social action. The increase in the ability of society to act upon itself is by no means restricted to a transformation in the social means of production but extends also to its relations of production. The unprecedented increase in the ability of society to transform itself increases the contingency of social, political, and economic relations and has the dual effect of implying both emancipation and the real danger of new forms of dependencies.

Science and technology are, therefore, not merely emancipatory forces, as has been one of the prevailing romantic images throughout history, but also socially constraining forces. One of the elementary constraints issuing from the "growth" of scientific knowledge is that it has no visible or conceivable term.

These transformations definitely imply that "all visions of a future without conflict and struggle are doomed to disappointment" (Richta, 1969:257), unless, of course, society uses its ability to change itself as a means to drastically inhibit changes which result in social and political conflicts. But such a program would be highly unrealistic. The source of the increase in the ability of society to act upon itself is, for the most part, the consequence of the expansion of scientific knowledge in the broadest sense of the term. The destinies of modern societies are inextricably bound to science and technology. Therefore, one can only reiterate the observations of Radovan Richta (1969:213), that science in advanced society does not operate merely

> as a factor in the production of things and as an instrument for satisfying wants; it serves equally as a source generating new types of human endeavor, as an initiator and producer of new wants. That is to say, it is a productive force that can create new demands, conflicts and outlooks.

The conception about knowledge in a knowledge society advanced here does not imply, therefore, that the expansion of knowledge encroaches somehow on "ideology" and produces a society less affected by ideological thinking. Science multiplies possibilities: "For every want satisfied and every advance in knowledge, it breeds a multitude of new questions, a spate of human dissatisfaction" (Richta, 1969:214).

Importantly, knowledge is not merely enabling, as many would want to stress, it is also constraining, as its critics are prompt to point out. Often the enabling and constraining features of knowledge are closely intertwined. The multiplicity of the consequences of knowledge may, for example, be seen in its effect on the social organization of work: On the one hand, the "information revolution" or the increased use of microelectronics in combination with "artificial" intelligence may indeed be viewed with alarm, since they enable a most sophisticated, centralized, and comprehensive capturing, monitoring, inexpensive storage, and transmitting of output data or even more generally work behavior, for example. On the other hand, the same artifacts also allow for a high degree of decentralization, local initiative, flexible location, personal responsibility and even the effective and inexpensive monitoring of the monitors.

I would like to complicate a matter which has often been rendered increasingly blunter in the history of much of *sociological* thought and research; that is, as I have indicated in the first chapter, proponents and opponents of modern science and technology agree that scientific knowledge transcends traditional knowledge, and in modern society, tends to take its place full stop

On the limits of the power of (scientific) knowledge

Zygmunt Bauman (1991:7) forcefully but also skeptically diagnoses that our existence is *modern*,

> in as far as it is effected and sustained by *design, manipulation, management, engineering*. The existence is modern in as fare as it is administered by

> resourceful (that is, possessing knowledge, skill and technology), sovereign agencies. Agencies are sovereign in as far as they claim and successfully defend the right to manage and administer existence: the right to define order and, by implication, lay aside chaos, as that left-over that escapes the definition.

The ordering of "raw existence", the radical elimination of ambivalence through (scientific) knowledge, and its derivative skills and technology, may be called *Bauman's law*. Bauman's law covers a social world in which expertise and power merged (Bauman, 1991:92).

Competition among forms of knowledge

In stark contrast, Thomas Luckmann (1983:72) stresses the *persistence* of traditional orientations:

> Because we are capable of turning on light-switch, using a camera, or driving a car, we are not more rational in the conduct of our lives than we were in horse-and-buggy times or, for that matter, before the "invention" of the wheel.

A useful illustration are the results of a national poll of registered votes in the United States from the Fall of 2012 which asked respondents whether the

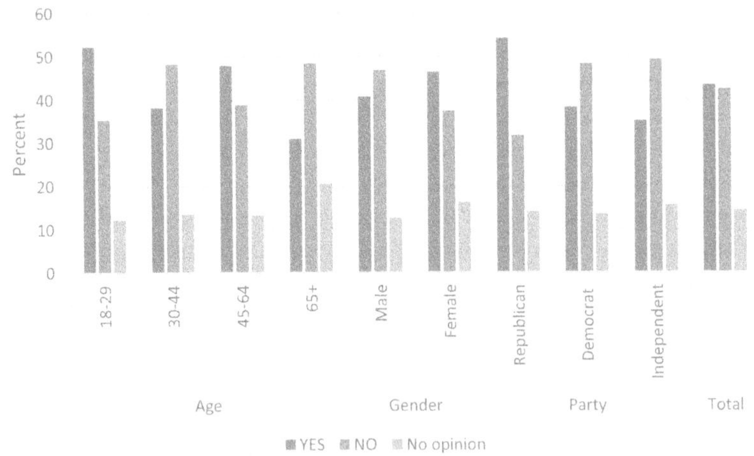

FIGURE 2.1 Percent of registered US who believe that Tim Tebow's success may be attributed to divine intervention by gender, age, and political affiliation.

Source: Poll Position 2012

https://web.archive.org/web/20120312191733/http://media.pollposition.com.s3.amazonaws.com/wp-content/uploads/Poll-Position-crosstabs-divine-intervention.pdf success of a professional football player Tim Tebow can be attributed to divine intervention.

If one follows the broad-based convictions about the power of scientific knowledge, the continuing robust dispute in everyday life about the value of a range of scientific knowledge claims, and not only since the dissent about the pandemic or global warming becomes incomprehensible. The idea of a competition among forms of knowledge, amounts, in the case of scientific knowledge, to inquire into the reasons for the limits of the power of scientific knowledge, especially in everyday life.

The vast majority of all everyday situations are unproblematic. Everyday constellations are repeated over and over again. The "solutions" to such settings "were stored in the stock of knowledge" and are routinely and unreflexively retrieved to master analogous situations reinforcing, in the process, the authority of such knowledge (Luckmann, 1982:257). The conditions of action are quite different, however, once routine orientations for example turn out to be insufficient. Which knowledge claims fulfill the need that leads to a satisfactorily *closure* of action in everyday life? Can scientific knowledge claims fill the void?

Society cannot wait

> At the practical level, any collective representation must serve individuals, in the sense that it must give rise to acts which are adjusted to things, to the realities to which the representation belongs.
>
> —Emile Durkheim, [1955] 1983:87

That closure is needed is one of the elementary contingencies of everyday life. Routine accounts relieve. Without an end no end. The attributes of scientific knowledge that live up to the need of reaching closure in everyday contexts are acquired and embedded or, better, are failed to be acquired and embedded in the course of the production of such knowledge.

What should be called the *material* attributes of scientific knowledge are effects produced for example under special conditions in real or fictitious *scientific laboratories* (i.e., *Gedankenexperimente*). Such effects can be reproduced or duplicated outside the laboratory *only* if the special conditions which allowed for such outcomes are reproduced as well. This requires *control* over the circumstances of the external social context (in the sense of a closed system).

In addition, *cognitive* attributes of knowledge claims are relevant. In most social contexts, there is, as Georg Simmel ([1890] 1989:115–116) commented, the need to act takes precedence over the need to know.[50] Thus, the suspension of the constraint to act within scientific discourse may be described, on the one hand, as a *virtue* of intellectual activity taking place under privileged conditions that moderate the effect that the pressing interests, rapidly passing opportunities and ambiguous dependencies of everyday contexts can have on the production of scientific knowledge claims. On the other hand, the result of this suspension of the pressure to act is that scientific knowledge takes on qualities of *incompleteness*, provisionality, fragmentariness, or expansiveness, which reduce its effectiveness as knowledge in circumstances in which the constraint to act (to get one with life) is the foremost requirement.

For as Emile Durkheim ([1912] 1965:479) observed so well: "Life cannot wait" (cf. also Gehlen, [1950] 1988:296–297). Incompleteness or the lack of any impetus to action is constitutive for scientific knowledge: "Faith is before all else an impetus to action, while science, no matter how far it may be pushed, always remains at a distance from this. Science is fragmentary and incomplete; it advances but slowly and is never finished" (Durkheim, [1912] 1965:479; cf. also Luhmann, [1986] 1989:77–83).[51] The scientific code de-anthropologizes scientific knowledge.

In his lectures on "Pragmatism and Sociology", Durkheim ([1955] 1983), discussing the scientific status of the discipline of sociology, refers to the same set of issues when he attempts to enumerate some of the reasons for the relative scientific backwardness of sociological knowledge. He underlines, for example, that the fragmentary and uncertain knowledge of sociology cannot but produce skepticism or doubt when confronted with the extensive contingencies of practical action in the social world. Such distance between contingencies of social contexts might be less of a problem for natural science knowledge, but we have to live in the social world, and to live means to act. "[S]ociety cannot wait for its problems to be solved scientifically. It has to make decisions about what action to take, and in order to make these decisions it has to have an idea of what it is" (Durkheim, [1955] 1983:90–91).

Where can we find in everyday life the collective representations that are appropriate, more, that are "indispensable for action and its life"? They are a complex of statements that are accepted without verification; it "is their collective character which confers on them the creative power that enables them to impose themselves on the mind" (Durkheim, [1955] 1983:86). There is but one solution if there is no "objective knowledge"; as Durkheim recognizes, the collective representations that work are those found in the lifeworld; perhaps they have to be treated as and called mythological representations. Representations which express the "unanimous conception . . . that gives them a force and authority which enables them to impose themselves without their being subject to verification or doubt" (Durkheim, [1955] 1983:90–91).

Expressions, assertions or, even broader, narratives (can) have multiple purpose. First and foremost, utterances or texts can often *stabilize*, even soothe, contingent social action. Whether utterances are true may well be another attribute utterances are seen to have. But depending on the circumstances of action, such an attribute may not be called for or inquired into in the first instance. As we have seen, it is the collective character of such statements that gives them authority. Other functions of narratives thereby recede into the background.

As a rule, scientific knowledge is, however, produced under conditions which consider waiting, distancing, careful reflection, provisionality, the elimination of time-bound constraints to reach a decision or even the deliberate abstention from a judgment until the "evidence" is in, describe at the same time the distinct attributes of the validity and the virtue of such knowledge claims. By reducing, and at times even eliminating, urgency as a part of the production process of scientific knowledge, gains for the point of view of epistemological ideals contrast with deficiencies from the perspective of everyday life in which urgency to act becomes a constitutive characteristic of action impossible to neutralize. Island within everyday life in which a provisionality of knowledge claims becomes a virtue are rare, I would surmise. In science, such circumstances are a distinct asset. Or, with respect to defining the fundamental purpose of the extension science, it is provisional discovery of new knowledge (cf. Drahos, 2020:334).

Novel, unusual, urgent, emotionally highly charged, or asymmetric circumstances of action in which routine knowledge cannot routinely be mobilized are typically extreme events, such as a serious accident, extraordinary dangers, presence of predators, fatal diseases, severe environmental conditions, extraordinary financial losses or even dramatic gains, threats of unknown origin, and so on. Extreme events multiply the urgency of orientation, that is, an immediate explanation that is socially as well as psychologically coherent and transcends habitual responses. Society must socially recognize and sanction orientations generated under extreme circumstances as appropriate by abstaining from doubt about the narrative that happens to be invoked. Precisely in circumstances of endangerment, scientifically based knowledge, given its particular characteristics, is without a relieving function.

The conditions I have described which led to a search for a narrative that accounts for the unusual event differs from conditions that are not unusual, for example, in the field of politics faced for example by the pandemic. Scientific or expert advice does not exonerate politics from arriving at a political decision because politicians explicitly command the decision or are expected to arrive at a decision. In that sense science has its limits. Science is not a substitute for politics. In many instances, science cannot solve the political dilemma faced by politicians. Too many interconnected outcomes to a particular course of action.

In critical situations, these existential pressures are very likely to be intensified, i.e., under the conditions of the National Socialist regime, for example, which represented a "particularly vicious form of social mythology and magical manipulation of society," Norbert Elias (1989:501) explains,

> the masses of the population, even in 'advanced' nations, feel threatened by dangers whose peculiarities they understand little better than simpler tribal societies understand the dangers of flood and thunderstorm. And like the latter, they tend to fill the gaps in their knowledge with half-truths and myths.

In addition to these considerations, and following Pierre Bourdieu ([1980] 1987), for example, it is possible to assign to everyday or practical contexts a logic which is less stringent than the logic of logic. The social scientific analysis of everyday contexts eliminates the urgency to act in such situations. The effect that is achieved might be called a *depragmatization* of everyday contexts or the elevation of practical circumstances to the level of theoretical contingencies. At the same time, the depragmatization of everyday contexts through social scientific discourse makes visible features of the former which offer resistance against theoretical transformation. Among them are aspects of a practical logic such as the ease of operation and control, subjective adequacy, economy and its practical persuasiveness represented in the union of a totality of judgments and their ambivalence. This opposition of practical and theoretical logic prompts Bourdieu to draw the radical conclusion that any theoretical reconstruction of practical situations amounts necessarily to a distortion of the "truth" of praxis. The peculiar character of practical circumstances happens to be that it resists theoretical reconstruction because the truth of praxis resides in its blindness to its own truth. Scientific discourse and praxis have different purposes and attempt to realize different functions. Practical knowledge must be above all "'*subjectively* adequate'. . . . It must be adjusted to the average limitations of experience and intelligence in an ordinary individual's life" (Luckmann, 1983:71).

The various considerations from sociological observers about the cognitive qualities' knowledge has to fulfil in order to be able to adequately respond to the peculiar contingencies of social contexts in which the urgency to get things done is the foremost task/expectation actors have to respond to, are exactly those characteristics of knowledge that make any further reflection unnecessary. Summarizing these observation, practical knowledge is knowledge that can be put to use immediately. And in this capacity, everyday knowledge or common sense is the "human way to maintain life in the face of obstacles which cannot be wished away" (Luckmann, 1983:761).

It is not the case, we can also summarize the observations about the lack of everyday applicability of scientific knowledge, that science cannot in principle successfully address many of the everyday dilemmas, risks, or moral choices and is in principle prevented from finding answers to causes of certain events. Science can indeed address many of these problems and find answers to everyday puzzles. There is a scientifically sound answer to the question of the causes of a traffic accident, as well as to why this or that person was spared injury. There are scientifically sound answers for the reasons of a plane crash. However, science often cannot immediately provide potent answers; the immediate answers that serve the "demand" are unhelpful for a number of reasons. In particular, the answers are unhelpful because they are not straightaway available to relieve the pressure of everyday action.

Thus, the problem is not the claim of an overwhelming objectivism of science, the assertion of a hegemonic, universally valid perspective that can rightly be criticized, but a "professional blindness and cultural limitedness" that, however, corresponds to the virtues and demands of scientific work. The unlimited claim of the power of scientific knowledge thus goes hand in hand with the systematic overestimation of the influence of science and many of the parallel, exaggerated criticisms, if not fear, of science. Not science has authored our world, knowledge has done so.

I now turn to the economic attributes of knowledge. The most general observation the economics of knowledge allows is that knowledge has a most complex economic status that varies, moreover, from historical epoch to epoch. Its status varies from being hardly an economic object to an era where its economic attributes stand out, for instance, with respect to the price of knowledge (for an extensive discussion, see Stehr and Voss, 2020:268–329).

The political economy of knowledge

The kinds of constraints which operate in a knowledge society differ from those analyzed in theories dealing with more traditional forms of power relations in general, and political power in particular. In the case of traditional notions of power, its possession and use are deliberate and intentional; responsibilities can be traced to its sources, and the benefits or costs associated with its employment are, in many instances, assigned quite unambiguously.

The kinds of emerging power in knowledge societies are not merely the constraints which issue from the exclusive possession and control over specific resources or persons, not to be minimized, however, as I will show which compel those subjected to the exercise of power to carry out certain actions or tasks. In knowledge societies, constraints circulate, as Rouse (1987:246) puts it convincingly,

> throughout our relations with one another and our dealings with things and pervade the smallest and most ordinary of our doings. They shape the practical configuration within which our action makes sense, both to ourselves and to one another. This shaping occurs most directly through their effects upon the kinds of equipment available to us, the skills and procedures required to use that equipment, the related tasks and equipment that use imposes upon us, and the social roles available to us in performing these tasks. Through this process, they change our understanding of ourselves and our lives.

The social and material contexts of social action are altered in fundamental ways. The choice of alternatives, especially sensible alternatives in a given situation, are affected and redesigned.

As Rouse (1987:246) puts it in the same context,

> it is not so much that these power relations compel specific actions from us (although they certainly do that), as that they configure the style and

> interconnectedness of what we do. There are still many possible actions and self-interpretations open to us. But these are drawn from a field of possibilities that increasingly displays characteristic features reminiscent of laboratory micro worlds.

But these changes are also related to changes in the fundamental characteristics of knowledge itself and the way knowledge is shaped by the means of its production and dissemination. The differences at issue concern the rise in the need to interpret knowledge and therefore the extent to which knowledge has lost, or appears to have lost, the characteristic of being secure, certain, definitive, and even truthful or not subject to obsolescence.[52]

The progressive elimination of time and space as relevant elements in the production of knowledge has paradoxically injected the importance of time and location in the interpretation or use of knowledge. Since the validation process of knowledge cannot refer back, except in rare circumstances, to the original author of the claim, the interpretative task once again becomes crucial. Anthony Smith (1986:162–163), ascribes the loss of authority of knowledge and the concomitant rise in the importance of processes of interpretation partly to the means of dissemination and production of augmented knowledge; that is, in

> an electronic era, . . . there is no longer any certainty in knowledge. In the new global Alexandria of computerized information there is no ultimate perceptual security, no ultimate validation of a text back to an original writer or to an original authority. It is a culture based upon a ceaselessly interpretative notion of knowledge. . . . There occurs a kind of paradigm shift when we move from the analog to the digital. It is a shift from the objective to the relative, from certainty through the representation of knowledge as objective to a different kind of certainty derived through a satisfying interpretation of varying reasons of information. It is a shift from precision to probabilism, and it echoes many other recent shifts in the sphere of science and culture.

In the view of some observers, part of the political economy of knowledge in modern societies concerns the possibility that knowledge becomes the basis for *class formation* in general or the emergence of a "knowledge class" in particular. Since I have already examined the relations between knowledge and inequality elsewhere (cf. Stehr and Machin, 2016), I will, at this point, restrict further observations about social inequality and knowledge to a few comments mainly intended to express skepticism toward the notion that we are witnessing the emergence of a "knowledge *class*" in modern society.

Peter Berger (1987:66), for example has argued that the modern middle class increasingly is divided into the old middle class consisting of the "business community and its professionals as well as clerical affiliates" and the newer part, namely the "knowledge class". In other words, the former segment of the middle class consists of individuals who derive their "livelihood from the production and distribution of material goods or services" while the knowledge class includes people whose occupations "deal with the production and distribution of symbolic knowledge".[53]

For the purposes of specifying this modern "middle-class" social stratum in greater detail, Berger refers affirmatively to Helmut Schelsky's description of the emerging group of knowledge-producers and knowledge-disseminators in modern society. Schelsky (1975:14), labels this group as the class of the "distributors and mediators of meaning and purposes" (*Sinn- und Heilsvermittler*). Given Berger's inclusive definition of social class, he maintains that the knowledge class has common material and political interests and a common consciousness. For Berger, the knowledge class tends to be, at least in the United States, on the left of the political spectrum while their economic interests include firm support for an extension of the welfare state—which happens to be the employer of the majority of the knowledge class. I believe that these claims about a knowledge class are exaggerated but also too restrictive. Individuals who are in the business of distributing and disseminating knowledge are by no means confined to the membership in the "middle class". The probability that this stratum develops a "class consciousness", or in fact has an incipient class consciousness, is remote. As a matter of fact, Schelsky maintained that the group of knowledge-producers and knowledge-disseminators has every interest in hiding its rule. Since the new class Schelsky discerns tends to dominate education, the media, and the public relations field—in short, all those spheres in modern society which somehow have to do with the formation of the public's consciousness and identity—it is relatively easy for this "class" to deceive the public about its inordinate influence and its interests. One of the most effective strategies employed in such a deceptive process is the maintenance of the old myth about the continued existence of the old class conflict between proletariat and capitalist. Such a stance precludes the formation of a novel class-based political organization and the explicit struggle for power. Finally, there is no certainty that this segment of the labor force will really grow any more.

Knowledge as a commodity

It would appear to be almost self-evident that in a society in which knowledge becomes the dominant productive force that knowledge, or certain types of knowledge at least, turns into a commodity and can be appropriated, recognized, treated and traded as property. And this despite the fact that knowledge may not have produced for the purpose of generating a marketable commodity. Of course, any effort to understand knowledge as a commodity is influenced or possibly hindered by the fact that knowledge has both market-relevant attributes and non-marketable values that do not disappear by treating knowledge as a commodity and having an exchange value.

It is a mistake to consider the question of knowledge as a commodity to be a modern question. In fact, the suspicion that knowledge is treated as a commodity has played a role in the 18th century. Exemplary for this are considerations by Adam Smith in a preliminary work of his classic *The Wealth of Nations*. Smith refers to the following context:

> Let any ordinary person make a fair review of all the knowledge which he possesses. . . . He will find that almost everything he knows has been acquired at second hand, from books, from the literary instructions which he may have received in his youth, or from the occasional conversations which he may have had with men of learning. A very small part of it only, he will find, has been the produce of his own observations or reflections. All the rest has been purchased, in the same manner as his shoes or his stockings, from those whose business it is to make up and prepare for the market that particular species of goods.

The acquisition of knowledge, in the end, does not differ according to Adam Smith from buying any other product; as "with the trade of material goods, there are individuals whose particular task it is to create knowledge and prepare it for the market" (Valenza, 2009:11). Not only can knowledge become a rival commodity, but there is a parallel intellectual division of labor between producers and consumers of knowledge. What is new, therefore, is the nature/logic of the modern *enclosure* of knowledge, i.e., its basis, which is predominantly based on *legal* restrictions.

Of course, knowledge has always had its price if only because it takes resources to adapt knowledge and knowledge was never available in an unlimited supply, that is, knowledge has been, not unlike other commodities, scarce/enclosed, and in order to utilize it, one had to sometimes buy it. What is new is the nature/logic of the modern enclosure, namely based predominantly on legal restrictions. However, what precisely determines the value of knowledge is by no means self-evident. The value of knowledge depends, for example, not merely on the utility it may represent to some individual or firm but is linked to the ability or inability of others actors, for example competitors, to utilize and exploit it to their advantage as well. In the context of traditional economic discourse, knowledge is treated in a peculiar and often less than plausible fashion ranging from assuming "perfect" knowledge of market participants to treating knowledge merely as an exogenous dimension or efforts to argue that knowledge can be treated in a reductionist manner, that is, as a conventional economic category to which orthodox concepts such as utility, fixed and variable costs apply with benefit and without restriction.[54]

It would seem that economists tend to prefer a conception of the value of knowledge which closely resembles their conception of value in the case of any other commodity, namely, value derives from the utility of the "product" knowledge (use-value), although there remains a considerable range of indeterminancy when it comes to the expected value of knowledge (e.g., Bates, 1988).

For a significant part, the service sector of society lives off selling knowledge. The educational system employs millions who make a living by disseminating socially necessary knowledge. The control of the free circulation of knowledge cannot only be hampered by limited access to the pre-conditions for its acquisition but also, in a legal way, by assigning property right to it. One only has to refer to, as will be examined in detail in the next chapter, patent and copyright laws. In many countries, patent and copyright laws are no longer confined to technical artifacts and processes but include intellectual ownership in art, music, literature, design and increasingly, scientific inventions.

In short, the fact that knowledge is treated as a commodity and is traded is not a new phenomenon. However, some observers would assert that we are witnessing, as the result of technological transformations, especially in conjunction with the proliferation of information-processing machines, a radical "exteriorization" of knowledge with respect to the "knower". With it, the relationship of the

> suppliers and users of knowledge to the knowledge they supply and use . . . will increasingly tend to assume the form already taken by the relationship of commodity producers and consumers to the commodities they produce and consume—that is, the form of value. Knowledge is and will be produced in order to be sold, it is and will be consumed in order to be valorized in a new production: in both cases the goal is exchange.
>
> (Lyotard, [1979] 1984:4)

What counts according to Lyotard, therefore, is the exchange and not so much the use-value of knowledge. Nonetheless, there is still not an economic theory of knowledge in analogy to a theory of location for land as a factor of production, capital, or labor. Economists have treated knowledge, as have most of their fellow social scientists, in a taken for granted manner and often introduced it as an exogenous or external factor, or put simply, as a black box.

The development of an economic theory of knowledge is by no means an easy task; for one thing, knowledge is, as I have argued, inherently a collective, rather than primarily a private good or property. Knowledge is embedded in social relations.[55] "Knowledge of various kinds, while it is differentially allocated and a scarce resource, is not, like so many other goods, diminished, decreased in value, or consumed in the process of exchange" (Holzner and Marx, 1979:23 9; see also Georg Simmel ([1907] 1978:438). The absence of any ready ways of dividing (in theory and practice) knowledge into separate "units" has perhaps also limited the enthusiasm of economists to treat knowledge as a commodity among other commodities (cf. Boulding, 1996). For the most part, the actual possession and legal definition of *property* is exclusive: "A thing over which I exercise the right of property is a thing which serves myself alone" (Durkheim, [1950] 1992:141).

The exclusive legal command and personal possession of knowledge or a kind of isolation of knowledge as an object is much more difficult to realize, if possible, at all. However, the legal system has provisions and presumably may evolve in the future, giving certain forms of knowledge an apparently exclusive status. More importantly, the (meta)-capacity to generate new increments of knowledge—which are most likely to confer comparative advantages—is not a collective property. In other words, knowledge is neither strictly comparable to property nor is without attributes which move it, under certain conditions, nearer to property and commodities.

Charles Derber and his colleagues arrive at a somewhat different conclusion in their analysis of the societal authority and influence of professional occupations in the United States. On the basis of the assumption of the enormous historical variability of what passes for and is accepted as knowledge and therefore the suspicion that almost anything may be sold as "knowledge" as long as this group is successful in persuading clients that they in fact have use and a need for the knowledge controlled by a certain occupation and that this knowledge is superior to everyday knowledge, "professional" knowledge takes on the typical attributes of the construct of "property". Knowledge becomes a commodity because the peculiar nature of the demand (as well as the needs it serves), and the strategies to meet the demand are fully controlled by those who offer the knowledge in question.

Among the crucial strategies is the privatization of knowledge. The prohibition barring lay practice is one of the most powerful strategies to "privatize" knowledge. In a kind of self-created enclosure and self-policed circle knowledge becomes a commodity (cf. Derber et al., 1990:16–18). Even if one assumes that it is relatively easy in practice to legitimize and monopolize knowledge, Derber and his colleagues overestimate the passivity of the consumer and the solidarity of the professional fraternities. A more significant drawback of their positions, it seems to me, is the fact that they once again discard any concrete analysis of the knowledge base of the professionals and rest their case with fairly formal attributes of the knowledge of professionals. The status of the attributes Derber and colleagues invoke appear to be applicable to any knowledge claim and the case boils down to a question of power enabling professionals to set and control cognitive agendas. It is not clear, for example, why scientific knowledge claims have displaced magic since both are functional equivalents as a source of control for the powerful. However, knowledge is not always identical.

The growing supply of and demand for knowledge

An issue which almost immediately follows on the heels of the question of knowledge as a commodity is how one accounts for the growth and therefore for a continuous *supply* of knowledge and, by the same token, how one explains any unrelenting *demand* for knowledge. The competing answers to the first question would see the answer as either resting with an inherent logic of scientific and technical progress[56] or with a specific demand for knowledge driven by socio-economic and socio-political requirements and needs. One of the fundamental questions which the emergence of knowledge societies in addition raises, concerns, of course, the very reason for the shift to knowledge as a crucial dimension in production. The theory of post-industrial society takes it for granted that the demand for theoretical knowledge increases to the point where it becomes the dominant dimension for production and fashions the kinds of skills required of labor (as a force of production) in a knowledge economy. Perhaps it is useful to review briefly some of the suggestions which go beyond trivial conclusions and indicate that the demand for knowledge simply reflects a shift or leap in the economic return of scientific research although the practical economic results from science may occur in a most roundabout fashion. Undoubtedly, this utilitarian argument is used most frequently, and it is the most persuasive one to justify the growing commitment of resources spent on scientific research by the state and business.

Conventional wisdom has it that the industrial revolution "was set in motion by a set of interests engendered by the self-expansion of capital" (Richta, 1969:70–71) and, more precisely, by the surplus value or profit generated by capital. While this is at least the motive force which holds for the owners of the means of production, others have theorized that the Protestant Ethic may well have propelled the industrial revolution. While this debate continues, the process or factors responsible for the dynamics of knowledge production remain largely unanalyzed. Daniel Bell (1973:26), suggests that

> a modern society, in order to avoid stagnation or "maturity" . . ., has had to open up new technological frontiers in order to maintain productivity and higher standards of living. . . . Without new technology, how can growth be maintained?

Radovan Richta's (1977:48), argument is quite similar, although he restricts his claims to socialist society and asserts a kind of pre-established harmony between scientific knowledge and "necessary" societal development. This assertion culminates in the plea and conviction that in socialist societies "there is an ever-growing need for further expansion and acceleration of scientific and technological progress" (also Richta, 1969:75–81). Thus, the question remains why it is that "where once science followed in the wake of industry and technology, the tendency today is for it to control industry and lead technology" (Richta, 1969:216).

Both Bell's and Richta's assertions about the rise of knowledge do not really claim that there is any novel motive force peculiar to post-industrial society which stimulates the expansion of science and its extensive use. The rise of knowledge is at best related negatively to factors that threaten the maintenance of certain motives, desires, and particularly economic (material) wants already prominent in industrial society. In this sense, post-industrial society represents but an extension of industrial society.

Similarly, the discussion of knowledge within the context of economic discourse does not appear to advance the matter much.[57] In order to critically examine the role of knowledge within the context of conventional economic discourse, I will confine myself at this point to an analysis of the ways in which economic investments are defined and measured. For the purposes of accounting for investments, economists employ a definition of what constitutes an investment which limits such expenditures to tangible capital, that is, to either machinery or physical plants. Knowledge cannot be an investment unless it is embedded in tangible capital. Knowledge as frozen into machinery (Weber, 1921:151) is an investment. Within conventional national accounting schemes, expenditures for research and development, for training and the purchase of certain types of services do not constitute an investment component. It follows that the purchase of a personal computer or acquisition of the hardware by a business represents, for the purposes of these national accounts, a capital investment while the purchase of the requisite software, perhaps a program tailored to the needs of the company and possibly much more expensive than the machine(s), itself, is considered a cost of doing business and not an investment.

Such a differentiation is a striking anomaly since "it is well known that software will play an ever-increasing role in the computer industry as hardware costs continue to decline" (Block, 1987:156–157). Not only is the number of people who are software developers growing at an exponential rate but so is the turnover of firms producing and selling software. The expenditures of individuals and corporation for advice, counseling and expertise also is growing at a rapid rate; however, such services are not treated as an investment.

Since economic discourse has treated knowledge mostly as an external variable and since the history of science has rarely inquired into the extent to which scientific progress is driven by or responds to economic forces, the possible impact of economic processes on the supply of scientific knowledge has hardly been investigated.

Despite the scarcity of analysis, one has little difficulty discerning two disparate positions: (1) It is asserted that scientific progress occurs in splendid isolation from economic demand and interests. The utilization of scientific knowledge for productive purpose is driven by the supply of knowledge which happens to be at hand. Utilization follows opportunistic principles; and (2), the growth in the supply of scientific knowledge is induced by the forces and the specifics of the demand for such knowledge. More specifically perhaps, one can assume that human needs, especially economic needs, as we have seen but also the desire to enhance foresight and the ability to control—through planning—the circumstances of social action, co-determine the path of scientific development.[58]

In his study *Invention and Economic Growth*, which is concerned with an economic account of inventions and their dissemination, Jacob Schmookler

(1966:184), for example, argues that economic demand "induces the inventions that satisfy it". Schmookler's assertion about the origins of inventions resonates quite closely with the well-known saying that "necessity is the mother of invention". The supply of inventions, it would appear, is almost totally elastic and independent of time and place. Each need generates almost concurrently the invention it requires.

One of the basic difficulties with this thesis, of course, is that you cannot really explain the perplexing persistence of many individual and collective needs. Why has it been impossible to satisfy these needs with appropriate scientific discoveries? Jacob Schmookler tries to escape this difficulty by concentrating on existing or successful inventions, more concretely, patents which have been issued. But this approach does not assure a clear separation and independence of the demand factors which are supposed to generate appropriate inventions.

Therefore, Nathan Rosenberg (1974:98) points out that it is only possible to explain the needs which might have been met by certain discoveries if one concentrates on the supply side and examines the available knowledge at any given time. Available knowledge is structured in a certain manner and not evenly distributed in relation to different external needs and requirements.

With respect to the assumption that scientific progress is not propelled by a specific self-regulating logic and that economic interest may well impinge upon scientific development, Rosenberg (1974:100), supports the idea that economic motives and processes "have played inevitably a major role in shaping the direction of scientific progress . . . but within the changing limits and constraints of a body of scientific knowledge growing at uneven rates among its sub component sub-disciplines".

Rosenberg's conclusion makes evident how important it is to base the analysis on a solid understanding of the nature and the function of knowledge. Schmookler's observations are too closely tied to the idea that knowledge puts things more or less directly into motion rather than that knowledge is the capacity for action and not yet identical with its realization. Knowledge also can be seen as the capacity for avoidance. However, Schmookler sets out from "successful" inventions, in the form of patents granted, and therefore is unable to identify and the role of demand forces "independently of the evidence that the demand was satisfied" (Rosenberg, 1974:97).

A very different hypothesis about the reasons for the growing need for knowledge in modern society is argued by Peter Drucker, who suggests that the impetus for the increasing demand has to do less with more difficult and complex job skills but more with the considerable extension in the working life span of individuals. Thus, it is not so much the demand for labor and particular skills, but the *supply* of highly skilled labor that underlies the transformation of society into a knowledge society. I will comment on this thesis in more detail later, designating it as *Drucker's Law*. Peter Drucker's (1969:278), thesis therefore is that the nature of work changed with the arrival of the highly educated workers. Because knowledge work is demanded by those who seek employment, knowledge jobs have to be created. Thus, Drucker proposes a "supply side explanation" of the transformation of industrial society into a knowledge society. The extension of education is itself a reflection of a drastic lengthening in the work life expectancy.[59]

A more conventional but also more realistic account is offered by Jean-Jacques Salomon (1973:49), who advances the suggestion that the change to post-industrial society is the result of a convergence, or much more directly, the result of a symbiosis between science and the public authorities (and the economy). Knowledge becomes the objective of power because power is nourished by knowledge. That is to say, the convergences of "their interests have set off a massive production of new knowledge and technologies of which the advanced societies make deliberate use." The convergence between state and science is derivative of the nature of modern science (it is quite expensive and basic research does not yield immediate economic returns), and the nature of modern society, especially the exercise of authority which comes to rely increasingly on knowledge.

For these reasons, Salomon (1973:67) is able to argue that the "pursuit of science fits the ends of power itself, however, remote it may be from any purpose outside itself and however remote its own purposes may be from those of the state." Salomon (1973:51) refers both to military research and research for civilian purposes, although he claims that "science policy is historically the child of war and not of peace." Basic science carried out to serve national interests and prestige, on the often-interdependent fronts of both the military and the economy, is viewed increasingly as a good investment by the state. The arms race in peace times leaves the pattern of science policy essentially unchanged.

Although the debate about the relative importance of different factors on the growth and the demand for knowledge is inconclusive, since one lacks a widely recognized standard of measurement, Jean-Jacques Salomon (1973:57), concludes that the economy "would not be so marked by technological innovation as it is today without the spur of military programs". Yet Salomon also recognizes that the spin-off from military and space research may well be less important in the future, or more generally, that not only research motivated by military designs may be the handmaiden of the demand for knowledge.

I now turn to the essentially contested issue of the *relation* information and knowledge. In the case of information, my focus is on the content conveyed by information rather than on information and communication technologies, as is more often the case in science and social science (e.g., Castells, 1996; Lash, 2002: Turkle, 2005).

The commonalities of knowledge and information are asserted in some of the discussions of information and knowledge, in other considerations such cohesions are denied vigorously. But what should not be contested is the extraordinarily expansive reach in the use of both concepts. In the case of information, the emergence of *Big Data* (for example, data from billions of sensors embedded in a widening range of objects, massive corporate and government databases, public and private surveillance data, non-market activities such as Google searches, Facebook likes, emails etc., or online economic transactions) is the latest installment. The difference between big data and knowledge is significant. Whereas knowledge

> has a natural tendency to expand and spread and is non-excludable (except where it is covered by intellectual property rights (IPRs) or kept secret from the public), the big data systematically collected, stored and used/reused by the Big Five [Google, Amazon, Facebook, Netflix and Microsoft] are under their exclusive control, even though it is not established that they own these data.
>
> (Hu, 2020:25)

The ownership of Big Data is a highly contentious matter and likely will be regulated by the state(s) in the foreseeable future.

Given the increasing availability of large volumes of structured data on the web, scholars are suggesting the possibility of a convergence of information and knowledge. Declarations could be found promising that big data and applied mathematics would replace every theory of human behavior. Accounting for human conduct is buried in the numbers. Mining big data would lead to the discovery of hidden knowledge (cf. Wellmon, 2021:133). However, such predictions are likely linked to the fallacy of conflating of information and knowledge. I will try to find robust arguments in favor of separating information from knowledge.

Knowledge and information

In the context of an examination of some of the important properties of knowledge, it is unavoidable to take up the contentious question of the relation/difference between knowledge and information. Before attempting to differentiate and explore the relations between knowledge and information, the initial puzzle that has to be addressed is whether, at this juncture of the much more typical insistence of the close affinity if not conflation of the two, is it even possible and sensible to distinguish between them? It would appear to be most difficult, if not impossible, to sustain any difference or a carefully constructed range of continuities between the two notions in light of the fact that the concepts are frequently employed as virtual equivalents: Information as knowledge and knowledge as information (for example, Hayek, 1937;[60] Faulkner, 1994; Stewart, 1997:426;[61] Lyotard, 1989; May, 2000a:1; Knorr-Cetina, 2010:172; Haskel und Westlake, 2017:64; Stiglitz, 2017:14).[62] In other words, information processes incorporate all the analytical dimensions such as interpretation, calculation, accounts, and explanation usually attributed primarily if not exclusively to knowledge (cf., Knorr-Cetina, 2010:172). I will make the point that these attributes should not be those of information.

I would like to argue in favor of the need and the benefits to arrive at a clear-cut differentiation. Such a clear-cut difference between knowledge and information is more than merely assigning a subordinate role to information, for example, by arguing that knowledge is the capacity necessary to use information to create new information (Benkler, 2006:313). It would be misleading to argue that there is *a single* distinction between information and knowledge. However, I would like to suggest that the dissolution of the unity of knowledge and information is of value. This is especially true in view of the fact that the importance of knowledge for the emergence and sustainability of democratic conditions is usually reduced to the importance of political information rather than knowledge of the actors. It is my contention that the substance of information primarily concerns the *properties of products or outcomes* while the stuff of knowledge refers to the qualities of *process or inputs*. It may be argued therefore that a user manual or operating instructions are a sophisticated example of information.

It is equally important to stress from the outset that knowledge and information have attributes in common. The most important common trait is that neither information nor knowledge is self-evident and free of context. But before I attempt to explicate the distinction between information and knowledge as the distinction between attributes of product and process, a discussion of the various alternative ways of *linking* the two concepts is in order.[63]

Conflating information and knowledge

Many dictionaries and scholarly treatises simply information as a certain kind of knowledge[64] or refer to the apparent ease with which knowledge is converted into information. A similar symmetry between information and knowledge is evident if one's information is expressed as "knowledge reduced and converted into messages that can be easily communicated among decision agents" (Dasgupta and David, 1994:493). In other definitions of information and knowledge, information is simply conceptualized as a subspecies, as an essential element or the raw material of a number of knowledge forms.[65]

For example, information is codified knowledge as well as indirect knowledge (see Borgmann, 1999b:49), or knowledge is defined as the cumulative stock of information (Burton-Jones, 1999:5), or "information is always only information in the light of certain knowledge" (Abel, 2008:17); similarly, knowledge in general is seen to extend to "tacit knowledge" (cf. Polanyi, 1967:204–206) and other categories of knowledge (Dosi, 1996:84). Jonathon Haskel and Stian Westlake (2017:64) defend a similar definition in which information and knowledge become Siamese twins:

> We define *knowledge* as connections made between pieces of information, supported by evidence, to form a coherent understanding. Knowledge cannot exist without information, and knowledge is required to fully understand and interpret information. Knowledge can, therefore, include

> theories, hypotheses, correlations, or causal relationships observed from information constituted by analyzable data.

But is there such a phenomenon as "tacit" information? The outcome of many efforts to knowledge and information appears always to remain the same: knowledge and information become indistinguishable (see Wikström and Normann, 1994:100–111).[66] As indicated, the extent to which such widespread indiscriminate usage of the terms information and knowledge has made them indistinguishable raises, last but not least, the problem of the futility of any alternative effort that aims not at conflating, but at distinguishing their meanings and referents (cf. Malik, 2005).

Nonetheless, from time to time efforts are launched to differentiate between information and knowledge. William Starbuck (1992:716), for example, suggests that knowledge refers to a stock of expertise and not a flow of information. Thus, knowledge relates to information in the way that capital or assets connect to income. Kenneth Boulding (1955:103–104) warns that we should not regard knowledge as a mere accumulation of information. Knowledge has, in contrast to information, a structure: sometimes it is a loose network, sometimes a quite complex set of systemic interrelations. Fritz Machlup (1983:644) refers to the possibility that one may acquire new knowledge without receiving new information. Summing up the distinction between knowledge and information, Machlup (ibid.) prefers to claim that

> information in the sense of telling and being told is always different from knowledge in the sense of knowing. The former is a process, the latter a state. Information in the sense of that which is being told *may* be the same as knowledge in the sense of that which is known, but *need* not be the same.

The act of delivering (information) is one side of the coin, the "object" that is being delivered (knowledge) the other (see also Machlup, 1979:63–65).

Brown and Duguid ([2000] 2002:119–120) stress that knowledge in contrast to information has at least three distinctive attributes. First, knowledge usually entails a knower; second, knowledge is harder to detach than information, and, third, knowledge requires a greater effort of assimilation: "knowledge is something we digest rather than merely hold." But only rarely does one find, in definitions designed to differentiate between information and knowledge, any reference to practical usefulness or correctness as salient characteristics of knowledge and information.

If there is another side to the ledger, it is the *unease* with the practice of liberally conflating information and knowledge both in everyday life and in scholarly reflections, and reducing or extending them to an all-inclusive "mental material". It is, of course, the case that one rarely finds in public places such as airports, shopping centers, or train stations a counter or booth marked "Knowledge", rather than "Information". It is likely, however, that prevailing practices of conflating knowledge and information, for example in legal discourse (cf. Easterbrook, 1982), will prove to be more persuasive than efforts designed to distinguish between them. After all, who is able to clearly distinguish between the information and the knowledge society?

An equally formidable barrier to any new or renewed attempt sociologically to separate knowledge and information (and/or point to their commonalities) is the almost insurmountable mountain of competing conceptions of knowledge and/or information embedded in and indebted to multiple epistemological perspectives or pragmatic purposes. Knowledge and information may be distinguished based on economic considerations or other social points of reference: the different ways in which they are produced, stored, diffused, consulted, and applied, their typical carriers, and the distinct social consequences they may be seen to have in society. I will refer to some relevant conceptions of knowledge *and* information, thereby recognizing the tremendous difficulties faced in efforts to sustain and codify differences between them.

Opposing knowledge and information

One of the more traditional distinctions among knowledge forms is the opposition between *knowledge of acquaintance* and *knowledge-about* (in theory). Though these terms appear to be somewhat clumsy in English, they signify an asymmetrical dichotomy available in many languages: for example, as the terms *connaître* and *savoir*, *kennen* and *wissen* or *noscere* and *scire* indicate. And as William F. James (1890:221) observes, with respect to this opposition of forms of knowing:

> I am acquainted with many people and things, which I know very little about, accept their presence in the places where I have met them. I know the color blue when I see it, and the flavor of a pear when I taste it; I know an inch when I move my finger through it; a second in time, when I feel it pass; an effort of attention when I make it; a difference between two things when I notice it; but *about* the inner nature of these facts or what makes them what they are, I can say nothing at all.

The differences between knowledge of acquaintance and knowledge-about by William James resonates in turn with Gilbert Ryle's ([1949] 2000) distinction between *knowing-that* and *knowing-how*. Knowing-that encircles the knowledge that one is able to articulate while knowing-how in addition includes what is best described as tacit knowledge and therefore the volume of the latter is more extensive than the *former* type of knowledge (e.g., Ryle, [1949] 2000:41). The distinctions by James and Ryle also suggest a possible difference between information and knowledge whereby information becomes less penetrating and consequential, a more superficial and fleeting cognizance of the attributes of a process or the instructions about an object.[67]

Knowledge of acquaintance or knowledge of attributes (World Bank, 1999:1)—for example, the quality of a product, the diligence of a worker, or the profitability of a company—refer to the presence or absence of information among market participants about relevant economic "data". "Information problems" such as product standards or credit reports—crucial to effective markets—therefore are defined by the World Bank as "incomplete knowledge of attributes". In this sense, economic discourse has always made reference to the importance of information, but also to incomplete information and its function in pricing mechanisms or market transparency, for instance. The attributes and instructions information in this sense conveys indicate that information plays an instrumental role in social conduct.

But the distinction between knowledge and information, even in its most elementary sense, is not only an asymmetrical dichotomy but also a difference that is supposed to have its dynamic, even progressive, elements.

For what might be called acquaintance-with becomes knowledge-about as knowledge develops, matures, or becomes more explicit and articulate. James (1890:221) indicates as much when he observes that the two kinds of knowledge are "as the human mind practically exerts them, relative terms". As a result, the distinction moves closer to the dichotomy of scientific knowledge in the sense of formal, analytic, rational, and systematic knowledge, and "information" as later interpretations of James (for example by Park, 1940) show as well.

Given the general attention paid to Daniel Bell's (1979) theory of post-industrial society and the extent to which knowledge for Bell is constitutive of such a society, it is worth giving some thought to his definitions of information and knowledge articulated within the context of that theory of modern society. First, Bell refers to what is an anthropological constant, namely that knowledge has been necessary for the existence of any human society. In other words, knowledge is a basic provision for social relations and social order.

What is therefore new and distinctive about the post-industrial society "is the change in the *character* of knowledge itself. What has now become decisive for the organization of decisions and the control of change is the centrality of *theoretical* knowledge—the primacy of the theory over empiricism, and the codification of knowledge into abstract systems of symbols that can be utilized to illuminate many different and varied circumstances. Every modern society now lives by innovation and growth and by seeking to anticipate the future and plan ahead" (Bell, 1968:155–156; Bell, 1973:343–344). And,

> just as the business firm was the key institution of the past one hundred years because of its role in organizing production for the mass creation of products, the university . . . will become the control institution of the next

> one hundred years because of its role as the new source of innovation and knowledge.
>
> (Bell, 1973:344)

However, the distinction between forms of knowledge that have run their course because they "informed" industrial society and theoretical knowledge constitutive of post-industrial society does not necessarily affect Bell's general differentiation between information and knowledge, to which I now turn.

By information, Bell (1969:168) suggests, "I mean data processing in the broadest sense; the storage, retrieval, and processing of data becomes the essential resource for all economic and social exchanges (in post-industrial society)." Bell's conception of information is indistinguishable from the technical conception of communication in which the meaning, exchange and transfer of a piece of information are independent of the carriers (source and receiver) of information.[68] By knowledge, in contrast, he means "an organized set of statements of fact or ideas, presenting a reasoned judgment or an experimental result, which is transmitted to others through some communication medium in some systematic form" (Bell, 1979:168).[69] Bell's definition of knowledge, however, lacks any elementary reference to the bearers of knowledge, or as I quoted Barry Barnes (1988:179) at the beginning of this chapter, "To talk about knowledge is to talk about people."

It would appear that the technical conception of communication applies to knowledge as well, although Bell makes implicit reference to the distinct epistemological status (or value) of knowledge and information, which results in a hierarchical and asymmetrical gradient between knowledge and information. As a result, information is easily dubbed "mere" information, while knowledge is methodically generated, sorted, and judged.

Nonetheless, the dichotomy has strong disembodied strains. That is, there is no reference to the contingent character of information and knowledge, or to the need to interactively render knowledge and information intelligible and negotiate whether it is valuable or appropriate. At least implicitly, the concepts depict innovation and fabrication of incremental knowledge as a fairly smooth, well-behaved process. Given Bell's scientific and technological conception of the communication and acquisition of knowledge and information, the strong assumption is that both knowledge and information travel virtually unimpeded. In addition, the linkages, if any, that may exist between information and knowledge remain ambivalent. At best, it would seem that Bell's conception of knowledge and information contains the claim that information is the handmaiden of knowledge. Moreover, this notion tends to be overly confident about the authority, trustworthiness, and power of information and knowledge. According to Bell, knowledge is primarily abstract, disembodied, formal, individual—and aspires to be universal (or knowledge in space). It seems to us that Bell's interpretation raises more questions than it answers.

Divorcing information and knowledge

Nonetheless, a discussion of the interrelation between knowledge and information provides an opportunity to summarily rehearse some of the comments I have made about the role of knowledge in social affairs. Knowledge, as I have defined it, constitutes a capacity for action. Knowledge is a model for reality. Knowledge enables an actor, in conjunction with control over the contingent circumstances of action, to set something in motion and to (re-)structure reality. Knowledge allows an actor or actors to generate a product or some other outcome. Knowledge is ambivalent, open, and hardly blind to the specific meaning knowledge claims contain. But knowledge is only a necessary, and not a sufficient, capacity for action. As indicated, in order to set something into motion or generate a product, the circumstances within which such action is contemplated to take place must be subject to the control of the actor. Knowledge that pertains to moving a heavy object from one place to the next is insufficient to accomplish the movement. In order to accomplish the transfer, one needs control over some medium of transportation useful for moving heavy objects, for example. The value that resides in knowledge, however, is relational in the sense that it is linked to its capacity to set something into motion. Yet knowledge always requires some kind of attendant interpretive skills and a command of the situational circumstances. In other words, knowledge—its acquisition (see Carley, 1986), dissemination and realization—requires an active actor; a knower that "has a particular history, social location and point of view" (Oyama, 2000:147). Knowledge involves an appropriation and transaction rather than mere consumption or assimilation. It demands that something be done within a context that is relevant beyond being the situation within which the activity happens to take place. Knowledge is conduct. *Knowing*, in other words, is (cognitive and collective acquiring) *doing* and the active accomplishment of multiple actors.

In contrast, the function of information is, as I would see it, both more restricted and more general. Information is something actors have and get. It can be reduced to "taking something in", as something whose function it is to *signify*. Information can be condensed into quantifiable forms.[70] It therefore is possible and sensible to conclude that someone has more information than another individual. It is much more difficult and contentious to conclude that someone commands more knowledge than another person.

In its compacted form, information can migrate more easily. Information does require sophisticated cognitive skills, but places fewer intellectual demands on potential users. Information is immediately productive but not necessarily politically neutral (Burke, 2000:116–148). This applies, for example, to a map, a timetable, legal records, charts, bibliographies, a census questionnaire, a directory, etc. Information amounts to the equivalent of a *document* (cf. Buckland, 2017:22–27).

In many instances, there is no need to be the master over the conditions of its implementation, as is the case for knowledge as capacity for action. Information is more general. Information is not as scarce as knowledge. It is much more self-sufficient. Information travels and is transmitted with fewer context-sensitive restrictions. Information is detachable. Information can be detached from meaning. It tends to be more discrete than knowledge. In addition, the access to and the benefits of information are not only (or not as immediately) restricted to the actor or actors who come into possession of information. Information is not as situated as knowledge.[71]

Information, in comparison to knowledge, can have a very high depreciation rate over time. The information that the share X is a good buy rapidly loses its value. The information about the value of purchasing the share quickly decreases in value, and does so not only as a result of its wide communication and the possibility that many will follow the advice. In other words, the marginal utility of information can be quickly reached. If, however, one wants to assure that information quickly depreciates, one should act and encourage others to act according to the information. For example, having been informed about a share price that may decline, acting on the information will likely prompt the price to fall even further, depending of course on the extent to which such shares are sold.

The use of knowledge can also be quite restricted and limited in its use-value, however, because knowledge alone does not allow an actor to set something into motion. Information may be a step in the acquisition of knowledge. The acquisition of knowledge is more problematic. In general, a simple and quite straightforward model of communication is appropriate for the purposes of tracing the "diffusion" or transfer of information. Whether it is even possible to speak of a transfer of knowledge is doubtful. The "transfer" of knowledge is part of a learning and discovery process that is not necessarily confined to individual learning.[72] Knowledge is not a reliable "commodity". It tends to be fragile and demanding, and has built-in insecurities and uncertainties.

Good examples of information are price advertising and other market information, such as the availability of products (*signaling* function). Such information is easy to get, unproblematic to have, and often robust, and can certainly be useful. In the context of the modern economy, it is very general and widely available, but the consequences of having such information as such are minimal. From the point of view of a consumer, price information combined with knowledge about the workings of the market place may constitute a capacity to realize some savings. But information about prices does not enable one to generate insights into the advantages or disadvantages of different economic regimes within which such prices are generated. A comparative analysis of distinct economic systems and the benefits it may have for different groups of actors requires special economic knowledge.

Not unlike language, information has attributes, especially on the supply side, assuring that it constitutes, certainly to a greater extent than is the case for knowledge, a public or free good. It is not enabling, in the sense of allowing an actor to generate a product. Information merely reflects the attributes of products from which it is and can be abstracted. In the economic context, more specifically in the context of market relations, information concerns characteristics of the commodities or services being transacted (see also Stiglitz, 2000:1447). The information of interest to the consumer or producer is of course by no means limited to the price of a product or service. Interest on the demand side of the transaction extends to many characteristics of the commodity as well as (often-hidden) behavior of the item paid for.

As I suggested at the outset of this chapter, knowledge refers to and specifies attributes of *process* or *input* whereas information refers to attributes of *product* or *output* (state). In other words, information is both input and output, while knowledge can be found only or primarily as an input element in the production process. It might now be clearer why I distinguish knowledge and information in this manner. As Charles Lindblom (1995:686) explains with respect to the attributes of commodities and services and the decisions consumers make about commodities and services: In many instances in the market place, "how and where the refrigerator was made, whether the work force was well treated, whether the process produced harmful wastes, and the like, you have no control over and little knowledge of." The consumer is typically informed about the price of the fridge, the energy efficiency, the life expectancy, the warranty, the colors, the volume it may hold, the size, and so on. None of the information about the refrigerator typically provided in one way or the other in the market place enables you to find out about the process of building the refrigerator, let alone the ability to construct it yourself.

Knowing and "not knowing"[73]

> The outstanding feature of a man's life in the modern world is his conviction that his life-world as a whole is neither fully understood by himself nor fully understandable to any of his fellow-men.
>
> —Alfred Schütz (1946:463)

> In the presence of the total reality upon which our conduct is founded, our knowledge is characterized by peculiar limitations and aberrations.
>
> —Georg Simmel (1906:444)

The quotes from Alfred Schütz and Georg Simmel summarize the typical hypothesis on the fuzzy phenomenon of non-knowledge well,[74] but the phenomenon is captured much more precisely by the economist Joseph Stiglitz's (2005:133) formulation about the "*invisible hand*" ostensibly operating in the market place. Asked why the invisible hand is invisible, Stiglitz gave a straightforward answer: because it does not exist. Similarly, I ask in this chapter why non-knowledge is difficult is difficult to grasp, in an elementary sense. And my response analogous to Stiglitz's response is: because there is no such thing as non-knowledge. By the same token, if we take the reference of "unknowability" to "realities and processes" (!) "that cannot be apprehended in any way . . . at all" (McGoey, 2020:198), one can only wonder about the robustness of the referent. Insofar as non-knowledge is a superstition, there is no need to engage in a discussion about whether non-knowledge has disadvantages or advantages.

My claim that non-knowledge is a myth contrasts more or less sharply with the conventional assumption about the phenomenon of non-knowledge. Wolfgang Krohn (1997:69, 84) offers a definition of non-knowledge that is shared among many observers and not only affirms the existence of non-knowledge but is inevitability as a by-product (not unlike, so it seems, the inevitable by-product of fishing) in any search for knowledge:

> On average, the discovery of new uncertainties is always greater than the construction of secured, confirmed stocks of knowledge. According to this law, the term knowledge society describes a society that learns to an ever-increasing extent about the extent and levels of its ignorance. . . . Ignorance is not at the beginning of a technological trial, but is worked out in the course of implementation. The dissolution of non-knowledge into workable problems and feasible solutions is connected with the generation of new non-knowledge.

Not wishing to capitulate already at this early point, I concentrate in this section on scholarly discourses in which their participants maintain that something like non-knowledge does indeed exist and, at the same time, do not relegate non-knowledge to a kind of black box by merely heroically claiming that there is the dichotomy of non-knowledge and knowledge. The knowledge/non-knowledge dichotomy appears in many discussions on the subject as a kind of performative speech act (Sartori, 1968). However, it recommends or affirms only one side of that which it designates, namely, knowledge.

Perhaps one of the most suspect features of the notion of non-knowledge is, to mention one of my objections at the outset that the definition of non-knowledge hints that there is such a thing as *a bit of knowledge* that can be isolated and carefully inspected and claimed to represent, as it were, non-knowledge. It would be much more adequate and realistic to imagine knowledge always to be part of a bouquet (neighborhood) of claims representing capacities to act. An isolation of a bit of knowledge is most difficult if not impossible. Hence to designate an aspect of knowledge as non-knowledge overshoots our capacity to breakdown the "network" of the ingredients of knowledge claims.

I cannot completely sustain my doubt about the existence of not-knowing in the following discussion; from time to time, I have to deviate from it and maintain that non-knowledge does exist. At the same time, I draw attention to other terms that are empirically and theoretically more productive than the naked assertion that non-knowledge exists. For instance, to Andrew Abbott's (2010) relational taxonomy of three types and levels of ignorance: expert, amateur, and professional that refers to the link between the social role of the "ignorant" person and the type of ignorance.[75] Finally, I will point to a number of intriguing, but rarely studied, topics relating to the question of the societal function or societal treatment of apparently insufficient knowledge.

Sigmund Freud and Friedrich Hayek: why quit?

The treatment of non-knowledge by Sigmund Freud and Friedrich Hayek is of particular interest in this context because their approach is, if I am not mistaken, quite representative for much of social scientific discourse. Both Freud and Hayek recognized that there can be no such thing as a researchable subject called non-knowledge, but, unimpressed by their own conclusion, they continued to examine something that does not exist. Their grappling with this perplexing issue gives me the opportunity to ask why the concern with the topic of non-knowledge appears to be typical especially for the German-speaking scientific community. Is it a sort of eccentricity?

Sigmund Freud's ([1924] 1963:100) theory of the dream as a psychic phenomenon is based on the primary conviction that the dreamer himself should "say what his dream means." But an evident fundamental obstacle to doing so is that the dreamer is, as a rule, firmly convinced that he does not know what his dream means. As Freud ([1924] 1963:101) notes, "the dreamer always says he knows nothing." The lack of information from the dreamer confronts Freud with an apparent scientific and methodological conundrum defying sound interpretation of dreams. "Since he [the dreamer] knows nothing and we [the psychoanalyst] know nothing and a third person could know even less, there seems to be no prospect of finding out [the dream's meaning]" (Freud, [1924] 1963:101).

Instead of accepting these findings as a sound conclusion and therefore forsaking any further search for the meaning of dreams, Freud ([1924] 1963:101) considered another possibility: "For I can assure you that it is quite possible, and highly probable indeed, that the dreamer *does* know what his dream means: *only he does not know that he knows it and for that reason thinks he does not know it*"). This interpretation seems to be confusing and self-contradictory. Freud even asked himself whether a contradiction in terms might exist in his hypothesis that there are "mental things in a man which he knows without knowing that he knows them" (Freud, [1924] 1963:101):

> Where, then, in what field, can it be that proof has been found that there is a knowledge of which the person concerned nevertheless knows nothing, as we are proposing to assume of dreamers? After all, this would be a

> strange, surprising fact and one which would alter our view of mental life and which would have no need to hide itself: a fact, incidentally, which cancels itself in its very naming and which nevertheless claims to be something real—a contradiction in terms.
>
> (Freud, [1924] 1963:102–103)

For Freud what followed from these observations was the conclusion that one ought to abandon this method of dream interpretation as lacking any substance. But Freud did not. After all, the knowledge does not really hide from the observer. One has only to search for it persistently. "It is very probable, then, that the dreamer knows about his dream; the only question is how to make it possible for him to discover his knowledge and communicate it to us" (Freud, [1924] 1963:104).

Hayek, confronted with a similar dilemma, decided, just like Freud, to ignore it. In his essay entitled "The Creative Powers of a Free Civilization" ([1960] 1978:22), in which the lack of knowledge is a question of the distribution of knowledge in markets, Hayek first notes that any progress in civilization is the result of an increase of knowledge. In the real world, according to Hayek, it simultaneously holds true that "the individual benefits from more knowledge than he is aware of," and he added that "this fundamental fact of man's unavoidable ignorance of much on which the working of civilization rests has received little attention" (Hayek, [1960] 1978:22) in science.[76] Human knowledge is far from being complete. More to the point, the knowledge that members of society have of society is *necessarily* incomplete, fragmentary, and imperfect. But note, it is not absent.

The key passage in Hayek's ([1960] 1978:22) analysis of the difference between what he called the "boundaries of ignorance" or man's "unavoidable ignorance" (Hayek, [1960] 1978:22) and "conscious knowledge" (Hayek, [1960] 1978:22) is: "It must be admitted, however, that our ignorance is a peculiarly difficult subject to discuss. . . . We certainly cannot discuss something intelligently about which we know nothing" (Hayek, [1960] 1978:23). Hayek takes recourse to a kind of Münchhausen maneuver: "We must at least be able to state the questions even if we do not know the answers. . . . Though we cannot see in the dark, we must be able to trace the limits of the dark areas". Nevertheless, as Hayek emphasizes, "If we are to understand how society works, we must attempt to the general nature and range of our ignorance concerning it" (Hayek, [1960] 1978:23).

The excessive prosperity (bubble) in non-knowledge

Despite of the problems that Freud and Hayek quite obviously had with the concept of non-knowledge, why has the term resonated so much in the contemporary cultural and social sciences, particularly in German-speaking countries? In the media and public discourse alike, the category of non-knowledge is increasingly becoming a prominent and trenchant monetary unit as the shady side of knowledge, but why is it gaining currency?

The boom in reflection on non-knowledge certainly has to do with the essentially controversial concept of knowledge as well as with the common understanding of the modern conditions for the production of knowledge, with the societal role often attributed to knowledge, and with the theory of modern society as a knowledge society. Is the difference between knowledge and non-knowledge an example of the typically static conceptual polarity of Old European philosophy? Or is that difference basically only the widespread cultural criticism that the individual—given the extensive and growing volume of objectified knowledge in modern societies and given the sophisticated new technical and complicated methods of accessing it—disposes over only a minute (and probably diminishing) share of all knowledge? Are the widely discussed findings on the average voter's alleged political ignorance, stupidity, and disenfranchisement and on the danger, it poses to democracy a cause of the topicality of the subject of non-knowledge?[77]

It is, on the other hand, unrealistic to assume that the average citizen, including the well-educated contemporary citizen, has (or should have) sufficient *technical* expertise to intervene, for example, in the complex decision-making on economic questions of the goal conflict between inflation and unemployment? At root, does the concept of non-knowledge merely mean the societally necessary *distribution* of knowledge? Does the concept of non-knowledge perhaps refer primarily to the future present, about which one is really little informed? Does the origin of the boom in observations about non-knowledge lie, under certain circumstances, in an overestimation of the societal role of allegedly unquestioned scientific knowledge and in an underestimation of the societal roles of knowledge?

In my view the societal phenomena perceived as non-knowledge can be better captured by other terms, such as "systemic ignorance" (Moore and Tumin, 1949:789), that express how a lack of knowledge or information is manifested in modern societies and how people can deal with knowledge gaps. In any case, two keys to recognizing the myth of non-knowledge are the concept of knowledge itself and the complicated question of distinguishing between information and knowledge.

Observing non-knowledge, and some of the questions one should ask

Repeating my observation about the distinction between knowledge and information: The content of information concerns the characteristics of products or results (output, condition, supply), whereas the stuff that science consists of refers primarily to the qualities of processes or resources (input, procedures, business enterprises), which are used in processes. Knowledge is the capacity to act, whereas information does not enable one to set anything in motion.

With these observations in mind, I try to ascertain what could or could not be meant when one speaks of non-knowledge. People's actions are guided by knowledge. Knowledge of others and self-knowledge are prerequisites for socialization. Hence, as Simmel (1906:441) noted, knowledge is an anthropological constant: "All relationships of people to each other rest, as a matter of course, upon the precondition that they know something about each other" (p. 441). There can be no societal actors without knowledge. One is just as far from being unknowing *without* knowledge as one is naked without a headscarf. A society without secrets is inconceivable. Ignoring knowledge and information is sensible, even rational. A society in which there is total transparency is impossible. Knowledge is never created out of nothing. Knowledge, or the revision of knowledge, arises out of already existing knowledge (not out of forms of non-knowledge). The existence of a *non*-knowledge society is just as questionable as that of a human society without language. Humans live in a complex society marked by a high degree of functional differentiation in which almost all of its members are non-knowledgeable about almost all knowledge. Knowledge in the broad sense meant in this chapter is not restricted to any particular social system in modern societies. Thus, knowledge is everywhere (Luhmann, 1990:147).

It is useful to ignore information and knowledge. Each individual knows that his or her knowledge is limited. Yet people profit a great deal from knowledge they are not acquainted with. What indicators could be used to characterize a non-knowledge society empirically? Almost half of the American population is convinced that the Earth is younger than 10,000 years old. Is the American society for that reason a non-knowledge society?

Who or what is the standard of comparison when one speaks of the duality of non-knowledge and knowledge or of the relationship of knowledge to non-knowledge (as *known unknowns*)? Is it the individual or rather a collective? Privileging the individual is common. To put it more stringently, does the concept of non-knowledge mean a single process, a single quality (information), or the prognosis of an occurrence? How long must (or can) non-knowledge be perceptibly recognizable in order to be non-knowledge? Can cluelessness, for example, last only for seconds? Does one refer to individual forms of knowledge (or information) that the isolated individual (e.g., a scientist) or a non-knowledgeable collective does not—and cannot—have because one always proceeds selectively or is forced to filter?

Knowledge, by contrast, is a variable societal phenomenon that lies on an indivisible continuum and points to the existence of the elementary distribution of knowledge in complex societies. No clear-cut difference between knowledge and non-knowledge exists. Knowledge is a total societal phenomenon.

There is no comprehensive knowledge; nobody can know everything. Acting under conditions of uncertainty is commonplace. Knowledge of these gaps is knowledge. but knowledge of gaps does not belong in the category of non-knowledge if it is a case of negative knowledge (to the extent that one finds this designation helpful). Actually, one can often close this gap quickly because it is possible to know or find out who might know it (a task fulfilled by the role of experts, for instance). On the other hand, there are things that everyone, or almost everyone, knows or about which almost everyone is informed (e.g., the fact that almost every human has two eyes or that there is such a thing as weather or climate). There are a number of expressions that are both empirically and practically more productive than *non-knowledge* and nonetheless illuminate the horizon of problems that non-knowledge allegedly comprises. In the following section I limit myself to just one of these possibilities.

Asymmetric information/knowledge

Economists have been at the forefront and for much of the time alone in examining asymmetric, limited or imperfect information resp. knowledge, with particular reference to competitive markets in which the characteristics of the commodities exchanged and other relevant contextual attributes are not fully known to at least one of the parties to the transaction (Rothschild and Stiglitz, 1976:629). The conflation of information and knowledge is for the most part taken for granted by economists in studies of asymmetric (multiple alternatives are available; the language is rich in this respect: for example, deficient, fractional, incomplete, implicit, tacit, deficient, lacking) market knowledge. In other social science disciplines, as far as I can see, perhaps with the exception of ethnography (e.g., Bauchet et al., 2019), the idea of imperfect information has not been taken up. Since knowledge and information always occur in an *aggregated state*, there can be no such thing as (complete) ignorance for this reason alone. George Akerlof's observation also draws attention to this connection.

In an influential article entitled "The Market for Lemons", the economist and later Nobel Laureate George Akerlof (1970) paved the way for a systematic analysis of asymmetric information by conducting an exemplary analysis of the respective information that buyers and sellers of *used cars* had at their disposal. An asymmetric state of information is one of the essential characteristics of various classes of participants in the used-car market. Asymmetry does not stand for non-knowledge, is not a stand-alone attribute of the intellectual status of an individual or a group face with the contingencies of her typical social context. Asymmetric knowledge refers to the situational based knowing; or, as Steve Rayner (2012:108) formulates it, asymmetric knowledge refers to "knowledge that exists somewhere else . . . but it not known here"; what we do not know we know.[78] Asymmetric knowledge refers to an axis of knowledge that may be located close or at a great distance from us. That the contingent distance or proximity of knowledge can have its advantages or disadvantages is obvious. Why should a houseowner have knowledge about the ways to construct a floor that is capable of carrying a certain weight? Is it therefore justified to call a lack of information an information deficit?

As a rule, the owner and the driver of the used car on sale have much more detailed knowledge about the dependability and history of the vehicle's mechanical problems than the potential purchaser does. In a credit agreement the debtor is guided by certain intentions to repay the credit or not. The lender usually has no access to that information. Nor can the lender be certain that the debtor's intended investment will actually be profitable. Generally speaking, asymmetric information on the part of market participants should lead to market failure.[79]

My interest in Akerlof's notion of asymmetric information does not extend, as would be typical for economists, to the effects limited knowledge has for market performance or, what would be primarily but not exclusively an ethical issue, should the seller tell the buyer about the "real" status of the car and thereby attempt to achieve a new balance of their information? Akerlof has answer to the latter question: The incentive of the seller to reduce the informational deficit of the buyer increases with valuable attributes of the commodity that is for sale.

Buyers and sellers, lenders and debtors are often conscious of the fact that there is or can be a state of asymmetric information. Moreover, "households and firms have incentives for creating information imperfections . . . they may gain from lack of transparency. So can managers . . . by creating an entry barrier to competitive managerial teams" (Stiglitz, 2017:7). It follows that the buyer or lender seeks indicators that diminish the mistrust in the available information or allow that information to be considered more or less reliable. Because the transaction costs of the acquisition of relevant information might be high, the very accessibility of the information on the seller's or debtor's social reputation will likely be an important indicator for the lender or buyer. The seller is not ignorant. In many social relationships, it is equally evident that we are not aware or only vaguely aware to have but asymmetric knowledge, for example, the skills needed to operate a machine.

From Akerlof's deliberations and those of other economists (e.g., Chappori and Salanie, 2000; Sharpe, 1990; Wang, 2012), I derive the following general lesson for my analysis of the antithesis of information and knowledge and the notion of non-knowledge: Because societal knowledge is scattered asymmetrically rather than evenly distributed, one has to assume a cognitive-societal functional differentiation in all societal institutions.[80] In science, such a cognitive division is not only perceived as a matter of course but is also generally understood to be a functional characteristic of science as an institution. Not every scientist can work on just any question. And the role of every scientist cannot be classified in relation to itself, but only in relation to that of other scientists. It is therefore natural to speak of a cognitive functional differentiation in all societal institutions including science. In other words, it makes sense to speak of a range of knowledge in groups of actors in comparison to symmetrically limited knowledge in other groups of actors, and not of knowledge and non-knowledge, especially since knowledge does not appear as a *piece* of the whole, but always in a selection or, better, in an aggregated state, which excludes something like a *tabula rasa* situation: In concrete circumstances there is always some knowledge available, even if it is only limited knowledge. One has to know a lot already before you can even begin to make sense of the notion of non-knowledge.[81] Following a formulation of Ludwik Fleck ([1935] 1979:20; my emphasis), I can also formulate my thesis on the reality of not-knowing as follows: "There is probably no such thing as *complete* error or complete truth."

The notion of asymmetric knowledge precisely captures such attributes and has the further advantage that it allows one to recognize "brakes" on the volume of asymmetric knowledge in economic relations, for example. Limits or brakes that have been institutionalized in law that ultimately correct asymmetric knowledge. I interpret patent law that can function as such a brake and serve as a correction to asymmetric knowledge. Patent law (the draft of patents) disclose and transfer knowledge about an invention and hence communicates knowledge that can eliminate a deficit in knowledge. In the next section, I will examine the function of asymmetric knowledge further.

On the virtues (advantages?) of non-knowledge

The functional meaning of non-knowledge differs from one societal institution to the next. In an institution such as science it is a state of development of knowledge that must be overcome, a condition that acts as an incentive. In a highly stratified societal institution (e.g., a total institution) differing states of knowledge are a constitutive characteristic feature (a functional necessity) that is defended by all means. A society in which complete transparency prevails would be, as Merton ([1949] 1968:345) emphasized, "diabolical". In practice, a mutually transparent, complex society is unrealistic.

In a modern society with its knowledge structure based on the division of labor, it is part of the reality accepted as self-evident that individuals, social groups, or social institutions have long since given up the desire for or hope of autarky of their knowledge as an illusion. Limited knowledge relieves. Knowledge is unequally distributed. Managers usually do not have the technical knowledge of their employed laboratory technicians, engineers, or assembly line workers. Managers become managers despite this lack of knowledge.

Gaps in knowledge or a kind of non-symmetrical distribution of knowledge, not ignorance, are constitutive for societies based on the division of labor. Asymmetrical knowledge stocks do not lead to social collapse. The ability to act competently in a society is not a function of the knowledge and information of isolated individual actors. A competent actor, for example as a politically active citizen, does not need to be fully informed as an individual. This actor can fall back on experts, advisors, and consultants who have the function of aggregating knowledge and making it available for "use" (Stehr and Grundmann, 2011).

Moore and Tumin (1949:787), in their classical functionalist analysis of the societal functions of ignorance, therefore pointed to what in their opinion is the widespread opinion that ignorance is the natural enemy of societal stability and of the possibility for orderly societal progress and that every increase in knowledge automatically increases human welfare. A generally positive public attitude toward new knowledge, which was widespread in the years immediately following World War II, is at present losing ground to growing skepticism about new scientific and technical knowledge. It is not unusual anymore to encounter the opinion that people know too much. Explicit knowledge politics, that is, efforts to police novel knowledge, commences once new capacities for action have been discovered (Stehr, 2003).

There is a multitude of convincing references to the virtues and advantages of ignorance, a lack of knowledge, and invisibility. The discussion and formulation of the novel moral principle for an individual's "right to ignorance" by Jonas (1974:161–163) is clearly germane to a discussion of the political and ethical dilemmas generated by the dynamics with which knowledge grows. Jonas' moral principle is opposed by equally formidable ethical demands that insist on a right to know, especially at the collective level or from a macro-perspective (Sen, 1981; Stiglitz, 1999). In everyday life, sentiments that support the virtue of not knowing find expression in such sayings as "What I don't know can't hurt me" and "Where ignorance is bliss, it is folly to be wise."

Opposition to excessive transparency of one's own behavior and that of other actors, as Merton ([1949] 1968:343) also emphasized, stems from certain structural characteristics of societal groups. To these features belong, for instance, the institutionally sanctioned, but in reality, also limited, negligence in complying with or enforcing existing social norms. The characteristics also include psychologically determined, variable opposition to maximum behavioral transparency (Popitz, 1968:8).[82] In modern society, technical and legal barriers and these conditions for opposition preclude an unlimited investigation of the behavior and convictions of individual actors—about whom one would like to know everything. The alleged goodwill or maliciousness of the thought police is irrelevant. For instance, new possibilities for avoiding technically mobilized monitoring keep turning up.

Popitz (1968:12), on the other hand, pointed to the *disencumbering* function that limited behavioral information has for the system of sanctions.[83] Limiting the available or requested behavioral information—a decision that is tantamount to relinquishing sanctions—is also a sort of "indeterminacy principle of social life". It "opens a sphere in which the system of norms and sanctions need not be taken literally without obviously giving up its claim to validity".

Lastly, there is a further (primarily cognitive) function of insufficient knowledge. It has repeatedly been claimed that knowledge arises from non-knowledge, or that non-knowledge can be transformed into knowledge. Just how this transformation is supposed to happen is scarcely addressed, however. The hypothesis that knowledge originates in non-knowledge as it were, in nothing (*ex nihilo*), completely overlooks the societal genealogy of knowledge, such as the close, even intimate relationship between scientific and practical knowledge. The birth of a scientific discipline is no parthenogenesis. The hypothesis of the transformation of non-knowledge into knowledge favors certain knowledge in that the origin of new knowledge is simply suppressed.

The societal differentiation of non-knowledge and knowledge gaps

Knowledge is unequally distributed. One of the self-evident realities in a modern society, with its functionally greatly differentiated cognitive structure, is that individuals, societal groups, and societal institutions have long since given up as an illusion the wish, the expectation, or the hope that their fundus of knowledge can be self-sufficient. As a matter of fact, limited knowledge relieves. As a rule, managers do not themselves have the technical knowledge of their employed laborers, engineers, or assembly-line workers.[84] Despite this lack of knowledge, managers still become managers and their restricted technical knowledge is not a burden.

Knowledge gaps, *not* non-knowledge, are a constitutive element of functionally differentiated societies. Asymmetrical stocks of knowledge do not lead to society's collapse. A society's ability to act competently is not a function of the knowledge and information of isolated individual actors or does not suffer from in its function from knowledge that I asymmetrical distributed. A competent actor, for instance, as a politically active citizen, need not be comprehensively informed as an individual nor is his legitimacy as a voter called into doubt, as a result.

A modern society, perhaps a collectivity per se without this fundamental limitation, without this cognitive functional differentiation, is inconceivable. No one has to know everything. But this elementary fact, which determines the way society is, does not justify the conclusion that that non-knowledge is the opposite of knowledge. A being constantly caught up in non-knowledge cannot exist. The more collective knowledge increases,

> the smaller the share of all that knowledge becomes that any *one* mind can absorb. The more civilized we become, the more relatively ignorant must each individual be of the facts on which the working of his civilization depends. The very division of knowledge increases the necessary ignorance of the individual and most of this knowledge.
>
> (Hayek, [1960] 1978:26)

Abandoning the hope/misconception for autarkic knowledge, especially for *individual* self-sufficiency of knowledge, and giving up the conviction that knowledge is not essentially limited (bounded), entails both costs and benefits. Asymmetric knowledge mitigates. The loss of autarky—assuming autarky ever existed, even in traditional societies—should never to be understood to amount to a form of non-knowledge. Societal innovations such as the markets, social hierarchies, age structures, the scientific community, different world views, aspirations, or political systems help manage knowledge gaps (Pérez et al., 2012).

Relevant functionally differentiated scales of knowledge differ according to facets such as their respective epoch, the type of society, the pattern of societal inequality, and the interests of the dominant world view.[85] In modern complex societies, the scale of knowledge is longer than in traditional societies. The distance to the sources of knowledge is often considerable. Personal acquaintance with the knowledge producer is not necessary. Only in exceptional cases does the knowledge that one does not have, but can obtain, include the knowledge that was necessary for the production, legitimation, and distribution of the knowledge acquired.

Outlook

The current intense debate among social scientists, with its radical polarization of knowledge and non-knowledge, is like an echo from a lost world or the wish to be able to live in this lost, but secure, world. It was a world in which knowledge was reliable, objective, ontologically well founded, truthful, realistic, uniform, undisputed, and anything but a social relation. It was a world in which scientific knowledge was unique and the profane world of nonscientific knowledge was largely disqualified. It was a world in which more knowledge alone—such as that which enables one to act successfully in practice—was always preferable than having no additional knowledge (knowledge bias). The world of unquestioned knowledge has vanished. Unclear is whether the disappearance of such knowledge is a real loss, as one is evidently supposed to believe from talk of the divide between non-knowledge and knowledge, or whether it is a form of intellectual emancipation.

The difference between knowledge and non-knowledge is an old European antithesis with an ancestry harking back to premodern cultures. The old European tradition of a dichotomy of non-knowledge and knowledge becomes apparent especially in the attribution of persons or groups to one of these two categories. Such ascription holds that the unknowing person or, more generally, the unknowing social class is not only helplessly exposed to the power of knowledge but also pitiable and backward. And inasmuch as the occurrence of non-knowledge applies to other societies and cultures, it is foreign knowledge—not one's own—that is non-knowledge.

The diagnosis to which attention is then usually drawn is to eliminate the alleged knowledge vacuum by tutoring. Brian Wynne (1992:39) has pointed out, as his own research efforts have shown, that this diagnosis of the knowledge vacuum does not go far enough. The stated (technical) ignorance is in contrast "a complex 'active' social construction which reflects a broader array of particular social relationships of dependency, trust, alienation, division of labor, etc., within which people constitute their moral identities." In other words, the so-called knowledge deficit or lack of knowledge must be understood as a strategy of adaptation to the particularities of the social context of people. It is this context that must serve as the key to understanding not only scientific knowledge in everyday life. Asymmetric knowledge is not something that stands on its own, in splendid isolation, but as an adaptation strategy for the contingencies in specific social situations.

As described by Ludwig Fleck (1935/1979:22): "Whatever is known has always seemed systematic, proven, applicable, and evident to the knower. Every alien system of knowledge has likewise seemed contradictory, unproven, inapplicable, fanciful, or mystical."

For that reason, these traditional deliberations on the great divide between knowledge and non-knowledge come nowhere close to resolving the dilemma described by Niklas Luhmann (1991:90; my translation): "Is the generally held assumption that more communication, more reflection, more knowledge, more learning, more participation—that more of all of this would bring about something good or, in any sense, nothing bad—at all justified?" The emerging political field of knowledge politics is dedicated to this societal dilemma posed by the risks of knowledge (Stehr, 2003).

One should not insist on an absolute antithesis of knowledge and non-knowledge—there is only less or more knowledge and those who know something and those who know something else. The practical problem is always to know how much or how little one knows in a given situation. A person is not either knowledgeable or unknowing. A person has more knowledge in one context than in another: A person may know a great deal about tax regulations but hardly anything about playing golf. Another person may know a lot about golf, but little else.

Actors (including scientists) react to complex societal forms by simplifying mental constructs of these relationships. The mental constructs are, in fact, incomplete inasmuch as they do not depict reality its full complexity. These simple models change, react to the unexpected, but are hardly non-knowledge. One of the advantages of liberal democracies is the consciousness that omniscience can be dangerous and that safeguarding privacy must remain a form of sanctioned ignorance.

One of the bold assertions about the *economy of knowledge societies*, as one may encounter them in reports by influential international organization, for example, the OECD (1996), is the idea that there is a *direct* link between developing "useful" or "practical" knowledge in research and development efforts, in turn based in increased educational investments, by both public and private organizations that then leads to enriched economic outcomes and competitive advantages of corporations and nations. Whether the assertion about the immediate productivity of practical knowledge is linked to the Neo-Marxian theory of science that knows no difference between "pure" and "applies" science is unclear (Polanyi, 1956). I assume that such an iron linkage does not exist. The search for practical knowledge is a separate enterprise.

The OECD (1996:7) along with other policy advice and political programs in many countries, emphasized that "governments will need more stress on upgrading human capital through promoting access to a range of skills, and especially the capacity to learn." But how should we imagine that useful or practical knowledge, let alone competencies and skills, look like? And is, assuming efforts are successful, the capacity of practical knowledge *as such* already a key to improved economic performance? We are capable to advance a solution to a problem. But how is this best done?

Practical knowledge

> If it is true that in subjects of great complexity we must rely to a large extent on . . . theories that are difficult to disprove, the elimination of inferior rival theories will be a slow affair, bound up closely with the argumentative skill and persuasiveness of those who employ them. There can be no crucial experiments which decide between them. . . . It is . . . because of the refractory nature of certain subjects that these difficulties arise.
>
> —Friedrich Hayek (1955:19)

In the present contentious climate of "post-truth politics", "alternative facts", a "crisis of science" (e.g. Fuller, 2019; Renn, 2019; Sim, 2019; Mcintyre, 2018: Collins et al., 2017) as well as the broad attention in the media and their affirmation in segments of the lifeworld given to "conspiracy theories" (see Popper, 1996), the question of what might make—outside of the social science community—social science knowledge trustworthy and legitimate has once more become a pertinent and pressing issue in society and science. For centuries, and well into the present day, the utilization of knowledge from all the sciences has been held up as the gold standard for appraising its importance. The by-product of the claim that a discipline is beneficial in society assures public attention and support. The road to legitimacy and trust of social science knowledge examined here occurs via the route of "practical knowledge". However, what exactly is practical knowledge? Practical knowledge represents scientific knowledge that is useable and, in this sense, "works", accomplishes something, makes a difference in the affairs of society by successfully attacking a social problem.

A knowledge framework that deserves the attribute of practical knowledge, it should be noted at the outset does not require that such knowledge structures everyday or popular discourse: The "popular appeal" of an idea does not always translate into his historical influence, and conversely, that unpopular ideas often have profound effects (Jewett, 2021:287).

If I am not mistaken, the dominant answer from social scientists—when pressed to identify attributes of practical knowledge—comes close in its major facets to Friedrich Hayek's response to the puzzle of the great complexity of social relations. Social scientists face considerable difficulties as they confront the extraordinary intricacy of social phenomena. The practical power of social science knowledge depends on constructing and validating social theories in relation to and assimilating the complexity of social phenomena. In other words, the approach is a conventional top-down approach: from theory to reality. My suggestions run exactly the opposite way: Practical knowledge, as I define it, is not identical with what passes for the corpus of validated scientific and technological knowledge and theory—not at any given time in history.[86]

Initially, it is important to repeat: Knowledge, as a generalized capacity for action, acquires an "active" role in the course of social action *only* under circumstances where such action does not follow purely stereotypical patterns, or is strictly regulated in some other fashion. Knowledge assumes significance under conditions where social action is, for whatever reasons, based on a certain degree of freedom in the courses of action that can be chosen. Structures of freedom of action tend to be stratified, of course. For this reason alone, there will always be, of course not with respect to all fields of action and problems, a surplus of knowledge. We often know more than we are able to deploy in order to influence, control or manipulate (cf. Borgmann, 1999b). Steve Rayner (2012:111) refers, using different words, to a comparable elementary fact: "Sense making is possible only through processes of exclusion." Rayner's assertion can be extended to another elementary lawlike observation, *action* is not possible without exclusion. Practical knowledge is always excluding.

The circumstance of action I have in mind may also be described as the capacity of actors to alter, transform or change a specific reality, a kind of "creative leeway" of social life, a "discretion to create" (*Gestaltungsspielraum*). The capacity to alter and affect reality is not symmetrical with the capacity to act (knowledge). Knowledge may be present but for a lack of the capacity to transform, knowledge cannot be employed. On the other hand, actors may have the necessary authority, power, or material resources to change reality, yet they lack the capacity to act. Practical knowledge is not, however, close to or even identical with *practical reason*. Practical reason refers to deliberations about what to do and to efforts, engaging with practical knowledge, in specific contexts, to realize the ambitions of practical reason.[87]

In the conceptual approach I advocate, the social phenomena and processes of knowledge and power are treated as distinct entities. Barry Barnes (1988:58) in his discussion of the *Nature of Power* assimilates knowledge and power much more closely; power is an aspect of the distribution of knowledge or, he offers the observation that "social power *is* the capacity for action in a society." Additional power is never equally distributed throughout society: "Social power is *possessed* by those with discretion in the direction of social action . . . to gain power is to gain such discretion." In this sense, my notion of *Gestaltungsspielraum* of actors is close to Barnes' conception of discretion. However, I would maintain that knowledge and discretion are not quite the same. *Gestaltungsspielraum* refers to the ability of actors to get things done because they control relevant circumstances of action. In order to get things done, one needs the power to command specific resources of action. Thus, the *deployment* of knowledge in particular social contexts cannot be detached from the *relations of power* in that context.

Karl Mannheim ([1929] 1936) defines, in much the same sense, the range of social conduct generally, and therefore contexts in which knowledge plays a role, as restricted to spheres of social life that have not been routinized and regulated completely. For, as he observes, "conduct, in the sense in which I use it, does not begin until we reach the area where rationalization has not yet penetrated, and where we are forced to make decisions in situations which have as yet not been subjected to regulation" (Mannheim, [1929] 1936:102).[88] Concretely to the point, and as Mannheim notes, the

> action of a petty official who disposes of a file of documents in the prescribed manner or of a judge who finds that a case falls under the provisions of a certain paragraph in the law and disposes of it accordingly, or finally of a factory worker who produces a screw by following the prescribed technique, would not fall under our definition of "conduct." Nor for that matter would the action of a technician who, in achieving a given end, combined certain general laws of nature. All these modes of behavior would be considered as merely "reproductive" because they are executed in a rational framework, according to a definite prescription entailing no personal decision whatsoever.

For Mannheim, the question of the relation of theory to practice is then restricted precisely to situations which offer a measure of *discretion* in social conduct, and which have not been reduced to a corset of strictly ordered and predictable patterns of social action. It cannot be ruled out, however, that even under these circumstances where situations are repeated with routine regularity, elements of "irrationality" (that is, openness) remain. The ability to deploy *new* knowledge (in the sense of additional knowledge or, in more conventional terms, invention and innovation) is just as crucial as is the process of finding knowledge for the evolution of society.

Thus, the question also arises as to what other situational factors trigger the search for the open characteristics of a context of action and hence for pragmatic knowledge? For Zygmunt Bauman (2001:141), the search is simply triggered by or brought to my attention "when something goes missing, or when it [my world] suddenly stops behaving as, monotonously, [as] it did before, loses its usefulness or shows itself to be 'unready' for my attempts to use it." Among the most important triggers are certainly *disappointed expectations and hopes*. But resistance (see also Luhmann, 2002:99), fear or doubts can also trigger reflections among the actors. Disappointed expectations, hopes, resistance, the need to justify oneself or doubts are essential incentives to search for opportunities, to mobilize and apply knowledge in order to establish a new balance that stabilizes expectations. Such "search" for open possibilities for action can also be triggered by external structures. In other words,

> if things always happen in the same way, habit is sufficient to control them; if, however, circumstances are constantly changing, habit must never serve as the ultimate guide. Only reflection makes it possible to discover useful new practices, because only reflection can anticipate the future.
>
> (Durkheim, 1991 [1950]:129)

For example, companies must adapt to their competitors, suppliers, and customers. The choice between alternative courses of action is obviously a complex matter, ranging from forced, habitual or random to carefully considered options. If the choice of a course of action is neither random nor forced, considerations of possible options for action are influenced and legitimized by, for example, world views, social symbolism (Taylor, 2004) or moral convictions.

At the macro-level the same point can be exemplified with reference to the power of Keynesian economic theory; a theory that has been noted to have saved capitalism from itself.[89] But first a brief reference to Daniel Bell's *Theory of Post-Industrial Society* and his solution to the inordinate complexity of social life.

Daniel Bell and the reduction of the indeterminacy of social conditions

Daniel Bell agrees with the traditional premise of the social sciences in his theory of post-industrial society: modern society is no longer the two-variable problem of the 18th or 19th century. On the contrary, the methodological promise of the 20th century is the "management of organized complexity (the complexity of large organizations and systems, the complexity of theory with a large number of variables) the identification and implementation of strategies for rational choice in games against nature and games between persons, and the development of a new *intellectual technology* which, by the end of the century, may be as salient in human affairs as machine technology has been for the past century and a half" (Bell, 1973:28). In other words, science through the development of an intellectual technology will be capable of handling large numbers of interacting variables; but this is looking towards the future. It is "the *hubris* of the modern systems theory that the techniques for managing these systems are *now* available" (Bell, 1973:29; my emphasis). Social scientists and intellectuals become managers of social progress, the conscious directors of social change within such a vision of overcoming social complexity.

There is no need in social science theorizing and research to reduce the "new" complexity of social affairs. The social sciences are quite capable of coping with the organized complexity of societal reality. One will not be too far off the mark to call such a vision a *technocratic* program. But what else is the imagined replacement of human judgment by algorithms. An intellectual technology, as Bell (1973:29–30) emphasizes is the "substitution of algorithms (problem-solving rules) for intuitive judgments. These algorithms may be embodied in an automatic machine or a computer program or a set of instructions based on some statistical or mathematical formula." The displacement of intuitive decisions solves the practical difficulties that come with the complexity of social life and therefore to manage the "ordering" (that is, stabilizing) of mass society.[90] These convictions of Bell go hand in hand with his confidence in the possibility of social planning and the idea of rational decision-making by means of futurology in order to alleviate the uncertainty of decisions in complex societies (cf. Andersson, 2019). The need for conscious social planning should not mean to "direct" society, but "to facilitate desired social changes" (Bell, 1973:313).

Daniel Bell (1973:337)[91] was aware of and rebelled against the charge of technocratic reasoning because, as he noted,

> the problems of the communal and post-industrial society are not technical, but political, for even though in the nature of the new complexities a large kind of new social engineering is involved, the essential questions are those of values. . . . The central question of post-industrial society, therefore, is the relation of the technocratic decision to politics.

It is not easy to see where the possibly subtle difference between a planned and a planning society might lie. A realistic and proven counter proposal to Daniel Bell's idea of a technocratic design of modern society is John Maynard Keynes' less ambitious but politically very successful *General Theory*.

The *General Theory* as practical knowledge

> I am sure that the power of vested interests is vastly exaggerated compared with the gradual encroachment of ideas.
>
> —John Maynard Keynes (1936:383)

I would like to stress at the outset that social scientists and their knowledge are extremely powerful in practice, as long as one bases such a judgment on the extent to which social scientists act as *producers of meaning* (meaningful narratives) taken on board in everyday life. Karl Polanyi ([1939]2014:114–115) refers precisely to these possibilities of influence of social science findings by pointing out that

> the social sciences have a massive influence on man's wishes and purposes . . . by creating the very phenomena on the existence of which they were insisting—such as the utilitarian psychology of the businessman, sex consciousness in psychoanalyzed persons, or class consciousness in social groups.

John Maynard Keynes would have agreed, as the motto from his famous conclusion to his *General Theory* demonstrates.[92]

However, what is left open, is exactly what ideas may prove to be more powerful than vested interests for example. In order to arrive at a response about to the question of exactly what social science narrative from among the multiplicity of meanings construed in social science prove to have a successful career in society, it is not sufficient to merely conjecture that social scientists produce narratives and that such a conception of social science labor is supported by the hermeneutic or interpretive theoretical tradition in social science (e.g., Bleakely, 2020:126).

In general, it is likely that social scientists are more successful in practical and political terms as producers of *meaning* than in their role as producers of (categorical) "new realities" (as a form of radical nominalism)—to the extent that the two possibilities of influence can be distinguished empirically and theoretically at all. Sociologists and economists who subscribe to a "performative understanding of economic theory" (see Çalışkan and Callon, 2009) follow closely the perspective of the social sciences as producers of categories produce the social world, in other words, as the producers of the economic world/reality by the social scientists. The categories of thought in the social sciences *contribute* to the constitution of the world. As meaning producers, the influence of social science discourse is only possible within the limits of their correspondence with pre-existing social structures (cf. Bourdieu, 1987:839).[93]

However, social scientists often subscribe to a *scientistic* version of their activity, and thus generally underestimate their influence in society. Granted: to trace the influence of social scientists as producers of meaning is extremely difficult—last but not least because the production of meaning is subject to the phenomenon of "obliteration by incorporation" (Merton, 1968:35–37) and its often-radical transformation by preachers, teachers, journalists, etc. as intermediators who are responsible for the ways social science knowledge travels in society.[94] For example, the sociological concept of "knowledge society" has been taken on board by many social institutions, political parties or international organizations. But few if any persons outside of the social sciences, that is, in these institutions would be able to identify the authors of the notion of knowledge society. I have made this test quite a few times. Their knowledge about the knowledge society stems from any of the intermediary sources that interpret the idea in their own way wherever and however they may have encountered it, in the first instance. The case of Keynesian economic theory as an example of powerful social science knowledge does not mainly draw on meaningful knowledge as the product of social science rather Keynesian theory represents the case of social science knowledge as instrumental knowledge. John Maynard Keynes' (1936) *General Theory of Employment, Interest and Money*, in spite of the "dry" title of his monograph, represents much more than a pure, narrow economic theory; his *General Theory* is a polemic against excessive saving, the stratum of *rentiers* who are not performing any productive work, and puritanism that had neglected the arts of production and the enjoyment of consumption.

The unique complexity of social phenomena

The assertion concerning the unique "complexity" or peculiarly intricate character of social phenomena has, at least in sociology, a long, venerable and virtually uncontested tradition. The classical theorists, for example Georg Simmel and Emile Durkheim, make prominent and repeated reference to this attribute of the subject matter of sociology and the extent to which it complicates the development of sociological knowledge generally and the production of practical knowledge in particular. At least for the last 100 years and more, this observation has been repeated almost without any further differentiation. In *The Elementary Forms of Religious Life* ([1912] 1965:31), Emil Durkheim stresses: "The social realm is a natural realm which differs from the others only by a far greater complexity."

The determination of the unprecedented complexity of social facts has of course not only a considerable influence on the difficulty and validity of formulating sociological findings, but also on the successful applicability of these findings to the solution of practical problems. The thesis about the reasons for the backwardness of social science findings—in theory and practice—has a positivistic genealogy. Otto Neurath ([1919] 1994:1589), who called himself without hesitation a social engineer, refers more than a hundred years ago to exactly this connection and the associated deficit as well as the way out of this deficiency:

> A social construction treats our whole society, especially our economy, like a huge enterprise. The social engineer, who understands his work and wants to deliver a construction that can be used as a first instruction for practical purposes, must take into account the mental characteristics of man, his desire for the novel, his ambition, his attachment to tradition, his obstinacy, his stupidity, in short, everything that is suitable for him and determines his social action within the framework of the economy, just as the engineer takes into account the elasticity of iron, the breaking strength of copper, the color of glass, and the like.

Otto Neurath continues, impressed but not resigned, "the levers and screws of the order of life are even more special and fine. But the difficulties of the task have never deterred a courageous thinker and man of action."

In short, no thoughtful social scientist seems to be prepared to deny the proposition that economic, political, and social systems are complex (Thrift, 1999). The assertion that social phenomena are complex and intricate is seen to affect all aspects of the search for robust social scientific knowledge and its application.

However, there is much less agreement about the precise nature of this complexity of social life; nor is there consensus about how deeply and for how long the intricate nature of social phenomena will affect the manufacture of social science knowledge. Finally, a closer examination of the repeated observation concerning the perplexing nature of social processes shows that social scientists have yet to find recipes, let alone uncontested measures, to overcome the limits this imposes on the reliability and validity of our reflections. In short, it would seem that the complexity of social reality has an especially inhibiting effect on the production of social science knowledge that is powerful in practice.[95]

The assertion that social phenomena happen to be complex phenomena is meant to sensitize social scientists, be it from an epistemological perspective or in a more mundane sense, to the purposes of practicing their craft, that is, to the kind of explanatory and methodological devices that are equal to the task of adequately capturing social reality.

Thus, complexity means that a particular social process, such as, for instance, exchange rates, is driven, re-produced, or modified by a multiplicity of interdependent factors and that it is most difficult to make a detailed and precise forecast about price movements. Since social systems exhibit properties of organized complexity, their structure includes, as Brewer (1973:75) suggests, "overlapping interaction among elements, positive and negative feedback control loops, and nonlinear relationships, and they are of high temporal order." Given the properties of complex social systems, does this mean that prediction and control are hopeless enterprises? In spite of our perhaps vague disciplinary awareness of the complexity of our existence, we have for centuries intervened and attempted to engineer social and ecological outcomes.

According to the conception of social systems as inordinately complex, any empirically valid representation, and therefore any effective and manageable control of such a complex process, requires, it would appear, a faithful and complete rendering and understanding of all the intricate factors involved as well as of their interconnections. Anything less constitutes or amounts to a sterile and, above all, deficient reflection of social reality. In short, as most social scientists would maintain, the most promising answer to the challenge of complexity is not to ignore the challenge but to devise ways of meeting it.

In his Nobel Memorial Prize in Economic Science lecture, entitled "The Pretence of Knowledge", presented in 1976, Fredrich Hayek ([1974] 1989) subscribes without hesitation to the idea that the social sciences, as far as I can tell, confront an inordinate complexity of social life and that a genuine *scientific* account would incorporate the full range of variables of such a complex realty. But he adds a novel concern. He adds the observation that unlike the physical sciences the social sciences suffer from an essential deficit, that is, "in economics and other disciplines that deal with essentially complex phenomena, the aspects of the events to be accounted for about which we can get quantitative data are necessarily limited and may not include the important ones."

For all intents and purposes, what is important in the physical sciences can be measured. In the social sciences, what is considered to be important often cannot be quantified. It is necessary to distinguish between facts that can be measured and are considered important and facts that cannot be measured but may be of relevance. Social scientists often try to follow or *appear* to follow the physical sciences assuming that only the variables that can be quantified are important. In fact, a wide range of social science variables cannot be quantified. This leads to a pretense of knowledge and amounts, as Hajek warns, to the specious claim of what the social sciences can accomplish, for example, in the policy advice generated on such a fragile basis.

Specifically, in the fields of the social sciences, there "are not only absolute obstacles to the prediction of specific events, but why to act as if we possessed scientific knowledge enabling us to transcend them may itself become a serious obstacle to the advance of the human intellect." The social are not scientific disciplines in the sense of the physical sciences. The social sciences are unable to capture the full empirical complexity of social structures such as the market. To pretend otherwise, for public policy, amounts to the very dangers Hayek enumerates.

Whether the claim to have full knowledge of the social complexity of social life really means complete knowledge of all the circumstances is perhaps an open question. However, if the idea indeed refers to the need to bring together all the relevant information needed to give a full, valid picture of a specific context, then what could be called the *social engineering fallacy* (scientism) would apply. A proposition that both Otto Neurath and Friedrich Hayek identified and rejected as an epistemic and practical aim. What speaks against such a lofty goal is the (1) division of knowledge in society which renders unavailable the full spectrum of knowledge to any individual or group, the (2) attachment of skills and know-how to local circumstances, and let alone the (3) uncertainly of the future conditions and desires (Hayek, 1937:1942–1944).

But what does one make of the typical social science knowledge generated under these demanding circumstances? Knowledge that fails to adequately capture the complexity of social phenomena may well be a precursor of the kind of knowledge which social science hopes to generate one day, and is therefore nevertheless necessary (e.g., Simmel, 1890:7–8). Immediate relevance, one might say, is sacrificed for ultimate relevance (cf. Lynd, 1940:2). If the subject matter of social science changes in ways which make it both more "complex" and, therefore, less able to capture its domain in frozen accounts, the debate about complexity will stay with us for a long time. The alternative is to reconsider the notion of complexity, as an obstacle to practical knowledge, in a quite radical sense.

It could be argued that the supposition concerning the temporary deficiencies of social science knowledge which can be repaired through incremental improvements and approximations to the "real" complexity of social phenomena itself suffers from serious deficiencies which originate not from any attributes of the domain of social science but are subject to the control of the social science community because they involve a deficient understanding of the nature of practical knowledge.

Is a reduction of societal complexity the prerequisite for powerful knowledge?

In his paper "Die 'Objektivität' sozialwissenschaftlicher und sozialpolitischer Erkenntnisse" ([1904] 1922:171; English [1904] 1949:72: " 'Objectivity' in Social Science and Social Policy"), published on the occasion of taking on—together Edgar Jaffe and Werner Sombart—the editorship of the *Archiv für Sozialwissenschaften und Sozialpolitik*, Max Weber refers to the intriguing and telling distinction between "Stoffhuber" and "Sinnhuber". The translation inherited from Edward Shils and Henry A. Finch ([1904] 1949:112) as "subject matter specialists" and "interpretative specialists" misses the German meaning by quite a distance.

A more appropriate translation of the dichotomy in knowledge-guiding interests Weber's terms capture would be a difference in orientation between "(data) accountant" and "meaning orientator"; the former refers to an endless and perhaps mindless effort to collect data upon data while the alternative interest deliberately limits inquiry and therefore data collection based on a specific meaningful orientation/goal.[96]

It may not have been Max Weber's intention, but his dichotomy opens up a path toward practical knowledge. However, only halfway because he does not specify the knowledge guiding interest that leads to useful knowledge.

Linking Weber's dichotomy to the issue at hand: the "Stoffhuber" aims to capture social reality in its full complexity while the "Sinnhuber" limits such a search based on a specific knowledge interest, in our case, locating dimensions of a social context that can be changed or are open to action/intervention. Weber's dichotomy therefore corresponds closely to alternative orientations in a search for practical knowledge. Simply collecting information does not lead to practical insights.

As far as I can see, Max Weber and Karl R. Popper are among the few well-known philosophers of (social) science who seem to be quite unimpressed by the assertion concerning the intricate and endless complexity of social phenomena.[97] Karl Popper ([1957] 1972:140) is convinced that the thesis about the extraordinary complexity of social phenomena actually constitutes a subtle form of a prejudice which has two origins: (1) The thesis is the result of a meaningless and inaccurate comparison of circumstances; for example, a comparison between the limited and controlled conditions found in a laboratory and the conditions of real-life social situations. (2) The thesis is the result of the orthodox methodological conception which holds that any adequate description of social phenomena requires a complete account of the psychological and material circumstances of all actors. Since humans tend to behave rationally in most situations, Popper maintains, social interaction can be re-constructed with the aid of relatively simple models which assume and reflect such rational conduct among the participants.

In the same essay on "Objectivity in Social Science and Social Policy", Max Weber emphasizes that the knowledge-guiding interest based on a "Stoffhuber" orientation is a meaningless social science undertaking because social science, as an *empirical science* of concrete *reality* (*Wirklichkeitswissenschaft*), can only portray *a fraction of the complexity* of social reality and, is therefore, unable to fully capture social reality: "Every knowledge of infinite reality achieved by the finite human spirit is therefore based on the tacit assumption that only a finite *part* of it should be object of scientific inquiry and 'essential' in the sense of 'worth knowing'." In other words, an epistemic interest that is deliberately limited is characteristic of the social sciences in general, and thus not just of the specific epistemic interest of seeking practical knowledge.

Let me, in addition, point to a couple of questionable premises of the orthodox position regarding the significance of capturing the full complexity of a specific social context as a precondition for generating powerful knowledge (Grundmann and Stehr, 2012; Stehr and Grundmann, 2001):

(1) "Mastery" and change of social conditions is not necessarily identical with and based on the *complete* intellectual control of the complex origins and processes of social situations. Whatever control may be possible under given circumstances is likely to be restricted to a few attributes of the context.[98]

(2) Efforts to raise the theoretical complexity of social science knowledge may therefore have the unanticipated effect of propelling such knowledge into an even greater distance from social action and its possibilities (cf. Luhmann, 1970).

I will illustrate these points with reference to what is possibly the most powerful and influential social science theory ever devised, namely John Maynard Keynes' theory of the modern economy (cf. Stehr, 1992).

Keynes' theory as an exemplary case

> Economics is fortunate among the social sciences in that many of its findings are directly applicable to public policy.
>
> —Paul A. Samuelson, 1959:183

Assuming Paul Samuelson's optimistic message is accurate, it remains an open question which economic insights are practical and why they are so. *One* answer to these questions can be found, as far as I can see, in the theory of John Maynard Keynes. Undoubtedly, the Keynesian theory of economic action is one of the most influential and important theoretical designs in economics in general and the economics of developed market economies in particular. Keynes positioned his theory in strict opposition to the ideas of the classical economists of the 18th and 19th centuries, arguing that the most important economic problem was not scarcity but economic policy mismanagement. Moreover, Keynes supported a much more active economic role of the state, for instance, as an investor to boost aggregate demand.

But does Keynesian economic reasoning also live up to the practical usefulness ascribed to much of economics by Paul Samuelson? It could be argued that Keynes saved capitalism from collapse and that economics today are largely "The House that Keynes Built". What makes Keynesian economic theory interesting as an exemplary model for an analysis of social science knowledge is, furthermore, the possibility to test the efficacy of this knowledge. Without entering into a painstaking exegesis of Keynes' (1936) *General Theory*, which was published toward the end of the global economic crisis of the 1930s, we can say that despite his intention, as expressed by the subtitle, to formulate a *general* theory of employment, interest, and money, Keynes' major work does not constitute such a general theoretical model.

That is, Keynes fails to enumerate and examine the intricate interrelation among innumerable attributes and processes of economic as well as other variables, any one of which may affect the employment rate, the monetary value, and the interest rate. The disappointment, given the widely shared standards for adequate knowledge and advances in knowledge over time, could hardly be greater.

Keynes' general theory of employment, money, and interest, above all, is rather parsimonious when it comes to identifying relevant theoretical dimensions for reflection and inquiry. His theory refers to *but a few* attributes of economic action. Keynes almost completely lacks an interest in foreign economic influences; therefore, his theory can rightly be described as an economic theory of the *nation-state* reflecting the exceptional political and economic realities of his time. The economic model theory we now need "would have to see the economy as 'ecology', 'environment', 'configuration', and composed of several interacting spheres: a 'micro-economy' of individuals and firms especially transnational ones; a 'macro-economy' of national governments; and *a world economy*" (Drucker, [1989] 2003:149–150; my emphasis).

As a matter of fact, for our purposes, Keynes' theory can even be summarized quite briefly by indicating that it represents, for the most part, the discovery of the relevance of *investment decisions* for the employment rate of a national economy. His theory therefore is about as far away as possible from attending to or capturing, as Seymour M. Lipset put it, the "total system behavior" of a major social phenomenon. On the contrary, Keynes' theory appears to be an intellectual "throwback" to the fallacies of classical social science theorizing with its abundance of limited factor theories.

Despite the fact that but few pertinent attributes of the full complexity of economic action appear to have been examined and taken into account by Keynes in his *The General Theory*, vigorous voices were raised almost immediately after its publication,[99] and certainly a chorus of voices in later years, that praised Keynes' theory and insisted that it may well have very important practical implications and benefits for the economic affairs of a nation.

In his new monograph "Capital and Ideology", Thomas Piketty ([2019] 2020:979–981) proposes an equally straightforward solution, that is, exempting it from the obvious complexity of the policy issue of attacking social inequality, to the question of tackling wealth inequality: every single person as a young adult should be given an inheritance of $120,000 financed by a progressive tax on private wealth, that is, ensuring "universal capital endowment" in society. This hardly captures, as many social scientists will complain, the complex ways of transcending social inequality in modern societies.

The constituents of practical knowledge

> Knowledge . . . changes something or somebody—either by becoming grounds for action, or by making an individual (or an institution) capable of different and more effective action. And this, little of the new "knowledge" accomplishes.
>
> —Peter Drucker ([1989] 2003:242)

Peter Drucker's skeptical observation that knowledge is not practical *a priori* is a useful reminder that the transformation of knowledge as a capacity to act requires congenial circumstances, for example, power or authority that commands conditions of action.

In general, I would like to submit, the search for practical knowledge has to be alert to the specificity of the (local) situation. It is a search for a problem than can be a problem. The lesson one may be able to draw from Peter Drucker's observation about the useful role of knowledge—knowledge that makes a difference—is that knowledge does not automatically apply or create its own momentum of usage. The question about what may make knowledge useful therefore remains open. In light of the value of Keynesian economic theory as a principally powerful intellectual tool for practical action (economic policy), I would like to suggest that reflections about the conditions or constituents of practical knowledge have to start out from the assumption that the adequacy (usefulness) of knowledge that is employed in a context different from that of its production can now be formulated in terms of the *relation* between knowledge and the *local* conditions of action. My observation about the centrality of the relation between knowledge and the local conditions of action leave the nature of the "relation" as a black box.

What exactly is local can of course be quite small social entity such as a firm or very large social unit such as the union of multiple states. Within the context of application, constraints, and conditions of action are apprehended as either open or beyond the control of the relevant actors. But who or what specifies what are open conditions of action? Invoking what is likely a simplistic dichotomy: it could be the authority of the scientific community or power of (local) politics. Andrew Jewett (2021:289) sees science as the "arbiter"; science

> is strategically central in societies that define politics in secular, depersonalized terms. In such societies, science is widely seen as the final arbiter within its own sphere, specifying which features of the world a political regime can seek to alter and which is cannot.

The legal scholar Cass Sunstein (2016:1607) prefers to attribute the power of the definition to the executive branch of government since "the executive is the most knowledgeable branch"; he adds,

> it often makes sense, within constitutional boundaries, to give it considerable discretion in both domestic and foreign affairs and to grant it considerable (though hardly unlimited) deference when it exercises that discretion. Both legislators and judges tend to be insufficiently aware of their epistemic disadvantage.

In less than a stringent binary attribution, the definition of the conditions that are open to action are an empirical matter. In specific instances the definition may be linked to the authority of science, in other cases, the power of politics may prevail and, not to be neglected, the decision may turn out to be hybrid matter.

Given this differentiation between conditions of action, practical knowledge pertains to open conditions of action, which means that theoretical knowledge has to be re-linked to the social context—be it large or small—in general and those elements of the situation that are actionable, in particular.[100]

A brief example may serve as a first illustration: A rather common social science knowledge claim, or a claim that at least appears to be central to a number of theoretical traditions within sociology, holds that there is a close relation between the degree of urbanization and the birthrate or the divorce rate (e.g., Yi and Vaupel, 1989). But such a knowledge claim clearly does not pertain, in all likelihood, to conditions that are open to action. Even very powerful politicians in a centralized state who are concerned about a decline in the birth or an increase in the divorce rate and looking for ways of effecting a slowing or even reversal of these rate would consider such a claim as highly irrelevant since the degree of urbanization is hardly an "open" dimension even within their context of political action. But that is not to say that this context of action is void of any attributes and conditions which are in relation to relevant actors, and in some sense, open and may in fact be capable of influencing the divorce and birth rates as the result of their political action. However, as we will see, these "fruitful" conditions of action are hardly on the radar of disciplinary-bound reflections, nor would they carry if taken on board much theoretical or disciplinary legitimacy.

In a complimentary sense, James Coleman (1972b) has suggested that "discipline research" knows but two types of variables, namely "independent" and "dependent" dimensions of social action, while social "policy research" must attend to three classes of variables. There are "policy outcomes", "policy variables", and "situational variables". The latter are part of the circumstances of action and cannot be affected by it, while policy variables, as Coleman calls them, correspond to what I have called attributes of action open to certain actors in a specific social context. Social policy research then is propelled by a consideration of "policy variables" or begins with a problem formulated outside the discipline but is executed within the discipline (Coleman, 1972b).

The social science literature generally and writings in the area of the methodology of the social sciences, scarcely contain any useful information about the systematic identification and use of attributes of social action which may be open in specific situations, or are perceived by the relevant group of actions as open to their control. For example, when Stanley Lieberson (1985:227), in his critique of dominant practices in social research, urges that "there is a need for knowledge about a basic cause that is sufficiently strong to overcome the existing entropy and, of course, that will change the outcome in the direction desired," he does not provide the sympathetic researcher with any useful hints about how such a contribution to policy questions might be achieved in social research.

Within much of social science discourse, the decision about which factors or attributes to select as objects of theoretical reflection and empirical study is, as a rule, dependent on disciplinary traditions. The selection or choice of factors for data collection and analysis which are subject to control in practical situations becomes a matter of mundane theories but, in contrast to scientific discourse, especially a question of the relative power of actors, their resources and resolve within their settings and with respect to the environment which also affects their context of action.

The fact is that many economic theories fail to address the question of power, resources, and features of economic action beyond the control for example of the specific corporate actors. Indeed, economic discourse has eliminated such considerations as a matter of *disciplinary* reasoning, constituting, for some economists at least, an explanation of the relative practical impotence of economic theorizing (e.g., Rothschild, 1971). In other words, economist often seem to assume erroneously that virtually all factors which are part of their theoretical models are somehow open to action or that the ability of actors to engage in economic action is insensitive the unique circumstances of action.

Gedankenexperimente

A somewhat different approach to the idea of practical knowledge are "real experiments", that is, in order to achieve a certain result in the laboratory, one has to screen out, simplify or reduce for example the complex impact of the natural environment on a process. For as Karl Popper ([1957] 1972:139) observes, "in general it is only by the use of artificial experimental isolation that one can predict physical events." Only then is one able to clearly determine or identify a specific relation that would be responsible for the observed or desired effect.

In order to successfully repeat/*translate into praxis* the observation made in the lab outside the lab, the artificial experimental isolation/set up has to be recreated. The transfer and implementation of such a laboratory result or, as the case maybe, in the social sciences, based on a *Gedankenexperiment*, into practice is of course encumbered with considerable difficulties, not to speak of various risks following the transformation of society into a laboratory (cf. Krohn and Weyer, 1989; Böschen et al., 2017) that might contaminate the effect or make it impossible to repeat it outside the laboratory. It is very likely that unanticipated intervening factors could occur, even with a certain delay which might jeopardize any effort to repeat the effect observed in the laboratory.

John Maynard Keynes' policy intervention

> Our final task might be to select those variables which can be deliberately controlled or managed by central authority in the kind of system in which we actually live.
>
> —John Maynard Keynes (1936:247)

The practical economic lessons drawn from Keynesian economic theory constitute a "system of political control over economic life" (Skikelsky, 1979:55). More specifically, a careful reading of *The General Theory* shows clearly that Keynes explicitly tried to devise practically sound answers for economic problems which were constructed with a certain corporate actor in mind: *The British Treasury*, an institution which he was personally familiar.

The policy conception advocated by Keynes was characterized by its simplicity and flexibility, though different concrete policy measures were consistent which its overall thrust. Keynes' theory and policy measures espouse the intervention of the state in an effort to balance the disequilibria of the capitalist economy. More specifically, these interventions should (1) create institutional conditions that lead to lower interest rates and contribute to expectations about economic growth that in turn should stimulate private investments, while (2) the state should support demand by increasing public expenditures. A crucial, if not decisive, premise of Keynes' advocacy of this type of economic policies is the *ability of the state to act/intervene* in the economy in the desired manner producing the expected results.

Today, any attempt to uncouple a nation from the global economy can only have serious, negative repercussions. Nationally compartmentalized economic policies are a strategy of the past. *National* economic goals can only be achieved on the basis of an international coordination and integration, which is of course associated with "costs" in terms of a loss of sovereignty. As far as I can see, since the mid-1960s, Keynesian economic policies are no longer effective. The Covid-19 pandemic may represent, if only temporarily, novel circumstances, for example, a lower volume of international economic ties that could partially reinstate the efficacy of Keynesian national economic policies.

One of the reasons for the decline in the practical usefulness of Keynesian economic thinking for economic policies is paradoxically the very success of Keynesian policies. Keynesian economic policies may well represent a peculiar case of self-elimination. That is, Keynes could not have anticipated that his theories would become part of economic common sense. Nor was he able to foresee the transformation of economic realities that resulted from the widespread practice of economic policies inspired by his ideas throughout the world. The far-reaching deficit spending programs by many states in response to the Covid-19 crisis is the most recent vindication of Keynes' insight.

Nonetheless, vigorous and passionate objections to his theory are often based on the argument that Keynes' ideas are totally useless or counterproductive when it comes to deriving policy lessons from them. Keynes was certainly aware that his ideas would one day be subject to heated political debates. In a letter to George Bernard Shaw, written in 1935, he says that "when my new theory has been duly assimilated and mixed with politics and feeling and passions, I can't predict what the final upshot will be in its effect on action and affairs. But there will be a great change" (Keynes, [1973] 1987:492–493). This prediction, at least, was fulfilled.

And one can surmise that the polemical style of Keynes' writings also fueled the public attention they attracted in many countries. The passionate debate, both in economics and the public, about Keynes' work continues until this day. Tragically, however, its initial penetration and acceptance among economists and practitioners occurred too late to prevent the "political disintegration in Central Europe [in the 1930s], let alone permit the Western world to arm itself in time, on the basis of its abundant superfluity of material resources, against the Nazi assault" (Balough, 1982:39; Stehr, 1992:98–100, 114).

The intellectual division of labor that has emerged within the social science in the last decades does not constitute a promising basis on which to build and develop social science knowledge that responds effectively to local conditions which, at times, can of course encompass man individuals and groups or a large territory for that matter. An analysis of research projects devoted to practical matter quickly confirms, on the whole, the disciplinary self-sufficiency (cf. Coleman, 1972a) of such research. The growing number and the growing tightness of cognitive boundaries of intellectual concerns and methodological practices of exclusion within social science are, for the most part, not a pre-condition, but a distinct barrier, as many have recognized, for the construction of social science knowledge which is practical knowledge. As long as the selection and incorporation of variables is driven by disciplinary or, even, subdisciplinary practices and traditions, then the probability is considerable that the outcomes of such cognitive efforts too are limited to the practitioners who inhabit and defend the territory within these boundaries. In principle, a broader integration of intellectual efforts for practical purposes is not impossible and may not even contradict further cognitive differentiation within the social science community. However, neither work on the legitimation of labor directed toward practical knowledge in social science is easy, nor is the optimistic conclusion justified that development in this direction will be without major difficulties. Entrenched intellectual and social forces within the social science community are very successful in operating in the opposite direction. Skepticism about the success of a program for practical knowledge is therefore in order. As a matter of fact, the description of the foundations of practical knowledge may have some affinity to Karl Popper's (([1957] 1972):428) praise for the need of "a social technology . . . whose results can be tested by piecemeal social engineering".

Instead of looking for the "correct" mix of policy levers which I take to mean in the dominant philosophical and methodological traditions to capture a fair rendering of the sheer number of working social parts, one should concentrate in detecting practical knowledge on those policy measures that work because they can be enacted in the relevant societal context. The method to be followed in the search for practical knowledge amounts to a trial-and-error approach.

A much more "powerful" but largely invisible effect of social science, as Michel Foucault or Helmut Schelsky, among others, have reminded us, is the impact it has on interpretations of reality in everyday life, that is, the extent to which the self-understanding of actors in modern society and the media through which such convictions come to be expressed are shaped by social science conceptions. Whether one is prepared to describe this process as a "social scientification" of collective and individual patterns of meaning is a contested question. However, it is not unwarranted to suggest that many of the current problems the social sciences face in practice are related to the fact that the self-understanding of many groups and actors is affected, often indirectly, by elements of social science knowledge. In this context, one may refer for example, to the discovery of climate change in everyday life and in politics. The empirical analysis of social problems by social science research therefore evolves into a form of self-reflection, or a reduplication of course altered social scientific conceptions.

The knowledge problem

The "knowledge problem" is closely allied with Friedrich Hayek's (1937) discussion of the significance of knowledge for economic conduct. In his 1937 essay, that constitutes the presidential address to the London Economic Club on November 10, 1936 and in the subsequent paper (Hayek, 1945) on "The Use of Knowledge in Society", Hayek describes what is and what is not the nature of the economic problem faced in society. That is, what is economic about the economic problem? Though an important step in the direction of a solution to the economic problem, it cannot be the *logical* problem and the calculus economists have developed to solve this logical problem.

The logical issue of the economic problem, or, static equilibrium theory, can best be described as one in which the models with which economists operate assume that there is *full transparency* of all relevant factors that make up the economic problem, for example, information about the preferences of all economic actors. It would follow that the economic choice individual make is a logical choice. The reason for our inability to address practical economic problems in society on such a basis is "that the 'data' from which the economic calculus starts are never for the whole society 'given' to a single mind which could work out the implications, and can never be so given" (Hayek 1945:519).

The empirical knowledge (and information—Hayek conflates the two terms, as I had already noted) one would need to command is not only widely dispersed but contradictory, incomplete and in the possession of many separate individuals. The economic problem of the modeler can therefore be described as a "the utilization of knowledge not given to anyone in its totality" (Hayek, 1945:520). The fact of the wide dispersal of different knowledges,[101] of "the knowledge of the particular circumstances of time and place" (Hayek, 1945:522)[102] raises the question of how really existing economic actors, each with limited knowledge, manage to carry out "rational" economic *exchanges* at all.

Hayek complains that recent (at this time) contributions by contemporary economists to economic theory as well as especially the extensive use of mathematics have obscured rather than clarified the issue. However, Hayek (1945:529) has an answer to the question what produced, in the first instance, the theoretical deficit he identifies: the "misconception . . . is due to an erroneous transfer to social phenomena of the habits of thought we have developed in dealing with the phenomena of nature."

But there is not only an epistemological, methodological, and theoretical issue. There also is a rational, moral, and political issue, after all, what is the most efficient way of "planning" to utilize the widely dispersed knowledge (*division of knowledge*) of economic actors? This is a core question of economic policy. In any case, as Stiglitz (2017:11) stresses,

> one of the important insights of the economics of information is that in the absence of good information, typically competition will be imperfect; and with imperfect competition, there is the possibility (likelihood) of firms exploiting market power, and indeed, with imperfect and costly information, of undertaking actions that enhance their market power.

Hayek's response to the core question of economic policy is a conservative counterattack to efforts to *politicize* the economy. In this respect, Friedrich Hayek opposed John Maynard Keynes, Joseph Schumpeter, as well as Ludwig von Mises in their tolerance for state intervention into the market place. Economic policy should not be based on the erroneous assumption that "we possess the knowledge and the power which enable us to shape the processes of society entirely to our liking, knowledge which in fact we do not possess, is likely to make us do much harm" (Hayek, 1974). Central economic planning by state authorities can only amount to a grave fallacy. It is the competitive *market* that is the director, it is the *price* that is the substance of communication and that serves to coordinate the limited knowledge of separated and dispersed individuals. It is surprising therefore how little the individual actor has to know in order to be able to make the right decision.

Market competition divulges "which goods are scarce goods, or which things are goods, and how scarce or valuable they are—these are precisely the things which competition has to discover" (Hayek, [1978] 2014:306). Knowledge of the market context transcends information about the price of a commodity. Knowledge of the market context also extends to many relevant attributes such as the legal issues, the size and geographic extension of the market, environmental regulations, innovative trajectories, preferences of other market participants, future price movements, etc. (cf. Caldwell, 2016).

Basically, however, markets organize economic action around information. But this leaves the question unanswered, exactly what information does the market transport? In general, the major deficit of the information markets communicate via the price of services and commodities excludes the social, ethical, political, and environmental externalities that economic interactions generate. These deficits in the price information produced by markets make it difficult for all economic actors to gain traction, for example with respect to ethical or sustainable conduct. But in concurrence with Hayek's conception, central planning authorities or agencies would not be able to overcome the deficits of the way in which markets are organized today.

Noteworthy in the context of a discussion of the knowledge problem and markets is the meta-observation about the modern economy as a knowledge-based economy where wealth is dependent on information and knowledge. Thus, counting and accounting for knowledge is a major political issue.

Hayek may not have solved the knowledge problem by producing a full theory of the ways in which markets allocate, distribute, and accumulate widely dispersed, unorganized knowledge/information among many different economic actors. However, what his interjection into the discussion of running a national economy made evident is a cautionary principle, namely that knowledge is widely dispersed, distinctive, difficult to assemble and accumulate for the purposes of policy intervention. As a result, Friedrich Hayek (1945:521) does not leave much room for the any hope for universal or global worlds of knowledge:

> practically every individual has some advantage over all others in that he possesses unique information of which beneficial use might be made, but

> of which use can be made only if the decisions depending on it are left to him or are made with his active cooperation.

The kind of knowledge Hayek has in mind is not the knowledge observers have in mind when they address the possibilities, benefits, or costs of globalizing knowledge regimes carried out for example by multinational corporations or scientific societies; as a matter of fact, Hayek refers to the knowledge of interest to him as "practical knowledge" (Hayek, 1945:522).

As I will discuss in the following section, the issue of practical knowledge that is globally available continues to be, despite Friedrich Hayek's efforts to show that that it does not make sense to expect anything approaching universal knowledge, a frequently discussed topic in the social sciences. What is meant with my analysis of global worlds of knowledge is not its *normative* reference, however significant such an orientation in certain contexts may well be, namely that global thinking is highly desirable, for example, in climate discourse and climate policies.

The problematization of global knowledge worlds depends on our understanding of knowledge, for example, if one decides to knowledge as "communicated as information" (Krohn, 2003:98–99), the global availability of knowledge must be unlimited and would appear to be hardly complicated. This means that we live in an information society, "because the networks of communication use all the knowledge in the world everywhere and at all times as information for decisions on action and for education of orientation patterns". However, Wolfgang Krohn's observation severely underestimates or hides that knowledge often lacks transparency, the resources that need to be mobilized in order to discover that knowledge maybe worthwhile, to learn and absorb knowledge, even if it reaches us as information (cf. Arrow, 1962). Conflating information and knowledge, given the assumption that information is abundant, easily leads to the erroneous conclusion that supports the idea that knowledge must global.

Anticipating a result of my inquiry into global worlds of knowledge, a global knowledge common in which its profits are not limited geographically or appropriated unequally exists at best theoretically. The concept of knowledge as a public good has been recognized for some time. More recently, as Joseph Stiglitz (1999:308; my emphasis) stresses, we "recognize that *knowledge* is not only a public good but also a global or international public good."[103] As far as I can see, empirically such a global knowledge common does not exist since knowledge cannot as easily travel as the World Bank appears to hope. The limits to the mobility of knowledge can be deliberately restricted, for example with the help of legal restraints and depend also on the kind of knowledge in question, for example, whether the knowledge in question amounts to additional or novel knowledge. In any case, the question THAT I would like to take up on the next section—"are there global worlds of knowledge?"—is a sensible puzzle given the broad understanding that knowledge is not an object that is *a priori* restricted to a particular physical space.

Global worlds of knowledge[104]

> What is common to all can only be the possession of who possesses less than anyone else.
>
> —Georg Simmel, [1917] 1970:44[105]

To what extent is, can—and maybe even should—knowledge generally be accessible around the world? Is global knowledge at best the minimum of globally shared knowledge? Is knowledge a public good whose opportunities for example in the field of health care can be *equitably* and globally exploited? Is knowledge universal? An affirmative answer, the knowledge of the knowledge society indeed is universal, obviously means that "knowledge in substance is abstracted from place and time. Knowledge, thus, is different from other types of meaning, which may be quite parochial" (Frank and Meyer, 2020:134).[106] One of the implications of the universality of knowledge assertion is the apparently close affinity of the knowledge society thesis and the idea of the unrelenting globalization process in the modern world. The related assertion that knowledge literally imposes itself, is realized independently of any social context or allows for a context-independent form of social exchange, is a fallacy of inappropriate concreteness. The economic implication of perfect mobility of knowledge would be a gradual but persistent trend toward full equality of knowledge capacities and human capital across countries. As Thomas Piketty ([2013] 2014:70) remarks with justification, "no small assumption".

Nonetheless, whatever convergence in the economic growth among countries may have taken place, the

> principal mechanism for convergence at the international as well as domestic levels is the diffusion of knowledge. In other words, the poor catch up with the rich to the extent that they achieve the same level of technological know-how, skill, and education, not by becoming the property of the wealthy.
>
> (Piketty, [2013] 2014:71)

However, successful convergence of knowledge depends on multiple factors; it does not occur more or less automatically transcending all social, economic, and political hurdles.

The conclusion of a laissez-faire global worlds of knowledge is of course diametrically opposed to the observation that knowledge is tacit and sticky and that such knowledge can be the source of a firm's competitive advantage because it is not accessible, copiable, or imitable. Knowledge is "reluctant" to travel because it clings to the knower. Knowledge is produced locally and remains local without efforts to overcome its parochial nature. The opinion that it should be otherwise is perhaps largely nourished by the ease with which data and information are believed to circulate. Nonetheless, knowledge as a non-rival good does leave its origins for obvious reasons; the producer desires that her creation departs, and not merely as "fugitive knowledge" but at times as a rival commodity.

In the following section, I will analyze more skeptically which factors and processes, immanent or not directly attributable to knowledge, impede and set limits to the dissemination of knowledge and its deployment, and, by the same token, if such confines fail to restrict the spread of knowledge around the world, would appear to enhance the world-wide accessibility and use of scientific knowledge, in particular. In other words, the issue of global world of knowledge is by no means settled by boldly asserting that knowledge knows no human boundaries. Specifically, in the next section, I will take up the question of the role of the "walling-in" of knowledge or the legal coding of knowledge as one of the key issues in the context of the evolution of knowledge societies into knowledge capitalism and, in particular, the knowledge economy.

How global is knowledge?

> Knowledge is like light. Weightless and intangible, it can easily travel the world, enlightening the lives of people everywhere. Yet billions of people still live in the darkness of poverty—unnecessarily.
>
> —World Bank (1999:1)

The quote from the World Bank Report (1919:1) in its report *Knowledge for Development* may serve as a first answer to the question of global worlds of knowledge.[107] There are apparently huge gaps and barriers to the actual dissemination of knowledge around the world. Poor countries and poor people, the World Bank Report (1999:1) concludes, "differ from rich ones not only because they have less capital nut because they have less knowledge. Knowledge is often costly to create, and that is why much of it is created in industrial countries." The unequal distribution of knowledge constitutes the comparative "knowledge gap". The sharpness of the knowledge divide may have increased in the last decades, but these disparities appear to constitute as far as the World Bank is concerned "only problems". The uneven distribution of knowledge may be overcome in principle.

And, as economist Kenneth Arrow notes (in Stiglitz and Greenwald, 2014:507; my emphasis), although "knowledge is a free good," "the biggest cost in its transmission is not in the production or distribution of knowledge, but in its *assimilation*." Knowledge is capability-dependent, that is, knowledge requires skills as well as the control of other circumstances of action for its effective use (cf. Drahos, 2004:331). Naturally,

> transmittal and receiving costs are lower the greater the similarities in the experience of the transmitting unit and the receiving unit; . . . the easier it is to transfer technology in codified form, such as blueprint, formulas, or computer languages. . . . The transfer of knowledge may be impossible in the absence of the transfer of people.
>
> (Teece, 1981:83–86)

In other words, the assumption that there are zero marginal costs in reproducing an additional "unit" of knowledge does not, in many cases, hold along the spectrum of knowledge claims.[108] Joseph Stiglitz (1999:309) therefore maintains, "to acquire and use knowledge, individuals may have to expend resources."[109]

On the basis of Arrow's observation alone it would be a fallacy to assert that either knowledge or information are subject to anything resembling a free-flowing process or an open access system. Discourse about the information society, for example, is often tied to discourse about a "shrinking world" or globalization theory with its assumption of an instantaneous/real time dissemination of knowledge and information as the motor of a global extension of social action.

The movement of knowledge is embedded in social relationships that can not only accelerate the movements but also successfully hinder the transmission of knowledge.[110] However, it is accurate to stipulate that efforts to hinder the flow of information and knowledge, for example, through the commodification of knowledge are effective, in principle.[111] Knowledge does not necessarily freely flow to the place where is might make the greatest profit. As in the case of "global capital", different social contexts may be organized and secured in a compatible network-like manner so that knowledge can "travel" largely unhindered, but then it travels in the interest of the power that has established and sustains these (legal) networks. Nonetheless, enclosing knowledge improves the chances that knowledge generates a profit.

Formulated in a different manner, knowledge is less transportable than physical equipment. Georg Simmel's sober observation about the minimum commonality of human attributes across collectivities, on the other hand, refers to a kind marginal law of its distribution, that is, the last individual who still shares in a specific knowledge determines the common world of knowledge in a population. It is not the middle or the average, but the lower limit of any "participation" that determines the degree of the dissemination of knowledge (also Luckmann, 1982:260–264).

However, as Joel Mokyr (2018:103) with justification points out,

> in the end, what each individual knows is less important than what society as a whole knows and can do. Even if very few individuals in a society know quantum mechanics, the practical fruits of the insights of this knowledge to technology may still be available just as if everyone had been taught advanced physics.

From an economic point of view, in particular, what counts for the welfare of society are the collective capacities of knowledge.

The most pertinent problem in achieving a global spread of knowledge or for any successful migration of knowledge across continents is, therefore, if we follow Kenneth Arrow, "learning" or the absorption/appropriation of knowledge that would have to be accomplished for knowledge to become widely disseminated, distant from its origins and capable of being deployed as a capacity to act in distant places. The reproduction of knowledge through learning may have the likely unintended consequence of a mutation (innovation) of an idea; more generally, "knowledge received and the knowledge transmitted are never quite the same" (Mokyr, 2018:96). But even the restrictions that Arrow acknowledges as impeding the ease with which global worlds of knowledge may emerge, and attributable to the need to learn and therefore to the straightforwardness with which knowledge may travel globally, neglects cultural, economic, and political factors that are part of the circulation and exchange of knowledge across boundaries. Everything else equal, the process and cost of generating an idea is different from the process and cost of re-producing an idea (e.g., research vs. teaching). Even in the absence of legal restrictions, diffusion and adoption of knowledge, not necessarily all knowledge, are costly and time-consuming.

Appropriating knowledge[112]

For economists, the attributes of non-rivalrous consumption and non-excludability of knowledge are critical attributes of knowledge. Such attributes of knowledge make it a prototypical example of an (even global) public good. If at least some of the profits of knowledge can be appropriated, using trade secrets or patents (at times labelled "private knowledge"), for example, it becomes an *impure* public good. Given these special characteristics of knowledge, the World Bank (1999:17) reiterates the conventional premise of neo-classical economic discourse about the inducement the legal encoding of knowledge, arguing that "public action is sometimes required to provide the right incentive for its creation and dissemination by the private sector, as well as to directly create and disseminate knowledge when the market fails to provide enough." In contrast to the dominant economic justification for legal ways of fencing in knowledge, the idea that knowledge is *self-protecting* summons up a very different perspective on knowledge and efforts to police knowledge. The idea that knowledge is self-protecting involves a *supply and demand* side argument, as Edmund Kitch (1980:711–715) outlines.

On the supply side, the point would be that knowledge is difficult to steal, or that no one has an interest in stealing knowledge because it is difficult to profit from stolen knowledge. The most common notion that knowledge does not travel well is, of course, the notion of the "tacitness" of knowledge properties (as a non-public aspect of knowledge), as first explicated by Michael Polanyi (1958,

1967). Profiting from non-public knowledge is possible without patent protection. The "stickiness" of knowledge (von Hippel, 1994) is related to the ways in which knowledge is organized: "Managers can avoid increasing the ease with which information can be transmitted by resisting the temptation to assemble the information in organized written form" (Kitch, 1980:712). On the supply side, the self-protection of knowledge would also be associated with the extent to which the command of scarce cognitive competencies is required for the appropriation of knowledge; the extent to which knowledge is embedded in specific socio-technical contexts or knowledge infrastructures (such as the ability to learn how to learn) that are not freely mobile or easily reconstituted; or the ability to mobilize capacities to effectively generate access to desired knowledge.

On the demand side, self-protective features of knowledge are related to a high depreciation rate, which means that knowledge, once it is acquired, has become worthless in relation to the cost of acquisition and to future benefits that may be derived from such knowledge. Moreover, in the case of some forms of knowledge, at least, the proprietary nature of such knowledge, not unlike a famous painting, can be easily identified by others and is therefore worthless except to its lawful owner. The exigencies that make it difficult to steal knowledge also protect it from unlawful distribution, since the thief may have difficulty establishing the necessary competence to offer any credible warranty of its efficacy and authenticity. Finally, the value of knowledge is related to its scarcity. Any dissemination or anticipation of dissemination of knowledge may reduce its value and therefore deter the incentive to obtain such knowledge. Such a depreciation of the value of knowledge occurs with greater likelihood among actors who compete in the same market or context. One can accelerate the depreciation of knowledge if one acts according to it and encourages others to do so. In short, a high depreciation rate means "by the time someone steals the information it is worthless which in turn means there is no incentive to steal it" (Kitch, 1980:714).

The sum total of the exigencies enumerated amount to *self-protecting* attributes of knowledge, indicating that knowledge is embedded in a "network" of cultural and structural attributes, for example, a scientific laboratory that affect the ease of its mobility and migration. The idea that knowledge is self-protecting, or can be "serviced" or protected in such a fashion that travel is bound to be difficult (e.g., avoiding its organization in written form), has implications for the very project of formulating knowledge policies. If a stringent case can be made for the existence of significant self-protecting features of knowledge, then restrictive knowledge policies would not have to be put in place, since the more or less unencumbered dissemination of knowledge is unlikely. However, rising voices, especially in the developing world, which see efforts by Western commercial interests to appropriate (traditional) public knowledge for private gain as a form of the theft of such knowledge would obviously oppose the notion that knowledge cannot be stolen and cannot be privatized easily. Vandana Shiva (2001:284–285), for example, defines "biopiracy" as "based on a false claim of creativity. It involves the appropriation of the cumulative, collective creativity of traditional societies and projects the theft as an 'innovation'." The appropriation and translation of public knowledge in traditional societies into forms of knowledge protected by patents signals that knowledge—although, in this case, devalued by treating it as a form of indigenous or even invisible knowledge—can move, can be transported into different social contexts while the original context is unable to protect its migration.

Considering the movement of knowledge into the opposite direction, from the developed to the developing world, a publication of the *International Monetary Fund* (IMF) boldly refers to the ease with which knowledge travels, now aided by the internet:

> With globalization and advances in information technology, however, the potential for knowledge to travel faster and further has increased dramatically, opening up greater opportunities for emerging market economies to learn from other, technologically advanced, countries and build their own innovation capacity.
>
> (Eugster et al., 2018:52)

Whether this is the case, will be the subject matter of the next section.

Knowledge knows no borders

The concept global knowledge as used here does *not* refer to already existing worldwide knowledge communities (for example, the aspiration of Mike Featherstone [2006] and his colleagues to create a "global archive of knowledge") or institutions of knowledge (examples could be cartels, universities, hospitals, libraries, museums [Frank and Meyer, 2020]), or assuming such worlds of *global* knowledge as part of a world society in fact already exists.[113] The *World Bank*, for example, claims for itself to be ready and prepared to be in the business, to sell ideas, to be a global knowledge actor representing a global Knowledge Bank: "Knowledge is the core of our DNA" (World Bank, 2009). Moreover, as indicated, I recognize that knowledge *embedded* in artifacts, for example, cell phones, is found almost universally, sells everywhere and does not require for its intended operation the know-how that went into its design and construction. Knowledge that spreads without or hardly any cognitive effort does not belong in this context to what I would like to call "global knowledge".

Instead, my focus is on the social and intellectual processes and obstacles knowledge as such has to master in order to become global in scope and overcome any unbalanced distribution across societies. The ease with which specialized knowledge (and information, given that these terms are often liberally conflated) is assumed to be able to travel is echoed in recent transnational treaties designed to protect intellectual property, for example, in the so-called TRIPS (trade-related aspects of intellectual property rights) treaty of the World Trade Organization (WTO).

One can only speak realistically of global worlds of knowledge if knowledge is *obligated* to travel, however such travel is directly or indirectly accomplished, that is, if the makers and the consumers of knowledge *are not* identical.[114] Something like a global world of knowledge exists only if a difference can be established between the groups of actors who represent the supply and those who constitute the demand, taking knowledge on board. That knowledge has to travel in order to become part of global worlds of knowledge is but one requirement; one could it as the necessary condition. The sufficient requisite is its intellectual effort and absorption requiring of course learning.

This separation is also valid for knowledge anchored in social constructions or embedded in technological artifacts: knowledge that indeed travels as part of a product, but whose content is not *directly* "consumed". Examples of this are the knowledge inscribed in material substances such as pharmaceuticals, foods, software, algorithms, and technological artifacts such as cars or cell phones, but also in pictures or symbols (for instance, in advertising; or in popular culture, especially as present in the media). Global worlds of knowledge relate to the "horizontal" and not the "vertical" (for instance, in the sense of class- or social stratum-specific or the one-sided downslope movement of knowledge from the expert to the layperson) distribution of knowledge. I also assume that we are dealing with forms of knowledge that, for whatever reason, are not subject to regulations—whether this be, for example, in the context of self-interested professional, commercially-motivated limits or restrictions generated by knowledge policies—placed on the circulation of ideas; or, as hotly debated recently, for reasons of so-called "national security".

At this point, I am not concerned with a range of topics that all would be at home under the umbrella of the global range and influence of scientific knowledge; specifically the worldwide dissemination of the *institution* of science including the global institution of particular *scientific fields and practices* as well as the *resistance* to the currently dominant boundaries of the cognitive authority of science, the structural convergence of scientific practice, or at the methodological level, the disciplining of observations as a precondition for his global mobility, the global dissemination of the role of the scientist/engineer and/or its integration into worldwide networks, global job markets, or that of the growing world-wide number of state-sponsored and non-governmental scientific institutions, and, last but not least, global evidence of self-interested science denial in many countries.

One of the early claims for the certain global reach of intellectual products, at least under the conditions of nascent modern capitalism may be found in Karl Marx and Friedrich Engels' *Manifest of the Communist Party*, which dates from 1848:

> In place of the old local and national seclusion and self-sufficiency, we have intercourse in every direction, universal inter-dependence of nations. And

> as in material, so also in intellectual production. The intellectual creations of individual nations become common property. National one-sidedness and narrow-mindedness become more and more impossible, and from the numerous national and local literatures, there arises a world literature.

The question of whether, among *modern* societies a "global" world of knowledge can exist is, from the viewpoint of sociology, a largely unexplored terrain. Thus, I take note of the widely taken-for-granted assertion that the origin of a *divided* world of knowledge is a modern phenomenon. Reference can be made, for example, to Emile Durkheim ([1955] 1983:76) who in his lectures on pragmatism stresses,

> it is in the very early ages that men, in every social group, all think in the same way. It is then that uniformity of thought can be found. The great differences only begin to appear with the very first Greek philosophers. The Middle Ages once again achieved the very type of the intellectual consensus. Then came the Reformation, and with it came heresies and schisms which were to continue to multiply until we eventually came to realize that everyone has the right to think as he wishes.

In the context of some discussions of globalization processes, the issues of globalizing worlds of knowledge, information, ideas, or policies are being considered. When we think of global knowledge, we tend to think, in the first instance, of the global dissemination of modern *technical and scientific knowledge* mainly originating, produced and validated in the Western world (cf. Connell, 2007) and not the global existence/presence of (different) traditional or indigenous forms of knowledge.

Among the basic and complicated questions that form part of any territory of inquiry into global knowledge would be: How dependent is the world-wide dissemination of knowledge systems on social structure (for example, "global" job markets) or "issues" that are considered to have a world-wide impact and "force" the global dissemination of associated forms of knowledge (for example, environmental, security or health issues)? Does knowledge change as it travels? Is an equal or uniform distribution of knowledge even possible in modern societies? Is knowledge the intellectual mark of an age of globalizing knowledge societies? If knowledge becomes global, what are its benefits or drawbacks? Why is new knowledge in demand worldwide? There also is a re-evaluation of the nature and the value of "local" or "indigenous" knowledge against the backdrop of globalization processes and their impact around the world.

But aside from distinct local or even global intentions to protect knowledge that threatens to become "placeless" and the vision that knowledge becomes effortlessly—in a technical sense—connected all over world, the question of the possibility or the nature of the limits to globalizing knowledge is an open matter.

Perhaps the matter can be put even more succinctly: Is "boundless knowledge" a matter of the growing "standardization" of organizational or social forms (e.g., states, firms and the scientific community) across the globe, or are there forms of knowledge (and its carriers) that increasingly transcend locality and actively promote converging social contexts around the world? The approach to and/or even the implementation of global or globalizing worlds of knowledge have hitherto been realized above all in normative and idealistic speculations, by decree, as a thought experiment, or in business plans. Similar premises, however, also underlie thoughts found in economic and/or management literature. Reflections on the development of a global world of knowledge without borders are found not only in discussions of the extension of a global knowledge-based economy (for instance, in the sense of global production networks), but also in studies or articles in the field of so-called knowledge management, which ever more frequently deal with global knowledge agendas, the institutionalization of global knowledge experts and global knowledge management strategies.

An important *inter*societal vehicle for the dissemination of knowledge and the development of globalizing worlds of knowledge is trade in services and products. An expansion of worldwide trade, particularly the dismantling of trade barriers for developing economies, could lead to an unintended worldwide diffusion of ideas and knowledge as easily as to the reduction of information and knowledge deficits in the world. To be sure, one ought not to imagine this as simply the transmission of knowledge and artifacts, but rather as the development of hybrid forms of knowledge.

In contrast, I will refer here to a couple of specific forms of constraints on the development of globalizing worlds of knowledge: (1) on intrasocial and intersocial limits, for example a society's legal practices, the cultural traditions of a country that resist any easy assimilation of new ideas, its inherent inequalities (forms of division of cognitive labor; incentives for asymmetrical access to knowledge, such as in order to defend the power of the market), the boundaries between social organizations (companies, laboratories; clusters and networks), and the trade barriers between societies;[115] and (2) on characteristics that can be traced directly back to certain characteristics of knowledge, for example, its embedded nature in complex bodies of ideas, commodities, and services.

Knowledge is often considered to be the public common property par excellence; the ethos anchored in the institution of science, for example, demands that knowledge—at least in principle—be accessible to all. Modern communications technologies and the spread of learning institutions seem to guarantee an easier access to knowledge and possibly contribute to rendering potentially still existing claims to ownership almost ineffective. To be sure the possibility, and the danger, also exist that it is not unhindered dissemination of knowledge that occurs, but rather concentration of knowledge. The conclusion to the host of questions raised about the existence or the prospect of global knowledge can only be those certain forms of knowledge, especially those embedded in projects and (physical) artifacts that transcend individuals may well be global but that most forms of knowledge will continue to struggle to be universal.

That knowledge is global because it represents and adds abstract, permanent, and universal value to the local context as David Frank and John Meyer (2020) emphasize is, however, doubtful. This also applies to the thesis of the inevitable globalization of knowledge through the loss of the power of the nation-state, as well as the increasingly globalized economy and information and communication technology that ignores all borders:

> Knowledge formation and power over knowledge in the global economy is moving out of the control of the nation state, because innovation is globalized, because the discourse on knowledge is outside the state's control, and because information is much more accessible than it was before thanks to technology and communications.
>
> (Carnoy and Castells, 2001:11)

Frank and Meyer's hypothesis about global world of knowledge underestimates the social construction as well the re-production of knowledge and the forces that impact on both processes. Imitation perhaps falls short of appropriation. Moreover, the observation of the global presence of scientific knowledge overlooks and misjudges the power relations involved. Global knowledge worlds usually go hand in hand with asymmetric power relations in which the power of the receiving groups and institutions is considerably limited in comparison to "sending" companies, for example. The colonization of other regions does not necessarily mean that indigenous forms of knowledge are impotent or are completely wiped out.[116] At the same time, it is not unheard of that indigenous knowledge is "expropriated" by foreign takeover. These realities indicate that a dominance of certain worlds of knowledge is not as yet realized.

Perhaps "knowledge as algorithm" moves closer to the vision of a knowledge society in which knowledge no longer knows local, parochial contexts, but is standardized across all borders? Algorithms resonate closely with the notion of "intellectual technologies" endorsed for example by Daniel Bell. Bell (1973:26) was convinced that post-industrial societies would be able to reach a "new dimension of societal change, the planning and control of technological growth" aided by the rise of a new intellectual technology. An intellectual technology represents "the substitution of algorithms (problem-solving-rules) for intuitive judgments" (Bell, 1973:29). Daniel Bell was correct in his anticipation of the ubiquitous presence of algorithms in the daily life of modern societies. The widespread employment of mobile technologies assisted in this development. Intellectual technologies promise, Daniel Bell expects, the reduction of indeterminacy in human affairs if not an anchoring of fairness and justice of human decisions. However, there is the not insignificant danger of encoding exactly the opposite, cementing inequality, for instance in the sense of an "empathy override". The fear even more generally is that AI systems will not do (whatever that may be) "what we want them to do".[117]

Knowledge in the age of the algorithm

It is helpful to ask, following immediately upon my discussion of the nature of practical knowledge as well as the prospect of global worlds of knowledge about the increasingly prominent role of algorithms (intellectual technology) in relation to knowledge, praxis and global aspirations of such tools. After all, algorithms are nothing but (*embedded*) practical knowledge;[118] however, the social context, for example, the decision rules, within which such capacities to act generate decisions to be executed are submerged. With algorithms, the (human) weighing, the search for decisions comes partially to an end. The decision is formalized, hence the earlier terminology for "artificial intelligence"—the "mechanization of thought".[119]

In other words, algorithms may be described as powerful tools in everyday life and as influential in decision-making in social institutions—for example, in law, by arriving at a decision by a judge on the length of a defendant's prison time,[120] in health, in the labor market, in the economy, and in politics—but simultaneously as largely undetected, opaque, and inaccessible to external critique. In order to "translate" knowledge into action, what is needed is, as I have shown, a particular context within which action is considered needed and then undertaken by mainly mobilizing knowledge. Algorithms are a non-rival good. Like a digital article, an algorithm may be used again and again without preventing someone else to study the article that recommends for example a certain restaurant to us.[121] However, under patent laws in many countries, algorithms are excluded from the sphere of patentable inventions (Abiteboul and Dowek, 2020:72). In general, progress in developing AI technology empowers those who have the data and computational capability to process and manage these resources, especially in companies such as Google, Amazon, and Facebook—entities that are for the time being for the most part outside external control—based on the huge amounts of business data generated. In these big corporations, AI proceeds apparently at a gradual pace rather than by leaps and bounds.

What mostly enhances the likelihood that knowledge is activated in response to a particular problem, command, or issue, for example, is the *social pressure to act*. But what is mainly needed are particular conditions of action, specifically, the ability (under the control of an individual or collectivity) to change elements/features of the social context in question in which pressure to act is perceived or brought to bear on the actor(s) in question. What prompts one to contemplate action is of course a "problem" (expectation, desire, goal attainment) and as a consequence the aspiration to achieve/prevent an outcome, to reach a goal, to hide something, to make a move, to eliminate the pressure to act, to complete a task, to eradicate the *status quo* etc.

Helmut Willke (2001:4) calls the resource mobilized upon under these circumstances "Intelligence"; intelligence describes solutions to problems that are incorporated, for example, in technologies:

> in tools, cars or telephones, means that as a user of these technologies, I don't usually must know more and no longer know how these technologies work, so what specific intelligence is built into them. It's enough that I know how I use these machines. Usage does not require an understanding of the built-in Intelligence.
>
> (Willke, 2001:10)

Intelligence could of course also be embedded in a recipe to prepare broccoli for dinner.

Joel Mokyr (2018:100) labels the ability to utilize embedded knowledge competence; in order to differentiate between knowledge

> needed to invent and design a new technique from that needed to execute it, I shall refer to the latter as *competence*. . . . Judgment, dexterity, experience, and other forms of tacit knowledge inevitably come into play when a technique [embedded knowledge] is executed. Another element of competence is the solution of unanticipated problems that are beyond the capability of the agent: knowing whom (or what) to consult and which questions to ask is indispensable for all but the most rudimentary production processes.

What Helmut Willke early in this century describes as intelligence could just as well be termed *algorithm*. A recipe is an algorithm. Algorithms make things happen. Following Ed Finn's (2019:561) definition of an algorithm, this becomes evident: "An algorithm is a recipe, an instruction set, a sequence of tasks to achieve a particular calculation or result." The chain of contemplation that leads to action is embedded in algorithms. As Robert Sedgewick, who is a leading researcher on computational algorithms, therefore points out, an algorithm is a "method for solving a problem" (cited by Finn, 2019:561).[122]

An algorithm is a bridge between knowledge as capacity to act and the solution to an issue at hand, or an algorithm represents the closure of the circle between knowledge and a goal. Finn (2019:561) quotes from a Google document that offers a similar definition: "Algorithms are the computer processes and formulas that take your questions and turn them into answers." The ability to get something done is in fact accomplished by algorithms; and it is accomplished relentlessly, faster, and without deviating from the coded path. Algorithms apply to virtually all phenomena. The foundations on which algorithms operate are not objective or raw information. As in similar cases of decision-making, algorithms employ socially constructed information. Whether algorithms are capable of learning is a contentious issue, however, for some observers, "algorithms can learn by repeating the same task and improving" (Abiteboul and Dowek, 2020:16).

The solution to the problem to which algorithms respond requires of course a judgment, possibly a series of compromises and presumptions about courses of action that may be available as solutions and their effectiveness. But once the solution is taken on board, once you have acquired the ability to cook a meal, the bridge between knowledge and action can be passed many times if not indefinitely. More and more actions become routine and virtually eliminate uncertainty, and we massively enlarge/create the volume of new kinds of temporality:

> As we blanket the planet in sensors, chips, and radio waves, the territory of "effective" is growing rapidly. In the past decade, we have made driving cars, playing Go, and conversing in natural language effectively computable, and the algorithms are marching on relentlessly to more ambitious and ambiguous challenges. The space of computability is growing most quickly in the dimension of time.
>
> (Finn, 2019:562)[123]

The risks and dangers associated with knowledge in the age of algorithms are considerable and certainly worthy of close attention as the first state-based efforts indicate to set standards for government and public agencies' use of algorithms. An article in *The Guardian* (July 28, 2020) summarizes the following concerns:[124]

> The increasing application of algorithms by governments around the world—particularly when they are deployed to profile or generate decisions about citizens by law enforcement, immigration, welfare and health agencies—has proved controversial in recent years. Critics claim that decision-making driven by lines of code can be inaccurate and discriminatory and that their use is often kept secret from the public.

Efforts to govern algorithms are therefore one of the more recent examples of knowledge politics engendered by "concerns about accountability, fairness, bias, autonomy, and due process—exacerbated by the widely bemoaned opacity and inscrutability of computational systems" (Ziewitz, 2016:4). The claims about the growing but hidden influence of embedded knowledge in the form of algorithms are extensive, as Diakopoulos (as quoted by Ziewitz, 2016:5) notes:

> We are now living in a world where algorithms, and the data that feed them, adjudicate a large array of decisions in our lives: not just search engines and personalized online news systems, but educational evaluations, the operation of markets and political campaigns, the design of urban public spaces, and even how social services like welfare and public safety are managed.

> But algorithms can arguably make mistakes and operate with biases. The opacity of technically complex algorithms operating at scale makes them difficult to scrutinize, leading to a lack of clarity for the public in terms of how they exercise their power and influence.

The claims made about the social, cultural, and economic impact indeed are extraordinary. It is quite easy to find such sweeping assertions about the coming extraordinary power of AI. For example, Stuart Russell, the initiator of the Center for Human-Compatible Artificial Intelligence, clearly expects that "machines more intelligent than humans would be developed this century"; obviously Russell anticipates such an enlargement as a potential danger and therefore now calls for "international treaties to regulate the development of the technology".[125] Similarly, the historian Yuval Noah Harari anticipates that "humans are at risk of becoming 'hacked' if artificial intelligence does not become better regulated"; to hack human beings means "to get to know that person better than they know themselves. And based on that, to increasingly manipulate you."[126] Even more radical are assertions claiming that AI *is already* manipulating us.[127]

It cannot be overlooked that narratives dealing with the characteristics and consequences of new technical developments often exhibit a technocratic drift. Technical discovery is expected not only to emancipate itself from its discoverers, but also to take dominion over its discoverers and developers as a phenomenon in its own right. As a result, people are urged to ensure that they do not squander control over the automation of the world of work or, indeed, AI.

So far, however artificial intelligence (AI) has not lived up to the buildup of its proponents or the fear engendered by its opponents. AI stirs excessive promises and existential doubts. Robots have not assumed power over humankind. Yet, there is real concern among some observers about the impact of AI and the extent to which it might emancipate itself from human control. Algorithms are viewed as social power that functions through algorithms as well as the cultural image such codes have in society. Algorithms are seen to occupy a central position in everyday life, the world of work as well as science. Algorithms are seen as a threat to jobs; they may limit civil liberties and/or spy on us on behalf of government and large corporations. But then there are or will be better outcomes as well. For instance, "algorithmic decisions are depicted as neutral decisions, algorithmic decisions are understood to be efficient decisions, algorithmic decisions are presented as objective and trustworthy decisions" (Beer, 2017:11).[128] Independent of outcomes, algorithms are still social constructs. In other words, they are phenomena that cannot be located beyond the control of all. Knowing about algorithms and their implications becomes an important capacity. But what does it mean to understand algorithms? The visibility of algorithms is obscured which allows for claims about its power that is doubly removed from the phenomenon. Courts will be increasingly confronted by claims that *decisions* that are more or less automated based on algorithms may be biased, lack transparency, are tough to change, and are difficult to subject to control, for example, in the field of welfare systems.[129]

Algorithms as repositories of knowledge, that is, of human choices that have an elective affinity to AI (*artificial intelligence*); this becomes clear when AI is defined as the ability "to make appropriate generalizations in a timely fashion based on limited data" (Kaplan, 2016:5–6). Exactly which goals, problem solutions and applications (choices) will be realized is open in principle. In other words, the application for repressive purposes is not excluded. AI can be used as a "less expensive" digital weapon; in fact, at lower cost in several respects compared to conventional methods of repression. Critical observers stress that AI is a "boon to authoritarian forces. . . . The advantage lies with the biggest information companies, such as Google, and the biggest authoritarian states, above all China" (Diamond, 2019:23).

Steven Feldstein (2019:41) refers also to the use of AI by autocratic political (and no longer by an informant system like the GDR) regimes:

> autocracies have achieved new levels of control and manipulation by applying advanced computing systems to the vast quantities of unstructured data now available online and from live video feeds and other sources of monitoring and surveillance. From facial-recognition technologies that cross-check real-time images against massive databases to algorithms that crawl social media for signs of opposition activity, these innovations are a game-changer for authoritarian efforts to shape discourse and crush opposition voices.

Political resistance in autocratically governed societies, which are at the same time undergoing a transformation to a knowledge society, is likely to come from the middle of society and not as rebellion by members of the ruling class. However, even democratic regimes are not immune to the lure of deploying surveillance instruments.

AI cannot only reduce the cost of repression but in addition has significant impacts on economic transactions, the globalization process, and, in its wake, global social inequality. As Anton Korinek and Joseph E. Stiglitz (2021:1) point out, "the new technologies [e.g., AI] have the tendency to be labor-saving, resource-saving, and to give rise to winner-takes-all dynamics that advantage developed countries." Inasmuch as developing economies reply for competitive advantages on lower labor cost, developing countries have especially reason to be concerned about the influence of AI and other automation technologies that they may lose the advantages that they now possess. "The worst-case scenario," Korinek and Stiglitz (2010:35) remind us,

> is the unravelling of much of the gains in development and poverty reduction that we have seen over the last half century. . . [and the] new advances

may arrest the convergence in standards of living between rich countries and developing countries.

At the same time, this is a useful point to reiterate that there is the danger that discourse about AI evolves into *technological determinism*. Technology is not a coercive power. Technology itself cannot tell us what to do. It is the power of a corporation and most likely the state that is a coercive power. Appropriate policy measure and the simple reminder that different choices are possible may be able to counter the developments Korinek and Stiglitz describe.

In the following chapter, I examine the question of transformation of knowledge societies into knowledge capitalism.

Notes

1. My chapter on our knowledge of knowledge has benefitted considerably from the pleasant and productive collaborative work on many of the facets of the topic of knowledge with Marian Adolf published for example as *Knowledge: Is Knowledge Power?* (Stehr and Adolf, 2017).
2. Depending on the research interest, the capacity to act may have a historical dimension, for example, in the sense of "culpability": what countries have contributed to greenhouse emissions more than other countries? The capacity to act may also refer to future conduct; for example, what country has the capability to contribute significantly to greenhouse gas mitigation?
3. As does the alleged distance between *knowledge and opinion* and its respective carriers, as Leo Strauss maintains: "Philosophy is the attempt to replace opinion by knowledge; but opinion is the element of the city, hence philosophy is subversive, hence the philosopher must write in such a way that he will improve rather than subvert the city" (cited in Benjamin Aides Wurgaft, "Against public philosophy," *Aeon*, 2021; https://aeon.co/essays/the-dangers-of-public-philosophy-according-to-leo-strauss).
4. Mariano Zukerfeld (2017:24) offers the following differentiation between mental and physical phenomena:

   > Life, in fact, constitutes a significant threshold separating different forms of being, placing on one side pure physical matter (atoms, molecules, etc.), and knowledge carriers on the other. Prior to the appearance of life on earth, there were only blind forces and inanimate masses: mute physical matter. After a certain moment, simple forms of knowledge emerged, carried by the first beings capable of reproducing them-selves. Much later, with the advent of humanity, knowledge was objectified in artefacts and codified in varied symbols.

5. A rather different conclusion is warranted once the issue turns to *scientific knowledge*. If one follows Niklas Luhmann (1990:124–124) in this regard, the question of scientific knowledge more urgently raises the question of truth: "Science is only science when concepts are used to determine whether certain statements are true (and not untrue), i.e., when the code of the scientific system directs the choice of distinctions with which the world is observed."
6. I am grateful to Stephen Turner for his reference to the aggregated condition of knowledge that *a priori* excludes the possibility of endlessly "dividing" forms of knowledge, enabling the possibility of arriving, in the final instance, at a "piece" of knowledge. This observation in turn has, as I will show, an important meaning for any reflection about the alleged existence of the phenomenon of non-knowledge or ignorance.

7. As is well-known, Karl Marx (1973:625–626) expresses the same idea in his *Grundrisse*:

> Nature builds no machines, no locomotives, railways, electric telegraphs, self-acting mules etc. These are products of human industry; natural material Grundrisse—625—transformed into organs of the human will over nature, or of human participation in nature. They are organs of the human brain, created by the human hand; the power of knowledge, objectified. The development of fixed capital indicates to what degree general social knowledge has become a direct force of production, and to what degree, hence, the conditions of the process of social life itself have come under the control of the general intellect and been transformed in accordance with it. To what degree the powers of social production have been produced, not only in the form of knowledge, but also as immediate organs of social practice, of the real life process.

8. The answer one economist, for example, provides, is that technology must be considered, in contrast to the convictions concerning scientific knowledge in the scientific community, a "private capital good". In the case of technology, disclosure is not the rule, and rents which can be privately appropriated for its use can be earned by its producers (cf. Dasgupta, 1987:10).
9. As Georg Simmel ([1907] 1978:437), indicates, the intellect (or, knowledge), stands in rather close relation and proximity to individualism, as does money. Reason has an individualizing property because it is the essence of its content that the "intellect is universally communicable and that, if we presuppose its correctness, every sufficiently trained mind must be open to persuasion by it. There is absolutely no analogy to this in the realms of the will and the emotions." In addition, the contents of the (objective), minds "do not possess the jealous exclusiveness that is common in the practical contents of life".
10. Compare for example the conflicting views of Harold Innis (1951), and Marshall McLuhan on this matter.
11. I realize that my definition of knowledge contradicts certain philosophical traditions, for example, the philosophical traditions of classical Greece. Classical Greek philosophers were of the opinion that to know does not mean the capacity to do; the capacity to do is *techne* (type of craft). The concept of *techne* resonates with a definition of technology advanced by Giovanni Dosi and Marco Grazzi. Dosi and Grazzi's (2010:173) technology functions

> as something like a 'recipe' entailing a design for a final product. . . . The recipe specifies a set of actions that need to be taken to achieve the desired outcome and identifies, if sometimes implicitly, the inputs that are to be acted on and any required equipment.

In the case of industrial technologies for example, the knowledge and skills are not typically in the possession of a single individual, but distributed across many individuals. Dosi and Grazzi's concept of technology as a "blue-print" differs from my definition of knowledge in significant respects. For example, knowledge as a capacity to act does not incorporate a particular built-in end that can be achieved given the means of the technological design. Dosi and Grazzi's concept of technology is also not close to what I consider to be "practical knowledge". Practical knowledge, given its construction, has a great probability to be realized; however, such knowledge depends for its realization on circumstances beyond its control. The technology Dosi and Grazzi have in mind appears to be a case of knowledge that realizes itself.

12. The *sociological* conception of knowledge advanced here resonates with Ludwig von Mises' (1922:14), definition of *property*, for von Mises suggests that as a sociological category, "property represents the capacity to determine the use of economic goods." Based on the idea that knowledge constitutes a capacity for action, one can of course develop distinctive categories or forms of knowledge depending on the enabling

function knowledge may be seen to fulfill. I believe Lyotard's ([1979] 1984:6) attempt to differentiate, in analogy to the distinction between expenditures for consumption and investment, "payment knowledge" and "investment knowledge" constitutes an example of such a functional differentiation of more or less distinctive forms of knowledge.

13. The definition of *scientific* knowledge as a capacity to act transcends the doctrine of the *intrinsic* value of scientific knowledge (cf. Tenbruck, 1974:317).
14. My translation of the German original. The existing translation into English uses a different German edition where the meaning, the assimilation of knowing and doing, to which I subscribe does not become quite as clear.
15. If, in contrast to my definition of knowledge, the focus is shifted to the process of the constitution/production of knowledge, as Helmut Willke (2001:5–6) for example maintains, knowledge from such a vantage point becomes "a communicatively constituted and confirmed practice. . . . Knowledge is the result of learning." This shift in the weight of analysis therefore moves to problems of epistemology.
16. An equally overextended definition of knowledge would be to suggest that knowledge has the following four components: hardware, software, skills, and ideas (Hage, 2020:14). Software in the sense of "operations", "techniques", and "methods", to take but one example of what is a definition of knowledge that excludes hardly anything, and certainly not information.
17. As a kind of discursive extension, the definition of knowledge as a capacity to act may invite reflections about the emergence of a New Class that commands special privileges grounded in their asymmetric "*individual* control of special cultures, languages, techniques, and of the skills resulting from these" (Gouldner, 1979:19). Whether the New Class is really a *new* class and, for that matter, a class is a contentious issue. In knowledge societies, pattern of inequality to put is rather ambivalently are definitely a function of the unequal access to and control of specialized knowledge.
18. As Simon Schaffer (as quoted in Chartier, 2016:333), for example points out:

    > The relationship between the values established in physics laboratories and those that supplied the basis for imperialism was even closer. Late nineteenth-century scientists joined networks that distributed machines, values, and standard practices across the entire world. Imperialism, mass production, and metrology dominated their universe.

19. For a more detailed discussion, see the following discourse on the competition of forms of knowledge.
20. Somewhat helpful in this context are Arnold Gehlen's ([1950] 1988:54) conception of *abilities*: an "analysis of the structure of skills reveals that these invariably involve an integration of perception and action to form an *ability*."
21. In this context, I refer, for example, to the thesis of Donald Schon (1967 [1963]; see also Adolf et al., 2013) of the displacement of concepts or, more specifically, to the proposal of Andrew Haldane (2013 [2009]) to understand financial circles at the beginning of this century from the perspective of the life sciences—especially epidemiology and ecology—and not according to the paradigm of economics.
22. Peter Drucker (1993: 52–53) argues that there has been a radical change in the global meaning of the term knowledge: "In both the West and Asia knowledge had always been see as applying to *being*. Almost overnight, it came to be applied to *doing*. It became a resource and a utility." I am not able to follow Drucker's differentiation of historical periods. Knowledge always had the function of doing. What has happened and has been transformative is that the volume of knowledge as a capacity to act has increased immeasurably in recent decades.
23. Norbert Elias ([1984] 2005: 252) also defines knowledge as that which "reflects the social meaning of man-made symbols, such as words or images, in their *capacity as means*

of orientation" (my emphasis and translation). Paul Romer's (1990:S72) definition of *technological change* also has an elective affinity to the definition of knowledge as a capacity for actions: "Technological change—[represents an] improvement in the instructions for mixing together raw materials—[and] lies at the heart of economic growth. . . . Once the cost of creating a new set of instructions has been incurred, the instructions can be used over and over again as no additional cost" and therefore represent economic goods that are inherently different from conventional economic goods.

24. It follows from my definition of knowledge that the social legitimacy of research, just like the legitimacy of scientific knowledge, is not least a function of the utility value of science. In many discussions in society about the usefulness of the knowledge generated in the research process, the ability of science to plan, construct or change the conditions of everyday life ranks first (see also Tenbruck, 1969: 63 and Elias, [1970] 2006).
25. The thesis that knowledge is a model for reality and that knowledge can change reality is also related to Albert Borgmann's (1999b: 1) definition of information, more precisely, to his concept of "recipe" as a "model of *information for reality*". However, no power is associated with knowledge "as such"—just as with technology as such. Only in connection with human action and under certain conditions of action does knowledge change reality and can influence it. Only then one can meaningfully speak of knowledge as power (see also Gehlen, 1993 [1940]: 341–354). Niklas Luhmann (2002b: 97–98) is not unfamiliar with this definition of knowledge when, for example, in his observations on society's education system ("education produces knowledge") he emphasizes that knowledge can be used to open up other possibilities—or that lack of knowledge can "block opportunities"—which "give direction to the further course of life". The special nature of knowledge can be understood even more precisely in Luhmann's (1990:714) description of the work of modern science:

    > Science can no longer see itself as a representation of the world as it is and must therefore also withdraw its claim to be able to teach others about the world. It carries out an exploration of possible constructions that can be inscribed in the world and thereby act as a form, i.e.: create a difference.

26. The concept of knowledge as *know-how* suggests that knowledge is a cultural resource, even if sometimes embedded in material objects. Paul DiMaggio (1997:267; see also Swidler, 1986) generally defines culture as a "toolkit of strategies", less so as a "clustering of cultural elements within social groups, less strong linkages among the elements, and weaker pressures for the exclusion of inconsistent elements".
27. The thesis of the immediate performance or persuasive power of knowledge exists in a number of assertions. First, and contrary to the notion of the essential limits of the power of knowledge, one thesis maintains, for example, that deficits in the ability to act in the world of politics or in everyday life can be compensated for simply by increasing or raising the supply of knowledge. Secondly, the idea of a technical-based interest in knowledge that aims at direct usability also implies the idea of direct ort immediate performance of knowledge. Third, the so-called technocracy thesis implies a creeping de-democratization of society.
28. For a detailed analysis of the different implications of Bacon's metaphor "scientia potentia est," see the study by José Garcia (2001). These implications include, in particular, the political demand, derived from Francis Bacon's thesis, for the rule of experimental "scientists" who, because of their expert knowledge based on practical insights, were much better suited for the exercise of political power than aristocratic rulers with their specific skills.
29. However, power etymologically refers to ability; and one of the most basic definitions of "ability" would be, "to make a difference". In this sense, and in the sense in which power is usually discussed in the context of social relations, namely as power exercised

to achieve something or over a person, the definition of power as ability echoes the notion of knowledge as enablement (cf. Dyrberg, 1997:88–99).

30. In their paper "Progress in know-how. Its origins and limits", Sarewitz and Nelson (2008) attempt to explain why the evolution of know-how is uneven and what factors make progress in some areas of human activity particularly difficult while in other human affairs the improvement of know-how has been much more rapid. According to Sarewitz and Nelson, the answer is linked to the differential capability in the development of know-how to generate standardized procedures at the level of management and policy-making for the purposes of implementing technological know-how (see also Nelson, 2003).
31. Perhaps I should point to a competing definition of "knowledge" that sets knowledge identical with action or conceives of knowledge as emerging from action. Peter Drucker (1969:269) observes that knowledge as

    > normally conceived by the "intellectual" is something very different from "knowledge" in the context of 'knowledge economy' or "knowledge work." . . . Knowledge, like electricity or money, is a form of energy that exists only when doing work. The emergence of the knowledge economy is not, in other words, part of "intellectual history" as it is normally conceived. It is part of the "history of technology," which recounts how man puts tools to work.

    In one of his studies, Drucker (1989:251) very much affirms this conception and defines knowledge as information that "changes something or somebody—either by becoming grounds for action, or by making an individual (or an institution), capable of different and more effective action. And this, little of the new 'knowledge' accomplishes."
32. The thesis that knowledge invariably is pushed to its limit, that is, is realized and implemented almost without regard for its consequences (as argued, for instance, by C.P. Snow [cf. Sibley, 1973]), constitutes of course a view which is quite common among observers, for example, of the nature of technological development. However, the notion that science and technology inherently and inevitably force their own realization in practice fails to give, for one thing, proper recognition to the context of implementation by assuming such automaticity in the realization of technical and scientific knowledge.
33. Compare Lazega's (1992) essay on the "information elaboration" in work groups and the relations between information and decision-making in and dependent on "local" contexts.
34. If knowledge indeed would "travel" almost without impediments and could be reproduced largely at will, the idea that the creators of what typically constitutes "new" knowledge in modern society, namely scientists and engineers, would have to be located at the apex of power in such societies certainly would make considerable sense.
35. Such a conclusion already follows from the theorem that knowledge is a kind of anthropological constant. But it also follows from conceiving of knowledge as a capacity for action because knowledge then becomes, as Lyotard ([1979] 1984:18), stresses,

    > a question of competence that goes beyond the simple determination and application of truth, extending to the determination and application of criteria of efficiency (technical qualification), of justice and/or happiness (ethical wisdom), of beauty of a sound or color (auditory and visual sensibility), etc.

36. Jürgen Habermas ([1968] 1970: 92) offers a comparable, general observation when he formulates that *skills* put us in a position to "solve problems".
37. In a somewhat different context, Jean-François Lyotard ([1979] 1984:18–19), describes the enabling social features of knowledge in a rather similar sense. Lyotard explicates the function of knowledge in postmodern society and emphasizes that knowledge is by no means limited to scientific, that is, instrumental knowledge. On the contrary, knowledge refers to a much more general and "extensive array of competence-building

measures and it is the only form embodied in a subject constituted by the various areas of competence composing it."

38. A *World Bank* (Lange et al., 2018:1) publication measures human capital as the *income* generated over a lifetime:

    > Human capital, measured as the value of earnings over a person's lifetime, is the most important component of wealth globally. Human capital wealth on a per capita basis is typically increasing in low- and middle-income countries. In some upper-middle- and high-income countries, aging and stagnant wages are reducing the share of human capital in total capital.

39. Much of the conventional discussion of human capital in economics does not capture the intergenerational value of human capital, for example, as a distinctive asset in perpetuating and locking in the family status. As Daniel Markovits (2020:120) points out for the inequality regime of the United States,

    > someone who wants an elite income—or, critically, even just an income sufficient to buy his children the schooling on which their own eliteness depends—must do one of a narrowly restricted class of jobs, heavily concentrated in finance, management, law, and medicine. Fewer than one in one hundred jobs, and virtually none in middle-class occupations—teaching, for example, or journalism, public service, or even engineering—pays even close to elite wages. And a person whose native interests lie in any of these fields, or indeed anywhere outside of whatever maximizes the return on her human capital, can pursue her calling only at the cost of sacrificing her own, and her children's, caste.

40. My focus resonates with that of Amartya Sen (1992), who concentrates on an examination of spaces of functioning or on the *capability* to achieve functioning as his focal variable for a normative analysis of inequality structures. The notion of capabilities, of course, is very broad indeed, as is the idea of knowledge as a general resource in the formation of inequality structures, and it therefore may suffer in the eyes of critics who prefer a less inclusive concept. Nonetheless, the capabilities approach differs, as Sen (1992:6), observes, quite substantially

    > from the more traditional approaches to equality, involving a concentration on such variables as income, wealth, or happiness. . . . In particular, judging equality and efficiency in terms of capability to achieve differs from the standard utilitarian approaches as well as from other welfarist formulations.

    The utilitarian and the welfarist perspectives employ a much more restrictive and narrow calculus of inequality.

41. If one proposes to retain, especially against those perspectives arguing that class location has declined in significance in recent decades as a source of ideological consciousness, the notion of a (subjective), "class consciousness" as relevant for modern society, it would follow that the formation and retention of such class consciousness should perhaps be more effected by factors other than solely the material status of individuals and households (cf. Evans, 1992 for an empirical critique of a narrow conception of factors linked to class consciousness in Great Britain).
42. In the United States, the social location of many of these activities can be found in what Peter Drucker (1989:187) calls the "third" sector of non-profit, non-governmental, "human change" institutions. The third sector is actually the "country's largest employer, though neither its workforce nor the output it produces show up in the statistics. One out of every two adult Americans—total of 90 million people—are estimated to work as volunteers in the third sector" (Drucker, 1989:197).
43. As Karl Marx ([1939–1941] 1973:706), observes,

    > nature builds no machines, no locomotives, railways, electric telegraphs, self-acting mules etc. These are products of human industry; natural material transformed into

organs of the human will over nature, or of human participation in nature. They are *organs of the human brain created by the human hand*; the power of knowledge, objectified.

44. For example, the idea that the social sciences are in the business of generating *Orientierungswissen* has in recent years been taken on board in the performative understanding of economic theory (Callon, 1968; Miller, 2008) pursuing an idea that Karl Polany ([1938] 2014:114–115) had already described. Friedrich Hayek (1942–1944:53) was less convinced about the immediate power of economic discourse on the way in which economic objects come to be defined or should be: an economic good, for example, food cannot be defined in physical terms ("objectivism") but only in terms of the ideas and beliefs economic actors have about them. Of course, Hayek's position about the viability of mental states in defining economic phenomena cannot rule out a normative understanding of such phenomena.
45. In the early Sixties, during the de-Stalinization period, orthodox Marxist philosophers, for example, in East Germany, discussed the notion of science as an "immediately productive force", last but not least as a corrective to the "undialectical" conception of science advanced by Joseph Stalin (cf. Klotz and Rum, 1963:27). But aside from the work the notion of science as an immediately productive force had to accomplish in the ideological struggle underway, the concept mainly referred, as far as I can tell, to the idea that production becomes the material realization of scientific discoveries (e.g., Stoljarow, 1963:835; it is claimed or had to be claimed for politically correct purposes that Walter Ulbricht initially employs the term, cf. Klotz and Rum, 1963:26). Later, somewhat more elaborate conceptions of the notion of science as an immediately productive force also are in evidence. For example, labor is described as a form of scientific work (e.g., Lassow, 1967:377); yet, such discussions continue to be embedded in the struggle against "narrow" Stalinist conceptions of the forces of production (see also Kosel, 1989).
46. Katharina Pistor (2020:101) explores how data in their processed variant become immediately productive "as a means of governance that will likely replace both markets and the law". Data become a tool "for governing others of a scale that rivals that of the nation states with their law". The rise of the Big Tech corporations "and their accumulation of vast amounts of data offers. . . [a] possibility: the rule by data".
47. Keeping in mind of course that this enlarged capacity to act is not necessarily evenly distributed throughout society and among institutions. I will discuss the stratified nature of knowledge and the consequences of extended capacities to act in a subsequent chapter entitled "The texture of knowledge societies".
48. The increasing capacity of society to act upon itself should, in the end, reduce the probability that knowledge societies will converge to form some kind of common form of society because the greater capacity to act, made possible by the growth of scientific and technical knowledge, has to "pass through" the filter of local conditions as it is being implemented. Such a process, under normal circumstances, assures that the variety of societies will not be limited to but a handful of exemplars (on the topic of convergence cf. Bell, 1979:110–112; Mills, 1958; Tinbergen, 1961; Levy, 1966; Meyer, 1970). In the context of describing and justifying his choice of the term "post-industrial society" rather than some other designation for the emerging form of society, Bell (1973:37), also notes that the new post-industrial societies will fail to achieve the kind of unity "of the economic system and character structure which was characteristic of capitalist civilization from the mid-eighteenth to the mid-twentieth century".
49. Compare our analysis of the interrelation of climate and society in Bray et al., 1993.
50. Though there is no direct textual evidence, Simmel's early observations may have been prompted by Goethe's dictum "Im Anfang war die Tat" ("In the beginning was the deed"), since Johann Wolfgang Goethe's sentiments about the priority of doing over knowing were no doubt well known to Simmel.

51. Niklas Luhmann (1986:154) specifies these attributes of scientific knowledge as the *code of science*:

> the code remains universal. It applies to everything, even to action. But it does not serve the communication that wants to carry out, cause or even recommend an action. It does not serve to select action. . . . It is this reduction to co-ordinate experience that differentiates the scientific code from morality and religion.

52. The obsolescence of the value of knowledge may occur as either a loss of the *exchange* or *use* value of knowledge.
53. The term "class" for Berger (1987:51) includes all those attributes which for Marxist's theorists constitute classes-for-itself *and* classes-in-itself.
54. In an effort to arrive at ways of determining the value of information as an economic good, Bates (1988:80), for example, argues that there is an inherent imbalance in the fixed cost and variable cost component of producing (and re-producing), information. The production of information has an exceptionally high component of fixed and a very low, even nonexistent variable cost component (the costs associated with the replication of the information), because information is infinitely reproducible and consumes all other resources. Such a treatment of "information", of course, is only plausible as long as one is convinced that reproduction is virtually unproblematic (e.g., transcends the initial conditions of production including the costs associated with it), and can be repeated at will because production is definitive and does not require any intermediaries or subsequent interpretation.
55. Daniel Bell ([1979] 1991:237–238) also observes that knowledge is as a "*codified theory is a collective good.* No single person, no single set of work groups, no corporation can monopolize or patent theoretical knowledge, or draw unique product advantage from it. It is a common property of the intellectual world." Bell's characterization of the main reasons why (codified) knowledge constitutes a collective rather than a private good allows the inference that such qualities derive, on the one hand, from their peculiar epistemological attributes and, on the other hand, from the effective operation of the ethos of the scientific community, especially its negative sanctions against secrecy. In contrast to Bell's views, I attempt to stress that it is the social nature of knowledge itself, its production and reproduction, which eliminates the possibility that it becomes the exclusive property of individual or of corporate actors.
56. Jerald Hage (2020:16) identifies the motives underlying (inevitable) the growth of (scientific) knowledge precisely in this sense: "The motivation for continual knowledge creation arises naturally because solving simple scientific and applied problems leaves more difficult and complicated issues that in turn require more complex social and institutional arrangements as the next logical step in knowledge production."
57. The problem of the economic theory of knowledge, for example in the sense of the theory of human capital, is critically analyzed in more detail in the third chapter.
58. Friedrich Tenbruck (e.g., 1972), a leading critic of widely accepted assumption or promise of the actual role of knowledge in social planning. The leading assumption indeed is that knowledge progress is a necessary prerequisite for any enhancement of "foresight" and hence toward an improved control of the conditions of social action. Tenbruck (1972:63) is convinced that the historical record of translating additional knowledge into action and thereby acquire a measure of control over the circumstances of action and organize action according to one's desires is poor if not non-existent. The more or less automatic association between additional knowledge, foresight and control is fragile. Social action is prompted by many motives. Knowledge can in fact represent as barrier to action; nor is rational action necessarily to most efficient form of action; and, foresight is not always equal to control.
59. An equally appropriate conception of Drucker's law is to point to the *secular* increase in human capital. The broad shift in employment from the agricultural into the manufacturing sector reflects, on the supply side, the competitive advantage of human capital growth which is more valuable out of agriculture (Porzio et al., 2021).

60. A few remarks by Friedrich Hajek (1937:49) in his classical paper "Economics and Knowledge" illustrates the liberal discursive fusion of information and knowledge:

    in our analysis, instead of showing what bits of information the different persons must possess in order to bring about that result, we fall in effect back on the assumption that everybody knows everything and so evade any real solution of the problem. . . . It has become customary among economists to stress only the need of knowledge of prices, apparently because—as a consequence of the confusion between objective and subjective data—the complete knowledge of the objective facts was taken for granted.

61. Thomas Stewart's definition of the "raw material knowledge" is also typical: the result is that the difference between knowledge and information becomes completely irrelevant. Stewart ([1997] 1998:27) emphasizes for example:

    It is sometimes very difficult to understand how knowledge influences our economic activity, because it appears in so many different forms. . . . Business reports, books, the electrons coursing through cyberspace, even gossip at the coffee machine: all forms of information exchange.

    Steswart seems to capitulate to the enormous variety of forms of knowledge or the heterogeneity of information, and decides to use them as interchangeable terms.
62. Joseph Stiglitz (2017:14) comments—in the context of an analysis of the "economics of information"—that "knowledge can be thought of as a particular form of information." Shoshana Zuboff (2021) claims

    on the strength of their surveillance capabilities [of the superstars of the tech industry; see also the following chapter] and for the sake of their surveillance profits, the empires engineered a fundamentally anti-democratic epistemic coup *marked by* unprecedented *concentrations of knowledge* about us and the unaccountable power that accrues to such *knowledge*.

    ("The coup we are talking about," *New York Times*, January 29, 2021; emphasis added)

    As I will argue what is collected is information and not knowledge; however, Information can still be turned into a profitable enterprise. As Zuboff (2015:75) explains the business model:

    "big data" is above all the foundational component in a deeply intentional and highly consequential new logic of accumulation . . . information capitalism aims to predict and modify human behavior as a means to produce revenue and market control.

    But in light of the conspicuous power and new control exercised the large corporations of the information capitalism, it is difficult to imagine how the observer is capable of escaping the powerful corporate veil to a meta-level of analysis?
63. Max Weber's ([1919] 1948:139; my emphasis) in his lecture "science as a vocation" emphasizes that the disenchantment of the world does not mean, that we have to have an idea, for example, when we take the streetcar "how the car happened to get into motion. And he does not need to *know*."
64. One example for the widespread conflation, even an essential unity of information and knowledge may suffice:

    "Information evolved as a category of knowledge . . . by comparison with knowledge it has been usually more detached from the theoretical context in which it was produced. . . . Information is characteristically more restricted to the technical practical surface of knowledge. . . . Information is often but thin knowledge.

    (Ezrahi, 2004: 257; also Rule and Besen, 2008)

Cultural critics of the power of newfound technological companies (Amazon, Apple, Facebook, Netflix. Microsoft) also tend to conflate knowledge and information. In the process of such an analysis, the volume of information—acquired by virtue of the surveillance of the activities of its users—is translated into unprecedented "concentrations of knowledge" which in turn leads to "unaccountable power that accrues to such knowledge" and the emergence of an "information civilization" and "surveillance empires" or "surveillance capitalism" (these terms can be found in the first two paragraphs of an essay by Shoshana Zuboff, "The coup we are not talking about", *New York Times*, January 29, 2021).

65. The abundance of definitions of information, knowledge and data is impressive. The best interpretation one may perhaps be able to offer in light of such a multiplicity of definitions is to suggest that the wealth of conceptions reflects the importance of data, information, and knowledge. Chaim Zins (2007) employing a Critical Delphi Study in 2003–2005 of leading scholars from 16 countries documents 130 definitions of knowledge, data, and information.
66. Wolfgang Krohn (2003:98–99) offers if I am not mistaken more sophisticated advice about the conflation of information and knowledge: information is knowledge transported as communication. Knowledge possessed by a producer of an object or an idea cannot pass on as knowledge but only as information. Knowledge is produced; knowledge is the primary source for the exchange of information. It is not quite clear whether knowledge and information are in a state of an *equilibrium*; for example, whether knowledge is information transported as communication and whether it is therefore "easy" to reproduce knowledge reduced to information?
67. However, Gilbert Ryle ([1949] 2000: 56) stresses that knowing-that does not necessarily entails or typically results in knowledge-how.
68. Daniel Bell's concept of information could also be defined very broadly, as Shapiro and Varian (1999: Chapter 1) suggest: "Essentially, anything that can be digitized—encoded as a stream of bits—is information. For our purposes, baseball scores, books, databases, magazines, movies, music, stock quotes, and Web pages are all *information goods*."
69. Bell (1973:175), in addition, offers an "operational" definition of knowledge when he indicates that knowledge "is that which is objectively known, an intellectual property, attached to a name or group of names and certified by copyright or some other form of social recognition".
70. The ability to easily reduce information to numbers, Liberti and Petersen (2018:1), in the context of analyzing information in financial markets, as "*hard information*". The new technologies of the last half century are more adapted to transmitting and potentially processing numeric information. Information that is difficult to completely summarize in a numeric score and where it is difficult to differentiate between collecting and using information, the authors call "*soft information*". The distinction between soft and hard information is not discrete.
71. If I am not mistaken, the description of the resource that information typically conveys and that is explicated here resonates with Gregory Bateson's (1972:482) definition of information as "news of a difference." Elsewhere, Bateson (1972:381) indicates that information is that which "*excludes* certain alternatives". That is, according to classical information theory, as Bruner (1990:4) also stresses, "a message is informative if it reduces certain alternatives." Pre-existing codes allow for the reduction of possible alternative choices. However, by defining information as pertaining to "any difference which makes a difference in some later event", Bateson moves the idea of information, it seems to me, closer to the notion of knowledge as a capacity for action, especially if one adds the questions, about what and for whom information makes a difference. Niklas Luhmann's (1997:198) central conceptual platform (see Bechmann and Stehr, 2002) allows him to follow Bateson's definition of information as a difference that makes a difference, in as much as the "news"—which could be an increase

in the population or a change in climatic conditions—alerts a system and thereby triggers new system conditions. But as Luhmann ([1984] 1995:67) therefore also stresses,

> a piece (!) of information that is repeated is no longer information. . . . The information is not lost, although it disappears as an event. It has changed the state of the system and has thereby left behind a structural effect; the system then reacts to and with these changed structures.

72. In a study of the diffusion of business computer technology, Attewell (1992:6) emphasizes that

> implementing a complex new technology requires both individual and organizational learning. Individual learning involves the distillation of an individual's experiences regarding a technology into understandings that may be viewed as personal skills and knowledge. Organizational learning is built out of this individual learning of members of an organization, but it is distinctive. The organization learns only insofar as individual insights and skills become embodied in organizational routines, practices, and beliefs that outlast the presence of the originating individual.

73. The discussion of non-knowing is indebted to our publication: Marian Adolf and Nico Stehr (2016), *Knowledge*. Second Edition. London: Routledge, S.69–99.
74. My usage of the term *non-knowledge* follows the convention in much of the literature that discusses the absence of knowledge in an affirmative sense. The term is synonymous with *not knowing* and has a close affinity but not identity with *ignorance*. The definition of "unknowability" also belongs into the category of non-knowledge: "Unknowability tends to refer to realities and processes that are not capable of being apprehended in any way—not simply by the 'uninitiated' but at all" (McGoey, 2020:198). In German, the relevant term is *Nichtwissen*.
75. Daniel Dennett (1986) identifies two additional categories of ignorance: (1) "excusable ignorance" (the model here is the country doctor) and (2) "unavoidable ignorance" (the model is our ancestors).
76. The German that Hayek chose as translations of two central concepts in his English original is of interest, and is, in my opinion, fully adequate. "The boundaries of his ignorance" and "man's unavoidable ignorance" are rendered as *Grenzen seines Unwissens* and *unvermeidlichen Unkenntnis des Menschen* (Hayek, [1960] 2005:31) In other words, there is no reference to non-knowledge (*Nichtwissen*).
77. The use of the term political ignorance, as in this context, is consistent with Linsey McGoey's (2020:198) relational definition of ignorance: "The phenomenon of 'ignorance' is related to but different than unknowability in that 'ignorance' of particular facts can be specific to a particular person or institution while those same facts are comprehensible to others."
78. In his paper, Steve Rayner (2012:108) explores

> unknown knowns of a particular sort: those which societies or institutions actively exclude because they threaten to undermine key organizational arrangements or the ability of institutions to pursue their goals. My interest is therefore in how information is kept out rather than kept in and my approach is to treat ignorance as a necessary social achievement rather than as a simple background failure to acquire, store and retrieve knowledge.

79. George Akerlof's empirical example of an asymmetric information condition in a market exchange involves what are best described as micro-economic relations. The concept of asymmetric information can, however, be extended to macro-economic relations and thereby show not only the broad significance of the asymmetry perspective but also that asymmetry pertains not to pieces of information and their deficiency but to a *bundle* of information. Frederic Miskin (1990:34) demonstrates, for example, how the

> asymmetric information approach to financial crises explains the timing patterns in the data and many features of these crises which are otherwise hard to explain.

> It also suggests why financial crises have had such important consequences for the aggregate economy over the past one hundred and fifty years. The evidence thus seems to favor an asymmetric information view of financial crises over a monetarist view.

80. In memory research, an extreme example of asymmetric information has recently come under study—the few people who have "superior autobiographical memory" (Parker et al., 2006:36), that is, the ability to recall every single day of their lives or to remember the occurrences of every single day.
81. At this point of the exposition, one beneficially needs to recall, Otto Neurath's (1932/1933:206, emphasis added) famous mariner's parable (*Schiffergleichnis*):

    > *There is no tabula rasa.* We are like skippers who have to rebuild their ship on the open sea without ever being able to disassemble it in a dock and rebuild it from solid components. Only metaphysics can disappear completely.

82. Inasmuch as the disregard and sanctioning of existing social norms by certain incumbents of societal positions of a group is known, it must be decided whether

    > the basic formal structure of a group is being undermined by the observed deviations of behavior. It is in this sense that authorities can have *excessive knowledge* of what is actually going on, so that this becomes dysfunctional for the system of social control.
    >
    > (Merton, [1949] 1968:343; emphasis added)

83. In this respect I note that the expression *non-knowledge* (*Nichtwissen*) in the title of Popitz's treatise does not appear a single time in the text. The work's title may be the work of the publishing house. The exposition shows that Popitz rightly avoided the term *non-knowledge* and more guardedly wrote of limited behavioral information and limited behavioral transparency.
84. Collinson's (1994:25) examination of labor resistance—based on two case studies—drew on the emphasis that Clegg (1989) placed on knowledge and information of subordinates and outlines generally "the importance of different forms of knowledge in the articulation of resistance". Collinson summarized his findings and pointed out that

    > specific forms of knowledge are a crucial resource and means through which resistance can be mobilized. Knowledge in organizations is multiple, contested and shifting. Employees may not possess detailed underpinnings of certain bureaucratic/political processes, but they often do monopolize other technical, production-related knowledges that facilitate their oppositional practices.
    >
    > (Collison, 1994:28)

85. The concept of the scales of knowledge has a parallel in the concept of the degrees of property rights, which are calibrated according to the labor, need, or performance, that is, the merits, of the owner (Neumann, 2009).
86. A prominent example of the position I would like to leave behind, are the views of Cass Sunstein and Adrian Vermeule's (2008:22) reflections, for example, on conspiracy theories and how social institutions might effectively oppose such views, on the ground. Sunstein and Vermeule propose to draw on the latest work/evidence in psychology and sociology as a form of considerable cognitive power in order muster a "cognitive infiltration of extremist groups" manipulating those individuals and groups that are proponents of conspiracy theories. The outcome ought to be a clear victory of the superior social science knowledge.
87. Peter Drucker ([1989] 2003:242; my emphasis) defines knowledge by combining or, even stronger, mixing, as far as I can see, practical reason and practical knowledge; in addition, he calls information knowledge: "Knowledge is information that changes something or somebody—either by becoming *grounds for action*, or by making an individual (or an institution) *capable of* different and more effective *action*."

88. Similar conceptions may be found in Friedrich Hayek's 1945 essay on the "Use of Knowledge in Society"; Hayek's essay is in fact a treatise in praise of decentralization, the importance of knowledge of local circumstances for action (knowledge in place), and the price system as an agency that communicates information and constitutes the answer to the question of coordinating local knowledges. Hayek ([1945] 1948:82) emphasizes in addition, "as long as things continue as before, or at least as they were expected to, there arise no *new problems* requiring a decision, no need to form a new plan" (my emphasis).
89. The suggestion that Keynes' is a savior of the capitalist system is based as far as I can see on the argument that the non-productive programs of public expenditures Keynes advocated help to solve the capitalist problem of underconsumption or overproduction. During the 1920s, output increased despite a decline in the amount of capital and labor used in production. Keynesian policy measures deal with these developments on two levels: On the one hand, the use of even more efficient means of production is slowed as a consequence of higher state expenditures because the economy is drained of investment funds. On the other hand, these expenditures produce additional demand which balances surplus supply of goods and services. However, the survival of the capitalist's economy Keynes' is credited with is only temporary according to some neo-Marxists (cf. Block und Hirschhorn, 1979:370–371).
90. The modern society as *mass society* repeatedly evoked by Daniel Bell (1973:313) is not characterized "by large numbers", but by a

    concentration and density. . . . It is when segmentation breaks down and people come into increasing contact and interaction with each other—in large urban concentrations in the past, or through mass communications today—that the features of a mass society appear.

91. Daniel Bell's position on the nature of the usefulness of the social science imagination has a family resemblance to the 1929 manifesto *The Scientific Conception of the World* of the *Vienna Circle*. In the view of the members of the Circle, scientific knowledge informs but does determine life.
92. John Dewey ([1927] 1954:1156) refers to the same perspective: "The doctrine of economic interpretation as usually stated ignores the transformation which meanings may effect." Robert Shiller (2019) in his *Narrative Economics* shows how popular economic stories arise, how they grow viral, and ultimately how they drive economic developments.
93. Pierre Bourdieu (1987:839–840) specifies the linkage for fully,

    the will to transform the world by trans- forming the words for naming it, by producing new categories of perception and judgment, and by dictating a new vision of social divisions and distributions, can only succeed if the resulting prophecies, or creative evocations, are also, at least in part, well-founded pre-visions, anticipatory descriptions. These visions only call forth what they pro- claim-whether new practices, new mores or especially new social groupings-because they announce what is in the process of developing. . . . Thus only a *realist* nominalism (or one based in reality0 allows us to account for the symbolic imposition of power, which only succeeds because it is fully based in reality.

    In other words, as in the case of knowledge as a capacity for action, certain conditions of action are required for language to be effective.
94. A current example is the vigorous complaint by the French President Emmanuel Macron and other prominent French politicians, intellectuals, and journalists that social theories entirely imported from the United States, especially on race, gender, and post-colonialism undermine the fabric of French culture and society. In a

struggle with younger cohorts in France who consider these theories enlightening and helpful, older intellectuals and politicians perceive these social theories as cognitive (meaning) contamination of established French cultural convictions. The French education minister, Jena-Michal Blanquer, Mr. Macron's education minister, Jean-Michel Blanquer,

> accused universities, under American influence, of being complicit with terrorists by providing the intellectual justification behind their acts. A group of 100 prominent scholars wrote an open letter supporting the minister and decrying theories 'transferred from North American campuses' in *Le Monde*.
>
> (In Norimitsu Onishi, "Will American Ideas Tear France Apart? Some of Its Leaders Think So," *New York Times*, February 9m, 2021)

95. Reflections on the nature and the ways of generating useful social science (policy) knowledge may focus, as is the case in more recent efforts (e.g. Powell et al., 2019) less on the kind of knowledge that might accomplish such a function and therefore more in policy and practice-oriented fields on the political negotiations between communities of social scientist and the desired audiences; hence, inquiry centers on "strategies of action and languages which create audiences and increase the value, legitimacy and thus, ultimately, the effects of particular interventions" (Williams, 2018:55).
96. The German language is full of neologisms; in contrast, the English language tends to abstain from neologisms. It is therefore impossible to find straightforward English equivalents for the at least slightly ironic "Stoffhuber" and "Sinnhuber". Short of retaining the German terms, I have attempted a translation that captures the spirit of Weber's dichotomy and links it to the purpose at hand.
97. John Kenneth Gailbraith (1975:123) had quite another suspicion about the widespread preference for the notion of "complexity" in economics: "The study of money, above all other fields in economics, is the one in which complexity is used to disguise truth or to evade truth, not to reveal it." Economists, particularly, in the field of monetary theory tend to invoke (unnecessary) complexity to mask the banality of their knowledge.
98. This thesis can be further illustrated with a reference to the term "uncomfortable knowledge" coined by Steve Rayner (2012): whereas uncomfortable knowledge refers to knowledge that exists but whose use proves to be less than purposeful or even counterproductive in light of the realities of a specific situation; knowledge that is not accessed is not uncomfortable knowledge, but knowledge that cannot contribute to solving a problem because the actors in question cannot—although these attributes are part of the relevant situation—influence/move these facets of a social context.
99. Compare the examination of "public ideas" by Hallett et al. (2019): The authors inquire into how *journalists* and other mediators (but not policy makers) between social science and the public use social science ideas. The specific focus is on social science ideas that become public ideas as they are used as objects of interest (being the news).
100. A different approach to the idea of practical knowledge are "real experiments", that is, in order to achieve a certain result in the laboratory, one has to screen out, simplify, or reduce for example the complex impact of the natural environment on a process. For as Karl Popper ([1957] 1972:139) observes, "in general it is only by the use of artificial experimental isolation that one can predict physical events." Only then is one able to clearly determine or identify a specific relation that would be responsible for the observed or desired effect. In order to successfully repeat/translate into praxis the observation made in the lab outside the lab, the artificial experimental isolation has to be recreated. The transfer and implementation of such a laboratory result or, as the case maybe, in the social sciences, a *Gedankenexperiment*, into practice

is of course encumbered with considerable difficulties, not to speak of various risks following the transformation of society into a laboratory (cf. Krohn and Weyer, 1989) that might contaminate the effect or make it impossible to repeat it outside the laboratory. It is very likely that unanticipated intervening factors could occur, even with a certain delay which might jeopardize any effort to repeat the effect observed in the laboratory.

101. Friedrich Hayek (1945:521) emphatically emphasizes that it false to assume that scientific knowledge is the sum total of all knowledge circulating in society; a

> little reflection will show that there is beyond question a body of very important but unorganized knowledge which cannot possibly be called scientific in the sense of knowledge of general rules: the knowledge of the particular circumstances of time and place. It is with respect to this that practically every individual has some advantage over all others in that he possesses unique information of which beneficial use might be made.

102. The knowledge Hayek (1945:524) of the knowledge problem has in mind that assures rapid adaptation to quickly changed circumstances of action is not the kind of knowledge that can

> enter into statistics and therefore cannot be conveyed to any central authority in statistical form. The statistics which such a central authority would have to use would have to be arrived at precisely by abstracting from minor differences between the things, by lumping together, as resources of one kind, items which differ as regards location, quality, and other particulars, in a way which may be very significant for the specific decision. It follows from this that central planning based on statistical information by its nature cannot take direct account of these circumstances of time and place, and that the central planner will have to find some way or other in which the decisions depending on them can be left to the "man on the spot".

Decentralization is the answer.

103. Stiglitz (1999:310) lists five global public goods (note: the first four public goods are not necessarily global public *knowledge* goods): "International economic stability, international security (political stability), the international environment. International humanitarian assistance and knowledge." The first four public goods are much more likely to fall into the category of "international conditions or circumstances for action", which in turn facilitate the implementation of capacities for action.
104. An earlier and detailed examination of the idea of global worlds of knowledge may be found in Stehr (2007) und Stehr and Ufer (2010).
105. The German quote of the Simmel citation reads: „Was allen gemeinsam ist, kann nur der Besitz des am wenigsten Besitzenden sein."
106. Frank and Meyer (202:134; emphasis added) explain, "what turns ability and skill into knowledge is *a single framework* offering a generalized understanding of abstract society, nature, and human personhood; and, of course, a schooled person may have the knowledge without possessing the actual skill."
107. However, one should have no illusions about the "right kind" of knowledge, which the World Bank (World Bank, 1999:2) classifies as eligible "knowledge for development":

> Considering development from a knowledge perspective reinforces some well-known lessons, such as the value of an open trade regime and of universal basic education. It also focuses our attention on needs that have sometimes been overlooked: scientific and technical training, local research and development, and the critical importance of institutions to facilitate the flow of information essential for effective markets.

The desired, correct neo-liberal form of knowledge—its promotion supported by large funds within the World Bank—already exists in the "first" world, the seat of the World Bank; the task that remains is to reduce the knowledge deficits in the rest of the world.

108. Even without patent protection, it is possible, at least temporarily, to benefit from an innovation for the following reasons:

> Because of lead times and the cost and time required for duplication and learning, and because of the availability of specific manufacturing facilities and sales networks, the first innovator can typically appropriate some return to his innovation, even without IPR.
>
> (Dosi and Stiglitz, 2014:8)

109. Joseph Stiglitz (1999:309) adds the claim that the transaction costs of acquiring and deploying knowledge does not itself alter the public good nature of knowledge as a public good: "Private providers can provide the 'transmission' for a charge reflecting the marginal cost of transmission while at the same time the good itself remains free."
110. Social relations, attributes, and capabilities that are mobilized in the course of producing something for example can only to a limited extent be imported into another country because these capabilities such a property rights, regulation, infrastructure or specific labor skills are not available across countries: It follows that the

> productivity of a country resides in the diversity of its available nontradable "capabilities," and therefore, cross-country differences in income can be explained by differences in economic complexity, as measured by the diversity of capabilities present in a country and their interactions.
> (Hidalgo und Hausmann, 2009:10570)

111. Labor, land, and money along with knowledge as a ("fourth") *fictitious* commodity: A commodification of knowledge signals that knowledge takes on the attributes of a commodity even though it was not produced in order to be for sale; that is, "the commodity description is entirely fictitious. . . . The postulate that anything that is bought and sold must have been produced for sale is emphatically untrue in regard to them" (Polanyi, 1944:75; Lyotard, 1984:4; Jessop, 2017). For a critique and an extension of Polanyi's conception of fictitious commodities, especially with reference to knowledge as a fictitious commodity that could serve as the basis for an understanding of capitalism based on the resource of knowledge, see Reitz, 2019.
112. This section relies on Marian Adolf and Nico Stehr (2017:108–111)
113. The theory of a "world society" in today's world often implies the concomitant presence of global knowledge although typically confined to highly rationalized, that is, scientific knowledge. John Meyer et al. (1997:166) in elaborating their notion of a world society postulate for example that "scientific and professional authority is rooted in universal, rationalized ultimate principles of moral and natural law. . . . Their rationalized knowledge structures constitute the religion of the modern world, replacing in good measure the older 'religions'."
114. It is for this reason that my analysis does not extend to what otherwise are important social roles in the transmission of knowledge across boundaries, for examples, exiles and expatriates whose contribution, often as creators of knowledge, to the mobility of ideas is significant throughout history (Burke, 2017:34–38).
115. Among the trade related barriers to the dissemination of knowledge across borders falls of course within the purview of patents, especially with the signing of the *Agreement on Trade-Related Aspects of Intellectual Property Rights* (TRIPS) in 1994. I will discuss the consequential issue for the control of knowledge of the agreement in detail in Chapter 4.

116. The value of indigenous cumulative cultural evolution (knowledge) follows from numerous

> natural experiments where explorers (usually European) arrived in a new location with more advanced technology but no cumulative knowledge of the local environment. These 'lost explorer experiments' have a remarkably similar storyline. . . . Despite having more scientific knowledge and more resources, including manufactured survival equipment, the explorers never fair well and often die. Without the benefits of cumulative cultural evolution, they are not able to survive let alone thrive in the new setting.
>
> (Nunn, 2020:14)

117. In 2015, a group of scholars and entrepreneurs issued a public letter urging that the developers of artificial intelligence systems aim "at ensuring that increasingly capable AI systems are robust and beneficial: our AI systems must do what we want them to do"; cf. https://futureoflife.org/ai-open-letter/.
118. The idea that algorithms are embedded knowledge resonates with the notion I mentioned already, namely that knowledge is embedded in social relations or objects. Algorithms are embedded in computational systems, platforms, and infrastructures; more specifically algorithms facilitate the sharing economy, assist in detecting diseases, are employed in efforts by government agencies to detect and control crime, and help us choose a television program or what to read. The social science literature on algorithm alone is enormous covering the entire range of possible issues from the assertion that algorithm control our romantic endeavors to decision-making about war and peace (cf. Lee and Larson, 2019 for an overview).
119. See also Joseph Weizenbaum's (1976) criticism of expectations or efforts to replace human thinking with computer programs. Weizenbaum's criticism is ignited by the attempt to leave human thinking to computers (to computerize humans) by simple operations.
120. The algorithm is designed to anticipate the likelihood that a defendant will commit future crimes (for a critique of the use of AI in legal matters, see Forrest, 2021)
121. A description of the kind of service AI systems offers to humans is Sue Halpern (2021) succinct observation that "most of us have encountered scripted, artificially intelligent customer service bots whose main purpose seems to be forestalling conversations with actual humans." The reason for the lack of further communication is of course that the decision at-hand has been made. No need to further engage in talk with anyone.
122. The Israeli military calls the May 2021 military conflict with Hamas the "first artificial intelligence war". The Jerusalem Post quotes a spokesman for the Israel Defense Forces (IDF) at the end of May 2021:

> For the first time, artificial intelligence was a key component and power multiplier in fighting the enemy. This is a first-of-its-kind campaign for the IDF. We implemented new methods of operation and used technological developments that were a force multiplier for the entire IDF.

In other words, military targets were determined using algorithms: One of these programs "Gospel", used AI to generate recommendations for troops in the research division of Military Intelligence, which used them to produce quality targets and then passed them on to the IAF to strike (see Anna Ahronheim, "Israel's operation against Hamas was the world's first AI war", Jerusalem Post, May 27, 2021; www.jpost.com/arab-israeli-conflict/gaza-news/guardian-of-the-walls-the-first-ai-war-669371).

123. The function algorithms appear to perform follow Alfred Whitehead's (1911) controversial observation in *An Introduction to Mathematics* that civilization advances "by

extending the number of important operations which we can perform without thinking about them".

124. See also the article by Jyoto Madhusoodanan, "Is a biased algorithm delaying health care for black people?" (*Nature* 588, December 24–31, 2020, pp. 564–547), reporting that "one million Black adults in the United States might be treated earlier for kidney disease if doctors were to remove a controversial 'race-based correction factor' from an algorithm they use to diagnose people, a comprehensive analysis finds."
125. Nicola Davies, "'Yeah, we are spooked': AI starting to have big real-world impact, says expert," The *Guardian*, October 29, 2021.
126. In an interview with CBS 60 minutes: www.cbsnews.com/news/yuval-harari-sapiens-60-minutes-2021-10-29/
127. It is notable that

> for the first time in history, [in 2019,] the United States Patent and Trademark Office (USPTO) received two patent applications listing an Artificial Intelligence (AI) powered computer named "DABUS" [short for Device for the Autonomous Bootstrapping of Unified Sentience] as an inventor. The filing of this patent application was significant because only a human or "natural person" can be listed as an inventor on a patent application. Although Title 35 of the United States Code does not explicitly state natural persons, the USPTO interprets the word "whoever" to suggest a natural person. The patent applications list DABUS as the inventor, and the AI's owner as the patent applicant and the prospective owner of any issued patents.
>
> (Hopes, 2021:120)

DABUS supposedly is a "creativity machine" that's able to generate ideas without human intervention.

128. The weaknesses of AI include, for example, the fact that AI decisions are largely based on the *status quo*, i.e., on existing—and accessible—data, that AI has no understanding of the content (meaning) of the data sets it uses, judgments are based on statistical correlations (reasoning), which in principle includes spurious correlations, and that decisions cannot be justified. Algorithmic decision-making, as a result, tends to reinforce prevailing biases by taken data sets on board that includes such established preferences/prejudices (see Michael Vogel, "Im Kopf einer künstlichen Intelligenz," Neue Zürcher Zeitung Sunday, July 4, 2021).
129. For a journalistic investigation of the use of algorithms and the welfare system, see "Digital dystopia: how algorithms punish the poor," *The Guardian* October 14, 2019.

3

FROM KNOWLEDGE SOCIETIES TO KNOWLEDGE CAPITALISM

The following chapter addresses the question of the nature and the evolution of knowledge societies head-on—specifically, the transformation of knowledge societies into knowledge capitalism assisted last but not least by the legal encoding of knowledge. Taking advantage of the legal encoding of knowledge are the digital giants (Big Tech). The digital giants are in the driver's seat of the transformation. The effects of knowledge capitalism extend well beyond the boundaries of the economy. The entire society is changed. The social structure and the culture of modern society are transformed.

I pay attention to the genealogy of the term "knowledge societies", its early usages in social science discourse, the reasons for the centrality of knowledge, especially within the economy of modern society and social inequality formation as a result of fencing in knowledge. Asking how *production* grows over time,[1] influential economic models proposed by Simon Kuznets (1955) and W. Arthur Lewis (1954) suggest that the main drivers of economic development are technological change and the spread of knowledge. The theoretical efforts by Daniel Bell and Peter Drucker are highlighted. Subsequently, I turn to multiple, best described as "soft" indicators of knowledge societies. Within the context of my inquiry, many of the soft indicators are nonetheless of considerable theoretical and practical interest. But the same indicators refer, in various ways, to rather contentious attributes of modern societies that are, for this reason alone, very difficult to quantify or locate adequate proxies, and fail to signify what could be called exclusive, relational attributes of the modern knowledge society.

In order to generate such attributes, I turn to the rise of *markets* for intellectual property, that is, the creation of an exchange value for knowledge—that is, knowledge as a fictitious commodity (Polanyi)—and stress, for example, the importance of investments in and rate of return to intangible assets as the core

DOI: 10.4324/9781003296157-3

economic activity of a knowledge-based economy. Historically, the production of new knowledge occurred outside of the market. Among the limits of the more restrictive notion of human capital, in this context, would be the recognition that not all knowledge becomes embedded in human capital and that creation of human capital depends not only on knowledge (Machlup, 1984:424).

The solidity of the attributes of knowledge societies is magnified by law, in particular, patent law, intellectual property rights law, copyright law, and other laws that resemble legal restrictions placed on cognitive phenomena that represent symbolic capital.[2] I will move the analysis of *the legal coding of knowledge*, in particular the role of patents into the foreground. My stress will be on the socio-economic consequences of patents, less on the derivative ideology and politics of patent systems or the relationship between patented inventions and advances in science. In general: Patents divide.[3] Patents control and direct the scarce human attention time. Hence patents yield more than merely economic power. What emerges as a crucial characteristic of knowledge-based societies is what I call "knowledge monopoly capitalism" or, for short, "knowledge capitalism". Knowledge monopoly capitalism refers to an economy based of course on the resource (non-rival) knowledge in production that is partially excludable (patentable) and effects a larger number of sectors of the economy that then are dominated by "superstar" firms (Rosen, 1981; Korinek and Ng, 2017).[4] The Google Group, for example, is responsible for over 90 percent of all internet searches. Superstar corporations amount to a growing concentration of economic success[5] based on a digital innovation, constant returns production technology, fixed costs, and an at least partially automated production process (see Korinek and Ng, 2019) and constantly enlarging their so-called (walled) "eco-systems". These developments represent secular trend toward an increase in the share of intangible in the value added of the final products. The marginal cost of an additional (almost unlimited) unit of production is practically zero. As is case for old-fashioned capitalism, knowledge capitalism is about ownership (property relations),[6] power, and profit.

In order not to be misunderstood that my analysis of knowledge societies amounts at best to a renewed corroboration of the classical premise that knowledge is power, I draw attention in this chapter to the limits of the power of knowledge. Although the right to intellectual property or, more generally, the legal encoding of knowledge or the commodification of knowledge provides the owner with extraordinary opportunities for profit and influence, which manifest themselves in a knowledge monopoly capitalism; however, privileges of this kind do not exclude the possibility of massive resistance from society and politics.

Early uses of the term "knowledge society"[7]

> The difficulty lies, not in the ideas, but in escaping from the old ones, which ramify, for those brought up as most of us have been, into every corner of our minds.
>
> —John Maynard Keynes (1936:viii)

The term "knowledge society" first appears, as far as I can see, in the name of "benevolent" societies in England in the 19th century. The purpose of one of these societies, the *Provident Knowledge Society* "under the patronage of Lord Derby, Lord Shaftesbury, and other distinguished men" is

> to make regular weekly saving a national habit, and so to increase the facilities for saving that it shall be as easy for a man to put by a small sum as it is now for him to spend that sum in beer or spirits. The Society has published a series of tracts upon *Penny Banks, Pensions, Insuring One's Life*, and other subjects, which are intended to promote thrift and forethought among the working classes; and of these tracts many thousands have been circulated.
>
> (The British Medical Journal, 1875:283; also, The Scottish Historical Review, 1920)

Inasmuch as the benevolent knowledge societies in England saw their mission to enlighten and educate the uninformed public, especially members of the working class, there is at least some resemblance to features of the modern-day knowledge societies that also rest on the broad dissemination of knowledge, information, and knowledgeability throughout society.[8]

The development and the growing usage of the idea of that *modern society* is a knowledge society dates to the early 1970s and more prominently and intensively to the 1980s and later decades.[9] One of the first social scientists to employ the term "knowledgeable society" is the political scientist Robert E. Lane (1966:650).[10] He justifies the use of this notion of the knowledgeable society by pointing to the growing societal relevance of *scientific knowledge* and defines a knowledgeable society, in a "first approximation", as one in which its members

> (a) inquire into the basis of their beliefs about man, nature, and society; (b) are guided (perhaps unconsciously) by objective standards of veridical truth, and, at the upper levels of education, follow scientific rules of evidence and inference in inquiry; (c) devote considerable resources to this inquiry and thus have a large store of knowledge; (d) collect, organize, and interpret their knowledge in a constant effort to extract further meaning from it for the purposes at hand; (e) employ this knowledge to illuminate (and perhaps modify) their values and goals as well as to advance them. Just as the "democratic" society has a foundation in governmental and interpersonal relations, and the "affluent society" a foundation in economics, so the knowledgeable society has its roots in epistemology and the logic of inquiry.
>
> (Lane, 1996:650)

Robert Lane's conception of a knowledgeable society is coupled rather closely to the promise of a particular theory of science and reflects, also, the great optimism or fear, as the case may be, in the early 1960s suggesting that science would somehow allow for the possibility of a society in which common sense would be radically replaced by scientific reasoning. That is, as Lane stresses in his definition, members of the knowledgeable society are guided in their "beliefs" and conduct, if only subconsciously, strictly by the standards of "veridical truth", the logic of inquiry and generally, the standard epistemology of science.

The very promise Lane attached to scientific knowledge as the motor that would transform modern society into a knowledgeable society is the reason for other social scientists to reflect about the emergence and the risks of a "*technical state*". At this point, I would just like to point out that the theory of the technical state, which continues to play a prominent role in discussions about modern society, associated, for example, to the accusation of a politicization of scientific findings (in discourse about the pandemic society) has an obvious affinity with Lane's ideas about the nature of a knowledge society.[11]

One prominent social scientist who warned about the dangers of the emergence of a technical state is Helmut Schelsky. Schelsky was one of the most well-known social scientists of the post-war era in Germany. His authority reached well beyond the narrow boundaries of academic social science. His influence was based on a distinctive understanding of the evolution of modern society and the terms he coined to capture core cultural and socio-structural developments. The theories he offered were distinctly middle-range and not of a grand design.

Robert Lane and Helmut Schelsky share in the dubious confidence that scientific knowledge will assume dominance throughout society. In the case of the political system, the deployment of scientific knowledge reduces political decision to mere technical matters. A brief quote from Schelsky [1961] 1965:459) transports the essence of the meaning of the notion of the technical state: "The 'technical state or government' deprives . . . democracy of its substance. Technical and scientific decisions cannot be subject to democratic decision-making, for in this manner they only become ineffective." Helmut Schelsky adds what is perhaps obvious, namely once political decisions are executed based on scientific/technical knowledge alone, the basic premise of democratic participation is eliminated: that is, the assumption that reason and reasoned judgments are equitably distributed throughout society. The citizen is deprived of her reasonably weighted judgement that would otherwise be attributed to her. Parliament becomes a mere control body of factual necessities.

Peter Drucker's and Daniel Bell's theory of the knowledge society

More than half a century ago, in *The Age of Discontinuity*, Peter Drucker explicitly and consistently employs the term *knowledge society* (cf. also Krohn, 2020:8140). The general knowledge society thesis places knowledge "as central to our society and as the foundation of economy and social action" (Drucker, [1968] 1992:349). In its broadest sense, Drucker's term of a knowledge society resonates closely with the emerging theory of modern societies as a knowledge society, as explicated in subsequent decades. Although Drucker's emphasis of knowledge is, in many ways, pioneering, it is not evident, however, whether he attributes to the *knowledge principle*, in the late 1960s at least, the same centrality for society as does, for example, at about the same time, Daniel Bell's notion of theoretical knowledge. Nor is there any direct evidence of a cross-fertilization between Drucker and Bell in their explication of their ideas of a knowledge society. Nonetheless, both theorists contributed with their reflections about the rise in the significance of knowledge as an economic resource to the displacement of the leading observation about the existence of a *managerial capitalism* immediately after World War II (cf. Chandler, 1977; Burnham, 1941).[12]

Drucker goes to considerable and informative lengths to describe some of the novel features and functions of contemporary knowledge. His definition of what counts as knowledge in a knowledge society is not restricted, as is the case for Lane's knowledgeable society, to scientific knowledge. Peter Drucker's account of the emergence of knowledge societies and the knowledge-based economy (also known as the symbolic or weightless economy) must be counted among the most original contributions to the theory of the knowledge society. However, Peter Drucker (1993:18) is reluctant to refer to our society as a knowledge society; "knowledge is now fast becoming the *one* factor of production, sidelining both capital and labour. It may be premature (and certainly would be presumptuous) to call ours a 'knowledge society'—so far we only have a knowledge economy."[13]

The popular response to questions about the origins of the knowledge society and the knowledge-based economy in particular typically refer (see Drucker, [1968] 1972:279) to the growth of more technically demanding and more complex tasks of jobs. However, this thesis leaves a significant social development of the labor market—that is not determined *a priori*—in the dark. Thomas Piketty (2006:68) rightly describes the dynamics of the labor market as a "race between the demand for skills and the supply of skills". It is entirely possible that the supply of skills is rising at a faster rate and is therefore the rising star in the world of work.

Drucker rejects the "demand" induced transformation of industrial society, that is, as Gary Becker (2013)[14] argues "economies . . . have increased their demand for knowledge workers at the expense of low skilled workers. The future is not likely to be kinder to workers with little education and few work skills." Becker's position implies in turn that school and colleges should teach the precise skills and concepts employers somehow want.[15]

Instead, Peter Drucker he points to what I would like to call "Drucker's law", namely that "the direct cause of the upgrading of the jobs is . . . the upgrading of the educational level of the entrant into the labor force"[16] and not, as the majority of social scientists such as Martin Carnoy and Manuel Castells (2001:7) stress, "globalization and information technology is transforming work." Drucker's law stresses that the transformation of the world of work is embedded in society.[17] What counts is the supply side. And the supply side is dependent on societal and political developments, for example, the ideological framing of education, that is, changing expectations education should of example play in the class relations of society, a commitment that high-quality education should be available for all but also the pressure from parents and political parties for more education. The realities of globalization and information technology, as we know and experience them today, do not assure an unimpeded and unconstrained flow of knowledge, goods, currencies, services, people, and capital investments.

Peter Drucker doubts that modern education reacts to the changes in the modern world of work. Skepticism about the traditional demand-driven view was also expressed in other ways, for example prominently by Randall Collins' (1977) discussion of functional and conflict theories of educational stratification. Collins is not convinced that schools and higher education provide the skills and technical knowledge that are actually relevant to the modern world of work. Collins (as cited by Gouldner, 1979:108) argues that an "increased requirements for schooling are not due primarily to the greater skills required by jobs, or to the skills transmitted by education." In fact, the function of increased schooling and the skills transmitted by education are primarily methods that "competing status groups [use to] monopolize jobs by imposing their standards on personnel selection" (Gouldner, 1979:108). Collins refers in this context to empirical studies that show that better schooling is not necessarily associated with greater labor productivity, although in the case of some professions such as law, medicine, or science, the acquisition of vocational skills is necessary. Thus, one of the primary functions of schools is seen as conveying status awareness by teaching status cultures, by establishing privileges and ensuring legitimation of inequality patterns.

Peter Drucker suggests that the stimulus for the increasing demand for knowledge-based work has to do less with the obviously changing technological regimes in the world of work, the growing complexity and specialization of the economy or an enhanced functional steering and coordination needs. The growth of knowledge workers has more to do with the substantial extension in the working life span of persons and the enhanced knowledge which individuals bring to the labor market in the first place. If we follow Drucker, it is not so much the *demand* for labor and particular skills as the result of more complex and exacting jobs, but a societal transformation that results in the *supply* of highly skilled labor that in turn triggers the observed transformation of the world of work. Support for Drucker's thesis may be found in growing investments of corporations in knowledge-based capital prior (and along) to major acquisitions of information and communication technology. Knowledge work must be considered a capital *asset*. Manual work as a *cost*. Given this frame, "cost need to be controlled and reduced. Assets need to be made to grow" (Drucker, 1999:87). Equally to the point is the idea that large antecedent investments in intangibles are the very stimulus that brought about the technological revolution in information technology (Beniger, 1986).

Among the surprising even startling properties of the original transformation of the labor market is that the American economy was able to

> satisfy the expectations of all these people with long years of schooling. . . . As a result of the change in supply, we now have to create genuine knowledge jobs, whether the work itself demands it or not. For a true knowledge job is the only way to make highly schooled people productive. . . . That the knowledge worker [Drucker first proposed the term knowledge worker in 1959 in his *Landmarks of Tomorrow*] came first and knowledge work second—that indeed knowledge work is still largely to come—is a historical accident. *From now on*, we can expect increasing emphasis on work based on knowledge, and especially skills based on knowledge and especially on skills based on knowledge.
>
> (Drucker, [1968] 1972:285–286; my emphasis; also, Drucker, 1992:91)[18]

There can be little doubt that knowledge for Drucker (1993:38) is the "*only meaningful resource today*. . . . And knowledge in this new meaning is knowledge as a utility, knowledge as the means to obtain social and economic results. . . . *Knowledge is now being applied to knowledge*." Knowledge is applied to *doing* (Drucker, 1993:17); it proves itself in *action* (Drucker, 1993:42). A central reference to one of the functions that knowledge occupies in all modern organizations and which, in contrast to Daniel Bell, Peter Drucker explicitly emphasizes is the role of knowledge in the "management revolution", i.e., the application of knowledge to the knowledge of work (see Drucker, 1993:68). The difference of owning the often-mobile means of production, in the case knowledge workers, and not owning the mobile means of production, in the case of the manual worker, has a significant bearing on the management of an organization. In many cases, the organization needs the knowledge workers more than they do the organization.[19]

Daniel Bell (1968:198) also employs the term "knowledge society" in the context of his discussion of the emergence of *post-industrial society*, a designation he ultimately prefers. Bell at times uses the concept knowledge society interchangeably with the notion of "post-industrial society". For example, he exclaims at one point in his discussion that "the post-industrial society, it is clear, is a knowledge society" (Bell, 1973:212). The basic justification for such an equivalence is, of course, that "knowledge is a fundamental resource" of post-industrial society. As a matter of fact, Bell (1973:37) indicates that he could have substituted "knowledge society" for "post-industrial society" because either term, and others, for example "intellectual society" (Bell, 1964:49), might be just as apt in describing at least some salient aspects of the emerging structure of society that he proposes to examine in his study of the structure and culture of modern society.

What is evident in both Peter Drucker's and Daniel Bell's designation of modern society as knowledge societies is their joint assumption that the significant transformations that bring about new constitutive principles of social relations and hence a new societal configuration are changes primarily within the economic system that then radiate throughout society and affirm the dominance of the economy. As a result, the emergence of knowledge or post-industrial societies out of industrial societies has not undermined in the eyes of Drucker and Bell the preeminence of the economy. In the course of further reflections about knowledge societies, however, hypotheses about a reversal of the equation of sub- (that is, the material foundations) to superstructure (the cultural or cognitive foundations) become my primary research agenda.

Radovan Richta's (1969) theory of the *scientific-technical revolution* constitutes the state socialist counterpart to Bell's theory of society. Bell (1973:212) argues that post-industrial society is a knowledge society for two major reasons: (1) "the sources of innovation are increasingly derivative from research and development (and more directly, there is a new relation between science and technology because of the centrality of theoretical knowledge)," and (2) "the weight of the society—measured by a larger proportion of Gross National Product and a larger share of employment—is increasingly in the knowledge field." The pace and scale of the translation of knowledge into technology provides the basis for the possibility of modernity.

Daniel Bell's theory of post-industrial society, Radovan Richta's theory of scientific-technological revolution, Helmut Schelsky's ([1961] 1965) *theory of scientific civilization*, or John K. Galbraith's (1967) *theory of the new industrial state* adopt quite readily those principles of theory construction characteristic of classical (sociological) theories of society. Among such principles is not merely a considerable aura of optimism about the future, and the conviction that there is a radical, even revolutionary, break in social relations but often also rather deterministic, lawlike assumptions about the tempo, the course, and the direction of social transformations.

As long as the emphasis is on the intellectual history of the idea of the knowledge society and theories that resemble the theory of the knowledge society, the historical account of the developments is not all that complicated, as we have seen. Much more complex and contentious is the effort to date the origins of the knowledge society on the ground. What empirical signals are there that would indicate modern societies are being enlarged to justify their designation as knowledge societies? I begin with various theories dating modern knowledge societies.

Dating modern knowledge societies

Radovan Richta (1969:276) and his colleagues date the beginning of the profound transformation of modern society, through the scientific and technological revolution, from the Fifties of the last century. Daniel Bell (1973:346) is less certain and argues, even though he points out that it really is foolhardy to give precise dates to social processes,[20] that the "symbolic" onset of the post-industrial society can be traced to the period since the end of World War II, for it was during this era that a new consciousness about time and social change began to emerge. This new awareness is due to scientific and technological developments, especially those of nuclear energy and computerization, which at the same time was accompanied by a new understanding of the relationship between science and the state, especially in the USA.

In contrast, Block and Hirschhorn (1979:368) in an effort to make a post-industrial argument within Neo-Marxism ask about the beginning of the emergence of the new productive forces typical for post-industrial society, namely knowledge, science, and technology, and in particular the period when they began to make a decisive difference in production, reach the conclusion that the 1920s already saw such a qualitative shift occurring in the production process—a shift in which a change in degree becomes a change in kind. In the 1920s, at least in the United States, the input of labor, time, and capital were constant or had begun to decrease while output had begun to rise. Industrial production increased by 65 percent while the amount of labor time in manufacturing fell. However, Block and Hirschhorn (1979:369) argue that it is more accurate to observe that in the 1920s both the input of human and physical capital declined indicating that in economic terms therefore, knowledge (the new productive forces) became the crucial source of (added) value.

If the growing use of a certain human capital, namely researchers, is taken as a distinguishing factor for the development of knowledge societies, the growing role of such specialized knowledge in large industrial laboratories is a crucial indicator. Knowledge as a resource in huge, sophisticated laboratories in industrial enterprises in the early 20th century, "staffed by thousands of researchers enabled the strategy of product diversification that characterized the chemical, electrical, automobile and machine industries" (Drahos and Braitwaite, 2002:41). American company names such as DuPont, Monsanto, IBM, Ford, AT&T, and General Electric are examples of a development towards knowledge-based corporations.

Steve Fuller (2005:83–84) is less concerned with dating the origins of the knowledge society by pointing to empirical changes in modern society, instead he claims to be able to locate intellectual precursors of the idea of the knowledge society and therefore is convinced that the social historians of the knowledge society suffer from a serious case of amnesia; as he observes, "the story of the knowledge society is one of large-scale historical deception." What justified this judgment is that "virtually all the intellectual components of the knowledge society were already in place by the eve of Nazism, although were only brought to fruition with the demise of communism." The intellectual originators were all located in Vienna in the 1930s: Friedrich Hayek, Alfred Schütz, Peter Drucker.

Any examination of the origins of the idea that modern society evolves into knowledge societies should, however, not overlook significant existential continuities or converging commonalties that reach far beyond the evolution of the modern economic systems. All modern societies, especially in comparison to earlier human civilizations, share key attributes that remain part of their structures despite "revolutionary" changes in the forces of production of these societies. Among these commonalities, I would count as a key attribute of modern societies the degree of social complexity of the social organization of societies, in particular, in terms of the population, capital population, life expectance, territory, social hierarchies, governance, division of labor, markets, money, social inequality, information infrastructure, specialization, and education (cf. Turchin et al., 2017).

The societal processes of enlargement and expansion—supported by a number of events and processes (be it due to military conflicts, the Cold War, economic growth, and crises, extending legal regulation), for example, of products and services or the speed and content of communication, proceed unhindered.

Mature theories of the knowledge society

From the late 1970s onward, the analysis of the modern society as knowledge societies became more sophisticated looking both backward to the existence of past knowledge societies as well as forward in time toward major social transformations of contemporary society (Böhme and Stehr, 1986). The theory of the knowledge society was developed alongside and competed with theories of modern society such as the *information society*, the *risk society*, *globalization theories*, or the *network society*.[21]

Of course, knowledge has always had a function in social life; as a matter of fact, one could speak justifiably of an anthropological constant: human action is knowledge-based. Humans are knowledge. Human is knowledge. Social *groups* and social roles[22] of all types depend on, and are mediated by, knowledge. Relations and communication among *individuals* are based on knowledge of each other.[23] Similarly, power and authority has frequently been based on advantages in knowledge, not only on physical strength. And, last but not least, societal reproduction is not merely physical reproduction but, in the case of humans, always cultural, i.e., reproduction of knowledge. In short, knowledge is not confined to a particular social system (Luhmann, 1990:147).[24] In retrospect, one is able to describe a variety of ancient societies as knowledge societies, for example, ancient Israel, which was a society structured by its religious-lawlike Torah-knowledge. Ancient Egypt was a society in which religious, astronomical, and agrarian knowledge served as the organizing principle and the basis of authority.

Contemporary society may be described as a knowledge society based on the penetration of all its spheres of social life by scientific knowledge as well as other forms of knowledge. Marxist theories of society have always assigned decisive importance to the forces or means of production for societal development since

> man's understanding of nature and his mastery over it by virtue of his presence as a social body . . . appears as the great foundation-stone (*Grundpfeiler*),

> of production and of wealth, so that general knowledge becomes a direct force of production.
>
> (Marx, [1939–1941] 1973:705)

Contemporary Marxist theories, especially through the notion of the Scientific-Technological Revolution developed by Radovan Richta and others, have analyzed scientific and technical knowledge as the principal motor of change. Max Weber's seminal inquiry into the unique features of Western civilization stresses the pervasive use of reason to secure the methodical efficiency of social action. The source of rational action and, therefore, of rationalization is found in particular intellectual devices. The theory of industrial society, as developed by Raymond Aron, that encompasses both socialist and capitalist forms of economic organization, stresses first and foremost the extent to which science and technology shape the social organization of productive activities and, therefore, other forms of life in society. More recent theories of post-industrial society and similar efforts at forecasting the course of social evolution of industrial society, in particular those by Daniel Bell, have elevated theoretical knowledge to the axial principle (the organizing principle) of society.

What justifies the designation of the emerging society as a knowledge society rather than, as is frequently the case, a science society (e.g. Kreibich, 1986), an information society (e.g. Nora and Minc, 1980; Duff et al., 1996; May, 2000; Webster, 2002), a network society (Castells, 1996; Schiller, 1999),[25] a post-industrial society (Bell, 1964), as technological civilization (Richta, 1969), Risk Society (Beck, [1986] 1992), post-capitalist society (Drucker, 1994), Audit Society (Power, 1997), cognitive capitalism (Vercellone, (2007),[26] digital capitalism (Nachtwey and Staab, 2015), finance capitalism (e.g. Fraser, 2017), "digital civilization", "Artificial Intelligence Society" (Inglehart, 2018), or the "algorithmic society" (Schuilenburg and Peeters, 2020)? A number of reasons are relevant for the choice of the term "knowledge society", last but not least the obvious reference to growing knowledge-based capital (also embedded, as it were, in huge financial markets)—in contrast to tangible capital—that is vital for a sustainable knowledge-driven economy. The role of tangible capital, however, does not vanish in knowledge societies. Yet, "wealth and might which depend on the size and the quality of hardware tends to be sluggish, unwieldy and awkward to move. . . . They grow by expanding the place they occupy and are protected by protecting that place" (Bauman, 2000:115).

But first a few remarks on the often-competing concept of modern society as an information society.

Much of the discussion about the axiomatic information society,[27] prominently taken on board by the UNESCO,[28] is, on the one hand, based on the idea—aside from the ambivalent observation that the present era is characterized by an abundance of information—that technological changes (new media, media products, internet) determine the nature of its economy, its organizational and cultural institutions; and, on the other hand, by a concern about the societal and personal consequences of a (control-) technology engaged in the "production, processing, and transmission of a very large amount of data about all sorts of matter—individual and national, social and commercial, economic and military" (Schiller, 1981:25).[29]

Modern technologies (e.g. in the form of the internet, smartphones, and artificial intelligence, algorithm, platforms, streaming services) are becoming the henchmen of dictators and other autocratic rulers (Kendall-Taylor et al., 2020)[30] or are controlled and exploited by the superstars of modern technology corporations (the largest corporations of the world:[31] Apple, Google/Alphabet, Amazon, Microsoft, Facebook, and Alibaba and Tencent)[32] with a *global* reach potentially undermining political liberty, stripping individuals of their free will, autonomy, individuality, and economic freedom in the name of unencumbered market forces. As an illustration of the economic power and the speed with which the superstar companies have risen to their dominant position, the market capitalization of these companies in 2021 may be taken as a comparison with the dominant corporations in terms of their market capitalization in 2006:

The advertising revenues of the superstar companies Facebook or Google account for by far the largest share of the company's revenues; in the case of Facebook, the share amounts to 98 percent. How effective such expenditures are is very much an open question. The powerful economic and societal position of superstar firms leads observers to speak of "platform capitalism" (Smizik, 2017), a "surveillance society" (Zuboff, 2019),[33] or "digital colonialism" (Kwet, 2021) and attempt to mobilize appropriate policy responses aimed at limiting nationally and internationally that very power. The coronavirus crisis has only boosted the economic status of "Big Tech" companies and enhanced the digitalization of society. The information society metrology I still in its infancy. It is not a foregone conclusion that the power of superstar corporations, insofar as their influence on the behavior of internet users depends on the influence of advertising, is really as extensive as their critics and the theorists of surveillance capitalism imply.

Every society has to transmit information. Less, or very little is said in theories of the information society about the genesis of the substance of information, the media of communication, especially human ones, ways of monopolizing information or the reasons for the demand for, and changes brought about by, the contents of the information which is communicated. Nor are discussions about the information society typically concerned with questions of solidarity, equality or domination in modern society and whether any economic effects of the spread of information and communication technologies cannot just as well be accommodated within more conventional economic discourse, namely "as phenomena best understandable in terms of long-established and familiar market-based criteria" (Schiller, 1981:xii).

The choice of the term "post-industrial society" is somewhat misleading because the "industrial sector" or manufacturing does not simply vanish in

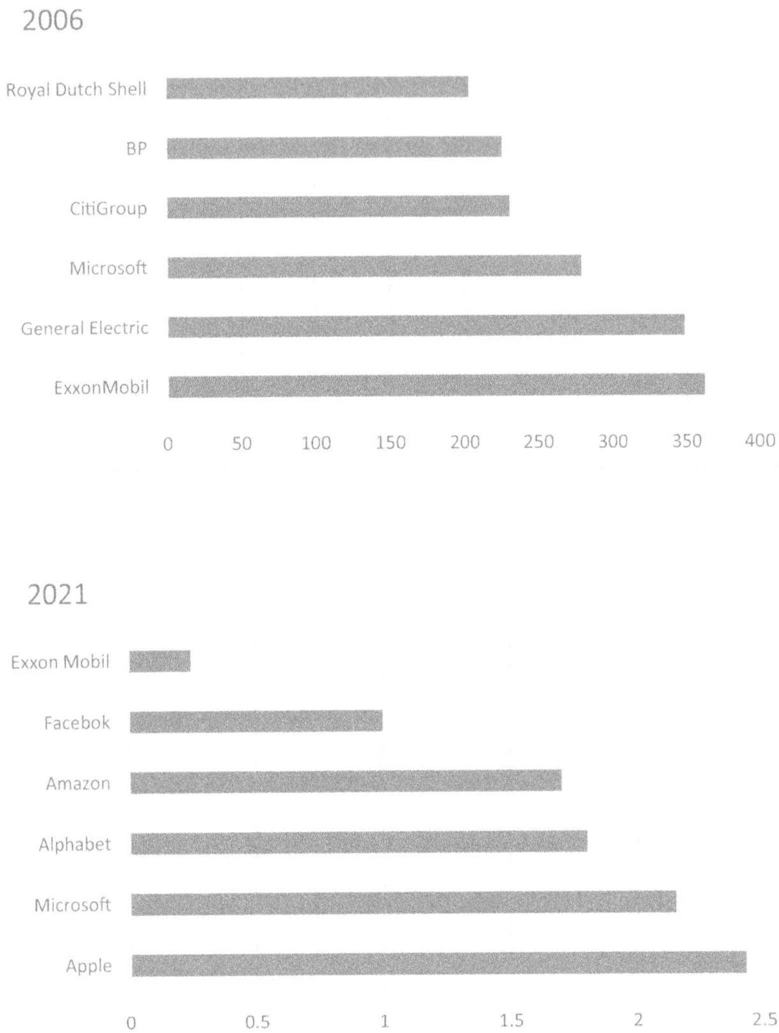

FIGURE 3.1 Market capitalization of the largest corporations in 2006 (in Billion US $) and 2021 (in Trillion US $).

Source: Yahoo Finance

modern societies. True, industry is transformed, it is host to many fewer jobs, but it is false to conclude that the industrial sector will disappear. The value added by the manufacturing sector in terms of its contribution, for example, to the national Gross National Product remains virtually unchanged. Moreover, one cannot really live without "industry", just as one cannot exist through leisure (*société des loisirs*), only (cf. König, 1979). The kinds of changes I will attempt to analyze here are the developments which occur with respect to the forms and dominance of knowledge itself. My focus is not merely on science, but on the relationships between scientific knowledge and everyday knowledge, knowledge as the foundation of scientific knowledge (cf. Luhmann, 1990:154), declarative and procedural knowledge, knowledge and "non-knowledge" or, better, asymmetric knowledge, and on knowledge as a capacity for social action.

Genealogy of knowledge societies

Past theories of society choose to designate, quite properly, those attributes of social relations which are constitutive of the specific nature of that society as identifying labels. Thus, such names as "capitalist" society or "industrial" society were created. For the same reasons, I choose to label the now emerging form of society as a "knowledge" society because the constitutive mechanism or the identity of modern society increasingly is driven by "knowledge". In the economy of the knowledge society, for example, value creation is increasingly based on the use of human capital rather than physical or natural capital.

The historical emergence of "knowledge societies" does not occur suddenly; it represents not a revolutionary development, but rather a gradual process during which the defining characteristic of society changes and a new one emerges. Even today, the demise of societies often is as slow as is their beginning. Social transformations rarely occur in spectacular leaps. Nonetheless, proximity to significant social, economic, and cultural changes seems to assure that what comes into view appears to be particularly significant and exceptional. The disruption of routines displaces orientations but it remains "difficult to pinpoint the actual crystallization of a new state of affairs so as to identify, both clearly and unequivocally, the emergence of a new society and its new modes of behavior" (Narr, [1979] 1985:32).

Knowledge societies do not come about as the result of a simple uni-modal unfolding and in an unambiguous fashion. Knowledge societies do not turn into some kind of one-dimensional social figurations. Knowledge societies become similar by remaining or even becoming dissimilar. New technological modes of communication and transportation break down the distance between groups and individuals but the isolation between regions, cities and villages remains. The world opens up and creeds, styles and commodities mingle, yet the walls between convictions of what is sacred do not come tumbling down. The meaning of time and place erodes while boundaries are celebrated.

Modern society was, until recently, conceived primarily in terms of property and labor. Labor and property (capital),[34] have had a long association in social, economic, and political theory.[35] Work is seen as property and as a source of emerging property (cf. Stehr and Voss, 2020) In the Marxist tradition, capital is objectified, encapsulated labor. On the basis of these attributes, individuals and groups were able or constrained to define their membership in society. In the wake of their declining importance in the productive process, especially in the sense of their conventional economic attributes and manifestations, for example as "corporeal" property such as land, natural capital, and manual work, the social constructs of labor and property themselves are changing.

My focus, therefore, is primarily on the role of labor, in the broad sense of human capital and property in generating added economic value and is less concerned with the distinguishing attribute of property or with the extent to which only labor may be viewed as the exclusive source of value.[36] While these features of labor and property certainly have not disappeared entirely, a new principle, "knowledge", has been added which, to an extent, challenges as well as transforms property and labor as the constitutive mechanisms of society.[37]

As Dietrich Rueschemeyer (1986:139–140), for example, underlines and cautions at the same time,

> taken together, the power sharing of the different knowledge-bearing occupations has probably diluted the concentrations of power based on property, coercion and popular appeal; but that is a far cry from saying that the power of partial interests and the conflicts between them have become irrelevant or even muted.

The types of societies, based on these core principles, reflect, of course, these constitutive mechanisms and their replacement. Bourgeois society was originally a society of owners. Later it became a "laboring society" (*Arbeitsgesellschaft*), and now, is transforming into a knowledge society. The decline of the societal importance of labor and property is associated with rising *sentiments of disaffinity* (Borgmann, 1992:20), toward those beliefs and convictions that center around the once dominant forces of production of industrial society. There is a growing feeling and need among individuals and groups to reinterpret the leading sentiments of the age.

The increased social significance of knowledge and of course science in *modern* society is the reason for analyzing its knowledge structure. The purpose of such a theoretical focus, therefore is, as Offe (1984:39), has described it in his discussion of the transformation of the "laboring society" (*Arbeitsgesellschaft*), to examine for what reasons

> the sphere of work and production evidently loses its capacity to structure and organize society and in the wake of the "implosion" of its ability to determine social action sets free new patterns of action with new actors and rationalities.

The knowledge referred to in many of the theories I have already mentioned, and the groups of individuals which acquire influence and control with it, tend to be conceptualized rather narrowly. The narrow consideration of what constitutes knowledge leads to the thesis that modern society is "science-determined" and not "knowledge-determined". The observation of the practical dominance of scientific knowledge contradicts reality.

Paradoxically perhaps, there is then a tendency to overestimate the efficacy of "objective" technical-scientific or formal knowledge. Theories of modern society lack sufficient detail and scope in their conceptualization of the "knowledge" supplied, the reasons for the demand of more and more knowledge, the ways in which knowledge travels, the rapidly expanding groups of individuals in society who, in one of many ways, live off knowledge, the many forms of knowledge which are considered as pragmatically useful, and the various effects which knowledge may have on social relations. The not insignificant resistance in society to scientific findings, such as skepticism about findings of climate research (see Stehr and Machin, 2020) or doubts about vaccination campaigns, must also remain mysterious.

The emergence of knowledge societies signals first and foremost a drastic transformation in the *structure of the economy*. At the end of this chapter, I will try to clarify whether in this case a kind of *tipping point* or precise timing for the transition from the industrial economic form to the economic structure of the knowledge society may be identified.

The political economy of knowledge societies

Productive processes in *industrial society* are governed by a number of factors, which appear to be on the decline in their significance as conditions for the possibility of a changing, particularly growing economy: The dynamics of the supply and demand for primary products or raw (natural) materials; the declining productivity of material inputs, the dependence of employment on production; the importance of the manufacturing sector which processes primary products; the role of labor (in the sense of manual labor), and the social organization of work; the role of international trade in goods and services; the function of time and place in production and of the nature of the limits to economic growth. The most common denominator of the changes in the structure of the economy seems to be a shift from an economy driven, valued, and governed, in large measure, by "material" inputs (*tangibles*) into the productive process and its organization to an economy in which transformations in productive and distributive processes are determined much more by "symbolic" (*intangible*) or knowledge-based inputs (especially as *nonrivalry* ideas that tend to raise the income of all individuals) and outputs (in more detail, see Stehr and Voss, 2020:22–78). Symbolic "products" based as intellectual property right and goodwill, which also have the great advantage that they can be extensively expanded (*scalable*) without further efforts, for example, the use of additional resources. An anti-virus program can be sold to another customer without the virus producer having to write a new program. Among the economic consequences observed as a result of the continuous expansion of the supply of immaterial goods are higher profits and often a growing market concentration. The transformation of what is important in the asset structure of a firm, the shift from fixed capital to intangible assets that typically do not depend for growth on size and spatial expansion, represents, at the same time, a shift from producing and selling commodities to collecting rent incomes (that is, excess of revenue over cost) derives from the ownership and control of assets.

Attributes of knowledge societies

The economy of industrial society is, in short, initially and primarily a *material economy*, an economy that relies primarily on investments in the physical apparatus of production and then changes gradually to a monetary economy; for example, Keynes' economic theory, particularly his *General Theory* (1936), society changes into an economy affected to a considerable extent by monetary matters. But as more recent evidence indicates, the economy Keynes described now becomes a (non-monetary), *symbolic economy*. Industrial societies had set out to overcome the widespread existential poverty and hardship of their populations. If we take the average economic success of households as a yardstick, we can indeed say that many industrial societies succeeded in achieving this goal from the mid-1980s forward, as already noted. Industrial societies had fulfilled its "historical mission".

The changes in the structure of the economy and its dynamics are increasingly a reflection of the fact that *knowledge* becomes the leading dimension in the productive process, the primary condition for its expansion and for a change in the limits to economic growth in the developed world but also for changes in the competitive structure of the economy. In the knowledge society, most of the wealth of a company is increasingly embodied in its creativity, innovativeness and human capital. In short, the point is that for the production of goods and services, with the exception of the most standardized commodities and services, factors other than "the amount of labor time or the amount of physical capital become increasingly central" (Block, 1985:95), to the economy of advanced societies.[38] Central attention of any sociological analysis of modern society, therefore, has to focus on the peculiar nature and function of knowledge in social relations and, of course, on the main carriers of such knowledge. The *United Nations Economic Commission for Europe* (UNECE, 2016:iii) and other national and international organizations charged with collecting statistical data on the structure of the modern economy is now officially recognizing this development that has been under way for some decades by emphasizing:

> Understanding and quantifying human capital is becoming increasingly necessary for policymakers to better understand what drives economic growth and the functioning of labour markets, to assess the long-term

sustainability of a country's development path, and to measure the output and productivity performance of the educational sector.

More concretely, and using what can only be called "*soft*" (mainly but not only economic but also one-dimensional) indicators, that is, indicators that in general are rather difficult to measure and where it is difficult to locate the boundaries of often overlapping indicators, here is a list of attributes that characterize *modern knowledge societies*:

- as the penetration of most spheres of social action, for example, production, education, policing by knowledge and scientific knowledge; knowledge activities subject to increasing returns[39] ("scientization", scientific knowledge as an instrument of political action); specifically,
- within the economic system, the emergence of the symbolic economy; investments in symbolic goods exceed investments in tangible goods both in households and corporations;[40]
- migration of social and economic activities to the internet;
- the limits of resources become a major dilemma;
- paradox of the knowledge economy (non-rival property is concerted into rival commodities, patent law, privatization; power generated by harnessing what is fenced in by the patent; Concentration in the application of knowledge advances in large private companies);[41]
- as conflicts and struggles that revolve around the control of knowledge and information (privacy, disclosure and transparency concerns);
- as the growing social importance of secondary education and higher education (production, transmission and certification of knowledge, discovery of problems)[42]
- as the growing significance of human capital (including "human consumption capital", that is, investments in capacities to enjoy); and, in recent years, the emergence of large corporations (superstars) who assets are mainly in human capital;
- as a sizable increase in real wages and a substantial decline in hours worked; and an increase in social inequality of income and wealth since the 1980s;
- as the displacement, although by no means the elimination of other forms of knowledge by scientific knowledge, mediated by the growing stratum of and dependence on experts, advisors and counselors, and the corresponding institutions based on the deployment of specialized knowledge;
- as the emergence of science as an immediately productive force;
- as the transformation of existing and the differentiation of new forms of political action (e.g., knowledge society policy; knowledge politics, science and educational policy; technology policy; patent politics);
- as the development of a new sector of production (the production of knowledge);

- as the change of power structures (technocracy debate; instrumentalization of science; concentration of markets; emergence of global superstar corporations);[43]
- as the emergence of knowledge, especially *proprietary* knowledge (based on policy choices) as the basis for social inequality[44] and social solidarity;
- as the foundation of new patterns of social inequality, especially as the increased spread of individual and collective income and wealth differences;[45]
- as the trend to base authority on expertise;[46] and
- as the shift in the nature of societal conflict from struggles about the allocation of income and divisions in property relations to claims and conflicts about generalized human needs,[47]
- and last but not least, the growing expectation that individuals are expected to be primarily responsible for the decisions they take, for assuming the consequences and risks of their actions (compare the contentious debate about responsibilities in the pandemic).

In the context of various discussions on the impact of science on society, including more recent theoretical efforts, for example as part of an attempt to devise an accounting scheme for the social impact of science (cf. Holzner et al., 1987), the nature of the impact of science on social relations tends to be conceptualized more restrictively than is the case here. In most conventional accounts, science is said to generate, first and foremost, if not exclusively, new types of practical action possibilities or constraints. The notion discussed in this context is much broader; science and technology not only allow for the possibility of new forms of action, but eliminate others and have an impact on the experience of action while also assuring the "survival" (in the sense of continued relevance) of existing forms of action and, in some way, even generating occasions which affirm traditional action.

Knowledge in knowledge societies

The concept of scientific knowledge elaborated here is therefore quite distant to any notion associated with technological or scientific determinism, especially the one-sided or unidirectional forms of determinism. The constraining features of science and technology are, however, by no means underestimated. But in contradistinction to most arguments in favor of technological and scientific determinism, and the theories of society associated with such views, the crucial point about knowledge societies is that science and technology simultaneously have strong features that allow for *resistance* to and defiance of homogeneous transformation. That is, science and technology have important enabling features which enlarge and extend social action, increase the number of available strategies, generate multiple centers of power in society, heighten flexibility or affect the ability of the powerful to exercise control and constraining forces which limit choices, reduce options, minimize the illusion of certainty, and impose penalties and risks.

It is therefore by no means contradictory to maintain that contemporaneous societal conditions of knowledge societies can become more standardized and more fragile at the same time. Generally, it is important to avoid overstating the extent to which science and technology are forces which merely are means of control, surveillance, supervision, and regulation and therefore constrain human agency and limit social action. Not unusual are therefore widespread and vigorous complaints or pervasive fears about the extraordinary power of machine learning, computational processes, or big data, often in the hands of the already powerful. Machines or technical artifacts are or will think for us.

Yet, regardless of "whether machines can think, the mechanics and computational processes of machine learning can obscure all-too human biases, prejudices, and power" (Wellmon, 2021:134). Computational processes on a massive scale consolidate social power, but that is only part of their consequences. The other part is represented by the "opposite" impact because science and technology enter relational fields of social action and can assume quite different values or outcomes especially for opposing social forces and purposes.[48] This means, at the same time, that the thesis advanced here does not imply that knowledge societies become uniform social and intellectual entities. It allows, for example, for the coexistence, even interdependence, of historically distinct forms of social organization and thought. Knowledge societies do not spell the end of ideology or irrationality. Nor is scientific knowledge, as a cultural ensemble, merely a way of deciphering the world; it is also a model for the world.

Although knowledge has always had a social function, it is only recently that scholars began to examine the structure of society and its development from the point of view of the production, distribution, and reproduction of knowledge.[49] Applied to contemporary society, the question becomes whether knowledge can provide the principle for social hierarchies and stratification, for the formation of class structure, for the distribution of chances of social and political influence and for the nature of personal life and, finally, whether knowledge may also prove to be a normative principle of social cohesion and integration even though the variations and alterations in the reproduction of knowledge appear to be enormous. Paradoxically, efforts to entrench necessity in history or eliminate chance from history has produced, at least at the collective level, it seems, its opposite outcome. The role of chance at the collective level continues to be part of the way society comes to be organized.

I will not attempt primarily to document, let alone provide an up-to-date and detailed empirical account of, trends in various societal sectors which emphasize that knowledge plays an increasingly important role in modern societies. Moreover, the precision with which the contribution of scientific and technical knowledge can be factored out is far from certain in most instances. For example, as the economist Heertje (1977:203), concludes,

> empirical analyses of the quantitative contribution of technical change to (economic) growth are indeterminate, partly because of the diversity of

> technical development and the difficulty of separating the development of technical possibilities from the expansion of technical knowledge. . . . Empirical observations in this field form a complex that cannot be unraveled without introducing arbitrary assumptions.

A typical example of the few existing contributions to the discussion of the nature and the emergence of a "knowledge society" may be found in the work of Fritz Machlup. His analysis is constituted by an elaborate apparatus of empirical, often census-type information about observable shifts and trends, such as in the occupational structure, intended to show that a knowledge society is indeed emerging and can therefore be documented in its own self-exemplifying terms, that is, in a quantitative (rational), manner. Today, we are able, in some sense at least, to take some of this documentary work for granted and can concentrate on what is, in my view, largely undocumented and unanalyzed in the same theoretical approaches.

Nor am I capable here of attending to many important theoretical issues which are clearly associated with any theory of society in general and of contemporary society in particular. But inasmuch as the knowledge society can be expected to restructure many existing societal configurations and to produce new social forms, all of social science is challenged to advance theoretical and empirical inquiry into knowledge societies.

I have to limit myself. My focus cannot be in detail on such otherwise important questions as the issue of political or moral bases of authority in knowledge societies (cf. Basiuk, 1977:266–274),[50] how the development of science and technology can be controlled (cf. Küng, 1976; Richta, 1977:27), the difficult measurement issues involved with attempts to estimate the changing size and contribution to the Gross National Product of what Fritz Machlup (1962), called the "Knowledge Industry" (also Machlup, 1981, 1984; Rubin and Taylor, 1986), the range of national and especially international policy questions raised in and by knowledge societies (cf. Bell, 1979:193–207), or whether a knowledge society must be a democratic society (cf. Lane, 1966:650; Richta, 1969; Merton, 1973; Bernal, 1954; nyinyi, 1962).

Most importantly, I am impressed by the degree to which modern society is becoming an "indeterminate" social configuration. The indeterminacy of modern society is the direct outcome of the growing importance of both a highly differentiated societal institution, namely the scientific and its impact of its products on society as well as the undifferentiated impact of knowledge generally—knowledge that is not confined to a single social system but is, as I have emphasized, everywhere. Knowledge societies are (to adopt a phrase by Adam Ferguson), the results of human action but not of deliberate human design. Knowledge societies emerge as adaptations to persistent but evolving needs and changing circumstances of human conduct. Among the most significant transformations in circumstances that face human conduct is the continuous "enlargement" of human action, with its unintended consequence to enlarge at the same time the fragility of contemporary societies.

The enlargement of human action is last but not least owed and tied to the historically unique enhancement of economic wealth, the emergence of the modern welfare state and the extent therefore to which "survival is secure" (Inglehart, 2018:1). In Europe and the United States, average real wages and standards of living have rapidly grown in a peaceful post-World War II decades, an unprecedented phenomenon since the onset of the industrial revolution.[51] The economic boom differed in its timing from country to country but, as Alan Milward (1992:21; see also Judt, 2005:324–353) has succinctly stated:

> By the end of this period the perpetual possibility of serious economic hardship which had earlier always hovered over the lives of three-quarters of the population now menaced only about one fifth of it. Although absolute poverty still existed in even the richest countries, the material standard of living for most people improved almost without interruption and often very rapidly for thirty-five years. Above all else, these are the marks of the uniqueness of the experience.[52]

Between 1950 and 1973 alone, per capita real income tripled in Germany, for example. In France, the three decades of the post-war period became known as *Les Trente Glorieuses*. The robust economic growth did deflate most aspirations for revolutionary change in Western societies: "Nowadays, in the richer countries, it is not so clear that the status quo represents the greatest possible evil" (Gorz, 1968:4). This historically unique increase in average prosperity or standard of living is becoming even more significant in society due to the "ageing" of many Western societies.[53] In spite of the general and unprecedent growth in economic well-being in the post-war years in many countries of the world, it is not the case, as some might have anticipated that concerns about inequality and poverty would vanish. In other words, for a long stretch during the second half of the 20th century, as the economy grew in many industrialize countries, productivity and wages grew almost at a similar rate. But inequality concerns were not beaten; and the relative position in the stratification structure continues to play an important role in how people see themselves (Stehr and Machin, 2016). Perhaps, it is the case, that after the end of the golden years of capitalism of the developed capitalist countries that represented three quarters of the world production (Hobsbawm, 1994:257–286), and as John Maynard Keynes ([1925] 1972:267) already described the success of capitalism in the decade of the 1920s in sober terms, "today [capitalism] is only moderately successful". The sustained promise and "continued crescendo of prospective successes" (Keynes, [1925] 1972:267) of capitalism today is highly asymmetric in its outcome.

The public perception of societal inequality patterns and "objective" inequality measures do not coincide in many countries. In many European countries, actual inequality is lower than perceived; in the United States, the actual inequality is higher than the public perception of inequality (see Niehues, 2016). The country differences tend to be fairly stable over time. In short, wealth formation continues to be less of a political and economic issue, than is wealth distribution.

In the decades that followed, output and productivity continued to advance, but wages did not keep pace; the proportion of the population that acquired its household wealth directly, or through inheritance, grew almost uninterrupted. With the growth of the average household prosperity, but not only due to increases in prosperity, certain normative notions are associated, such as a sense of existential security or, as Ronald Inglehart (2018:1–2) calls it, a post-materialistic world view

> which was part of an even broader [cultural] shift from Survival values to Self-expression values. . . . Self-expression values emphasize gender equality, tolerance of gays, lesbians, foreigners and other outgroups, freedom of expression and participation in decision-making in economic and political life.

A comprehensive existential security also promotes the secularization of society while the opposite development mobilizes an "Authoritarian Reflex" (Inglehart, 2018:5).

Since this development is not cast in concrete, massive disappointments may also occur, followed by financial and emotional insecurity. In the social science literature, the question of a society's wealth often refers only to the undoubtedly highly stratified distribution of material resources and assets and therefore primarily asks about the concentration of property. A blind spot of research, on the other hand, is the impact of the collective and individual increase in prosperity on people's behavior and expectations.

The widespread emancipation from economic vulnerability and subjugation, unforeseen by Karl Marx and Friedrich Engels, but anticipated by Maynard Keynes ([1930] 1935) amid the global slump in the late 1920s, does not occur to the same extent and at a similar pace in all industrialized countries. As it is, it provides the basis not only for the material foundation of new forms of inequality (see Stehr, 1999), political conduct, but also for morally coded markets.

The growth of economic well-being

The more recent renewal of interest by economists inquiring into the foundations of economic growth can be linked to the so-called new growth theory as developed by the 2018 Nobel price recipient Paul Romer (1984)[54] and Robert Lucas (1988), the Nobel Prize winner in economics in 1995. However, exactly at the same time in the early 1980s of the last century, Wassily Leontief (1983:3–4), Nobel Prize winner in 1973, appears to express exactly the opposite concern and draws attention to what can best be described as the specter of technological unemployment: "The role of humans as the most important factor of production is bound to diminish—in the same way that the role of horses in agricultural production was first diminished and then eliminated by the introduction of tractors." I will return to the issue of technological unemployment in Chapter 4.

For the time being, it is sufficient to point out the observations of Romer and Lucas and Leontief are not at odds with each other. Leontief expects a decline in the volume of socially necessary labor as the result of technological "progress"; Romer and Lucas advance the idea that knowledge makes a critical contribution to long-term economic growth in advanced economies. The idea of the knowledge-based economy was born. However, the origins of the ideas of the modern knowledge-based economy have its intellectual predecessor in classical economic theory. Adam Smith ([1789] 1978:87) stresses that

> man educated at the expense of much labour and time . . . may be compared to one of those expensive machines. . . . The difference between the wages of skilled labour and those of common labour, is founded upon this principle.

Similar observation about the centrality of human labor in economic affairs may be found in the works of Karl Marx or David Ricardo, not to mention more contemporary economists interested in in the history of the economy. And, in the early decades of the 20th century, the English economist Alfred Marshall (1920:115) declared with emphasis: "Knowledge is our most powerful engine of production."

What therefore accounts in recent decades for the growth of welfare, in particular, for a growing general well-being in knowledge societies? Perhaps it is possible to locate in response to this issue at the same time a more precise, that is, hard indicator for the origin, the salient attributes of knowledge societies and its sustainable features by asking about the economic foundation of knowledge societies and its peculiar shapes? In any case, according to standard economic theory, "sustained increases in standards of living, at least within developed countries, are largely associated with investments in capital and people that move the frontier outward" (Stiglitz and Greenwald, 2014:41).

My question is, is it possible to quantify which investments—and their results—in which factors of production have priority in modern economies and, as far as this is possible, to determine what is the decisive contribution to maintaining or improving living standards? And does this only apply to certain economic systems? The basic assumption I would like to test is that the nature of investment behavior has changed gradually but increasingly in significant ways. The type of investment that is typical for knowledge societies is investment in intangibles; that is, investment in ideas, skills, and knowledge or knowledge capacities. Intangible assets[55] such as patents (rights in useful ideas), copyrights (rights in expression), plant varieties,[56] and trademarks (rights in identifiers) are inherently more mobile, for example, in response to tax laws than the traditional physical factors of production.[57] Profits from patents can easily be moved to low-tax jurisdictions, that is, the current global tax regime permits "multinational firms to avoid much taxation—often paying taxes at rate markedly lower than local small business" (see Korinek and Stiglitz, 2021:31–32). Globally, intangible investments (and profits from such investments) have seen a steady and lasting increase in recent years as have larger surpluses in intangible trade by core countries, especially the United States (Fu and Ghauri, 2020). Although the agreement among economists about the increasing importance of investments in intangible capital for economic growth is significant, it also is the case that intangible forms of investment often have escaped the statistical net (cf. Corrado and Hulten, 2010).[58] Most intangible assets, such as research and development (R&D), organizational capital, and features of human capital have not been treated as investment in national statistical or (partly) corporate accounts. It is unavoidable therefore, to refer, from time to time, in the course of my discussion of the role immaterial capital, to the extent to which it continues to be difficult to obtain valid data about the nature and the volume of investments in intangible capital.

My interest concerns *long-term investment patterns*. Obviously, overall investments and investments in different forms of capital shift depending on secular political and economic developments; recent examples are the financial crisis of the year 2007–2008; changing trade or tax policies and the global political climate.

In general, given the role of knowledge not only in the economy but throughout modern societies,

> we should consequently expect knowledge (or "human capital") to be an especially important "test case" of both the power and limits of economic expertise to render the contemporary world governable in its terms, as it expands beyond macroeconomics and high finance into pressing post-industrial governance issues such as sustainability, inequality, automation and wellbeing.
>
> (Yarrow, 2020:6)

By stressing the human capital notion in general and the role of intellectual property in particular in the following sections of my inquiry, it is important to emphasize that my inquiry does *not* amount to a theoretical perspective of *economic determinism*. The impression of pursuing a perspective that "naturalizes" economic attributes, diminishing many other features of the knowledge society already elaborated, is enhanced by virtue of the fact that the human capital notion has been discovered by economists and is mainly elaborated as part of an economic discourse. Research that employs the notion of human capital is virtually the monopoly of economists. Efforts to measure and critically interrogate such statistics, and develop policy advice based on an understanding of the value of human capital for the development of the modern economy in particular and society in general (e.g., education policy and vocational training) remains squarely within the domain of economic discourse. Economic determinism in the case of human capital analysis is made "attractive" or appealing by virtue of the many efforts to turn human capital and thereby the complex entity of knowledge in a quantifiable social phenomenon.

(Hard) Indicators of knowledge societies

Apart from the various nonspecific attributes of knowledge societies that I have listed so far, it should be possible to find more precise indicators, perhaps even quantitative indicators, that signal both the origin and the characteristic transformational features of knowledge societies. The attributes I have already listed are rather vague characteristics, since they do not contain a precise beginning or a clear reference to the transformation of knowledge societies. However, all the attributes listed so far are consistent with the thesis of the simultaneity of the non-simultaneous: professional occupations along more traditional jobs existed in industrial societies as well as science and technology policies. Even the knowledge policy of knowledge societies highlighted in the next chapter is not necessarily a new field of political activity: church-dominated and other, earlier societies had their own knowledge policy.

But the lack of precise indicators is also analytically useful and plausible, precisely because they lack of specificity makes direct reference to the essential fragility of modern knowledge societies as well as possible reversal in societal trajectories, the perpetual transition of knowledge societies' attributes as the result of a changing relevance of such attributes over time and the persistent emergence of novel attributes including the meaning attributed to such traits. Since the prevailing economic discourse is strongly "biased", i.e., according to its self-understanding prefers quantitative modes of argumentation, it is probably only within the boundaries of economic discourse defined in this way that it is possible to locate hard indicators of both the specifics and the origins of and changes in the knowledge society.

Statistical information about the *volume* of investments in knowledge-based capital or tangible capital may well be a primary method in a search for hard indicators of knowledge societies and therefor for differentiating epochs of economic activity. However, the essential or unavoidable difficulty in pursuing such a criterion is a probable error of tautological reasoning: *tangible* wealth or capital, for example, machines, embody in various forms past labor including past efforts in natural and social science. The reference to an "automation" of the production process implies, so it seems, if only without further reflection, the substitution of capital for labor (cf. Acemoglu et al., 2020:2). Such an account suggests that corporations have substituted expenditures on labor inputs into production for investments into physical capital inputs into production. However, automation is exactly an expenditure that relies on dual resources, tangible and intangible capital. Automation reduces the labor share of value but raises the value added by employees. Assuming we are referring to industrial robots, the investment in automation should not be counted solely as an investment in physical capital because such a definition eliminates any recognition of the investment in human capital that leads to the robot, in the first instance.

We are forced to correlate, in light of the nature of typically available statistical information, common means of production with each other arriving at what amounts to a tautology; we correlate for example labor with labor. In short, it is important to keep in mind that official statistics tend to underestimate (mismeasure) the contribution of labor, if we, if only implicitly, falsely assume that tangible capital is void of labor. On either side of the "divide" between physical and human capital, we encounter the complex contribution of labor, also not easy to infer let alone estimate. For instance, how much "upskilling" is there in contemporary physical capital?

Measures that attend to the *productivity* of economic activity, often understood by economist as the engine of economic growth, may be of particular relevance for the development of hard indicators for knowledge societies. Productivity in terms of economic discourse is, so it seems, a simple concept. Productivity is supposed to reflect the output produced per unit input. However, modern-day economic productivity is notoriously difficult to measure for "in today's economy, value depends increasingly on product quality, timeliness, customization, convenience, variety, and other *intangibles*" (Brynjolfsson and Hitt, 1998:49; emphasis added).

The difficulties of attaining a valid measure of such values are exemplified for example by Ikujiro Nonaka's (1991) well-known suggestion—in the context of describing a "knowledge-creating company"—that it is the successful conversion and organizational interaction between "explicit knowledge" and "tacit knowledge" which represents a major source of innovation, expanding productivity and quality in firms. Upon closer examination, it will become evident that it is very difficult to generate robust indicators or proxies for hard values of productivity success in order to gain a measure of certainty that one is in fact dealing with a knowledge-based corporation.

Individuals as capital

> The acquisition of . . . talents during . . . education, study of apprenticeship, costs a real expense, which [is] capital in [a] person. Those talents [are] part of his fortune [and] likewise that of society.
>
> —Adam Smith ([1776] 1937, book 2, chap.1),

It is only within the more narrowly defined boundaries of modern economic discourse[59] that one encounters quantitative indicators of knowledge as a bundle of competencies and skills. Investments in *human capital* are defined as investments in knowledge. The statistical technology of measuring and accounting for knowledge-based capital has become a core undertaking of national and multinational statistical agencies and organization, for example, the World Bank or the OECD. The UN's Economic Commission for Europe (UNFEC, 2016:iii) describes the importance of obtaining information about the volume and the value of human capital, pointing out:[60]

> Understanding and quantifying human capital is becoming increasingly necessary for policymakers to better understand what drives economic growth and the functioning of labour markets, to assess the long-term sustainability of a country's development path, and to measure the output and productivity performance of the educational sector.

Economists tend to stress that investments in human capital are undertaken by the state, families, and corporations for their *instrumental* value of generating income. But it is valuable to recall that investment in human capital produces major dividends in other social institutions and everyday life.[61] As Mathew Collin and David Weill (2020:77) for example reiterate pointing also to a blind spot in research,

> education that results from more years and/or higher-quality schooling allows individuals to lead more fully actualized lives and to participate more actively in their societies. And better health, which we have considered solely in terms of making workers more productive, also allows people to enjoy more years of life.

However, the notion of human capital that is modeled on the valuation of fixed capital has been developed and deployed primarily within economic discourse (Schultz, 1961)[62] and, more specifically, the economics of education.[63] In his ground-breaking article on investment in human capital, Theodore W. Schultz (1961, 1981; also, Stehr and Voss, 2020:276–281) emphasized the importance of human capital as a contributor to national wealth. Moreover, the press release announcing his selection as a Nobel prize laureate in economics states "Schultz and his students have shown that, for a long time, there has been a considerably higher yield on 'human capital' than on physical capital in the American economy" (Nobel Foundation, 1979).

Human capital theory places the working person (as a presumed rationally acting subject motivated by *future* returns) at the center of its considerations. A variant of human capital theory, or its development in terms of incorporating empirical indicators of skills (for example, cognitive skills such as math, science, and literacy skills across countries), is what Eric Hanushek and Ludger Woessman

(2015:16) call *knowledge capital theory*. In any case, in human capital theory education plays a crucial role.

As Gary S. Becker (1994b:16) in a subsequent revisit of human capital theory therefore summarizes,

> expenditures on education, training, medical care, etc., are investments in capital. However, these produce human, not physical or financial, capital because you cannot separate a person from his or her knowledge, skills, health, or values the way it is possible to move financial and physical assets while the owner stays put.

My personal human capital, can however be defined in a broader sense than Becker's definition, and as Michel Feher ([2007] 2009:26) describes it succinctly,

> is me, as a set of skills and capabilities that is modified by all that affects me and all that I affect. . . . [Human capital] now refers to all that is produced by the skill set that defines me. Such that everything that I earn—be it salary, returns on investment, booty, or favors I may have incurred—can be understood as the return on the human capital that constitutes me.

Thus, it is not only the length and substance of formal education that counts as the input of a person's human capital, but also influences of a societal nature, taken on board outside the channel of formal education, such as the family background, the social strata of origin or the historical era of socialization should count as element of one's human capital. The *value* of human capital is set by the future income streams (discounted rate) of an individual (as an entrepreneur) or a group (company or even state) that skills can generate.[64]

Expenditure for the acquisition of human capital, it is important to note here, is not usually borne *directly* by the organizations that benefit from employing people to whom a particular human capital can be attributed. In general, however, the individual, the family or the state initially assume these expenditures. An exception may be the costs of subsequent company-based training of the employees. And the accounting rules of institutions or companies leave it at that. However, corporations (at times universities) are usually quick to endorse the slogan "our employees are our best and most important asset." For the state, corporations and the economy information about the value of human capital becomes a resource for political decision-making, financial reporting, fiscal management, and decision-making (for universities in efforts to shift priorities and values).

Investments in human skills

One of the obvious manifestations of a growing investment in human skills are data that confirm the increasing proportion of the labor force with "elevated/enlarged" skills. Aggregate data about the growing "skill level" of the population in most OECD countries confirm the thesis. According to Johnson (1997:42), the relative skill supply measured as a ratio in the population of high school to college equivalency in the US has risen from .105 in 1940 to .496 in 1993. In only five decades, the proportion of the population in the United States with a college education has increased fivefold. The increase of college educated labor is particularly strong in 1970s, reflecting a growing share of college students in the age cohorts in the latter half of the Sixties. It would be far too simple to suggest however that the tremendous increase in the collective skill level of the work force is in direct response to market forces. Although individuals will respond to perceived market opportunities, the fit not only in terms of time between perceived market opportunities and education could hardly be expected to be exceptionally close. Too many other social factors and forces impinge upon those choices and only after many years of education perhaps result in "higher" collective skill levels.

One of the major drawbacks of working with the hypothesis about the yield of different types of investment are the limitations of available data of investment regimes (cf. Black and Lynch, 1996) in relation to productivity outcomes including the feedback loops that should exist among types of investments mediated for example by income. It is likely that higher income that results from investing in human capital in turn generates additional investments in human capital (cf. Collin and Weil, 2020:69); higher income can also generate more physical capital.

It is now an established fact that economic growth is a function of the investments a country is capable of lifting. Similarly, there is a strong, positive empirical link between income/wages and productivity. Investments made can either target the material foundations of the production process which is fairly straightforward to account, for example, the infrastructure of production and the material means needed to produce; or, investments may be undertaken in human capital, albeit they are far less easy to establish let alone to quantify. After all, one needs to take into account more than merely the years of schooling; in the past, years of schooling was the main proxy for human capital. More recently, economists have broadened the measures designed to account for levels of human capital. For example, test scores as a measure of the quality of the school, school attendance records, and health inputs and outcomes as a measure of the physical well-being of the working population. The extension in the number of attributes taking into account of human capital represents an advance compared to standard measures dominant in the past. However, the relative contribution of each indicator toward the overall value of human capital is a contested matter.

Also contested is whether investments in human capital can be seen to generate "greater knowledge". At least Peter Drucker (1993:185) was convinced that such a link does not exist: "There is no shred of evidence that greater *investment* in the economy leads to greater knowledge." The lead time, as is the case of the linkage between market conditions and educational outcomes is too long to expect robust results.

A recent World Bank project by Aart Kraay (2019; the methodology is described in Kraay, 2018) developed the *Human Capital Index* (HCI). The index incorporates information on school attendance rates, test scores, and combined health data. The quantification of each of the elements of the index is difficult as is their aggregation (see Kraay, 2018:4). The weighting assigned to each element of the index is based on empirical information of the impact of schooling and health on wages along with an assessment of the mapping from test scores into school year equivalents. The index takes human capital investments through the end of secondary schooling into account.

Given the *Human Capital Index*, the gap among countries' investments in the human capital of their citizen is considerable; investment rates into human capital are highly correlated with the average income across countries as is, at the other end, their poverty (cf. Collin and Weil, 2020:75). However, there is not a close linkage between HCI and income in all countries.[65] The issue of the simultaneity of the non-simultaneous plays a role in assessing the profits for a country of investing in human capital, not least because it takes a long time before the "profits" become evident. It takes "a long time to produce a new worker and even longer time before existing workers, who were subject to lower human capital investments during their youth, cycle out of the labor force" (Collin and Weil, 2020:75).

Growing, stagnating, or declining investments in human capital can occur in any of the types of modern societies although modern knowledge societies should in general have a high human capital index. The dynamic nature of human capital, for example, over the lifetime of the individual elements that make up a human capital index is not adequately reflected in the present version of the index; skills can depreciate, lie dormant (useless knowledge), but also appreciate in value over time. Consequently, and for the time being, the human capital index *per se* is not an adequate hard indicator of the emergence and change of knowledge societies.

Investments in knowledge societies, in human or physical capital, benefits all segments of the labor force not only workers who are highly skilled or who are employed in industries with disproportional investments. Therefore, as Edward Lazear (2020:27; emphasis added) notes and as I apply it to the issue at hand:

> The fundamental question . . . is not whether changes in average productivity affect a high wage worker's wages more than changes in average productivity affect the wages of a low wage worker. It is whether changes in a high wage worker's productivity affects a high wage worker's wages *and* whether changes in a low wage worker's productivity affect the wages of a low wage worker.

Lazear undertakes a comparison of the productivity gains (value added, hours worked, and productivity per hour worked) by industry that employ highly educated workers (some college or college graduates) with those that employ less educated workers (some high school or high school graduate) between the years of 1989 and 2017 for the United States. The findings show that the return on education increased for the period under consideration and that *all parts* of the income distribution seem to benefit from increases in aggregate productivity: "The mean wage rises as does the wage of the lowest wage earners and highest wage earners when productivity increases" (Lazear, 2020:38).[66] Over a 30-year time period, the gap between higher-paid and lower-paid workers increased (Lazear, 2020:23–34). Productivity is higher in industries with more highly educated workers. The difference in productivity between the two groups of workers is more significant than the gap in wages and more explain wage differences.

Edward Lazear's study on productivity and wages does not answer my main question about the differential productivity of human capital or material capital investments. The increase in productivity and wages Lazear observes could be due to a number of factors, for example, technological change that generates increased productivity, labor elasticities leading to higher labor participation rates or that human capital itself has seen a (differential) increase. What is also possible, as Lazear (2020:36) mentions, is that an exogenous increase in wages leads to an increase in productivity. But such a link is rather unlikely.

Investments in physical and human capital

> A nation's real capital does not consist so much of buildings, machines, railways and the like, as of the industrial and technical knowledge which the members of the community possess, handed down from generation to generation, diffused by education and increased by the advances of science. Our knowledge and our science are infinitely more precious possessions that the whole aggregate of our accumulated capital.
>
> —Allyn Young, 1929:237

My hypothesis for a more precise determination of the *origins* as well as for some of the essential attributes and significant changes of knowledge societies in general and the economy of knowledge societies in particular[67] involve an examination of the *relations* (rather than single, stand-alone measures) between investments a society undertakes into physical forces of production (non-human; that is, natural capital,[68] infrastructure, buildings, plant, and equipment) compared to investments in human capital or knowledge-based capital (people, skills; rather than merely investment in labor).

Efforts to generate answers to my question are made difficult because there is not a standard definition of knowledge-based capital or material capital. Moreover, on the surface, the difference between human capital and physical capital assets seems clear. However, the difference hides the fact that physical capital contains "embedded" human capital. A fact that already prompted Max Weber (1921:151) to refer to machines as "geronnenem Geist" and Karl Marx (Kritik der politischen Ökonomie, 1953:594) to characterize the machine and industry in general as "vergegenständlichte Wissenskraft". A "realistic" calculation of the total contribution of knowledge skills to the prosperity of a nation or a corporation should therefore include all parts of knowledge. This would have the consequence of calculating those parts of knowledge that are internal and *external* to the enterprise and that are used to produce physical or immaterial capital.[69]

Since the 1950s, and much earlier as the previous citation from American economist Allyn Young (18976–1929) demonstrates, it has been taken for granted in economics that the growing productivity of the economy in the long run is only to a smaller and declining extent due to the accumulation of physical capital. A stronger and stronger source of productivity growth must be attributed to the human capital forces of production, including the increase in human knowledge (see Solow, 1956, 1957). Various estimates dating from the 2010s indicate that the contribution of intangible capital to the entire volume of corporate assets in the United States tends to be around one half of all assets (for example, Ewens et al., 2019).

These general observations on the growing importance of knowledge as the engine of economic growth/wealth are at the same time the path toward the essential answer to the question why it is that knowledge and not the conventional factors of production are superseded by knowledge that then, in turn, transcend an otherwise inevitable stagnation of economic life. It should be noted, however, that most intangible capital assets, as I will discuss in more detail, never appear on corporate balance sheets, leading to both a growing mis-measurement of books assets (Elsfeldt et al., 2020:1)[70] as well as to an under-illumination of the societal and economic significance of knowledge.

A major, *novel hypothesis* toward a characterization of the uniqueness of knowledge societies and the emergence of knowledge capitalism involves the idea that *rents on intellectual capital* legally formalized for example in the sense of *patents* (knowledge embedded in original ideas), *copyrights* (knowledge embedded in novel expressions or effort),[71] *trademarks* (knowledge embedded in symbolic material), and *trade secrets* (no requirement for novelty) are at the center of returns to human capital and inequality regimes in modern economic systems (cf. Stiglitz, 2015:3);[72] returns—in the form of an extraction revenue mechanism—that often exceed the cost of the production of the *patented knowledge*[73] and lead to a (digital) monopoly rent.

My stress will be on the socio-economic consequences of patents and patent portfolios; less directly on the ideology and politics of patent systems (Haunss, 2013:11–51; Parthasarathy, 2017; Khan, 2020:20–21).[74] Patents and their rigid enforcement are not merely economic phenomena, patents distribute power and wealth and impact political relations. The corporate ownership of embedded knowledge in the form of patents constitutes a major element of the forces of production of knowledge societies and a significant source of its economic inequality. Patents divide, and patents rule. Patents divide even if corporations patent and then decide to bury the invention. It is estimated that half or more than half of all patents are never commercialized (see Miller, 2019:85–86).[75]

The difficulty of calculating the multiple yields of patents—not only in monetary terms—is obvious. Patent analysis should greatly aid in an analysis of the modern economy; as a matter of fact, it has become one of the dominant methods of examining innovation and scientific-technical advance. A vital question of patent analysis becomes not only whether patenting decelerates innovativeness but also whether patents are the motor of economic concentration, rising social inequality within and among societies around the globe and a change in the geopolitical regime?

As Fritz Machlup (1984:164), one of the most astute students of patents confirms (cf. Machlup, 1960), one should not labor under the illusion that it will be possible to offer precise answers to these questions: "Both the benefits society stands to gain and the losses it stands to suffer [from granting patents] can be appraised only by comparing actual with fictitious situations, with no clues, let alone evidence, available for such comparisons." But this is not to say that we are completely at a loss estimating, even in a quantitative sense, the impact of the patent system.

Attention to the role of patent law in knowledge societies, even though patents are not an invention of the 21st century, should extend not only to its effects on the legal ordering of the economic order and related outcomes, for example, on the world of geopolitics (that is, the new imbalance between countries and regions of the globe)—which is the focus in this analysis. Patent law has also significant consequences in the field of social justice (cf. Feeney et al., 2018) since it shapes domains such as medicine, education, or citizenship and who in fact participates in science, technology, and markets (Vats, 2020). Just as the growing importance of knowledge as a productive force has an impact on society as a whole, developments in the field of patenting intellectual property have consequences not only for the economy, but also for many areas of society, for example. politics or our civil liberties. Intellectual property rights determine what we can read and who can say what. By the same token, intellectual property rights are political creatures since their "make-up" are the outcome of political and regulatory decisions about what are patentable or copyright-able phenomena, the rules under which their legal encoding can be contested and for how long the protection is granted.

For Werner Sombart (1927:518), there can be no doubt that the age of *high capitalism* is the age of *material capital*: "lease of a plot of land, construction of a factory, purchase of raw materials and machinery, etc.". My assertion is that the age of the symbolic or knowledge economy, the action of knowledge on knowledge, is, by the same token, the age of *immaterial capital*. Within the context of symbolic capital, the matter of patents and copyrights as a *negative* right excluding third parties from practicing and benefitting from the invention defined by the knowledge claims of the patent and copyright-protectable material looms large.

In the public relations work of so-called superstar companies, the industry's public idealism tends to be proclaimed and, in the media, by investors, politics and science its economic value, innovativeness and profitability are admired; in short, the praise of their worldwide success that enhances the authority of large corporations is a major part of the public discourse about these companies, and rarely are serious challenged, so far.

Patents, property, scarcity, and monopolies

> The right of property consists in essence. In the right to withdraw a think from common usage. The owner may use it or not use it; that is a minor consideration. . . . The right of property can be far better defined negatively than in terms of positive content.
>
> —Emile Durkheim ([1950] 1992:142)

Patents are a most peculiar entity whose major attributes as *property* Emile Durkheim already portrayed usefully. Knowledge as another peculiar entity shares attributes with patents. This is not surprising because patents consist for the most part of knowledge (expressions of capacities to act). The right of exclude others from the use of knowledge *enables* the organization of markets and, as I have noted, the creation of *exchange-value* for knowledge. There is not a natural relation between knowledge and property or patents and property; patent law awards an artificial monopoly and impedes free riding. The commodification of knowledge or the knowledge embedded in patents means to construct what is not *a priori* part of knowledge, namely *scarcity*. Scarcity can be created.[76] Property generates scarcity (Arrow, 1996:125). For there is no purpose to property where there is abundance. Since patents are property, it would make sense to analyze patents through an analysis of power and *economic power* in particular. Whether the creation of an acritical monopoly is justified is a highly contentious issue.[77] Classical liberal economic discourse would of course deny that any intervention in a *laisser-faire* regime is defensible.

The desire/need to use patented knowledge if one is not the owner of the patent comes with a price. Patents not only assure that knowledge comes with a price, but that the owner of the commodity patent will be in charge when it comes to control the price or the use of the patent, in the first instance. Ultimately, it is the legislature, or more precisely, politics that determines the price of knowledge. Patents generate *political prices*. The exact economic advantages of the patent holder are determined by the way the patent is formulated and how easy or difficult patent rules make it is to obtain a patent. From the fact that patents are political prices, it can be inferred that government action, for whatever reason, will not lose access to patent pricing, even in the face of political opposition and that of affected companies.

How significant the "unearned income" (i.e., extracted on the basis of owning capital assets or, non-labor income) of patent holders happens to be, especially for the observed *growth* of inequality since the late 1970s, it not an easy matter to determine. Perhaps in the case of pharmaceutical patents that calculation may be possible since the expiration of pharmaceutical patents often means that such medicines will be produced and sold as generics.[78] I will return to this issue.

Arnold Platt (1934:31) has effectively summarized some of the essential attributes of patents:

> It is a peculiarity of property rights in patents (and copyrights) that they do not arise out of the scarcity of the objects which become appropriated. . . . They are the deliberate creation of statute law. . . . Whereas we might expect that public action concerning private property would normally be directed at the prevention of the raising of prices, in these cases the object of the legislation is to confer the power of raising prices by enabling the creation of scarcity. The beneficiary is made the owner of the entire supply of a product for which there may be no easily obtainable substitute. It is the intention of the legislators that he shall be placed in a position to secure an income from the monopoly conferred upon him by restricting the supply in order to raise the price.

The monopoly created by statute derives some of its justification—and this becomes a crucial question—from the theory of public goods and the expectation that the benefits of practicing the knowledge enclosed in a patent will facilitate spillover effects that benefit not only the owners of the patents but society as a whole. Competitive markets, in contrast, encourage the underproduction of knowledge, since the production of knowledge is usually costly but "inexpensive" to copy. In short, in a knowledge-based economy patents represent a *strategic asset* for corporations and individuals, as the case may be although the assignment of a patent typically means that social control over knowledge in companies is removed from the realm of the inventor and shifted to the world of management.

Moreover, policy makers, managers, and corporations tend to stress the success story of the enlarged global protection of the patent system. In fact, the very success in protecting patents has led to major asymmetrical economic and political results widening the gap between the powerful and less powerful. Few patents are profitable. Profitable patents allow the owner to extract extraordinary profits while resisting improvements in the quality of the product. Such asymmetries enhance, for example, the concentration of research and development in the hands of a few large corporations rather than small firms or start-ups.[79]

For corporations, the strategic nature of patents assets manifest itself in obtaining as many patents as possible, even if some or many of the patents are essentially worthless.[80] In the field of complex technologies, such as the smartphone, a large bouquet of patents will make it virtually impossible for a rival firm to enter market since the cost can be prohibitive. For instance, "the roughly 250,000 patents enforced by the dominant smartphone companies have rendered it nearly impossible for others to challenge the iPhone or Samsung Galaxy" (Day and Schuster, 2020:119). Holders of a large number of patents, for instance in the Bluetooth market, can threaten infringement litigation.[81] In the United States, the cost of defending an infringement lawsuit can amount to three million dollars and thereby ensure that potential competitors resist research and, of course, are kept from entering the market.[82] Moreover, if "infringers" lose a case, they can be assessed punitive damages, which further reduces any incentive to enter a market saturated with patents.[83]

In the case of patents as strategic assets what counts are not the quality but the quantity of patents,[84] although the number of patents is not altogether irrelevant.[85]

A tipping point?

How much productivity growth originates in knowledge societies from working smarter rather than from the deployment of any of the material forces of production? The picture is mixed. My proposition will be that the origins of a modern, established knowledge society, that is, knowledge capitalism, its *tipping or critical point*, can be traced to a time-range when investments in human capital not only exceed investments in physical capital but investments in human capital became more productive and profitable than investments in physical capital.

One estimate puts this critical date in the 1990 years (e.g., Alexander and Eberly, 2018).[86] In knowledge-based economies, in the era of "light modernity" in which software rules (Bauman, 2000:118), the proportion of knowledge to physical matter in production is one of the most significant variables that determines the kind of society in which we live. But it is important to stress that a symbolic or immaterial economy (see Stehr and Voss, 2020:22–78) will not inevitably lose its nature as a *capitalist* economic system, as the choice of the term knowledge capitalism already signifies.

Nor is it the case that we should expect a *linear* transformation of investment activities throughout the economy. The proportion of investments in tangible and intangible capital differs sector by sector of the economy.[87] The relation of investment in human capital versus physical capital in corporations within each sector of the economy will not converge. Some corporations even in the service industry will have a significant volume of their investments in physical capital; for example, corporations that dominate the material infrastructure of the internet such as fiber optic submarine cables, Internet Exchange Points (IXPs), or Autonomous system numbers (ASNs) have mainly assets in tangible capital. The modern superstar corporations (e.g., Apple, Google, Netflix, Facebook) have mainly investments in intangible capital.[88] The control of the material foundations of the internet is more dispersed that is the control of the symbolic activities of the internet.

The response of corporations and other institutions to the pressure to stay competitive today, to retain or enlarge market share, is to be at the forefront of innovative activities. The key to innovativeness is found in knowledge-based capital. Raw materials are being eclipsed in the knowledge economy. The decline in natural capital is also due to an exhaustion of such finite resources and for environmental policies that demand that natural capital remain in the ground. Investments in fossil fuel requires more tangible capital than renewable energy that tends to be more knowledge-based. An OECD (1996) report estimates that more than half of the Gross Domestic Product (GDP) in most OECD countries in the last decade of the 20th century is already knowledge-based. In the automobile sector, for example,

> it is estimated that 90% of the new features in cars have a significant software component (innovative start-stop systems, improved fuel injection, on-board cameras, safety systems, etc.). Valuable trade secrets now lie in the electronic controls that regulate the operation of motors, generators and batteries. Hybrid and electric vehicles require huge volumes of computer code.
>
> (OECD, 2013:25)

Nations, social strata, corporations, and individuals that are capable in mobilizing knowledge capacities, for example, exploiting discretionary opportunities or the ability to generate new and persuasive ideas, are more likely to accumulate and defend financial gains within the frame of the knowledge economy (see Stehr, 2016:101–108). The combination of dynamic knowledge capabilities—which enhance the complexity of the economy and its products—are strongly correlated with the level of development of an economy, its income per capita and future growth potential (Hidalgo and Hausmann, 2009).

The outcome may be called the *paradox* of the knowledge economy; knowledge as a *nonrival* phenomenon (that can be utilized or sold infinitely and that are not depleted by use) is widely available or can be widely available, it Is "potentially democratic and egalitarian but, at the same time, it is offering corporations and financial capital unprecedented opportunities to concentrate on wealth and monopoly power" (Pagano, 2018:355). Finally, many intangible investments can be scaled many times in many locations (e.g., Starbucks, Airbnb, Uber, or McDonald's), It follows those large markets and the globalization represent more attractive investment opportunities (cf. Haskel and Westlake, 2017:34) that further enhance the economic power of large corporations. The key is that rival goods, in principle, offer constant returns while nonrivalry gives rise to increasing returns to scale. With nonrivalry, "growth in income per person is tied to growth in the total stock of ideas (i.e., an aggregate) not to growth in ideas per person" (Jones, 2019:861).

However, profitability does not happen automatically, for example, in the sense that new technology, complex software or clever design alone assure the flow of profits to the inventing corporation. For it is in this context that the ability of corporations in the United States and elsewhere to *legally fence in* novel knowledge (through the institutional arrangements surrounding intellectual property rights) thereby creating virtual monopolies becomes a dominant pattern within the symbolic economic system—assuring also that a disproportionate share of national and international profits flows to superstar firms that horde such rights to knowledge. In other words, intellectual property law turns nonrival goods into excludable goods. Without their legal protection, new findings and their use by other companies would be non-excludable and non-rival. Although the piracy of protected intellectual property is not uncommon, this fact but moderately affects the profitability of intellectual property owners (cf. Schwartz, 2019:511).[89]

After the tipping point, the development of the knowledge society becomes a self-reinforcing process. The timing/payoff of the two investments methods are different. Benefits from physical investment manifest themselves in productivity gains earlier than investment in human capital. The comparison I would like to undertake requires a full accounting of all investments in human and physical capital; i.e., not only the investments that can be directly attributed to an organization, but also societal investments, such as public investments.

The changes in the volume of investments (factor inputs)—rather than productivity growth—I have in mind should overlay and should not be a direct reflection of changing patterns of productivity growth, for example, more recently, as the result of a financial crisis or a Euro Area slowdown (twelve economies) in the first decade of this century. A distinction that might be of value is the measurement of the increase of investments in factor inputs versus the overall value of capital and labor stocks minus depreciation. But this approach raises the complex issue of how to calculate the depreciation of capital, let alone labor assets (Dinerstein et al., 2010). The labor productivity growth whether static, declining, or growing is not at the center of the analyses. If productivity figures are taken into consideration, the contrast in the productivity of factors would be of interest. What is of particular interest is the volume of investments in different input factors. It would also be helpful to have information on the relations between investments made in different sector of the economy as well as trend data beyond the statistics for a few years only. Information about factor inputs raises difficult measurement issues, for example, in the field of Information and Communication (ICT) capital; what part of the ICT assets fall into the labor category and what investments are material capital? It is evident, however that investments in ICT assets require complimentary intangible investments.

Likely even more complicated is to empirically assess the value of "unique" attributes that may be ascribed to knowledge-based in contrast to tangible capital. Jonathan Haskel and Stian Westlake (2017:58) list the following attributes of knowledge-based capital: *scalability*, *sunkenness*, *spillovers*, and *synergies*. Scalability refers to ability of re-employing an intangible asset again and again without little cost and significant depreciation, for example, of a software program or an algorithm. Intangible-intensive production compared to tangible-intensive production may require a significant (start-up) initial investment but requires at times negligible marginal cost to keep the production going. The outcome is that intangible-intensive production offer almost infinite returns to scale. Infinite returns to scale annuals the iron law of diminishing marginal returns that governed industrial society.

Sunkenness refers to the costs of a project that cannot be recovered once the project has been discontinued. Spillovers refer to the possibility that some intangible assets, such as organizational processes, training, or marketing campaigns, are difficult to protect. Synergies suggest that it is relatively easy for competitors to copy intangible assets. The combination of these attributes means that knowledge-based capital is inherently uncertain and essentially contested (Haskel and Westlake, 2017:87–88).

What exactly is knowledge-based capital?

The beginnings of efforts by economists and statisticians to (quantitatively) determine the knowledge capital of an economy or a company can be traced back to the not-so-distant invention of gross national product (GDP) in the 1940s (Masood, 2016). Knowledge was not part of these initial efforts to determine the extent of a country's economic performance. With the publication of Fritz Machlup's (1962) *The Production and Distribution of Knowledge in the United States*, heroic efforts to empirically determine knowledge capital began. In the 1980s, the economists' interest was strengthened by the invention of the computer. The question of the value of software also arouses interest in an effort to arrive at an exact compilation of parts of the overall economic performance to which no material character could be ascribed.

It is now obvious that the assets of a firm, an organization, or an institution (schools, universities, museums, media) of *knowledge-based capital* (KBC) are significant economic attributes that have only recently come to the attention of economist and the official regimes of national accountants (see Haskel and Westlake, 2017:43). A deficiency that is only gradually recognized and removed is that "most intangible assets . . . such as research and development (R&D), organizational capital, and training are to date not treated as investment in national accounts" (Niebel et al., 2017:S50). For economists, what in the end counts as investments in knowledge-based capital are nominal values or what actually has been spend or purchased and what is expected to generate a profit. An additional deficit, until recently, of the discourse on knowledge-based capital by many economists is the failure to attend to the legal coding of intangible assets, in particular grafting patent legislation to knowledge (cf. Pistor, 2019:116–117).

One widely accepted definition, as an OECD Report (2013:22) notes, identifies three types of knowledge-based capital:

> computerised information (software and databases); innovative property (patents, copyrights, designs, trademarks); and economic competencies ([refers to investments that do not directly involve computers or innovation:] including brand equity, firm-specific human capital, networks of people and institutions, and organisational know-how that increases enterprise efficiency).[90]

In any case, it can be said that investment in knowledge-based capital includes more "labor" than the labor share of physical capital. As a result, labor-intensive services will become more expensive compared to products that are mainly produced with physical capital. The typology generates the following table that also

TABLE 3.1 Classification of the forms of KBC and their effects on output growth.

Type of KBC asset	Mechanisms of output growth for the investor in the asset
Computerised information	
Software	Improved process efficiency, ability to spread process innovation more quickly, and improved vertical and horizontal integration.
Databases	Better understanding of consumer needs and increased ability to tailor products and services to meet them. Optimised vertical and horizontal integration.
Innovative property	
Research & Development	New products, services and processes, and quality improvements to existing ones. New technologies.
Mineral explorations	Information to locate and access new resource inputs - possibly at lower cost - for future exploitation.
Copyright and creative assets	Artistic originals, designs and other creative assets for future licensing, reproduction or performance. Diffusion of inventions and innovative methods.
New product development in financial services	More accessible capital markets. Reduced information asymmetry and monitoring costs.
New architectural and engineering designs	New designs leading to output in future periods. Product and service quality improvements, novel designs and enhanced processes.
Economic competencies	
Brand-building advertisement	Improved consumer trust, enabling innovation, price premia, increased market share and communication of quality.
Market research	Better understanding of specific consumer needs and ability to tailor products and services.
Worker training	Improved production capability and skill levels.
Management consulting	Externally acquired improvement in decision making and business processes.
Own organisational investment	Internal improvement in decision making and business processes.

Source: left column, Corrado, C.A, Hulten, C.R and Sichel, D. (2005), *Measuring Capital and Technology: An Expanded Framework*. in C. Corrado, Haltiwanger, J. and Sichel, D. (eds), *Measuring Capital in a New Economy*, National Bureau of Economic Research and University of Chicago Press.

Source: OECD (2013:23) Report: *Supporting Investment in Knowledge Capital, Growth and Innovation*

considers the "contribution" of the specific asset for economic growth but is at the same time silent about the interaction and complementarities of the individual knowledge assets:

The category "*Economic competencies*" includes according to the OECD definition of the classification of knowledge-based capital:

> Knowledge emb1edded in a firm's human and structural resources, such as firm-specific training, organisational capital, and brand equity and measured mainly by using secondary sources of data and a set of provisional assumptions. This asset category represents the biggest challenge in terms of definition, measurement and modelling.
>
> (OECD, 2013:183)

What is remarkable about the OECD typology of knowledge-based assets and the table of its economic benefits is what it omits but what could very well constitute the most precious knowledge-based capital of a corporation. The common attribute of the account of knowledge-based assets found in the table are *expenditures* of the organization. In other words, price information is important in order to capture the volume and the value of the asset. Hence each item *purchased* is justified by virtue of its determinable contribution to growth. For example, "new product development in financial services" is expected to result in "more accessible markets. Reduced information asymmetry and monitoring costs". Investments undertaken by a corporation or institution are only an investment if it can show that *spending* took place. It hardly needs to be emphasized that *it is easy* to locate the nominal value for what is treated as an investment in non-knowledge and knowledge-based capital. However, this approach has the disadvantage that internally generated knowledge-based capital is not necessarily counted.

Missing in the OECD classification is the most significant symbolic (immaterial) resource of a firm, namely, the skills and abilities of its employees or, what is usually understood to represent the *human capital* of the corporation and institution. The assets missing differ from the assets incorporated in that they tend to have a longer life expectancy and depreciate slower manner. In a study on sectoral productivity of knowledge capital in the EU by Thomas Niebel and colleagues (2017:S51), there is a casual reference to "workforce training is necessary to gain productivity benefits", for example through the adaptation of information technologies, but probably only because this attribute can be directly related to company expenditures. In other studies, even investment in in-house education and continuing training is not taken into account (Belitz et al., 2018:64). Other smaller items that can be attributed to knowledge capital, such as financial innovations or design, are also usually missing (see Belitz and Gorning, 2019:532). The narrow definition of knowledge-based capital and its attendant interest in the often-short-lived depreciation of such assets, for instance, the "productive live" of branding is judged to be 2.8 years results in a significant underestimation of the value in human skills. Of course, human capital expenditures are not directly charged to the organization, nor do they become the property of the corporation (except in a slave economy). The omission is perhaps therefore justified for accounting and tax purposes or the idea that the knowledge capital is the "property" of the employees.[91]

The narrow definition of the volume and the values of intangibles explains why the "contribution of intangibles to labor productivity growth [tends] to be higher in manufacturing than in services" because in manufacturing there is high share of intangible investment (expenditure) that falls into the category of Research & Development (Niebel et al., 2017:S64-S65).

The approach I have criticized for determining investments in knowledge-based capital follows the rules of the "UN System of National Accounts", which is not only closely followed by many authors, but is also called "the bible of national accounting" (Haskel and Westlake, (2017:20) and is therefore given precedence in defining intangible investments: Investment "is what happens when a producer either acquires a fixed asset or spends resources (money, effort, raw materials) to improve it" (SNA, 2008, para 10.32). This definition shows that all prior investments in the human capital of an individual are irrelevant for the calculation of the value of the intangible capital of an enterprise and therefore cannot show up in the balance sheet of an organization. Of course, this also applies to exogenous knowledge that may be freely available (*common knowledge*), but which nevertheless contributes to the productivity of a company and increases the prosperity of a society.

I had already referred to the growing qualification level of the population in developed societies in the past decades. The higher and growing level of skills affects the productivity of the knowledge capital of a society or individual enterprises, for example, the type and number of innovations and patents filed and the extension of additional knowledge. Highly specialized human intangible assets probably are less mobile and therefore more firm-dependent, for example within the financial sector than tangible assets. The restrictive definition of the volume and value of intangibles explains why the contribution "of intangibles to labour productivity growth [tends] to be higher in manufacturing than in services", because manufacturing industries have a high proportion of intangible investment (expenditure) that falls into the category of research and development (Niebel et al., 2017:S64-S65).

The problematic issue of measurement of knowledge-based capital, given for instance the contestable definition of what exactly counts as the boundary of intellectual property and the growing significance of ideas for economic growth (cf. Jones, 2021) receives more and more attention. The OECD (2013:180) reports for example that is has invested considerably and made advances in developing methods and obtaining data on the volume and the nature of knowledge-based capital as well as advancing the international harmonization of such estimates.

Markets for intellectual property

> It is hardly possible to discuss the functioning of a market without considering the right system, which determines what can be bought and sold and which, by influencing the cost of carrying out various kinds of market transactions, determines what is, in fact, bought and sold, and by whom.
>
> —Ronald Coase (1978:210)

The difference of investment in tangible and knowledge-based assets for private businesses (excluding real estate, health, and education) in the United States for the period between 1973 and 2011 shows that investment in knowledge-based capital was approximately equal as a percentage of adjusted GDP to tangible investments before knowledge investment began to exceed tangible investment consistently. Tangible investments declined while investments in knowledge-based capital steadily increased year by year; hence the difference increased significantly until the year 2011, the last year for which data are available (cf. OECD, 2013:24; Corrado and Hulten, 2010:99–104; Chen, 2018). If the data are accepted as valid and my definition of the boundaries of the transition of the economy of industrial to knowledge societies, then the American economy would be a fully developed knowledge-based economy since the beginning of the new century. In Europe, this applies, in the same time period, only to Sweden.

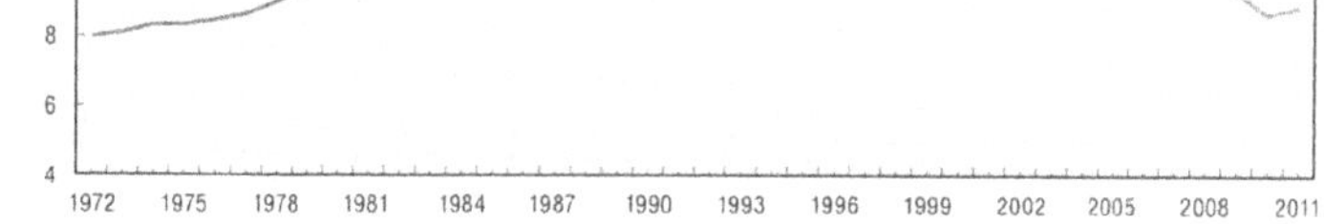

Note: Estimates are for private industries excluding real estate, health and education.

Source: Unpublished update on Corrado, C.A. and C.R. Hulten (2010), "How do you Measure a 'Technological Revolution?", *American Economic Review: Papers & Proceedings 100* (May 2010): 99–104.

FIGURE 3.2 Business investment in KBC and tangible capital, United States, 1972–2011 (% of adjusted GDP).

Source: OECD (2013:24)

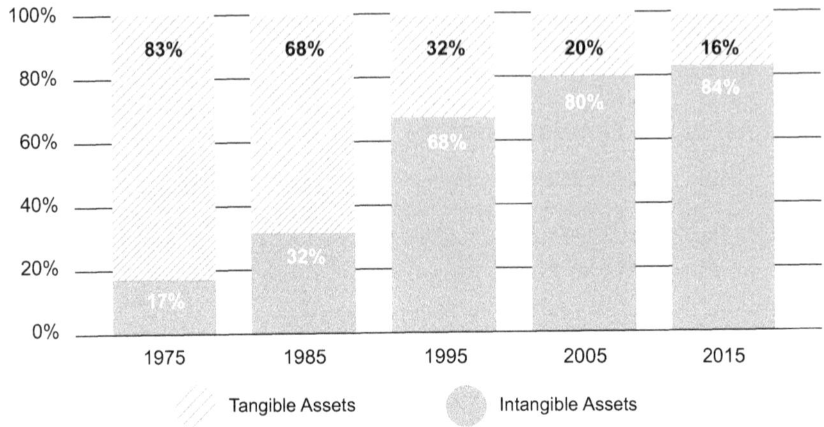

FIGURE 3.3 Components of market capitalization of the S&P 500 firms, 1975–2015.[92]

Source: Intangible Asset Market Value Study www.oceantomo.com/intangible-asset-market-value-study/

Another relevant statistic compares the ratio of the *market value* of (tangible) physical to (intangible) human capital in the years 1975–2005 for the 500 companies included in the American Standard & Poor Index.

The statistics of the company *Ocean Tomo* support the thesis that human capital has become the most important capital asset, at least in the United States. The intangible capital (intellectual assets) of the 500 S&P companies amounts to 80 percent of the total value of the companies in 2015. Twenty years earlier, this value was several times exceeded by the value of the companies' tangible assets. Korinek and Ng (2019:12) report, for the United States that investments in intangible assets have risen as a share of total assets for most industries since around 1990. More significant, however, is their finding that the growth of intangibles occurs and is *concentrated* in the top four firms by sales in each industrial sector.[93] However, the values in question are a function of the controversial definition of intellectual capital; in this case, the value of intangibles is the market value of the company (on the stock market) minus the value of physical capital.

The development, the widening of the gap between physical and human capital does not apply to the entire German economy. On the contrary, the volume of investment in both material and immaterial capital has been stagnant since 2009 in Germany. A general intensification of investment in knowledge-based capital in recent years is not observable. According to estimates by Heike Belitz and colleagues (2018:64–65), gross investments in knowledge-based capital in Germany in 2015 amounted to around 202 billion euros, whereas in tangible assets they amounted to 323 billion euros:

> Of the total investments in knowledge-based capital in 2015, the majority were in R&D (38.5 percent) and organizational capital (20.8 percent).

> These elements were followed by advertising and marketing (14.3 percent), software and databases (12.4 percent), and architectural and engineering design (9.5 percent). Smaller investments were made in copyrights, mineral exploration, and new financial products.

Available information indicates that investments in knowledge-based assets also increases in many emerging economies, for example, China's rate of investment in KBC is comparable to Germany and France; however, the ratio of investments of tangible vs intangible capital is significantly lower in China compared the United States or the United Kingdom. In China, "the ratio of investment in KBC to investment in tangible capital is around 0.3. By contrast, in Finland, France, the United Kingdom and the United States this ratio is near to, or above, 1" (OECD, 2013:25).

One statistic of particular interest to economists is the question of the distribution of income between the various production factors and the distribution of income and wealth among individuals. I will try to shed some light on these questions. Answers to these classical questions of economics also allow a look at social inequality in knowledge societies. In the middle of the last century, the answer advocated by many economists was that the success of capital as well as the relative share of production factors was relatively constant.

Labor and capital share of income

An important question for which that I cannot supply a detailed answer at this point is the relationship between investment in physical and human capital in its effect on the income of employees. Does the so-called "rising capital hypothesis" apply to the income of society as a whole? This question arises in particular in view of the empirical trend described by Thomas Piketty in his study *Capital in the Twenty-First Century* to reduce the share of labor in society's income. Piketty ([2013] 2014:223) asks, "has the apparently growing importance of human capital over the course of history been an illusion?" His answer is that the function of and income from human capital has not disappeared even in an economy that paradoxically relies more and more on human skills (cf. Piketty, ([2013] 2014:224). The increase in the need for human competence is accompanied by an increased need for investments in nonhuman capital (Piketty, [2013] 2014:234). In modern economies, the deep structure of capital relative to labor has not been lost.[94] In any case, the definition of what constitutes part of human capital is crucial.

Based on an analysis the national income and fixed assets data from the recent 1999 and 2013 data of the U.S Bureau of Economic Analysis (BEA), Koh et al. (2015:2; my emphasis) conclude that

> the prolonged secular decline of the LS [labor share] is driven by IPP [intellectual property products capital]. . . . Removing, in an accounting sense,

> the effects from IPP on aggregate capital accumulation, depreciation and the price of investment in a parsimonious investment model, we recover a LS that is trendless from 1947 to the present. That is, the shift in the speed at which aggregate capital accumulates and depreciates due to *the increasing importance of IPP capital* in the US economy fully accounts for the observed decline of the LS.[95]

Florian Hoffmann and his colleagues (Hoffmann et al., 2020:53) empirically confirm the observation about the declining share of labor income in its impact on social inequality, "capital income [especially after 2000] has magnified the growth in US earnings inequality over time as the capital to labor income ratio disproportionately increased among high-earnings individuals." However, confirming the simultaneity of the non-simultaneous as well, labor income remains the main driver of inequality during the last few decades. Hidden within these statistics and studies of social inequality is sustained decline in high income countries (Germany, United Kingdom, United States among other nations) of real income of employees with low educational qualifications during the last four decades.

What is classified as intellectual property products includes software, R&D, and artistic products. IPP products are therefore greatly knowledge-based and labor-intensive. In the United States, the share of IPP in aggregate investment has increased from 8 percent in 1947 to 26 percent in 2013 (cf. Koh et al., 2015). It is somewhat misleading to conclude, as these authors do, that the increase in IPP capital income over time accounts for the entire secular decline in the LS that has started in the late 1940s. After all, the intellectual property products are immediately and entirely a function of human capital; capital that may be linked to outside financing, for example, public money and, of course, legal restrictions to the access of knowledge.[96]

In the following section, I turn to one of the widely underexposed consequences of the knowledge society. The consequences in question are not directly related to knowledge advances and accumulated knowledge capital, but rather to an unequal accumulation of knowledge capital and the benefits that owners can realize from their *monopoly position* or from preventing other actors from using the same or related knowledge productively;[97] if the "monopoly power of firms increase, it will show up as an increase in the income of [the owner of] capital" (Stiglitz, 2015:24) or, more precisely, the income from "human" capital which, paradoxically perhaps, represents the realization of a political demand issued a long time ago, namely "a redistribution of the national product in a way that favors work" (Touraine, [2010] 2013:3). As Susan Lund and Laura Tyson (2018:137; emphasis added) stress, "because of the rise of digital flows is increasing competition in knowledge-intensive sectors, the importance of intellectual property is growing, generating *new forms of competition around patents*."

I suggest that this development amounts to *knowledge monopoly capitalism* or shorter, *knowledge capitalism*, a winner-take-all phenomenon (cf. Frank and Cook, 2010). Ugo Pagano's (2014) conception of the recent transformation of the global economy into an "*intellectual monopoly capitalism*" has a rather close affinity to the idea of knowledge capitalism:[98] The emergence and legitimacy of knowledge monopoly capitalism rests less on technological innovations. It is dependent on political and legal action by the state or multi-state action that allows for the emergence of monopolies.

> The main characteristic of intellectual monopoly capitalism is that monopoly is not simply based on the market power due to the concentration of skills in machines and management; it becomes also a *legal monopoly* over some items of knowledge, which extends well beyond national boundaries. In this respect, a model of capitalism based on the ownership of knowledge is fundamentally different from the one on which Marx and Braverman focused their analysis
>
> (Pagano, 2014:1413).

It is only in the mid-1990s that these intellectual monopolies become well defined and enforceable in the global economy, and "since then intellectual monopoly capitalism has become the dominant form of organisation of big business" (Pagano, 2014:1410). As Ugo Pagano's definition also signifies, I favor the term "*knowledge* capitalism"—rather than the broader "*intellectual* capitalism"[99] and its characteristic attribute as a non-rival and non-excludable phenomenon that becomes legally encoded through patents and assumes commodity form for which markets emerge. This implies of course that income from ideas can be highly stratified. The majority of all goods are rival and therefore do not require special protection.

As I noted at the outset, within knowledge capitalism a larger number of (superstar) firms emerge that have a constant returns production technology, fixed cost and an at least a partially automated production process. The marginal cost of an additional (almost unlimited) unit of production is practically zero. Knowledge monopoly capitalism is closely linked to, and strongly, embedded within the context of international trade and trade agreements (cf. Durand and Milberg, 2020). Knowledge monopoly capitalism generates societal inequality that is very difficult to undo; as a result, knowledge capitalism has major repercussions for societal engagement, ideological hardening, and political disenchantment in a society.

Knowledge capitalism favors the most productive firms of an industry. Favoring often mean that these "superstar firms" (Autor et al., 2020:648) control the relevant knowledge needed to produce their products. Given the legal encoding of knowledge, firms rise to superstar status and can exclude others from employing the innovation they have developed and protected. In other words, the rise of superstar companies is promoted and, subsequently, fortified by patent laws. As Herman Mark Schwartz (2019:511–512) points out, the

> legal infrastructure makes it possible for US firms to construct global commodity chains in which they operate the high profit, human capital-intensive parts of the production chain, while delegating physical capital-intensive production to mostly non-US rich country firms (which in turn absorb considerable capital into that immobile, asset specific and thus vulnerable physical base) and delegating labor intensive assembly steps to developing economies. . . . On the other hand, concentrating on transforming ideas into IPRs also creates some risk of the loss of actual manufacturing capacity and it also drives rising income inequality in the US domestic economy.

It is significant, however, that the superstar status of U.S corporations is measurably enhanced by a favorable balance of migration of inventors to the Unites States as the following Figure 3.4 (for the time span between 2000–2010) demonstrates.

The geopolitics of the knowledge-based economy extends, in other words, to the competition/recruitment among countries and corporations of highly skilled employees and not only the competition to achieve national, regional, or global

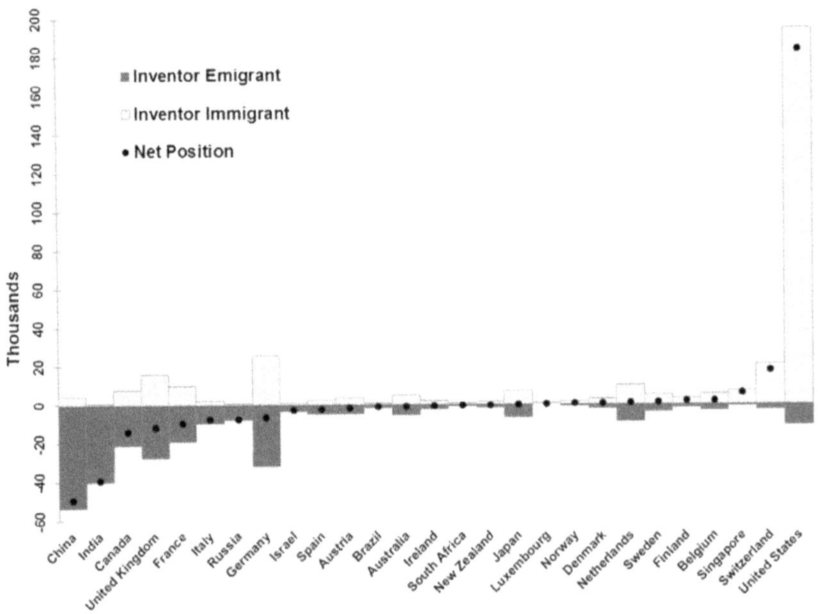

FIGURE 3.4

Source: Kerr et al. (2016)

domination among forms of knowledge controlled by states and firms (cf. Kerr, 2020).[100]

However, knowledge-based capitalism contains significant attributes of the territorial state, for example, efforts of state-based or regional-based legal systems such as the EU to control large multinational corporation such as Google. By the same token, not all but certain nations, for example, the United States, continue to exercise a significant measure of control over the external value of their currencies and thereby retain the centrality their monetary system has as a global power. Not insignificant in this context, for example, as a management strategy and a lever of power may also be the fact that patents do not convey the right or responsibility to actually exercise the invention the patents certify.

An additional management strategy is to link corporations not in the sense of a cartel but in the sense of jointly exploiting software standards, controlling a key part on the internet. A major case in point would be the cooperation between superstars Google and Apple. The agreement between the two companies extends to featuring Google's search engine as the *preselected* choice on Apple devices. According to an investigation by the *New York Times*,[101] Apple now receives an estimated $8 billion to $12 billion in annual payments (up from $1 billion a year in 2014) from Google. These so-called "licensing revenue" amount to 14 to 21 percent of Apple's annual profits. The US Justice Department is now—in the Fall of 2010—targeting the partnership between Apple and Google analyzing whether their conduct has anticompetitive effects.

The essential difference between *knowledge* capitalism and *monopoly capitalism* is the fact that the monopolistic position is *not* primarily due to the market power of a company[102] but to the *legally* secured cross-border control over knowledge; knowledge becomes a *commodity*. The economic significance of the legalization of knowledge in the form of patents and the concentration of patents, especially profitable patents in the hands of a few companies, is also illustrated by how selective patenting is. Most companies in the US have no patents and have never applied for a patent. This is a development that classical Marxist social theory did not anticipate or could not anticipate.[103] A prominent example would be the control of GM products and its accompanying fertilizers, seeds, and herbicides, however, controversial in its application, in the hands of a few biotech corporations such as Bayer, DuPont, and Syngenta.

The importance of legal control (legal encoding) of intellectual property is made even more evident given the general, massive growth in the share of knowledge in new products in recent years: an OECD (2013:25–26) study draws attention to the following connection:[104]

> Many products are themselves becoming more knowledge-intensive. For instance, in the automotive sector, it is estimated that 90% of the new features in cars have a significant software component (innovative start-stop systems, improved fuel injection, on-board cameras, safety systems, etc.).

> Valuable trade secrets now lie in the electronic controls that regulate the operation of motors, generators and batteries. Hybrid and electric vehicles require huge volumes of computer code: the Chevrolet Volt plug-in hybrid uses about 10 million lines of computer code. And a major part of the development costs for entirely new vehicles is also software-related (while manufacturers guard the exact figures closely, estimates of around 40% are not uncommon).

The OECD (2013:163) endorses as indispensable, based on these considerations, a strong intellectual property rights (IPR) legislation as an integral part of the development and use of knowledge-based capital.

Knowledge capitalism

> Monopolistic rights are the only sustainable competitive advantage. So, from the point of view of business, intellectual property rights are the ultimate key to success.
>
> —Employee of a Patent & License Exchange Firm[105]

Under the unwieldy keyword "knowledge monopoly capitalism" I would like to examine the question of the private (i.e., also that of companies') appropriation of the profit of knowledge and its consequences, for example on the labor market and social inequality but not so much on class formation, in more detail. The term *capitalism* is justified in this context because the *ownership* of property, in this instance, of course, the ownership of patented knowledge and, in relation, to those who own their labor power, remains an essential attribute of the social relations of knowledge societies.

Another feature typically attributed to the economic order of capitalism also persists under knowledge capitalism, namely the tendency to a *concentration* of market power. The great majority of patents granted are applied for and awarded compared to the past by (large) corporations.[106] Continuity rather than distinctiveness is the case, representing an enlargement of social Gestalt of capitalism. The reach of intellectual property law extends beyond IPRs in the narrow legal sense, that is, knowledge that constitutes output and is embedded in objects that can be patented, for which copyright can be obtained and that are trademarked.

One of the typical and massive consequences of the inequality regime of the knowledge society is the possibility that social inequality shifts in favor of corporate actors, especially the large multinational corporations and their managers and capital owners (superstars). The crucial question is, what role does the law play and what knowledge is being privatized and how sustainable are monopolies of this kind?

A central role in this context is played by the way in which the law allows additional knowledge (as well as definitions of what exactly is additional, patentable knowledge) to be protected and by which attributes additional knowledge is typically characterized? Undoubtedly, it is in the interest of a company to institutionalize the hurdles of patentability as low and as broad as possible: At the same time, the search for new knowledge extends to the pursuit of a monopoly (Drahos and Braithwaite, 2000:52).

The desire to use patents as weapons leads companies (such as Apple, Microsoft, and Google),[107] with the corresponding financial capital, to invest larger sums in the purchase of patents and in legal disputes to defend against patent infringements than in research and development. Intellectual state-based property rights policies, territorially limited until this day, that originated in the century between 1770 and 1870 in western and central Europe and spread to America[108] stand in a possibly sharp conflict with competition policies. The latter designed to enhance competition, the former by definition limiting competition (cf. OECD, 2013:162–171).

There are, however, other increasingly used legal possibilities of enclosure that do not so much concern the results (output), but rather what knowledge is used for (input)—such as "skills, experience, know-how, professional relationships, creativity and entrepreneurial energies" (Lobel, 2015:790)—further substantiating knowledge monopoly capitalism. The legally legitimized protection of knowledge by patents is increasingly supported by accompanying, again legally based, control measures over knowledge (for instance in the sense of human capital) of a company's employees in addition to the specific patentable innovation. The result of these changes is the extension of the legal coding of individual and collective knowledge: knowledge that cannot be contained by copyright, patents, or trademarks will be accessed by employers through so-called "nondisclosure agreements"—that can go back in time.

Patents, used as a sword

> Immediately and directly the patent right must be considered a detriment to the community at large, since its purport is to prevent the commumty from making use of the patented innovation, whatever may be its ulterior beneficial effects or its ethical justification.
>
> —Thorstein Veblen (1908:116)

A restrictive, strongly limiting protection, in the sense of low hurdles of patentability, of new knowledge through patents can have the result, provided that such patented knowledge is not evenly distributed globally (1) that monopoly-like conditions quickly develop in certain organizations and societies. In such a case, economic control lies in the hands of organizations that can afford to be innovative. (2) It is important to point out that the innovations that are typical today and then patented are not "revolutionary", stand-alone inventions, but cumulative technologies that are interdependent with existing technologies and their realization in production. The legal framework in question and the typical innovation process, can lead organizations and companies to specialize in those business areas in which they historically have initial advantages—in the form of existing patents. The owner of a patent can thus prevent competitors and interested parties from using this (complex) technology. Filippo Belloc and Ugo Pagano (2012:445) draw attention to the economic and social consequences of an internationally enforceable patent law:

> at the macro level . . . countries rich of IPRs [Intellectual Property Right] can prevent countries poor of IPRs from using their knowledge for production, with the possible consequence of generating a "snowball dynamics" according to which IP-rich countries exploit larger investment opportunities and acquire new (proprietary) knowledge, and IP-poor countries tend to stagnate in a low-investments/low-patents equilibrium.

Societies without control over sufficient intellectual property have no choice but to gain economic advantages over countries that have accumulated a more extensive knowledge capital through low wage levels. By the same token, countries and corporations with a dipropionate share, perhaps even a near monopoly of lucrative patents protected world-wide will capture a disproportionate share of the global profits and a disproportionate share of the national share of economic benefits.

Global profits in recent years are dominated by US firms with robust Intellectual Property Rights. The profits generated are disproportionally large compared to the share of the United States of the global economy; by the same token, the share of the German and Chinese firms is in relation small:

> US firms account for 33.9% of cumulative profits generated by the 3795 firms ever appearing on the Forbes Global 2000 list from 2006 to 2018 and firms in sectors characterized by robust IPRs account for a disproportionate 26.6% of those profits. This disproportionate share of global profits ensures that US firms—though not necessarily average US incomes or even less so worker incomes—have differential growth relative to foreign competitors.
>
> (Schwartz, 2019:507)

The increase in the *collective* wealth of a society can, under certain circumstances, result disproportionately from the increase in the *private* wealth of a society. In any case, such a development cannot be ruled out. Private prosperity that is both favored and protected by the evolution of the legal and tax systems in a society. This development can include the private acquisition of knowledge advances.[109]

Insofar as it is possible to document that income from capital (non-human factors) and income from labor (human factors) develop in opposite directions in favor of capital assets, this casts a skeptical light on the so-called Kuznets (1955:1) hypothesis, which is dedicated to the topic of the "character and causes of long-term changes in the personal distribution of income"—a prognosis that Simon Kuznets (1955:26–28) himself considered fragile, despite the extensive empirical data he mobilized for the first time. In short, the hypothesis formulated by Kuznets with explicit caution states that income inequality in capitalist societies will stabilize at an acceptable level, regardless of national characteristics. Sooner or later, in an optimistic view, the entire population will benefit from economic growth. At the beginning of industrialization, the concentration of incomes grows, only to decrease and level off as the economy develops. The course of inequality thus follows a kind of Bell curve. The development described earlier is the result, for example, of the shift of workers from the generally low-paying agricultural sector to the better paying industrial sector: "In a sense, Kuznets' theory can be viewed as a sophisticated formulation of the standard, trickle-down view of development: innovations first benefit a few individuals and eventually trickle down to the mass of the people" (Piketty, 2006:64).

Thomas Piketty (2006) criticizes Kuznets' explanation.[110] In contrast, Piketty observes a growing social inequality since the 1970s in economically developed countries. He is convinced that capitalism shows a natural, system-immanent trend toward growing inequality. More recently, the course of the profit rate has crossed the growth rate of the economy, only to become increasingly larger than the growth rate. This trend was typical until the First World War and is likely to be repeated in the coming decades and may even be enhanced (Piketty, [2013] 2014:358).

What does this mean for our question about the distribution of the profit that knowledge generates? Not very much. Unless we suspect that the increase in the profit rate of capital is due to a greater or lesser extent to the use of privatized additional knowledge, highly specialized skills and that the profits of the profit rate may be unequally distributed. At the same time, knowledge can also be embedded in the (statistical) growth rate. The crucial question I have already analyzed is, is there such a thing as a global world of knowledge (global common of knowledge)? I have answered this question in the negative.

Patents and knowledge capitalism[111]

> Patent systems in their present form represent deep concentrations of power and dominance in which networks of big businesses, patent attorneys and patent offices cooperate to produce an insider governance of the system.
>
> —Peter Drahos (2010:288)

Patent laws that regulate property rights to knowledge play a decisive role in the context of the transformation of knowledge societies into knowledge capitalism.[112]

This includes in particular the international legal regulations that have existed since the 1980s and the world-wide network of patent offices that "increasingly think in terms of business opportunities and less in terms of providing public goods" (Drahos, 2010:303).

Keeping in mind that the sheer number of patents supplies but limited information: A brief word on the volume of patents granted worldwide in recent decades and the number of recent "active" patents:[113] the number of patents granted in 2005 was about 700,000; in 2019, it has increased to 1,400,000. In 2019, 3,224,200 patents were applied for worldwide; almost half of them from China (43.4 percent).[114] Asia's patent offices received 65 percent of all patent applications. In 2019, 15 million patents were "active" worldwide; the largest number in the US (3.1 million), followed by China (2.7 million), Japan (2.1 million), and South Korea (1 million). More than half of the patents active in the US are from foreign patent holders; China's comparable number in 2019 was 72.1 percent of all active patents. American citizens/companies filed the majority of all patent applications outside their home country. Patents typically have a term of 20 years. Patent holders must pay a fee to keep a patent active. Only 18.6 percent of all patents according to the *World Intellectual Property Organization* were protected for the full 20-year term. Not surprisingly, given the rise in the general economic significance of knowledge and the massive increase in the number of active patents, the legal disputes over intellectual property rights have exploded in recent years: "No field of law is in greater ferment. And no field of law have judges and scholars more experienced difficulty recently in getting their bearings" (Posner, 2002:5).

A simple definition of a patent would be, as indicated already that it grants property rights to the inventor (for the time being in almost all countries, a human being) for a limited period of time (17 years in the USA, 20 years in Germany) and a certain geographical area, in analogy to the legal regulations that generally apply to property.[115] In many countries, the patent holder is under the obligation to pay patent taxes during the term of the patent. Subsequently, the knowledge of the patent becomes *apart* from the knowledge commons despite the fact that the knowledge of the patent draws, in many instances, to a significant degree on publicly financed knowledge. For example, the genealogy of the production of new discoveries in the pharmaceutical industry makes it clear time and again that large, multinational corporations are late in the development of new drugs (see Pfizer and the Corona vaccine). Large pharmaceutical corporations tend to concentrate their activities not on basic research but on the last phases in the development of the new medicines, that is, large scale testing (for example, the third phase and application process in order to gain market access). The rapid, much-praised market introduction of the Covid vaccine is based on decades of research on mRNA agents in publicly funded university research institutions.[116]

The owner of the invention acquires a legal title that prevents others from producing, using, or selling the invention, but at the same time grants him/her the right to sell his/her "immaterial" good for money. A patent—often acquired only after a lengthy administrative process involving highly specialized experts—gives its owner the right to make practical use of the invention described in the patent. The time it takes to acquire a patent, for example, in the domain of pharmaceuticals[117] implies that the delay before a new drug is launched may be lengthy. Therefore, the often-articulated demand in the case of the Covid vaccine that its knowledge/technology should be more widely shared in order to expedite the production of the vaccine in the short run and the development of similar pharmaceuticals in the long run. Even in a global health crisis, patent holders were not prepared to forgo the profits of the patents they owned.

A patent covers a new invention, not a discovery (genes cannot be patented; see Contreras, 2021). In return for the legal enclosure, the patent holder has to disclose the knowledge that is protected. Patents reduce competition.

Depending on the patented resource and in terms of economic impact, patents on knowledge capacities confer

(1) *market power*—markets without *exclusion* are not markets[118] (extracting [monopoly] rents; concentration, decline of competition, productivity growth constant or decline; concentration of research and development; significant coronally (concurrent) benefits; global imbalances);[119] patents can
(2) impede the ability to produce new knowledge by effectively blocking market access by protecting relevant, needed knowledge with patents, that is, by privatizing knowledge (see Drahos and Braithwaite, 2002).
(3) Market power influences the risk behavior and investment in research and development of these companies. In addition, patents can
(4) influence on the labor market up to the possibility of *monopsies*, i.e., only one buyer for certain special knowledge skills emerges (e.g., in biotechnology, computer science, artificial intelligence). The power over the labor market, in turn, has a number of economic and social consequences, which can range from determining the income of employees to consequences for the educational system. Patents can
(5) increase the degree of market concentration and a lack of competition for access to the market (across the world which makes international taxation and competition policy especially important, cf. Korinek and Stiglitz, 2021);[120] for example, under conditions of a health emergency such as the pandemic of 2020 and 2021, patent enforcement restricted the ability of poorer nations to gain timely access to vaccines produce vaccines locally.[121]
(6) Patent have an impact on the economic cycle: shrinking investment opportunities through the growing impact of knowledge privatization contributed to the 2008 financial crisis (see Pagano, 2014:1419–1420);
(7) Patents represent a *financial asset*;[122] patents increase the differentiation of individual earnings; *income* inequality between wage earners and those who own shares in corporations increases (see Korinek and Ng, 2019:3);

TABLE 3.2 Charges for the use of intellectual property receipts (BoP, current US $), 2019.*

	2000	*Δ*	*2010*	*Δ*	*2019*
World	80.746.000	+190%	234.207.000	+67%	390.537.402
Korea	701.500	+780%	3.188.000	+142%	7.742.000
Sweden	1.414.000	+311%	5.813.000	+42%	8.246.575
France	3.974.000	+243%	13.625.000	+17%	15.960.506
Germany	2.536.000	+885%	24.972.000	+45%	36.170.561
China	80	+1000%	830.483	+695%	6.604.705
UK	6.749.000	+270%	24.972.000	+1%	25.257.130
Japan	10.227.000	+161%	26.680.000	+76%	46.853.098
Netherlands	2.170.000	+1051%	24.972.000	+68%	41.842.127
Canada	2.324.000	+21%	2.814.000	+92%	5.396.142
USA	43.476.000	+118,5%	94.968.000	+24%	117.401.000
RoW	7.900.000	+444,5%	43.000.000	+84%	79.500.000

(ROW = Rest of the World; World minus total of charges of the listed, selected counties)

Source: World Bank *https://data.worldbank.org/indicator/BX.GSR.ROYL.CD.* Own calculations.

**Charges for the use of intellectual property are payments and receipts between residents and nonresidents for the authorized use of proprietary rights (such as patents, trademarks, copyrights, industrial processes and designs including trade secrets, and franchises) and for the use, through licensing agreements, of produced originals or prototypes (such as copyrights on books and manuscripts, computer software, cinematographic works, and sound recordings) and related rights (such as for live performances and television, cable, or satellite broadcast). Data are in current US dollars.*

(8) internationally sanctioned patents help co-determine *wealth* inequality of modern society through *unearned income*. The wealthy classes of society earn a substantial part of their income not as a result of their work, but as a function of their assets. The significance of these earnings has increased after the year 2000 (Piketty et al., 2018). Asset-based income which is more skewed than labor income and therefore magnifies economic inequality (cf. Hoffmann et al., 2020:56–60).[123]

In addition to the various consequences of the legalization of knowledge in the form of patent rights, there is the social mobilization function, which finds its expression in social movements of resistance against a monopolization of knowledge (for example open source and open access activities). The economic significance of intellectual property rights and its stratification by country can be cleaned from the following table which documents the highly uneven benefits different countries gain from the rights they command. The United States in 2019 is by far the largest beneficiary, while Russia hardly receives funds from abroad for the intellectual property the country controls.

At the same time, patents have the effect that the production of additional knowledge, research, and development, for example, can be *separated* from the application of newly gained knowledge in production or elsewhere. Knowledge is converted into private property by patents and is scarce in the legal sense. A meaningful argument can be made that internationally enforced patent law is one if the engines of contemporary economic globalization. Patents can accelerate but also delay the global diffusion of new drugs, for example. Extensive patent protection speeds up diffusion while price regulation policies for new drugs delays the marketing of new drugs. In short, patent rights have an important impact on the diffusion of innovations across the world. One large study shows that "all else equal, longer and more extensive patent protection strongly accelerated diffusion, while price regulation delayed it. Health policy institutions, and economic factors that make markets more profitable, also sped up diffusion" (Cockburn et al., 2014):

It is the patent owner who must ensure that his patent is not "abused". In principle, this is particularly difficult under the conditions of globalization. A sustainable legal enforcement of patent rights was not possible until the 1980s.[124] With the TRIPS (*Trade-Related Aspects of Intellectual Property Rights*) agreement, as a prime example of the extension of social action,[125] signed in Marrakesh, Morocco April 15, 1994—representing a solidification of a global economic order that had been in the making for decades—mandatory for all members of the WTO (World Trade Organization), patent law moved from an arcane law and legal analysis to the forefront of global *policy/politics* and should move as well into the center of the societal analysis of geopolitics, inequality, and globalization (cf. Sinnreich, 2019).

The adoption of TRIPS as a multilateral, enforceable, global intellectual property protection regime can justifiably be called "one of the most dramatic instances of international market regulation in the twentieth century" (Sell, 2010:762) that continues to be of growing significance beyond the last century. One if the highly contested issues of the TRIPS agreement is that it only requires countries to provide "minimum" standards of intellectual property protection.[126] This meant that signatories to the agreement were able to flexibly support enforcement. To enhance stricter protection of intellectual property rights, bilateral and regional preferential trade agreements increasingly included IP provisions. However, this matter continues to be an essentially contested issue last but not least because encircling knowledge is a contest about different value-commitments.

A decision perhaps almost comparable in importance to the TRIPS agreement for patent law was the 1988 legal opinion of the US Supreme Court to grant patents on life, the so-called "onco mouse" (see Shiva, 2001:1–3). The patentability criteria have generally been relaxed during the last 40 years. In the United States, the intellectual property rights regime opened up to software patents and business models, on the one hand, and living matter, on the other hand.

During the Uruguay Round (from 1986 to 1994 involving 123 contracting parties), well-organized groups of (multinational) corporations, who are the most likely to benefit from the treaty, in Europe and Japan as well as the United

States lobbied policy makers heavily in favor of ensuring that Intellectual Property Rights (IPR) would be part of the agreement.[127] The corporate lobby also succeeded in putting much of the oversight of the treaty in private hands. Corporations filed complaints which then taken up by official bodies (cf. Richards, 2004:13–16). More than 100 countries signed the treaty. Today, most countries in the world, no matter how tiny, have patent offices.[128] The drafting and enactment of the TRIPS treaty generally manifests the influence of the nation-state as a motor of globalization.

Developing countries signed TRIPS in return for the promise of liberalizing world trade. In spite of the broad assent to the TRIPS rules, the standards continue to remain controversial. Critics from peripheral states, for example, complain that the special economic and political interests of the developed world and its multinational corporations are protected rather than global health and economic prosperity.[129] Important to note is in addition that the TRIPS agreement extends the life of a patent over what many countries stipulated; the patent protection is granted for 20 years. As Maggi and Ossa (2020:5) note with the respect to the contemporaneous politics of TRIPS:

> A common concern is that stronger IPRs benefit developed countries at the expense of developing countries, and possibly at the expense of efficiency, by allowing firms from developed countries to charge higher prices and preventing firms from developing countries from catching up. Some observers even see TRIPS as a key reason for the current stalemate at the WTO.

The genealogy of TRIPS exemplifies the iron tenet that global rules tend to favor high-income countries and are often set in accordance with the special interests within large powerful countries. The developing countries are shut out from effectively participating in writing global rules (cf. Korinek and Stiglitz, 2021:31–32).

The end of the Soviet Empire politically promoted this development. In order to participate in world trade and be present in foreign markets, each member country must create a legal framework that corresponds to the patent law in the economically dominant countries of the world. In addition, the transnational association of the largest patent offices of the United States, Europe and Japan has created a global network of knowledge governance, which leads to a "clandestine" alignment of patent law (Drahos, 2010).[130] In 1996, the *World Intellectual Property Organization* (WIPO) of the UN was established as an "appendage" to the WTO. WIPO (www.wipo.int/portal/en/index.html) developed a copyright agreement based on TRIPS, which further tightened copyright regulations. It is hard to overestimate the importance of TRIPS rules; Vandana Shiva's (2001:3) broad classification of the consequences of global treaties is therefore accurate:

> The universalization of patents to cover all subject matter, including life forms, has resulted in patents invading our forest and farms, our kitchens,

> and our medical plan gardens. Patents are now granted not just for machines but for life forms and biodiversity; not just for new inventions but for the knowledge of our grandmothers.

The sheer number of patents provides only limited information: Nevertheless, a brief word on the volume of patents granted worldwide over the past decades and the number of recent "active" patents (patents in force):[131] the number of patents granted in 2005 was about 700,000; in 2009, it has increased to 1,400,000. In 2019, 3,224,200 patents were applied for worldwide; almost half of them from China. Asia's patent offices received 65 percent of all patent applications. In 2019, 15 million patents were "active" worldwide; the largest number in the US (3.1 million), followed by China (2.7 million), Japan (2.1 million), and South Korea (1 million). More than half of the patents active in the US are from foreigners; China's comparable number in 2019 was 72.1 percent of all active patents. American citizens/companies filed the majority of all patent applications outside their home country. Patents typically have a term of 20 years. Patent holders must pay a fee to keep a patent active. Only 18.6 percent of all patents were protected for the full 20-year term.

The relevant question for me arising from the consequences of the TRIPS Agreement as well as subsequent agreements is, what are the consequences of globally effective patent law or the enclosure of the knowledge commons (Boyle, 2003), i.e., the privatization of knowledge capital, the knowledge asymmetries for the distribution of the benefits from the rights to knowledge capital? One assumption would be that massive inequality in income/wealth as well as in other benefits, such as individual and collective access to knowledge, can result from the containment of intellectual property and the (exploitation) rents such a patent regime permit. The fencing in of additional knowledge results in an increase of wealth of those who have been assigned the control of the property rights. Beginning in the 1980s, a significant portion of the wealth of large corporations which tend to be the main beneficiaries of the new global patent system derives "not so much by their machines and building as by their intellectual monopolies. Patents, copyrights, and trademarks now constitute the bulk of the big corporations' assets" (Pagano, 2018).

Linked to the establishment of TRIPS is, in its wake, a significant enlargement of global value chains trade (GVC; for example, Gereffi, 2014; Durand and Milberg, 2020). Stricter International Property Rights enables not only more and more GVC trade but also that the rents from the expansion would largely go to the large firms; that is, the encasing tent in of additional knowledge leads to an increase in the wealth of those who have been given control over property rights. This also applies to the employees of companies that benefit disproportionately from knowledge monopolies:

> firms endowed with a greater amount of intellectual capital not only earn much greater returns on the capital that they invest but also, by investing

> more in the firm-specific skills of their workers, they pay higher wages. In turn, the possibility of making investments in human capital specific to private intellectual property is an important reason for the high return on invested capital.
>
> (Pagano, 2018:363)

A general theme that follows on from these observations concerns the transformation of the economic system itself given its widely acknowledged and growing dependence on knowledge and the legal encoding of large sways of additional knowledge, the motor of economic growth in knowledge societies, and of course knowledge capitalism.

One broad-based answer to my question about the societal attributes of knowledge capitalism is made more consequential by virtue of the fact that patent protection is not merely a technical, legal, or economic matter, but that patent rights have global, social, economic, and political effects, and in particular, to a significant extent, on social inequality and the balance of power between companies, regions and countries. This problem of inequality can be reinforced by a more comprehensive definition of what is in principle patentable, for example business practices, designs, or biotechnological products (living matters). A kind of multiplier function is provided by the fact that additional knowledge that is then patented by private companies was originally financed by the public sector: "Much of the research that really matters to the biotechnology industry and pharmaceutical industry goes on taxpayer expense in public universities" (Drahos and Braithwaite, 2002:15).

The protection of intellectual property in the sense of intellectual property law (copyright and related rights; Intellectual Property Rights, IPR) should, if this is indeed the case, create incentives for innovation (Stiglitz and Greenwald, 2014:429–456). The counterpart to copyright-protected intellectual property is the public domain, intellectual property as common property or, as I called it, it is part of the global commons of knowledge. However, there is the not unjustified suspicion or even fear that companies have an interest in promoting exactly the opposite (Stiglitz, 2002:245), namely the increased monopolization of knowledge advances. This suspicion is reinforced by the fact that additional knowledge is the most important resource for future inventions and profits in knowledge capitalism.

Belloc and Pagano (2012:473), for example, refer to so-called "patent pools" (collectively supported by several companies) and anticipatory patenting, which only large companies can afford to do in order to avoid being hindered in their business practices (specialization restrictions) by lawsuits from other companies. More recently have,

> 11 firms, including Sun Microsystems, Motorola, Hewlett-Packard, Verizon Communications, Cisco Systems, Google and Ericsson, . . . become

> members of AST (*Allied Security Trust*), a joint trust which is a patent holding company that helps protect members against patent infringement lawsuits.

Patent cartels take over the function of traditional cartels that are strongly opposed by law in many countries. In both cases, the protection of their own patents and the application of new, patented knowledge, small companies hardly have a chance.

In short, attention to patents should occupy a central role in the analysis of modern societies as knowledge societies turn into knowledge-based monopolies; and within as well as across knowledge societies, patents should play a crucial role in the analysis of the knowledge-based economy, social inequality, geopolitics, innovation, the motive structure of knowledge societies, and the politics of knowledge societies. One of the foremost moral and political dilemmas the knowledge capitalism faces are that patents as expressions of capacities to act may far too rigorously encode knowledge and, as a result, fail to consider the rights of societies and individuals who have a profound need of using the encoded knowledge; the context of a pandemic would furnish a prime example but so would be threat of environmental damage and withholding knowledge and technological inventions that may prove to be essential for adaptive measures. On the other side, the actual financial benefits that accrued to either the organization or the individuals for inventions that transformed our lives, for example, in the case of the inventions that led to computing, the green revolution, the television or antibiotics were small. The principal motives of the inventors were not, so it seems, financial in nature (Cf. Kay, 2003:258). Many of the most consequential discoveries were initiated, supported, and developed by government agencies and public funding. It follows that the question that is not new but appears to be on solid grounds: Is it time to fix patent law? But first, a brief reference to a blind spot and the reasons for the blind port in the usual narrative of the power of knowledge and thus the power of patents; this view can be located in a kind of magic triangle: Power, Knowledge, and Patents.

A blind spot: the limits of the power of patents

The blind spot in the analysis of the power of patents results, on the one hand, from the close theoretical interlocking of the phenomena of knowledge and power, symbolized by the classic metaphor "knowledge is power," and, on the other hand, is reinforced in this particular case by the legal enclosure of the knowledge embedded in patents.

The formula of the fusion of knowledge is power is ever present in everyday life, civil society and the scientific community and points, as a rule, to the following equation: Power is knowledge. Those who claim that success is linked to knowledge claim that power is knowledge and that success is linked to knowledge or that power is legitimized by knowledge. This is a thesis that is particularly closely associated with Michel Foucault's theory and empirical work in the social sciences (see Stehr and Adolf, 2018:324–334).

One of the most famous, significant and consequential analyses of the authority of (instrumental as well as one-dimensional) knowledge and technical expertise is, of course, Max Weber's [1922] 1964:339) theory of bureaucracy, or more generally, his theory of the intrinsically rationalizing instruments of modern political power, for

> bureaucratic administration means fundamentally the exercise of control on the basis of knowledge ("*Herrschaft kraft Wissen*"). This is the feature of it which makes it specifically rational. This consists on the one hand in technical knowledge which, by itself, is sufficient to ensure its position of extraordinary power. But in addition to this, bureaucratic organizations, or the holders of power who make use of them, have the tendency to increase their power still further out of experience in the service. For they acquire through the conduct of office a special knowledge of facts and have available a store of documentary material peculiar to themselves.

Bureaucracy constitutes a form of "domination based on knowledge". It is capable of attaining levels of efficiency, reliability, precision, or modes of rational control, however, only as the administrative apparatus of the state that no other form of authority is able to attain. However, the authority of the administrative apparatus derives, in the final analysis, from impersonal legal norms[132] and continuous procedurally correct work carried out by officials in offices with clearly circumscribed spheres of competence; and this authority is based on technical knowledge.

Thus, there is a *convergence or even symbiosis of legal norms, sanctions, and knowledge*; the effective application of general, standardized legal norms requires the use of general, abstract knowledge. Domination by legal norms routinizes and strengthens domination by technical knowledge. In its classical 19th-century vision, the primary object of knowledge within the state bureaucratic organization in particular "was the legal system, particularly those parts of it establishing the governmental and administrative apparatus, controlling its activities, and regulating its relations to private individuals. Law was seen as the speech itself of the state" (Poggi, 1982:356).

Weber knew, of course, that the effective agency of the state and the relative superiority of rational, bureaucratic knowledge is also somehow limited. But these limits play at best a secondary role in the analysis of rule by virtue of knowledge.

A parallel to the rule by virtue of knowledge, based on legal regulations, can be seen in the assumptions of the power of patents as described here. In this case, too, it is difficult to imagine that weak individuals and groups can mobilize resistance against the legally legitimized power of patents or can offer resistance against an almost unlimited transfer of power by corporations whose assets are based on the ownership of patents.

It is in this tradition, therefore, that it is not conceivable that social and cultural scientists today would follow advice formulated more than a century ago by the Protestant theologian and liberal politician Friedrich Naumann (1909:626–627):

> Perhaps it is not altogether incorrect to begin the discussion of political powers with a consideration of the power of apolitical people. . . . These people are governed, taxes are taken from them, if possible, they are punished if they ride on the footpath or if they do not have their children vaccinated, but that they are a political power occurs to them least of all themselves [my emphasis].

Naumann's observations point emphatically to what can only be described as the power of the weak; and power that by no means has to renounce knowledge. The power of the weak lies in the collective, despite their common lack of knowledge.

"Headwinds" against the power of patents, for example, come from very different directions: academia, politics, science, and civil society; resistance to monopolies interlocks, reinforces each other, and can even lead to monopolies breaking apart:

(1) The thesis of the desirable feedback between patent protection and private-sector innovation is questioned. The existing system of intellectual property protection was institutionalized when the innovation system was structured differently than it is today: interlocks, reinforces each other, and can even lead to the breakup of monopolies: "Innovation now occurs in collaborative networks, often linking the public and private sector," in contrast to an era in which "innovations were produced by corporate laboratories or individual inventors" (Block and Keller, 2012:98). Hinzu kommt eine wachsende Rolle des öffentlichen Sektors bei der Finanzierung kommerziell wertvoller Innovationen (vgl. Vallas et al., 2011). In addition, there is a growing role of the public sector in the financing of commercially valuable innovations (cf. Vallas et al., 2011).
(2) The monopoly privileges of superpower corporations are viewed more skeptically by policymakers in nation-states and internationally (for example, through the EU). Policy measures in tax legislation, a relaxation of patent law[133] or data protection[134] are among the demands that are being made more and more frequently and may ultimately lead to a limitation of the power and private profit margins of large corporations. In any case, awareness of the problem has reached the global political level. As a result, competition regulators in the United States and Europe are seeking national but also concerted action against the economic power of the large tech corporations. The Chinese government is also targeting its tech corporations in an effort to regain its lost power.
(3) Resistance from civil society against the asymmetric power of corporations owed to patent legislation is becoming more typical and generally results in "Moral Markets" (Stehr, 2008).

Has the time therefore come to repair patent legislation?

Time to fix patents?

> Long-range investing . . . especially under . . . the impact of new commodities and technologies. . . [make it] necessary to resort to such protecting devices as patents or temporary secrecy of process.
>
> —Joseph Schumpeter (1942:88)[135]

Joseph Schumpeter (1942:84–88) is one of the prominent modern economists who defends monopolies as essential to economic growth based on innovative activities. A strong patent system would be a helpful, especially in industrial sectors that are subject to "new things and methods".[136] Schumpeter's central premise in his defense of the legal containment of knowledge points to the motive, which at least in a capitalist economic order are entirely legitimate, of expecting and/or realizing a profit as a reward for investing financial resources in a particular future-oriented process (the reward theory).[137] Joseph Schumpeter (1942:88) emphasizes that while patents are not without alternatives as a means of protecting an investment, alternatives serve the same purpose and have the same economic consequences: "If a patent cannot be secured or would not, if secured, effectively protect, other means may have to be used in order to justify the investment." These alternatives of protecting an investment include, for example, a certain pricing policy for the innovative product that ensures that financial expectations are not disappointed. Self-critically, Schumpeter (1942:88) notes that his position may be difficult to understand. But the critic is simply unable to understand that "restrictions of this type . . . are unavoidable incidents, of a long-run process of expansion, which they protect rather than impede." In other words, both macroeconomic reasons and motives of the risk-taking entrepreneur as investor and hero of neo-liberalism speak strongly in favor of patenting knowledge: "intellectual property is understood self-referentially as both a driver of value creation as well as an indicator of innovation, the latter positively interpreted to be a determinant of economic growth and therefore assumed to be of value" (Kang, 2020:51). It is often observed that companies, in their own self-interest, and through intense lobbying, show solidarity with Schumpeter's observations, and that politicians follow suit by adopting appropriate rules to fence off the market.

Joseph Schumpeter's endorsement of patents as an essential element of a capitalist economic system echoes rather similar conclusions that can be traced at least to the 15th century. A Venetian statue from 1474 (cited in Brown and Rushing, 1990:1) for example asserts as does Schumpeter that the lack of a patent system equals the lack of motives to be inventive:

> We have among us men of great genius, apt to invent and discover ingenious devices. . . . Now, if such provision were made for the works and devices discovered by such persons, so that others who may see them could not build them and take the inventor's honor away, more men would then

> apply their genius, would discover, and would build devices of great utility to our commonwealth.

For decades, Joseph Schumpeter's advocacy of at least a temporary limit to the free play of the market met with the approval of prominent economists. William Nordhaus' (1969:19) influential model of innovation, for example, has as an essential component the temporary monopoly position of the discoverer of a new product or process: The discoverer "can either produce out or license the invention to other producers. After T years, his monopoly vanishes, and anyone can use the invention." On the other hand, the demystification of Schumpeter's position continues to this day (e.g., Diamond, 2015) and makes but slow progress.

As far as I can see, Schumpeter's advocacy of at least temporary monopolies is indiscriminate as to the phenomenon to be protected. In contrast to Schumpeter, Friedrich Hayek ([1947] 1958:113–114) in a lecture before the *Mont-Pèlerin Society* on "'Free' enterprise and competitive order", at about the same time, vehemently opposes patent protection for and thus a "mechanical" extension of the concept of property to intellectual "products". It is precisely the legal enclosure of intellectual property that hinders competition:

> The problem of the prevention of monopoly and the preservation of competition is raised much more acutely in certain other fields to which the concept of property has been extended only in recent times. I am thinking here of the extension of the concept of property to such rights and privileges as patents for inventions, copyright, trade-marks. . . . It seems to me beyond doubt that in these fields a slavish application of the concept of property as it has been developed for material things has done a great deal to foster the growth of monopoly and that here drastic reforms may be required if competition is to be made to work.

However, at the end of the century, under the strong influence of the Chicago Economics, the weight of the argument shifted again; now, economists rejected the idea that intellectual property rights (IPRs) produce monopoly powers. Attention shifted to *prices and markets*. Edmund Kitch (2000:1730), for example, makes the case that IPRs only create monopolies if the patent covers a good whose "economically distinctive features" fall within the claims of the patent. Often this is not the case; competitors are able to create works with the same functional characteristics, be it dictionaries, novels, television shows or competing software translation programs or a technology is available, and often at a lower price (Kitch, 2002:1734). Edmund Kitch adds, in most instances of trademarks, copyrights, and patents this is the case. On the basis of the patent, the patent holder may be able to monopolize but a slice of the market. The market may therefore well extend much beyond the expression of the patent.

During the course of the pandemic and the crucial role vaccination played as a means of combatting the spread of the virus, the debate about the merit of patenting saw its most recent iteration. Especially during the initial phases of vaccination and the widely felt shortage of vaccines, demands to suspend patents on Covid-19 vaccine were issued. In countering such demands, the Director of the Max-Planck Institute for Innovation and Competition, Reto Hilty,[138] defended the patent restriction repeating some of Joseph Schumpeter's argument:

> The mutating Covid 19 viruses in particular call for caution. For it will again primarily be those players who have developed the vaccines that are now available and who can also modify them. Whether they will go to such lengths again after the protective possibilities for their previous developments have been knocked out of their hands seems more than questionable.

Only the pharmaceutical companies that own the relevant patents of the vaccines can decide whether their intellectual property remains their exclusive property, whether they grant licenses, or whether they make their findings available without payment. Unless the basic legal rights are changed by government action. The *United Nations*, as well as the *International Science Council*, has been concerned that developing societies in the South have limited access to vaccines.[139] In the early phases of the vaccination effort, 'high income countries represent only 16% of the world population, . . . purchased more than half of all COVID-19 vaccine" (Yarney, 2021:529); of course, this can change and probably will change, after all, in is in the interest of all societies to assure a *globally* equitable vaccination process.

In contrast, the critique of the Schumpeterian position draws attention to what appears to be a widely recognized dilemma: there is little robust empirical evidence to prove that barriers or other strategies mobilized against competition lead to productivity growth. The criticism of these assumptions, which apply to the entirety of products and services traded on the market, further points out that the market-based protection of knowledge through patents leads to research and development focusing on products or processes that promise above-average profits by looking for inventions that are aimed at a wealthy clientele that can afford a high price.

But more fundamentally, as I have argued, patents divide. Patents control and direct the scarce human attention time. Patents impose knowledge limits.[140] Patents are expensive. Patents protection is spreading. Patent concentration is increasing.[141] Patents yield more than merely economic power, although it is evident that patents redistribute economic resources toward patent holders. In contrast to Schumpeter's favorable view, patents tend to lock in the advantages of corporate incumbents of patents. As is case for old-fashioned capitalism, knowledge monopoly capitalism is about power and profit.

There is no doubt that monopoly practices are incentives to innovate. However, the arguments for a fundamental revision, if not abolition, of patent law, if one follows the critics, are very strong (see also the next chapter on patent policies).[142] The arguments in favor of loosening patent enclosure make use of a number of considerations:

(1) even without patent rights, inventors benefit from their innovations (Boldrin and Levine, 2005);
(2) there is no evidence that patents promote innovation and thus productivity gains (Boldrin and Levine, 2013:4–7);
(3) there are strong incentives to temporary extend monopoly practices;
(4) deincentivizing knowledge-creation: future innovative behavior is stymied by active patents and their legal, defensive accompaniment; under using ideas (Quah, 2004);
(5) marginalizing research, for example, in the humanities and the social sciences that are not considered to have a market or at best a small exchange value;
(6) the purported dissemination of information or promotion of discourse through patents is minimal;
(7) intellectual property reservations cannot be absolute;
(8) the societal exploitation of ideas has fewer disadvantages compared to the societal exploitation of physical capital;
(9) not all discoveries need long-term protection;
(10) there are too many patents; and
(11) inventions (as cumulative developments) depend on preceding creative ideas, hence patents slow the construction of additional knowledge or prevent it altogether, that is, if such a calculation is possible at all.

In a report on the patent system written for the Subcommittee on Patents, Trademarks, and Copyrights of the Committee on the Judiciary, United States Senate, Fritz Machlup (1958:80) makes the following realistic recommendation to the members of the Senate Committee, which is probably still valid today:

> If one does not know whether a system "as a whole" (in contrast to certain features of it) is good or bad, the safest "policy conclusion" is to "muddle through"—either with it, if one has long lived with it, or without it, if one has lived without it. If we did not have a patent system, it would be irresponsible, on the basis of our present knowledge of its economic consequences, to recommend instituting one. But since we have had a patent system for a long time, it would be irresponsible, on the basis of our present knowledge, to recommend abolishing it.

The legal containment of the dissemination of knowledge through national and international legislation is the lever that enables the transformation of the knowledge society into knowledge capitalism. The warranted suspicion is that knowledge capitalism exerts a significant influence *on society as a whole*. However, in this context it is also useful to point out that there were also influential monopolistic companies in industrial society, such as John D. Rockefeller's Standard Oil Company or Friedrich Krupp's steel group. However, the corporations that exemplify knowledge capitalism cannot call on a solid political base, as the powerful corporations of the industrial age were able to do.

The suspicion that Big Tech in particular, in the guise of digital corporations, is causing a significant impact on the culture and social structure of modern society at the present time is voiced mainly by critics of big tech companies (see, for example, Foer, 2017; Taplin, 2017).

Given its importance and complexity, the analysis of the social culture and social structure of knowledge capitalism requires a separate study. Such an analysis is still missing. At this point, I can only briefly draw attention to selected societal changes triggered or, for that matter, not induced by knowledge capitalism.

The society of knowledge capitalism

I have noted a number of attributes of knowledge societies that should represent germane departures for a theoretical examination of the motive structure of knowledge societies. But first, I want summarize the ways in which modern individuals are characterized by social theorists of modern society: Social theory of liberal capitalism employs terms such as *liquidity*, *flexibility*, *immateriality*, *creativity*, *reflexivity* to describe the abilities and expectations of modern individuals. All designations I have listed point to the newfound dominance of *individual decision* and choices. The present social world is, as a result, and as Zygmunt Bauman (2000:7–8; emphasis added) sums it up, "an individualized, privatized version of modernity, with the burden of patterns weaving and the responsibility for failure falling primarily on the *individual's shoulders*". The modern world is a world of "fluid or liquid modernity". Do the same characterizations somehow apply to the main *social institutions* of modern society?

Zygmunt Bauman's characterization of the liquid world contrast sharply, perhaps most strongly, with the enlargement of social action of *small groups* such as the management of the world of superstar corporations that I have described as benefitting enormously from the legal encoding of knowledge and how these firms exploit and profit from the protection the law grants. The superstar firms draw up regulations in the style of the state and are tolerated in their conduct, for the time being, by the state. The superstar firms tend to mimic major social institutions, foremost of course, the state. Corporations, such as Amazon, "behave like government because they want to invest their decisions with that sense of procedural legitimacy. But they do it for the purpose of warding off government."[143]

The motives that prompt the management of the large tech corporations are, in the end, conventual motives enlarging and protecting the profitable enterprise. A reference to Max Weber's ([1904/1905] 1992:117) incomparable description of the power of the Puritan conception of life or frame of mind should be of assistance here. The Puritan outlook

> extended, under all circumstances—and this is, of course, much more important than the mere encouragement of capital accumulation—it favoured the development of a rational bourgeois economic life; it was the most important, and above all the only consistent influence in the development of that life. It stood at the cradle of the modern economic man.

Not every person of the Puritan age and its followers also managed not to be seduced by the temptations of wealth, i.e., to avoid the secularizing effect of possessions.

The economic order of the Puritan conception of life has taken on a life of its own. While the Puritan wanted to be a professional man, "we are forced to do so" (Weber, [1904/1905] 19:123). The Puritan way of life helped in this, not only a century ago, but to the present day, Weber predicted [1904/1905] 1992:123),

> For when asceticism was carried out of monastic cells into everyday life, and began to dominate worldly morality, it did its part in building the tremendous cosmos of the modern economic order. This order is now bound to the technical and economic conditions of machine production which to-day determine the lives of all the individuals who are born into this mechanism, not only those directly concerned with economic acquisition, with irresistible force. Perhaps it will so determine them *until the last ton of fossilized coal is burnt*" [emphasis added].

Rational capitalism is based on irrational motives; and this in view of the inner uncertainty and restlessness of man through a bond to a higher "calling" ("*Berufung*"). Contemporary capitalism, against the background of this extraordinary origin, is now, as it was in Max Weber's time, an "iron cage"; it no longer needs, since it rests on a mechanical-machine basis, the support of the spirit of a religious world view. And this is exactly the dilemma of the existing age. A pure utilitarianism is spreading (cf. Tenbruck, 1974).

Critics of the overall social consequences of knowledge monopoly capitalism are not sparing with references to the serious, negative influences of the digital power of the large tech companies. The critics often feel personally affected by the monopoly power of the digital corporations. They hold these companies responsible for a radical cultural change, namely for

> everything from growing incivility and political polarization to a declining faith in facts and truth, from the addictive manipulations of our attention to the secretive exploitation of our user data. If all that were not bad enough, some of these critics suggest, the growing monopolistic power of the largest tech companies threatens to limit the creativity, autonomy, and earnings

> of artists, writers, and intellectuals, thus diminishing the mind and soul of our larger culture.
>
> (Tenner, 2018:70)

The salient issue in the politics of knowledge societies, to which the following capital is devoted, concerns the increasing, broad societal mobilization of knowledge as an agency/ability, and thus the expansion of the choices available to members of society. It would be a mistake, however, to assume that the expansion of agency—the ability to make a difference—involves a transformation that follows a linear pattern, i.e., applies at all levels of action and to all actors.

Let's jump to the present, the age of the deselection of mechanical-machine production and the transition to a symbolic, knowledge-based economic order. Is there or can there be a new motivational structure, a kind of new enchantment of the world? Highly unlikely.

Countermodels

In the last decades, there have been numerous diagnoses that we are living in a great variety of advanced societies rather than an emerging, comprehensive knowledge society, let alone knowledge capitalism. In most instances, I will simply list the term that signifies the proposed foundation or the fundamental features of advanced society:

However, I will focus on explicating two of the theoretical counter-models of modern society: (1) the network society and (2) the creative society. The choice of the network society and the creative society is based on one attribute of these theories they share with the theory of the knowledge society, namely their common emphasis on the transformation of the economic system and the stress both theories place on creative minds, innovation, and, in the last analysis, knowledge. Manual Castell's theory of the network society and Richard Florida's theory of the creative class are also characterized by the fact that both theories are strongly influenced by the work of Daniel Bell and Peter Drucker. Theories that may be perceived as alternative theories, in this respect, the post-industrial and the information society have already been critically discussed in some detail.

The discussion of the counter theories of society allows, at the same time, to refer to some of the salient objections that have been raised in opposition to the idea of modern society as a knowledge society. I will begin with the list of alternative terms, devised to capture the uniqueness of modern society, in no particular order; however, I cannot claim to not have overlooked one or the other term.[144]

The creative society

In his *The Rise of the Creative Class*, published in 2002 (revisited in 2011; also 2014), Richard Florida describes its purpose as the empirical analysis of the emergence of a *new class*, the purveyors of creativity centered and clustered in cities whose class basis continues to be, as was the case for prior classes, an economic one. Florida (2014:197) relates that he was strongly influenced by Peter Drucker and Daniel Bell's work on the rise of the "post-industrial knowledge economy" but that his "own interest began to shift from knowledge, per se, to innovation and ultimately creativity. . . . Creativity is an underlying construct or skill that links what were thought of as separate and distinct fields of science and technology." Florida's description of the cognitive attributes of creativity resonates with one of my features of the knowledgeability that I describe (Stehr, 2016:106), namely the *ability to generate new and persuasive ideas or opinions*, for example, on the basis of the capacity to apply knowledge to knowledge that may find its place on the basis of unforced persuasion, for example, on the political agenda of the day. Creativity and innovation require an openness to ideas (cf. Haskel and Westlake, 2017:142). Creativity, as far as I can see, demands a social context free of most constraints. Therefore, writing still under the impression of the multiple fallout of the financial crisis of 2008/2009, Alain Touraine declares in 2012 that "creativity has ceased to count." Instead, we are surrounded by the "poisonous proximity of immense wealth, financial collapse and social crisis" (Touraine ([2012] 2014:16). The socio-political and economic circumstances Touraine describes in the wake of the financial crisis are not presumably conducive to creative action.

Since neither knowledge, as the capacity to act, nor information describe features of a person or a thing contain specific references to what to do, let alone the circumstances and commitments that would allow for them to be set it in motion, ideas have the unique ability to recommend and mobilize action by virtue of the diagnosis of a state of affairs contained in the statement of ideas. Ideas ("the basis of social inequality is unjust") contain kernels of a call for action. As is the case for all of the parts of the bundle of competencies I have enumerated, the benefits for the individual or a collectivity that come with opinions and ideas can of course have their direct or indirect downside; they do not only confer status and satisfaction and bring about social and political change.[145]

Among the major theorist who anticipates Florida's perspective is Alain Touraine (]1969] 1971:4–6; my emphasis), who indicates that the

> most widespread characteristic of the programmed society [post-industrial society] is that economic decisions and struggles no longer possess either the autonomy or the central importance they had in an earlier society which was defined by the effort to accumulate and anticipate profits from directly productive work. . . . Nowadays, it depends much more directly than ever before on *knowledge*, and hence on the capacity of society to call forth *creativity*.

A major attribute of "shared" creativity is that it is a resource that is not subject to a persistent decline. On the contrary, "unlike land, capital, and labor, creativity is not a stock of things that can be depleted but an unlimited resource that is constantly renewed and improved by education, on-the-job experience, and the stimulation that is provided by human interaction" (Florida, 2014:197). Florida thereby mixes or conflates the labor factor of production and, as he would like to conceptualizes the production function, creativity. Accounting for labor and creativity as separate phenomena becomes a major challenge (compare Florida, 2014:198–201). After all, creativity is embedded in capital goods and to some degree also in cultivated land.

The (intellectual) professions or occupations Florida lists as members of the creative class are scientists and engineers, architects, designer, writers, artists, and musicians working for example in education, law, business. However, missing from the catalogue of professions and jobs in the creative field are the million free lancers, artists, and musicians in the United States and other countries who have a difficult time, not only in the pandemic, carving out a living. The growing shift to digital has likely made the livelihood of creative individuals even more precarious. The internet has, in addition, make possible the persistent increase in "unpaid [creative] labor" involved, for example, in the creation, maintenance, and extension of social networks and the circulation of cultural content. The distribution of creative products and the social and economic power that comes with it is now more and more often controlled by large conglomerates. The missing link in Florida's class analysis is social inequality.

Daniel Bell's (1973:344) similarly had identified as the dominant figures of the post-industrial society not those who ruled industrial society, the entrepreneur, the businessman, and the industrial executive but the "new men" who are scientists, mathematicians, economists, and engineers of the rising intellectual technology. Eventually, Bell adds, new groups assume power in society and the entire complex of prestige and status will be rooted in the intellectual and scientific communities.

In the United States, Florida estimates that some 30 percent or more than 40 million members of the total work force are part of the creative class. The estimate by Florida is a useful reminder, how difficult it is to operate with a *static binary* of creative and non-creative professions, firms and industries. It would be preferable to work with a dynamic relationship between creativity and the ability to generate new ideas and processes that form the foundation for innovation and ultimately, in the case of the economic system, to bring novelty to the market. And since creativity is the foundation of economic growth in modern society, the new class has become the dominant class. Florida's account of the rise of the creative class represents one of the most widely adopted urban growth strategies in decades. This allows for the inference that his theory represents or is interpreted as powerful practical knowledge.

However, it is unavoidable to note at this point that the concept of the new social class is a convoluted one. It is both a sociological and linguistic muddle. In the theoretical understanding of post-industrial society, a new stratum of knowledge-intensive occupations is indeed expected to appear on the horizon. This idea, as diagnosed early on by Joseph Schumpeter and Friedrich Hayek, refers to an intellectual occupational stratum. Whether the term "class" applies to this stratum must be doubted. As Daniel Bell (1979:144) critically remarks, this term is an inappropriate mixture of two characteristics of a class: a class-by-itself and a class-for-itself. Class can be a path for organizing class-based interests and subsequent political action. Florida's creative class is neither one nor the other (see Stehr and Adolf, 2009).

Richard Florida (2002:318) refers to the shift of employment from manufacturing toward higher-value-added creative sectors. He neglects to indicate, as Daniel Bell had done in his exposition of employment patters in the shift toward post-industrial society that the value added by manufacturing to the societal returns remains strong or, even unaffected, in spite of the decline in employment. Many of the jobs in manufacturing are highly skilled jobs. The research and development carried out in manufacturing is, in many countries, higher than in the service sector. The create class as Florida indicates can often be found in the manufacturing sector.

Creativity

The fundamental but unseen and unrecognized economic driver is creativity: "Creativity is truly a limitless resource; it is something we all share. Scientists like to say that they "stand on the shoulders of giants. So do we all. . . . What sets us apart from all other species is our collective creativity, something that is innate in each of us and shared by every one of us" (Florida, 2011:xi). Although creativity is seen by Florida as a kind of anthropological constant, it is only now, for the first time that creativity becomes the central driver of the economy:

> creativity is pervasive and ongoing: it drives the incremental improvements in products and processes that keep them viable just as much as it does their original invention. Moreover, technological and economic creativity are nurtured by and interact with artistic and cultural creativity. This kind of interplay is evident in the rise of whole new industries, from computer graphics to digital music and animation. Creativity also requires a social and economic environment that can nurture its many forms.
>
> (Florida, 2011:6)

It is obvious therefore that creativity takes on many and varied forms highlighted in the optimistic claim "only when we unleash that great reservoir of overlooked and under-utilized human potential, will we truly enjoy not just sustained economic progress but a better, more meaningful, and more fulfilling way of life" (Florida, 2012:xiv). In the end, creativity becomes a most ambivalent concept. Moreover, the theory of the creative class creativity gives rise to in the New Age is impossible to falsify; creativity is manifest in wherever we look, in whoever works for a living and in whatever we consume. Thus, which one does not want to deny, "creativity in the world of work is not limited to members of the Creative Class. Factory workers and even the lowest-end service workers have always been creative in valuable ways" (Florida, 2011:10). It would appear to be very difficult if not impossible to create an asymmetric creative regime. Creativity seems to be freely available but does not show up on anybody's balance sheet and hence on accounts that are supposed to reflect the prosperity of a society.

Creative capital

Richard Florida (2002:319–320) stresses the importance of investing in "creative capital" versus physical capital. Both private and public funds available for investment should shift toward investments in creative capital. Create capital, as far as I can tell, involves investment in education and skill development but also in research and the arts. Such investments have the highest rate of return. In the final analysis, the creative capital theory, Florida advocates is about investments in people. A regional concentration of creative capital is beneficial. Florida's (2002:223) theory amounts to the claims that "regional economic growth is driven by the location choices of creative people—the holders of creative capital—who prefer places that are diverse, tolerant and open to new ideas."

But what is the difference between human and creative capital theory? Florida (2002:223) suggests that his theory of creative capital differs from human capital theory in two respects:

> 1. It identifies a type of human capital, creative people, as key to economic growth; and 2. It identifies the underlying factors that shape the locations decisions of these people, instead of merely saying that regions are blessed with certain endowments of them.

Florida's has little to say about the intellectual history and development of human capital theory but insists that there is a significant difference between the two approaches. Not surprisingly Florida's critics were quick to point out, there is no difference (e.g. Glaser, 2005).

In the revised edition of his monograph (2011:194), Florida concedes that his

> own theory shares much in common with human capital theory; I certainly agree that skilled and talented people are the keys to city and regional growth. . . . Where human capital theory uses education as a proxy for skills, I look at the kinds of work that people actually do.

In this respect, Florida may be seen as a proponent of the supply-aside theory of changes in the world of work. After all, the new class comes to the world of work with creative skills and preferences for certain environments.

The more recent and more sophisticated theories of human capital go much beyond the use of the education variable as a proxy for human capital; as a matter of fact, the reference increasingly is to knowledge capacities and their combination (see Stehr and Voss, 2021). The key, innovative idea Florida claims to advance does not so much involve human capital (endowment of skill and talent), but the reference to the flow of "human capital" that is induced through "the openness of a given place to human capital" (Florida, 2011:263). An assertion that is neither new nor controversial.

The network society

In a series of imaginative and empirically grounded studies, Manual Castells (1996; enlarged 2000) suggests that modern society from the 1980s onwards constitutes a *network society*[146] and that the unity in the diversity of global restructuring has to be seen in the massive deployment of information and communication technologies (ICT) in all spheres of modern social life. Information and communication technology (ICT) refers to both different types of communications networks and the technologies used in them. The ICT sector combines manufacturing and services industries whose products primarily fulfil or enable the function of information processing and communication by electronic means, including transmission and display. The ICT sector contributes to technological advance, output, and productivity growth. Its impact can be examined in several ways: directly, through its contribution to output, employment or productivity growth, or indirectly, as a source of technological change affecting other parts of the economy, for instance.

The innovations in the field of communication and information technologies therefore represent not unlike the 18th century industrial revolution a major historical event and a fundamental change in the material as the social structure and culture of society (Castells, 1996:30). Echoing what has been generally stated in its most uncompromising form by Marx, the transformation of the "material culture" of modern society on the basis of the information revolution since the decade of the 1980s amounts to a historically new formation of capitalism (cp. Castells and Henderson, 1987). But the reshaping of advanced capitalism Castells also emphasizes cannot be reduced to a manifestation of mere capitalist interests. In his network theory, Manuel Castells (1996:17) explicitly takes on board Daniel Bell's concept of theoretical knowledge as his own definition of the relevant type of knowledge of network societies.

In this brief description and critique of the theory of the network society or informational capitalism,[147] I like to address two basic and related fundamental questions posed by Castell's theory: First, there is what can only be described as the puzzling issue of "*technological determinism*" as well as the associated question of how the notion of a network society differs from designating modern society an information society; after all, both terms rely to a crucial extent the convergence between information and communication technologies and on references to efforts to decipher the social and economic impact of more efficient "information processing" on social conduct. Second, there is what economists have called the puzzle of the *productivity paradox*. Castells (1996:17) makes it the very premise of his observations that the source of productivity in the new form of capitalism "lies in the *technology* of knowledge generation, information processing, and symbol communication" (emphasis added).

In social science discourse, the first issue I have identified is, depending on one's perspective, hardly a novel theoretical dilemma or promise; however, the second question represents a unique challenge because as the economist Robert Solow (1987) expressed it: "You can see the computer age everywhere but in the productivity statistics." The challenge at this time is the inability of economists, marshalling conventional indicators of economic success to trace any significant financial payoff from the massive corporate and state investments in information and communication technologies, at a time when the acquisition price of IT equipment fell rapidly (from 1990 to 1996 the price of IT equipment for *investment* fell 16.9 percent in the United States; cf. Jorgenson and Stiroh, 1999:110).

Although Manuel Castells in his own study continually stresses the enormous efficacy and impact of the new technological means as the major productivity inducing factors in modern nations, he fails to refer to as far as I can tell to the productivity paradox[148] and the extensive literature that has grown up around this topic.[149] The reference to the productivity paradox does not mean that investments in information technologies have been ineffectual. Increased productivity is indeed of major importance not only for the competitive advantages of firms and countries but also for wages and salaries paid, the ability of the state to maintain entitlement regimes and standards of living.

The theory of the network society belongs to more general observation about the motor of social change in modern societies, namely a new age that is driven by its distinctive technological apparatus. Various accounts are seen as responsible for the dawn of the "information age"; for example, as part of a self-description of the multinational corporation, IBM advertising in 1977 stressed that the new age to which they have made significant contributions in the form of machines from computers to copiers best represents the new "information Age". Competing accounts attribute the notion of the information age to the Marshal McLuhan.

The information age

> We define our time by technology. Until recently have taken material power as the singular measure of the advance of civilization.
>
> —Daniel Bell ([1975] 1991:4)

According to Manuel Castells, the new society or network society in which the state continues to occupy a decisive function, similarly originates as the result of a new technological paradigm and therefore a dynamic process that is propelled by information processing or informationalism: "the information technology revolution was instrumental in allowing the implementation of a fundamental process of restructuring of the capitalist system from 1980s onward" (Castells, [1996] 2000:13). In this respect, Manuel Castells' theory of modern society is a classical theory of society as described by Daniel Bell. Given Castells' description of the network society with its essential dependence on the operation of communication technologies, the question that arises is in what way if at all does his term of the network society differ from that of the more frequently used concept of modern society as an information society?

The difference to which Castells himself points and which in his self-assessment constitutes a progressive conceptual step in our analytical understanding of modern society as well as the theoretical model of the information society, can be explicated in analogy to the distinction between "industry" and "industrial". At first glance, such a differentiation would not appear to yield much in the way of differences. Information (society) and informational (society) results, Castells (1996:21) suggest, are distinct ways of viewing and knowing. The concept of information or, as he also calls it, the "communication of knowledge" implies nothing more or less than the assertion that information is of importance in all possible social formations or represents an anthropological constant found in all human societies. In contrast to information, "the term informational indicates the attribute of a specific form of social organization in which information generation, processing, and transmission become the fundamental sources of productivity and power, because new technological conditions emerging in this historical period". In other terms, information becomes an immediately productive force.

The close alliance of Castells' theory of society to the development of information and communication technologies as well as his conscious conflation of knowledge and information[150] makes it rather difficult to detect any decisive and robust differences between the notion of an information and a network society.[151] After all, for most observers, the information revolution is understood as a *technical* one, in the first instance. The gadgets change but not the socio-cognitive frames, immediately productive knowledge, the language of entitlements and scientific regimes.

Although Castells is not a strict, open proponent of technological determinism, it is almost unavoidable that one discovers a number of theses in his study that tend to resonate directly with the paradigm of technological determinism stressing, as it does, context-insensitive consequences of technical products rather than the social processes of innovation, deployment, and use. Technology along with knowledge (information) is often treated as a black box; that is, as stable and robust entities or processes whose embeddedness into the circumstances of their production and use are hidden. It is self-evident that technology plays a crucial role in the modern life world and in the course of economic "progress". However, technology needs to be examined not from "disembodied" perspective but from one that is cognizant of the social conditions within which it emerges and is employed.[152] A narrow or central focus on the use of ICTs severely restricts our relational understanding of technology, context, and agency (cf. Liu, 2010). And as Alain Touraine ([1984] 1988:104) has therefore argued persuasively, the specificity of a particular society should not hinge on a given technology:

> It is just as superficial to speak of a computer society or of a plutonium society as it is of steam-engine society or an electric motor society. Nothing justifies the granting of such a privilege to a particular technology, whatever its economic importance.

Castells' skeptical presentation of the politics of the network society emphasizes the form of *symbolic politics* with its concentration on individual policy fields such as environmental issues or human rights, as well as a growing "tension between political participation, social demands, and the responsiveness of democratic institutions" (Castells, [1997] 2004:413). The legitimacy of the democratic system is fading. The democratic regime is not able to find convincing answers to the questions of the day, answers that are also credible among the public. The state's ability to carry out its will is diminishing. Although democracy is not fundamentally challenged, at best by politically extreme minorities, approval of the democratic model is eroding. As matter of fact, according to Castells, political democracy has become an empty shell. In other words, democracy is apparently a political system unsuitable for the network society.

The productivity paradox

Manuel Castells (1996:80) reiterates throughout his study that "productivity is the source of the wealth of nations." Global competition represents the linkage path that connects information technology, organizational change, and productivity growth. However, in the last two decades of the last century, as some accounts have it between 1974–1994 and 1995–2004, economists have been puzzled about the apparent lack of measurable productivity gains in industry and services in OECD countries in response to or conjunction with the immense investments in recent years in information and communication technologies. Between 1947–1973, labor productivity in the USA grew by 2.7 percent annually. In the period 1974–1994, however, labor productivity fell by 1.5 percent annually. Between 2005–2015, labor productivity increased again by 1.3 percent annually. The slowdown in productivity growth is not peculiar to the US economy. The slowdown is also observable in other developed national economies. In any case, these figures were cause to ask, was this perhaps even the end of the centuries-long productivity revolution? (Drucker, 1993:29–36)? The slowdown "is statistically and economically significant" and does not appear to represent a cyclical economic process (Syverson, 2017:165).

The choice of the label of the animated and to this day inconclusive discussion of the massive dipping of labor productivity fell on the concept of a *productivity paradox*. The choice of the concept of a productivity paradox results from the disjuncture between the immense economic expectations and promises that have been engendered by the "computer age", on the one hand, and the apparent lack of economic payoffs resulting from the enormous investments by corporation and the state in information and communication technologies, on the other hand.

The productivity paradox is of interest for several reasons. In the context of the analysis of knowledge capitalism, the paradox again draws attention to the fragility and the difficulty at the same time of statistically capturing intangible capital and recognizing it according to its importance. A much more comprehensive accounting of growth factors would be valuable. Nicolas Crouzet and Janice Eberly (2021:1; my emphasis) flesh out this deficit in the discussion of the productivity paradox by pointing out that

> how the presence of *intangible capital and market power*, which have also grown over this time period [in the period following the financial crisis], leads to *underestimates of productivity growth*. The effect of either alone is relatively small, but together . . . their effect is magnified. Empirically reasonable values of markups and unmeasured capital can account for about half of the measured productivity slowdown in the 2000s.

Manuel Castells (1996:78) also took the view that the measurement methods that are utilized to represent the output of the economy are subject to measurement error and that these errors conceal the productivity growth that is "really" taking place (cp. Diewert and Fox, 1997):

> It may well be that a significant proportion of the mysterious productivity slowdown results from a growing inadequacy of economic statistics to capture movements of the new informational economy, *precisely because of the broad scope of its transformations under the impact of information technology and related organizational changes*. . . . So maybe after all, productivity is not really vanishing but is increasing through partly hidden avenues, in expanding circles.

Castell's explanation of the productivity paradox as the result of measurement deficits lacks precision, however: Exactly which movements of the information economy are responsible for the lack of measurement of "actual" labor productivity? This cannot be deduced from Castell's observations, as far as I can see.

David Attewell (1994:24), however, sums up previous research by economist on the productivity paradox by *affirming* the validity of its existence and comments generally "no study documents substantial IT effects on productivity." What remains open or contested are explanations for the existence of the paradox. Another observation would simply assert—with Manuel Castells—that the increase in productivity is hidden or invisible because it has not been adequately detected and measured (also Jorgension und Stiroh, 1999:114).

A robust, measurable increase in productivity did not occur in response to the significant investment in computer technology, one could for example maintain because the personal computer *did not* enhance the division of labor (cf. Newport, 2021). Following one of the elementary laws of economic reasoning, at least since Adam Smith, calls for productivity gains to occur in accordance with an increase in the division of labor; but as Smith (1776:21) stresses, "men are much more likely to discover easier and readier methods of attaining any object, when the whole attention of their minds is directed toward a single object, than when it is dissipated among a great variety of things" (also Drucker, 1999). Our own experience with personal computers would perhaps easily support the idea that the computer has not assisted us in focusing or reducing our attention on just a single or a few tasks.[153]

If the lack of productivity as a result of heavy investments by corporations in information- and communication technologies in the decades of the 1980s and 1990s is real, what mechanisms possibly account for the productivity paradox? My answer is that the productivity paradox can help us to understand that we are not faced with a technology-driven transition from industrial to informational society or something of that kind, but rather with a societally driven transition from an industrial to a knowledge society.

One answer to the search for the reason of the paradox focuses on the "mismeasurement" of the *output*; for example, gains have not been reflected because of low or even zero prices of many new goods (Google searches, Facebook; cf. Syverson, 2017:183). The alternative approach concentrates on a mismeasurement of *inputs* into services and commodities, for example, population growth, enlarged educational attainment, increased labor force participation due to the entry of women, and rising research intensity; all of which may stagnate or even decline in the future (cf. Jones, 2021).

Technology, labor, and the knowledge capitalism

As Kenneth Arrow (1974:47) observes with respect to the conditions for the possibility of innovation, "innovation by firms is in many cases simply a question of putting an item on its agenda before other firms do it." What counts and what increasingly drives the transformation of the modern economy is the quality of the *supply* of labor or the extent to which not merely technological change but the transformation of work and the structure of the labor force is skill-based. Charles Jones (2021: 12) calculates for the United States, without specifying the contribution of the individual factors, that "*the ultimate source of long-run economic growth is population growth, historical growth accounting suggests that population growth accounts for only around 20% of U.S. growth in recent decades.* The remaining 80% is accounted for by rising educational attainment, increases in the fraction of the population devoted to R&D, and declines in misallocation." My emphasis is on the increase in the skills (knowledge assets) of the labor force.[154,155]

Investments in communication and information technologies in the decades of the Eighties and Nineties has been accompanied, perhaps even precipitated by a noticeable substitution of skilled labor. The additional assumption is (1) of the difficult appropriability of knowledge capital, and (2) of the easier appropriability of physical assets. Technological determinism basically fails to acknowledge the agency in the discovery, deployment, and use of technology. The use of material investment in information and communication technologies are "never absolutely proper or intrinsic to their bearers, as they are the result of appropriations or attributions" (Cooren, 2018:281). Empirical work supports such a contention:

Using a cross-sectional empirical study at the level of individual manufacturing firms and using individual rather than aggregate data for the American economy, Doms et al. (1997) for example have examined the relationship between technology use, the education, occupation and wages of the employees in the manufacturing sector. On the basis of the data collected the authors of the study conclude that there is a growing covariance between the degree of technology use in firms, that is to say, the progress made in automating both the development and the production process, and the educational level of the employees. The conclusion therefore is not only is that "skilled workers and advanced manufacturing technologies are complements" but also that the proportion of employees "in skilled occupations rises significantly with the number of technologies employed" (Doms et al., 1997:261, 263; also Berman et al., 1994) *and, as* the volume of technology use increases, the proportion of employees not directly active in the production process increases as well. More concretely, "the positive relationship between technology use and the percent of skilled workers is primarily due to a dramatic increase in the percent of scientists and engineers in the most technologically advanced plants" (Doms et al., 1997:263). A variety of controls confirm these findings. In addition, the authors report that employees in firms with extensive technology deployment earn higher wages and salaries.

It is entirely possible that the "causal" relation runs in the oppositive direction than often assumed, especially among employers: that is, highly skilled or educated employees produce the "scientification" and technological modernization of their workplaces and therefore of the world of work. It is the growing supply of highly qualified workers, as Peter Drucker surmises, and in what I chose to call the Drucker paradox, rather than the growing complexity or the pre-existing skill requirements of the world of work that constitutes the motor and the motivating force behind the transformation of work.

Both the idea of network society and information society rests on premises that resonate strongly with technological determinism. Moreover, both perspectives are insufficient because they do not deal adequately with the productivity paradox. The productivity paradox can be better understood if one recognizes three empirical facts—in addition to the difficulties of adequately taken the role of immaterial capital into account: First, highly skilled labor appears on the scene before information technology. Second, the increasing importance of highly skilled labor is not a reaction to demand for such labor, but rather there is an autonomous (i.e., societally driven) supply shift. And third, information technology actually helps entrepreneurs and managers to catch up with and reverse the rising labor costs implied by this supply shift. Therefore, the productivity paradox can help us to understand that we are not faced with a technology driven transition from industrial to informational society or something of that kind, but rather with a societally driven transition from an industrial to a knowledge society.

In the following section, I will explore the question of the extent to which the world stage is a corrective or an accelerator of knowledge capitalism. A corrective to a strengthening of knowledge capitalism might be, for example, regulatory efforts by national governments or multinational political institutions that check asymmetric profit rate of large companies or monitoring efforts that reign into the ability of superstar corporations to defend their competitive advantages.[156] Whether the power of the markets or state intervention, for example, with the help of a global minimum tax, is still sufficient today to heal massive inequalities becomes a central and open question.

Geopolitics, inequality, and patents

The geopolitics of industrial and post-industrial societies with their plurality of nation-states has, according to the majority of analyses of the modern world, been replaced by geopolitics of the shrinking world that had its origins in the 1970s due to historically unique changes in military, communication, and transport technology. The concept of *globalization* which outpaced the term of modernization plays a central role in these reflections. The emphasis of the developments in question is on the disappearance of boundaries; apparently easily transcending old hurdles of time and space of the old world. Whereby it remains an open question whether the globalization process has already reached its peak, whether it proceeds more or less unhindered or whether it is reversible (see Ericson and Stehr, 2000; Stehr, 2009)?

The globalization process is an outstanding example of what I have described the expansion and extension of social action as the epitome of modernization. In this sense, Ulrich Beck ([2002] 2005:52) underlines the globalization as "a creeping, post-revolutionary, epochal transformation of the national and international state-dominated system governing the balance of power and the rule of power". But it is not clear exactly what is operating as the engine of this trend: is it the economy, politics, law, culture, science, civil society, or all of these institutions?

However, it is not clear that globalization is necessarily characterized by a trend in only one direction: the loss of the diversity of social relations and the dissolution of the boundaries of social action. As many observers critically state, for example, the globalization process is associated with the inexorably growing worldwide influence of American culture, through its films, popular music, television, software, tastes, and so on. The worldwide expansion of the influence of these cultural standards is at the same time, as the critics point out, a decisive shortening of diversity. However, the expansion of social action, co-determined by globalization, can also be interpreted as a conscious reaction precisely to this development, that is, to the strengthening and expansion of diverse local traditions, for example, the everyday viability and presence of dialects.

Until recently, the praise or the fear of the consequences of an apparently unstoppable process of economic globalization formed much of the center of the globalization perspective or, even more generally, a transition to a mature form of modernization. Both critics and proponents of globalization, although fundamentally at odds in their judgments, both among themselves and across the divide of their verdicts about the nature and the consequences of globalization, deploy similar metaphors and are in the main convinced, as is Ulrich Beck that significant consequences of globalization already are irreversible and inevitable, constituting a profound transformation, even revolution not only of ordinary life around the world.

The peculiar consensus about the effects of globalization is then seen as either profoundly harmful or as of great utility to humanity. It is worth citing Anthony Giddens ([1999] 2002:4), who shares in the general judgment about the consequences of the globalization process and writes under the title of the "Runaway World" at the dawn to the 21th century that

> globalisation is restructuring the ways in which we live, in a very profound manner. It is led from the west, bears the strong Imprint of American political and economic power, and is highly uneven in its consequences. But globalisation is not just the dominance of the West over the rest; it affects the United States as it does other countries.

One of the at one time welcome but in the meantime doubtful consequences of globalization, as Giddens ([1999] 2002:5) summarized it, is that democracy is [currently] spreading worldwide.

However, history[157] provides much evidence that such widely celebrated sweeping and undifferentiated judgments are either self-destructing prophecies, quickly surpassed by events or just plain wrong. Increased trade and growing foreign direct investment and technological developments were seen as the motor of ever-closer ties among nations, mostly it was hoped for to the benefit of all concerned. As a side effect, democratic governance was expected to be exported around the world. In the case of inequality, the expectation was the growing integration of the world economy would also lead to a decrease in the unequal distribution of incomes across nations. The strict adherence to the TRIPS agreement in all countries, including in the poorest regions of the world, was expected, in addition, to stimulate the creation of additional knowledge and its dissemination. The protection of intellectual property rights more generally would lead to the global dominance of the symbolic economy, knowledge, and human capital as the driving force of economic welfare, now only present in the richer parts of the world.

What the upbeat or fearful examination of globalization did not take into account were the impact of the TRIPS agreement or the emergence of knowledge monopoly capitalism on geopolitics, the pattern of globalization and inequality. As a result, the reported returns from employing intellectual property rights, especially, in the case of large firms, superstar corporations, is extraordinary.[158]

> The insight that "free trade is good" is no longer sufficient as a guide to evaluating the efficiency of international agreements. In a world of shallow agreements that focuses on tariff cooperation, a good rule of thumb is that if an agreement leads to lower tariffs, it has done a good job. But in a world where governments strive to cooperate on *regulatory policies*, for example, the ultimate objective of an international agreement is more complex, since regulations are typically imposed for more than just protectionist motives.
>
> (Maggi and Ossa, 2020:3; emphasis added)

The critics of economic globalization foresaw exactly the opposite development; the gains from the now dominant force of production, knowledge, were situated in the richer regions of the world and only enhanced the divergence in economic development.

I have already noted and discussed what has been called Piketty's law of capitalism, namely that the modern capitalist economic order generates persistent, even accelerating inequality. More specifically, Thomas Piketty (2006) observes a growing social inequality since the 1970s in economically developed countries. He is convinced that capitalism shows a natural, system-immanent trend toward growing inequality. More recently, the course of the profit rate has crossed the growth rate of the economy, only to become increasingly larger than the growth rate. This trend was typical until the First World War and is likely to be repeated in the coming decades and may even be enhanced (Piketty, [2013] 2014:358).

The interesting question becomes and one that Piketty with his emphasis on the results markets produce has not investigated, what is the role of internationally valid law in these inequality developments and hence to want extent knowledge monopolies legitimated by patent law pay a role in the formation of new geopolitics regimes?

The salient problematic of the politics of knowledge societies as knowledge capitalism, to which the following chapter is devoted, concerns the increasing, broad societal mobilization of knowledge as an agency/capability and thus the expansion of the choices of society's members, though it would be a mistake to assume that the expansion of agency—the ability to make a difference—involves a transformation that follows a linear pattern, i.e., applies at all levels of action and to all actors.

In the following chapter, I will examine a number of remarkable features of the dynamics of knowledge societies as they have evolved into the *Gestalt* of knowledge capitalism, in particular some of the central *policy fields* of knowledge societies: knowledge politics, patent policies, technological unemployment,t and climate change. In each of the four policy fields, I enumerate specific policy challenges.

The policy problems knowledge societies face now often include *"wicked" problems*, that is, problems that cannot really be "solved". From a theoretical perspective, I will ask how a couple of the salient features of the knowledge society, the fragility of knowledge societies and the fact that the agency of individuals and small groups of individuals, for example, the management of superstar corporations, small investors, political activists, or the leadership of new social movements, has expanded their influence and affect the typical political processes of knowledge societies.

My thesis of the broad societal mobilization of knowledge as an opportunity/ability to act, the power of the weak and thus the expansion of choice for members of society, must not be misunderstood; it would be a mistake to assume that the expansion of agency—the ability to make a difference—involves a societal transformation that follows a linear pattern, i.e., applies at all levels of action and to all actors.

First, however, the following chapter is concerned with outlining the circumstances of action in which the politics of knowledge capitalism take place.

Notes

1. It should be noted that the central and consistent reference throughout the chapter is indeed on the production side of economic relations rather than the consumption side; however, this does not signal a kind of silent acceptance of the Say's theorem that a given value of supply must create an equivalent value of demand and that consumption issues are an irrelevant issue.
2. It is worth noting that the generalizing term "intellectual property rights" is of recent origin covering a wide range of cognitive phenomena, as Mark Blaug (2005:71–72) under scores:

   > It never occurred to anyone before, say the 1980s, that such disparate phenomena as patents for mechanical inventions, industrial products and processes (now extended to biotechnology, algorithms and even business methods), copyrights for the expression of literacy and artistic expressions in fixed form and trademarks and trade names for distinctive services, *could be generalized under the heading of property rights*, all conferred by the legal system in relation to discrete items of information resulting from some sort of appropriate intellectual activity.

3. More precisely, as in the case of social phenomena in general, patents bind different, contradictory or opposing elements and layers: patents not only separate but can also unite; for example, patents can both protect and disclose knowledge. Patents (the patent specification) can disclose knowledge and thus inducing an interest in the knowledge in question, patents may eventually initiate entrepreneurial partnerships or valuable transactions in the form of royalties. Michael Polanyi (1944:64) supports the idea that patents made knowledge available;

   > patents afford—at the least—a most important source of information concerning the ideas which inventors have pursued in the past and reveal to a considerable extent the trend of their current interests. They disclose also, at least in part, what has actually been achieved in practice. . . . This publicity is an altogether indispensable advantage of the patent system.

   However, my thesis will be that the work of patents, especially in economically highly relevant patents, consists mainly in their separation, fencing off and compartmentalization of knowledge; that is, embedded in patents is an unequal distribution of advantages or power.

4. Anton Korinek und Ding Xuan Ng (2017:1) define Superstar-corporations as

   > arising from digital innovations, which replace a fraction of the tasks in production with information technology that requires a fixed cost but can be reproduced at zero marginal cost. This generates a form of increasing returns to scale. To the extent that the digital innovations are excludable, it also provides the innovator with market power.

   Anton Korinek and Ding Xuan Ng's definition of a superstar company should add at least two criteria; that of globally operating companies and the exceptionally low tax burden associated with it—that is, taking advantage of international tax laws. Amazon generated a profit of $24 billion globally in 2020. The profit was offset by a tax burden of $2.9 billion. That represents a burden of 11.8 percent, relatively less than the tax burden of the average wages of a worker.
5. An April 2019 report issued by McKinsey, focusing on profits as the sole criterion, comes to the conclusion that

   > among the world's largest companies . . . economic profit is distributed unequally along a power curve, with the top 10 percent of companies capturing 80 percent of positive economic profit. . . . As economic profits grow larger, so do economic losses at the other end of the distribution. The bottom 10 percent of companies destroy as much value as the top 10 percent create. . . . A growing number are turning into zombie companies, unable to generate enough cash flow even to sustain interest payments on their debts. The impact of these economic losses goes beyond these companies' investors, managers, and workers: it drives down the returns for healthy companies that compete for the same resources or profits.

   See: www.mckinsey.com/featured-insights/innovation-and-growth/what-every-ceo-needs-to-know-about-superstar-companies.
6. Peter Drucker (1994:67) calls attention to a profound transformation in the nature of property relations in what he as a result calls the post-capitalist society: In the knowledge society all workers have a stake in post-capitalism because collectively, "the employees own the means of production . . . whether through their pension funds, through mutual funds, through their retirement accounts, and so on. . . . The 'capitalist' have thus themselves become employees." Drucker (1997:23–24) later formulates an alternative or, as they case may be, an additional thesis about the changing property relation in post-capitalist societies: "Knowledge workers, unlike manufacturing workers, own the means of production: they carry their knowledge in their heads and therefore can take it with them."
7. I rely on Nico Stehr (2015) for a discussion of the history of the idea of the theory of knowledge societies.
8. A perhaps even earlier use of the term "knowledge society" may be found in the title of an "Church Missionary Society" in the United States: "The Evangelical Meeting—The Evangelical Knowledge Society—American Church Missionary Society—The Education of Young Men for the Ministry". The account of the annual (nineteenth) Meeting of the "Evangelical Knowledge Society" of the Church of Ascension on November 8, 1865 may be found in the *New York Times*, November 9, 1865.
9. The critique of the theory of the knowledge society was partly animated by the dating of the genesis of the knowledge society, as well as by the allegedly abridged conception of the science system; for example, it is criticized that, in addition to an unhistorical and static concept of science, a further weakness of the "theory lies in the misconception that the comparatively marginal treatment of knowledge in the classical economic literature actually points to a lesser importance [of knowledge] in the

industrial society of the 19th and 20th centuries" (Vogel, 2004:634). The following explanations, however, make it clear that there was and is indeed ample discussion of the industrial society as being determined by knowledge and science, however, without a detailed history of the economic significance of science and technology.

10. James Rule and Yasemin Besen (2008:321) comment laconically upon Robert Lane's discovery of the modern knowledge society as

    > Lane's sweeping ideas did no more than articulate a swelling current of educated opinion in the 1960s on relations between expert knowledge and governance. This was, after all, the period in which a number of noted intellectuals discerned the extinction of ideology in favor of applications of expertise in the management of public affairs.

    As is well known, Daniel Bell (1960) thesis of the end of ideology in modern societies in the seventies of the last century was a prominent proponent of the rational transformation of governance and the controversial disappearance of a significant part of everyday (ideological) political beliefs.
11. The idea of the technical state also has some resemblance to the observation of a change in the hierarchy of social systems in modern society, in particular to Luhmann's (1975:63) idea of a "change in leadership" from social systems that reply on normative expectations (that is, values, regulations, purposes) to cognitive expectations (economy, science, and technology).
12. In an interview with Peter Drucker published in the *Wilson Quarterly* in 1993, Drucker confirms the lack of interchange with Daniel Bell, "Daniel Bell and I—I in 1969, he four years later—started at very different points but came out at pretty much the same place."
13. Jürgen Renn (2020:146) uses the concept "knowledge economy" in a more general sense than most economists and sociologists

    > when they refer, for instance, to the transition of the global economy from a labor-intensive economy to a knowledge economy. In my usage here, a knowledge economy is the ensemble of all societal practices, including institutions, concerned with the production, reproduction, transfer, distribution, sharing, and appropriation of knowledge in a given society.

    Renn's a-historical term of the knowledge economy refers as far as I can see to knowledge an anthropological constant and its social organization.
14. Becker, Gary "The dismal future for workers with few skills," The Becker-Posner Blog, University of Chicago Law School, March 17, 2020; see also "Bridge builders"
15. www.stradaeducation.org/report/bridge-builders/ offers and support this very reasoning. It is of course mute to ask how *employers* know what skills exactly are needed to prepare for and ensure a *great future* in the job market.
16. I suspect (because this is not an entirely robust observation by the authors of the Report) that the OECD Report (2013:25) *Supporting Investment in Knowledge Capital, Growth and Innovation* support Drucker's law. In an effort to account for the rising investment in knowledge-based capital across OECD countries in the new century, the report notes:

    > With rising educational attainment, OECD economies have accumulated a larger stock of human capital. The stock of human capital in turn enables and complements the production and use of KBC (for instance, patents are a means of securing the intellectual property associated with innovations emanating from human capital).

17. Daron Acemoglu (2019:7), in a search for "good jobs" (well-paying and secure jobs) in an era of automation and artificial intelligence emphasizes that the "market, innovators

included will undervalue good jobs. . . . This is all the more so when part of the social benefits from high-wage jobs does not accrue to the firms supplying those jobs." Striving for good jobs is also a matter embedded in society.

18. For a contemporary contrast and comparison between Peter Drucker's notion of the knowledge society and self-organizing knowledge labor as *cognitive capitalism* (cf. Boutang, [2007] 2011) and the more recent Italian Marxist inspired analysis of capitalism's cognitive phase see Hardt and Negri (2000) and Peters and Reveley (2012).
19. The role of the management of an organization is not altogether trivial. Drucker (1999:93) anticipates that the comparative advantages in the world economy will go to countries and industries that "have most systematically and most successfully raised knowledge-worker productivity".
20. The interest in accurately dating a particular social formation is itself a modern cultural phenomenon, as Daniel Bell (1973:346) points out: "Our self-consciousness about time, which is itself an aspect of modernity, urges us to seek some symbolic points that mark the emergence of a new social understanding."
21. Ulrich Beck ([1986] 1992:46) views his (industrial) risk society perspective as converging with or even in a close family resemblance with the "science society, the media and the information society".
22. Florian Znaniecki (1940:23), for example, emphasizes that "every individual who performs any social role is supposed by his social circle to possess and believes himself to possess the knowledge indispensable for its normal performance."
23. Compare Georg Simmel's ([1908] 1992: 383–455), analysis of "The secret and the secret society" in his *Soziologie*.
24. "It can be assumed," Luhmann (1990:247) summarizes this idea, "that knowledge today as in the past is a freely floating quality of expectation, which can neither be differentiated nor assigned to a special system for exclusive production and use. Knowledge exists everywhere—and more than one can know."
25. Robert Darnton (2000:1) puts forward the universal thesis that every age has been an information age, "each in its own way, and that communication systems have always shaped events."
26. The "cognitive capitalism" perspective is one of a range of strained and parallel neo-Marxist efforts to rescue and highlight the originality and actuality of Karl Marx's contribution to the analysis of contemporary capitalism (e.g., Moulier-Boutang, [2007] 2011).
27. Osmo Wiio (1985) claims that the term "information society" first appeared in 1972 in a report written for the Japanese government. Often, however, analyses and discussions of the information society ultimately refer to a vocabulary typical of the concept and theory of post-industrial society (e.g., Lyon, 1986). Frank Webster (2002:22) who has written extensively on the theory of the information society, however, is ready to give up in the term as of little use to social science; for example, based on the "unsupportable supposition of information society theorists that quantitative increases in information lead to qualitative social changes". One can add to this critical point of view that the "empty" reference to modern society as an information society can hardly be justified by the fact that "social processes based on innovative information uses, and especially the transformation of information into authoritative knowledge, manifestly represented the distinguishing feature of the age" (Rule and Broom, 2007:317). Whether information can be transformed more or less directly into knowledge has to be marked with a big question mark, just like the implicit assertion that this is new.
28. In 2003, the UNESCO organized the first *World Summit on the Information Society* (WSIS) that took place in Geneva in December of that year. In a sober assessment, Joux (2006:193) notes, despite a lack of "positive" results and confusion about the vague term "information society", the UNESCO stuck to the term in subsequent years.

29. If the conception or development of a technological apparatus that processes data determines whether a society is an information society, then its origins can perhaps be traced to Gottfried Wilhelm Leibnitz (1646–1716), who postulated a machine that might be able to manipulate mathematical representations of human thought.
30. One result from the study by Kendall-Taylor, Frantz, and Wright (2020:106–107) may serve as an example of the political consequences of modern surveillance technology in autocratic systems:

    > Our analysis using data from Varieties of Democracy's data set (which covers 202 countries) and the Mass Mobilization Project shows that autocracies that use digital repression face a lower risk of protests than do those autocratic regimes that do not employ these same tools. Digital repression not only decreases the likelihood that a protest will occur but also reduces the chances that a government will face large, sustained mobilization efforts, such as the "red shirt" protests in Thailand in 2010 or the anti-Mubarak and antimilitary protests in Egypt in 2011. The example of Cambodia illustrates how these dynamics can play out.

31. Kean Birch and D.T. Cochrane (2021) designate the Big Tech companies "ecosystems" and not "platforms". Ecosystems "are heterogenous assemblages of technical devices, platforms, users, developers, payment systems, etc. as well as legal contracts, rights, claims, standards, etc. . . . They are techno-economic in character, co- constructed with socio-legal orders."
32. Notwithstanding differences between Big Tech firms one

    > can draw two critical parallels. The first is their largely unchecked corporate power, and the second is their highly financialised nature. . . . They have more financial assets at their disposal and follow a business model that relies more strongly on *intangible assets* such as patents, data and related analytics, or goodwill.
    >
    > (Fernandez et al., 2020:10; emphasis added)

    Apple is unique among the superstars. Apple does not mainly rely on copyright law but has surrounded itself by a bouquet of expensive technologies—the Mac, the iPod, the iPhone, the iPad and the AirPod Max (and maybe soon a car). None the less, iTunes dominates global digital music sales, with around 75 percent of the market.
33. Shoshana Zuboff (2019:331) tries to avoid the thesis to what extent the so-called surveillance society is a form of totalitarianism ("We can have democracy, or we can have a surveillance society, but we cannot have both." Shoshana Zuboff, "The coup we are not talking about," New York Times, January 29, 2021) by stating that there is no convergence between totalitarianism and surveillance society, especially since, as she rightly points out, "totalitarianism impedes our understanding as well as our ability to resist, neutralize, and ultimately vanquish its potency." This is certainly but a very faint hope of escaping the pervasive and unchecked power of the relentless information gathering of the big tech corporations. But there remains—in spite of her protest—is a strong measure of ambivalence in her analysis: "There is no escape from Big Other [a largely uncontested societal power]. There is no place to be where the Other is not" (Zuboff, 2015:82).
34. As Albert Borgmann (1992:61), notes and as every (small), bank customer also knows well, "Capital is less real than land; it is relatively mobile and, as financial capital, quite intangible. But the latter is always within hailing distance on being properly balanced with material goods."
35. Nineteenth-century social theory, for example, paid close attention to property and labor and was convinced that we are about to enter an era in which property would become obsolescent and in which labor would take on a very different social, political, and economic status. My immediate focus, however, is not on the nature of the totality of changes in these social constructs, conceived as independent entities nor on the

ways in which labor and property can be used to identify major social formations in modern society. I will be more concerned with the reduced economic and therefore societal relevance of these constructs as forces of production. It is of course likely that the social, legal, and political conception and the predominant symbolic function of these phenomena will be transformed *in response* to their lesser status in production (cf. also Luhmann's, 1988:151–176 discussion of the cognitive significance and decline of capital and work as salient categories of social theory).

36. In his examination of the *Economy of Society* (*Die Wirtschaft der Gesellschaft*), Niklas Luhmann (1988:164–166) attributes the decline of the theoretical and practical relevance of capital and labor to their neglect of the demand and consumption side of modern economic activity. Patterns of social inequality of workers (*Lebenslagen*), for example, are much more driven by consumption activities than by wages (see also the later chapter on the economic structure of knowledge societies and the discussion of the transformation of the employment society into a consumption society).
37. In the course of past waves of economic developments and failures, the transformation of nature by man in the course of, for example, the last two centuries of modern societies, has resulted in the fact that the preeminent natural landscape is a man-made environment. From an economic point of view therefore, it has become almost impossible to distinguish between the rent which may accrue to property due to its natural advantage and the quasi-rent of the same property due to man's transformation.
38. See especially Peter Drucker (1986), and Richard Lipsey (1992).
39. "The use and application of knowledge give rise to increasing returns because of the non-subtractability of knowledge (resulting in the fact that use of knowledge generates more and/or new knowledge); because of the increasing division of knowledge; because of circular and cumulative causation between use and capacity; and because knowledge, though not a sufficient condition, helps and promotes creativity." (Hu, 2020:21)
40. In the United States, for example, financial assets of households in 2019 now make up nearly 72 percent of total assets, compared to 65 percent in 2009. The bottom 50 percent of the households owned only 2.3 percent of financial assets, compared to 35 percent by the top one percent (cf. https://www2.deloitte.com/us/en/pages/financial-services/articles/how-us-household-balance-sheets-changed-since-the-financial-crises.html According to figures Manuel Castells (2000:54) cites, "In 1997, for the first time, a higher proportion of US households' assets were in securities than in real estate."
41. Nikolas Zolas et al. (2020:71) report that AI adoption rate varies greatly by firm size. Using data from a 2018 survey of US businesses, more than 60 percent of companies that have 10,000 and more employees use AI technologies. Companies with 100–249 employees, for example, indicate that less than 20 percent use these technologies. It would appear to be self-evident that the concentration in the use of new knowledge and technologies will potentially have significant implications on topics such as inequality, competition and the rise of "superstar" firms (cf. Footnote 31 "The economic importance. . .).
42. Compare the study by David Frank and John Meyer (2020:122), *The Expanded University and the Knowledge Society*, in which the authors present their hypothesis that "the contemporary knowledge society is filled with rationalized roles and articulated cultural domains that derive fundamentally from the university."
43. The economic importance of large firms is of course hardly a new phenomenon; however, internationally enforceable patent laws and the advent of digital platforms has brought about a new quality of market concentration. The World Bank (2019:37) reports that

    > large firms dominate the global economy: 10 percent of the world's companies are estimated to generate 80 percent of all profits. Superstar firms shape a country's

> exports. One study of 32 developing countries found that, on average, the five largest exporters in a country account for a third of its exports, nearly half of export growth, and a third of growth due to export diversification.

The concentration is most notable for corporations that rely on technological innovations and in markets that are rapidly changing due to technological innovations.

44. And in a much narrower sense, as the emergence of *intellectuals* as a new social class. Such a transformation has been identified as a characteristic feature of advanced societies in which science and technology assume a powerful role (cf. Konrád and Szelényi, 1979; Gouldner, 1979). Whether this "class" constitutes a power elite or not depends on more detailed theoretical reflections and is by no means uncontroversial, as remarks by Daniel Bell (1979:204), addressing this question, for example, indicate, "such an elite has power within intellectual institutions . . . but only influence in the larger world in which policy is made". But possible limits to the power of this new class have not discouraged others from sketching the dawning of a new age as a result of the development of "political knowledge":

> As engagement in the world is encouraging the appearance of a new breed of politicians-intellectuals, men who make it a point to mobilize and draw on the most expert, scientific, and academic advice in the development of political programs. . . . (So), the largely humanistic-oriented, occasionally ideologically-minded intellectual-dissenter, who saw his role largely in terms of proffering social critiques, is rapidly being displaced by experts and specialists, who become involved in special government undertakings, or by generalist-integrators, who become in effect house-ideologues for those in power, providing overall intellectual integration for disparate action.
>
> (Brzezinski, 1968:22)

45. Thomas Piketty ([2013] 2014:332; also, Song et al., 2015) for examples observes, that

> wage inequalities increased rapidly in the United States and Britain because U.S. and British corporations became much more tolerant of extremely generous pay packages after 1970. . . . This change in senior management compensation has played a key role in the evolution of wage inequalities around the world.

In other words, it is well established now that income and earnings differences, especially in the United States since the late 1970s have increased substantially. The explanations for the rise in social inequality remain a matter of debate, especially among economists. Moreover, the experience is not identical in all developed societies: "Existing studies show that earnings inequality has increased in Germany, the United Kingdom, and Italy but remained stable in France" (Hoffmann et al., 2020:53).

46. The shift of authority toward expertise is, at the same time, accompanied by disputes about the legitimacy and basis for expertise. Expertise becomes therefore an essentially contested attribute and the self-evident quality of expert knowledge is not always easily established and maintained (e.g., Smith, 1985; Stehr and Grundmann, 2011).
47. Alain Touraine ([1984] 1988: 111), captures the change I have in mind as well. He observes that in mercantile societies, the

> central locus of protest was called *liberty* since it was a matter of defending oneself against the legal and political power of the merchants and, at the same time, of counterposing to their power an order defined in legal terms. In the industrial epoch, this central locus was called *justice* since it was a question of returning to the workers the fruit of their labor and of industrialization. In programmed [or, post-industrial] society, the central place of protest and claims is *happiness*, that is, the global image of the organization of social life on the basis of the needs expressed by the most diverse individuals and groups.

Touraine ([1969] 1971: 3), employs the term "programmed" society for the emerging type of modern society in order to identify the "nature of their production methods and economic organization".

48. Not unlike the demand the demand for a "balanced" form of surveillance Yuval Noah Harari (*Financial Times*, February 26, 2021) advocates:

> surveillance must always go both ways. If surveillance goes only from top to bottom, this is the high road to dictatorship. So whenever you increase surveillance of individuals, you should simultaneously increase surveillance of the government and big corporations too.

49. For example, Malinowski (1955), and Fritz Machlup (1962).
50. Such a restriction in foci extends to the questions of the range of rights and duties of individuals and corporate actors concerning the management and diffusion of knowledge. This implies, more concretely, deferring discussions of questions pertaining to "informed consent", confidentiality or publicity of information, the obligation to transmit or prevent the transmission of knowledge, and the problem of secrecy in exchange processes of information in knowledge societies. In the concluding chapter of this study, however, I will examine, in quite a general manner, the social control of knowledge in modern societies.
51. See Morgan Housel, "How this all happened", www.collaborativefund.com/blog/how-this-all-happened/ which is a short story about what occurred to the economy in the United States since the end of World War II. Robert Gordon (2016) has written an economic history of the United States that covers the period where real wages rose rapidly. He calls the time between 1870 and 1979 "the special century". His conclusion about the future of economic growth is more circumspect. Gordon does not expect a repeat performance.
52. Terms such as "prosperity", "wealth", and "abundance" are, of course, and this does not need to be described in more detail, highly controversial terms. They refer to phenomena that are difficult to quantify, have different meanings depending on place and time, and in their different meanings are in turn closely interwoven with different moral discourses in which prosperity is understood, for example, as a virtue or as a symbol of a profound social injustice. Quantitatively speaking, my distinction between wealth and affluence of a population is based on the average household income.
53. A detailed discussion of the term "standard of living" and its origins can be found in Coffin, (1999). The concept of living standards first appeared in the literature when economists and other social scientists increasingly turned their attention to the hitherto neglected topic of consumption at the beginning of the 19th century. An examination of the concept of living standards that does not follow a materially determined definition but understands it as a form of freedom is found in Sen, 1984. The definition of living standards used by Sen (1984:78) emphasizes the ability to live well and assigns high priority to the ability to deal with economic affairs in the specific economic context of living standards.
54. Given Romer's emphasis on ideas and knowledge as the levers of economic growth, in the 1990s, the magazine *Wire* labelled him "an economist for the technological age". A designation, the management Silicon Valley corporations would not repeat today since Romer has become a critic of superstar firms (cf. Steve Lohr, "One tech's favorite economist, now a thorn in its side," *New York Times*, May 20, 2021; www.nytimes.com/2021/05/20/technology/tech-antitrust-paul-romer.html?action=click&module=Top%20Stories&pgtype=Homepage)
55. Legal and sociological classifications of the various items that are part of the bouquet of intangible assets—assuming that the law or scholars can even agree on the range of items that belong—are difficult to establish and give rise to multiple contests about the proper definition and boundaries.

56. The World intellectual Property Organization (WIPO, 2020:231) defines a plant variety grant, under the UPOV (*International Union for the Protection of New Varieties of Plants*) as "the breeder's right [to be] granted (title of protection is issued) only when the variety is new, distinct, uniform, stable and has a suit- able denomination." In 2019, China received 36.6 percent of all plant variety applications filed worldwide:

    > Around 21,430 plant variety applications were filed worldwide in 2019, up 7.8% on 2018—a fourth con- secutive year of growth. The China [patent] office contributed the majority of global growth, followed by the offices of Argentina, Israel and Turkey.

57. It may come as a surprise, but one can receive a patent

    > in many jurisdictions without implementing an invention in practice and demonstrating that it works as expected. Instead, inventors applying for patents are allowed to include predicted experimental methods and results, known as prophetic examples, as long as the examples are not written in the past tense.
    >
    > (Freilich and Quellette, 2019:1036)

    In other words, patent applications resemble, in some instances, an application for research funding in science.
58. Wen Chen has compiled a database of the volume of investment in intangible capital for 60 countries for the period 1995–2011. Based on his database, Chen (2018:627–628) concludes that investments in intangible capital "have become [globally] increasingly the more important forms of investment in the modern economy [and that] there is a strong positive association between the level of economic development of a country and its investment intensity in intangibles."
59. Modern economic discourse is not as was the case in classical liberalism—as the quote from Adam Smith indicates—interested in the societal (social) capital that human capital represents. This extensive meaning has to be rediscovered (World Bank, 2019:51).
60. An extensive, helpful and informative genealogy of human capital accounting may be found in Yarrow (2020:7–14).
61. The contest among the relative weight of those shares of collective income that are generated by different forms of capital has significant repercussions beyond economic performance, for example, for the formation of social inequality in a society. Thomas Piketty ([2013] 2014: 21) notes, "the progress of technological rationality is supposed to lead automatically to the triumph of human capital over financial capital and real estate, capable managers over fat stockholders, and skill over nepotism." But, as he adds in a cautionary remark, "inequalities would thus become more meritocratic and less static (though not necessarily smaller): economic rationality would then in some sense automatically give rise to democratic rationality" (Piketty, [2013] 2014: 21).
62. In sociology, there are many precursors and parallel perspectives in which the importance of education for social stratification is emphasized. Reference may be made to one of Max Weber's observations ([1917] 1994: 103–104):

    > the way the modern state and economy are organised ensures that a privileged position is permanently given to *specialised training* and thereby to "education" (*Bildung*) which is not identical with specialised training but promoted by it for purely technical educational reasons, this being one of the most powerful factors in status group (*ständisch*) differentiation in modern society.

63. An early critique of the image of the individual within human capital theory that views individuals not as moral or ethical beings but driven by the logic of rational economic discourse, may be found in Shaffer (1961). Harry Shaffer objects that the term "investment" is not really applicable to the issue of human capital; "investment" in individual employees should not be used as a basis for policy formation. A fundamental criticism of the human

capital theory is therefore also prompted by the (implicit?) idea that a more comprehensive school education is associated with productivity gains and that a higher income of these groups is seen as a function of these productive gains (for example, Gouldner, 1979: 108). Randall Collins (1971) notes, and Gouldner (1979:108) agrees and emphasizes that "the main activity of schools . . . is to teach status cultures, thus socializing persons to gain admission to status groups and their privileges" (see also Stehr, 2000).

64. Human capital knows no demographic differences (gender, age, race) and most certainly no social class (cf. Paltrinieri, 2019:160). However, by linking the notion of human capital to the well-being of the national collectivity, the economic theory of human capital acquires a selective affinity to eugenics philosophy.
65. The correlation between HCI and GDP per capita shows that there are countries that score highly in the HCI but low on per capita income (Cuba, China, Vietnam) and countries with a high per capita income that score low on the index (mainly oil producing countries).
66. In comparing both groups, "the college-high school premium in wages has increased by much less than the college-high school premium in productivity has increased over the past almost-three decades" (Lazear, 2020:39).
67. One of the significant attributes of what Herman Schwartz (2020:9) choses to call the "IPR economy" (intellectual property economy) relates to the typical employee structures of high-tech corporations:

    > The contemporary IPR economy thus has a three-tier structure, in ideal typical terms. Human capital-intensive, low employee headcount, low physical capital firms comprise the high profit volume top tier. Physical-capital-intensive firms comprise the moderate profit volume middle tier. High employee headcount firms with little physical or human capital are the bottom tier. The tech world precisely exhibits this structure: consider the iPhone value chain with Apple and Qualcomm in level 1, Intel, Toshiba or Corning in level 2, and Hon Hai Precision (aka Foxconn), Pegatron or Flextronics in level 3. The first group typically does only chip and software design, the second group uses capital-intensive processes to produce parts based on those designs and the last group assembles those parts. Apple produces nothing physical for its phones, though it owns many of the sophisticated tools used to make its products.

68. Compare the essay "The world's wealth is looking increasingly unnatural," *The Economist*, July 18th edition 2020, providing observations about the extent to which that the world's natural capital (oil, natural gas, and as well as minerals) is being drawn down over the next decades. Natural capital diminishes because it is increasingly exhausted and/or deliberately left in the ground. One scenario quoted in the essay has the natural capital of the typical person in today's high-income countries at their disposal in 2040 decline by 21 percent. In poorer countries, they will have 17 percent less. It follows that there ought to be a greater reliance on human capital for wealth creation.
69. As Thomas Piketty ([2019] 2020:664) points out that the private appropriation of public knowledge or knowledge produced with the assistance of public financial support, is not deducted (or displayed) from the immaterial value of a firm:

    > The stock market value of technology firms includes patents and knowhow that might not exist were it not for basic research financed with public money and accumulated over decades. Such private appropriation of common knowledge could increase dramatically in the coming century. What happens will depend on the evolution of legal and tax systems and on the social and political response.

    The development of the *corona virus vaccine* by multiple large pharmaceutical corporations is a most recent example of the private appropriation (by corporations and shareholders) of the economic benefits of inventions that depended for their development on public finds (cf. Achmal Prabbala, Arjun Jayadev and Dean Baker, "Want vaccines fast? Suspend intellectual property rights," *New York Times*, December 7, 2020 as well as the contest between the US Governments NIH over the patent rights to the Moderna Covid-19 vaccine: Sheryl Gay Stolberg and Rebecca Robbins, "Moderna and U.S. at Odds over Vaccine Patent Rights, *New York Times* November 9, 2021).

70. The research results of Elsfeldt et al. (2020:17) indicate that

> asset pricing researchers should consider adjusting the value factor and accompanying test assets to incorporate intangible capital. Practitioners can also use the intangible value factor to implement a profitable relative value strategy, especially in recent years when traditional value has underperformed.

71. In the case such rights are granted to an individual writer, artist or musician, copyright governs the relation between a collective and the individual—and signifies that society places a high value on the individual. Copyright is highly contested matter; even more so in the age of the internet. One day, copyright provisions will also matter in the case of material reproductions, as the 3D-printers signal.
72. The discussion of the role of patents has a venerable tradition of legislation. As Fritz Machlup (1984:163), for example, notes:

> Special monopoly grants by kings and other rulers to private inventors and innovators were known in the fourteenth century. The first general promise of exclusive rights to inventors was made in a statute enacted in 1474 by them Republic of Venice. In the sixteenth century, patents were issued by German princes, some of whom had a well-reasoned policy of granting privileges on the basis of a careful consideration of the utility and novelty of the inventions and of the burden that would be imposed on the country by excluding others from the use of these inventions and by enabling the patentees to charge higher prices.

73. The authors of the US Constitution (Article I, section 8, clause 8) already stipulated, in an ambivalent sense, that Congress shall have the power to establish patent and copyright laws to "promote the progress of science and the useful arts by securing for limited times to Authors and Inventors the exclusive right to their respective writings and discoveries". Congress passed patent law in 1790. Rarely recalled in the story of U.S. patent laws is the fact that the protection of the patent law only extended to inventions of free individuals. The legal frame for intellectual copyrights cannot settle and has not settled the question whether such laws actually promote science and serve as incentives to add to the volume of knowledge (cf. Machlup, 1961).
74. Patent systems have existed for decades (and longer) in many countries. The patent systems of the United States, France, and England are significantly different. The patent systems reflect different national motivations and accordingly differ in their emphasis on different standards. These differences, in turn, have an impact on knowledge production and what is understood as useful knowledge as well as economic growth patterns (Khan, 2020:20–25).
75. That patents were not actively exploited is already a concern in the 19th century: In a paper presented to the Annual Meeting of the *American Association of Inventors and Manufacturers* entitled "Needed modifications in our patent laws" concern was expressed that patents lie idle for years. The law should compel patents owners to put them to use or it should compel them to grant a license to another person, appointed by the government perhaps, who should have the right to use it (see "Papers on patens," *New York Times*, January 17, 1894).
76. More generally, scarcity is not an anthropological constant, as James Suzman (2020:6–7) argues in his history of work. On the contrary, the "economic problem" for most

of human history is abundance; that is, the life of hunter-gatherers revolves not around scarcity but abundance;

> there is good reason to believe that because our ancestors hunted and gathered for well over 95 per cent of *Homo sapiens*' 300,000-year-old history, the assumption about human nature in the problem of scarcity and our attitudes to work have their roots in farming.

In other words, patents are historically one of the more recent social constructions of scarcity.

77. Kenneth Arrow (1996:125; emphasis added) maintains—in agreement with the then prevailing consensus in economics—that it is difficult to turn information (for Arrow knowledge and information converge) into property but

> if information is not property, the *incentives* to create it will be lacking. Patents and copyrights are social innovations designed to create artificial scarcities where none exist naturally. . . . These scarcities are intended to create the needed incentives for acquiring information.

78. Dean Baker (2018) refers to a calculation that is enlightening in this context:

> According to data from the [US] Association for Accessible Medicines (AAM), the trade group for the generic industry, brand drugs accounted for 74 percent of spending even though they were only 11 percent of the prescriptions sold. By contrast, generic drugs accounted for just 26 percent of spending even though they were 89 percent of sales. This implies that the average generic prescription cost just 3.6 percent of the price of the average brand prescription, or $29.70 per prescription. This figure would mean that we could save 96.4 percent of the money spent on brand drugs if we immediately got rid of protections and allowed them to be sold as generics.

79. The role of the patent system as a motor of the industrial revolution is a separate research field and a contentious matter; there are, on the one hand, strong assertions that assign a crucial role to the contribution of patents, as foremost examples of how *institutions* fostered the industrial revolution. Joel Mokyr (2009:350) points out that

> the number of patents filed in Britain . . . seems at first glance to track the history of the Industrial Revolution. Yet the question remains if this can be taken as evidence of the role that patents played in incentivizing and stimulating the processes that eventually generated modern economic growth.

The implementation of the patents law in Britain appear to tell a different story as does the function of incentives for innovation other than financial rewards such a honor or reputation:

> The objections were not so much against the system in general as against the way the law was written and carried out in Britain, especially the high cost of patenting and the sense that even the granting of a patent was 'almost wholly illusory' until the patent had been sustained by a court of law, at an even higher cost.
>
> (Mokyr, 2009:351)

80. Observers of patent activity noted more than a century ago that but the smallest portion of all patents acquired should be considered valuable. Lord Moulton (1844–1921) in an interview in 1919 ("Publishing patents: Interview with Lord Moulton. Useless ideas", *The Observer*, August 3, 1919) observed: 40 percent of thousands of all patents

issued annually are rubbish and worthless; only 4 to 5 percent of patents survive over the lifetime of the period for which the patent is granted.

> Inventors . . . are peculiarly prone to imagine that their particular geese are swans, and behave accordingly. Disillusionment comes later and the inventor has not realised the fortune he anticipated. Edison and Maconi do not visit the Patent Office every day of the year.

81. A profitable and at times highly profitable venture now has become patent litigation also known as "patent trolls" or "patent sharks": The term "patent trolls" "is a colloquialism that denotes what the trolls themselves prefer to call "patent-assertion entities." A patent troll buys patents (sometimes thousands) with the aim not of making the patented product or process or licensing it to others to make but of finding companies or individual inventors that the troll can claim with more or less plausibility are infringing one or more of his inventories of patents. The troll demands a license fee from every such allegedly infringing company or inventor (Posner, 2013—from the Becker Posner Blog; http://uchicagolaw.typepad.com/beckerposner/).
82. In 2012, almost two-thirds of all legal disputes (in the US) involving patents were related to patent trolls. Additional successful patents shark cases can be found in Henkel and Reitzig, 2008). Furthermore, it is possible that some corporations will focus their resources on defending their original innovations rather than developing new products, mainly engage in "quit politics/lobbing" (Schwartz, 2021:2) and therefore limiting their output below socially desirable levels leading to negative consequences on consumer welfare (Shapiro and Hassett, 2005).
83. The United States patent office is, as Dean Baker (2018) notes in paper on intellectual property and inequality, "is notoriously lax in the standards it applies to patents". This in turn empowers the patent holders; for example, in the pharmaceutical industry:

> If a pharmaceutical company claims a dubious patent on some aspect of a drug that is about to lose protection from its main patent, a generic competitor would take a considerable risk in entering the market. It is also important to recognize the fundamental asymmetry in this sort of contest: the brand producer is fighting to be able to continue to sell the drug at the monopoly price, the generic competitor is trying to get the right to sell it at the free market price. In recent years, AI is deployed more and more often to find drugs that are just as effective as existing patented drugs, but different. This is relevant because when a drug patent expires, a corporation may still own patents on numerous chemical steps needed to manufacture the drug, then requiring payments to the original firm.
>
> (Joshia Howgego, "AI knows to bust drug patents," *New Scientist* January 29, 2019, 15).

84. For this reason, a recent *Bertelsmann* study (Overdiek et al., 2020) of "world-class patents" is of minor value if any value. The authors focus exclusively on the number of patents granted. The method chosen does not reflect the economic value of the patents, the fact, as I have noted that half of all patents granted are never commercialized or the power of different corporations in different regions of the world and for the world based on the patens they command. Moreover, as Fred Block and Matthew Keller (2012:81) have pointed out,

> patent rates are a problematic proxy for effective innovation, and there is a danger that reliance on this proxy is producing a distorted understanding of the circumstances under which innovation occurs and the intellectual property regimes that might best facilitate such innovation.

A patent policy that follows the results of the Bertelsmann study is bound to be an impotent policy.

85. The number and the growing number of patents granted worldwide does shed a light on, on the one hand, the expansion of the patentability domain and, on the other, on what might be called patent politics; for example, as Dosi and Stiglitz (2014:11–12) point out:

> One by-product of the recent surge in patenting is that, in several domains, knowledge has been so finely subdivided into separate but complementary property claims that the cost of reassembling constituent parts/properties in order to engage in further research imposes a heavy burden on technological advance.

It likely is very difficult to separate these causes of the expansion in the number of patents statistically and to record them separately.

86. Alexander and Eberle (2018) report that at industry level in the United States, intangible assets have risen as a share of total assets for most industries since 1990.
87. For a quantitative model of the difference in knowledge intensity by sector of the economy see the Table 5.A.1.1. in OECD (2013:245) "Knowledge intensity of 18 industries" proxied by the share of labor compensation of employees with tertiary education.
88. The Apple corporation is the best known and most successful *factory-less producer* of devices well-known around the world (Barnard and Fort, 2015):

> A complex and well-managed value chain is a key asset of Apple suppliers must comply to get access to their enormous consumer end market. The value chain process allows Apple to capture the lion's share of value produced in the chain.
> (Durand and Milberg, 2019:416–417)

Another distinguishing element of large technology companies is what Rikap and Lundvall (2020:1449) call the *Corporate Innovation System* (CIS). Rikap and Lundvall define the CIS as a

> system organized and controlled by a dominant firm but constituted also by a multitude of more or less subordinate firms and knowledge institutions that participate in multiple production and innovation processes. Unlike other productive and innovation structures, in CIS not only the resulting value but also the collectively created knowledge is mostly appropriated by the dominant firm acting like a predatory intellectual monopoly.

89. Apple filed a patent in 2006 "for a rudimentary version, a headset that would let users see a 'peripheral light element' for an 'enhanced viewing experience', able to display notifications in the corner of your vision. That was finally granted in 2013, at the time of Google's own attempt to convince people about smartglasses," which failed commercially ("Part human, part machine: Is Apple turning us all into cyborgs?" *The Guardian* November 25, 2020).
90. The authors of the OECD Report refer to Corrado, Hulten, and Sichel, 2005 as their authority of the reproduced typology of knowledge-based capital.
91. The statistically unrecorded intangible assets of firms are not only of interest in determining the changing ratio of an economy's investments in physical and human capital, but the missing data are furthermore of weight in their impact on other important economic measures, such as the productivity figures (of a corporation or of the economy as a whole). The controversial discussion among economists about the decline in aggregate productivity (see also my discussion of the so-called productivity paradox in the next chapter) in recent decades and the search for the causes of this development is tangential to the problem of collecting the intangible capital value. The weak productivity figures, at least in the USA, which were observed even before the so-called financial crisis, turn out to be far less significant as soon as it is possible to capture the unrecorded intangible capital more completely. An empirically valid capture of "markups and unmeasured capital can account for about half

of the measured productivity slowdown in the 2000s" (Cerouzet and Eberle, 2021:1. More precisely, Crouzet and Eberly (2019), "show that intangibles can explain 30 to 60 percent of the decline, when looking at firm- level and industry-level data, respectively".

92. *Ocean Tomo* (www.oceantomo.com/intangible-asset-market-value-study/) indicates that their definition of "intellectual capital" "refers generally to traditional Intellectual Property assets—patents, trademarks and copyrights. At Ocean Tomo, we uniquely include within the definition of 'intellectual capital' special client intangible assets, especially corporate and government preference rights."
93. It follows as the authors of the same study (Korinek and Ng, 2019:12; also, Crouzet and Eberly, 2019) expect that the

    rise in concentration of ownership of intangible assets suggests that the largest firms are owning increasing shares of assets that have the potential to replace traditional factor inputs in the production process. Firm owners of the largest firms can then reap the yields on intangible assets, to the exclusion of traditional factor inputs and smaller firms.

94. David Autor et al. (2020:650) not only doubt the principle of a general declining share of labor, but also indicate based on their firm level empirical analysis that "the fall in the labor share is largely due to the reallocation of sales and value added between firms rather than a general fall in the labor share for the average firm." Competition has changed with the advantages now going to large corporations with superior, innovative quality of commodities and services, and lower costs who disproportionally garner greater benefits compared to past market conditions. Superstar firms have higher
    mark-ups and a lower share of labor costs in relation to sales and value-added accounting for the overall declined in labor share (Autor et al., 2020:702–703). Gilbert Cette, Lorraine Koehl and Thomas Philippon (2020) also express doubt about the validity of the declining labor share based on three issues: (1) the failure to include real estate income, (2) accounting for self-employment and the (3) starting point of the statistical account.
95. In the meantime, a vast literature identifying a range of factors has emerged that attempts to measure and explain the decline in the labor share in national income that has occurred in recent times not only in the United States but also elsewhere (see Grossman and Oberfield, 2021).
96. Thomas Piketty ([2019] 2020:665) notes that the value of technology companies listed on the stock market "includes patents and know-how that might not exist were it not for basic research financed with public money and accumulated over decades. Such appropriation of common knowledge could increase dramatically in the coming century."
97. Katharina Pistor (2020:103) defines the basis of asymmetric power of big tech companies as monopolizing and monetizing the information content and power of disposal over data by granting them only selective access to the data they obtain.
98. Another, perhaps competing concept is that of "technoscientitic capitalism" advanced by Kean Birch (2020):

    technoscientific capitalism is characterized by the (re) configuration of a range of "things" (e.g., infrastructure, data, knowledge, bodies) as assets of capitalized property. . . . Technoscientific capitalism is increasingly underpinned by rentiership or the appropriation of value through ownership and control rights.

    The concept of technoscientitic capitalism inherits, so it seems, the difficulties of the perspective of technological determinism, the failure to differentiate between information (data) and knowledge as well as between tangible and intangible property. Economic historians, as is well known, have repeatedly and for a long time highlighted the role of technological change for economic development.

99. Not all or many intellectual constructs can become legal constructs where encoding and control rests on the intervention of the state.
100. A paper on the future of American power (Nye, 2010) refers to the strong correlation

 between the number of H-1B visas and the number of patents filed in the United States. In 1998, Chinese- and Indian-born engineers were running one-quarter of Silicon Valley's high-tech businesses, and in 2005, immigrants were found to have helped start one of every four American technology start-ups over the previous decade.

 Despite the efforts of the Trump administration of the day, the linkages have not much changed to this day.
101. "Apple, Google and a Deal That Controls the Internet," *New York Times*, October 25, 2020.
102. Although market power and monopoly power are linked, they are not the same thing. The conventional definition of market power includes the ability to achieve prices that are higher than those that would be achieved on an unrestricted competitive market. Monopoly power is conventionally understood as the power to control market-wide prices or to exclude others from competition. In other words, market power can be defined as power over one's own price, while monopoly power can be defined as power over market prices.
103. And in this respect, knowledge monopoly capitalism is a novel development of capitalism that differs significantly from the capitalism model analyzed by Karl Marx or, more recently, by Harry Braverman (1974). In my model of knowledge monopoly capitalism, patents (knowledge capital) are used as the sword. As one executive threatened another executive in 2008 during a dispute about voice recognition software: "I have (voice recognition) patents that can prevent you from practicing in this market." The company defended itself in court; and won the case. It was too late, however, because the cost of $3 million of the lawsuit drove the company into financial ruin and sold the company to the opponent (*New York Times,* "Tech Giants' Legal Warfare Takes Toll on Innovation," October 8, 2012).
104. According to calculations by Japanese scientists, the *knowledge advantage* of the TESLA automobile company over its most important competitors VW and Toyota amounts to approximately six years:

 > The module—released last spring and found in all new [Tesla] Model 3, Model S and Model X vehicles—includes two custom, 260-sq.-millimeter AI chips. Tesla developed the chips on its own, along with special software designed to complement the hardware. The computer powers the cars' self-driving capabilities as well as their advanced in-car "infotainment: system. The Model 3's :full self-driving computer: consists of two boards: one with custom AI chips for autonomous driving, and a media control unit for the "infotainment" system. A water-cooled heat sink is installed between the two boards. (Nikkei xTech). This kind of electronic platform, with a powerful computer at its core, holds the key to handling heavy data loads in tomorrow's smarter, more autonomous cars. Industry insiders expect such technology to take hold around 2025 at the earliest. That means Tesla beat its rivals by six years.
 >
 > (*Source*: https://asia.nikkei.com/Spotlight/Most-read-in-2020/Tesla-teardown-finds-electronics-6-years-ahead-of-Toyota-and-VW)

105. Source: "Patents; Putting a value on the intangible: Patents," *New York Times* (online), December 18, 2000.
106. However, patents awarded to smaller companies can of course have major drawbacks for large corporations if they are found by the courts to be in violation of the patent of a small company: The experience of the Daimler corporation is a relevant example. A heating system installed in the head part of the seating system

of a series of convertible cars lead to a legal challenge of the patent holder of the heat system. In 2016, Daimler had to suspend the production of the cabriolet. Only after paying a hefty sum to the patent holder was Daimler able to resume selling the cabriolet (cf. "Patente mit Drohpotential," *Frankfurter Allgemeine Zeitung*, February 23, 2021). The case may contribute to a change in the patent law: the German Ministry of Justice is contemplating a change that would prohibit a patent holder from insisting of the range of their rights if the consequences on the other side are disproportional.

107. Apple is, in 2020, the most valuable publicly traded company in the world by a considerable margin: 2 trillion dollars vs. 1,6 trillion in the case of Microsoft.
108. An informative "anatomy of patents" can be found in Morrison (2019: 14–15).
109. Major acquisitions of patent pools include Google's (defensive) purchase of roughly 17,000 patents from Motorola Mobility for $12.5 billion and Microsoft's acquisition of Nokia's patents for $5.4 Billion.
110. Thomas Piketty ([2013] 2014:14–15) counters Kuznets, "the theory of the 'Kuznet curve' was a product of the cold war" and explains instead that

> the sharp reduction of income inequality that we observe in almost all the rich countries between 1914 and 1945 was due above all to the world wars and the violent economic and political shocks they entailed (especially for people with large fortunes). It had little to do with the tranquil process of intersectoral mobility described by Kuznets.

A research question that at least some economists have been asking recently is whether a kind of second wave of the Kuznets Theorem might possibly occur; out of the persistently increasing social inequality, a new alignment of social differences could follow in the future (e.g., Milanovic, 2016).

111. See also the section on patents and the price of knowledge in Stehr and Voss, 2020:287–293.
112. There is also the by no means insignificant case that knowledge does not need to be protected separately, that knowledge protects itself; I have analyzed this possibility in more detail elsewhere (Stehr, 2005:40–43)
113. The following figures are all taken from the annual report of the *World Intellectual Property Organization* (WIPO, 2020).
114. It should be noted that an international treaty

> administered by WIPO, the Patent Cooperation Treaty (PCT) allows applicants to seek patent protection for an invention simultaneously in a large number of countries by filing a single PCT international application. The granting of patents remains under the control of national and regional patent offices and is carried out in what is called the "national phase" or "regional phase." International patent applications filed via the PCT grew by 5.2% (265,800 applications) in 2019, representing a tenth consecutive year of growth. Applicants residing in China (58,990) filed the greatest number of PCT patent applications in 2019, followed closely by applicants from the U.S. (57,840) and Japan (52,660). Germany and the Republic of Korea ranked fourth and fifth, respectively, with 19,353 and 19,085 applications.
> (World Intellectual Property Organization, 2020:20)

115. Perhaps not surprisingly, aside from the possibility in certain countries that allow for an regular extension of the patent, there are (clever) long practiced ways of legally encoding the life span of knowledge beyond the limitations specified in patent law (cf. Pistor, 2019:108; also known as "zombie" patents); for example, through a what is called a "chain patent": A study of "Cartels, patents and politics" from 1945 (Hamilton, 1945:587–588) notes,

> As inventions runs thin, numbers make up for a dearth of novelty and through the "chain patent" a continuity is given to the legal sanction. In respect to the

telephone, shoe machinery and the recording of music, the foundation patents expired several times 17 years ago. But by piling improvements upon improvements upon improvements, these processes of production are more adequately guarded than ever before.

116. According to the *New York Times*, the company Moderna which has not previously brought a product to market, received $10 billion in government funds to develop the corona vaccine (cf. Sheryl Gay Stolberg and Rebecca Robbins, "Moderna and U.S. at Odds over Vaccine Patent Rights, *New York Times* November 9, 2021).
117. Until recently,

> allowing pharmaceutical patents was the exception and not the rule around the world. . . . Many countries in the "Global South" resisted making patents available for pharmaceutical products. . . . Drug companies and their representatives were among the leading advocates of TRIPS.
>
> (Shadlen et al., 2020:78–79)

118. David Autor et al. (2020:703) report that the increase in market concentration is most noticeable "in industries that experience more rapid technological change as measured by the growth of patent intensity". Simcha Barkar (2010:2460) results demonstrate, that "increases in industry concentration are associated with declines in the labor share. Taken as a whole, my results suggest that the decline in the shares of labor and capital are due to a decline in competition." Michele Boldrin and David Levine (2013:3), who have extensively made the case against patents laws, argue "there is no empirical evidence that [patents] serve to increase innovation and productivity, unless productivity is identified with the number of patents awarded—which, as evidence shows, has no correlation with measured productivity."
119. Concurrent or by-products benefit for patent holders, especially derived from internet dominance or control (algorithms), in the for harvested from the use of the internet by customers of hard devices or from the use of software on hard devices that can be utilized for business purposes but do not have to be shared. Concrete figures that illustrate the dominance of the superstars on the internet traffic: "The big five internet giants—Google, Amazon, Facebook, Netflix and Microsoft—currently account for nearly 60 percent of all 'prime-time' [identical with the classical prime-time television period] traffic" (Winseck, 2019:106). Whether the internet is—as once was the consensus a source of emancipation or, as now increasingly feared, a source of repression and control is a function of who monopolizes access to the information of the internet (see Stehr and Adolf, 2017:175–187).
120. The number of "triadic family patents" (that is, "A triadic patent family is defined as a set of patents registered in various countries (i.e., patent offices) to protect the same invention. Triadic patent families are a set of patents filed at three of these major patent offices: the European Patent Office (EPO), the Japan Patent Office (JPO) and the United States Patent and Trademark Office (USPTO). Triadic patent family counts are attributed to the country of residence of the inventor and to the date when the patent was first registered. This indicator is measured as a number") has been steadily and significantly on the increase since 1985 (cf. the OECD calculation: https://data.oecd.org/rd/triadic-patent-families.htm).
121. The United States, Britain, Canada, Switzerland, Norway, and the European Union, among others, are blocking a proposal from October 2020 at the *World Trade Organization* "put forward by India and South Africa in October, [that] calls on the W.T.O. to exempt member countries from enforcing some patents, trade secrets or pharmaceutical monopolies under the organization's agreement on trade-related intellectual property rights, known as TRIPs." As reported by Achmal Prabbala, Arjun Jayadev and Dean Baker, "Want vaccines fast? Suspend intellectual property rights" (*New York Times*, December 7, 2020),

> The U.S. trade representative is reported to have said that protecting intellectual property rights and otherwise "facilitating incentives for innovation and

competition" was the best way to ensure the "swift delivery" of any vaccines and treatments. The European Union has argued that there was "no indication that intellectual property rights issues have been a genuine barrier in relation to Covid-19-related medicines and technologies.

The British mission to the W.T.O. agrees, characterizing the waiver proposal as "an extreme measure to address an unproven problem."

122. As financial assets, what counts in the case of patents is the property right itself as a financial vehicle and not the patented invention, that is, "the future return expected on the intellectual property right as a forward-looking investment vehicle" (Kang, 2020:53).
123. Saez and Zucman (2016) tax data show that 90 percent of wealth (or capital income) in the United States is owned by the top 10 percent and approximately 50 percent by the top 1 percent.
124. Until about the middle of the 1980s, the number of patents applied for in the USA was largely stable. In 2015, the number of patent applications and the number of patents granted in the USA increased six-fold. This explosive development in patent numbers likely due to TRIPS also applies to many other countries (see also table). Jeffrey Funk (2018:50) estimates that the cost for applying for a patent on the United States could reach $50,000—perhaps distracting many companies from applying, in the first instance.
125. Aram Sinnreich (2019:155–156) list the most important legal extensions of patent law that the TRIPS agreement generated as well as the enforcement measures and sanctions that are part of the agreement:

> The new laws imposed by TRIPS included new forms of intellectual property (such as semiconductor chip rights), new categories of protected expression (such as software, databases, and sound recordings for copyright and "virtually all subject matter" other than living organisms for patents), longer minimum terms for both copyrights (life plus fifty years) and patents (twenty years), mandatory enforcement protocols within member states and at borders, and mandatory criminal punishment, including imprisonment, for some forms of infringement (historically, IP has been considered more of an issue for civil law, which seeks compensation rather than punishment from those who have violated it).

126. Article 7 (Objectives) of the TRIPS agreement states:

> The protection and enforcement of intellectual property rights should contribute to the promotion of technological innovation and to the transfer and dissemination of technology, to the mutual advantage of producers and users of technological knowledge and in a manner conducive to social and economic welfare, and to a balance of rights and obligations.

Article 8.2. adds:

> Appropriate measures, provided that they are consistent with the provisions of this Agreement, may be needed to prevent the abuse of intellectual property rights by right holders or the resort to practices which unreasonably restrain trade or adversely affect the international transfer of technology.

127. Joseph Stiglitz (2006:105) is very explicit in his judgment about whose interests were at stake in negotiating of the TRIPs agreement: TRIPs "had been long sought by the United States and other advanced industrial countries in order to force other countries to recognize their patents and copyrights . . . TRIPs was designed to ensure higher -prices medicines." A US Consular official in China who preferred to remain anonymous is quoted in an essay in the *New York Times*: "Nothing has a higher priority in our trade policy than the fight to protect American intellectual property. It is every bit as important an effort for us as the war against weapons of mass destruction" (Ted Fishman, "Manufaketure," *New York Times*, January 9, 2005, p. 40).

128. See "Inventor challenges a sweeping revision in patent law," *The New York Times*, August 26, 2012.
129. Writing on the history of intellectual property laws, Hannes Siegrist (2019:32; also, Machlup, 1958) notes, that the

    concept of intellectual property emerges from the formative periods of modern culture, science and economics. It was developed in the eighteenth and nineteenth centuries in American and European culture-producing states with the objective of protecting the individual creative and commercial work of certain groups of the affluent and educated middle classes and protecting their special entitlements and special position during the transition from traditional aristocratic and profession-based society to modern class society.

    Whether patent legislation from an analog age can still fulfill its function in a digital age is an open question.
130. For American universities it is in addition relevant that they were allowed to patent research successes achieved with the help of state funding under the Bayh-Dole Act passed in 1980. However, the number of patents granted to US universities had already increased before 1980, but after 1980 it rose by 300 percent (see Berman, 2008).
131. The following figures are all taken from the annual report of the *World Intellectual Property Organization* (WIPO, 2020).
132. The "belief in the 'legality' of patterns of normative rules and the right of those elevated to authority under such rules to issue commands" constitutes the foundation of legal authority (Weber, [1922] 1964: 328).
133. Compare Nico Stehr, „Wie das globale Impfstoff-Wissen das Ende der Pandemie beeinflusst" ("How global vaccine knowledge is influencing the end of the pandemic"), *Frankfurter Allgemeine Zeitung*, 30. April 2021; www.faz.net/aktuell/feuilleton/debatten/wie-das-globale-impfstoff-wissen-das-ende-der-pandemie-beeinflusst-17318991.html; and „EU-Ratspräsident sieht in Patentfreigabe für Impfstoffe ‚keiner Wunderlösung" ("EU Council President sees 'no miracle solution' in patent release for vaccines"), *Der Standard*, Mai 8, 2021; www.derstandard.at/story/2000126498480/eu-ratspraesident-sieht-in-patentfreigabe-fuer-impfstoffe-keine-wunderloesung
134. One should not underestimate the flexibility of large tech companies—as owners of the tech infrastructure—in the face of civil society's demand for more privacy, to use AI to find ways to circumvent privacy measures in order to continue to be profitable while seemingly reaching out to their critics.
135. Joseph Schumpeter's apology of temporary monopolies referred, of course, to a time when the balance of private and public interests in knowledge content was different than it is today. The scope of corporate interests in the totality of (productive) knowledge has grown exponentially since the 1940s (see Burlamaqui, 2012).
136. Joseph Schumpeter's perspective is anticipated by classical economists; John Stuart Mill ([1848] 2004:849) for example defends temporary monopolies:

    The condemnation of monopolies ought not to extend to patents, by which the originator of an improved process is allowed to enjoy, for a limited period, the exclusive privilege of using his own improvement. This is not making the commodity dear for his benefit, but merely postponing a part of the increased cheapness which the public owe to the inventor, in order to compensate and reward him for the service.

137. The "reward theory" is an expression introduced, as far as I can see by Edmund Kitch (1977:266). Joseph Schumpeter's reward theory clashes strongly with Benjamin Franklin's sentiments:

    In 1742, Benjamin Franklin invented a new type of stove, for which he was offered a patent. Franklin refused it, arguing in his autobiography that because "we

> enjoy[ed] great advantages from the inventions of others, we should be glad of an opportunity to serve others by any invention of ours."
>
> (cited in *The Economist*, "Patents that kill," August 8, 2014)

138. Reto Hilty, "Patente sichern schnelle Impfung," *Frankfurter Allgemeine Zeitung*, February 24, 2021.
139. The *International Science Council* (February 2021) draws attention to this issue in a news release:

    > Significant developments are being made in relation to IP domains. These unprecedent efforts by governments should help ensure patents don't obstruct the fight against the pandemic and ensure access for the South. These developments also shine a light on future possibilities that could lead to further technological advancements and tackle the strong need for equitable and inclusive access to innovations for the wider community.

140. Patents limit, for example, in the choice of the kind of scientific research that is followed, that is, is permissible (cf. Sarewitz, 2010).
141. Worldwide, there were approximately 15 million active patents in 2019. In the years from 2005 to 2017, the number of active patents (patents in force) increased from 434,663 to 657,749 in Germany and from 1,683,968 to 2,984,825 in the United States; the top five patent offices (China, USA, South Korea, Japan, EU) accounted for 84.7 percent of the 3.2 million patent applications filed worldwide in 2019. This is 8.3 percentage points higher than their combined share in 2009 a decade earlier. China's office alone received 43.4 percent of the global total in 2019.
142. Such a case is advanced by Hans Radder (2019): Moving from commodification to the common good. His focus is mainly the commodification of academic research examined from the perspective of the philosophy of science and technology.
143. Binyamin Appelbaum, "Why are tech companies pretending to be governments?", *New York Times*, May 19, 2021; www.nytimes.com/2021/05/19/opinion/amazon-facebook-government.html?action=click&module=Opinion&pgtype=Homepage
144. Not part of this brief discussion of alternative diagnoses are at times widely discussed notion such as the "transformation society", "experience society" (*Erlebnisgesellschaft*), "liquid modernity", "learning economy/society".
145. In the context of discussing ways of measuring the quality of life that transcend the conventional economic indicator of the GNP, Albert Hirschman (1989) asks whether "having an opinion" is a good that should be incorporated into a measure of the quality of life of a country. Hirschman (1989:77) offers the following assessment employing the language of economics:

    > The forming and acquiring of opinions yields considerable utility to the individual. At the same time, if carried beyond some point, the process has dangerous side effects—it is hazardous for the functioning and stability of the democratic order. Under present cultural values these side effects do not enter the individual calculus—they are like external diseconomies.

146. The term *network society* may be found in Peter Drucker's 1995 (March 29) article in the *Wall Street Journal*, "The Network Society", in which he describes a trend in employment patterns that finds a large minority of employees, especially among those that are part of the knowledge work force, working for an organization but who are not employed by the organization—hence the stress on networking tasks.
147. Manuel Castells' theory of informational capitalism has a close affinity to the idea of "digital capitalism" (Nachtwey and Staab, 2015) or "digital economics" (Goldfarb and Tucker, 2919)—already in existence, the claim is, within major multinational corporations; "research in digital economics examines whether and how digital technology changes economic activity" (Goldfarb and Tucker, 2019:3).However, it is noteworthy that the authors are able to advance their technology centered theory

without any reference to patent laws as one of the central foundations of the power of large modern corporations Neither theoretical approach therefore requires a new economic theory: "Digital economics explores how standard economic models change as certain costs fall substantially and perhaps approach zero: (Goldfarb and Tucker, 2019:3).

148. In an essay in a collection of essays from 2000, Castell (2000:61–63) deals with the invisible productivity surge and blames two reasons (1) the lack of adequate statistical data and (2) the time lag between investments and manifest revenues. The first obstacle continues to exist, as Castells emphasizes in the same context; the returns on investment in modern computer technology are observable, with the expected delay in case of the US economy.

149. In a justification for assigning a core function to the new information of communication technologies in economic restructuring, Castells and Henderson (1987:5), using Colin Clark's (1940) likely obsolete three economic sector hypothesis, precisely stress the contribution to a "*qualitative* increase in productivity, across the board, in manufacturing, agriculture . . . and services. In fact, productivity growth is particularly crucial in the service sector of the economy" (emphasis added). The qualification of a merely "qualitative" rise in productivity by Castells and Henderson can of course be interpreted to constitute a cautionary but deliberate qualification of their universal thesis of a productivity growth in response to corporate and state investments in information technologies.

150. Manuel Castells (1996:17) emphasizes for example why he cannot detect any persuasive reasons for disagreeing with the reductionist definition of (theoretical) knowledge advocated by Daniel Bell (1973:175) in his theory of post-industrial society. "Information technology" is defined by Castells (1996:30) in such a fashion that is in important respects identical with scientific work: "I also include in the realm of information technologies genetic engineering"; perhaps one could add climate science, cognitive science, econometric modeling, impact assessment as further examples and therefore scientific fields that resonate strongly with Bell's conception theoretical knowledge.

151. One ambivalent reference designed to explain why an informational society should be called a network society may be found hidden in a footnote: "one of the key features of informational society is the networking logic of its basis structure" (Castells, 1996:21).

152. As David Nye (1997:180) in his enlightening examination of the deployment of narratives to understand technology in this 20th century observes,

> the misleading sense of determinism so common to technological narratives is fostered in part by the Cartesian sense of space, which seems to predicate linear developments seen in log perspective. In this neutral space, the world is raw material, waiting to be worked up, and it offers only temporary resistance to what seems an inexorable sequence of events.

153. Cal Newport (2021:103) advances the following thesis, written in *future* tense, called the "attention capital principle": "The productivity of the knowledge sector can be significantly increased if we identify workflows that better optimize the human brain's ability to sustainably add value to information."

154. Charles Jones (2021:12) calculates for the United States, without specifying the contribution of the individual factors in more detail, that

> the ultimate source of long-run economic growth is population growth; historical growth accounting suggests that population growth accounts for only around 20% of U.S. growth in recent decades. The remaining 80% is accounted for by rising educational attainment, increases in the fraction of the population devoted to R&D, and declines in misallocation.

My emphasis is on the increase in the skills (knowledge capabilities) of the workforce.

155. According to the *Washington Post*, in December of 2020, the Chinese Government, for example, announced

> a multi-pronged antitrust investigation Thursday into its most successful Internet company, making moves that could potentially break up Alibaba's sprawling e-commerce business or splinter its highly lucrative financial services affiliate. While it has grown into the dominant player in Chinese online shopping—now raking in $50 billion a year in revenues—Alibaba in the last decade has steadily encroached on China's tightly controlled financial sector through its Ant Group spin-off. Ant Group, a $16 billion-a-year business, has been chipping away at powerful state banks' market share and unnerving regulators with investment and lending products that have become so popular that Ant sometimes acts as a lender to government banks—not the other way around. . . . China's State Administration for Market Regulation said it would look into complaints from online merchants about Alibaba's demands for exclusivity deals. In a simultaneous announcement, banking regulators said they were summoning Ant Group executives for discussions about the financial platform's competitive and consumer protection practices.
> ("China launches antitrust investigation into Alibaba, its most successful Internet company", Washington Post, December 24, 2020)

156. In the Fall of 2021, the European Commission proposed a "Digital Market Act" (DMA) that aims at preventing superstar firms from misusing their market power. In contrast to typical anti-trust legislation which tends to look to the past deeds, the DMA attempts to be forward looking (*ex ante* rules) by outlawing certain types of conduct that tend to cement Superstar market power (cf. https://ec.europa.eu/info/strategy/priorities-2019-2024/europe-fit-digital-age/digital-markets-act-ensuring-fair-and-open-digital-markets_en
157. The most recent history as well as the ongoing impact of Covid-19 on economic globalization shows how fragile as well as resilient globalization can be. The question remains whether the Covid-19 pandemic will have lasting structural effects on the global economy or rather short-term financial and economic consequences.
158. A report for the European Union (June 2015) concludes:

> The study shows that large companies are four times more likely to own IP rights than smaller companies—40% of larger firms have registered rights, compared with 9% of SMEs. It also shows that companies that own IP rights perform better than those that do not. This is a particularly significant finding for the 1.8 million SMEs [small and medium sized enterprises] that have registered IP rights, since they represent such an important part of the EU economy. The results demonstrate that businesses that own Intellectual Property Rights generate more revenue per employee than those that do not, have more employees and pay higher salaries to their workers and that this relationship is particularly strong for SMEs.

4

THE POLITICS OF KNOWLEDGE CAPITALISM

> Mankind thus inevitably sets itself only such tasks as it is able to solve, since closer examination will always show that the problem itself arises only when the material conditions for its solution are already present or at least in the course of formation.
>
> —Karl Marx [1859] 1977

In the Preface to *A Contribution to the Critique of Political Economy*, Karl Marx writes that the problems the politics of societies take on board are restricted to those that it can solve. It would appear that we are entering a different age if the diagnosis Marx provided was even adequate for the times he had in mind.

In the following chapter, I will describe and critically examine a number of remarkable features of the dynamics of knowledge societies as they have evolved into the *Gestalt* of knowledge capitalism, in particular some of the central policy fields of knowledge societies that all appear to defy Marx's restrictive observation. The policy problems knowledge societies face now often include *"wicked" problems*, that is, problems that cannot be "solved". From a theoretical perspective, I will ask how one of the salient features of the knowledge society, the fact that the agency of individuals and small groups of individuals, for example, the management of superstar corporations, small investors, political activists, or the leadership of new social movements, has expanded considerably, see for example the success of individual politicians in *democratic* societies, affects the political processes of knowledge societies. For example, one of the significant emerging fields of political activity of knowledge societies are a virtually new field of politics, namely *knowledge politics*, that is, *efforts to nationally and/or internationally control additional or incremental knowledge.*

DOI: 10.4324/9781003296157-4

A UNESCO (2016) report entitled *Knowledge Societies Policy Handbook* also identified—but in anticipatory support—the emergence of knowledge *policies* as a new field of public policy. The Report (UNESCO, 2016:14–15) observes that

> knowledge policies are becoming a progressively significant element of Knowledge Societies, and the knowledge economies. Such policies make available institutional grounds for creating, managing, and using organizational knowledge as well as social foundations for harmonizing global competitiveness with social order, social welfare, environmental sustainability and diverse cultural values.

More specifically, the Report (UNESCO, 2016:15) adds, "social knowledge policies represent equilibrium between technological evolution, and advancement in the knowledge economy to promote global competitiveness with social values, such as transparency, equity, unity, freedom of expression, and the well-being of citizens."

In other words, the description of the UNESCO refers to (conventional) science and technology policies, educational policy, or competition policies, and therefore the extension of public policies well entrenched in industrial societies These policies, as a result, are not new and cannot be described as an emerging field of public policy activity in knowledge societies. What is novel although not entirely unique are policy proposals or efforts to regulate and control additional knowledge.[1]

From a *practical political* point of view, I would like to draw attention above all to one policy field that is not necessarily relevant in the short term, but is largely new, namely how society and the state deal with new knowledge (*knowledge politics*). In stressing that my analysis of the politics of knowledge societies is not primarily tied to what appear to be pressing issues of the contemporary theoretical and practical agendas of the day, for example, whether democracies are in decline, populism has attained a central status in the political processes of the present, *Völkerwanderungen* (mass migrations) are at the helm of ongoing political conflicts, whether pandemics are at the helm of massive societal changes or the end of triumphant globalization will give way to the solidarity of the societies of the world, I want to signal that I am more concerned with certain political issues that are on the horizon, for example climate change, knowledge politics, patent policies and the transformation of the world of work. This is not to say that echoes of political conflicts of the present will not persist well into future and continue to be part of emerging political struggles, for example that the immense, existing societal power and economic monopolies of the *Superstar corporations* will not continue to be one of the critical political issues of the coming years. Although motivation may differ, different jurisdictions, the European Commission, the United States Administration headed by President Biden and China have in 2021 started to reign into the power of superstar corporations announcing that they would unveil far-reaching regulations and legal norms to somehow limit technologies powered by *artificial intelligence* (AI).

It is worth repeating that the politics of knowledge societies revolve around, more than any other factor, the generalized enlargement of the capacities to act of (almost) all members of modern societies. The overall enlargement of the capacity to act is uneven as are the capacities to act itself and they therefore sustain and cement one of the elementary facets of human society, their essential inequality. Although the enlargement of the capacity to act—currently further expanded by the possibility of digital activism—is a fundamental attribute of the members of modern society; its real efficacy occurs in conjunction with the command of other basic social attributes such as power, authority, energy, social control, knowledge, charisma, or wealth and at the same time signals the importance of knowledge monopoly capitalism as a framework for this societal development. The politics of knowledge societies are further linked to and embedded in the widely discussed issue of the general emancipation of members of society through knowledge and the possibility that modern societies as knowledge societies are fragile entities, that is, knowledge societies are increasingly the result of human activity rather adaptations to processes over which they had little if any control.

Actors with capacities to act

The more comprehensive, disproportionate increase in the chances for action (compared to earlier forms of society) can be observed particularly for the lower status groups in society who in earlier forms of society where mainly victims, i.e. especially in the case of individual actors and/or intermediary social groups. The new reality of politics is pluralism and diversity; the body politics is that "of the new 'mass movements': small, highly organized minorities, single cause or single interest in their focus, and totally political" (Drucker, [1989] 2003:55). The new reality of the political is a function or consequence of the massive expansion of the capacity of citizens in society to act, and the new reality of politics makes for novel and different demands on the political elite.

In this context, it is important to stress that the expansion of individuals' opportunities for action, for example, in the sense of *civil society* networks/aggregates, does not correspond to a parallel increase in the opportunities for action of the *major social institutions* (state, economy, religion, science). On the contrary, in historical comparison there is an imbalance in the development trend of the abilities of institutions and individuals to assert their will.

The description of modern society in terms of its liquidity, creativity, flexibility, reflexivity and similar terms therefore does not primarily apply to major social institutions but to the openness of individuals and small groups of actors which in turn contributes to a decline in the influence of major societal institutions. Therefore, from the point of view of the large social institutions, one can rightly speak of the *fragility (instability) of modern societies* (Stehr, 2001). However, this cannot mean that the state, science, religion, or the economy of society are completely powerless. It means that their conventional richness of societal power is significantly curtailed. Perhaps not surprisingly, large social institutions, in the process, have lost public confidence. Trust in social institutions is not least a function of their real possibilities for shaping the future.

From the point of the individual, the experience of the fragility of modern societies is tempered by the experienced facticity that collective actions assure that the basic existential conditions individuals face are attended to successfully by large social intuitions, the state, science, economy, religion, or education. Experiences of the failure and the limits of planning are often hidden from the individual.

On the other hand, Zygmunt Bauman's (2001:149) observation that the confidence "of being in control of one's destiny, is what men and women in our type of society most conspicuously lack" is not mistaken. The lack of conscious self-assertion, however, does not apply without qualification to the totality of individuals in modern society. The sense of being without control over important elements of one's lifeworld is just as politically significant as is the awareness of having control over one's lifeworld. That is, the incisive reference to the simultaneity of the non-simultaneous applies. With this necessary caution, we can nevertheless observe a tendency (the balance) to expand the individual's ability to act in knowledge societies.

The enlargement of the ability to make one's voice politically heard represents, more precisely, the *condition for the possibility* of gaining political influence. The extension of the capacity to act of individuals and small groups of actors does not by itself assure success the of the desired goals. It takes more that the enhancement of capacities for action to actually to succeed in the body of politics. Three examples from business, politics, and law may serve as illustrations of the importance and complexity of expanding the scope of action for members of society. The stories, briefly recounted later, about the Arab Spring, the Friday's for Future movement, and the GameStop rebellion are all stories about the allegedly weak in society who organize against the powerful of society.[2]

However, examples from the social sphere do not exhaust the ways in which our enhanced capacity to act impact on society. Discoveries made in the natural sciences as they become active in society can be powerful examples as well. The recently discovered technology for making precise changes to the genome is maturing quickly, most notably with the (heritable) gene editing tool CRISPR (=clusters of regularly interspaced short palindromic repeats)—for which Jennifer Doudna and Emmanuelle Charpentier won the 2020 Nobel Prize in Chemistry—would be such an example. At the same time, the editing tool CRISPR is a perfect example, as I will note, for the nature of knowledge politics, the pressure to politically reign into the use of novel scientific or technical knowledge. The challenge of knowledge politics in the case of the CRISPR technique extend, for example, to the question whether and to what extent the technology should be patented or not.[3] The possibility of targeted molecular intervention, probably not only in the case of diseases, will provoke societal reactions and eventually politically sanctioned regulations and sanctions of the application of this new knowledge.[4]

The common attributes of the three cases, more directly linked to a social science perspective, are that the social movements—engendered by the enhancement of capacities to act—are not initiated, led and organized by elites, supported by undemocratic leadership with democratic ambitions (as described by Robert Michels) or a set of powerful, dogmatic ideas; nor are these movements and rebellions always successful.

The origins and the ultimate failure of the ambitions of those in Middle Eastern societies who struggled to realize the political and economic aims of what became known as the Arab Spring more than a decade ago, are good examples of the dilemma of the enlargement of capacities to act of certain strata of society and their ability to translate these skills into lasting political and economic enhancements for themselves.

Robert Barro and Lee Jong Wha (2010) have documented in what way the rapid increase in schooling (as a proxy for capacities for action) in these countries of the Middle East affected the political upheavals:

> Egypt and Tunisia, for instance, all registered large gains in total years of schooling among the population aged 15 and above, respectively rising from 2.6 to 7.1 years and from 3.2 to 7.3 years between 1980 and 2010. Out of the top 20 countries in the world as ranked by increases in general schooling during this period, there were eight Arab League countries.
>
> (Campante and Chor, 2011:1)

By the same token, the participation of women—not only well-educated women appear to have been a significant part of the move toward a democratic polity in these countries.

The significant and rapid increase in the schooling of large cohorts of the younger population of course as well as their access to global information streams raises the question to what extent these skills, and their allied expectations about adequate economic rewards are translated into gainful employment—or into political activities, should a country fail to provide satisfactory financial compensation and jobs that require the skills gained. Campante and Chor's (2012) study offers a compelling answer to the question of the impact of schooling on political activities and economic expectations in societies with a low-skilled economy, but a rapid increase in the skill levels of significant portions of their population: the economies of the Middle East are, as yet, typically not skill-intensive economies. The Arab world for the most part lags behind other world regions in building knowledge-based economies. Thus, it would appear that "an interaction between individual skills and the dearth of economic opportunities that reward those skills lies at the heart of the political turmoil that has shaken the Arab world" (Campante and Chor, 2012:8422). The evidence presented by Campante and Chor (2011:20) shows that "individuals whose income underperforms what would have been predicted given their level of schooling are more inclined to use their human capital in political activities such as demonstrations, strikes, and occupation of buildings."

The 2021 *GameStop* rebellion by small investors against large hedge funds is another example—and as "Economist Mohamed El-Erian said the Reddit-fueled trading phenomenon against Wallsteet players has all the elements of the Arab Spring, and he totally gets where the anger comes from."[5] None of the large stock market investors, pension fund, banks, hedge funds, or wealthy individuals, let alone regulating agencies of the financial markets or politicians, had in early 2021 seen this development coming or had seen anything like this hectic trading of millions of traders.[6] The event that made headlines around the world and rattled large stock market investors and regulators alike is a prime example of the enlargement of the capacity to act of individuals *organizing* using the social media of the day. Until a few years ago, it was hardly conceivable that small investors could have a say in stock market events, let alone influence them.

The rebellion stylized or framed itself as a novel culture of investing—a culture in opposition to the established norms of Wall Street. Wall Street investing is primarily oriented to achieve a profit based on the fundamental value of the underlying corporate activity. The value orientation of the rebellion, perhaps accelerated by the social consequences of the pandemic, was based much more on turning a profit by manipulating the stock market, driving share prices up or down quite independent of the fundamental value of a listed corporation. The self-conception of the rebellion was to focus on what might be called a democratization of investing. The reaction of the conventional culture of investment was one of confusion, chaos, and perhaps accelerating opportunities for the oppositional culture.

Until December of 2020, the shares of GameStop were a relatively lethargic stock on the US market, bouncing around between $15 and $20 a share, as the company in the business of retailing video game struggled to stay to avoid bankruptcy. GameStop was still better than some other failing companies whose business was unfavorably affected not only by the corona pandemic, for example, Nokia or AMC, a movie theater chain. But then in the month of January 2021, small scale, amateur investors (Kleinanleger) using free trading platforms like Robinhood (and the "weapons" of the larger investors) started wagering on this pool of otherwise unremarkable stocks. What happened to GameStop was the tipoff the iceberg.

GameStop trading mania was sparked by members of a popular Reddit investing community who said they hoped to strike back at the Wall Street elites who had long dismissed them as "dumb money". But growing evidence casts doubt on the idea that the episode mostly benefited small-time investors.[7]

At one point, the company's share price was up more than 1,700 percent for the month—a stratospheric rise that made the company worth roughly the same amount as the large corporations of Tyson Foods and Valero Energy. Among the noticeable and intended results was what's known as a short squeeze—an effort to raise the stock's price and pressure the investors who had bet against it. GameStop was suddenly one of the most-traded stocks in the market. Some of the investors, especially hedge funds that had bet against GameStop were forced to close out their positions against the stock at enormous losses. When GameStop's share price took off, the company's on-paper value soared. Its market capitalization—essentially its share price multiplied by its number of shares—rose by billions at a time. A month after it was valued at roughly $2 billion, it was worth nearly $23 billion. The only thing that had really changed was investor interest.

While the investor activities surrounding GameStop and related shares, signaled activities of many thousands of individuals, numerous attracted for the time to become speculators, the downfall of *Archegos Capital Management*, led by Bill Hwang, shortly thereafter, represent the immense ability to act of but a small group of individuals that in turn produced major financial repercussions. As the *New York Times* (March 29, 2001)[8] points out:

> Turmoil surrounding a little-known firm run by a onetime star trader rippled through Wall Street on Monday, exposing banks to billions of dollars in losses and highlighting yet again the potential of individual players to hobble an intricately connected but largely opaque financial system. . . . The impact of Archegos's stumble underscored the risks to the financial system from sophisticated investors who work with Wall Street banks to make bets using leverage. When the going is good, leverage can amplify returns. But on the flip side, it can enlarge relatively minor market setbacks and force a run of selling that takes on a life of its own.

On the surface, the extension of the capacity to act, representing the growth of knowledge (knowledge capacities) in modern society has overlapping consequences classified, in a very preliminary manner as genuine social and individual advances (for example, the extension of life expectancies, the growth of social welfare, advances in physical and mental health, genome editing) or, has created, as Jerald Hage (2020:12) notes, "many of. . . [the] disruptions that are tearing the social fabric of society apart" (alienation, powerlessness, social isolation and social inequality). Whether the terms of the diagnosis are correct and some of the policies that are recommended in response to the assessment of the state of modern society are leitmotifs of the following chapter.

The uneven, non-linear pace at which capacities to act are enlarged generates a new contradiction of knowledge societies: An increasingly large proportion of the public in modern societies for example acquires political skills while the ability of the state and its agencies to "impose its will" or to exercise its sovereignty is arrested, even decreases. More than three decades ago, Ronald Inglehart (1977:317–32; 1990:335–370) examined the enlargement of political skills of the public in Western societies in terms of a shift from "elite-directed" to "elite-challenging" politics to such an extent that "petitions, boycotts and other forms of direct action are no longer unconventional but have become more or less normal actions for a large part of the citizenry of post-industrial societies"). And, contrary "to assumptions that the public is becoming more apathetic, both political interest and discussion have increased in many nations" (Inglehart and Catterberg, 2002:300). The institutions that facilitated political participation in industrial (and perhaps post-industrial) society—for example, political parties, labor unions, and associations—all have weakened and are in decay; increasingly the institutions of past participation are replaced as Inglehart notes by single issue broad based social movements, small scale spontaneous organizations less closely linked to intensive political partisanship, organizations associated with the professions, or civic- and community-based and -oriented collectivities.

The state or government are no longer the sole power center of society. In the sense of the simultaneity of the non-simultaneous, state activities do not simply disappear or cannot even vanish; in the case of some activities, the state becomes "committed to yesterday, to the obsolete, to the no longer productive" (Drucker [1989] 2003:59).

The evolving clash is not between, as was the case in (low-skilled biased) industrial society, culture and civilization resulting in a cultural lag, or between subjective and objective culture ensuing in a cultural tragedy but between individual and collective capacities to act. This certainly would appear to lead to a much more fragile and volatile form of legitimate authority and power of the state and possibly other major social institutions in modern society.

And in that sense, it may be said that the growth and the broader dissemination of knowledge paradoxically produces greater uncertainty and contingency rather than a resolution of disagreements or the basis for a more effective domination by central societal institutions. At least in this sense, it can therefore be concluded that the growth of knowledge and its increasing social dissemination paradoxically produces greater uncertainty and contingency, rather than a resolution of disagreements or a basis for more efficient governance of central social institutions.

This development is thus in strict contradiction to the dire warnings about the emergence and the rule of the so-called "technical state" in the 1960s. Herbert Marcuse (1964:x) for example, anticipating the dawn of the technical state, made the following depressing observation, which on the one hand was true but on the other hand was a misinterpretation: "The capabilities (intellectual and material) of contemporary society are immeasurably greater than ever before—which means that the scope of society's domination over the individual is immeasurably greater than ever before." Undoubtedly, and in comparison, over time, societal institutions gained in influence but the "power" of the dominated gained even more significantly.

In the Sixties, although these conceptions had their intellectual predecessors, both conservative and neo-Marxist thinkers conjured up the image of the impending spiritless technical state and society as technical rationality extends its relentless influence to all sectors of modern life. The domination and closure achieved by science and technology mark the beginning of a singular type of society and the end of individual freedom and of subjectivity. Individuals are in danger of being totally absorbed into a repressive set of productive relations and absolute domination exercised by the state with the help of new forms of control. The predictions of the overwhelming power of scientific-technical knowledge and in its undertow of the state have been realized neither in the social reality nor as self-fulfilling prophecy.

I interpret the considerable modern enlargement of the life expectancy, the informal economy, health, crime, corruption, the success of new political parties and movements, as well as the growth of wealth in modern society as evidence of the diverse capacity of individuals, households, and small groups to take advantage of and benefit from contexts in which the degree of social control exercised by larger (legitimate), social institutions has diminished considerably.

However, much of social science discourse has been fascinated by exactly the opposite phenomenon, namely the probable and dangerous enlargement of the ability of modern social institutions, especially various state institutions but also of large corporations/organizations within the economic sector, the education field, or the health sector to ever more ruthlessly impose its will on its citizens, workers, consumers, tourists, students, or patients. Thus, social theorists were concerned with discovering the conditions that produce and reproduce domination and repression rather than greater autonomy, freedom, and independence. Modern science and technology often were viewed, in the context of such analyses, as the handmaidens of these regressive civilizational developments.

Emancipation through knowledge

A peculiar feature of the heterogeneous discussion of the role of knowledge, information and skills in modern society is how slanted it happens to be, that is, reflections very often are skewed toward and preoccupied with concerns about the repressive potential of growing human knowledge, especially as it enters the "employ" of powerful aggregate agents, be it a social class, the state, a multinational cooperation, the intellectuals, the military-industrial complex, the professions, the estate of science, the Mafia, political parties, the managerial class, and so on. Similarly, at the opposite end of the spectrum, discussions about the social distribution of knowledge in modern society often tend to be concerned with the dispossession of the individual from access to expertise and technical competence reducing him to play the role of helpless victim, exploited consumer, alienated tourist, colonized viewer, bored student, deskilled worker, and directed voter. For example, Zygmunt Bauman (2000:76) supports the idea that the postmodern society is mainly populated by manipulated and powerless consumers rather individuals capable of mounting agency and the ability to produce: "Life organized around consumption . . . must do without norms: it is guided by seduction, ever rising desires and volatile wishes—no longer by normative regulation". Bauman's dark description of a regulated consumer society has only undermined any hopes for democratic conditions. It would indeed be more than merely shortsighted to dismiss the enlargement of the repression in modern societies and the extent to which the repression is based on an extension of the capacities to act by large social institutions. But it would equally imprudent to overlook the socio-political emancipation of ordinary citizens made possible by its enlargement of capacities to act.

If one disregards the ease with which of the repressive effect of knowledge in many interpretations of the social consequences of findings foregrounded, it is striking on the other hand how unreflective knowledge is understood as the immediate foundation of democratic relations and of short-range and long-term policy measures (e.g. in the sense of political planning) in democratic societies. Highlight of such utopian is perhaps the image of a scientific civilization. The limits of the power of scientific knowledge are not a relevant issue within such the context of such a conviction. Our ability to plan—with the toolkit of the sciences—the future of major features of society (based for example on a plan for entire social institution) is, in contrast, limited but not entirely impossible, a discussed in Chapter 2 in the context of the idea of "practical knowledge". Selective access is certainly conceivable. Subsequent planning is often necessitated as the result of a failure of earlier planning (cf. Tenbruck, 1977:139).

Not only have predictions about the pending assent to almost monolithic power and authority of any of these large social formations so far proven to be illusions as history up to this point anyhow demonstrates, discussions about the social role of knowledge have been, for the most part, state-centered, class-centered, profession-centered, science-centered, and so on.

Reflections about the social role of knowledge therefore have rarely invoked that tradition of the Enlightenment which saw knowledge as a strong and peculiar force in the liberation of individuals, citizens, workers, women, and men. Obviously, if it is the case, as Hans Morgenthau (1970:38), for example observes that people have the feeling that they now live in "something approaching a Kafkaesque world, insignificant and at the mercy of unchangeable and invisible forces . . . a world of make-believe, a gigantic hoax", then the Enlightenment project that attributed liberating qualities to knowledge to date has failed miserably and, at best, is a utopian promise that may hardly be closer to realization than in the distant past.

A realistic appraisal, an assessment without illusions, however, has to accept that on balance the enlargement of our capacity to act for some has produced not only elements of liberation but also threatening and risk-rich attributes for the same individuals as well as others, as the critics of the growing role of science and technology have long been able to enumerate.[9] The main barrier to a realistic assessment of the impact of knowledge in modern society has been its taken for granted image as an instrument that "naturally" centralizes power, that has virtually uncontested features suppressing any chance of launching effective resistance, and that sieves off local knowledge and easily succeeds to fill the vacuum.[10]

This image of knowledge as easily controlled underestimates the influence of various factors on the production of knowledge and the difficulties knowledge encounters as it travels across social and cultural contexts. But such difficulties are opportunities for actors encountering authoritative knowledge or "expertise" (cf. Smith and Wynne, 1989). That is to say, the need to continually reappropriate knowledge alone leaves it marks on knowledge and the agents engaged in reappropriation. As actors acquire more and more skills in reappropriating knowledge, they also acquire a greater capacity to act. Setting specific pressures and interests further heighten the possibilities of critically "deconstructing" and reassembling knowledge claims. The social distribution of knowledge is not a zero-sum game. The extension of aggregate knowledge actually may lead, in comparative terms, to an explosion in the capacity of individuals and groups to reappropriate knowledge for their ends, and therefore represent a movement from a situation in which a *few* control circumstances of action to a condition in which *many* exercises some influence.

All this does not mean that ordinary citizens, students, voters, and consumers acquire a strong sense of control over either the circumstances of their day-to-day existence or any secure feeling of comprehension of the events beyond local contexts (cf. Giddens, 1990:146). In short, the general extension of the capacity to act should not be mistaken to mean an abolition of anxiety, risk, luck, and especially conditions of conduct over which only limited control is exercised. However, such is a far cry from virtual individual impotence in the face of conditions of action controlled by a powerful few.

The fragility of knowledge societies

In light of the potential climate change to come, one is well advised to not only keep the congenital frailty of human beings when compared to the immense forces of nature in mind (cf. Braudel, [1979] 1992:50), but also the essential fragility of social structures, especially when judged against the background of the widely imagined and promised stability of our designs directed toward maximizing prediction and control by and for the powerful.

The degree of the fragility of social structures and human constructs in knowledge societies generally increases. This already follows from the observation that knowledge societies are increasingly human constructs with its massive self-induced risk and dangers. For example, there is now an immense stock of objectified knowledge which mediates our relation to nature and to ourselves. Nature is and can scarcely be experienced other than as a human product or within human products, and social relations are mediated by an increasing stock of arrangements of an administrative, legal, or technical kind. The material appropriation of nature means that nature as a whole has gradually been transformed into a human product by super-imposing on it a social structure. This structure is in essence objectified knowledge, namely, an explication and realization of what we know to be the laws of nature extended by engineering design and construction. The self-appropriation of society occurs through an analogous process, namely, by way of the social production and construction of data that are social facts and that constitute the social and political reality, the enforcement of rules that govern social conduct and the bureaucratization of community life.

One of the first characterizations one is able to give of our contemporary societal condition is a mere quantitative diagnosis: the superstructure of society and nature is now so immense that the greater part of the overall social activity is not production but reproduction; in particular, reproduction of knowledge itself, and that means of the conditions which make specific effects and processes possible in the first place. At the same time, the overall level of knowledgeability of each and every individual in society is elevated while the distribution of knowledge is far less concentrated. Thus, one of the better images symbolizing and summing up the nature of the change from industrial to knowledge societies would be to refer to the former as communities and societies organized and controlled in a pyramid-like fashion while the latter type of societies more closely resemble delicate mosaics without definite centers. And this shifts the source of the risks of modern societies or the causes of the growing fragility of knowledge societies. Increasingly, it is the unintended consequences of intentional social action. The new policy fields of the knowledge society are thus often responses to the results of intentional social action that lead to unanticipated hazards and risks; one has to think in this context of global warming. The recognition and the Interpretation of the new field of political conduct brought new actors and movements onto the political scene and contributes to a decline in the interpretive authorly of the large societal institutions,

But first, and for the purpose of contrast, I like to look back to the design and the texture of post-industrial societies as sketched by Daniel Bell. That is, Daniel Bell's *The Coming of Post-Industrial Society* still stands, in many ways, for an intellectual and political era animated by enthusiastic support for and expectation of the benefits which will accrue from planning utopias.

It will be possible, Bell (1973:344), asserts, for example, "to plot alternative futures in different courses, thus greatly increasing the extent to which we can choose and *control* matters that affect our lives". If this proposition has a ring of truth at all, see Afghanistan as a negative example, at least from the perspective of the forces attempting to install democratic governance, it might be accurate, but even in this instance only to a limited degree, at the individual or micro-social level, but that is not necessarily what Bell has in mind. The thesis about the ability to realize planning efforts points much more at the social realities of the collective level. At this level, the assertion about more efficacious planning and, therefore, control over alternative courses of action—take, for example, the goal to significantly alter the structure of inequality in society, bringing democracy to another society or the desire to reduce and perhaps even eliminate certain patterns of conduct—is likely mistaken.

But most of all, one gets such a strong sense of optimism about our ability to construct, plan and control collective relations from above, by governmental and administrative agencies at all levels, and by business or other major social institutions. That this might well be a proposition with dubious assumptions becomes evident even from Bell's own account of the design of post-industrial society. For Bell (1973:159) underlines, for example, that social life in post-industrial societies is that of a "communal society" rather than a "market society". This means that the share of goods and services allocated by public mechanisms or public choice, rather than the market or individual preferences, grows significantly. A communal society also is one in which the number and range of "rights" multiplies as does concern and public responsibility for the externalities of the market place. But as a game between persons social exchanges become much more difficult since "political claims and social rights multiply, the rapidity of social change and shifting cultural fashion bewilders the old, and the orientation to the future erodes the traditional guides and moralities of the past" (Bell, 1973:123).

In addition, as Bell underlines in the same context, in post-industrial society increased public participation of individuals and groups is likely, however,

> the very increase in participation leads to a paradox: the greater the number of groups, each seeking diverse or competing ends, the more likelihood that these groups will veto one another's interests, with the consequent sense of frustration and powerlessness as such stalemates incur.

In other words, any design to plan and control social conduct becomes rather difficult under these circumstances. Moreover, the conditions Bell anticipates in this instance are likely a more realistic description of the essential fragility of future social structures and conduct.

Nonetheless, Bell's account of post-industrial society is also and perhaps more strongly animated by expectations and the promise of the possibility of much better and effective "management of organized complexity" in advanced society. Since the notion of complexity about the nature of social reality and the difficulty in intellectually reconstructing such reality effectively is one which has been a pervasive thesis for decades in social scientific discourse (cf. Stehr, 1992), it is not surprising to see Bell assert that social science and its kindred disciplines are about to conquer what many have felt has held them back in the past, namely, the difficulties in manipulating a greater bundle of "variables". In fact, Bell explicitly talks about the progress made in science since the 18th and 19th century as advances made in terms of the number of *variables* which can be handled simultaneously.

The move is from two variable problems, to a small number of interdependent variables and, finally, reflecting the very intellectual and sociological problems of post-industrial society, to a large number of interacting variables. Bell stresses approvingly (1973:29) that "it is the *hubris* of the modern systems theorist that the techniques for managing these systems are now available." The cognitive techniques designed to manipulate a large bundle of variables at one time represents the emergence of an *intellectual technology*. Intellectual technologies are defined as the substitution of algorithms for intuitive judgments. Problem solving rules may be embodied, Bell (1973:29–30), explains, in "an automatic machine or a computer program or a set of instructions based on some statistical or mathematical formula". Intuitive judgments are replaced by formalized decisions. The computer is particularly suited to implement and execute efficiently such problem-solving rules. In short, what is distinctive about intellectual technology, as far as Bell is concerned, is the clear separation of means and ends in social action and therefore the calculation of the risks and costs associated with alternative means, and, ultimately the pre-situational assignment of particular means to pre-set goals. In all situations, the desirable action would be a strategy that ensures the "best" solution. What Bell therefore has in mind, with his notion of intellectual technology, is merely a re-statement of long-standing ambitions (or fears), to "automate" decisions for which means (more or less independent of goals), and ends are known in advance. In other words, Bell's metaphor of an intellectual technology amounts to a heightened "rationalization" process in and of modern society as we know it from Max Weber's extensive discussion, except that the computer now enters the equation as a *tool* of such "technology" which presumably multiplies its efficiency.

In a distinctive contrast and in opposition to these images, knowledge societies are societies characterized, to an unprecedented degree, by self-made social relations and a self-produced future including, of course, the capacity to destroy themselves. But this does not imply that such capacities, in whatever fashion one might depict such cumulative or additive outcomes, may not add up to the ability to control and manipulate social conduct to a greater and in a more efficient manner as the emergence of knowledge capitalism and technologically based surveillance activities of the state demonstrates. On the contrary, the greater capacity to act may also have the inverse consequence in that it reduces the ability of administrative bodies for example to plan, recast, and repress, or, from the perspectives of the potential targets of planning and manipulation, it heightens the capacity to resist these very efforts.

Knowledge is both a constant source of change and a principle of social organization. Knowledge societies offer unprecedented means and instruments empowering social actors to add to the self-transforming capacity of society (heightened "historicity" of society, see Touraine, [1984] 1988:11). The capacity of society to intervene and act upon itself is exceptional. As political entities too, knowledge societies appear to be rather fragile. They are politically fragile, not because they are liberal democracies, as some might argue but because they are knowledge societies. Knowledge societies potentially enhance the democratic character of liberal democracies. But as the potential for meaningful political participation is enlarged, some traditional attributes associated with the political system, especially its ability to "get(s), things done" or, to impose its will, increasingly is diminished.

In the remainder of this section and in the next section, under the heading of the governability of knowledge societies, I would like to explore the thesis of the unequal enhancement of the capacity to act in knowledge societies in some detail. Initially, I primarily will examine it from the perspective of the individual or small groups of actors. That is, from the perspective of a range of subjects in past analysis who have been treated mainly as the objects of the action of large institutions and corporations that succeed in reducing them to victims, by-standers or otherwise incapacitated persons. In the next section, I plan to discuss its impact on larger collectivities including the state.

This thesis about the uneven promotion of capacities to act and its consequences for society needs to be explicated and explored in more detail for a number of reasons. It is a thesis central to this analysis, but it is also a thesis which can be easily misconstrued. In order to avoid any misconceptions which are easily introduced, first, it does not follow from the general thesis about the increased contingency of social reality that there is a coalescence of social relations toward some center. On the contrary, social conflicts, for example, are generalized, which means that they lose their previous identity as primarily economic conflicts. Second, this malleability and tenuousness of social relations should not be seen to result invariably in greater social inequality, even more effective forms of social control, and more demands for social discipline, which then may be enforced even more efficiently compared to societies in which the powerful have fewer and less effective means to impose their will and exploit others for their own ends. Third, the prevailing fears, at least among those who have examined critically the spread of technology and technical rationality, has been that what we have called the increased contingency of social reality will in fact be employed for the most part in the partial interests of then even more powerful groups and will increase immeasurably the social, cultural, and political cleavages in modern society. Symptomatic and representative of this view is, perhaps, the conclusion that advanced technological institutions are agencies of highly centralized and intensive social control, that their logic defies and drives out any other values, that technology creates, therefore, its own politics, is resistant to intervention on other terms, imposes its own roles and values, and serves, in the final instance, the interests of a ruling elite (who appear to be capable of defying its constraints; e.g. McDermott, 1979).

I already have referred to the more sophisticated account of the self-propelled and then irresistible transformation of society through *technical rationality*. These accounts of the dawning of the "technical state" are compatible with conservative and more liberal political philosophies. Both Helmut Schelsky and Herbert Marcuse have, as indicated, each in their own terms of course, developed theories of the victorious and apparently almost irreversible spread of the imperatives of technical rationality. However, the inevitable allegiance between technological rationality and domination in advanced industrial societies, in Schelsky's theory of scientific civilization or Marcuse's treatment of the one-dimensional man, is at best one-sided. At worst, it fails to capture the crucial features of advanced society. Fourth, the increased contingency of social reality is, perhaps paradoxically, associated with a strong sense of a lack of malleability or even of helplessness and impotence, rather than emancipatory possibilities in the face of existing societal arrangements.

As Johannes Berger (1986:91), describes the association in question, for example,

> everything is highly contingent in modern societies but, at the same time, embedded in interest-laden 'systematic' contexts, it appears, therefore, nothing goes anymore. What can possibly be changed: the automobile traffic, the distribution of income or, at least, the laws governing the closing hours of stores? The experience of a resilience of social conditions is in a confusing sense linked to the consciousness of contingency.

However, the relevant issue is not merely or even mainly the question of the self-centered operation of societal subsystems, for example, of the neglect of the economy of goals other than economic interests. Even within subsystems, though there may be an increase in the range of options available, in the capacity to mobilize resources for action and in the ability to anticipate outcomes, there may well be a much greater autonomy. The fields of action and circumstances of action that can be influenced or controlled by actors are expanding; and with them the "power" of actors to realize knowledge as the ability to act. And of course, this also applies to the executive suite of big tech companies.

The degree and the consequences to which social action has become malleable in the consciousness of many citizens is an outflow of the availability of reflexive knowledge about the nature of social reality and the nature of nature and how to re-make both for ends which are socially constructed and known to be man-made. However, the effects this has are quite opposite to those anticipated by scholars who have warned about the dawn of the technical state or similar iron cages for social relations brought about by the social impact of science and technology. Of course, science and technology are creating cages, but they are of a very different sort than the theories of society produced in the 1960s. The dissemination of such knowledge means that the capacity of traditional institutions to enforce discipline or compliance declines. Or, what is but the same, resources increase to effectively resist central agencies of social coercion. Hermann Lübbe's (1987:95), observation about our ability to anticipate future conditions is therefore quite accurate. That is, the inaccuracies of predictions have increased manifold as the result of increased knowledge: "Every earlier period of history enjoyed, in relation to its future, the culturally significant advantage to be able to offer much more accurate pronouncements about the future than we today are capable to do." The reasons for our inability to anticipate future conditions, and for the increase in the fragility of social conditions in this sense, are attributed by Lübbe directly to the increase in the quantity of knowledge. Although Lübbe focuses mainly on technical knowledge, he asserts for this realm that the volume of events which change the structural conditions of life grows directly with the quantity of available knowledge. The probability of anticipating and controlling the future declines, rather than improving with the growth of knowledge. But the thesis about the fragility of social structure in the sense of the unpredictability of future conditions is more than merely a restatement of the Popperian theorem that one cannot know what we will know in the future.[11]

Nonetheless, the extension of the capacity to act in the case of individuals and small groups is considerable, especially since the enlargement of options to act can be quite small and still have a major impact, for example, in situations of conflict with corporate actors. As Dorothy Nelkin (1975:53–54), has shown in her study of the competitive use of technical expertise in two major controversial political decisions to extend a large airport and to site and develop a power plant in the United States, "those opposing a decision need not muster equal evidence." That is to say, "it is sufficient to raise questions that will undermine the expertise of a developer whose power and legitimacy rests on his monopoly of knowledge claims or claims of special expertise." In much the same spirit, Adolph Lowe (1971:576), describes, using terms perhaps somewhat more appropriate for another age, that what is at issue is that

> growing affluence, cumulative technology, government interventions, and most of all a widening and deepening knowledge of social reality has imparted a new "freedom" to the elements that make up the social system—that is, a capacity to determine for themselves what shall be their patterns of behavior, their reactions to stimuli, their goals.

Loss of fear—especially in relation to the state, the state administrative apparatus and other positions of authority and power—coincide with considerable gains in fear, in particular, in relation to environmental problems, the fallout of technological artifacts, the realization that not all action can be subjected to rational planning and control, and the element of unanticipated consequences of social action initiated by fellow human beings. In the social context of this loss of trust in government institutions, as well as in science, which is seen as a stooge of the state, conspiracy theories thrive particularly well and are one of the offensive responses to the scientific and government narratives in, for example, the Covid vaccination case. Distrust may be so deeply entrenched that any news source other than sources close to the government is believed. This relationship holds true in both developing and lesser developed societies.[12] However, such gains in fear and concerns can, at times, lead to a heightened resolve to employ one's gains in capacity for social action to influence the balance of risks and gains favorably.

The gain many individuals experience in their capacity to act does not mean that the social distribution of knowledge in knowledge societies is equal or displays a greater degree of equality than was the case in industrial society. The distribution of knowledge is reason for and the result of social inequalities. Those who are powerful have fewer difficulties gaining access to knowledge, especially

> additional knowledge and gain control of relevant conditions of action. Nonetheless, what is of particular interest here is that in recent years knowledge, perhaps in the role of knowledge-based occupations or experts, has increasingly come to the assistance of grassroots pressure groups and other elements of the general public and local communities. And it is equally true that the grassroots have learned how to deploy expertise, and have exploited it with some success in furthering their interests and in embarrassing the establishment.
>
> (Barnes, 1985:111)

In sum, the rise in the general level of knowledge accessible and available to larger segments of the population than ever before contributes simultaneously to an enlargement of the fragility of modern social structures.

The political challenges of modern knowledge societies

The growth of knowledge and the growing societal importance of knowledge forces society to confront at least dual contingencies directly linked to the enlargement of modern knowledge. There is (1), the contingency of knowledge itself and (2), the heightened contingency of social relations as the result of the growing penetration of knowledge into society. For these reasons, the future, more than ever, is much harder to visualize. It is more difficult to imagine than even Daniel Bell still reckoned in his treatise on post-industrial societies in the mid-1970s. Social, economic and intellectual strains that undoubtedly will attend the dual contingency are not resolved by reverting to the now largely discredited deference for a scientific politics, a return to whatever "foundations", the image of "progress", or technocratic solutions of societal problems. However, setting specific opportunities, strains, ambitions, pressures, and traditions will lead to very different forms of knowledge societies, when compared to the image of post-industrial societies.

The image of the logic of science from which all individuals and groups associated with the production and dissemination of scientific knowledge directly or indirectly have benefited in the past, has been dismantled and replaced by a perspective which comprehends the construction of scientific knowledge as a social and intellectual endeavor and not as a meta-social enterprise progressively approximating a recalcitrant objective reality. The social construction of scientific claims to knowledge or scientific facts and theories, as examined by ethnographic studies of laboratories, public controversies involving scientific expertise and the socio-historical reconstruction of the emergence, establishment and decline of scientific theories (e.g. Mulkay, 1979; Knorr-Cetina and Mulkay, 1983; Stehr and Meja, 1984b; Zuckerman, 1988), strongly attributes a contingency to knowledge. In the past, the eradication of contingency (or disagreements), was seen as the hallmark of the scientific enterprise.

As a result, the harnessing of knowledge will be accompanied not only by continuing concerns about past threats that are persistent fears, for example, the horror of global destruction through nuclear weapons or a major environmental catastrophe, but by a decline in the authority of experts and growing skepticism toward the possibility of disinterested expertise. Nonetheless, in the countries of the West and Asia, despite decidedly distinct political systems and histories, reliance on knowledge will increase as well and the ways in which scientists, experts, advisors and knowledge-based occupations generally are able to maintain cognitive authority in the face of uncertainty, political conflict, and skepticism toward expertise represents one of the main challenges for these occupations in knowledge societies (cf. Gieryn, 1983; Janasoff, 1990; Stehr and Grundmann, 2011). But despite such misgivings and any sustained demystification of knowledge, the alternative cannot be to randomly invoke any odd belief as an equivalent. The challenge is to cope with contingency, not labor under the illusion that it merely is a temporary aberration.

The following sections address a range of socio-political challenges faced by knowledge societies. Under the heading of economic policies, I refer to (1) revisions of the patent law; (2) meaning, taxation, automation and artificial intelligence in light of the specter of technological unemployment; and (3) climate politics. None of these policy matters is ever the issue of but one scientific discipline. Knowledge politics are intersystem as well as wicked matters.

Knowledge politics

Our knowledge of the human genome is growing rapidly and will continue to develop in the future. Hundreds of thousands of human genomes can be analyzed in the wake of the decreasing cost of genomic sequencing, making it almost routine. Selection of embryos for complex polygenic diseases is very likely one day. Although there are many reasons not to implement such heritable interventions, it is conceivable that in the future we will use CRISPR technology to make dozens of changes in the genome of a human embryo (cf. Kozubek, 2017; Darnovsky, 2019; Lemma, 2019). A parallel development in human embryo research that awaits political and scientific guidelines is stem cell research delineating for example which experiments are acceptable both legally and to society.

Eric Lander and Françoise Baylis (2019:165) and other scientists have published a call in *Nature* for a global temporary halt to all applications of the "human germline moratorium on all clinical uses of human germ-line editing—that is, changing heritable DNA (in sperm, eggs or embryos) to make genetically modified children". The call in *Nature* makes it clear that the application of CRISPR technology is not automatic or inevitable, but requires a societal decision as to whether the new knowledge should be applied. This is precisely the new field of knowledge policy.[13] Ethical, social, and political questions need to be addressed. One of the social consequences of genome editing is almost certainly that it will reinforce and increase social inequality. Genome editing will be expensive. One therapy (non-CRISPR), already approved to correct congenital vision loss, costs $850,000.

As I have discussed in some detail with respect to the successive legal encoding of knowledge in patent law, in the course of the development of industrial society, liberal democracies successively instituted increasingly elaborate legal frames pertaining to the social status and use of property and labor. The freedom of economic actors to exercise power and authority by virtue of their individual assets or collective ownership over the means of production increasingly is in many countries constrained and circumscribed by a host of legal norms. Ownership is restrained not only spontaneously, for example, by the market but by the state. Deliberate and anticipatory legal constraints on the use of property and labor are not neutral. Legal norms convey, from the point of view of certain actors, especially for those who feel impotent in acquiring ownership and in affecting the legal rules pertaining to their disposition, privileges while they signal (natural), rights to those who control property and labor. Unequal access to ownership and therefore any stratification of effective influence on the construction of the legal restraints and rights, in turn, often is, but not always exclusively, based on an unequal distribution of labor and property in industrial society, elements that are constitutive for its social and economic existence.

It is almost self-evident that informal, political, and *legal* efforts in the form of legislation in knowledge societies will be directed more and more toward the ways of *controlling* both the development and to a more significant extent the deployment and employment of knowledge. The politics of knowledge are ubiquitous amounting for example to an analysis of the circulation, reception, re-interpretation and application of knowledge in society. The general social control of knowledge examines the traffic of knowledge between social institutions or, the prestige of different discourses. The emphasis in the section is less expansive. I focus on a new field of political activity, knowledge politics, that is, *efforts to control of additional or incremental knowledge*,[14] for example, to look toward a likely future, laboratory grown meat (in a bioreactor) that may, permission granted, one day replace conventional meat.[15] A likely even more contentious future site of knowledge politics will be the invention and possible utilization of CRISPR (clusters of regularly interspaced short palindromic repeats) that captured the attention of researches beginning some two decades ago. CRISPR represents a DNA sequence that occurs in bacteria and constitutes the bacterial immune system protecting the cells from infection: It is "a tool that will allow real manipulation of disease-causing genes"[16] not only in humans but also plan (Davies, 2020; Isaacson, 2021). As a field of *broader* public policy, knowledge politics cuts across the many fields of public policy activities, for example, economic supervision and regulation, innovation, competition, knowledge generation and international trade.

Within the context of the new arena of politics, I emphasize one strand of knowledge politics, namely legislative efforts to control new scientific knowledge rather than more tenuous forms of informal, popular or spontaneous social control, for example, driven by social movements because the latter simply is part and parcel of the conventional state of affairs of science and its relation to society, namely the standard selectivity with which knowledge develops, is utilized, rejected and resisted. Vigorous opposition to political ventures to limit the considerable autonomy of the modern scientific community and to control knowledge will be as common as was opposition to efforts to control the use of property or the ways in which labor power might be utilized by the owners of the means of production.

The most powerful modern policy designed to protect knowledge legally defined as *intellectual property* (patents, trademarks, copyrights) in particular is as, I have discussed it in the previous chapter, the Agreement on *Trade-Related Aspects of Intellectual Property Rights* (TRIPS) signed in 1980 as part of the constitution of the *World Trade Organization* (WHO).

While the legal constructs pertaining to labor and property evolved at a time when the "distance" to the empirical manifestations of these constructs for those who demanded, enacted and sanctioned legal rules was hardly a major concern, today, however, the "loss of contact" (Holton, 1986:92), itself between science, the public and its representatives is a salient attribute in the dynamics of the interrelation between knowledge and society.

It is possible, in fact in some controversies already manifested, that discussions, demands and efforts to legislate selectivity in the ways in which knowledge is developed and employed are linked to strong disaffections with science and will be branded as part of an anti-science crusade or movement. The term anti-science is vague and potentially lumps together a broad range of things that perhaps "have in common only that they tend to annoy or threaten those who regard themselves as more enlightened" (Holton, 1992:104). Moreover, disaffection with science and technology not only extends to scientific knowledge claims or the scientists but also to the reputation and standing of governmental institutions that generate information about scientific knowledge and often are in charge of certifying the deployment if knowledge, for example, the Center for Disease Control or the Environmental Protection Agency. The growth of scientific knowledge has of course always been accompanied by skepticism of some groups.

This is also true of public reaction to vaccines developed during the pandemic. In societies with comparably high levels of public trust in science and in scientists, as shown in a comparative study of attitudes toward science and vaccines in 126 countries (Sturgis et al., 2021), societal trust in science correlates, not surprisingly, with trust in vaccines. On the other hand, there are quantitatively by no means small minorities in all societies, typically up to 25 percent of the adult population, who refuse to be vaccinated.

The social control of science and technology that has successfully moved from the stage of being-in-progress to some form of societal control is already extensive. In all modern societies, we now find elaborate drug regulation agencies are in existence that register, test, control or permit pharmaceutical substances to enter the market as drugs. Only a few decades ago, decisions about the production and marketing of chemicals as drugs was in the hands of corporations, individual pharmacists or physicians (c.f. Bodewitz et al., 1987). As scientific knowledge is "applied" it becomes embedded in social contexts external to science. As a part of such embeddedness, knowledge is subject to the kinds of control mechanisms found in these social contexts. Knowledge simply cannot escape the selectivity that issues from such external constraints and be it only in efforts designed to generate trust toward a certain artifact or solution offered by novel knowledge.

The whole area of national and international intellectual property and copyright protection is another arena in which legislation to control the deployment of scientific and technical knowledge already is extensive. In many ways, such controls date back to at least the 1883 Paris Convention for patents and related industrial matters and the 1886 Berne Convention for copyrights. The acceleration in the speed with which inventions reach the market, their shortened economic life span and the extent to which recent inventions, for example, in the field of microelectronics, the organization of production, medical treatments, and biotechnology are difficult to protect from copying efforts, will increase pressures to enact further protective legislation (cf. Vaitsos, 1989).

But to legislate and attempt to closely control science-in-progress is a most difficult if not impossible enterprise. In addition, efforts to do so would have the unintended consequence of reducing the authority of science as an asset to politics. Perhaps the most significant barrier to extensive measures to impose external social control mechanisms on science-in-progress is the size and organization of the scientific enterprise today as well as its competitive and its international texture.[17]

The politics of science should not be conflated with the politics of society. The politics of knowledge are not or cannot merely be reduced to the politics of societal power, nor does science only generate knowledge that is essentially political and therefore perhaps eminently practical.

The institution generating knowledge and the institution contemplating and executing political action were once, although this now appears to have been the case in the distant past, seen to be completely detached domains. At the beginning of this century, the dilemmas of the indispensable separation of science and politics found one of its most appealing expressions in Max Weber's ([1921] 1948:77–128, [1922] 1948:129–156), essays on science and politics as a vocation. Today, the intellectual foundations which allowed Weber to legitimize the fundamental division between the practice of knowledge and politics have fallen into disrepute. While the scientific community and polity still have professional roles and vocations with ideals and career patterns which are at odds, any remaining confidence in the neutral, purely instrumental, and apolitical character of science has eroded significantly. At the present time, therefore, any reference to the politics of knowledge does not any longer constitute a profound break or violation of precious norms of scientific action and essential attributes of scientific knowledge. Science is deeply implicated in social action and political agendas hold sway over science. Precisely how dependent or interdependent science and politics are is a matter of genuine debate and continued empirical analysis. But the widespread disenchantment with science in some countries and the extensive material dependence of the scientific community on the state should not give rise to the equally unrealistic proposition that the boundaries between politics and science have vanished without a trace. Science is embedded in particular political realities, and as long as it is situated and implanted in a specific form of civil and political society, in particular one free of totalitarian strains, scientific activity benefits. By the same token, as long as the traffic across the boundaries of science and the rules which govern such transactions remain open in principle and negotiable, both science and society stand to gain.

Inasmuch as knowledge becomes the constitutive principle of modern society, the production and distribution of knowledge can no longer escape, if it ever could, explicit political struggles and conflicts. The production and distribution of knowledge will increasingly also become a domain of more explicit legislation and generally become the target of political and economic decisions. On the one hand, such a development is inevitable because "as the institutions of knowledge lay claim to public resources, some public claim on these institutions is unavoidable" (Bell, 1968:238). But in addition, and in some ways perhaps more consequential, as the importance of knowledge as a central resource in modern society increases, its social, economic, and political consequences for social relations generally grow rapidly and so will demands to regulate the production, the utilization and access to knowledge.

A significant part of a politics of knowledge will have to be concerned with the consequences of the social distribution of knowledge, especially the stratified access to knowledge. To what extent any dispossession of knowledge, for example, may generate social conflicts and in what ways such struggles may manifest themselves, is an open question. However, Daniel Bell (1964:49), warned as early as 60 years ago that right-wing extremism may "benefit" from any exclusion of social groups from access to and acquisition of technical expertise.

The political challenges in the field of knowledge politics are impossible to anticipate since specific political action, for example. legislation depends on the discovery of novel capacities for action and the resulting (at times enormous) pressure to act; on the other hand, ongoing controversies about discoveries already made and political response on the record indicate that political action with the contours of these discoveries are not exhausted but will continue to generate controversial debates:

- GM food technologies and biotechnology
- Geroscience[18]
- Regulation of the deployment of artificial intelligence; for example, AI hacking;[19]
- Specifically: Regulation of artificial intelligence with which you can supposedly recognize and measure emotions; but so far, AI is without a consciousness;
- Application and governance of CRISPR ("Clusters of Regular Interspaced Short Palindromic Repeats"). CRISPR is a powerful tool for modifying DNA in any type of human cell and in plants. Efforts of the World Health Organization: www.who.int/publications/i/item/9789240030381.[20]
- (Reproductive and therapeutical) Human cloning
- Hybrid human–animal embryos; "human–nonhuman" creatures.
- Reconstruction of the genomes of extinct species based on fragments of DNA retrieved from fossils.[21]

In the case of encoding knowledge, among numerous issue that may be surveyed under the general heading of knowledge politics, the perhaps fundamental issue is the question of the "tragedy of the anti-commons" (Heller, 1998), that is, patent law and how to overcome the alleged underutilization of knowledge in the wake of fencing in capacities of action.

Patent policies

The *profitability* of knowledge-intensive firms depends on the control of the range (both quantity and quality) of excludable intellectual property rights (IPRs—patents, copyrights, trademarks, brands) rather than—as was the case in industrial societies—production costs. The legal system, that is, the state defines, creates, and enforces excludability. It follows that the development of patent law is of central importance for the evolution of the economy and the social structure of knowledge societies, for example, the inequality formation in these societies.

During the pandemic, concern that the prevailing international system of intellectual property rights offers excessive protection to patent holders has not been voiced for the first time; but under the contingencies of vaccinating the global population speedily, the demand to keep know-how about vaccines in the public domain grew more persistent and louder. Not only favors the global patent regime patentholders; the major share of the benefits of the patents typically go to corporations in the rich countries, hence

> In a globally integrated economy—from which developing countries and emerging markets have benefited enormously in many ways—global rules matter. The global rules have always been set to favour high-income countries; they are, to a large extent, set by the large powerful countries, and frequently by powerful special interests within them, whereas developing countries don't have a seat at the table, or are at least underrepresented.
>
> (Korinek and Stiglitz, 2021:341)

A similar controversial discussion will be sparked in the coming years by the question of the extent to which the widespread patenting of technical (and other) innovations in the field of climate protection and the protection of society from climate change is justified. This fact, in turn, makes the question of legal restrictions on access to this knowledge a contentious issue in which familiar political, economic, and legal positions will then clash again (see Biddle, 2016): How important is patent law for additional knowledge?

An initiative of the non-governmental organization *Third World Networks*[22] takes up this issue and opposes the prevailing legal regime of intellectual property protection by emphasizing the urgency of disseminating relevant findings:

> Evidence suggests a mismatch between the urgency of climate challenges as set out by the Intergovernmental Panel on Climate Change and the time taken historically for technology systems to evolve under business-as-usual practices. Thus continuing to promote and advocate such approaches to facilitate technology development and transfer is essentially a recipe for a worldwide climate disaster.

What can be done to ensure that the inequities in place do not grow further or can even be redistributed more equally, perhaps short of keeping technological and scientific advances in the public domain? In other words, what would the optimal (and dynamic) form of intellectual property rights (IPR)? The demand for the latter is easily advanced but most difficult to implement. But the change in patent law could adhere to the basic premise of patent law advocated by Michael Polanyi (1944:63): "Patent protection must not abandoned altogether," nor should it be without its exceptions (as I note later): The following political issues await resolution within patent politics:[23]

- Keep technological advances and early financial benefits in the public domain[24]

- Should some patent questions be decided with respect to moral not economic issues? How does one define a need for knowledge (cf. May, 2002:142–143)?
- Should patents be assigned to entities other than "natural human beings" (the language of the US Patent and Trademark Office) as required in most jurisdictions (cf. Rosen, 2021)?;
- if based on publicly funded research;[25]
- Reduce the length of the patent protection (cf. Korinek and Stiglitz, 2019)?[26]
- Solution of the so-called "patent troll" problem (for instance the "barred enforcement of a patent that was not reduced to practice within a specified time after the patent was granted" (Posner, 2013)
- Patent sharks[27]
- Definition of a patent too broad; what should not be eligible for patent protection?
- The relation of patents for the supply of green innovation (cf. Reichmann et al., 2014)
- Strengthening of patent offices (quantitatively and qualitatively).
- Patent offices should be required/empowered to produce, on a regular basis, a regulatory impact statement; for example, do patents are more likely to harm/aid innovation (Lessig, 2001:259).
- Exempt certain inventions from patent protection, for example, in the area of climate adaptation and life-saving intellectual property[28] (that is, patents designed to attend to global emergencies such as the pandemic or global warming; patents [need for knowledge] pertaining to global public goods, cf. Frow, 1996)[29]
- Tax law: (a) erosion of tax basis[30] and (b) taxing large financial benefits (monopoly rents) gained from protected patents and use funds to support research and development, thereby
- Separating incentives to innovate from rewards due to exploitation of additional knowledge
- Earnings for inventions are paid by the state (cf. Polanyi, 1944:65)?[31]
- Different patent protection in developing and lesser developed countries (cf. Korinek and Stiglitz, 2021:33)
- Should IPR protection policy ensure that superstar corporations lose their monopoly rents?
- Innovations should remain an indispensable part of societal activity
- IPR relation of developing and lesser developed nations: The uneven distribution of intangible assets.
- Alternatives to patents (in order to stimulate innovation; pricing for example[32]

In any event, "society faces a difficult trade-off in determining how to engineer the optimal level of innovation" and determine the optimal length if any and scope of patents (Korinek and Stiglitz, 2019:366; Acemoglu and Akcigit, 2012; Arrow, 1962b).

The next section addresses the challenge of the development of what Daniel Bell called "intelligent technologies" for the world of work, in at least a dual sense: First, the impact of what is widely perceived to amount to labor-replacing innovation and, second, on the kind of skills and competencies what will be foremost in demand under the effects of intelligent technologies both as conditions for the continued evolution of technological change and in response to the technological advances. The widely applicable observation about the simultaneity of the non-simultaneous is a useful reminder that technological advances in the world of work creates both winners and losers.

And this ambivalence is not a recent discovery: John M. Keynes ([1930] 1984:325) emphasized, the specter of technological unemployment was, in his view, a "new disease" which meant that "unemployment due to our discovery of means of economising the use of labour outrunning the pace at which we can find new uses for labour." However, in an ambiguious—or realistic appraisal that persisted aside from Keynes during the next century, he quickly added, "this is only a temporary phase of maladjustment . . . in the long run. . . *mankind is solving its economic problem*."[33] The utopian conclusion Keynes'reached in 1930—without the slightest recognition, in the contemporary scientific community, of anthropogenic climate change on the horizon—about the pursuit to end scarcity, following the business-as-usual approach, today is, in stark contrast seen not as the solution to the economic problem but as a certain path to historically unprecedented catastrophe.

Given centrality of work as a crucial part of one's life interest, the changes that might impact both the volume of socially necessary labor, the changes of the kind of competences required and, in the meaning, work represents in the design of life, already indicate how significant economic policies designed to attend to the issues these changes imply.

The specter of technological unemployment

The fear in modern societies against a massive loss in the socially necessary volume of work (aggregate labor demand in a society), and even a society without work, is, on the one hand, at the center of any discussion about the future of work in knowledge societies, just as, for example, the technical transformations of the world of work, most recently through the evolution of robotics and artificial intelligence or the loss of tax revenue of governments, depending of course on the scenario that is seen to be most realistic.[34] On the other hand, a persistent economic and political issue from past societies will carry over into knowledge societies as it implements the most recent set of technological advances in the economic system and beyond: the distribution of income. If the volume of socially necessary labor declines and the application of robotics an AI broadens, what will happen to the distribution of incomes? Since recessions tend to strengthen or impose new trends, will the pandemic—as companies reduce reliance on human labor and contact between workers—only exacerbate many of these developments in the labor market? Will AI mitigate or reinforce the trend toward greater social inequality? And, finally, will AI create a 21st century "Lumpenproletariat"?[35] Or, are these misplaced fears that repeat such fears in the past that remained fears and perhaps turned into self-defeating prophecies?

These developments in and beyond labor market transformations—mostly articulated by economists—which appear to have picked up speed in the recent past, perhaps also in response to the pandemic are supposed to cause major changes not only regarding needed skills, the attractiveness, the organization, and the general nature of labor but also massive future social disruptions. In instance of some observations, the very future of humanity is seen at stake (Reese, 2018).[36]

The paradox explored in past and present investigations of the impact of technological change on the world of work is the extent to which "technological change threatens social welfare not because it intensifies scarcity but because it augments abundance" (Autor, 2015b:1) and thereby often sustains as well as enhances social inequality. But the contradictions do not end there.

There are significant examples of productivity-enhancing technologies that increase employment rather than reduce the volume of work. Automation or information technologies increase employment for some groups without reducing net employment (see Bessen, 2017). These observations point to the fact that in the past many of the fears associated with automation turned out to be false. As George Borjas and Richard Freeman (2019:2) surmise, "today we see robots taking job from humans in the media but not in real world labor markets."

However, in contrast, the *new* canonical narrative concerning the use of computers, robots, and artificial intelligence has given new impetus to the fear that machines will replace human beings and create considerable unemployment and with it the prospect of "idleness without work [that] is a torment" (Benjamin, [1938] 2006:127). Optimistic economists say no. Other economists warn that the new technological developments that at times are labeled part of the fourth industrial revolution (cf. Soete, 2018:29) will replace not only human muscles but also human skills and minds and enhance polarization and wage inequality (cf. Frey and Osborne, 2017). Daron Acumoglu and Pascual Restrepo (2021) document that between 50 percent and 70 percent of the changes in the income structure in the US over the past four decades (1980–2016) are the result of the relative income loss of workers whose routine jobs have been altered by rapid automation (i.e., displacing certain work-groups from employment opportunities for which they originally had comparative advantage).

In contrast, a survey (and not a prognosis) on what happened to jobs defined at risk of automation over the past decade 21 countries carried out for the OECD (Georgieff and Milanez, 2021) arrives at a much more sober conclusion,

> there is no support for net job destruction at the broad country level. All countries experienced employment growth over the past decade and

> countries that faced higher automation risk back in 2012 experienced higher employment growth over the subsequent period. At the occupational level, however, employment growth has been much lower in jobs at high risk of automation (6%) than in jobs at low risk (18%).

It is also striking that Japan, Singapore and South Korea, which are among the countries with the highest levels of automation, also had low unemployment rates. Perhaps it is the lack of workers that is the driving force? The findings of the OECD study exemplify, in my view, a further confirmation of Drucker's law, namely that changes to employment are not merely linked to technological developments and the motive structure of capitalist enterprises but societal transformations, policies and human preferences. However, pessimistic views about future employment patterns persist:

Ronald Inglehart (2018:4) stipulates the coming of an "Artificial Intelligence [AI] Society", a kind of "advanced" phase of the knowledge society, as a result of a further dramatic technological transformation of the labor market in which "virtual(Inglehart, 2018:200) ly anyone's job can be automated" and which "tends to produce a winner-takes-all society" (Inglehart, 2018:200). AI may be seen as a "continuation of a long process of automation" of labor (Korinek and Stiglitz, 2019:349); other observes are convinced that AI differs fundamentally from past inventions (also Acemoglu, 2021).

No matter how we may interpret AI in a longer historical perspective, AI makes it likely that many jobs, even those with high skills and advanced education, will be replaced by "computer programs" written by computer programs.[37] Unless the state or other institutions intervene, the market should ensure that the gains will go largely to those with the appropriate skills or ownership of properties that benefit disproportionally from a change toward an Artificial Intelligence Society. The ensuing economic struggle in society is no longer between the working class and the middle class but between the top one percent and the remaining 99 percent. The Artificial Intelligence Society is not producing significant numbers of secure, well-paying jobs (Inglehart, 2018:203). This statement by Inglehart takes us right in the heart and heat of a long-standing discussion about the impact of technological change on the volume of socially necessary labor.

One of the most important unresolved problems is therefore that neither collective bargaining nor statutory compensation of individual persons who lose their jobs and thus suffer significant economic disturbances is on the policy agenda in most countries. Nor are reflections about the political impact of a sustained loss of jobs. Generous compensation may allow an occupational reboot although past experience in this regard does not give rise to optimism. But who pays for the transition costs and the shortfall of tax revenue?

One idea to compensate for the loss of tax revenue as the result of the displacement of workers by robots is proposed by a member of the European Parliament in 2016, endorsed by Bill Gates and supported by Robert Shiller, [38] who suggest to tax robots. A major part of the economic value of robots is made up of the embedded knowledge it takes to design, produce and program the robot. In contrast, the

> physical vessel of the robot constitutes physicals capital in the traditional sense. . . . We should refrain from taxing the robot as a physical vessel but should tax the design of the robot und the programs that are running on it because those are information goods that generate rents.
>
> (Korinek, 2020:256)

When robots replace workers, the company should incur taxes equivalent to that worker's income taxes.[39] Right now, Gates notes,

> the human worker who does, say, $50,000 worth of work in a factory, that income is taxed and you get income tax, social security tax, all those things. If a robot comes in to do the same thing, you'd think that we'd tax the robot at a similar level.[40]

But even if there might be widespread political agreement about the desirability of a tax on robots in the future, the implementation of a *new* tax would face enormous formal (e.g. constitutional) and political push back let alone the systemic issues (given the nature of tax systems in different countries) and the attendant socio-economic consequences (for instance, the impact of societal inequality, see Guerreiro et al., 2017). More generally, as David Autor (2015a:8, 28) cautiously emphasizes,

> rapid automation may create distributional challenges that invite a broad policy response. . . . If machines were in fact to make human labor superfluous, we would have vast aggregate wealth but a serious challenge in determining who owns it and how to share it.

The probable profound changes due to technological progress (automation and artificial intelligence) in the world of work imply, above all, the possibility of a significant decrease in the volume of socially necessary work. How can these challenges to the world of work be met in their multiple consequences for society? The policy implications are complex:

- Human labor, including highly skilled labor, may become redundant (see Korinek, 2020:246). Under these circumstances, the need to create well-paying and secure jobs arises (for policy implications, see Acemoglu, 2019). The potential decline in the number, scope, and quality of available jobs and associated income also implies,

- Compensating for the loss of meaning that accompanies the loss of work for those who can no longer find work.
- Promoting competencies and professional skills
- A decline in tax revenues for governments that assume that taxing work, especially when this revenue is the main source of government tax revenue.
- In the face of lower tax revenues from labor, an increase in needed tax revenues to support those who do not have jobs
- A more radical step would be to eliminate taxation on labor altogether (see Korinek, 2020:248) and focus instead on taxing nonrenewable resources or negative externalities (such as pollution)

Next, I turn to the perhaps most significant policy challenges of the next decades: Following—prior to the pandemic—a warning not only of the World Health Organization, climate change will be the biggest threat to human societies in the 21st century. Climate change propel policy issues of a different human and ecological future toward the center of political attention, likely pushing all the other policy issues listed here into the background. The retention time of greenhouse gases in the atmosphere, rarely publicly discussed as it where, lasting for centuries if not longer depending of the greenhouse gas are but one of the robust indicators of the dramatic difference of the future confronting societies. Yet greenhouse gas emissions continue to rise rapidly.

Climate change and the future of societies[41]

> Our reconstructions demonstrate that the modern global temperature has exceeded annual levels over the past 12,000 years and probably approaches the warmth of the last interglacial period (128,000 to 115,000 years ago).
>
> —Samantha Bova et al. (2021:548)

> Adaptation is "an important part of the underlying problem. Do we have so much faith in our own adaptability that we will risk destroying the integrity of the entire global ecological system? If we try to adapt to the changes, we are causing rather than prevent them in the first place, have we made an appropriate choice?"
>
> —Al Gore (1992:240)

An unprecedented, accelerating societal challenge:[42] For example, landscapes viewed as utterly stable entities become dynamic. The changeability of nature leads to wholly different tasks faced by humankind. But the climate crisis is just as much an economic and cultural crisis (see Ghosh, [2016] 2021).

A survey carried out by *Nature* of leading climate scientists, the author of the most recent IPPC Report, expect that the average global temperature will increase

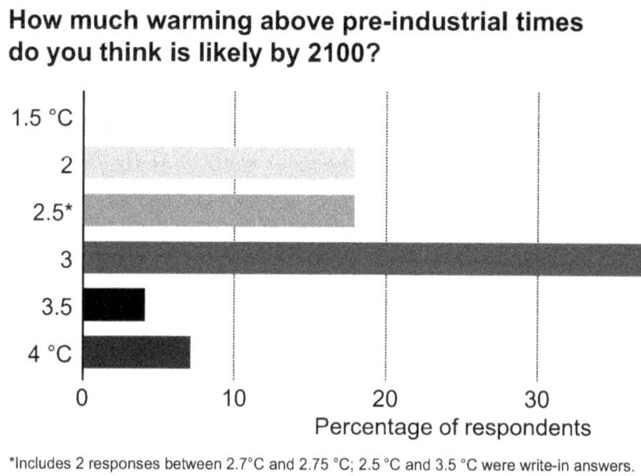

FIGURE 4.1

Source: Nature, November 4, 2021, Volume 599, Issue 7898

by 3 degrees Celsius compared to pre-industrial times. Unless massive, preventive adaptation measures are realized, such an increase would have disastrous consequences. Our planet already is hotter now than it has been for at least 12,000 years, a period spanning the entire developmental phase of human civilization (with the start of hunter-gathering societies), as research by Samantha Bova and her colleagues demonstrates. Progress toward decarbonization has been dismal. Whether humans have the collective capacity to reverse the carbonization process remains unclear.

On a smaller scale, Katey Walter Anthony has studied some 300 lakes across the tundra of the Alaska Arctic.[43] But sitting on the mucky shore of her latest discovery, the Arctic expert said she'd never seen a lake like this one. Set against the austere peaks of the Western Brooks Range, the lake in the Arctic Circle of Alaska is about 20 football fields in size, looked as if it was boiling. Its waters hissed, bubbled and popped as a powerful greenhouse gas escaped from the lake bed. Some bubbles grew as big as grapefruits, visibly lifting the water's surface several inches and carrying up bits of mud from below. This was methane. As the permafrost thaws across the fast-warming Arctic, it releases carbon dioxide, the top planet-warming greenhouse gas, from the soil into the air. Sometimes, that thaw spurs the growth of lakes in the soft, sunken ground, and these deep-thawing bodies of water tend to unleash the harder-hitting methane gas. But not this much of it. This lake, which Walter Anthony dubbed Esieh Lake, looked different. And the volume of gas wafting from it could deliver the climate system another blow. If lakes like this turn out to be widespread in the permafrost zones of the earth. Methane is a greenhouse gas with a far greater impact on global warming than CO2. It has a much longer retention time in the atmosphere.[44]

Despite all the world-wide policy efforts in the last decade directed at *Klimaschutz* (protecting the climate), a.k.a. reducing greenhouse gas emissions, the WMO (World Meteorological Association) reports that in 2020 the *increase* in the concentration of greenhouse gases the atmosphere is higher than the average in the last decade and that the total has reached a new record. If the same trend continues, the WMO observers, the 2015 in Paris agreed to goal of an increase in the average temperature by the end of the century between 1.5 and 2 degrees Celsius will surely be missed.

Well before global warming became of significant interest to scientific research and subsequently a major public issue, at least some historians displayed considerable fascination with the interrelation of climate, cultural, demographic, and economic processes. It appears that the results of such inquiries into long-term social transformations in response to climate changes generally are negative, at least as far as historians are concerned. The well-known French historian Le Roy Ladurie ([1967] 1988:119), for example, in his treatise *Times of Feast, Times of Famine* (a book published in 1967 that carries the subtitle "A History of Climate since the Year 1000") concludes that "in the long term" the human consequences of climate appear "to be slight, perhaps negligible, and certainly difficult to detect". It seems obvious that we are about to enter an era in which both the effect of climate on human conduct and of human behavior on climate change are granted a status opposite from the conclusions Le Roy Ladurie's has advanced.

Exceptional circumstances

The threats to democracy in the modern era are many. Not least is the risk posed by the widespread feeling among different segments of the public in contemporary democracies that no one from the political class is listening. Such discontent reaches from the Tea Party in the United States, UKIP in the United Kingdom, the AfD in Germany, to the National Front in France (see Guriev and Papaioannou, 2020). Freedom House in London reports that according to their calculations, there have now been 14 consecutive years during which democracy has been in retreat globally.[45] Perhaps surprisingly, similar voices of democracy skepticism can also be found in the scientific community.

On the other hand, most of us are well informed that the robustness and the consensus in the science community about human-caused climate change has in recent years not only increased in strength but that a number of recent studies point to far more dramatic consequences such as increased weather extremes and long-lasting consequences of global warming than previously thought. Moreover, it is highly likely that the sophistication and depth of our knowledge about global and regional climates will substantially increase in the next decades. Under such circumstances, how is it possible, many scientists ask, that such evidence does not or, at least, much more promptly motivate significant political action in all societies around the world?

Climate scientists, social scientists concerned with climate change, segments of civil society (NGO's) and the media refer to a "future present" of "exceptional circumstances". However, the same groups often assert, too, that no one is listening to their diagnosis of potential, incomparable dangers. An elite of climate scientists believes they are reading the evidence much more fully that others fail to acknowledge and know truths that others lack the courage to fully confront. In light of the extraordinary dangers to human civilization posed by climate change, democracy quickly becomes an inconvenient form of governing.

Surprisingly perhaps, discourse about the disenchantment with democracy and the need to suppress political liberties in the wake of profound future environmental changes has not received much systematic attention in social science.

In this section, therefore, I will bring this disenchantment under the spotlight. I will argue that there is no contradiction between democratic governance and knowledge. Rather than lamenting about the inconvenience of democratic governance, it is important to reflect upon enhancing democracy, not despite but *especially* in light of the massive challenges of a changing climate. The section reframes our changing climate as an issue of political governance and not as an environmental or as an economic issue.

I will advance my argument in a number of steps I address, first, the growing assertion of "exceptional circumstances" by elites. Second, I describe the growing sentiment of an *inconvenient democracy* among climate scientists, other scholars, and the media. Third, I consider the proposed shift in role for climate scientists as policy makers. Fourth, I examine the serious faults in the assertion of "an inconvenient democracy". Finally, I will draw attention to some of the policy implications of these observations.

The rise of exceptional circumstances

In the past, war-like conditions and major disasters typically were seen to justify the abolition of democratic liberties, if only temporarily. The present appeal to exceptional circumstances—which from time to time could also be observed in the face of the pandemic[46]—echoes this sentiment, demanding the elevation of a single socio-political purpose to ultimate political supremacy. The position can also be summed up arguing that the existential threat of climate change to society is simply too real and too massive to discuss, that is, waste time discussing civil liberties and human rights when the basic survival is at stake.

We are confronted with an entirely novel situation: Climate change is locked in. Most of the scientific discourse has been devoted to establishing the phenomenon that there is anthropogenic climate change. That issue has been settled. What is not settled in science are a range of important questions such as the speed of warming or the nature of the consequences of climate change, in various regions of the world, on various significant attributes of human existence.

Except for reference to singular historical events, for example war, for example the World War II intervention in the economy, there are no large-scale human experiences to which the claims of the climate science community can appeal as it begins to reflect about a "future present" as massive impacts of climate change have set in. Governing the consequences of climate change refers to a time scale and societal transformations that are clearly beyond the human imagination and current political institutions to cope with.

Appeal is therefore made to extraordinary circumstances or a war-like footing that necessitates the suspension of freedoms and the political ascent of climate scientists. In *The Vanishing Face of Gaia*, James Lovelock (2009) explicitly compares climate change to war, emphasizing that we need to abandon democracy in order to meet the challenges of climate change head on. We are in a state of war. In order to pull the world out of its state of lethargy, the equivalent of a global warming speech, "nothing but blood, toil, tears and sweat" is urgently needed. The central state is seen as the source of security in the face of radical risk (cf. Rosanvallon, [2011] 2013:184). It is the hope that an appeal to extraordinary circumstances, that is, to a threat to the very existence of humankind "alone might be able to give capacity and . . . energy back to a failing or hampered [political] will", as a French political scientist argues.

But how does one govern well under exceptional circumstances? Governing well under exceptional circumstances is allied to a couple of assertions: that of an *inconvenient mind* that justifies imposing one's (superior) ideas on citizens and *inconvenient social institutions* that justify a strong state in the form of a command society.

The implication of the position is that good governance of society must be subordinated to the defeat of the exceptional circumstances. It is the single purpose of defeating the exceptional circumstances that legitimizes the suspension of freedoms. But for how long can one defer liberties? At least in the case of war, in democratic societies, the answer is that "it is sensible temporarily to sacrifice freedom in order to make it more secure in the future" (Hayek, 1944:189). However, is any massive absorption of powers in the hand of the state and its representative's reversible, in the long run? And, are the potential consequences of climate change the equivalent of (abrupt) war-like conditions? How can one pinpoint the onset of exceptional circumstances?

The deficiencies of and the short term as well as long term challenges faced by democratic governments indeed are many and far exceed of course the issue of climate change[47] and its societal consequences but is it therefore justified to reach such a disparaging conclusion as is the diagnosis of an inconvenient democracy? After all, authoritarian and totalitarian governments do not have a record of environmental accomplishments; nations that have followed the path of "authoritarian modernization" such as China or Russia cannot claim to have a better record. Nonetheless, the disenchantment with democracies continues to be advanced, perhaps is becoming even more vocal as entrenched climate policies fail to live up to their promise.

The erosion of democracy

The assertion of "exceptional circumstances and the concomitant promotion of an "inconvenient democracy" derives its intellectual sustenance from a range of considerations:

- a deep-seated pessimism about the "the psychological make-up of human beings"; the temporality of human thought;
- the intellectual competence of individuals to grasp complex issues—if not the extent to which most politicians and the electorate are scientifically illiterate; the capability to govern is an irrelevant criterion, as one of the early critics of democracy (Plato) already noted: there is prerequisite to rule
- the failure to mobilize individuals generally for the cause of politics and more specifically for the cause of effective climate policies;
- the inability of government given constitutional constraints to attend to long term goals, even as the result of "too much democracy" (see Fukuyama, 2014);
- the fragility of the political order;
- the failure of the political institutions to internally generate effective "governing knowledge"[48]
- the influence of vested interests on the political agendas of the day;
- the addiction to fossil fuel;
- and, last but not least, the futility of the climate science community itself to ensure that their message does not a fall on deaf ears.
- Although the affinity—not by accident—of the argument about an inconvenient democracy rarely spells out its ideological closeness to the ideas of the legal scholar cum political philosopher Carl Schmitt, a kinship is quite evident. Schmitt believed that the supreme leadership and not the rule of law should always have the last word. Following the rule of law only undermines the effectiveness of decision-making, especially under extraordinary circumstances.

Daniel Kahneman (in Marshall, 2014:57) sums up the growing skepticism regarding citizen motivation when he states:

> the bottom line is that I'm extremely skeptical that we can cope with climate change. To mobilize people, this has to become an emotional issue. It has to have the immediacy and salience. A distant, abstract, and disputed threat just doesn't have the necessary characteristics for seriously mobilizing public opinion.

The mass of citizens, it seems, simply cannot be won over to endorse and follow the course of scientifically based policy options. The large majority of citizens is basically inclined to act irrationally.[49] As the climate scientist Hans-Joachim Schellnhuber (2011)[50] relates, "my own experience and everyday knowledge illustrate that comfort and ignorance are the biggest flaws of human character. This is a potentially deadly mix." The well-known climate researcher James Hansen, who first alerted the American Congress to the phenomenon of global warming, summaries the general frustration in stating: "the democratic process does not work."

Not just citizens, but their politicians seem unlikely to implement satisfactory policy; activist climate scientists, NGOs, politicians and many other observers agree that past climate summits in Copenhagen, Cancun, Durban and Warsaw were failures. The summits did not result in a new global agreement to cope effectively with the emissions of greenhouse gases. Whether the 2015 Paris Accord will fare better remains to be seen.

The nature of the relation between temporality and democracy justifies doubts about the effectives of democratic governance in the face of future risks and dangers of climate change. Issues of temporality refer to at least a couple of significant matters driven by distinctive but related conditions of democratic governance. On the one hand, democratic governance is captivated by the immediacy of frequently changing "events" that come and go often rapidly as much as it is affected, on the other hand, by constitutional rules of representation that prescribe relatively short frames of temporality.[51]

Is democracy and societal institutions constrained by short-term constitutional frames and governed by principles of liberty such as the market place capable of dealing with harms and risks to society that are located in the future? How can democracies sustain interest in a future present a couple of decades away thereby escaping the typical attention circle of events?

The discussion in the climate science community about the shortcomings of democratic governance converges with assessments of the present state and future of democracy in the social sciences that reach similar discouraging conclusions about the efficacy of democracy in many nations. In contrast to decades of optimism in the post-war world about the trajectory and the spread of democratic governance, assisted if not triggered by economic expansion, social science observers see contemporary democracy—whether by design or at the outcome of structural economic, political, and moral changes—on the way to autocratic forms of governance. The lack of trust, shattered confidence and the erosion of democracy manifests itself for example "in a hollowing out of citizenship, the marketization of the public sector; the soul-destroying targets and audits that go with it; the denigration of professionalism and the professional ethic; and the erosion of public trust" (Marquand, 2004:172), de-politicization, the restriction of the public sphere or the replacement of politics by techniques of management (cf. Rosanvallon, 2006:228). At the same time, it can be stated that the hesitant attitude towards Covid vaccines is a characteristic of the broken relationship of the opponents of vaccination towards the state. In some societies, democratic governance is increasingly replaced by a rapid abolition of democratic rights and values of ordinary citizens and hence autocratic forms of governance.

What distinguishes the discussion about the poor health of democracy among professional social science observers of contemporary forms of democratic governance from the diagnosis of democracy at the center of our analysis is the remedy that is advocated: On the one hand, efforts are discussed that should restore the vitality of the core function of democracy, for example, restoring "a society of similar individuals" (Rosanvallon, [2011] 2013) though the active participation of large numbers of citizens in shaping the agenda of public life (cf. Crouch, 2004); on the other hand, climate scientists and other observers of global climate change disparage about the very vitality of democratic governance in coping effectively with the large scale environmental problems. Hence, the very abolition of democracy is considered a virtue and the establishment for example of a "benevolent despotism" considered desirable. In some of the images of "post-democracy" as such a state of the state—a return to aristocratic society—has already been achieved: Self-appointed elites claim to carry out the wishes of the masses.

The conclusion drawn by many is that democracy itself is inappropriate, that the slow procedures for implementation and management of specific, policy-relevant scientific knowledge leads to massive, unknown risks and dangers. The democratic system designed to balance divergent interest has failed in the face of these threat.

Enlightened leadership

Until recently, it has been rare to observe an open and explicit expression of doubt about the virtues of democracy, with the obvious exception of certain leaders of decidedly undemocratic nations. In particular, it has traditionally been the case that scientists rarely have raised serious misgivings in public about democracy as a political system, most surely in post-war Germany.

But times are changing. Within the broad field of climatology and climate policy one is able to discern growing frustration with the virtues of democracy and a mounting appeal to exceptional circumstances and the promotion of the role of scientists and experts in policy making. The impatience with democracy and the shifting understanding of the role of scientists goes hand-in-hand with a change in the function IPCC. Increasingly IPCC no longer considers itself a scientific organization with the mandate to offer alternative policy options for political discussion and decision but as a body demanding that options for political action it identifies be realized.

Leading climate scientists insist that humanity is at a crossroads. A continuation of present economic and political trends leads to disaster if not a collapse of human civilization. To create a globally sustainable way of life, we immediately need, in the words of German climate scientist Hans Joachim Schellnhuber, a "great transformation". What that statement exactly means is vague. Part, if not the core of the required great transformation is a new political regime and forms of governance: For example, as expressed by the Australian scholars David Shearman and Joseph Wayne Smith in their book *The Climate Change Challenge and the Failure of Democracy*: "We need an authoritarian form of government in order to implement the scientific consensus on greenhouse gas emissions."

Clearly therefore as Shearman and Smith (2007:4) conclude, "humanity will have to trade its liberty to live as it wishes in favor of a system where survival is paramount." Another Australian scholar, Mark Beeson agrees with Shearman and Smith's political conclusion and adds, "forms of 'good' authoritarianism, in which environmentally unsustainable forms of behavior are simply forbidden, may become not only justifiable, but essential for the survival of humanity in anything approaching a civilised form." Moreover—although existing research is methodologically weak, a recent study using a web-based survey of residents of the Province of British Columbia concludes that citizens' support for climate change policies is not only weak, but that citizen knowledge of policy is not associated with higher policy support "providing information on likely policy effectiveness . . . did not translate into higher support." Hence, the conclusion of this group of researchers is that "*widespread knowledge and well-informed citizen support* are not necessarily required for implementation of effective climate policies" (emphasis added; Rhodes et al., 2014:92). Along with other observers, this can only mean that present political conditions in China, especially the preeminent role of the state and the party in climate policies regimes, ought to become exemplary and attain global significance, as the New York Times columnist Thomas Friedman for example recently observed; the dictatorship of the party is superior to chaotic democratic governance.

The following statement by Robert Stavins, director of Harvard's Environmental Economics Program and a co-author of the IPCC (Intergovernmental Panel on Climate Change) WG 3 report exemplifies the case at hand. Stavins notes a

> bottom-up demand which normally we always want to have and rely on in a representative democracy, is in my view unlikely to work in the case of climate change policy as it has for other environmental problems. . . . It's going to take enlightened leadership, leaders that take the lead.[52]

The social scientist Evelyn Fox Keller (2010), for example, makes the strong case for an immediately effective, absolute political role of climate science that confers a special political status on the holders of such knowledge (philosophers-kings)—in light of the seriousness of the problem of global warming:

> there is no escaping our dependence on experts; we have no choice but to call on those (in this case, our climate scientists) who have the necessary

> expertise. . . . Furthermore, for the particular task of getting beyond our current impasse, I also suggest that climate scientists may be the only ones in a position to take the lead. . . . [and] given the tacit contract between scientists and the state which supports them on the other, I will also argue that climate scientists are not only in a position to take the lead, but also that they are obliged to do so.[53]

But what kind of competences is one exactly prepared to turn over to the then ruling elite of experts and the state? Does is perhaps even include the extreme competence to "not to permit to live" ("Nicht-leben-lassen"; cf. Blumenberg, 2006:553)? Not only such a competence but also many others would clearly be indicative of authoritarian governance.

Science, knowledge, and democracy

What should be the role of climate science knowledge in political deliberations about climate policy? *Can science tell us what to do*? The strong desire to reach specific policy outcomes, spelled out by the scientific community lead many scientists to at least sympathize with the suspension of democratic process. However, there are a number of weaknesses with this position:

First, a flawed understanding of knowledge; scientific knowledge is not immediately performative (knowledge equals control or represents practical reason), nor is it immediately persuasive (that is, knowledge convinces unencumbered).[54] One of the fundamental flaws in the portrait of an inconvenient democracy is the failure to recognize the social character of knowledge in general and the essentially contested nature of political knowledge in particular.

Second, the dominant political approach concentrates almost to the exclusion of other forms and conditions of action, on a single *effect* that governance ought to achieve, namely a reduction of greenhouse gas emissions. By focusing on the goals of political action rather than its conditions, the contentious issue of climate change is reduced to scientific or technical issue from a sociopolitical issue and a depoliticization of climate change and the politicization of climate science. Sheila Jasanoff (2012) asserts that support for such a conversion comes with the societal ascendency of science and technology generally; matters relevant to the public's participation have been permanently taken out of politics.

Third, the generally pessimistic assessment of the ability of democratic governance to cope with and control exceptional circumstances is if only implicitly linked to the optimistic assessment of the potential of large-scale social planning. The capacity not only of governments but societies *to plan* its future present is rather limited, perhaps absent (see Tenbruck, 1977:138; also Scott, 1968). Public consciousness about the limits of state planning continues to be, despite even recent relevant historical experiences, limited. Plans as we all know only too well, turn into dreams. Democracies, not civilizations, of course with the exceptions we all only know too well have an impressive capacity to overcome tensions engendered by political, economic, and cultural change and manage to adopt to novel circumstances. When one approach doesn't work, democracies tend to try another. One of the basic similarities between science and democracy therefore is that their effectiveness as a social organization is linked to their modesty based on their competence of self-criticism and self-doubt.

Aside from the paradoxical fact that, after all, the thesis of our limited capability of social planning is itself a prognosis about our ability to manage the future, a variety of powerful perspectives are unenthusiastic about the disposability of conditions. The social planning conception widely discussed a couple of decades ago in the controversies about centralized economic policies has fallen into disrepute. Similarly, the once active program of and enthusiastic support for Futurology about desirable futures has vanished. More recently, the social systems perspective developed by Niklas Luhmann's stresses the de-centering of modern, functionally differentiated societies that precludes de-differentiated social planning.

Fourth, in the reasoning of the impatient critics of democracy, one notes an inappropriate fusion of the nature of nature and the nature of society. The uncertainties that the science of the natural processes (climate) claims to have eliminated and the consensus the sciences have thereby acquired, is simply transferred to the domain of societal processes. Consensus on the evidence, it is argued, should motivate a consensus on political action. The constitutive uncertainties of social, political, and economic events, the difficulty of anticipating the future present is treated as minor obstacles that can be encircled as soon as possible—of course by a top-down approach—by implementing policies that knowledge prescribes. This undermines the plurality and conflict that inevitably features in contemporary societies.

There is but one political system, namely democratic practices designed to rationally cope with divergent political interests, attend to distributive conflicts within and among nations, deal with different policy options (for example, adaptation and/or mitigation) and generally advance the aspirations of different segments of the population. The challenge that remains is enhancing rather than abolishing democracy.[55] And as Albert Einstein[56] reminded us in the case of the nuclear age policies, not every citizen has to become a nuclear physicist but "the nuclear age concerns every person in the civilized world. . . . Choices about survival depend ultimately on decisions made in the village square." Responses to the extraordinary consequences of climate change require democratic decisions.

Enhancing democracy

Governing under exceptional circumstances of a changing climate appears to be an intractable problem; although C.P Snow (1962:61) does not refer to the issue of climate change, perhaps one can generally agree that it is "one of the most intractable problems that organized society has thrown up" (Snow, 1962:61). Can good governance of exceptional circumstances be democratic governance?

The discourse of the impatient scientists in their disenchantment with democracy privileges hegemonic players such world powers, states, transnational organizations, and multinational corporations. Participatory strategies on how to involve citizens are only rarely in evidence. More despairingly, a large segment of the public has given up on politics altogether, for example, convinced that those in political office do not really about those who have declared themselves to be absent. Perhaps a "social contract" between politics and citizen/voters is an initial, effective intellectual and organization answer (cf. Willis, 2020:82).

Likewise, global mitigation has precedence over local adaptation.[57] A unitary *Anthropocene* gains over regional circumstances. "Global" knowledge triumphs over "local" knowledge. However, the simplistic global view neglects the fact of a highly stratified world, for example, in terms of responsibility for greenhouse gas emissions or highly divergent lifestyles. Societal trends appear to operate into the opposite direction. The ability of large institutions to impose their will on citizens is declining. As a result, people mobilize around local concerns and efforts including those of the consequences of climate change—thereby enhancing the democratic in democratic governance. The local/regional coupling of the climate change discourse, for example by referring to the local consequences of extreme weather events and benefits of adaptation, has among voters a greater persuasive power in principle.

The discussion of options for future climate policies supports the impression that the same failed climate policies must remain in place and are the only correct approach; it is simply that these policies have to be become more effective and "rational". It follows that international negotiations must lead to an agreement for concrete, but much broader emission reduction targets. Only a super-Kyoto can still help us. But how the noble goals of a comprehensive emission reduction can be practically and politically enforced remains in the fog of general declarations of intent and only sharpens the political skepticism of scientists.

The still-dominant line of attack to climate policy shows little evidence of success either at the state or at the global level. One result of the recent global recession may well have an unintended reduction of the increase of CO_2 emissions. The worldwide reaction to the economic crisis, for example during the G20 meeting in Australia in November of 2014, however, shows very clearly that governments do not conceive of a reduction in the growth of their wealth of their populations as a useful mechanism toward a reduction of emissions. On the contrary, everything is set in motion worldwide aimed at a resumption of economic growth. Jump-starting the economy means emissions will raise again.

An alternative model is therefore needed, and it is possible that it will only be found through revitalized democratic interaction in which alternative perspectives can be presented. Democracy is likely to enhance active environmental citizenship. Environmental citizenship should be supportive of ambitious climate policies, for example, by carefully monitoring policies generated and supported by states and large social institutions.

Proponents of an inconvenient democracy perspective tend to draw the wrong conclusion, namely that only authoritarian political states,[58] preferably guided by scientists make effective and correct decisions on the climate issue. History teaches us that the opposite is the case. The emergence and broad-based support for environmental concerns and subsequently regulations came about in open democratic argument about the value of nature for humanity (cf. Purdy, 2010). Therefore, today's China let alone past Eastern European state socialist societies cannot serve as a model.

Climate policy must be compatible with democracy; otherwise the threat to civilization will be much more than just changes to our physical environment. The alternative to the abolition of democratic governance as the effective response to the societal threats that likely come with climate change is more democracy, that is making not only democracy and solutions more complex but also to enhance the worldwide empowerment and knowledgeability of individuals, groups and movements that labor on environmental issues. A war-like footing has exactly the opposite effect. A war-like approach reduces the complexity of social and political life inasmuch as war "nationalizes people's life. Private activities. . . [are] largely shaped by collective constraints" (Rasonvallon, [2011] 2013:183). Under modern conditions, especially the heightened cognitive and social abilities of ordinary citizens require their political participation for successful policies and good governance.

Moreover, a further denationalization of governance will assist in producing new, multiple forms of social solidarity and obligations, strengthens local/regional responses to climate change and enhances the understanding of social interdependence. Another important socio-political process that enhances democracy and political participation is the systematic reduction of patterns of social inequality in modern societies.

In addition, the self-sufficiency of social institutions wherever it still exists and is practiced efforts have to be re-made in order to transcend boundaries, joining allegedly distinctive motives and practices of different social institutions, for example, joining economic and moral incentives and enhancing the complexity of needs.

The erosion of democracy might seem to be "convenient" to some, but surely is an unnecessary suppression of social complexity and rights. Friedrich Hayek ([1958] 1960:25) pointed a paradoxical development that appears to manifest itself in the present context: As science advances it tends to strengthen the observation that we should "aim at more *deliberate and comprehensive control of all human activities*". Hayek pessimistically adds, "It is for this reason that those intoxicated by the advance of knowledge so often become the enemies of freedom".

The political and cultural challenges of a comprehensive climate policy are not easy to enumerate; I therefore refer to the following (incomplete) list of research goals, policy fields, and normative demands in the wake of a heating world:

- Higher priority to the policy and practical field of "adaptation" (protecting society; enhancing resilience) in everyday life, research and policy; "localized climate-risk information should be invested in as a *public good*" [Hill, 2021:9] my emphasis)
- Adaptation will be costly, e.g., necessitates energy and requires a more comprehensive examination of the actual threats of the *consequences* of climate change (cf. Albert, Christoph et al., 2021; Chakrabarty, 2017),
- Climate change, *global* inequality, and climate policies.
- A more persuasive narrative toward a transition and social organization of a resilient society.
- Climate change narratives that are not supported by reference to the mere economic value of adaptation/mitigation.
- Food security and climate change
- Health and climate change (cf. *New England Journal of Medicine*, September 3, 2021: "Call for emergency action to limit global temperature increases, restore biodiversity, and protect health."
- Inviting nature back into the urban landscape
- The vulnerability of (our classical and digital) infrastructure due to climate change[59]
- What exactly is meant by net-zero carbon pledges? Does is apply to all greenhouse emissions? Concrete steps? Fairness?
- Biodiversity and Global Warming
- Rise of sea level[60]
- Geoengineering[61]
- Public participation in climate policies
- Restorative stewardship
- Linking climate policy and social policies;[62] organizing the resources for climate policies, and, most required and most difficult to enact
- "democratisation of democracy" (e.g. Giddens, 1999)

I end my observations about modern societies as knowledge societies with highlighting selected conclusions as well as some reflections about the dilemma of theorizing about the future of knowledge societies. The present of the future cannot be anticipated in the present; but we can learn from the recollection of the past in the present, as has been done here, and draw benefits for our future. Whether these benefits will result, as they perhaps must, in a fundamental revolution of the ways we live is open. But our enlarged capacities to act ensure that we have a measure of control about the path of the revolution ahead.

Notes

1. For the purpose of an illustrative example, I refer to an example of a knowledge policy proposal from the 1930s: In an analysis of the societal role of technology that reiterated his earlier critique of and distance from modern technology (Sombart, 1911; Grundmann and Stehr, 2001), Werner Sombart (1934: 266) called for the creation of a *Kulturrat,* or Cultural Affairs Commission, whose mandate would be to decide whether "an invention should be discarded, passed on to a museum, or . . . realized in practice" (also Lenger, 1996: 366–377). Engineers were supposed to have an advisory role in the commission. Sombart's choice of the name of the commission is not accidental, but rather programmatic. The term "cultural" refers, of course, to the difference between mere civilization and culture—implying that the difference between the civilizational and the cultural sphere is not symmetrical but hierarchical. Although threatened by civilizational developments, culture is superior and is in charge of determining the fate of purely civilizational products. Sombart's aims for the realization of cultural policies were deeply embedded in ideologies of the merits of mere civilizational accomplishments, designed to regulate new technological inventions. But have new knowledge and new technical capacities ever been relegated to a "museum," and therefore not utilized?
2. According to an account repeated in the *Guardian* (January 29, 2021; "The Guardian view on the Arab Spring, a decade on: a haunting legacy"), the Chinese premier Zhou Enlai, when asked in 1972 about the influence of the French Revolution, replied: "Too soon to tell." Zhou Enlai was correct if he meant that the assessments of historical events tend to change much of the time—but that may not be what he meant.
3. An editorial in Nature (Sept. 9, 2021) takes the position that the patent holders of CRISPR techniques—they are primarily universities, only one-third of the patents for these techniques belong to the private sector—should make the techniques with an enormous potential available for free for non-profit purposes: The time has come, the *Nature* editorial demands,

   > for all universities that hold CRISPR patents, along with public funders and international institutions such as the World Intellectual Property Organization, to consider how they might join forces so that IP on CRISPR can be more easily accessed free of charge for research, under clear and transparent rules.

4. The Journal *Nature* (29 June 2021) reports that

   > preliminary results from a landmark clinical trial suggest that CRISPR—Cas9 gene editing can be deployed directly into the body to treat disease. . . . The study is the first to show that the technique can be safe and effective if the CRISPR—Cas9 components—in this case targeting a protein that is made mainly in the liver—are infused into the bloodstream. . . . The treatment was developed by Intellia Therapeutics of Cambridge, Massachusetts, and Regeneron of Tarrytown, New York. They published the trial results in *The New England Journal of Medicine*[1] and presented them at an online meeting of the Peripheral Nerve Society on 26 June [2021].

5. Cited in *Business Insider*, February 4, 2021. https://markets.businessinsider.com/news/stocks/mohamed-el-erian-reddit-war-wall-street-elements-arab-spring-2021–2–1030042395
6. This account is based on a *New York Times* Article, January 29, 2021, "Behind the Stock Market's Wild Ride This Week," www.nytimes.com/interactive/2021/01/29/business/stock-market-gamestop-amc.html?action=click&module=Spotlight&pgtype=Homepage
7. Cf. ("How the rich got richer: Reddit trading frenzy benefited Wall Street elite," Washington Post, February 9, 2021)

8. www.nytimes.com/2021/03/29/business/archegos-hwang-viacomcbs-discovery.html
9. Notably Karl Popper ([1961] 1992:141), expresses an opinion skeptical about overall benefits for mankind as the result of the advancement of science:

   > The progress of science—itself partly a consequences of the ideal of self-emancipation through knowledge—is contributing to the lengthening and to the enrichment of our lives; yet it has led us to spend those lives under the threat of an atomic war, and it is doubtful whether it has on balance contributed to the happiness and contentment of man.

10. As Michel Foucault famously noted in the introduction to the *History of Sexuality* "Where there is power, there is resistance."
11. However, it is a comment on the sensibility of claims made on behalf of "future studies" as relevant to future conduct.
12. See Nesrine Malik, "Vaccine hesitancy is a symptom of people's broken relationship with the state," The Guardian, August 15, 2021; www.theguardian.com/commentisfree/2021/aug/15/vaccine-hesitancy-broken-relationship-state-conspiracy-theorists
13. Lander and Baylis (2019:567) make a concrete, rather liberal suggestion of how to deal with genome editing in practice:

   > The governance model we present would intentionally leave room for nations to take differing approaches and reach different conclusions, informed by their history, culture, values and political systems. Still, the common principle would be all nations agreeing to proceed deliberately and with due respect to the opinions of humankind.

14. I have devoted a separate study (Stehr, [2005] 2015) to the emergence of the new field of political activity, knowledge politics.
15. As noted by the *Scientific American* (September 14, 2018):

   > If widely adopted, lab-grown meat, also called clean meat, could eliminate much of the cruel, unethical treatment of animals raised for food. It could also reduce the considerable environmental costs of meat production; resources would be needed only to generate and sustain cultured cells, not an entire organism from birth.
   > (www.scientificamerican.com/article/lab-grown-meat/)

16. Compare "A conversation with Jennifer Doudna & Walter Isaacson", *Washington Post*, March 15, 2021: www.washingtonpost.com/washington-post-live/2021/03/15/transcript-conversation-with-jennifer-doudna-walter-isaacson/
17. The enlargement of the scientific community into a genuine international or even global community is beginning to become a focus of reflection and research in science studies (e.g., Schott, 1988, 1993).
18. According to the US National Institute of Health, geroscience "seeks to understand molecular and cellular mechanisms that make aging a major risk factor and driver of common chronic conditions and diseases of older adulthood".
19. As Bruce Schneier (2021) alerts us, one, artificial intelligence systems will be used to hack us. Specifically, two,

   > AI systems will themselves become hackers: finding vulnerabilities in all sorts of social, economic, and political systems, and then exploiting them at an unprecedented speed, scale, and scope. It's not just a difference in degree; it's a difference in kind.

   To which one should add, three, AI systems can be deployed to hack AI systems.
20. "In December 2018, WHO established a global, multidisciplinary expert advisory committee (the Expert Advisory Committee on Developing Global Standards for

Governance and Oversight of Human Genome Editing, hereafter called the Committee) to examine the scientific, ethical, social and legal challenges associated with human genome editing (somatic, germline and heritable). The governance framework on human genome editing, along with the recommendations of the Committee, form a set of two publications that provide advice and recommendations on appropriate institutional, national, regional and global governance mechanisms for human genome editing. A position paper on human genome editing provides a summary of these two publications." See www.who.int/publications/i/item/9789240030060.

21. See "A new company with a wild mission: Bring back the woolly mammoth," *New York Times*, September 14, 2021; www.nytimes.com/2021/09/13/science/colossal-woolly-mammoth-DNA.html
22. *Climate Change & Technology Transfer: Addressing Intellectual Property Issues* (Third World Network, 2012); available via http://go.nature.com/pCOhCT
23. The "sweeping" executive orders signed by President Biden in early of July 2021 (compare "Biden urges more scrutiny of big business, such as Tech Giants," *New York Times*, July, 2021) intended to increase competition will have little if any impact if implemented—as far as I can see—on the key level of the monopoly power of tech giants, namely the institutional framework of international intellectual property law.
24. A proposal by Senator Russel B. Long in 1965 ensuring that the Government should keep the proprietary right to drug discoveries inventions it finances, failed to receive the necessary majority in the US Senate. A representative of the pharmaceutical firm of Eli Lilly argued that all companies should retain the rights to discoveries they make under Government research and development contracts (cf. "Exception indicate in drug patent policy," *New York Times*, July 8, 1965). Since the mid 1960s, the matter has become more urgent: Fred Block and Mathew Keller (2012:98; also Teece, 1992) underline the need to re-examine the knowledge governance in the case of (increased) publicly financed innovations: "A new regime of knowledge governance is necessary to recognize the important role of the public sector in facilitating innovation and to minimize the negative consequences on technological advance of the current restrictive regime of intellectual property rights."
25. According to a *Guardian* (April 15, 2021) (www.theguardian.com/science/2021/apr/15/oxfordastrazeneca-covid-vaccine-research-was-97-publicly-funded) inquiry, researchers report that

    > at least 97% of the funding for the development of the *Oxford/AstraZeneca Covid-19 vaccine* has been identified as coming from taxpayers or charitable trusts, according to the first attempt to reconstruct who paid for the decades of research that led to the lifesaving formulation.

    Using two different methods of inquiry, researchers were able to identify the source of hundreds of millions of pounds of research grants from the year 2000 onwards for published work on what would eventually become the novel technology that underpins the jab, as well as funding for the final product (emphasis added).
26. As Christopher May (2002:143) observers,

    > the problem . . . is not so much the lack of balance between private and public rights over knowledge, but rather that the acceleration . . . of innovation has disturbed a previously legitimized balance. By leaving term limits where they are, . . . the current regime of protection for intellectual property has essentially extended and expanded the advantages for owners.

27. See Henkel and Reitzig, 2008:129: "Technology companies have been attacked by *patent sharks,* firms with hidden intellectual property that surface, threatening to sue, when their rights are *inadvertently* infringed."

28. An editorial in *Nature* (April 1, 2021) reports

> around 100 countries, led by India and South Africa, are asking fellow World Trade Organization members to agree a time-limited lifting of COVID-19-related intellectual-property (IP) rights. The main vaccine suppliers, they argue, should share their knowledge so that more countries can start producing vaccines for their own populations and for the lowest-income nations [and endorses the idea]. This idea needs to be considered seriously because a temporary IP waiver could have a role in accelerating the end of the pandemic.

"The fear is," as Joseph Stiglitz ("A better way to crack it," *New Scientist, September 16, 2006*) observes that "a focus on profits for the rich corporations amounts to a death sentence for the very poor in the developing world."
An alternative to lifting IP restriction would be

> for companies to increase the licensing of their product designs in exchange for payment. This would allow vaccines to be made by many more companies. In addition, the World Health Organization is setting up a facility for companies to share their vaccine technology, skills and other know-how.
> (*Nature,* "It's time to consider a patent reprieve for COVID vaccines," April 1, 2021)

See also Joseph Stiglitz (2006:120–124) proposals for revising patent law, particularly in the area of life-saving drugs.

29. Note the discussion of "curbing climate change" as a "global public good" (GPG): "Key GPGs include curbing climate change, instituting universal regulatory practices, eradicating infectious diseases, preserving world peace, discovering scientific breakthroughs, and limiting financial crises" (Buchholz and Sandler, 2021:488).
30. A related issue concerns the weakening of the national capacity to tax due to a lack of harmonization of international tax regimes (see Durand and Milberg, 2020:422–423).
31. Michael Polanyi (1944:65) argues for the case for "socializing" the rewards for inventions: "In order that inventions may be used freely by all, we must relieve inventors of the necessity of earning their rewards commercially and must grant them instead the right to be rewarded from the public purse."
32. Joseph Stiglitz, "A better way to crack it," *New Scientist*, September 16, 2006.
33. The solution to the economic problem, the struggle for subsistence, Keynes anticipated to occur in a hundred years from 1930; and it would confirm that the economic problem is not a permanent affliction of the human race. The most recent installment of the ambiguous future may be found in an *Economist* article ("Riding high in a workers' world as jobs rebound, shifting politics and technological change could bring a golden age for labour in rich countries", April 10, 2021) that predicts, "today, as the economy emerges from the pandemic, a reversal of the primacy of capital over labour beckons—and will come sooner than you think."
34. A more extensive discussion of the changes and prospect of transformations affecting labor may be found in the chapter on "The Price of Labor" in Stehr and Voss (2020:179–267).
35. This is an assertion that appears to be the message of an article in the *New York Times* on "The tech industry is building a vast digital underclass," July 24, 2020.
36. During the last four decades, as a study by Jaimovich, Saporta-Eksten, Siu, and Yedid-Levi (2020) shows, the US has

> experienced a fall in the employment in middle-wage, "routine-task-intensive," occupations. We analyze the characteristics of those who used to be employed in such occupations and show that this type of individual is nowadays more likely to be out of the labor force or working in low-paying occupations.

37. See Kevin Roose, "The robots are coming for Phil in accounting," *New York Times*, March 6, 2021 describes a transformative trend in employment called "robotic process automation" (RPA), "liberating" many people from their jobs; with RPA one is able to build "a bot that costs $10.00 a year and take out two to four humans". Workers with the highest exposure to AI are the most vulnerable. The question remaining is how many business jobs can be automated?
38. www.theguardian.com/business/2017/mar/22/robots-tax-bill-gates-income-inequality. See the draft report by the member of the European parliament Mady Delvaux from the committee on legal affairs published in May of 2016.
39. www.theguardian.com/commentisfree/2017/feb/26/robots-make-sure-pay-taxes
40. www.theguardian.com/commentisfree/2017/feb/26/robots-make-sure-pay-taxes
41. This account draws on a number of my previous reflections on the relation between governance and climate change: cf. Stehr (2015, 2016, 2020).
42. Jarmo S. Kikstra (2021) and his colleagues make an effort to estimate the future cost of climate change;

    > A key statistic describing climate change impacts is the 'social cost of carbon dioxide' (SCCO2), the projected cost to society of releasing an additional tonne of CO2. Cost-benefit integrated assessment models that estimate the SCCO2 lack robust representations of climate feedbacks, economy feedbacks, and climate extremes.

    Nonetheless, their results emphasize the significant economic impacts of climate change if future adaptation does not exceed historical trends. The authors conclude that, on average—across different scenarios—global gross domestic product (GDP) *would fall by around 37 percent this century* due to climate change. This is six times as much as previously assumed. The dangerous mix of the consequences of weather extremes such as fires, floods and droughts would be accompanied by losses in labor productivity due to higher temperatures.
43. This account is based on a *New York Times Article* from May 5, 2012 about the research carried out by Professor Katey M. Walter Anthony of the University of Alaska at Fairbanks (see Anthony et al., 2012).
44. More than 100 countries including the members of the European Union and the United States but not China, Russia, and India agreed during the COP26 meeting in Glasgow in November of 2021 to cut the methane emissions by 30 percent by 2030. Methane is 80 times more potent in warming the planet than carbon dioxide. Methane is not the only "superpollutant"; so are hydrofluorocarbons and black soot. Attending to these pollutants should have policy priority (see Prins et al., 2009).
45. https://freedomhouse.org/article/new-report-freedom-world-2020-finds-established-democracies-are-decline
46. Kriszta Kovács (2020:257) refers to the Hungarian response to the pandemic and reports,

    > on March 23, 2020, the Hungarian parliament debated a piece of legislation so similarly sweeping that Hungarians now informally call it the "Enabling Act." Seizing as a pretext the threat to public health caused by the spread of COVID-19, government members tabled a draft act on protecting against the coronavirus in accord with articles 48–54 of the Hungarian constitution. The act enables the government led by Prime Minister Viktor Orbán to issue decrees independently of the parliament.

47. Opinion polls from around the world have documented that the support for democratic institutions is declining. A Cambridge University report (2020)

    > analyzed data collected across 154 countries, 3,500 surveys covering more than 4 million respondents, and half a century of social-science research. Satisfaction with democracy, according to the report, has eroded in most parts of the world,

with an especially notable drop over the past decade. Public confidence in democracy is at the lowest point on record in the United States, the major democracies of Western Europe, sub-Saharan Africa, and Latin America. In some countries, including the United States, this metric is now reaching an important threshold: The number of people who are dissatisfied with democracy is greater than the number of people who are satisfied with it

(cf. www.theatlantic.com/ideas/archive/2020/01/confidence-democracy-lowest-point-record/605686/)

48. Marija Bartl (2017:152) defines governing knowledge as knowledge "produced by governing institutions in order to make sense of the outer world, to articulate the problems and solutions."
49. The observation of the minimal intellectual competencies of the vast majority of the population and the consequences this should have for their participation in governance can be found in reflections by some of the greatest advocates and skeptics of democracy, for example, Joseph Schumpeter (1950:chapter 21).
50. The climate scientist Hans Joachim Schellnhuber in an interview with DER SPIEGEL (Issue 12, 21. March 2010, p. 29) in response to the question why the messages of climate science fail to reach society. A similar assertion about the "know nothings" voters can be found in an exasperated comment by the economist Paul Krugman trying to account for the state of mind of portions of the American voters who at the time put Donald Trump well ahead in surveys of likely Republican presidential voters: "People can't tell the difference between someone who sounds as if he knows what he's talking about and someone who is actually serious about the issues" ("From Trump on down, the Republicans can't be serious" *New York Times,* August 7, 2015). Moreover, the GOP deserves the impoverished candidates they get.
51. C.P. Snow (1962:73) calls the *administrative* class of the state "the masters of the short-term solution".
52. As quoted in Andrew Revkin, "A Risk Analyst Explains Why Climate Change Risk Misperception Doesn't Necessarily Matter," *New York Times* April 16, 2014.
53. Evelyn Fox Keller (2010; also 2011) arrives at her conclusion about the inseparability of science and politics and the political authority of climate science by suggesting "where the results of scientific research have a direct impact on the society in which they live, it becomes effectively impossible for scientists to separate their scientific analysis from the likely consequences of that analysis."
54. For a more detailed discussion of knowledge and power, see Stehr, 2015.
55. I agree with the insights of Karl Otto Hondrich (2001:215) in this respect,

> the successes of the national, the democratic, and the free-market principle have one and the same reason: all three mechanisms are collective learning via trial and error. Not with fixed solutions, but with alternatives, they steer society into a world of open problems [wicked problems].

56. Quoted in Frederick A. O. Schwarz Jr. (2015), *Democracy in the Dark:* The Seduction of Government Secrecy. New York: New Press, p. 110.
57. Reducing greenhouse gas emissions yields benefits that are (not perfectly) non-rival and non-excludable; eliminating one ton of greenhouse gas emissions is a perfect substitute for any other ton of greenhouse gases. If global emission reductions lead to fewer weather extremes, the benefits tend to favor some countries more than others, for example, in the case of a reduction of the frequency and intensity of hurricanes. Successful adaptation, in contrast, tends to yield benefits that are rival and excludable.
58. Indeed, the state continues to be the main player even as governance may become more global (cf. Jordan and Huitema, 2014).
59. What is the next Covid? An attack on our digital infrastructure is a leading candidate. It took several months for coronavirus to spread through the world and infect millions

of people. Our digital infrastructure might collapse in a single day. And whereas schools and offices could speedily shift online, how much time will it take you to shift back from email to snail-mail? For instance,

> a cyberattack forced the shutdown of one of the largest pipelines in the United States, in what appeared to be a significant attempt to disrupt vulnerable energy infrastructure. The pipeline carries refined gasoline and jet fuel up the East Coast from Texas to New York. . . . The breach comes just months after two major attacks on American computer networks—the SolarWinds intrusion by Russia's main intelligence service, and another against a Microsoft email service that has been attributed to Chinese hackers—that have illustrated the vulnerability of the networks on which the government and corporations rely.
>
> (*New York Times*. May 8, 2021; www.nytimes.com/2021/05/08/us/cyberattack-colonial-pipeline.html?action=click&module=Top%20Stories&pgtype=Homepage)

The problem of obsolescence of digital infrastructure, such as fiber optic cables, is also a largely unaddressed issue.

60. Gilbert, Ella and C. Kittel (2021), "Surface melt and runoff on Antarctic ice shelves at 1.5°C, 2°C and 4°C of future warming," *Geophysical Research Letters*, 48, e2020GL091733. https://doi.org/10.1029/2020GL091733
61. Compare: National Academies of Sciences, Engineering, and Medicine (2021), *ReflectingSunlight*: Recommendations for Solar Geoengineering Research and ResearchGovernance. Washington, DC: The National Academies Press.https://doi.org/10.17226/25762
62. The vice-president of the EU commission, Frank Timmermans, is quoted by the *Guardian* (May 1, 2021) linking the urgent need to couple climate and social policies:

> Older people will have to make sacrifices in the fight against climate change or today's children will face a future of fighting wars for water and food, the EU's deputy chief has warned. . . . If social policy and climate policy are not combined, to share fairly the costs and benefits of creating a low-carbon economy, the world will face a backlash from people who fear losing jobs or income, stoked by populist politicians and fossil fuel interests.

He said:

> It's not just an urgent matter—it's a difficult matter. We have to transform our economy. There are huge benefits, but it's a huge challenge. The biggest threat is the social one. If we don't fix this, our children will be waging wars over water and food. There is no doubt in my mind.

WINDS OF CHANGE

Conclusions

> One task of human thought is to try to perceive what the range of possibilities may be in a future that always carries on its back the burden of the present and the past.
>
> —Barrington Moore Jr. (1969)

More than ever before, my central hypothesis was, knowledge is the basis and guide of human action in all areas of our society. This inquiry into knowledge societies has therefore been written in response to the fundamental observation that modern science is by no means only, as is still much assumed today, the key and access to the mysteries of nature and human behavior, but above all the becoming of a world. At the same time, as I have tried to underline, knowledge societies are not a social formation at a standstill. The dynamics of the economic system of knowledge societies hand in hand with the juridification of knowledge as the most important resource of knowledge societies leads directly to the transformation of the knowledge society into knowledge capitalism. The legal containment of the dissemination of knowledge through national and international legislation is the lever that enables the transformation of the knowledge society into knowledge capitalism. The fencing-in of knowledge has an impact not only on the dissemination of knowledge, but also on its production. Observers have a justified suspicion that the confinement of knowledge impairs the work on additional knowledge or makes it economically unattractive. Knowledge capitalism also has distinct effects on intra- and inter-societal inequality. Although knowledge capitalism is primarily an economic development, there is a reasonable suspicion that the digital giants who occupy the driver's seat are having significant effects on the social structure and culture of modern society.

DOI: 10.4324/9781003296157-5

In other words, science and technology are fundamentally changing our social institutions: work, education, politics, economics, everyday life, physical, and cultural reproduction are all affected. Basically, there are hardly any social, economic, and cultural conditions that are immune to scientific and technological knowledge. This unprecedented importance of scientific knowledge does not mean, however, that it will succeed in simply overrunning traditional ways of life and attitudes, as hoped or as seriously feared again and again.

Despite these facts, the rather undifferentiated treatment or even non-treatment of knowledge itself is the greatest theoretical deficit of existing theories of modern society in which knowledge is assigned a central role.

I have defined knowledge as the ability to act (*Handlungsvermögen*), as the possibility to "set something in motion". However, the special, almost outstanding status of scientific and technical knowledge in modern society does not result from the fact that scientific knowledge, for instance, is still largely treated as a truthful, objective standard or as an indisputable instance, but from the fact that scientific knowledge, more than any other form of knowledge, permanently fabricates and constitutes additional (incremental) possibilities of action. Scientific knowledge thus represents possibilities of action that are constantly expanding and changing, producing novel opportunities for action that can even be "privately appropriated", if only temporarily. The process that transforms knowledge into a rival (private) good relies primarily on the establishment of patents. In short, in modern society, knowledge is the basis and motor of progressive modernization as an extension process. New realities require a new language. This is also true for the fundamental transformation of the economic structure of modern society. I have tried to outline the major changes in the economy in knowledge societies and their consequences for society, especially as a result of the emergence of knowledge as an immediate productive force.

Knowledge monopoly capitalism

My hypothesis for a determination of the *origins* and for some of the essential *features* of knowledge societies was based on an examination of the *relations* (rather than single, stand-alone measures) between investments a society undertakes into physical forces of production (non-human; that is, natural capital, infrastructure, buildings, plant, and equipment) compared to investments in human capital or knowledge-based capital (people, skills; rather than merely investment in labor). It was noted that most intangible capital assets never appear on corporate balance sheets, leading to both a growing mismeasurement of book assets as well as to an under-illumination of the societal significance of knowledge. If intellectual property items show up as intangible asset on the balance sheets of corporations they tend to be "valued at its cost of production rather than its profit generating capacity" (Schwartz, 2020:3).

A major, novel hypothesis involved the idea that rents on intellectual capital formalized for example in the sense of *patents* (knowledge embedded in original ideas), *copyrights* (knowledge embedded in novel expressions or effort), *trademarks* (knowledge embedded in symbolic material), and *trade secrets* (no requirement for novelty) may be at the center of returns on human capital and inequality regimes in modern economic systems; returns—in the form of an extraction revenue mechanism—that exceed the cost of the production of the patented knowledge and lead to a monopoly rent.

I emphasized the socio-economic consequences of patents and patent portfolios; less the ideology and politics of patent systems. Patents and their rigid enforcement are not merely economic phenomena, patents distribute power and wealth and impact political relations. The corporate ownership of embedded knowledge in the form of patents constitutes a major element of the forces of production of knowledge societies and a significant source of its economic inequality. Patents divide and patents rule. Patents divide even if corporations patent and then decide to bury the invention.

How much productivity growth originates in knowledge societies from working smarter rather than from the deployment of any of the material forces of production? My proposition is that the origins of a modern, established knowledge society, *the tipping or critical point*, can be traced to a time-range when investments in human capital not only exceed investments in physical capital but investments in human capital became more productive and profitable than investments in physical capital. As Susan Lund and Laura Tyson (2018:137; emphasis added) stress, "because of the rise of digital flows is increasing competition in knowledge-intensive sectors, the importance of intellectual property is growing, generating *new forms of competition around patents*."

I suggest that this development amounts to *knowledge monopoly capitalism*, a winner-take-all phenomenon. Knowledge monopoly capitalism favors the most productive firms of an industry. Favoring often mean that these "superstar firms" (Autor et al., 2020:648) control the relevant knowledge needed to produce their products. Given the legal encoding of knowledge, firms rise to superstar status and can exclude others from employing the innovation they have developed and protected. In other words, the rise of superstar companies is promoted and, subsequently, fortified by the action of states through patent laws.

Compared to the tangible-intensive production of *industrial society*, the marginal cost of the production of intangibles—as scalable assets—in *knowledge societies*, i.e., software, standards, organization know-how, platforms, and texts, approaches zero. Returns on tangible capital, given their physical nature and the diseconomies of scale, tend to be finite. Returns on intangible assets are almost infinite. Infinite returns to scale annul the iron law of diminishing marginal returns that governed industrial society. Corporate reliance and strategy in knowledge societies is therefore largely directed toward the generation and purchase of *Intellectual*

Property Rights (IPRs—patents, copyrights, trademarks, brands, digital platforms). IPRs, in turn, are political creatures, that is, they are based on politically constructed exclusion.

Knowledge, uncertainty, and contingency

The new language that becomes necessary should also, in contrast to the orthodox image of modern society, emphasize above all, however, the newly acquired capacities of actors to act, the flexibility, heterogeneity, volatility of social structures, and the possibility that a greater number of individuals and groups have the capacity to influence and reproduce these structures in their own sense. The basis of this reversal in relation to inequality, from passive actor to active co-creator, is the use of the knowledge-based competencies I have described, and their influence on the structure of social inequality in modern society.

An examination of the modern social role of science, however, should by no means result only in a scientific utopia or degenerate into an apology of scientific knowledge. Rather, I have attempted to draw attention to the limits of the power of scientific knowledge in modern society, which have been largely neglected by the contemporary social sciences.

Not only Western industrial societies but industrial societies in other parts of the world have been quite successful in enlarging the material well-being of their citizens. The same economic transformation allows for the possibility of the expansion of modern science and technology, education, occupational skills, social security provisions, or the welfare state (and with it, a reduction in long economic insecurity), political participation, the increase of other state activities as well as cultural shifts that often invert meanings and orientations associated with what appear to be entrenched political platforms. In the process of "solving" its problems which industrial society both inherited and saw as its own peculiar agenda, industrial society not only produced new problems and conflicts but exhausted the sources as well as the organizational frames that were crucial for the resolution of old problems; at the same time, industrial societies reached the limits of enlarging its capacities in the same direction and in the same fashion. The economy of industrial society is undergoing a mutation. The sources of its wealth or added value have been exhausted, and a new force of production takes the place of the productive factors of labor and property that had dominated industrial society.

These transformations propel industrial society on its way to form a knowledge society. However, these changes do not occur as revolutionary transformations. They evolve gradually and re-write what is constitutive for society. New phenomena require new perspectives, as I have argued. Knowledge *societies* as highly self-transformative social constructs differ in important ways from industrial societies. The core of classical social discourse is directed to the analysis of industrial society. Within such analysis, as it were, there is, as Alain Touraine ([1984] 1988:4), has argued convincingly,

> scant room left for the idea of social action. The more one speaks of society, the less one talks of social actors, since the latter can be conceived only as the bearers of the attributes that are proper to the place they occupy in the social system: whether they are at the center or at the periphery, at the top or at the bottom, they take part, to a greater or lesser extent, in the values of modernity.

The agency and intentionality of actors and intermediate social groups are subservient to the logic of social collectivities and institutions that dispense with the often-repressive cement of social life ensuring that social order prevails despite the many pressures to the contrary. Whether or not such a perspective ever accurately portrayed social reality, or was primarily an ideological conviction, this conception now is disqualified.

In a knowledge society, the capacity of individuals to disengage themselves from the pressures of institutions and collectivities grows immeasurably. Contrary to Adorno ([1972] 2021:239), the spell which the system as a whole casts "over its members has been strengthened by greater social integration," has actually lessened as a result of the widening dissemination of social capacities of action throughout society. But the rise in the level of knowledge as a whole "does not mean by any means . . . a general leveling, but rather the opposite" (Simmel ([1907] 1978:440). New forms of social inequality based on knowledge emerge and are firmly institutionalized, creating and extending advantages as well as forms of deprivation. The unity of collectivities now derives from the fact that they are arenas of contests of knowledgeable actors. However, knowledge does not have some of the crude and cruel qualities of those factors (of production) that are constitutive of industrial societies. Just as "industrialization transformed societies in a fashion that empowered subordinate classes and made it difficult to politically exclude them" (Rueschemeyer et al., 1992:vii), the core of the economic transformation of knowledge societies further empowers those groups and individuals in democratic societies still marginalized even in the face of universal suffrage.

But the transition from industrial to knowledge society is not without serious problems. The likelihood that the loss of full employment will in the future also be associated with economic growth is one of the salient features of an economy in which the major source of added value is knowledge and in which more production will be possible with less labor.

As the proportion of the gross national product that is appropriated and distributed by governments, for example, reaches well above 50 percent, there would appear to be no further room for a continuation of enlarging state activities. Further growth of state activities not only reaches a point of diminishing returns but effectively curbs those sources of economic expansion taking the place of forces of production that prevailed in industrial society.

The growth of knowledge and the growing societal importance of knowledge forces society to confront at least dual contingencies directly linked to the enlargement of modern knowledge. There is (1) the contingency of knowledge itself and (2) the heightened contingency of social relations as the result of the growing penetration of knowledge into society. For these reasons, the future, more than ever, is much harder to visualize. It is more difficult to imagine than even Daniel Bell still reckoned in his important treatise on post-industrial societies in the mid-1970s.

Social, economic and intellectual strains that undoubtedly will attend the dual contingency are not resolved by reverting to the now largely discredited deference for a scientific politics, a return to whatever "foundations", the image of "progress" or, technocratic solutions of societal problems. However, setting specific opportunities, strains, ambitions, pressures, and traditions will lead to very different forms of knowledge societies.

The image of the logic of science from which all individuals and groups associated with the production and dissemination of scientific knowledge directly or indirectly have benefited in the past has been dismantled and replaced by a perspective which comprehends the construction of scientific knowledge as a social and intellectual endeavor and not as a meta-social enterprise progressively approximating a recalcitrant objective reality. The social construction of scientific claims to knowledge or scientific facts and theories, as examined by ethnographic studies of laboratories, public controversies involving scientific expertise and the socio-historical reconstruction of the emergence, establishment, and decline of scientific theories strongly attributes a contingency to knowledge. In the past, the eradication of contingency (or disagreements) was seen as the hallmark of the scientific enterprise.

As a result, the harnessing of knowledge will be accompanied not only by continuing concerns about past threats that are persistent fears, for example, the horror of global destruction through nuclear weapons or a major environmental catastrophe, but by a decline in the authority of experts and growing skepticism toward the possibility of disinterested expertise. Nonetheless, reliance on knowledge will increase as well and the ways in which scientists, experts and knowledge-based occupations generally are able to maintain cognitive authority in the face of uncertainty, political conflict and skepticism toward expertise represents one of the main challenges for these occupations in knowledge societies.

But despite such misgivings and any sustained demystification of knowledge, the alternative cannot be to randomly invoke any odd belief as an equivalent. The challenge is to cope with contingency, not labor under the illusion that it merely is a temporary aberration. The essential fragility of knowledge societies leads to the following conclusions.

Conclusion

The diagnosis of a turning point in history as a conclusion of this study would not only be an exaggeration, but also far from credible, insofar as one expects from such a diagnosis a precise description of the present of the future. Is our lack of knowledge about the specifics of future society really the only knowledge we have about the present of the future? The future of society is not a random event but occurs "on the shoulders of past societies" just as much as the development of science occurs "on the shoulders of giants". Our ideas about the future are past and present views. But they are therefore not powerless.

There can no doubt that social upheavals, unexpected events, shifts in equilibrium, risk and dangers, etc. will be a permanent concomitant of the course of the present of the future. What is even more certain is that societies, their large social institutions, the state, the economy and science are unprepared for a variety of disaster but also for more pleasant scenarios.

Trigger and amplifier of this future social development, this much can be said, is a multiple and manifold extension of the capacities for action of individuals and small social groups. The extension of the ability to act is both a risk and a virtue for the knowledge society, that is, growing capacities for action lead to both toxic populism and necessary sustainability. It is in this context that the encircling of knowledge as intellectual property is "not merely some arcane technical legal issue" (May, 2002:144) but allows for the transformation of knowledge societies into knowledge capitalism.

The promise, challenge, and the dilemma knowledge societies pose for every individual and the collectivity derives from the need to cope with and even welcome greater transience and volatility, the recognition that uncertainty is a necessary by-product of the search for any elimination of disagreements and the need to accept the transitoriness and ambiguity of virtually all social constructs. Efforts to arrest, cure or reserve these predicaments are likely to result in conditions worse than the alleged disease. The only certainty is that the future will surprise us. As a matter fact, we have to make sure that our future will allow for surprises. And that future—as John M. Keynes ([1930] 1984:331) hoped—may even "value ends above means and prefer the good to the useful". However, it is not possible at this time to even imagine a sustainable future society that is not a comprehensive knowledge society. Nonetheless, the way things are they are now, do not have to be that way in the future.

BIBLIOGRAPHY

[TX] Under each author's name the most recent works are listed first. In the case of translations, revised or later editions, the original date of publication is also shown, within square brackets.

Aaron, Henry J. and Charles L. Schultze (eds.) (1992), *Setting Domestic Priorities. What Can Government Do?* Washington, DC: The Brookings Institution.

Abbott, Andrew (2010), "Varieties of ignorance," *The American Sociologist* 41:174–189.

Abiteboul, Serge and Gilles Dowek (2020), "The end of employment: The hitchhiker and the pencil sharpener," pp. 53–60 in *The Age of Algorithms*. Cambridge: Cambridge University Press.

Acemoglu, Daron (2019), "It's good jobs, stupid," Research Brief: Economics for Inclusive Prosperity.

Acemoglu, Daron (2021), "Harms AI," NBER Working Paper No. 29247. www.nber.org/papers/w29247

Acemoglu, Daron and Ufuk Akcigit (2012), "Intellectual property rights policy, competition and innovation," *Journal of European Economic Association* 10:1–42.

Acemoglu, Daron, Claire LeLarge and Pascual Restrepo (2020), Competing with robots: Firm-level evidence from France," NBER Working Paper No. 26738.

Acemoglu, Daron and Pascual Restrepo (2021), "Tasks, automation, and the rise in US wage inequality," NBER Working Paper No. 28920. https://www.nber.org/papers/w28920

Acemoglu, Daron and James A. Robinson (2019), *The Narrow Corridor. States, Societies and the Fate of Liberty*. London: Viking.

Acham, Karl (2020), "Cultural relativity, ethical relativism and the immutability of human nature: Some considerations on philosophical anthropology," *Aoristo* 1:43–66.

Adams, Samuel (2008), "Globalization and income inequality: Implications for intellectual property rights," *Journal of Policy Modelling* 30:725–735.

Adelstein, Jennifer and Stewart Clegg (2013), "And rewind! Recycling discourses of knowledge work and knowledge society," *Management & Organization* 9:3–25. http://doi.org/10.1080/17449359.2013.821023

Adolf, Marian and Nico Stehr (2017), *Knowledge. Is Knowledge Power?* 2nd edition. London: Routledge.

Adorno, Theodor W. (1969), "Spätkapitalismus oder Industriegesellschaft," pp. 12–26 in Theodor W. Adorno (ed.), *Spätkapitalismus oder Industriegesellschaft. Verhandlungen des 16. Deutschen Soziologentages*. Stuttgart: Ferdinand Enke [English translation: Theodor W. Adorno, "Late capitalism or industrial society," pp. 232–247 in Volker Meja, Dieter Misgeld and Nico Stehr (eds.) (2021), *Modern German Sociology*. London: Routledge].

Adorno, Theodore W. ([1966] 1973), *Negative Dialectics*. London: Routledge and Kegan Paul.

Adorno, Theodor W. ([1967] 2019), *Aspekte des neuen Rechtsradikalismus*. Berlin: Suhrkamp.

Adorno, Theodor W., Else Frankel-Brunswick, Daniel J. Levinson and R. Nevitt Sanford ([1950] 2019), *The Authoritarian Personality*. London: Verso.

Adorno, Theodor W. and Max Horkheimer ([1947] 1987), "Dialektik der Aufklärung," pp. 13–290 in Max Horkheimer (ed.), *Gesammelte Schriften*. Band 5. Frankfurt am Main: Fischer.

Akerlof, George A. (1970), "The market for "lemons": Quality uncertainty and the market mechanism," *Quarterly Journal of Economics* 84:488–500. http://doi.org/10.2307/1879431

Albert, Christoph, Paula Bustos and Jacopo Ponticelli (2021), "The effects of climate change on labor and capital reallocation," NBER Working Paper No. 28995.

Alexander, Jeffrey C. (1983), *Theoretical Logic in Sociology. Volume Four: The Modern Reconstruction of Classical Thought: Talcott Parsons*. Berkeley, CA: University of California Press.

Alexander, Jeffrey C. (1990), "Differentiation theory: Problems and prospects," pp. 1–15 in Jeffrey C. Alexander and Paul Colomy (eds.), *Differentiation Theory and Social Change. Comparative and Historical Perspectives*. New York: Columbia University Press.

Alexander, Jeffrey C. (1992a), "Durkheim's problem and differentiation theory today," pp. 179–204 in Hans Haferkamp and Neil J. Smelser (eds.), *Social Change and Modernity*. Berkeley, CA: University of California Press.

Alexander, Jeffrey C. (1992b), "The promise of a cultural sociology: Technological discourse and the sacred and profane information machine," pp. 293–323 in Richard Münch and Neil Smelser (eds.), *Theory as Culture*. Berkeley, CA: University of California Press.

Alexander, Jeffrey C. and Paul Colomy (eds.) (1990), *Differentiation Theory and Social Change. Comparative and Historical Perspectives*. New York: Columbia University Press.

Alexander, Lewis and Janice Eberly (2018), "Investment hollowing out," *IMF Economic Review* 66:5–30.

Allport, Gordon W. (1958), *The Nature of Prejudice*. New York: Doubleday.

Anthony, Katey M. Walter, Peter Anthony, Guido Grosse and Jeffrey Chanton (2012), "Geologic methane seeps along boundaries of Arctic permafrost thaw and melting glaciers," *Nature Geoscience* 5:419–426.

Arendt, Hannah (1958), *The Human Condition*. Chicago, IL: University of Chicago Press.

Arendt, Hannah (1961), *Between Past and Future: Eight Exercises in Political Thought*. New York: Penguin.

Arendt, Hannah ([1960] 1981), *Vita activa, oder vom tätigen Leben*. München: Piper.

Aron, Raymond ([1950] 1953), *Deutsche Soziologie der Gegenwart*. Stuttgart: Kröner.

Aron, Raymond (1962), *Eighteen Lectures on Industrial Society*. New York: Free Press.

Aron, Raymond (1964a), *La lutte de classes*. Paris: Gallimard.

Aron, Raymond ([1966] 1968), *The Industrial Society. Three Essays on Ideology and Development*. New York: Praeger.

Aron, Raymond ([1983] 1990), *Memoirs. Fifty Years of Political Reflection*. New York: Holmes & Meier.

Arrow, Kenneth (1962a), "The economic implications of learning by doing." *Review of Economic Studies* (3)29: 155–173.

Arrow, Kenneth (1962b), "Economic welfare and the allocation of resources for invention," pp. 609–626 in Richard R. Nelson (ed.), *The Rate and Direction of Inventive Activity: Economic and Social Factors*. Princeton, NJ: Princeton University Press.

Arrow, Kenneth (1974), *The Limits of Organization*. New York: W.W. Norton.

Arrow, Kenneth (1996), "The economics of information: An exposition," *Empirica* 23:119–128.

Attewell, Paul (1987), "Big brother and the sweatshop: Computer surveillance in the automated office," *Sociological Theory* 5:97–99.

Attewell, Paul (1992), "Technology diffusion and organizational learning: The case of business computing," *Organization Science* 3:1–19.

Attewell, Paul (1994), "Information technology and the productivity paradox," pp. 13–53 in Douglas H. Harris (ed.), *Organizational Linkages: Understanding the Productivity Paradox*. Washington, DC: National Academy Press.

Attewell, Paul (2001), "The first and the second digital divide," *Sociology of Education* 74:252–259.

Autor, David H. (2013), "The 'task' approach to labor markets: An overview," IZADP No. 7178. *Journal for Labour Market Research* 46.3: 185–199.

Autorenkollektiv (1972), *Die gegenwärtige wissenschaftlich-technische Revolution. Eine historische Untersuchung*. Berlin: Akademie Verlag.

Badham, Richard (1984), "The sociology of industrial and post-industrial societies," *Current Sociology* 32:1–141.

Badham, Richard (1986), *Theories of Industrial Society*. London: Croom Helm.

Baldamus, Wilhelm (1976), *The Structure of Sociological Inference*. London: Martin Robertson.

Balough, Thomas (1982), *The Irrelevance of Conventional Economics*. London: Weidenfeld and Nicolson.

Barber, Bernard (1968), "Social stratification: Introduction," pp. 288–295 in David Sills (ed.), *International Encyclopedia of the Social Sciences*. Volume 15. New York: Crowell Collier and Macmillan.

Barkar, Simcha (2020), "Declining labor and capital shares," *Journal of Finance* 75:2421–2463.

Barnes, Barry (1972), "On the reception of scientific beliefs," pp. 269–291 in Barry Barnes (ed.), *Sociology of Science*. Harmondsworth: Penguin.

Barnes, Barry (1974), *Scientific Knowledge and Sociological Theory*. London: Routledge and Kegan Paul.

Barnes, Barry (1985), *About Science*. Oxford: Blackwell.

Barnes, Barry (1988), *The Nature of Power*. Urbana and Chicago, IL: University of Illinois Press.

Barnes, Barry (2000), *Understanding Agency. Social Theory and Responsible Action*. London: SAGE.

Barnes, Barry and David Bloor (1982), "Relativism, rationalism and the sociology of knowledge," pp. 21–47 in Martin Hollis and Steven Lukes (eds.), *Rationality and Relativism*. Oxford: Blackwell.

Barnes, Barry and David Edge (eds.) (1982), *Science in Context: Readings in the Sociology of Science*. Cambridge, MA: MIT Press.

Barth, Paul (1922), *Die Philosophie der Geschichte als Soziologie*. Leipzig: Reisland.

Bartl, Marija (2017), "Contesting austerity: On the limits of EU Knowledge governance," *Journal of Law and Society* 44:150–168.

Basiuk, Victor (1977), *Technology, World Politics and American Policy*. New York: Columbia University Press.

Bates, Benjamin J. (1988), "Information as an economic good: Sources of individual and social value," pp. 76–94 in Vincent Mosco and Janet Wasko (eds.), *The Political Economy of Information*. Madison, WI: University of Wisconsin Press.

Bateson, Gregory ([1972] 2000), *Steps Toward an Ecology of the Mind*. Chicago, IL: University of Chicago Press.

Bauchet, Jonathan, Amy Damon and Brian Hunter (2019), "Asymmetric information in microinsurance markets: Experimental evidence from Mexico," *Economic Development and Cultural Change* 68:165–188.

Bauman, Zygmunt (1987), *Legislators and Interpreters. On Modernity, Post-modernity and Intellectuals*. Ithaca, NY: Cornell University Press.

Bauman, Zygmunt (1991), *Modernity and Ambivalence*. Ithaca, NY: Cornell University Press.

Bauman, Zygmunt (1992), *Intimations of Postmodernity*. London: Routledge.

Bauman, Zygmunt (2000), *Liquid Modernity*. Cambridge: Polity Press.

Bauman, Zygmunt (2012), "Times of interregnum," *Ethics & Global Politics* 5:49–56.

Bean, Charles (1990), *European Unemployment: A Survey*. Centre for Economic Performance Working Paper No. 35. London: London School of Economics.

Beck, Ulrich (1986), *Risikogesellschaft. Auf dem Weg in eine andere Moderne*. Frankfurt am Main: Suhrkamp.

Beck, Ulrich ([1986] 1992), *Risk Society. Toward a New Modernity*. London: SAGE.

Beck, Ulrich ([2002] 2005), *Power in the Global Age. A New Global Political Economy*. Cambridge: Polity Press.

Beck, Ulrich (2006), "Europäisierung—Soziologie für das 21. Jahrhundert," pp. 513–525 in K.-S. Rehberg (Hrsg.), *Soziale Ungleichheit, kulturelle Unterschiede: Verhandlungen des 32. Kongresses der Deutschen Gesellschaft für Soziologie in München. Teilband 1 und 2*. Frankfurt am Main: Campus Verlag.

Beck, Ulrich (2016), *The Metamorphosis of the World*. Cambridge: Polity Press.

Beck, Ulrich und Michael Brater (1978), *Berufliche Arbeitsteilung und soziale Ungleichheit. Eine gesellschaftlich-historische Theorie der Berufe*. Frankfurt am Main: Campus.

Becker, Egon (2001), "Die postindustrielle Wissensgesellschaft: ein enormer Mythos?" *Zeitschrift für kritische Theorie* 7(12):85–106.

Beer, Carel S. de (2010), "The Knowledge Society: Refounding the Socius," pp. 266–277 in Miltiadis D. Lytras, Patricia Ordonez de Pablos, Ernesto Damiani, David Avison, Ambjörn Naeve and David G. Horner (eds.), *Organizational, Business, and Technological Aspects of the Knowledge Society: Communications in Computer and Information Science*. Berlin and Heidelberg: Springer.

Beer, David (2017), "The social power of algorithms," *Information, Communication* 1–13.

Belitz, Heike and Martin Gornig (2019), "Deutsche Wirtschaft muss mehr in ihr Wissenskapital investieren," *DIW Wochenbericht* 31:527–534.

Belitz, Heike, Marie Le Mouel and Alexander Schiersch (2018), "Produktivität der Unternehmen steigt mit mehr wissensbasierten Kapital," *DIW Wochenbericht* 85(4):63–70. www.econstor.eu/bitstream/10419/174600/1/1011558696.pdf

Bell, Daniel (1960), *The End of Ideology*. Glencoe, IL: Free Press.

Bell, Daniel (1964), "The post-industrial society," pp. 44–59 in Eli Ginzberg (ed.), *Technology and Social Change*. New York: Columbia University Press.

Bell, Daniel (1965), "The disjunction of culture and social structure," pp. 236–251 in Gerald Holton (ed.), *Science and Culture*. Boston, MA: Houghton Mifflin.

Bell, Daniel (1967a), "Notes on the post-industrial society," *The Public Interest*: 24–35.

Bell, Daniel (1967b), "Notes on the post-industrial society," *The Public Interest* 7:102–118.

Bell, Daniel (1968), "The measurement of knowledge and technology," pp. 145–246 in Eleanor B. Sheldon and Wilbert E. Moore (eds.), *Indicators of Social Change. Concepts and Measurements*. Hartford, CT: Russell Sage Foundation.

Bell, Daniel (1971), "Technocracy and politics," *Survey* 16:1–24.

Bell, Daniel (1972), "Labour in the post-industrial society," *Dissent* 19:163–189.

Bell, Daniel (1973a), *The Coming of Post-Industrial Society. A Venture in Social Forecasting*. New York: Basic Books.

Bell, Daniel (1973b), "A rejoinder to Timothy A. Tilton," *Social Research* 40:745–752.

Bell, Daniel (1973c), "Technology, nature and society. The vicissitudes of three worlds views and the confusion of realms," *The American Scholar* 42:385–404.

Bell, Daniel (1974), "A reply to Peter N. Stearns," *Society* 11:11, 23–24.

Bell, Daniel (1975a), "The disjunction of culture and social structure: Some notes on the meaning of social reality," *Daedalus*: 208–222.

Bell, Daniel (1975b), "Toward the great restoration: Reflections on culture and religion in a postindustrial age," *Social Research* 42:381–413.

Bell, Daniel (1976a), *The Cultural Contradictions of Capitalism*. New York: Basic Books.

Bell, Daniel (1976b), "Welcome to the post-industrial society," *Physics Today* :46–49.

Bell, Daniel (1977), "Teletext and technology. New networks of knowledge and information in post-industrial society," *Encounter* 48:9–29.

Bell, Daniel (1979a), "The social framework of the information society," pp. 163–211 in Michael L. Dertouzos and Joel Moses (eds.), *The Computer Age: A Twenty-Year View*. Cambridge, MA: MIT Press.

Bell, Daniel (1979b), "The new class: A muddled concept," pp. 169–190 in B. Bruce-Biggs (ed.), *The New Class*? New Brunswick, NJ: Transaction Books.

Bell, Daniel ([1975] 1979), *Die nachindustrielle Gesellschaft*. Frankfurt am Main: Campus.

Bell, Daniel ([1975] 1980), "Technology, nature, and society. The vicissitudes of three world views and the confusion of realms," pp. 3–33 in Daniel Bell (ed.), *The Winding Passage. Essays and Sociological Journeys 1960–1980*. Cambridge, MA: Abt Books.

Bell, Daniel ([1979, 1980] 1982), *The Social Science Since the Second World War*. New Brunswick, NJ: Transactions Books.

Bell, Daniel (1987), "The world and the United States in 2013," *Daedalus* 116:1–31.

Bell, Daniel ([1975] 1991), "Technology, nature, and society. The vicissitudes of three world views and the confusion of realms," pp. 3–33 in Daniel Bell (ed.), *The Winding Passage. Sociological Essays and Journeys*. New Brunswick, NJ: Transaction Publishers.

Bell, Daniel ([1979] 1991a), "Liberalism in the postindustrial society," pp. 228–244 in Daniel Bell (ed.), *The Winding Passage. Sociological Essays and Journeys. With a New Foreword by Irving Louis Horowitz*. New Brunswick, NJ: Transaction Books.

Bell, Daniel ([1979] 1991b), "The new class: A muddled concept," pp. 144–164 in Daniel Bell (ed.), *The Winding Passage. Sociological Essays and Journeys*. New Brunswick, NJ: Transaction Publishers.

Bell, Daniel and Virginia Held (1969), "The community revolution," *The Public Interest* 16:142–177.

Belloc, Filippo and Ugo Pagano (2012), "Knowledge enclosures, forced specializations and investment crisis," *European Journal of Comparative Economics* 9:445–483.

Ben-Yehuda, Nachman (1985), *Deviance and Moral Boundaries. Witchcraft, the Occult, Science Fiction, Deviant Scientists and Scientists*. Chicago, IL: University of Chicago Press.

Benkler, Yochai (2006), *The Wealth of Networks: How Social Production Transforms Markets and Freedom*. New Haven, CT: Yale University Press.

Berger, Johannes (1983), "Die Wiederkehr der Vollbeschäftigungslücke—Entwicklunglinien des wohlfahrtstaatlichen Kapitalismus," pp. 309–320 in Joachim Matthes (ed.), *Krise der Arbeitsgesellschaft? Verhandlungen des 21. Deutschen Soziologentages in Bamberg 1982*. Frankfurt am Main: Campus.

Berger, Johannes (1985), "Der Kapitalismus-Ein unvollendbares Projekt?," pp. 485–496 in Burkart Lutz (ed.), *Verhandlungen des 22. Deutschen Soziologentages*. Opladen: Westdeutscher Verlag.

Berger, Johannes (1986), "Gibt es ein nachmodernes Gesellschaftsstadium? Marxismus und Modernisierungstheorie im Widerstreit," pp. 79–96 in Johannes Berger (ed.), *Die Moderne. Kontinuitäten und Zäsuren. Sonderband 4 Soziale Welt*. Göttingen: Otto Schwartz and Co.

Berger, Johannes (1988), "Modernitätsbegriffe und Modernitätskritik in der Soziologie," *Soziale Welt* 39:224–236.

Berger, Peter (1987), *The Capitalist Revolution. Fifty Propositions about Prosperity, Equality, and Liberty*. New York: Basic Books.

Berger, Peter A. ([2006] 2014), "Soziale Milieus und die Ambivalenzen der Informations- und Wissensgesellschaft," pp. 77–105 in Helmut Bremer and Andrea Lange-Vester (eds.), *Soziale Milieus und Wandel der Sozialstruktur, Sozialstrukturanalyse*. Wiesbaden: Springer.

Berman, Elizabeth Popp (2008), "Why did universities start patenting?," *Social Studies of Science* 38:835–871.

Bernal, John D. (1954), *Science in History*. London: Watts.

Biddle, Justin B. (2016), "Intellectual property rights and global climate change: Toward resolving an apparent dilemma," *Ethics, Policy & Environment* 19:301–319.

Birch, Kean (2020), "Technoscience rent: Toward a theory of *rentiership* for technoscientific capitalism," *Science, Technology & Human Values* 45:3–33.

Birch, Kean and David T. Cochrane (2021), "Big Tech: Four Emerging Forms of Digital Rentiership," *Science as Culture*. http://doi.org/10.1080/09505431.2021.1932794

Birnbaum, Norman (1971), "Is there a post-industrial revolution?," pp. 393–415 in Norman Birnbaum (ed.), *Toward a Critical Sociology*. New York: Oxford University Press.

Birnbaum, Norman (1971b), "Is there a knowledge elite?," pp. 416–441 in Norman Birnbaum (ed.), *Toward a Critical Sociology*. New York: Oxford University Press.

Black, Sandra E. and Lisa M. Lynch (1996), "Human-capital investments and productivity," *The American Economic Review* 86:263–267.

Blaug, Mark (2005), "Why Did Schumpeter Neglect Intellectual Property Rights?" *Review of Economic Research on Copyright Issues* 2:69–74.

Bleakely, Jason (2020), *We Built Reality. How Social Science Infiltrated Culture, Politics, and Power*. Oxford: Oxford University Press.

Block, Fred (1985), "Postindustrial development and the obsolescence of economic categories," *Politics and Society* 14:416–441.

Block, Fred (1985), "Postindustrial development and the obsolescence of economic categories," *Politics and Society* 14:71–104.

Block, Fred (1987), *Revising State Theory: Essays in Politics and the Contradictions of Contemporary Capitalism*. Philadelphia, PA: Temple University Press.

Block, Fred (1990), *Postindustrial Possibilities. A Critique of Economic Discourse*. Berkeley, CA: University of California Press.

Block, Fred and Larry Hirschhorn (1979), "New productive forces and the contradictions of contemporary capitalism," *Theory and Society* 17:363–395.

Block, Fred and Mathew R. Keller (2012), "Where do innovations come from? Transformations in the U.S. economy, 1970–2006," pp. 81–103 in Leonardo Burlamaqui, Ana Célia Castro and Rainer Kattel (eds.), *Knowledge Governance. Reasserting the Public Interest*. New York: Antham Press.

Bodewitz, Henk J.H.W., Henk Buurma and Gerard H. de Vries (1987), "Regulatory science and the social management of trust in medicine," pp. 243–259 in Wiebe E. Bijker, Thomas P. Hughes and Trevor Pinch (eds.), *The Social Construction of Technological Systems: New Directions in the Sociology and History of Technology*. Cambridge, MA: MIT Press.

Böhme, Gernot and Nico Stehr (Hrsg.) (1986), *Knowledge Societies. The Growing Impact of Scientific Knowledge on Social Relations*. Dordrecht: D. Reidel.

Böhme, Gernot, Wolfgang van den Daele and Wolfgang Krohn (1978), "The 'scientification' of technology," pp. 219–250 in Gernot Böhme, Wolfgang van den Daele and Wolfgang Krohn (eds.), *The Dynamics of Science and Technology*. Dordrecht: D. Reidel.

Boiset, Max H., Ian C. Macmillan and Kyeong Seok Han (2007), "Data, information, and knowledge: Have we got it right?," pp. 15–47 in Max H. Boiset, Ian C. Macmillan and Kyeong Seok Han (eds.), *Explorations in Information Space: Knowledge, Actors, and Firms*. Oxford: Oxford University Press.

Boldrin, Michele and David K. Levine (2013), "The case against patents," *Journal of Economic Perspectives* 27:3–22.

Boreham, Paul (1983), "Indetermination: Professional knowledge, organization and control," *Sociological Review* 31:693–718.

Borgmann, Albert (1992), *Crossing the Postmodern Divide*. Chicago, IL: University of Chicago Press.

Böschen, Stefan, Matthias Groß and Wolfgang Krohn (2017), "Experimentelle Gesellschaft: Das Experiment als wissensgesellschaftliches Dispositiv," pp. 7–25 in Stefan Böschen, Matthias Groß and Wolfgang Krohn (eds.), *Experimentelle Gesellschaft: Das Experiment als wissensgesellschaftliches Dispositiv*. Baden-Baden: Nomos.

Bottomore, Tom B. (1960), "The ideas of the founding fathers," *European Journal of Sociology* 1:33–49.

Boulding, Kenneth (1965), *The Meaning of the Twentieth Century. The Great Transition*. New York: Harper & Row.

Boulding, Kenneth (1966), "The economics of knowledge and the knowledge of economics," *American Economic Review* 56:1–13.

Bourdieu, Pierre (1975), "The specificity of the scientific field and the social conditions of the progress of reason," *Social Science Information* 14:19–47.

Bourdieu, Pierre (1979), "Les trois etats du capital culturel," *Acûtes de la recherche en sciences sociales* 30:3–6.

Bourdieu, Pierre (1983), "Ökonomisches Kapital, kulturelles Kapital, soziales Kapital," pp. 183–198 in Reinhard Kreckel (ed.), *Soziale Ungleichheiten. Soziale Welt, Sonderband 2*. Göttingen: Verlag Otto Schwartz & Co.

Bourdieu, Pierre ([1979] 1984), *The Distinction: A Social Critique of the Judgement of Taste*. Cambridge, MA: Harvard University Press.

Bourdieu, Pierre (1986), "The forms of capital," pp. 241–258 in John G. Richardson (ed.), *Handbook of Theory and Research for the Sociology of Education*. New York: Greenwood Press.

Bourdieu, Pierre ([1980] 1987), *Sozialer Sinn. Kritik der theoretischen Vernunft*. Frankfurt am Main: Suhrkamp.

Bova, Samantha, Yair Rosenthal, Zhengyu Liu, Shital P. Godad and Mi Yan (2021), "Seasonal origin of the thermal maxima at the Holocene and the last interglacial," *Nature* 589:548–553.

Boyle, James (2003), "The second enclosure movement and the construction of the public domain," *Law and Contemporary Problems* 66:33–73.

Braudel, Fernand ([1979] 1992), *The Structures of Everyday Life. The Limits of the Possible. Volume 1: Civilization and Capitalism 15th–18th Century*. Berkeley, CA: University of California Press.

Braun, Ernst (1984), *Wayward Technology*. London: Pinter.

Braverman, Harry (1974), *Labor and Monopoly Capital: The Degradation of Work in the Twentieth Century*. New York: Monthly Review Press.

Brennan, Geoffrey (2010), "The Division of Epistemic Labour," *Analyse & Kritik* 32(2):231–246.

Breslau, Daniel (2013), "Designing a market-like entity: Economics in the politics of market formation," *Social Studies of Science* 43:829–851.

Brewer, Garry D. (1973), *Politicians, Bureaucrats, and the Consultant. A Critique of Urban Problem Solving*. New York: Basic Books.

Brick, Howard (1986), *Daniel Bell and the Decline of Intellectual Radicalism. Social Theory and Political Reconciliation in the 1940s*. Madison, WI: University of Wisconsin Press.

Britton, Stephen (1990), "The role of services in production," *Progress in Human Geography* 14:529–546.

Brooks, Harvey (1965), "Scientific concepts and cultural change," *Daedalus* 94:66–83.

Brown, John Seeley und Paul Duguid ([2000] 2002), *The Social Life of Information*. Cambridge, Massachusetts: Harvard Business School Press.

Brown, Carole Ganz and Francis W. Rushing (1990), "Intellectual property rights in the 1990s," pp. 1–15 in Francis W. Rushing and Carole Ganz Brown (eds.), *Intellectual Property Rights in Science, Technology and Economic Performance*. Westview.

Bruce-Biggs, Barry (ed.) (1979), *The New Class?* New Brunswick, NJ: Transaction Books.

Bruyn, Severyn T. (1991), *A Future for the American Economy. The Social Market*. Stanford, CA: Stanford University Press.

Brynjolfsson, Erik and Lorin M. Hitt (1998), "Beyond the productivity paradox. Computers are the catalyst for bigger changes," *Communications of the ACM* 41:49–55.

Brzezinski, Zbigniew (1968), "America in the technetronic age. New questions of our time," *Encounter* 30:16–26.

Bucher, Rue and Anselm Strauss (1961), "Professions in process," *American Journal of Sociology* 66:325–334.

Buchholz, Wolfgang and Todd Sandler (2021), "Global public goods: A survey," *Journal of Economic Literature* 59:488–545.

Buckner, William (2017), "Romanticizing the Hunter-Gatherer," *Quillette*, December. http://quillette.com/2017/12/16/romanticizing-hunter-gatherer/

Buckland, Michael (2017), *Information and Society*. Cambridge, MA: MIT Press.

Burke, Peter (2017), *Exiles and Expatriates in the History of Knowledge, 1500–2000*. Brandeis University Press.

Burlamaqui, Leonardo (2012), "Knowledge governance: An analytical approach and its policy implications," pp. 3–26 in Leonardo Ana Célia Castro and Rainer Kattel (eds.), *Knowledge Governance. Reasserting the Public Interest.* New York: Antham Press.

Burnham, James (1941), *The Managerial Revolution. What Is Happening in the World?* New York: John Day.

Burton-Jones, Alan (1999), *Knowledge Capitalism. Business, Work, and Learning in the New Economy.* Oxford: Oxfords University Press.

Burton-Jones, Alan (2003), "Knowledge capitalism. The new learning economy," *Policy Futures in Education* 1:143–159.

Caldwell, Bruce (2016), "FA Hayek and the economic calculus," *History of Political Economy* 48:151–180.

Caldwell, Bruce (2020), "The *Road to Serfdom* after 75 years," *Journal of Economic Literature* 58:720–748.

Çalışkan, Koray and M. Michel Callon (2009),"Economization, part 1: Shifting attention from the economy towards processes of economization," *Economy and Society* 38:369–398.

Callon, Michel (1994), "Is science a public good?" *Science, Technology, & Human Values* 19:395–424.

Campante, Filipe R. and Davin Chor (2011), "'The people want the fall of the regime': Schooling, political protest, and the economy," Harvard Kennedy School Faculty Research Paper 11–018. https://voxeu.org/article/how-schooling-investments-facilitated-middle-east-uprisings?quicktabs_tabbed_recent_articles_block=0

Campante, Filipe R. and Davin Chor (2012), "Schooling, political participation, and the economy," *Review of Economics and Statistics* 94:841–859.

Carley, Kathleen (1986), "Knowledge acquisition as a social phenomenon," *Instructional Science* 14:381–438.

Carnoy, Martin and Manuel Castells (2001), "Globalization, the knowledge society, and the Network State: Poulantzas at the millennium," *Global Networks* 1:1–18.

Carr-Saunders, Alexander M. and P.A. Wilson (1933), *The Professions.* Oxford: Oxford University Press.

Castells, Manuel (1989), *The Informational City. Information Technology, Economic Restructuring, and the Urban-Regional Process.* Oxford: Basil Blackwell.

Castells, Manuel (1996), *The Information Age: Economy, Society and Culture. Volume I: The Rise of the Network Society.* Oxford: Blackwell.

Castells, Manuel (2000), "Information technology and global capitalism," pp. 52–74 in Will Hutton and Anthony Giddens (eds.), *On the Edge. Living with Global Capitalism.* London: Jonathan Cape.

Castells, Manuel ([1996] 2000), *The Information Age: Economy, Society and Culture. Volume I: The Rise of the Network Society.* 2nd edition. Oxford: Blackwell.

Castells, Manuel (2001), "Bausteine einer Theorie der Netzwerkgesellschaft," *Berliner Journal für Soziologie* 4:423–439.

Castells, Manuel ([1997] 2004), *The Information Age: Economy, Society and Culture. Volume II: The Power of Identity.* 2nd edition. Oxford: Blackwell.

Castells, Manuel (2009), *Communication Power.* Oxford: Oxford University Press.

Castells, Manuel and Jeffrey Henderson (1987), "Introduction. Techno-economic restructuring, socio-political processes and spatial transformation: A global perspective," pp. 1–17 in Jeffrey Henderson and Manuel Castells (eds.), *Global Restructuring and Territorial Development.* London: SAGE.

Cette, Gilbert, Lorraine Koehl und Thomas Philippon (2020), "Labor share," *Economic Letters* 188.

Chakrabarty, Dipesh (2017), "The politics of climate change is more than the politics of capitalism," *Theory, Culture and Society* 34:25–37.

Chandler, Alfred D. (1977), *The Visible Hand. The Managerial Revolution in American Business*. Cambridge, MA: Harvard University Press.

Channell, David F. (1982), "The harmony of theory and practice: The engineering science of W.J.M. Rankine," *Technology and Culture* 23:39–52.

Chappori, Pierre-Andre and Bernard Salanie (2000), "Testing for asymmetric information in insurance markets," *Journal of Political Economy* 108:56−78.

Chartier, Roger (2016), "Science and knowledge," *HSS (English Edition)* 71:321–335.

Chen, Wen (2018), "Cross-country income differences revisited-accounting for the role of intangible capital," *Review of Income and Wealth* 64:626–647.

Coase, Ronald H. ([1977] 1978), "Economics and contiguous disciplines," *The Journal of Legal Studies* 7:201–211.

Cockburn, Iain M., Jean O. Lanjouw and Mark Schankerman (2014), "Patents and the global diffusion of new drugs," NBER Working Paper No. 20492. Revised October 2014 w20492. https://www.nber.org/papers/w20492

Coleman, James S. (1972a), "Integration of sociology and other social sciences through policy analysis," pp. 162–174 in James C. Charlesworth (ed.), *Integration of the Social Sciences Through Policy Analysis. Monograph 14 of the American Academy of Political and Social Science*. Philadelphia, PA: The American Academy of Political and Social Science.

Coleman, James S. (1972b), *Policy Research in the Social Sciences*. Morristown, NJ: General Learning Press.

Collin, Mathew and David N. Weil (2020), "The effect of increasing human capital investment on economic growth and poverty—A simulation exercise," *Journal of Human Capital* 14:43–83.

Collins, Harry M. (1982), "The replication of experiments in physics," pp. 94–116 in Barry Barnes and David Edge (eds.), *Science in Context. Readings in the Sociology of Science*. Cambridge, MA: MIT Press.

Collins, Harry M. (1985), *Changing Order*. Beverly Hills, CA: SAGE.

Collins, Harry M. (1993), "The structures of knowledge," *Social Research* 60:95–116.

Collins, Harry M., Robert Evans and Martin Weinel (2017), "STS as science or politics?," *Social Studies of Science* 47:580–586.

Collins, Randell ([1981] 2019), "In retrospect: 1981," *Contemporary Sociology* 48: 388–391.

Collison, David (1994), "Strategies of resistance: Power, knowledge and subjectivity in the workplace," pp. 25–68 in J.M. Jermier, D. Knights and W.R. Nord (eds.), *Resistance and Power in Organizations*. London: Routledge.

Connell, Raewyn (2007), *Southern Theory: The Global Dynamics of Knowledge in Social Science*. Cambridge: Polity Press.

Contreras, Jorge L. (2021), *The Genome Defense: Inside the Epic Legal Battle to Determine Who Owns Your DNA*. Chapel Hill, NC: Algonquin.

Cooren, François (2018), "Materializing communication: Making the case for a relational ontology," *Journal of Communication* 68(2):278–288.

Corrado, Carol A. and Charles R. Hulten (2010), "How do you measure a technological revolution?" *American Economic Review* 100:99–104.

Corrado, Carol A., Charles R. Hulten and Daniel Sichel (2005), "Measuring capital and technology: An expanded framework," pp. 114–146 in John Haltiwanger, Carol A. Corado and Daniel Sichel (eds.), *Measuring Capital in the New Economy*. Chicago, IL: University of Chicago Press.

Corrado, Carol A., Charles R. Hulten and Daniel Sichel (2009), "Intangible capital and US economic growth," *Review of Income and Wealth* 55:661–685.

Coser, Lewis A. (1970), *Men of Ideas: A Sociologist's View*. New York: Free Press.

Crouch, Colin (2004), *Post-Democracy*. Cambridge: Cambridge University Press.

Crouzet, Nicolas and Janice C. Eberly (2012), "Intangibles. Markups, and measurement of productivity growth," NBER Working Paper No. 29109. https://www.nber.org/system/files/working_papers/w29109/w29109.pdf

Crouzet, Nicolas and Janice C. Eberly (2019), "Understanding weak capital investment: The role of market concentration and intangibles," National Bureau of Economic Research Paper w25869. www.nber.org/papers/w25869

Cummings, Alex Sayf (2016), "Of sorcerers and thought leaders: Marketing the information revolution in the 1960s," *The Sixties* 9:1–25.

Daele, Wolfgang van den (1977), "Die soziale Konstruktion der Wissenschaft," pp. 129–182 in Gernot Böhme et al. (eds), *Die gesellschaftliche Orientierung wissenschaftlichen Fortschritts*. Frankfurt: Suhrkamp.

Dahrendorf, Ralf ([1957] 1959), *Class and Class Conflict in Industrialized Society*. Stanford, CA: Stanford University Press.

Dahrendorf, Ralf (1969), "The intellectual and society: The social function of the "fool" in the twentieth century," pp. 53–56 in Phillip Rieff (ed.), *On Intellectuals*. New York: Anchor Books.

Dahrendorf, Ralf ([1967] 1974), "Soziologie und industrielle Gesellschaft," pp. 64–73 in Ralf Dahrendorf (ed.), *Pfade aus Utopia. Arbeiten zur Theorie und Methode der Soziologie*. München: Piper.

Dahrendorf, Ralf (1977), "Observations on science and technology in a changing socio-economic climate," pp. 73–82 in Ralf Dahrendorf et al. (eds.), *Scientific-Technological Revolution*. London: SAGE.

Dahrendorf, Ralf (1980a), "Effectiveness and legitimacy: On the governability of democracies," *Political Quarterly* 51:393–410.

Dahrendorf, Ralf (1980b), "Im Entschwinden der Arbeitsgesellschaft. Wandlungen in der sozialen Konstruktion des menschlichen Lebens," *Merkur* 34:749–760.

Dahrendorf, Ralf (1987), "Changing perceptions of the role of government," pp. 110–122 in Organisation for Economic Co-Operation and Development (ed.), *Interdependence and Co-Operation in Tomorrow's World*. Paris: OECD.

Dahrendorf, Ralf (1988), *The Modern Social Conflict. An Essay on the Politics of Liberty*. Berkeley, CA: University of California Press.

Darnovsky, Marcy, et al. (2019), "CRISPR regulation," *Issues in Science and Technology* 35:5–12.

Darnton, Robert (2000), "An early information society: News and Media in eighteenth-century Paris," *The American Historical Review* 105:1–35.

Dasgupta, Partha (1987a), "The economic theory of technology policy," pp. 7–23 in Partha Dasgupta and Paul Stoneman (eds.), *Economic Policy and Technological Performance*. Cambridge: Cambridge University Press.

Dasgupta, Partha and Paul Stoneman (1987b), "Introduction," pp. 1–6 in Partha Dasgupta and Paul Stoneman (eds.), *Economic Policy and Technological Performance*. Cambridge: Cambridge University Press.

Dasgupta, Partha S. and Paul A. David (1994), "Toward a new economics of science," *Research Policy* 23: 487–521.

Davies, Kevin (ed.) (2020), *Editing Humanity. The CRISPR Revolution and the New Era of Genome Editing*. London: Pegasus.

Day, Gregory R. and Michael Schuster (2019), "Patent Inequality," *Alabama Law Review* 71:117–162.

Del Guidice, Manlio, Maria Rosaria Della Peruta and Vincenzo Maggioni (2013), "The 'right' knowledge and spin-off processes: An empirical analysis of knowledge transfer," *Journal of Knowledge Economy* 4:304–318.

Denison, Edward (1979), *Accounting for Slower Economic Growth*. Washington, DC: Brookings Institution.

Dennett, Daniel C. (1986), "Information, technology, and the virtues of ignorance," *Daedalus* 115:135–153.

Derber, Charles (1982), "Toward a new theory of professionals as workers: Advanced capitalism and postindustrial labour," pp. 193–208 in Charles Derber (ed.), *Professionals as Workers: Mental Labour in Advanced Capitalism*. Boston, MA: Hall.

Derber, Charles, William A. Schwartz and Yale Magrass (1990), *Power in the Highest Degree. Professionals and the Rise of a New Mandarin Order*. New York: Oxford University Press.

Dewey, John ([1927] 1954), *The Public and Its Problems*. Athens, OH: Swallow Press.

Diamond, Arthur M. (2015), "Seeking the patent truth: Patents can provide justice and funding for inventors," *The Independent Review* 19:325–355.

Diamond, Larry (2019), "The threat of postmodern totalitarianism," *Journal of Democracy* 30:20–24.

DiMaggio, Paul J. (1997), "Culture and cognition," *Annual Review of Sociology* 23:263–287.

Doms, Mark, Timothy Dunne and Kenneth Troske (1997), "Workers, wages and technology," *The Quarterly Journal of Economics* 253–290.

Dosi, Giovanni (1982), "Technological paradigms and technological trajectories: A suggested interpretation of the determinants and directions of technical change," *Research Policy* 11:147–162.

Dosi, Giovanni (1984), *Technical Change and Industrial Transformation. The Theory and an Application to the Semiconductor Industry*. London: Macmillan.

Dosi, Giovanni (1988), "The nature of the innovative process," pp. 221–238 in Giovanni Dosi, Christopher Freeman, Richard Nelson, Gerald Silverberg and Luc Soethe (eds.), *Technical Change and Economic Theory*. London: Pinter.

Dosi, Giovanni, Christopher Freeman, Richard Nelson, Gerald Silverberg and Luc Soethe (eds.) (1988), *Technical Change and Economic Theory*. London: Pinter.

Dosi, Giovanni and Marco Grazzi (2010), "On the nature of technologies-knowledge, procedures, artifacts and production inputs," *Cambridge Journal of Economics* 34: 173–184.

Dosi, Giovanni and Joseph H. Stiglitz (2014), "The role of intellectual property rights in the development process, with some lessons from developed countries: An introduction," pp. 1–53 in Mario Cimoli, Giovanni Dosi, Keith E. Maskus, Ruth L. Okediji, Jerome H. Reichmann and Joseph E. Stiglitz (eds.), *Intellectual Property Rights*. Oxford: Oxford University Press.

Drahos, Peter (2004), "The regulation of public goods," *Journal of International Law* 7:321–339.

Drahos, Peter (2010), *The Global Governance of Knowledge: Patent Offices and Their Clients*. Cambridge: Cambridge University Press.

Drahos, Peter (2020), "Responsive science," *Annual Review of Law and Social Science* 16:327–42.

Drahos, Peter and John Braithwaite (2001), "Intellectual property, corporate strategy, globalization: TRIPS in context," *Wisconsin International Law Journal* 20:451–480.

Drahos, Peter and John Braithwaite (2002), *Information Feudalism. Who Owns the Knowledge Economy?* London: Earthscan.

Drucker, Peter (1968), "Worker and work in the metropolis," *Daedalus* 97:1243–1262.

Drucker, Peter (1993a), *Post-Capitalist Society*. New York: Harper Business.

Drucker, Peter (1997), "The future has already happened," *Harvard Business Review* 75:20–24.

Drucker, Peter (1999), "Knowledge-worker productivity: The biggest challenge," *California Management Review* 41:79–94.

Drucker, Peter ([1989] 2003), *The New Realities. With a New Preface by the Author*. New Brunswick, NJ: Transaction Publishers.

Drucker, Peter ([2001] 2011), "Die Wissensgesellschaft," pp. 20–48 in Jochen Steinbicker (ed.), *Zur Theorie der Informationsgesellschaft*. Wiesbaden: Springer.

Drucker, Peter F. (1951), "Labor in industrial society," *The ANNALS of the American Academy of Political and Social Science* 274:145–151.

Drucker, Peter F. (1953), "The employee society," *American Journal of Sociology* 58:358–363.

Drucker, Peter F. (1965), *The Future of Industrial Man*. New York: The John Day.

Drucker, Peter F. (1967), "Technological trends in the twentieth century," pp. 10–33 in Melvin Kranzberg and Carroll W. Pursell Jr. (eds.), *Technology in Western Civilization*. Volume II. New York: Oxford University Press.

Drucker, Peter F. ([1968] 1972), *The Age of Discontinuity. Guidelines to Our Changing Society*. New York: Harper & Row.

Drucker, Peter F. (1986), "The changed world economy," *Foreign Affairs* 64:768–791.

Drucker, Peter F. (1989), *The New Realities: In Government and Politics/In Economics and Business/In Society and World View*. New York: Harper & Row.

Drucker, Peter F. (1993), "The rise of the knowledge society," *The Wilson Quarterly* 17(2):52–71.

Duff, Alistar S. (1998), "Daniel Bell's theory of the information society," *Journal of the Information Sciences* 24:373–393.

Durand, Cédric and William Milberg (2020a), "Intellectual monopoly in global value chains," *Current Studies Series A*, No. 9.

Durand, Cédric and William Milberg (2020b), "Intellectual monopoly in global value chains," *Review of international Political Economy* 27:404–429.

Durkheim, Emile ([1950] 1957), *Professional Ethics and Civic Morals*. London: Routledge and Kegan Paul.

Durkheim, Emile ([1893] 1964), *The Division of Labor in Society*. New York: Free Press.

Durkheim, Emile ([1912] 1965), *The Elementary Forms of Religious Life*. New York: Free Press.

Durkheim, Emile ([1955] 1983), *Pragmatism and Sociology*. Cambridge: Cambridge University Press.

Dyer, Maxine (2012), "Network or net worth? Deconstructing the knowledge society," *E-Learning and Digital Media* 9:335–344.

Dyrberg, Torben Bech (1997), *The Circular Structure of Power*: Politics, Identity, Community. London: Verso.

Dyson, Freeman (2011), "How we know," *The New York Review of Books* 58(4). www.nybooks.com/articles/archives/2011/mar/10/how-we-know/

Economist (2014), "The onrushing wave. The future of jobs," 18 January 2014. https://www.coursehero.com/file/22891750/Economist-2014-The-onrushing-wave-The-future-of-jobs-Economist-140118/

Eder, Klaus (1989), "The cognitive representation of social inequality: A sociological account of the cultural basis of modern class society," pp. 125–146 in Hans Haferkamp (ed.), *Social Structure and Culture*. Berlin and New York: de Gruyter.

Eder, Klaus (1992), "Contradictions and social evolution: A theory of the social evolution of modernity," pp. 320–349 in Hans Haferkamp and Neil J. Smelser (eds.), *Social Change and Modernity*. Berkeley, CA: University of California Press.

Ehrlich, Paul (1968), *The Population Bomb*. New York: Ballentine.

Eisenstadt, Shmuel N. (1973), "Post-traditional societies and the continuity and reconstruction of tradition," *Daedalus* 102:1–27.

Elias, Norbert (1984), "Knowledge and power," pp. 251–291 in Nico Stehr and Volker Meja (eds.), *Society and Knowledge. Contemporary Perspectives on the Sociology of Knowledge*. New Brunswick, NJ: Transaction Books.

Elias, Norbert (1987a), "The retreat of sociologist into the present," *Theory, Culture & Society* 4:223–247.

Elias, Norbert (1987b), "The retreat of sociologists into the present," pp. 150–172 in Volker Meja, Dieter Misgeld and Nico Stehr (eds.), *Modern German Sociology*. New York: Columbia University Press.

Elias, Norbert ([1987] 1991), *The Society of Individuals*. Oxford: Blackwell.

Elkins, Paul (ed.) (1986), *The Living Economy. A New Economics in the Making*. London: Routledge and Kegan Paul.

Ellul, Jaques (1954), *The Technological Society*. New York: Vintage.

Emden, Christian J. (2006), "Die Gleichzeitigkeit des Ungleichzeitigen—Walter Benjamins" Archäologie "der Moderne," *KulturPoetik* 6:200–221.

Engster, Johannes, Giang Ho, Florence Jaumotte and Roberto Piazza (2018), "How knowledge spreads. More rapid diffusion of know-how is an important benefit of globalization," *Finance and Development* 55:52–55.

Ennals, Richard (2004), "Europe as a knowledge society Integrating universities, corporations, and government," *Systematic Practice and Action Research* 17:237–248.

Enns, Charis (2015), "Knowledge in competition: Knowledge discourse at the World Bank during the Knowledge for Development era," *Global Social Policy* 15:61–80.

Ericson, Richard V. and Nico Stehr (2000), "Globalization and governance: Introduction," pp. 29–41 in Richard V. Ericson and Nico Stehr (eds.), *Governing Modern Societies*. Toronto: University of Toronto Press.

Esping-Anderson, Gosta (1992), "Three postindustrial employment regimes," pp. 149–188 in Jon E. Kolberg (ed.), *The Welfare State as Employer*. Armonk, NY: M.E. Sharpe.

Esquith, Stephen L. (1987), "Professional authority and state power," *Theory and Society* 16:237–262.

Etzioni, Amitai and Clyde Nunn (1974), "The public appreciation of science in contemporary America," *Daedalus* 103:191–205.

Eulau, Heinz (1973), "Skill revolution and consultative commonwealth," *American Political Science Review* 62:169–191.

Evans, Geoff (1992), "Is Britain a class-divided society? A re-analysis and extension of Marshall et al.'s study of class consciousness," *Sociology* 26:233–258.

Ewens, Michael, Ryan H. Peters and Sean Wang (2019), "Acquisition prices and the measurement of intangible capital," Technical report, National Bureau of Economic Research.

Farrington, David P. (2000), "Explaining and preventing crime: The globalization of knowledge—the American Society of Criminology 1999 Presidential Address," *Criminology* 38(1):1–24.

Faulkner, Wendy (1994), "Conceptualizing knowledge used in innovation: A second look at the science-technology distinction and industrial innovation," *Science, Technology & Human Values* 19:425–458.

Featherstone, Mike (1989), "Postmodernism, cultural change, and social practice," pp. 1–22 in Douglas Kellner (ed.), *Postmodernism*. Washington, DC: Maisonneuve Press.

Feeney, Oliver, Julian Cockbain, Michael Morrison, Lisa Diependaele, Kristof Van Assche and Sigrid Sterckx (2018), "Patenting foundational technologies: Lessons from CRISPR and other core biotechnologies," *The American Journal of Bioethics* 18:36–48.

Feigenbaum, Edward A. and Pamela McCorduck (1983), *The Fifth Generation. Artificial Intelligence and Japan's Computer Challenge to the World*. Reading, MA: Addison-Wesley.

Feldstein, Steven (2019), "How Artificial Intelligence is reshaping repression," *Journal of Democracy* 30:40–52.

Feller, Irwin (1987), "The economics of technological change filtered through a social knowledge system framework," *Knowledge* 9:233–253.

Ferguson, Niall (2017), *The Square and the Tower. Networks and Power, from the Freemasons to Facebook*. New York: Penguin.

Ferkiss, Victor (1979), "Daniel Bell's concept of post-industrial society. Theory, myth and ideology," *The Political Science Reviewer* 9:61–99.

Fernandez, Rodrigo, Illke Adriaans, Tobia J. Klinge and Reijer Hendrickse (2020), *The Financialisation of Big Tech*. Amsterdam: Somo.

Feuer, Lewis S. (1976), "What is an intellectual," pp. 47–58 in Aleksander Gella (ed.), *The Intelligentsia and the Intellectuals*. Beverly Hills, CA: SAGE.

Feyerabend, Paul ([1994] 2019), "Potentially every culture is all cultures," *Common Knowledge* 25:13–20.

Field, Frank (ed.) (1983), *The Wealth Report-2*. London: Routledge and Kegan Paul.

Finn, Ed (2019), "The black box of the present: Time in the age of algorithms," *Social Research* 86:557–579.

Fisher, Allen G.B. (1939), "Production–primary, secondary and tertiary," *The Economic Record* 15:24–38.

Flanagan, Scott C. (1987), "Value change in industrial societies," *American Political Science Review* 81:1303–1319.

Flechtheim, Ossip (1972), "Der Prager Frühling und die Zukunft des Menschen," pp. 9–31 in Radovan Richta et al. (eds.), *Technischer Fortschritt und industrielle Gesellschaft*. Frankfurt am Main: Makol.

Fletcher, Michael-Shawn, Rebecca Hamilton, Wolfram Dressler and Lisa Palmer (2021), "Indigenous knowledge and the shackles of wilderness," *PNAS* 118(40):e2022218118.

Florence, P. Sargant (assisted by W. Baldamus), (1948), *Investment, Location, and Size of Plant*. Cambridge: Cambridge University Press.

Florida, Richard (2002), *The Rise of the Creative Class. And How It's Transforming Work, Leisure, Community and Everyday Life*. New York: Basis Books.

Florida, Richard (2014), "The creative class and economic development," *Economic Development Quarterly* 28:196–205.

Floud, Jean (1971), "A critique of Bell," *Survey* 16:25–37.

Forrest, Katherine B. (2021), *When Machines Can Be Judge, Jury, and Executioners. Justice in an Age of Artificial Intelligence*. Singapore: World Scientific.
Forstner, Helmut and Robert Ballance (1990), *Competing in a Global Economy. An Empirical Study of Specialization and Trade in Manufactures. Prepared for the United Nations Industrial Development Organization*. London: Unwin Hyman.
Foster, George M. (1973), *Traditional Societies and Technological Change*. New York: Harper & Row.
Foucault, Michel (1957), "La recherche du psychologue," *Des chercheurs Francais s'interrogent*.
Foucault, Michel (1970), *L'Ordre du Disours*. Paris: Gallimard.
Foucault, Michel (1977), *Discipline and Punish*. New York: Random House.
Foucault, Michel (1983), "The subject and power," pp. 208–226 in Hubert Dreyfus and Paul Rabinow (eds.), *Michel Foucault: Beyond Structuralism and Hermeneutics*. Chicago, IL: University of Chicago Press.
Fourasti, Jean (1950), *Le Grand Espoir du XX sicle*. Paris: PUF.
Fourasti, Jean ([1951] 1960), *The Causes of Wealth*. Glencoe, IL: Free Press.
Fox, Renee C. (1967), "Training for uncertainty," pp. 20–24 in Mark Abrahamson (ed.), *The Professional in the Organization*. Chicago, IL: Rand McNally.
Frank, David John and John W. Meyer (2020), *The University and the Global Knowledge Society*. Princeton, NJ: Princeton University Press.
Frank, Jürgen (1973), "Die postindustrielle Gesellschaft und ihre Theoretiker," *Leviathan* 1:383–407.
Frank, Robert H. and Philip J. Cook (2010), *The Winner Take All Society. Why the Few at the Top Get So Much More Than the Rest of Us*. New York: Random House.
Frankel, Boris (1987), *The Post-Industrial Utopians*. Madison, WI: University of Wisconsin Press.
Fraser, Nancy (2017), "A new form of capitalism," *New Left Review* 106:57–65.
Freilich, Janet and Lisa Larrimore Quellette (2019), "Science fiction: Ficticious experiments in patents," *Science* 364:1036–1037.
Frenkel, Sheera and Cecilia Kang (2021), *An Ugly Truth. Inside Facebook's Battle for Domination*. London: The Bridge Street Press.
Freud, Sigmund (1930), *Das Unbehagen in der Kultur*. Wien: Internationaler Psychoanalytischer Verlag.
Freud, Sigmund ([1924] 1963), *Introductory Lectures on Psycho-analysis* (Vol. 15, Parts I and II, 1915–1916), Translated from the German under the General Editorship of James Strachey in collaboration with Anna Freud. Assisted by Alix Strachey and Alan Tyson. London: Hogarth Press.
Freud, Sigmund ([1924] 2010), *Vorlesungen zur Einführung in die Psychoanalyse*. Hamburg: Nikol.
Frey, Carl Benedikt and Michael A. Osborne (2017), "The future of employment: How susceptible are jobs to computerisation?," *Technological Forecasting and Social Change* 114:254–280. https://doi.org/10.1016/j.techfore.2016.08.019.
Freyer, Hans (1960), *Über das Dominantwerden technischer Kategorien in der Lebenswelt der industriellen Gesellschaft*. Mainz: Academie der Wissenschaften.
Freyer, Hans, Johannes Chr Papalekas and Georg Welppert (eds.) (1965), *Technik im technischen Zeitalter. Stellungnahmen zur geschichtlichen Situation*. Düsseldorf: Schilling.
Friedman-Ekholm, Kajsa und Jonathan Friedman (1995), "Global complexity and the simplicity of everyday life," pp. 134–168 in Daniel Miller (Hrsg.), *Worlds Apart. Modernity through the Prism of the Local*. London: Routledge.

Friedman, Jonathan (1992), "General historical and culturally specified properties of global systems," *Review* 15:335–372.
Friedmann, George (1953), *Zukunft der Arbeit. Perspektiven der industriellen Gesellschaft.* Köln: Bund Verlag.
Friedmann, Georges (1955), *Industrial Society.* Glencoe, IL: Free Press.
Friedmann, George ([1956] 1992), *The Anatomy of Work. Labor, Leisure and the Implications of Automation. With a New Introduction by Donald C. King.* New Brunswick, NJ: Transaction Books.
Friedmann, John (1987), *Planning in the Public Domain: From Knowledge to Action.* Princeton, NJ: Princeton University Press.
Frow, John (1996), "Information as gift and commodity," *New Left Review* 219:89–108.
Fu, Xiaolan and Pertez Ghauri (2020), "Trade in intangibles and the global trade imbalance," *World Economy* 44:1448–1469.
Fuchs, Victor (1968), *The Service Economy.* New York: Columbia University Press.
Fukuyama, Francis (1999/2000), "Getting it right," *The National Interest* 58:130–132.
Fuller, Steve (2005), *The Knowledge Book. Key Concepts in Philosophy, Science and Culture.* Stocksfield: Acumen.
Fuller, Steve (2019), "Against academic rentiership: A radical critique of the knowledge economy," *Postdigital Science and Education* 1:335–356.
Funk, Jeffrey (2018), "Beyond patents," *Issues in Science and Technology* 34:48–54.
Galbraith, John K. (1967), *The New Industrial State.* New York: Houghton Mifflin.
Gehlen, Arnold ([1957] 1980), *Man in the Age of Technology.* With a Foreword by Peter L. Berger. New York: Columbia University Press.
Gehlen, Arnold ([1940] 1988), *Man. His Nature and Place in the World.* New York: Columbia University Press.
Gellner, Ernest (1987), *Culture, Identity and Politics.* Cambridge: Cambridge University Press.
George, Frank H. (1970), *Science and the Crisis in Society.* New York: Wiley.
Georgieff, Alexandre and Anna Milanez (2021), "What happened to jobs at high risk of automation?," OECD Social, Employment and Migration Working Papers No. 255. Paris: OECD Publishing. https://doi.org/10.1787/10bc97f4-en.
Gereffi, Gary (2014), "Global value chains in a post-Washington Consensus world," *Review of International Political Economy* 21:9–37.
Ghosh, Amitav ([2016] 2021), *Uncanny and Improbable Events.* London: Penguin Random House.
Giddens, Anthony (1971), *Capitalism and Modern Social Theory.* Cambridge: Cambridge University Press.
Giddens, Anthony ([1973] 1980), *The Class Structure of the Advanced Societies.* London: Hutchinson.
Giddens, Anthony (1981), *A Contemporary Critique of Historical Materialism.* Volume 1. London: Macmillan.
Giddens, Anthony (1984), *The Constitution of Society: Outline of the Theory of Structuration.* Cambridge: Polity Press.
Giddens, Anthony (1990a), "R.K. Merton on structural analysis," pp. 97–110 in Jon Clark et al. (eds.), *Robert K. Merton: Consensus and Controversy.* London: Falmer Press.
Giddens, Anthony (1990b), "Sociology, modernity and utopia," *New Statesman & Society* 3(125):20–22.
Giddens, Anthony (1990c), *The Consequences of Modernity.* Stanford, CA: Stanford University Press.

Giddens, Anthony (1991), *Modernity and Self-Identity. Self and Society in the Late Modern Age*. Stanford, CA: Stanford University Press.
Giddens, Anthony (1999), *Runaway World. The 1999 Reith Lectures*. London: Routledge.
Giddens, Anthony ([1999] 2001), *Entfesselte Welt. Wie die Globalisierung unser Leben verändert*. Frankfurt am Main: Suhrkamp.
Giddens, Anthony (2011), *The Politics of Climate Change*. 2nd edition. Cambridge: Polity Press.
Gieryn, Thomas F. (1983), "Boundary-work and the demarcation of science from non-science: Strains and interests in professional ideologies of scientists," *American Sociological Review* 48:781–795.
Glaser, Barney G. (1964), *Organizational Scientists: Their Professional Careers*. Indianapolis, IN: Bobbs-Merrill.
Goldfarb, Avi and Catherine Tucker (2019), "Digital economics," *Journal of Economic Literature* 57:3–43.
Goldhamer, Herbert (1978), *The Adviser*. New York: Elsevier.
Goldthorpe, John H. (1971), "Theories of industrial society: Reflections on the recrudescence of historicism and the future of futurology," *European Journal of Sociology* 12:263–288.
Gore, Al (1992), *Earth in the Balance: Ecology and the Human Spirit*. Boston, MA: Houghton Mifflin.
Gouldner, Alvin W. (1976), *The Dialectic of Ideology and Technology. The Origins, Grammar, and Future of Ideology*. New York: Seabury Press.
Gouldner, Alvin W. (1979), *The Future of Intellectuals and the Rise of the New Class*. New York: Seabury Press.
Grossman, Gene M. and Ezra Oberfield (2021), "The elusive explanation for the declining labor share," NBER Working Paper No. 29165. https://www.nber.org/system/files/working_papers/w29165/w29165.pdf
Grundmann, Reiner and Nico Stehr (eds.) (2009), *Society. Critical Concepts in Sociology*. 4 Volumes. New York: Routledge.
Grundmann, Reiner and Nico Stehr (2012), *The Power of Scientific Knowledge. From Research to Public Policy*. Cambridge: Cambridge University Press.
Guellec, Dominique and Caroline Paunov (2017), "Digital innovation and the distribution of income," NBER Working Paper No. 23987. https://www.nber.org/system/files/working_papers/w23987/w23987.pdf
Guriev, Sergei and Elias Papaioannou (2020), "The political economy of populism." Available at SSRN 3542052. https://www.hks.harvard.edu/sites/default/files/centers/mrcbg/programs/senior.fellows/20-21/populism_oct2020.pdf
Habermas, Jürgen (1968), *Toward a Rational Society*. London: Heinemann.
Habermas, Jürgen ([1973] 1976), *Legitimation Crisis*. London: Heinemann.
Habermas, Jürgen ([1980] 1981), "Modernity versus postmodernity," *New German Critique* 22:3–14.
Hage, Jerald (2020), *Knowledge Evolution and Societal Transformation. Action Theory to Solve Adaptative Problems*. New York: Antham Press.
Halpern, Sue (2021), "The human cost of AI," *New York Review of Books*, October 21.
Hallett, Tim, Orla Stapleton and Michael Sauder (2019), "Public ideas: Their varieties and careers," *American Sociological Review* 84:545–576.
Hamilton, Walton (1945), "Cartels, patents and politics," *Foreign Affairs* 23:582–593.
Hansen, James (2009), *Storms of My Grandchildren*. London: Bloomsbury.

Haskel, Jonathan and Stian Westlake (2017), *Capitalism without Capital*. Princeton, NJ: Princeton University Press.
Haug, Marie R. and Marvin B. Sussman (1969), "Professional autonomy and the revolt of the client," *Social Problems* 17:153–161.
Haunss, Sebastian (2013), *Conflicts in the Knowledge Society. The Contentious Politics of Intellectual Property*. Cambridge: Cambridge University Press.
Hayek, Friedrich A. (1938), "Freedom and the economic system," *The Contemporary Review* 153:434–442.
Hayek, Friedrich A. ([1945] 1948), "The use of knowledge in society," pp. 77–91 in Friedrich A. Hayek (ed.), *Individualism and Economic Order*. Chicago, IL: University of Chicago Press.
Hayek, Friedrich A. (1960), *The Constitution of Liberty*. Chicago, IL: University of Chicago Press.
Hayek, Friedrich A. (1967), *Studies in Philosophy, Politics, and Economics*. Chicago, IL: University of Chicago Press.
Hayek, Friedrich A. ([1960] 1978), *The Constitution of Liberty* (reprint ed.). Chicago, IL: University of Chicago Press. www.libertarianismo.org/livros/tcolfh.pdf
Hayek, Friedrich A. ([1974] 1989), "The pretence of knowledge," *The American Economic Review* 79:3–7.
Hayek, Friedrich A. ([1960] 2005), "Die schöpferischen Kräfte einer freien Zivilisation [The creative powers of a free civilisation]," pp. 31–50 in Friedrich A. von Hayek (ed.), *Gesammelte Schriften in deutscher Sprache, Abteilung B: Vol. 3. Die Verfassung der Freiheit*). Tübingen: Mohr Siebeck.
Hayek, Fredrich A. ([1978] 2014), "Competition as a discovery procedure" pp. 304–13 in Bruce Caldwell (ed.), *The Market and Other Orders, Vol. 15 of The Collected Works of F. A. Hayek*. Chicago, IL: University of Chicago Press.
Hayek, Friedrich August (1938), "Freedom and the economic system," *The Comparative Revue* 434–442.
Hayek, Friedrich August (1944), *The Road to Serfdom*. London: George Routledge & Sons.
Heidegger, Martin (1977), *Gelassenheit*. Pfullingen: Neske.
Heidegger, Martin (1978), *Vorträge und Aufsätze*. Pfullingen: Neske.
Held, David (1991), "Democracy, the nation-state and the global system," *Economy and Society* 20:138–171.
Heller, Michael (1998), "The tragedy of the anticommons. Property in transition from Marx to markets," *Harvard Law Review* 111:698–701.
Helm, Dieter (2009), "Climate-change policy: Why has so little been achieved?," pp. 9–35 in Dieter Helm and Cameron Hepburn (eds.), *The Economics and Politics of Climate Change*. Oxford: Oxford University Press.
Henderson, Jeffrey and Manual Castells (eds.) (1987), *Global Restructuring and Territorial Development*. London: SAGE.
Henkel, Joachim and Markus Reitzig (2008), "Patent sharks," *Harvard Business Review* (June):129–133.
Herder, Johann Gottfried (1774), *Ideen zur Philosophie der 'Geschichte der Menschheit*. Carlsruhe: Christian Gottlieb Schmieder.
Heyden, Günter (1969), "Industriegesellschaft," p. 520 in Georg Klaus and Manfred Buhr (eds.), *Philosophisches Wörterbuch*. 6th edition. Leipzig: VEB Bibliographisches Institut.
Hidalgo, César and Ricardo Hausmann (2009), "The building blocks of eco nomic complexity," *PNAS* 106:10570–10575.
Hill, Alice C. (2021), "Covid's lesson for climate research: Go local," *Nature* 595:9.

Hippel, Eric von (1994), "'Sticky information' and the locus of problem solving: Implications for Innovation," *Management Science* 40:429–439.

Hirschman, Albert O. (1997), *The Passions and the Interests. Political Arguments for Capitalism before Its Triumph*. Princeton, NJ: Princeton University Press.

Hobson, John A. (1910), *The Industrial System. An Inquiry into Earned and Unearned Income*. London: Green.

Hoffmann, Florian, David S. Lee and Thomas Lemieux (2020), "Growing income inequality in the United States and other advanced economies," *Journal of Economic Perspectives* 34:S52–S78.

Holton, Gerald (1992), "How to think about the 'anti-science' phenomenon," *Public Understanding of Science* 1:103–128.

Holzner, Burkart, William N. Dunn and Muhammad Shahidullah (1987), "An accounting scheme for designing science impact indicators," *Knowledge* 9:173–204.

Holzner, Burkart and John H. Marx (1979), *Knowledge Application: The Knowledge System in Society*. Boston, MA: Allyn and Bacon.

Hondrich, Karl Otto (1984), "Der Wert der Gleichheit und der Bedeutungswandel der Ungleichheit," *Soziale Welt* 35:267–293.

Hondrich, Karl Otto (2001), *Der Neue Mensch*. Frankfurt am Main: Suhrkamp.

Hong, Eunsook (2014), "Liberal education reconsidered: Cultivating humanity in the knowledge society," *Asia Pacific Education Revue* 15:5–12.

Hopes, Briana (2021), "Right for robots?," *Tulane Journal of Technology & Intellectual Property* 23:119–135.

Hradil, Stefan (1983), "Die Ungleichheit der "sozialen Lage": Eine Alternative zu schichtungssoziologischen Modellen der sozialen Ungleichheit," pp. 101–118 in Reinhard Kreckel (ed.), *Soziale Ungleichheiten. Soziale Welt, Sonderband 2*. Göttingen: Verlag Otto Schwartz & Co.

Hu, Yao-Su (2020), "The impact of increasing returns on knowledge and big data: From Adam Smith and Allyn Young to the age of machine learning and digital platforms," *Prometheus* 36:10–29.

Hubig, Christoph and Wolfert von Rahden (eds.) (1978), *Konsequenzen kritischer Wissenschaftstheorie*. Berlin: De Gruyter.

Hübner, Kurt ([1978] 1983), *Critique of Scientific Reason*. Chicago, IL: University of Chicago Press.

Hübner, Kurt (1988), "Warum gibt es ein wissenschaftliches Zeitalter?" pp. 93–109 in Wolfgang Kluxen (ed.), *Tradition und Innovation. XIII. Deutscher Kongress für Philosophie*. Hamburg: Felix Meiner.

Hughes, Everett C. (1958), *Men and Their Work*. New York: The Free Press.

Huntington, Samuel P. (1974), "Postindustrial politics: How benign will it be?," *Comparative Politics* 6:163–191.

In't Veld, Roeland Jaap (2013), "Sustainable development within knowledge democracies: An emerging governance problem," pp. 3–35 in Louis Meulema (ed.), *Transgovernance*. Heidelberg: Springer.

Inglehart, Ronald (1977), *The Silent Revolution*. Princeton, NJ: Princeton University Press.

Inglehart, Ronald (2018), *Cultural Evolution. People's Motivations Are Changing and Reshaping the World*. Cambridge: Cambridge University Press.

Inglehart, Ronald and Gabriela Catterberg (2002), "Trends in political action: The developmental trend and the post-honeymoon decline," *International Journal of comparative Sociology* 43:300–316.

Innerarity, Daniel (2013), "Power and knowledge: The politics of the knowledge society," *European Journal of Social Theory* 16(1):3–16.

Innis, Harold A. (1951), *The Bias of Communication*. Toronto: University of Toronto Press.

International Labour Office (1987), *World Labour Report: Incomes from Work*. Volume 3. Geneva: International Labour Organisation.

International Monetary Fund (1992), *World Economic Outlook*. Washington, DC: The Fund.

Isaacson, Walter (2021), *The Code Breaker. Jennifer Doudna, Gene Editing, and the Future of the Human Race*. New York: Simon & Schuster.

Jackman, Richard and S. Roper (1987), "Structural unemployment," *Oxford Bulletin of Economic and Statistics* 49:9–36.

Jaimovich, Nir, Itay Saporta-Eksten, Henry E. Siu and Yaniv Yedid-Levi (2020), "The macroeconomics of automation-data, theory, and policy analysis," NBER Working Paper No. 27122. https://www.nber.org/system/files/working_papers/w27122/w27122.pdf

Jessop, Bob (2017), "Knowledge as a fictitious commodity: Insights and limits of a Polanyian perspective," pp. 115–133 in A. Bugra and K. Agartan (eds), *Reading Karl Polanyi for the Twenty-First Century*. Basingstoke: Palgrave Macmillan.

Jewett, Andrew (2021), "On the politics of knowledge: Science, conflict, power," pp. 285–304 in Haberski Raymond (ed.), *American Labyrinth. Intellectual History for Complicated Times*. Ithaca, NY: Cornell University Press.

Joas, Hans (1992), *Die Kreativität des Handelns*. Frankfurt am Main: Suhrkamp.

Jonas, Hans (1974). *Philosophical Essays: From Ancient Creed to Technological Man*. Englewood Cliffs, NJ: Prentice Hall.

Jones, Charles I. (2019), "Paul Romer: Ideas, nonrivalry, and endogenous growth," *Scandinavian Journal of Economics* 121:859–883.

Jones, Charles I. (2021), "The past and future of economic growth: A semi-endogenous perspective," NBER Working Paper No. 29126. https://www.nber.org/system/files/working_papers/w29126/w29126.pdf

Jordan, Andrew and Dave Huitema (2014), "Policy innovation in a changing climate: Sources, patterns, and effects," *Global Environmental Change* 29:387–394.

Joux, Alexandre (2006), "Theoretical approaches of the knowledge society at UNESCO," *Communications* 31:193–214.

Jünger, Friedrich Georg (1946), *Die Perfektion der Technik*. Frankfurt am Main: Vittorio Klostermann.

Kakaomerlioglu, Dllek Cetindamar and Bo Carlsson (1999), "Manufacturing in decline? A matter of definition," *Economics of Innovation and New Technology* 8:175–196.

Kang, Hyo Yoon (2020), "Patents as assets: Intellectual property rights as market subjects and objects," pp. 45–74 in Kean Birch and Fabian Muniesa (eds.), *Assetization: Turning things into assets in technoscientific capitalism*.

Kay, John (2003), *The Truth about Markets. Their Genius, Their Limits, Teir Follies*. London: Allen Lane.

Keller, Evelyn Fox (2010), "Climate science, truth and democracy," unpublished manuscript.

Keller, Evelyn Fox (2011), "What are climate scientists to do?," *Spontaneous Generations. A Journal for the History and Philosophy of Science* 5:19–26.

Kellner, Douglas (1984), *Herbert Marcuse and the Crisis of Marxism*. Berkeley, CA: University of California Press.

Kern, Horst and Michael Schumann (1983), "Arbeit und Sozialcharakter: Alte und neue Konturen," pp. 353–365 in Joachim Mattes (ed.), *Krise der Arbeitsgesellschaft. Verhandlungen des 21. Deutschen Soziologentages in Bamberg 1982*. Frankfurt am Main: Campus.

Kerr, William (2020), "The gift of global talent: Innovation policy and the economy," *Innovation Policy and the Economy* 20:1–37.

Kerr, William, Çağlar Özden and Christopher Parsons (2016), "Global talent flows." *Journal of Economic Perspectives* 30(4):83–106.

Keynes, John Maynard (1936), *The General Theory of Employment, Interest and Money*. London: Macmillan.

Keynes, John Maynard ([1925] 1972). "A Short View of Russia," pp. 253–271 in the *Collected Writings of John Maynard Keynes*. Volume 9.London: Macmillan.

Keynes, John Maynard ([1930] 1984), "Economic possibilities for our grandchildren," pp. 321–332 in John M. Keynes (ed.), *Essays in Persuasion*. London: Palgrave Macmillan.

Keynes, John Maynard ([1973] 1987), *Collected Writings. Volume XIII: The General Theory and After. Part I: Preparation*. Edited by Donald Moggridge. London: Macmillan.

Khan, B. Zorina (2020), *Inventing Ideas. Patents, Prices, and the Knowledge Economy*. Oxford: Oxford University Press.

Kikstra, Jarmo S., et al. (2021), "The social cost of carbon dioxide under climate-economy feedbacks and temperature variability," *Environmental Research Letters* 16:094037.

Kitch, Edmund W. (1977), "The nature and function of the patent system," *Journal of Law and Economics* 20:265–290.

Kitch, Edmund W. (1980), "The law and the economics of rights in valuable information," *Journal of Legal Studies* 9:683–723.

Klein, Sherwin (1993), "Drucker's knowledge society and socratic sōphrosyné," *Business & Professional Ethics Journal* 12(4):51–71.

Klotz, Hans and Klaus Rum (1963), "Über die Produktivkraft Wissenschaft," *Einheit* (2):25–31.

Knorr-Cetina, Karin (1981), *The Manufacture of Knowledge: An Essay on the Constructivist and Contextual Nature of Science*. Oxford: Pergamon Press.

Knorr-Cetina, Karin (1988), "The internal environment of knowledge claims: One aspect of the knowledge-society connection," *Argumentation* 2(3):369–389.

Knorr-Cetina, Karin (2007), "Culture in global knowledge societies knowledge cultures and epistemic cultures," *Interdisciplinary Science Reviews* 32:361–375.

Knorr-Cetina, Karin (2010), "The epistemics of information. A consumption model," *Journal of Consumer Culture* 10:171–201.

Knorr-Cetina, Karin and Michael Mulkay (eds.) (1983), *Science Observed. Perspectives on the Social Study of Science*. Newbury Park, CA: SAGE.

Knutsson, Beniamin (2012), "The 'making' of knowledge society in Rwanda? Translations, tensions and transformations," *Globalisation, Societies and Education* 10:181–199.

Koch, Claus and Dieter Senghaas (eds.) (1970), *Texte zur Technokratiediskussion*. Stuttgart: Europäische Verlagsanstalt.

Koh, Dongya, Raül Santaeulàlia-Llopis and Yu Zheng (2015), *Labor Share Decline and Intellectual Property Products Capital*. San Domenico di Fiesole: European University Institute.

Köhnke, Klaus C. (1986), *Entstehung und Aufstieg des Neukantianismus. Die deutsche Universitätsphilosophie zwischen Idealismus und Positivismus*. Frankfurt am Main: Suhrkamp.

Kolberg, Jon E. and Gosta Esping-Anderson (1992), "Welfare states and employment regimes," pp. 3–35 in Jon E. Kolberg (ed.), *Between Work and Citizenship*. Armonk, NY: M.E. Sharpe.

Kolberg, Jon E. and Arne Kolstad (1992), "Unemployment regimes," pp. 171–192 in Jon E. Kolberg (ed.), *Between Work and Citizenship*. Armonk, NY: M.E. Sharpe.

König, René (1955), "Die Begriffe Gemeinschaft und Gesellschaft bei Ferdinand Tönnies," *Kölner Zeitschrift für Soziologie und Sozialpsychologie* 7:348–420.

König, René (1958), "Gemeinschaft," pp. 83–88 in René König (Hrsg.), *Soziologie*. Frankfurt am Main: Fischer.

König, René ([1956] 1965), "Masse und Vermassung," pp. 479–493 in René König (ed.), *Soziologische Orientierungen. Vorträge und Aufsätze*. Köln: Kiepenheuer & Witsch.

König, René ([1962] 1965), "Die Gesellschaft von heute zwischen gestern und morgen," pp. 79–91 in René König (ed.), *Soziologische Orientierungen. Vorträge und Aufsätze*. Köln: Kiepenheuer & Witsch.

König, René (1965), "Bemerkungen zur Sozialpsychologie," pp. 45–78 in René König (ed.), *Soziologische Orientierungen. Vorträge und Aufsätze*. Köln: Kiepenheuer & Witsch.

König, René (1979), "Gesellschaftliches Bewußtsein und Soziologie: Eine spekulative Überlegung," pp. 358–370 in Günther Lüschen (ed.), *Deutsche Soziologie seit 1945*. Sonderheft 21 der *Kölner Zeitschrift für Soziologie und Sozialpsychologie*. Opladen: Westdeutscher Verlag.

König, René ([1984] 1987), "Vom vermeintlichen Ende der deutschen Soziologie vor der Machtergreifung des Nationalsozialismus," pp. 343–387 in René König (ed.), *Soziologie in Deutschland. Begründer, Verächter, Verfechter*. München: Hanser.

König, René (1987), "Kontinuität oder Unterbrechung. Ein neuer Blick auf ein altes Problem," pp. 388–440 in René König (ed.), *Soziologie in Deutschland. Begründer, Verächter, Verfechter*. München: Hanser.

Konrád, Gyoergy and Ivan Szelényi (1979), *The Intellectuals on the Road to Class Power: A Sociological Study of the Role of the Intelligentsia in Socialism*. Brighton: Harvester Press.

Korinek, Anton (2019), "Labor in an age of automation and artificial intelligence," *Research Brief: Economist for Inclusive Prosperity*. https://econfip.org/policy-briefs/labor-in-the-age-of-automation-and-artificial-intelligence/

Korinek, Anton, and Ding Xuan Ng (2019), "Digitization and the Macro-Economics of Superstars, Working Paper. https://www.ecb.europa.eu/pub/conferences/shared/pdf/challenges_dig_age/ecb.digitalisation_conf_KORINEK_Digitization_and_the_Macro_Economics_of_Superstars_Presentation.pdfhttps://drive.google.com/file/d/1inCe3I17YeWY177U8GA93wB6IkJPMyrc/view

Korinek, Anton (2020), "Taxation and the vanishing labor market in the age of AI," *The Ohio State Technology Law Journal* 244–257.

Korinek, Anton and Joseph E. Stiglitz (2019), "Artificial intelligence and its implications for income distribution and unemployment," in Aja Agrawal, Joshua Gans and Avi Goldfarb (eds.), *The Economics of Artificial Intelligence: An Agenda*. Chicago, IL: University of Chicago Press.

Korinek, Anton and Ding Xuan Ng (2017), "The macroeconomics of superstars," *Mimeo*. www. korinek.com/download/Superstars.pdf

Korinek, Anton and Joseph E. Stiglitz (2021), "Artificial intelligence, globalization, and strategies for economic development," NBER Working Paper No. 28453. w28453. https://www.nber.org/system/files/working_papers/w28453/w28453.pdf

Kornhauser, William (1962), *Scientists in Industry: Conflict and Accommodation*. Berkeley, CA: University of California Press.

Kosel, Gerhard (1989), *Unternehmen Wissenschaft. Die Wiederentdeckung einer Idee*. Berlin: Henschelverlag Kunst und Gesellschaft.

Koselleck, Reinhart (1977), "Neuzeit," pp. 300–348 in Reinhard Koselleck (ed.), *Vergangene Zukunft*. Frankfurt am Main: Suhrkamp.

Koselleck, Reinhart (1989), *Vergangene Zukunft. Zur Semantik geschichtlicher Zeiten*. Frankfurt/Main: Suhrkamp.

Koselleck, Reinhart (2003), *Zeitschichten. Studien zur Historik*. Frankfurt am Main: Suhrkamp.

Kovács, Kriszta (2020), "Democracy in lockdown," *Social Research* 87:257–264.

Kozubek, James (2017), "Crispr-Cas9 is impossible to stop," *Georgetown Journal of International Affairs* 18:112–119.

Kraay, Aart (2018), "Methodology for a World Bank Human Capital Index," Policy Research Working Paper No. 8593. Washington, DC: World Bank. https://openknowledge.worldbank.org/handle/10986/30466 License: CC BY 3.0 IGO

Kraay, Aart (2019), "The World Bank Human Capital Index: A guide," *World Bank Research Observer* 34:1–33.

Kracauer, Siegfried (1968), "General history and the aesthetic approach," pp. 111–129, 559–881 in Hans Robert Jauss (ed.), *Die nicht mehr schönen Künste*. München: Fink.

Kraft, Claudia (2009), "Die Gleichzeitigkeit des Ungleichzeitigen: Die Rolle der Kategorie Geschlecht in den Demokratisierungsprozessen in Ost-und Westeuropa seit 1968," *L' homme: Zeitschrift für feministische Geschichtswissenschaft* 20:13–30.

Král, Jaroslav and Michal Zemlicka (2010), "Crucial barriers of knowledge society," pp. 85–93 in Miltiadis D. Lytras, Patricia Ordonez de Pablos, Ernesto Damiani, David Avison, Ambjörn Naeve and David G. Horner (eds.), *Organizational, Business, and Technological Aspects of the Knowledge Society. Communications in Computer and Information Science*. Berlin and Heidelberg: Springer.

Krämer, Sybille (1982), *Technik, Gesellschaft und Natur: Versuch über ihren Zusammenhang*. Frankfurt am Main: Campus.

Kratochwil, Friedrich (1994), "Changing relations between state, market and society, and the problem of knowledge," *Pacific Focus* 9(2):43–59.

Kreckel, Reinhard (1983), "Theorien sozialer Ungleichheit im Übergang," pp. 3–12 in Reinhard Kreckel (ed.), *Soziale Ungleichheiten. Soziale Welt, Sonderband 2*. Göttingen: Verlag Otto Schwartz & Co.

Kreibich, Rolf (1986), *Die Wissenschaftsgesellschaft. Von Galilei zur High-Tech Revolution*. Frankfurt am Main: Suhrkamp.

Krohn, Wolfgang (1981), " 'Wissen ist Macht': Zur Soziogenese eines neuzeitlichen wissenschaftliches Geltungsanspruchs," pp. 29–57 in Kurt Bayertz (Hrsg.), *Wissenschaftsgeschichte und wissenschaftliche Revolution*. Köln: Pahl-Rugenstein.

Krohn, Wolfgang (1997), "Rekursive Lernprozesse: Experimentelle Praktiken in der Gesellschaft. Das Beispiel der Abfallwirtschaft," pp. 65–89 in Werner Rammert und Gotthard Bechmann (Hrsg.), *Technik und Gesellschaft. Jahrbuch 9: Innovation—Prozesse, Produkte, Politik*. Frankfurt am Main and New York: Campus.

Krohn, Wolfgang (2002), "Knowledge societies," pp. 8139–8142 in Neil J. Smelser and Paul B. Bakes (eds.), *International Encyclopedia of the Social and Behavioral Sciences*. Oxford: Blackwell.

Krohn, Wolfgang (2003), "Das Risiko des (Nicht-) Wissens. Zum Funktionswandel der Wissenschaft in der Wissensgesellschaft," pp. 97–118 in Stefan Böschen and Ingo

Schulz-Schaefer (eds.), *Wissenschaft in der Wissensgesellschaft*. Wiesbaden: Springer Fachmedien.

Krohn, Wolfgang and Werner Rammert (1985), "Technologieentwicklung: Autonomer Prozess und industrielle Strategie," pp. 411–433 in Burkart Lutz (ed.), *Soziologie und gesellschaftliche Entwicklung. Verhandlungen des 22. Deutschen Soziologentages*. Frankfurt am Main: Campus.

Krohn, Wolfgang and Johannes Weyer (1989), "Gesellschaft als Labor: Die Erzeugung sozialer Risiken durch experimentelle Forschung," *Soziale Welt* 40:349–373.

Krugman, Paul (1991), *Geography and Trade*. Cambridge, MA: MIT Press.

Küchler, Susanne (2017), "Differential geometry, the informational surface and ocean IC art: The role of pattern in knowledge economy," *Theory, Culture & Society* 43:75–97.

Kuhn, Thomas S. ([1962] 1970), *The Structure of Scientific Revolutions*. Chicago, IL: University of Chicago Press.

Kumar, Krishnan (1978), *Prophecy and Progress. The Sociology of Industrial and Post-Industrial Society*. Harmondsworth: Penguin.

Kumar, Krishnan (1989), "The limits and divisions of industrial capitalism," pp. 16–43 in Richard Scase (ed.), *Industrial Societies: Crisis and Division in Western Capitalism and State Socialism*. London: Unwin Hyman.

Küng, Emil (1976), *Steuerung und Bremsung des technischen Fortschritts*. Tübingen: J.C.B. Mohr (Paul Siebeck).

Kupfer, Antonia (2011), *Bildungssoziologie*. Wiesbaden: Springer.

Kuznets, Simon (1955), "Economic growth and income inequality," *American Economic Review* 45:1–28.

Kuznets, Simon (1966), *Modern Economic Growth*. New Haven, CT: Yale University Press.

Kwak, Duck-Joo and Paul Standish (2014), "Introduction. Cultivating humanities and transforming the knowledge society," *Asia Pacific Education Review* 15:1–3.

Kwet, Michael (2021), "Digital colonialism: The evolution of the American empire," *Roar*, March 3. https://roarmag.org/essays/digital-colonialism-the-evolution-of-american-empire/?utm_source=feedburner&utm_medium=feed&utm_campaign=Feed%3A+roar

La Follette, Marcel C. (ed.) (1983), *Creationism, Science and the Law. The Arkansas Case*. Cambridge, MA: MIT Press.

Ladd, Everett C. Jr. (1970), *American Political Parties. Social Change and Political Response*. New York: W.W. Norton.

Lakoff, Sanford A. (ed.) (1966), *Knowledge and Power. Essays on Science and Government*. New York: Free Press.

Lam, Alice (2002), "Alternative societal models of learning and innovation in the knowledge economy," *International Social Science Journal* 54:67–82.

Lander, Eric S., et al. (2019), "Adopt a moratorium on heritable genome editing," *Nature* 567:165–168.

Landes, David (1980), "The creation of knowledge and technique: Today's task and yesterday's experience," *Daedalus* 109:111–120.

Lane, Robert E. (1966), "The decline of politics and ideology in a knowledgeable society," *American Sociological Review* 31:649–662.

Lane, Robert E. (1978), "Markets and the satisfaction of human wants," *Journal of Economic Issues* 12:799–827.

Lanier, Jaron (2013), *Who Owns the Future?* New York: Simon & Schuster.

Lapp, Ralph E. (1965), *The New Priesthood: The Scientific Elite and the Uses of Power*. New York: Harper & Row.

Larson, Magali Sarfatti (1977), *The Rise of Professionalism*. Berkeley, CA: University of California Press.

Larson, Magali Sarfatti (1984), "The production of expertise and the constitution of expert authority," pp. 28–80 in Thomas L. Haskell (ed.), *The Authority of Experts*. Bloomington, IN: Indiana University Press.

Larson, Magali Sarfatti (1990), "In the matter of experts and professionals, or how impossible it is to leave nothing unsaid," pp. 24–50 in Rolf Torstendahl and Michael Burrage (eds.), *The Formation of Professions. Knowledge, State and Strategy*. London: SAGE.

Lasch, Christopher (1972), "Toward a theory of post-industrial society," pp. 36–50 in M. Donald Hancock and Gideon Sjoberg (eds.), *Politics in the Post-Welfare State. Responses to the New Individualism*. New York: Columbia University Press.

Lash, Scott (1990), *Sociology of Postmodernism*. London: Routledge.

Lash, Scott (2002), *Critique of Information*. New York: W.W. Norton.

Lassow, Ekkhard (1967), "Problem der Produktivkrafttheorie in der Periode des umfassenden Aufbaus des Sozialismus und der technisch-wissenschaftlichen Revolution," *Deutsche Zeitschrift für Philosophie* 15:373–398.

Latour, Bruno (1983), "Give me a laboratory and I will raise the world," pp. 141–170 in Karin D. Knorr-Cetina and Michael Mulkay (eds.), *Science Observed. Perspectives on the Social Study of Science*. London: SAGE.

Latour, Bruno (1991), "The impact of science studies on political philosophy," *Science, Technology, Human Values* 16:3–19.

Latour, Bruno (2002), *Wir sind nie modern gewesen. Versuch einer symmetrischen Anthropologie*. Frankfurt am Main: Suhrkamp.

Lauder, Hugh, Phillip Brown and David Ashton (2008), "Globalisation, skill formation and the varieties of capitalism approach." *New Political Economy* 13:19–35.

Lave, Jean (1988), *Cognition in Practice. Mind, Mathematics and Culture in Everyday Life*. Cambridge: Cambridge University Press.

Layard, Richard and Stephen Nickell (1985), *The Causes of British Unemployment*. London: National Institute of Economic and Social Research.

Layard, Richard, Stephen Nickell and Richard Jackman (1991), *Unemployment. Macroeconomic Performance and the Labour Market*. Oxford: Oxford University Press.

Layton, Edwin T. (1976), "American ideologies of science and technology," *Technology and Culture* 17:688–701.

Lazear, Edward P. (2020), "Productivity and wages: Common factors and idiosyncrasies across countries and industries," NBER Working Paper No. 26428 2019, Revised June 2020. https://www.nber.org/system/files/working_papers/w26428/w26428.pdf

Lazega, Emmanual (1992), *Micropolitics of Knowledge. Communication and Indirect Control in Workgroups*. New York: Aldine de Gruyter.

Lazonick, William (1979), "Industrial relations and technical change: The Case of the self-acting mule," *Cambridge Journal of Economics* 3:231–262.

Lazonick, William (1983), "Technological change and the control of work. The development of capital-labour relations in US mass production industries," pp. 111–136 in Howard F. Gospel and Craig R. Littler (eds.), *Managerial Strategies and Industrial Relations. An Historical and Comparative Study*. London: Heinemann.

Lederer, Emil ([1931] 1938), *Technical Progress and Unemployment: An Inquiry into the Obstacles of Economic Expansion*. London: P.S. King & Son.

Lee, Francis and Lotta Björklund Larsen (2019), "How should we theorize algorithms? Five ideal types in analyzing algorithmic normativities," *Big Data & Society*. http://doi.org/10.1.2053951719867349.

Lehnert, Detlev (2016), "Ungleichzeitigkeit des Gleichzeitigen," *Indes* (Sonderheft):12–20.

Lemma, Bonny (2019), "CRISPR dreams: The potential of gene editing," *Harvard International Review* 40:6–7.

Lenk, Hans (1987), *Zwischen Sozialpsychologie und Sozialphilosophie*. Frankfurt am Main: Suhrkamp.

Lenk, Hans and Günter Ropohl (1978), "Technik im Alltag," pp. 265–298 in Kurt Hammerich and Michael Klein (eds.), *Materialien zur Soziologie des Alltags. Sonderheft 20 der Kölner Zeitschrift für Soziologie und Sozialpsychologie*. Opladen: Westdeutscher Verlag.

Lenski, Gerhard (1970), *Human Societies*. New York: McGraw-Hill.

Leontief, Wassily (1983), "National perspective: The definition of problems and opportunities," in National Academy of Engineering (ed.), *The Long-Term impact of Technology on Employment and Unemployment. National Academy of Engineering Symposium*. Volume 30. Washington, DC: National Academy Press.

Leontief, Wassily (1985), "The choice of technology," *Scientific American* 252:37–45.

Leontief, Wassily et al. (1977), *The Future of the World Economy*. New York: Oxford University Press.

Lerner, Allan W. (1976), *The Politics of Decision-Making. Strategy, Cooperation, and Conflict*. Beverly Hills, CA: SAGE.

Lessig, Lawrence (2001), *The Future of Ideas*. New York: Random House.

Lethen, Helmut (2018), *Die Staatsräte. Elite im Dritten Reich. Gründgens, Furtwängler, Sauerbruch, Schmitt*. Berlin: Rowohlt.

Leubner, Jens (2012), "Franz L. Neumann und das Recht der Wissensgesellschaft," pp. 203–222 in Frank Schale, Ellen Thümmler und Michael Vollmer (eds.), *Intellektuelle Emigration*. Wiesbaden: Springer.

Levy, Marion (1966), *Modernization and the Structure of Societies*. Princeton, NJ: Princeton University Press.

Lewis, W. Arthur (1954), "Economic Development with Unlimited Supplies of Labour," *Manchester School* 22:139–191.

Liberti, José María and Mitchell A. Petersen (2018), "Information: Hard and Soft," *The Review of Corporate Finance Studies* 8:1–41.

Lieberman, Jethro K. (1970), *The Tyranny of Experts: How Professionals are Closing the Open Society*. New York: Walker.

Lieberson, Stanley (1985), *Making It Count. The Improvement of Social Research and Theory*. Berkeley, CA: University of California Press.

Lipset, Seymour M. (1960), *Political Man. The Social Basis of Politics*. Garden City, NY: Doubleday.

Lipset, Seymour M. ([1960] 1962), *Soziologie der Demokratie*. Neuwied: Luchterhand.

Lipset, Seymour M. (1968), "Social class," pp. 296–315 in David Sills (ed.), *International Encyclopedia of the Social Sciences*. Volume 15. New York: Crowell Collier and Macmillan.

Lipset, Seymour M. (1981), "Whatever happened to the proletariat? An historic mission unfulfilled," *Encounter* 56:18–34.

Lipsey, Richard G. (1992), "Global change and economic policy," pp. 279–299 in Nico Stehr and Richard V. Ericson (eds.), *The Culture and Power of Knowledge: Inquiries into Contemporary Societies*. Berlin and New York: de Gruyter.

Liu, Gang and Barbara M. Fraumeni (2020), "A brief introduction to human capital measures," NBER Working Paper No. 27561. https://www.nber.org/system/files/working_papers/w27561/w27561.pdf

Liu, Jun (2020), "Information and communication technologies as contentious repertoire," *European Journal of Sociology* 61:1–31.

Livingstone, David N. (2003), *Putting Science in Its Place. Geographies of Scientific Knowledge*. Chicago, IL: University of Chicago Press.

Livingstone, David W. (1999), "Lifelong learning and underemployment in the knowledge society: A North American perspective," *Comparative Education* 35:163–186.

Livingstone, David W. and Antonie Scholtz (2016), "Reconnecting class and production relations in advanced capitalist 'knowledge economy': Changing class structure and class consciousness," *Capital & Class* 40:469–493.

Lobel, Orly (2015), "The new cognitive property: Human capital law and the reach of intellectual property," *Texas Law Review* 93:788–851.

Lopata, Helena Z. (1976), "Expertization of everyone and the revolt of the client," *The Sociological Quarterly* 17:435–447.

Lor, Johan P. and Johannes Jacobus Britz (2007), "Is a knowledge society possible without freedom of access to information?," *Journal of Information Science* 33(4):387–397.

Lowe, Adolph (1971), "Is present-day higher learning 'relevant'?," *Social Research* 38:563–580.

Lowe, Adolph (1986), "The specter of technological unemployment," Workings Papers: Forschungsgruppe 'Technologischer Wandel und Beschäftigung. Bremen: Universität Bremen.

Lübbe, Hermann (1987), "Der kulturelle Geltungschwund der Wissenschaften," pp. 89–108 in Helmut de Rudder and Heinz Sahner (eds.), *Wissenschaft und gesellschaftliche Verantwortung*. Berlin: Arno Pitz.

Lucas, Robert E., Jr. (1988), "On the mechanics of economic development," *Journal of Monetary Economics* 22:3–42.

Luckmann, Thomas (1982), "Individual action and social knowledge," pp. 247–266 in Mario von Cranach and Rom Harré (eds.), *The Analysis of Action*. Cambridge: Cambridge University Press.

Luckmann, Thomas (1983), "Common sense, science and the specialization of knowledge," *Phenomenology & Pedagogy* 1:59–73.

Luhmann, Niklas (1986), *Ökologische Kommunikation*. Wiesbaden: Westdeutscher Verlag.

Luhmann, Niklas (1970), "Soziologische Aufklärung," pp. 66–92 in Niklas Luhmann (ed.), *Soziologische Aufklärung. Aufsätze zur Theoriesozialer Systeme*. Opladen: Westdeutscher Verlag.

Luhmann, Niklas ([1973] 1975), "Weltzeit und Systemgeschichte," pp. 103–133 in Niklas Luhmann (ed.), *Soziologische Aufklärung*. Volume 2. Opladen: Westdeutscher Verlag.

Luhmann, Niklas (1980), "Temporalisierung von Komplexität. Zur Semantik neuzeitlicher Zeitbegriffe," pp. 235–300 in Niklas Luhmann (ed.), *Gesellschaftsstruktur und Semantik. Studien zur Wissenssoziologie der modernen Gesellschaft*. Volume 1. Frankfurt am Main: Suhrkamp.

Luhmann, Niklas (1981), "Gesellschaftsstrukturelle Bedingungen und Folgerungen des naturwissenschaftlich-technischen Fortschritts," pp. 113–134 in Reinhard Löw et al. (eds.), *Fortschritt ohne Mass*? München: Piper.

Luhmann, Niklas (1984), *Soziale Systeme. Grundriß einer allgemeinen Theorie*. Frankfurt am Main: Suhrkamp.

Luhmann, Niklas ([1973] 1986), "Über Beziehungen zwischen Zeithorizonten und sozialen Strukturen gesellschaftlicher Systeme," pp. 103–133 in Niklas Luhmann (ed.), *Soziologische Aufklärung*. Volume 2. Wiesbaden: Westdeutscher Verlag.

Luhmann, Niklas (1988), *Die Wirtschaft der Gesellschaft*. Frankfurt am Main: Suhrkamp.

Luhmann, Niklas ([1986] 1989), *Ecological Communication*. Chicago, IL: University of Chicago Press.

Luhmann, Niklas (1990a), *Die Wissenschaft der Gesellschaft* [The science of society]. Frankfurt am Main: Suhrkamp.
Luhmann, Niklas (1990b), "Gleichzeitigkeit und Synchronisation," pp. 95–123 in Niklas Luhmann (ed.), *Soziologische Aufklärung*. Volume 5. Opladen: Westdeutscher Verlag.
Luhmann, Niklas (1991), "Verständigung über Risiken und Gefahren," *Die politische Meinung* 36:86–95.
Luhmann, Niklas (1991), *Soziologie des Risikos*. Berlin and New York: de Gruyter.
Luhmann, Niklas ([1984] 1995), *Social Systems*. Stanford, CA: Stanford University Press.
Luhmann, Niklas (1997), *Die Gesellschaft der Gesellschaft*. Frankfurt am Main: Suhrkamp.
Luhmann, Niklas (2000), *Die Politik der Gesellschaft*. Frankfurt am Main: Suhrkamp.
Luhmann, Niklas (2002), *Das Erziehungssystem der Gesellschaft*. Frankfurt am Main: Suhrkamp. March 31, 2022
Luke, Allan (2004), "Teaching after the market: From commodity to cosmopolitan," *Teachers College Record* 106(7):1422–1443.
Lundvall, Bengt-Ake and Björn Johnson (1994), "The learning economy," *Journal of Industry Studies* 1:23–42.
Lynd, Robert (1940), *Knowledge for What? The Place of Social Science in American Culture*. Princeton, NJ: Princeton University Press.
Lyon, David (1986), "From 'post-industrialism' to 'information society': A new social transformation?," *Sociology* 20:577–588.
Lyotard, Jean-François ([1979] 1984), *The Postmodern Condition: A Report on Knowledge*. Minnesota, MN: University of Minnesota Press.
Maasen, Sabine ([2006] 2013), "Wissensgesellschaft," pp. 279–286 in Albert Scherr (ed.), *Soziologische Basics*. Wiesbaden: Springer.
Machlup, Fritz (1958), *An Economic Review of the Patent System. Study of the Subcommittee on Patents, Trademarks, and Copyrights of the Committee on the Judiciary, United States Senate, Study No. 15*. Washington, DC: Government Printing Office.
Machlup, Fritz (1960), "The supply of inventors and inventions," *Weltwirtschaftliches Archiv* 85:210–254.
Machlup, Fritz (1961), "Patents and inventive effort," *Science* 133:1463–1466.
Machlup, Fritz (1962), *The Production and Distribution of Knowledge in the United States*. Princeton, NJ: Princeton University Press.
Machlup, Fritz (1979a), "Uses, value, and benefits of knowledge," *Knowledge* 1:62–81.
Machlup, Fritz (1979b), "Stocks and flows of knowledge," *Kyklos* 32:400–411.
Machlup, Fritz (1981), *Knowledge and Knowledge Production*. Princeton, NJ: Princeton University Press.
Machlup, Fritz (1984), *The Economics of Information and Human Capital*. Princeton, NJ: Princeton University Press.
Machlup, Fritz and Trude Kronwinkler (1975), "Workers who produce knowledge: A steady increase 1900 to 1970," *Weltwirtschaftliches Archiv* 3:752–759.
MacIntyre, Alasdair (1981), *After Virtue. A Study in Moral Theory*. Notre Dame, IN: University of Notre Dame Press.
MacIver, Robert (1931), *Society: Its Structure and Changes*. New York.
MacKenzie, Donald and Judy Wajcman (eds.) (1985), *The Social Shaping of Technology: How the Refrigerator Got Its Hum*. Milton Keynes: Open University Press.
MacRae, Duncan (1976), "Technical communities and political choice," *Minerva* 14:169–190.

Magalhães, António and Stephen Stoer (2003), Performance, Citizenship and the Knowledge Society: A new mandate for European education policy," *Globalisation, Societies and Education* 1:41–66.

Maggi, Giovanni and Ralph Ossa (2020), "The political economy of deep integration," NBER Working Paper. www.nber.org/papers/w28190

Malik, Suhail (2005), "Information and knowledge," *Theory, Culture & Society* 22:29–49.

Malinowski, Bronislaw (1955), *Magic, Science and Religion*. Garden City, NY: Doubleday Anchor.

Mannheim, Karl (1932), *Die Gegenwartsaufgaben der Soziologie*. Ihre Lehrgestalt. Tübingen: J.C.B. Mohr (Paul Siebeck).

Mannheim, Karl (1936), "Ferdinand Tönnies," *The Sociological Review* 28:313–314.

Mannheim, Karl ([1929] 1936), *Ideology and Utopia. An Introduction to the Sociology of Knowledge*. London: Routledge and Kegan Paul.

Mannheim, Karl ([1935] 1940), *Man and Society in an Age of Reconstruction. Studies in Modern Social Structure*. London: Routledge and Kegan Paul.

Mannheim, Karl ([1928] 1952), "The problem of generations," pp. 278–320 in Karl Mannheim and Paul Kecskemeti (eds.), *Essays on the Sociology of Knowledge*. London: Routledge & Kegan Paul.

Mannheim, Karl ([1928] 1970), "Das Problem der Generation," pp. 509–565 in Karl Mannheim (ed.), *Wissenssoziologie. Auswahl aus dem Werk. Hrsg. v. Kurt H. Wolff. 2. Auflage*. Neuwied and Berlin: Luchterhand.

Mannheim, Karl ([1980] 1982), *Structures of Thinking*. Edited and introduced by David Kettler, Volker Meja and Nico Stehr. London: Routledge and Kegan Paul.

Mannheim, Karl ([1925] 1986), *Conservatism. A Contribution to the Sociology of Knowledge*. Edited and introduced by David Kettler, Volker Meja and Nico Stehr. London: Routledge and Kegan Paul.

Mannheim, Karl ([1928] 1990), "Competition as a cultural phenomenon," pp. 53–85 in Volker Meja and Nico Stehr (eds.), *Knowledge and Politics. The Sociology of Knowledge Dispute*. London and New York: Routledge and Kegan Paul.

Mannheim, Karl ([1936] 2001), *Freedom, Power and Democratic Planning*. London: Routledge Kegan Paul.

Mansell, Robin (2002), "From digital divides to digital entitlements in knowledge societies," *Current Sociology* 50(3):407–426.

Mansell, Robin (2015), "Futures of knowledge societies—destabilization in whose interest?," *Information, Communication & Society* 18:627–643.

Marcuse, Herbert (1941), "Some social implications of modern technology," *Studies in Philosophy and Social Science* 9:414–439.

Marcuse, Herbert (1964), *One-Dimensional Man. Studies in the Ideology of Advanced Industrial Society*. Boston, MA: Beacon Press.

Marquand, David (2004), *The Decline of the Public. The Hollowing Out of Citizenship*. Cambridge: Polity Press.

Marshall, Alfred (1920), *Principles of Economics*. London: Macmillan.

Marshall, George (2014), *Don't Even Think About It. Why Our Brains Are Wired To Ignore Climate Change*. New York: Bloomsbury.

Marshall, Gordon, Howard Newby, D. Rose, C. Vogler (1988), *Social Class in Modern Britain*. London: Hutchinson.

Marshall, Thomas H. (1939), "The recent history of professionalization in relation to social structure and social policy," *Canadian Journal of Economics and Political Science* 5:128–155.
Marshall, Thomas H. (1965), *Class, Citizenship, and Social Development*. Garden City, NY: Doubleday Anchor Books.
Martin, Randy (2010), "Specters of finance: Limits of knowledge and the politics of crisis," *Journal of Communication Inquiry* 34(4):355–365.
Marx, Karl ([1867] 1967), *Capital*. Volume 1. New York.
Marx, Karl ([1939–1941] 1973), *Grundrisse. Introduction to the Critique of Political Economy*. New York: Vintage Books.
Marx, Karl ([1848] 1977), *Selected Writings*. Oxford: Oxford University Press.
Marx, Karl ([1859] 1977), *A Contribution to the Critique of Political Economy*. Moscow: Progress Publishers.
Marx, Karl and Friedrich Engels ([1848] 1954), *Manifest der kommunistischen Partei*. Berlin: Dietz.
Marx, Karl and Friedrich Engels ([1932] 1960), *Die deutsche Ideologie*. Berlin: Dietz.
Marx, Karl und Friedrich Engels ([1867] 1968), *Werke. Band 23: Das Kapital*. Berlin: Dietz Verlag,
Marx, Leo (1989), "Developing a national science culture under free trade. What kind of knowledge do we need?," *Technology in Society* 11:203–211.
Maryanski, Alexandra and Jonathan H. Turner (1992), *The Social Cage. Human Nature and the Evolution of Society*. Stanford, CA: Stanford University Press.
Masood, Ehsan (2016), *The Great Invention. The Story of GDP and the Making and Unmaking of the Modern World*. New York: Simon and Schuster.
Mausner, Bernard and Judith S. Mausner (1955), "A study of the anti-scientific attitude," *Scientific American* 192:35–39.
Mauss, Marcel ([1925] 1990), *The Gift. The Form and Reason for Exchange in Archaic Societies*. London: Routledge.
May, Christopher (2000a), *A Global Political Economy of Intellectual Property Rights. The New Enclosures*. London: Routledge.
May, Christopher (2000b), "The information society as mega-machine," *Information, Communication & Society* 3:241–265.
May, Christopher (2002), "Unacceptable costs: The consequence of making knowledge property in a global society," *Global Society* 16:123–144.
Mazur, Allan (1973), "Disputes among experts," *Minerva* 11:243–262.
Mazur, Joseph (2020), *The Clock Mirage: Our Myth of Measured Time*. Princeton, NJ: Princeton University Press.
Mazzucato, Mariana (2018), *The Value of Everything: Making and Taking in the Global Economy*. London: Allen Lane.
McDermott, John (1969), "Technology: The opiate of the intellectuals," *New York Review of Books* 13(2):25–35.
McElhinney, Stephen (2005), "Exposing the interests: Decoding the promise of the global knowledge society," *New Media & Society* 7:748–769.
McIntyre, Lee (2018), *Post-Truth*. Cambridge, MA: MIT Press.
McKinley, John B. (1982), "Toward the proletarianization of physicians," pp. 37–62 in Charles Derber (ed.), *Professionals as Workers: Mental Labor in Advanced Capitalism*. Boston, MA: Hall.
McLain, Raymond (2002), "Reflexivity and the sociology of practice," *Sociological Practice* 4:249–277.

Meadows, Donella H., Dennis L. Meadows and Jürgen Randers (1992), *Beyond the Limits*. Post Mills, VT: Chelsea Green.

Meadows, Donella H., Dennis L. Meadows, Jürgen Randers and William W. Behrens III (1972), *The Limits to Growth*. New York: Universe Books.

Meertje, Arnold (1977), *Economics and Technical Change*. London: Weidenfeld and Nicolson.

Mehta L (2001), "The World Bank and its emerging knowledge empire," *Human Organization* 60:189–196.

Meier, Andreas (2012), "Knowledge Society," pp. 191–204 in Andreas Meier (ed.), *eGovernment & eDemocracy. Stages of a Democratic Knowledge Society*. Berlin and Heidelberg: Springer.

Meja, Volker and Nico Stehr (1992), "Social scientific and epistemological discourse: The problem of relativism," pp. 1–13 in Diederick Raven, Lieteke van Vucht Tijssen and Jan de Wolf (eds.), *Cognitive Relativism and Social Science*. New Brunswick, NJ: Transaction Books.

Melachroinos, Konstantinos A. and Nigel Spence (2019), "The spatial footprint of the knowledge economy: The role of intangible investment in shaping regional inequalities in great brit," *Tijdschrift voor Economische en Sociale Geografie* 110:442–471.

Mendelsohn, Everett (1983), "Science, power and the reconstruction of knowledge," pp. 49–71 in Gunnar Bergendal (ed.), *Knowledge and Higher Education*. Stockholm: National Board of Universities and Colleges.

Merton, Robert K. (1936a), "Civilization and culture," *Sociology and Social Research* 21:103–113.

Merton, Robert K. (1936b), "The unanticipated consequences of purposive social action," *American Sociological Review* 1:894–904.

Merton, Robert K. (1947), "The machine, the worker and the engineer," *Science* 105:79–84.

Merton, Robert K. (1949), "The role of applied social science in the formation of policy: A research memorandum," *Philosophy of Science* 16:161–181.

Merton, Robert K. ([1945] 1957), "Role of the intellectual in public bureaucracy," pp. 207–224 in Robert K. Merton (ed.), *Social Theory and Social Structure*. Revised and Enlarged Edition. New York: Free Press.

Merton, Robert K. ([1949] 1968), *Social theory and social structure*. Revised and enlarged edition. New York: The Free Press.

Merton, Robert K. (1968). *Social theory and social structure* (revised and enlarged edition). New York: The Free Press. (Original work published 1949)

Merton, Robert K. (1970), "Preface 1970," pp. vii–xxix in Robert K. Merton (ed.), *Science, Technology, and Society in Seventeenth-Century England*. New York.

Merton, Robert K. (1973), *The Sociology of Science*. Theoretical and Empirical Investigations. Chicago: University of Chicago Press.

Merton, Robert K. ([1938] 1973), "Science and the social order," pp. 254–266 in Robert K. Merton (ed.), *The Sociology of Science. Theoretical and Empirical Investigations*. Chicago, IL: University of Chicago Press.

Merton, Robert K. ([1942] 1973), "The normative structure of science," pp. 267–278 in Robert K. Merton (ed.), *The Sociology of Science. Theoretical and Empirical Investigations*. Chicago, IL: University of Chicago Press.

Merton, Robert K. ([1970] 1973), "Social and cultural contexts of science," pp. 173–190 in Robert K. Merton (ed.), *The Sociology of Science. Theoretical and Empirical Investigations*. Chicago, IL: University of Chicago Press.

Merton, Robert K. (1975a), "Structural analysis in sociology," pp. 21–52 in Peter Blau (ed.), *Approaches to Social Structure*. New York: Free Press.
Merton, Robert K. (1975b), "The uses of institutionalized altruism," pp. 105–113 in *Seminar Reports. Program of General and Continuing Education in the Humanities*. New York: Columbia University.
Merton, Robert K. (1985), *Entwicklung und Wandel von Forschungsinteressen. Aufsätze zur Wissenschaftssoziologie*. Frankfurt: Suhrkamp.
Meuleman, Louis (ed.), *Transgovernance. Advancing Sustainability Governance*. Heidelberg: Springer.
Meyer, Alfred G. (1970), "Theories of convergence," pp. 313–341 in Chalmers Johnson (ed.), *Change in Communist Systems*. Stanford, CA: Stanford University Press.
Meyer, John, John Boli, George M. Thomas and Francisco O. Ramirez (1997), "World society and the nation state," *American Journal of Sociology* 103:144–181.
Mikl-Horke, Gertraude (2011), "Entfremdung und WIssensgesellschaft," pp. 173–187 in Gertraude Mikl-Horke (ed.), *Historische Soziologie—Sozioökonomie—Wirtschaftssoziologie*. Wiesbaden: Springer.
Milanovic, Branko (2016), *Global Inequality. A New Approach for the Age of Globalization*. Cambridge, MA: Harvard University Press.
Miller, S. Michael (1975), "Notes on neo-capitalism," *Theory and Society* 2:1–35.
Miller, Stephen (2019), "What do patents mean," *Issues in Science and Technology* 84–87.
Mills, C. Wright (1958), *The Causes of World War Three*. New York: Simon & Schuster.
Mills, C. Wright ([1955] 1967), "On knowledge and power," pp. 599–613 in Irving L. Horowitz (ed.), *Power, Politics and People: The Collected Essays of C. Wright Mills*. New York: Oxford University Press.
Mills, C. Wright ([1959] 1970), *The Sociological Imagination*. Harmondsworth: Penguin Books.
Mincer, Jacob (1958a), "Investment in human capital and personal income distribution," *Minerva* 43:297–309.
Mincer, Jacob (1958b), "Investment in human capital and personal income distribution," *Journal of Political Economy* 66:281–302.
Mingione, Enzo (1991), *Fragmented Societies. A Sociology of Economic Life Beyond the Market Paradigm*. Oxford: Basil Blackwell.
Mirowski, Philip and Edward Nik-Khan (2017), *The Knowledge We Have Lost in Information. The History of Information in Economics*. New York: Oxford University Press.
Mises, Ludwig (1922), *Die Gemeinwirtschaft. Untersuchungen über den Sozialismus*. Jena: Gustav Fischer.
Miskin, Frederic S. (1990), "Asymmetric information and financial crisis: A historical perspective," NBER Working Paper 3400.
Mitchell, Timothy (2014), "Ecomentality: How the future entered government," *Critical Inquiry* 40:479–507.
Mokyr, Joel (2009), "Intellectual property rights, the industrial revolution, and the beginnings of modern economic growth," *American Economic Review* 99:349–355.
Mokyr, Joel (2016), *Culture and Growth. The Origins of the Modern Economy*. Princeton, NJ: Princeton University Press.
Mokyr, Joel (2018), "Science, technology, and knowledge—What economic historians can learn from an evolutionary approach," pp. 81–119 in U. Witt and A. Chai (eds.), *Understanding Economic Change*. Cambridge: Cambridge University Press.
Montagu, Ashley (ed.) (1984), *Science and Creationism*. Oxford: Oxford University Press.

Montgomery, David (1979), *Worker's Control in America. Studies in the History of Work, Technology and Labour Struggles*. Cambridge: Cambridge University Press.
Moore, Barrington Jr. (1969), "Revolution in America," *The New York Review of Books*, January 30.
Moore, John A. (1974), "Creationism in California," *Daedalus* 103:173–189.
Moore, W. and M.M. Tumin (1949), "Social functions of ignorance," *American Sociological Review* 14:787–796. www.jstor.org/stable/2086681
Moore, Wilbert E. (1967), *Order and Change. Essays in Comparative Sociology*. New York: John Wiley.
Moore, Wilbert E. (1970), *The Professions: Roles and Rules*. New York: Russell Sage Foundation.
Moore, Wilbert E. and Melvin M. Tumin (1949), "Some social functions of ignorance," *American Sociological Review* 14:787–795.
Morgenthau, Hans (1970), "Reflections on the end of the republic," *New York Review of Books* 15:38–41.
Morrison, David E. (1978), "The beginning of modern mass communication research," *European Journal of Sociology* 14:347–359.
Moscovici, Serge ([1981] 1985), *The Age of the Crowd. A Historical Treatise on Mass Psychology*. Cambridge: Cambridge University Press.
Mósesdóttir, Lilja (2011), "Gender (in)equalities in the knowledge society," *Gender, Work and Organization* 18(1):30–72.
Moulier-Boutang, Yann ([2007] 2011), *Cognitive Capitalism*. Cambridge: Polity Press.
Mulkay, Michael (1979), *Science and the Sociology of Knowledge*. London: Allen & Unwin.
Mulkay, Michael (1984), "Knowledge and utility: Implications for the sociology of knowledge," pp. 77–98 in Nico Stehr and Volker Meja (eds.), *Society and Knowledge. Contemporary Perspectives on the Sociology of Knowledge*. New Brunswick, NJ: Transaction Books.
Mumford, Lewis (1962), *Technics and Civilization*. New York: Harcourt Brace Jovanovich.
Mumford, Lewis (1964), "Authoritarian and democratic technics," *Technology and Culture* 5:1–8.
Mumford, Lewis (1970), *The Myth of the Machine: The Pentagon of Power*. New York: Harcourt Brace Jovanovich.
Münch, Richard (2011), "Globales Wissen, lokale Lebenswelten, Reflexive Modernisierung in der Wissensgesellschaft," pp. 135–161 in Andrea Maurer und Uwe Schimank (eds.), *Die Rationalitäten des Sozialen*. Wiesbaden: Springer.
Myles, John (1990), "States, labor markets, and life cycles," pp. 271–298 in Roger Friedland and A. F. Robertson (eds.), *Beyond the Marketplace. Rethinking Economy and Society*. New York: Aldine de Gruyter.
Myles, John and Gail Fawcett (1990), *Job Skills and the Service Economy*. Working Paper No. 4. Ottawa: Economic Council of Canada.
Nachtwey, Oliver and Philipp Staab (2015), "Die Avantgarde des digitalen Kapitalismus." *Mittelweg* 36:1–21.
Narr, Wolf-Dieter ([1979] 1985), "Toward a society of conditioned reflexes," pp. 31–66 in Jürgen Habermas (ed.), *Observations on 'The Spiritual Situation of the Age'*. Cambridge, MA: MIT Press.
Nassehi, Armin (1993), *Die Zeit der Gesellschaft. Auf dem Weg zu einer soziologischen Theorie der Zeit*. Wiesbaden: Westdeutscher Verlag.
National Science Board (1989), *Science and Engineering Indicators-1989*. Washington, DC: U.S. Government Printing Office.

Naumann, Friedrich (1909), "Von wem werden wir regiert?," *Neue Rundschau* 20:625–636.
Needham, Joseph (1974), "Science and society in East and West," pp. 102–122 in Sal Paul Restivo and Christopher K. Vanderpool (eds.), *Comparative Studies in Science and Society*. Columbus, OH: C.E. Merrill.
Nelkin, Dorothy (1975), "The political impact of technical expertise," *Social Studies of Science* 5:35–54.
Nelson, Richard R. (1981), "Research on productivity growth and productivity differentials: Dead ends and new departures," *Journal of Economic Literature* 19:1029–1064.
Nelson, Richard R. and Sidney G. Winter (1982), *An Evolutionary Theory of Economic Change*. Cambridge. MA: Harvard University Press.
Nelson, Robert H. (1987), "The economics profession and the making of public policy," *Journal of Economic Literature* 25:49–91.
Nettl, J. Peter and Roland Robertson (1968), *International Systems and the Modernization of Societies. The Formation of National Goals and Attitudes*. New York: Basic Books.
Neumann, Michael (2009), "Degrees of property," Think, 8(22), 75-91. doi:10.1017/S1477175609000104
Neurath, Otto ([1932] 1933). "Protokollsätze," *Erkenntnis* 2/3:204–214.
Neurath, Otto (1944), *Foundations of the Social Sciences*. Chicago, IL: University of Chicago Press.
Neurath, Otto ([1919] 1994), "Die Utopie als gesellschaftstechnische Konstruktion," pp. 157–160 in Paul Neurath and Elisabeth Nemeth (Hrsg.), *Otto Neurath oder die Einheit von Wissenschaft und Gesellschaft*. Wien: Böhlau.
Neuser, Wolfgang (2013), "Wissen begreifen," p. 17, *Zur Selbstorganisation von Erfahrung, Handlung und Begriff*, Wiesbaden: Springer.
Newfield, Christopher (2019), "Unbundling the knowledge economy." *Globalisation, Societies and Education* 17:92–100.
Newman, Rhona and Julian Newman (1985), "Information work: The new divorce?," *British Journal of Sociology* 34:497–515.
Nicol, Lionel (1985), "Communications technology: Economic and spatial impacts," pp. 191–209 in Manuel Castells (ed.), *High Technology, Space and Society*. Beverly Hills, CA: SAGE.
Niebel, Thomas, Mary O'Mahony and Marianne Saam (2017), "The contribution of intangible assets to sectoral productivity growth in the EU," *Review of Income and Wealth* 63:S49-S67.
Niehues, Judith (2016), "Wahrnehmung und Wirklichkeit—ein internationaler Vergleich, 'Vergleich,'" *Wirtschaftsdienst* 96:13–18.
Nietzsche, Friedrich ([1878] 1984), *Human, All-Too-Human*. Lincoln, NE: University of Nebraska Press.
Niklas, Luhmann ([184] 1995), *Social Systems*. Stanford, California: Stanford University Press.
Nimkoff, Meyer F. (1957), "Obstacles to innovation," pp. 56–71 in Frances R. Allen et al. (eds.), *Technology and Social Change*. New York: Appleton Century-Crofts.
Nisbet, Robert A. (1970), *The Social Bond. An Introduction to the Study of Society*. New York: Alfred A. Knopf.
Nobel Foundation (1979), "Press Release: This Year's Economics Prize Awarded to Developing Country Research," *The Royal Swedish Academy of Sciences*, October 16.
Noble, David F. (1977), *America by Design: Science, Technology, and the Rise of Corporate Capitalism*. New York: Alfred A. Knopf.

Noble, David F. (1984), *Forces of Production: A Social History of Industrial Automation*. New York: Alfred A. Knopf.

Nolte, Ernst (1993), 'Die Fragilität des Triumps. Zur Lage des liberalen Systems nach der neuen Weltordnung," *Frankfurter Allgemeine Zeitung* 151.

Nolte, Paul (2002), "Gleichzeitigkeit des Ungleichzeitigen," pp. 134–137 in Stefan Jordan (Hrsg.), *Lexikon Geschichtswissenschaft*. Stuttgart: Hundert Grundbegriffe.

Nora, Simon and Alain Minc (1980), *The Computerisation of Society*. Cambridge, MA: MIT Press.

Nordhaus, William D. (1969), "An Economic Theory of Technological Change," *The American Economic Review* 59:18–28.

Nordhaus, William D. (2006), "Baumol's diseases: A macroeconomic perspective," NBER Working Paper 12218.

Norris, Pippa (2013), *Democratic Deficit. Critical Citizens Revisited*. Cambridge: Cambridge University Press.

Norris, Pippa und Ronald Inglehart (2019), *Cultural Backlash. Trump, Brexit and the Authoritarian Populism*. Cambridge: Cambridge University Press.

North, Douglas C. (1981), *Structure and Change in Economic History*. New York: W.W. Norton.

Nowotny, Helga (1979), *Kernenergie: Gefahr oder Notwendigkeit? Anatomie eines Konflikts*. Frankfurt am Main: Suhrkamp.

Nowotny, Helga (1993), *Eigenzeit. Entstehung und Strukturierung eines Zeitgefühls*. Frankfurt am Main: Suhrkamp.

Nowotny, Helga, Peter Scott and Michael Gibbons (2003), "Re-Thinking Science: Mode 2 in Societal Context," http://comparsociology.com/wp-content/uploads/2013/02/Mode2-Science-Gibbons-Nowotny.pdf

Nun, Nathan (2020), "History as evolution," NBER Working Paper 27706. www.nber.org/papers/w27706

Nunn, Nathan (2021), "History as evolution," pp. 41–91 in Alberto Bisin and Giovanni Federico (eds.), *The Hand book of Historical Economics*. London; Elsevier.

Nye, David E. (1997), *Narratives and Spaces. Technology and the Construction of American Culture*. New York: Columbia University Press.

Nye, Joseph, Jr. (2010), "The future of American power. Dominance and decline," *Foreign Affairs* 89(6):2–12.

O'Carroll, A. (2015), *Working Time, Knowledge Work and Post-Industrial Society. Unpredictable Work*. London: Palgrave MacMillan.

OECD (2013), *Supporting Investment in Knowledge Capital, Growth and Innovation*. Paris: OECD Publishing. https://doi.org/10.1787/9789264193307-en

Offe, Claus (1968), "Technik und Eindimensionalität: Eine Version der Technokratiethese?," pp. 73–88 in Jürgen Habermas (ed.), *Antworten auf Herbert Marcuse*. Frankfurt am Main: Suhrkamp.

Offe, Claus (1983), "Arbeit als soziologisches Schlüsselkategorie," pp. 38–65 in Joachim Mattges (ed.), *Krise der Arbeitsgesellschaft*. Verhandlungen des 21. Deutschen Soziologentages in Bamberg 1982. Frankfurt am Main: Campus.

Offe, Claus (1984), *Arbeitsgesellschaft: Strukturprobleme und Zukunftsperspektiven*. Frankfurt am Main: Campus Verlag.

Offe, Claus ([1979] 1984), "Ungovernability: On the renaissance of conservative theories of crisis," pp. 67–88 in Jürgen Habermas (ed.), *Observations on 'The Spiritual Situation of the Age'. Contemporary German Perspectives*. Cambridge, MA: MIT Press.

Offe, Claus (1986), "Die Utopie der Null-Option. Modernität und Modernisierung als politische Gütekriterien," pp. 97–117 in Johannes Berger (ed.), *Die Moderne. Kontinuitäten und Zäsuren*. Sonderband 4. Soziale Welt. Göttingen: Schwartz & Co.

Ogburn, William F. ([1922] 1950), *Social Change, With Respect to Culture and Original Nature*. New York: Viking.

Ogburn, William F. (1957a), "Cultural lag as theory," *Sociology and Social Research* 41:167–174.

Ogburn, William F. (1957b), "Social forces affecting the future of the United States," *India Quarterly* 13:23–32.

Ogburn, William F. (1964), *On Culture and Social Change*. Selected Papers. Chicago, IL: University of Chicago Press.

Oja, Gail (1987), *Changes in the Distribution of Wealth in Canada, 1970–1984. Income Analytic Report No. 1. Statistics Canada, Labour and Household Surveys Division*. Ottawa: Statistics Canada.

Olssen, Mark (2006), "Understanding the mechanisms of neoliberal control: Lifelong learning, flexibility and knowledge capitalism," *International Journal of Lifelong Education* 25(3):213–230.

Olssen, Mark and Michael A. Peters (2005), "Neoliberalism, higher education and the knowledge economy: From free market to knowledge capitalism," *Journal of Education Policy* 20(3):313–345.

Oppenheimer, Martin (1973), "The proletarianization of the professional," pp. 213–227 in Paul Halmos (ed.), *Professionalization and Social Change*. Sociological Review Monograph 20. Keele: University of Keele.

Organisation for Economic Co-Operation and Development (1985), *Labour Force Statistics, 1963–1983*. Paris: OECD.

Organisation for Economic Co-Operation and Development (1987), *Historical Statistics 1960–1985*. Paris: OECD.

Organisation for Economic Co-Operation and Development (1991a), *Employment Outlook*. Paris: OECD.

Organisation for Economic Co-Operation and Development (1991b), *Labour Force Statistics, 1969–1989*. Paris: OECD.

Organisation for Economic Co-Operation and Development (1991c), *Technology and Productivity. The Challenge for Economic Policy*. Paris: OECD.

Organisation for Economic Co-Operation and Development (1992a), *Economic Outlook. Historical Statistics, 1960–1990*. Paris: OECD.

Organisation for Economic Co-Operation and Development (1992b), *Employment Outlook*. Paris: OECD.

Organisation for Economic Co-Operation and Development (1992c), *National Accounts: Detailed Tables, 1978–1990*. Volume 2. Paris: OECD.

Organisation for Economic Co-Operation and Development (1992d), *Quarterly Labour Force Statistics*. Number 3. Paris: OECD.

Organisation for Economic Co-Operation and Development (1992e), *Structural Change and Industrial Performance. A Seven Country Growth Decomposition Study*. Paris: OECD.

Organisation for Economic Co-Operation and Development (1996), *The Knowledge-Based Economy*. Paris: OECD.

Organisation for Economic Co-Operation and Development (2013), *Supporting Investment in Knowledge Capital, Growth and Innovation*. Paris: OECD.

Organisation for Economic Co-Operation and Development (2017), *How's life? Measuring well-being*. Paris: OECD.

Orhangazi, Özgür (2019), "The role of intangible assets in explaining the investment-profit puzzle," *Cambridge Journal of Economics* 43:1251–1285.

Osberg, Lars, Edward N. Wolff and William J. Baumol (1989), *The Information Economy: The Implications of Unbalanced Growth*. Halifax: The Institute for Research on Public Policy.

Osborne, Thomas (2004), "On mediators: Intellectuals and the ideas trade in the knowledge society," *Economy and Society* 33:430–447.

Pagano, Udo (2018), "Knowledge as a global common and the crisis of the learning economy," pp. 353–373 in Martin Guzman (Hg.), *Joseph Stiglitz and the Twenty-First Century Economics*. New York: Columbia University Press.

Pagano, Ugo (2007), "Cultural globalisation, institutional diversity and the unequal accumulation of intellectual capital," *Cambridge Journal of Economics* 31:649–667.

Pagano, Ugo (2009), "The crash of the knowledge economy," *Cambridge Journal of Economics* 33:665–683.

Pagano, Ugo (2014), "The crisis of intellectual monopoly capitalism," *Cambridge Journal of Economics* 38:1409–1429.

Paltrinieri, Luca (2019), "Neoliberal selves. Human capital between Bourdieu and Foucault," pp. 157–180 in Stephen W. Sawyer and Daniel Steinmetz-Jenkins (eds.), *Foucault, Neoliberalism, and Beyond*. London: Rowman & Littlefield.

Parkin, Frank (1979), *Marxism and Class Theory: A Bourgeois Critique*. London: Tavistock.

Parsons, Talcott (1937), *The Structure of Social Action*. New York: McGraw-Hill.

Parsons, Talcott (1939), "The professions and social structure," *Social Forces* 17:457–467.

Parsons, Talcott (1951), *The Social System*. Glencoe, IL: The Free Press.

Parsons, Talcott (1954), "A revised analytical approach to the theory of social stratification," pp. 386–439 in Talcott Parsons (ed.), *Essays in Sociological Theory*. New York: Free Press.

Parsons, Talcott ([1942] 1954), "Democracy and social structure in pre-Nazi Germany," pp. 104–123 in Talcott Parsons, *Essays in Sociological Theory*. New York: Free Press.

Parsons, Talcott (1968), "Professions," pp. 536–547 in David Sills (ed.), *International Encyclopedia of the Social Sciences*. Volume 12. New York: Macmillan.

Parsons, Talcott (1969a), *Politics and Social Structure*. New York: Free Press.

Parsons, Talcott (1969b), "The intellectual," pp. 3–26 in Phillip Rieff (ed.), *On Intellectuals*. New York: Anchor Books.

Parsons, Talcott (1970), "The impact of technology on culture and emerging new modes of behavior," *International Social Science Journal* 22:607–627.

Parsons, Talcott (1977), *The Evolution of Societies*. Englewood Cliffs, NJ: Prentice-Hall.

Parsons, Talcott ([1973] 1990), *Die amerikanische Universität. Ein Beitrag zur Soziologie der Erkenntnis*. Frankfurt am Main: Suhrkamp.

Parsons, Talcott and Gerald M. Platt (1973), *The American University*. Cambridge, MA: Harvard University Press.

Parsons, Talcott et al. (eds.) (1961), *Theories of Society*. New York: The Free Press.

Parthasarathy, Shobita (2017), *Patent Politics. Life Forms, Markets, and the Public Interest in United States and Europe*. Chicago, IL: University of Chicago Press.

Peláez, Antonio L. (2014), "From the digital divide to the robotics divide? Reflections on technology, power, and social change," pp. 5–24 in Antonio L. Peláez (ed.), *The Robotics Divide. A New Frontier in the 21st Century?* London: Springer.

Peláez, Antonio L. and Sagrario Segado Sánchez-Cabezudo (2014), "From 'singularity' to inequality. Perspectives on the emerging robotics divide," pp. 195–217 in Antonio L. Peláez (ed.), *The Robotics Divide. A New Frontier in the 21st Century?* London: Springer.

Pellegrino, Giuseppina (2012), "Beyond an IT-driven knowledge society: Knowledge management as intertwined sociotechnical circulation," *European Review* 20(2):164–172.

Penty, Arthur J. (1917), *Old World for New: A Study of the Post-Industrial State*. London: Allen and Unwin.

Percy, Arnold (1983), *The Culture of Technology*. Cambridge, MA: MIT Press.

Perl, Martin L. (1971), "The scientific advisory system: Some observations," *Science* 173:1211–1215.

Perlmutter, Howard V. (1991), "On the rocky road to the first global civilization," *Human Relations* 44:897–920.

Perrole, Judith A. (1986), "Intellectual assembly lines: The rationalization of managerial, professional, and technical work," *Computers and the Social Sciences* 2:111–121.

Perrow, Charles (1984), *Normal Accidents*. New York: Basic Books.

Peters, Michael A. and James Reveley (2012) "Retrofitting Drucker: Knowledge work under cognitive capitalism," *Culture and Organization*. DOI:10.1080/14759551.2012.692591.

Peters, Sybille, Kai Reinhardt und Holger Seidel (2006), "Globalisierung und Wissensgesellschaft," pp. 7–33 in *Wissen verlangen. Risiken und Potentiale von Standortverlagerungen*. Wiesbaden: Gabler.

Pfaffenberger, Bryan (1992), "Technological dramas," *Science, Technology, and Human Values* 17:282–312.

Piketty, Thomas (2006), "The kuznets curve yesterday and tomorrow," in S. Abhijit Vinayak Banerjee, Roland Bnabou und Dilip Mookherjee (eds.), *Understanding Poverty*.

Piketty, Thomas ([2013] 2014), *Capital in the Twenty-First Century*. Cambridge, Massachusetts: Harvard University Press.

Piketty, Thomas ([2019] 2020), *Capital and Ideology*. Cambridge, MA: Harvard University Press.

Piketty, Thomas, Emmanuel Saez and Gabriel Zucman (2018), "Distributional national accounts: Methods and estimates for the United States," *Quarterly Journal of Economics* 133:553–609.

Pinch, Trevor and Wiebe J. Bijker (1987), "The social construction of facts and artifacts, or how the sociology of science and technology might aid each other," pp. 17–49 in Wiebe E. Bijker, Thomas P. Hughes and Trevor Pinch (eds.), *The Social Construction of Technological Systems: New Directions in the Sociology and History of Technology*. Cambridge, MA: MIT Press.

Piore, Michael J. and Charles F. Sabel (1984), *The Second Industrial Divide*. New York: Basic Books.

Pistor, Katharina (2019), *The Code of Capital*. Princeton, NJ: Princeton University Press.

Pistor, Katharina (2020), "Rule by data: The end of markets?," *Law and Contemporary Problems* 83:101–124.

Plant, Arnold (1934), "The economic theory concerning patents for inventions," *Economica New Series* 1:30–51.

Poggi, Gianfranco (1982), "The modern state and the idea of progress," pp. 337–369 in Gabriel A. Almond, Marvin Chodorow und Roy Harvey Pearce (Hg.), *Progress and Its Discontents*. Berkeley, CA: University of California Press.

Polanyi, Karl ([1944] 2001), *The Great Transformation. The Political and Economic Origins of Our Time*. Boston, MA: Beacon Press.

Polanyi, Karl (2014), *For a New West: Essays, 1919–1958*. Cambridge: Polity.

Polanyi, Michael (1944), "Patent reform," *The Review of Economic Studies* 11:61–76.

Polanyi, Michael (1956), "Pure and applied science and their appropriate forms of organization," *Dialectica* 10:231–242.

Polanyi, Michael (1958), *Personal Knowledge. Towards a Post-Critical Philosophy*. London: Routledge & Kegan Paul.

Polanyi, Michael (1962), *The Republic of Science, Its Political and Economic Theory*. Chicago, IL: Lecture at Roosevelt University.

Polanyi, Michael (1967), *The Tacit Dimension*. New York: Doubleday.

Popitz, Heinrich (1968), *Über die Präventivwirkung des Nichtwissens: Dunkelziffer, Norm und Strafe [On the Preventive Effect of Not Knowing: Number of Unreported Cases, Norm, and Punishment]*. Tübingen: J. C. B. Mohr (Paul Siebeck).

Popitz, Heinrich (1986), *Phänomene der Macht*. Tübingen: J.C.B. Mohr (Paul Siebeck).

Popper, Karl R. ([1957] 1972), *The Poverty of Historicism*. London: Routledge and Kegan Paul.

Popper, Karl R. ([1991] 1992), "Emancipation through knowledge," pp. 137–150 in Karl Popper (ed.), *In Search of a Better World. Lectures and Essays from Thirty Years*. London: Routledge.

Popper, Karl R. (2020), *The Open Society and Its Enemies*. Princeton, NJ: Princeton University Press.

Porat, Marc U. and Michael R. Rubin (1977), *The Information Economy*. Washington, DC: Government Printing Office.

Porzio, Tommaso, Federico Rossi and Gabriella V. Santangelo (2021), "The human side of structural transformation," NBER Working Paper No. 29390. https://www.nber.org/papers/w29390

Portes, Alejandro and Saskia Sassen-Koob (1987), "Making it underground: Comparative material on the informal sector in Western market economies," *American Journal of Sociology* 93:30–61.

Portello, Eduardo (2003), "Introduction: Indications of the Knowledge Society, *Diogenes* 50(1): 5–7.

Portwood, Derek and Alan Fielding (1981), "Privilege and the professions," *Sociological Review* 29:749–773.

Posner, Richard A. (1977), *Economic Analysis of Law*. New York: Little Brown and Company.

Posner, Richard A. (2002), "The law & economics of intellectual property," *Daedalus* 131:5–12.

Posner, Richard A. (2013), "Automation and Employment," *The Becker-Posner Blog* http://www.becker-posner-blog.com/2013/03/automation-and-e

Powell, Alison, Huw T. O. Davies and Sandra M. Nutley (2018), "Facing the challenges of research-informed knowledge mobilization: 'Practising what we preach'? *Public Administration* 96:36–52.

Power, Michael (1997), "From risk to audit society," *Soziale Systeme* 3:3–21.

Price, Derek J. de Solla (1961), *Science since Babylon*. New Haven, CT: Yale University Press.

Price, Derek J. de Solla (1963), *Big Science, Little Science*. New York: Columbia University Press.

Price, Don K. (1965), *The Scientific Estate*. New York: Oxford University Press.

Priddat, Birger P. (2004), "2nd-order democracy. Politikprozesse in der Wissensgesellschaft," pp. 72–89 in Peter Collin und Thomas Hostmann (eds.), *Das Wissen des Staates. Geschichte, Theorie und Praxis*. Baden-Baden: Nomos.

Prins, Gwythian, Isabel Galiana, Christopher Green, Reiner Grundmann, Mike Hulme, Atte Korhola, Frank Laird, Ted Nordhaus, Roger Pielke Jr., Steve Rayner, Daniel Sarewitz, Michael Shellenberger, Nico Stehr, Hiroyuki Tezuka (2009), *The Hartwell Paper*. London: London School of Economics.

Prins, Gwythian, Isabel Galiana, Christopher Green, Reiner Grundmann, Mike Hulme, Atte Korhola, Frank Laird, Ted Nordhaus, Roger Pielke Jr., Steve Rayner, Daniel Sarewitz, Michael Shellenberger, Nico Stehr, Hiroyuki Tezuka (2013), *The Vital Spark. Innovating Clean and Affordable Energy for All*. London: LSE Academic Publishing.

Purdy, Jedediah. (2010), "The politics of nature: Climate change, environmental law, and democracy," *Yale Law Journal* 119:1122–1209.

Quah, Danny (2003), *Digital Goods and the New Economy*. London: London School of Economics, Centre for Economics Performance.

Quéau, Philippe (2002), "Global governance and knowledge societies," *Development* 45:10–16.

Quinn, Sara (2008), "The transformation of morals in markets: Death, benefits, and the exchange of life insurance policies," *American Journal of Sociology* 114:738–780.

Rabin-Havt, Ari and Media Matters for America (2016), *Lies, Incorporated. The World of Post-Truth Politics*. New York: Penguin Random House.

Radder, H. (1986), "Experiment, technology and the intrinsic connection between knowledge and power," *Social Studies of Science* 16:663–683. https://doi.org/10.1177/030631286016004005

Ramesh, Sangaralingam (2023), "China's transition to a knowledge economy," *Journal of Knowledge Economy* 4:473–491.

Rasonvallon, Pierre ([2011] 2013), *Society of Equals*. Cambridge, MA: Harvard University Press.

Ravetz, Jerome R. (1971), *Scientific Knowledge and Its Social Problems*. New York: Oxford University Press.

Ravetz, Jerome R. (1987), "Usable knowledge, usable ignorance," *Knowledge* 9:87–116.

Rayner, Steve (2012), "Uncomfortable knowledge: The social construction of ignorance in science and environmental policy discourses," *Economy and Society* 41:107–125.

Reichmann, Jerome H., Arti K. Rai, Richard Newell, und Jonathan B. Wiener (2014), "Intellectual property and alternatives: Strategies for green innovation," pp. 358–391 in Mario Cimoli, Giovanni Dosi, Keith E. Maskus, Ruth L. Okediji, Jerome H. Reichmann und Joseph E. Stiglitz (eds.), *Intellectual Property Rights*. Oxford: Oxford University Press.

Reitz, Tilman (2019), "Knowledge," pp. 191–212 in Gareth Dale, Christopher Holmes and Maria Markantonatou (eds.), *Karl Polanyi's Political and Economic Thought*. Newcastle: Agenda Publishing.

Renn, Jürgen (2020), *The Evolution of Knowledge. Rethinking Science in the Anthropocene*. Princeton, NJ: Princeton University Press.

Renn, Ortwin (2019), *Gefühlte Wahrheiten. Orientierung in Zeiten postfaktischer Verunsicherung*. Opladen: Barbara Budrich.

Rhodes Ekaterina, Jonn Axsen and Mark Jaccard (2014), "Does effective climate policy require well-informed citizen support?," *Global Environmental Change* 29:92–104.

Richards, Donald G. (2004), *Intellectual Property Rights*. Armonk, NY: M.E. Sharpe.

Richards, Stewart (1983), *Philosophy and Sociology of Science*. Oxford: Basil Blackwell.

Richta, Radovan (1977), "The scientific and technological revolution and the prospects of social development," pp. 25–72 in Ralf Dahrendorf et al. (eds.), *Scientific-Technological Revolution: Social Aspects*. London: SAGE.

Richta, Radovan et al. (1969), *Civilization at the Crossroads: Social and Human Implications of the Scientific and Technological Revolution*. White Plains, NY: International Arts and Sciences Press.

Rickson, Roy E. (1976), "Knowledge management in industrial society and environmental quality," *Human Organization* 35:239–251.

Rieff, David (2013), "The singularity of fools: A special report from the utopian future," *Foreign Policy*. www.foreignpolicy.com/articles/2013/04/29/the_singularity_of_fools?

Riesman, David (1950), *The Lonely Crowd. A Study of the Changing American Character*. New Haven, CT: Yale University Press.

Riesman, David ([1953] 1954), "Some relationships between technical progress and social progress," *Explorations in Entrepreneurial History* 6:131–145.

Riesman, David ([1958] 1964), "Leisure and work in postindustrial society," pp. 162–183 in David Riesman (ed.), *Abundance for What? And Other Essays*. Garden City, NY: Doubleday.

Rifkin, Jeremy (2014), *The Zero Marginal Cost Society. The Internet of Things, the Collaborative Commons, and the Eclipse of Capitalism*. New York: Palgrave Macmillan.

Rikap, Cecilia and Bengt-Åke Lundvall (2020), "Big tech, knowledge predation and the implication for development," *Innovation and Development* :1–28.

Roach, Stephen S. (1991), "Pitfalls on the "new" assembly line: Can services learn from manufacturing?" pp. 119–129 in Organisation for Economic Co-Operation and Development (ed.), *Technology and Productivity. The Challenge for Economic Policy*. Paris: OECD.

Robertson, Roland (1990), "Mapping the global condition: Globalization as the central concept," pp. 15–30 in Mike Featherstone (ed.), *Global Culture. Nationalism, Globalization and Modernity*. A Theory, Culture & Society Special Issue. London: SAGE.

Robson, Kevin and Frank Webster (1989), *The Technical Fix. Education, Computer and Industry*. New York: St. Martin's Press.

Rogers, Everett M. (1972), *The Diffusion of Innovation*. Glencoe, IL: Free Press.

Romer, Paul M. (1986), "Increasing returns and long-run growth," *Journal of Political Economy* 94:1002–1037.

Ropohl, Günter (1991), *Technologische Aufklärung. Beiträge zur Technikphilosophie*. Frankfurt am Main: Suhrkamp.

Rorty, Richard (1984), "Habermas and Lyotard on post-modernity," *Praxis International* 4:32–44.

Rosanvallon, Pierre (2006), *Democracy Past and Future*. New York: Columbia University Press.

Rosanvallon, Pierre ([2011] 2013), *The Society of Equals*. Cambridge, Massachusetts: Harvard University Press.

Rose, Günther (1971), "*Industriegesellschaft' und Konvergenztheorie. Genesis, Strukturen, Funktionen*. Berlin: VEB Deutscher Verlag der Wissenschaften.

Rose, Richard (1978), "Ungovernability: Is there fire behind the smoke?" *Political Studies* 27:351–370.

Rose, Richard (1979), "Pervasive problems of governing: An analytic framework," pp. 29–54 in Joachim Matthes (ed.), *Sozialer Wandel in Westeuropa*. Verhandlungen des 19. Deutschen Soziologentages, Berlin and Frankfurt: Campus.

Rose, Steven (1986), "The limits of science," pp. 26–36 in Steven Rose and Lisa Appignanesi (eds.), *Science and Beyond*. Oxford: Blackwell.

Rosen, Michael M. (2021), "AI invents—But should it get patents, too?" *Issues in Science and Technology*.

Rosen, Sherwin (1981), "The economics of superstars," *American Economic Review* 71:845–858.

Rosenberg, Hans ([1958] 1966), *Bureaucracy, Aristocracy and Autocracy: The Prussian Experience*. Boston, MA: Beacon Press.

Rosenberg, Nathan (1974), "Science, invention and economic growth," *The Economic Journal* 84:90–108.

Rosenberg, Nathan (1982), *Inside the Black Box: Technology and Economics*. Cambridge: Cambridge University Press.

Roski, Melanie B. (2011), "Wissensgesellschaft und Wissensarbeit," pp. 87–111 in Melanie B. Roski (ed.), *Spin-off-Unternehmen zwischen Wissenschaft und Wirtschaft*. Wiesbaden: Springer.

Roszak, Theodore (1972), *The Making of a Counter Culture*. New York: Doubleday.

Rothman, Robert A. (1974), "Problems of knowledge and obsolescence among professionals: A case study in dentistry," *Social Science Quarterly* 55:743–752.

Rothschild, Kurt W. (1971), *Power in Economics*. London: Penguin.

Rothschild, Michael and Joseph E. Stiglitz (1976), "Equilibrium in competitive insurance markets: An essay in the economics of incomplete information," *Quarterly Journal of Economics* 90:624–649.

Rouse, Joseph (1987), *Knowledge and Power. Toward a Political Philosophy of Science*. Ithaca, NY: Cornell University Press and Princeton University Press.

Rubin, Michael R. and Mary Taylor Huber (1986), *The Knowledge Industry in the United States, 1960–1980*. Princeton, NJ: Princeton University Press.

Rueschemeyer, Dietrich (1986), *Power and the Division of Labor*. Stanford, CA: Stanford University Press.

Rueschemeyer, Dietrich, Evelyne Huber Stephens and John D. Stephens (1992), *Capitalist Development & Democracy*. Chicago, IL: University of Chicago Press.

Rule, James B. and Yasemin Besen (2008), "The once and future information society," *Theory and Society* 37:317–342.

Sabel, Charles F. (1982), *Work and Politics. The Division of Labor in Industry*. Cambridge: Cambridge University Press.

Sabel, Charles F. (1991), 'Moebius-strip organizations and open labor markets: Some consequences of the reintegration of conception and execution in a volatile economy," pp. 23–54 in Pierre Bourdieu and James S. Coleman (eds.), *Social Theory for a Changing Society*. Boulder, CO: Westview Press.

Sachs, Jeffrey and Laurence J. Kotlikoff (2012), "Smart machines and long-term misery,c NBER Working Paper 18629. https://www.nber.org/system/files/working_papers/w18629/w18629.pdf

Saez, Emmanuel and Gabriel Zucman (2016), "Wealth inequality in the United States since 1913: Evidence from capitalized income tax data," *Quarterly Journal of Economics* 131:519–578.

Saez, Emmanuel (2021), "Public Economics and Inequality: Uncovering Our Social Nature," *AEA Papers and Proceedings* 111:1–26).

Sahlberg, Pasi (2010), "Rethinking accountability in a knowledge society," *Journal of Educational Change*.

Sala, Roberto (2013), "One, two, or three cultures? Humanities versus the natural and social sciences in modern Germany," *Journal of Knowledge Economy* 4:83–97.
Salomon, Albert (1936), "The place of Alfred Weber's Kultursoziologie in social thought," *Social Research* 1:494–500.
Salomon, Jean-Jacques (1973), *Science and Politics*. Cambridge: Cambridge University Press.
Salz, Arthur (1932), "Die Kontrolle des technischen Fortschritts: Technischer Fortschritt und Arbeitslosigkeit," *Der Deutsche Volkswirt* 6:1607–1609.
Samuelson, Paul A. (1959), "What economists know," pp. 183–213 in Daniel Lerner (ed.), *The Human Meaning of the Social Sciences*. Cleveland, OH and New York: Meridian Books.
Sarewitz, Daniel (2010), "Normal science and limits on knowledge: What we seek to know, what we choose not to know, what we don't bother knowing," *Social Research: An International Quarterly* 77:997–1010.
Sarewitz, Daniel and Richard R. Nelson (2008), "Progress in know-how. Its origins and limits," *Innovation* 1:101–117.
Sartori, Giovanni (1968), "Democracy," pp. 112–121 in D. L. Sills (ed.), *International Encyclopedia of the Social Sciences: Vol. 4*. New York: Macmillan and Free Press.
Sartori, Giovanni (1971), "Technological forecasting and politics," *Survey* 16:60–68.
Sassen, Saskia (2002), "Towards a sociology of information technology," *Current Sociology* 50:365–388.
Scase, Richard (ed.) (1989), *Industrial Societies: Crisis and Division in Western Capitalism and State Socialism*. London: Unwin Hyman.
Schäfer, Wolf (1994), *Ungleichzeitigkeit als Ideologie. Beiträge zur historischen Aufklärung*. Frankfurt am Main: Fischer.
Scharpf, Fritz W. (1987), *Sozialdemokratische Krisenpolitik in Europa*. Frankfurt am Main: Campus.
Scharpf, Fritz W. (1988), "Strukturen der post-industriellen Gesellschaft oder: Verschwindet die Massenarbeitslosigkeit in der Dienstleistungs- und Informations-Ökonomie?" *Soziale Welt* 38:3–24.
Scheler, Max ([1925] 1960), "The forms of knowledge and culture," pp. 13–49 in Max Scheler (ed.), *Philosophical Perspectives*. Boston, MA: Beacon Press.
Scheler, Max ([1926] 1980), *Problems of a Sociology of Knowledge*. London: Routledge and Kegan Paul.
Schelling, Thomas C. (1990), "Global environmental forces," *Technological Forecasting and Social Change* 38:257–264.
Schelsky, Helmut (1954), "Zukunftsaspekte der industriellen Gesellschaft," *Merkur* 8: 13–28.
Schelsky, Helmut (1955), *Wandlungen der deutschen Familie in der Gegenwart. Dritte, durch einen Anhang erweiterte Auflage*. Stuttgart: Ferdinand Enke.
Schelsky, Helmut (1956), "Gesellschaftlicher Wandel," *Offene Welt* 41:65.
Schelsky, Helmut (1961), *Der Mensch in der wissenschaftlichen Zivilisation*. Köln/Opladen: Westdeutscher Verlag.
Schelsky, Helmut ([1953] 1965), "Die Bedeutung des Schichtungsbegriffes für die Analyse der gegenwärtigen deutschen Gesellschaft," pp. 331–336 in Helmut Schelsky (ed.), *Auf der Suche nach der Wirklichkeit. Gesammelte Aufsätze*. Düsseldorf: Diederichs.
Schelsky, Helmut ([1961] 1965), "Der Mensch in der wissenschaftlichen Zivilisation," pp. 439–480 in Helmut Schelsky (ed.), *Auf der Suche nach der Wirklichkeit. Gesammelte Aufsätze*. Düsseldorf: Diederichs.

Schelsky, Helmut (1975), *Die Arbeit tun die Anderen*. Klassenkampf und Priesterherrschaft der Intellektuellen. Opladen: Westdeutscher Verlag.

Schieder, Theodor (1977), "Einmaligkeit oder Wiederkehr. Historische Dimensionen der heutigen Krise," pp. 22–42 in Wilhelm Hennis, Peter Graf Kielmansegg and Ulrich Matz (eds.), *Regierbarkeit. Studien zu ihrer Problematisierung. Band 1*. Stuttgart: Klett-Cotta.

Schiller, Dan (1993), "Capitalism, information, and uneven development," pp. 386–406 in Stanley A. Deetz (ed.), *Communication Yearbook. Vol. 16*. Newbury Park, CA: SAGE.

Schiller, Dan (1999), *Digital Capitalism*. Networking the Global Market System, Cambridge, Massachusetts: MIT Press.

Schiller, Herbert I. (1981), *Who Knows: Information in the Age of the Fortune 500*. Norwood, NJ: Ablex.

Schimank, Uwe (1985), "Der mangelnde Akteurbezug systemtheoretischer Erklärungen gesellschaftlicher Differenzierung—Ein Diskussionsvorschlag," *Zeitschrift für Soziologie* 14:421–437.

Schmieder, Falko (2017), "Gleichzeitigkeit des Ungleichzeitigen. Zur Kritik und Aktualität einer Denkfigur," *Zeitschrift für Sozialtheorie und Philosophie* 4:325–363.

Schmookler, Jakob (1966), *Invention and Economic Growth*. Cambridge, MA: Harvard University Press.

Schneider, Louis (1962), "The role of the category of ignorance in sociological theory. An exploratory statement," *American Sociological Review* 27:492–508.

Schneier, Bruce (2021), *The Coming AI Hackers*. Cambridge, MA: Belfer Center at the Harvard Kennedy School.

Schoomaker, Mary G. and Elias G. Carayannis (2013), "Mode 3: A proposed classification scheme for the knowledge economy and society," *Journal of Knowledge Economy* 4:556–577.

Schott, Thomas (1988), "International influence in science: Beyond center and periphery," *Social Science Research* 17:219–238.

Schott, Thomas (1993), "World science: Globalization of institutions and participation," *Science, Technology, Human Values* 18:196–208.

Scott, J. C. (1998). *Seeing like a state: How certain schemes to improve the human condition have failed*. New Haven, CT: Yale University Press.

Schroeder, Ralph (2007), *Rethinking Science, Technology, and Social Change*. Stanford, CA: Stanford University Press.

Schroyer, Trent (1974), "Review of Daniel Bell, the Coming of Post-Industrial Society," *Telos* 19:162–176.

Schuilenburg, Marc und Rik Peeters (2020), *The Algorithmic Society: Technology, Power, and Knowledge*. London: Routledge.

Schultz, Theodore W. (1961), "Investment in human capital," *American Economic Review* 51:1–17.

Schultz, Theodore W. (1981), *Investing in People*. Berkeley, CA: University of California Press.

Schumm-Garling, Ursula (1972), *Herrschaft in der industriellen Arbeitsorganisation*. Frankfurt am Main: Suhrkamp.

Schumpeter, Joseph A. ([1942] 1950), *Capitalism, Socialism and Democracy*. New York: Harper Torchbooks.

Schütz, Alfred (1946), "The well-informed citizen: An essay on the social distribution of knowledge," *Social Research* 13:463–478. www.jstor.org/stable/40958880

Schwartz, Barry (1981), *Vertical Classification. A Study in Structuralism and the Sociology of Knowledge*. Chicago, IL: University of Chicago Press.

Schwartz, Herman M. (2019), "American hegemony: Intellectual property rights, dollar centrality, and infrastructural power," *Review of International Political Economy* 26:490–519.

Schwartz, Herman M. (2020), "Intellectual property, technorents and the labour share of production," *Competition & Change*. https://doi.org/10.1177/1024529420968221

Schwartz, Herman M. (2021), "Global secular stagnation and the rise of intellectual property monopoly," *Review of International Political Economy*. https://doi.org/10.1080/09692290.2021.1918745

Schwemmer, Oswald (1987), *Handlung und Struktur. Zur Wissenschaftstheorie der Kulturwissenschaften*. Frankfurt am Main: Suhrkamp.

Scott, James C. (1990), *Domination and the Arts of Resistance: Hidden Transcripts*. New Haven, CT: Yale University Press.

Scott, J. C. (1998). *Seeing like a state: How certain schemes to improve the human condition have failed*. New Haven, CT: Yale University Press.

Scott, Peter (2005a), "The academic profession in a knowledge society," *Wenner Gren International Series* 83:19.

Scott, Peter (2005b), "Universities and the knowledge economy," *Minerva* 43:297–309.

Seefried, Elke (2015), *Zukünfte*. Aufstieg und Krise der Zukunftsforschung 1945–1980. (Quellen und Darstellungen zur Zeitgeschichte, Band 106.) Berlin/München/Boston: De Gruyter Oldenbourg.

Sell, Susan K. (2010), "The rise and rule of a trade-based strategy: Historical institutionalism and the international regulation of intellectual property," *Review of International Political Economy* 17:762–790.

Sen, Amartya (1981), "Ingredients of famine analysis: Availability and entitlements," *Quarterly Journal of Economics* 96:433−464. https://doi.org/10.2307/1882681

Sen, Amartya (1985), "The moral standing of the market," *Social Philosophy & Policy* 2:1−19.

Sen, Amartya (1992), *Inequality Reexamined*. Cambridge, MA: Harvard University Press.

Shadlen, Kenneth C., Bhaven N. Sampat und Amy Kapczynski (2020), "Patents, trade and medicines: Past, present and future," *Review of International Political Economy* 27:75–97.

Shaiken, Harley (1985), *Work Transformed: Automation and Labor in the Computer Age*. New York: Holt, Rinehart & Winston.

Shannon, C. (1949), "Communication theory of secrecy systems," *Bell System Technical Journal* 28:656−715.

Shannon, Claude and Warren Weaver ([1949] 1963), *The Mathematical Theory of Communication*. Urbana, IL: University of Illinois Press.

Shapin, Steve and Simon Schaffer (1986), *Leviathan and the Air-Pump*. Princeton, NJ: Princeton University Press.

Shapiro, Carl and Hal R. Varian (1999), *Information Rules. A Strategic Guide to the Network Economy*. Boston, MA: Harvard Business School Press.

Shapiro, Robert J. and Kevin A. Hassett (2005), "Healthy returns: The economic impact of public investment in surface transportation," *American Public Transportation Association*.

Sharma, Ravi S., Elaine W. J. Ng, Mathias Dharmawirya and Chu Keong Lee (2008), "Beyond the digital divide: A conceptual framework for analyzing knowledge societies," *Journal of Knowledge Management* 12:151–164.

Sharpe, S. A. (1990), "Asymmetric information, bank lending and implicit contracts: A stylized model of customer relations," *The Journal of Finance* 45:1069−1087.

Shearing, Clifford and Richard V. Ericson (1991), "Culture as figurative action," *British Journal Sociology* 42:481–506.

Shils, Edward (1982), "Knowledge and the sociology of knowledge," *Knowledge: Creation, Diffusion, Utilization* 4:7–32.

Shiva, Vandana (2001), *Protect or Plunder? Understanding Intellectual Property Rights*. London: Zed Books.

Sibley, Mulford Q. (1973), "Utopian thought and technology," *American Journal of Political Science* 17:255–281.

Sica, Alan (1988), *Weber, Irrationality, and Social Order*. Berkeley, CA: University of California Press.

Sieferle, Rolf P. (1984), *Fortschrittsfeinde? Opposition gegen Technik und Industrie von der Romantik bis zur Gegenwart*. Munich: C.H. Beck.

Siegrist, Hannes (2019), "Intellectual propertry rights and the dymamics of propertization, nationalization, and globalization in modern cultures and economies," pp. 19–47 in Hannes Siegrist and Augusta Dimou (eds.), *Expanding Intellectual Property*. Budapest: Central European University Press.

Sillitoe, Paul (1998), "The development of indigenous knowledge," *Current Anthropology* 39:223–252.

Silvestrini, Giuseppe Vittorio (2013), "Toward knowledge societies," pp. 9–13 in Anne-Marie Bruyas and Michaela Riccio (eds.), *Science Centres and Science Events: A Science Communication Handbook*. Springer.

Sim, Stuart (2019), *Post-Truth, Scepticism & Power*. Cham: Springer.

Simmel, Georg (1906), "The sociology of secrecy and of secret societies," *American Journal of Sociology* 11:441−498. www.jstor.org/stable/2762562

Simmel, Georg (1890), *Über sociale Differenzierung. Sociologische und psychologische Untersuchungen*. Leipzig: Duncker & Humblot.

Simmel, Georg ([1900] 1907), *Philosophie des Geldes. 2. vermehrte Auflage*. Leipzig: Dunker & Humblot.

Simmel Georg ([1911] 1968), "On the concept and the tragedy of culture," pp. 27–46 in Georg Simmel (ed.), *The Conflict in Modern Culture and Other Essays*. New York: Teachers College Press.

Simmel, Georg ([1919] 1968), *The Conflict in Modern Culture and Other Essays*. Translated, with an Introduction by K. Peter Etzkorn. New York: Teachers College Press.

Simmel, Georg ([1917] 1970), *Grundfragen der Soziologie*. Berlin: de Gruyter.

Simmel, Georg ([1907] 1978), *The Philosophy of Money*. London: Routledge and Kegan Paul.

Simmel, Georg ([1909] 1984), "Die Zukunft unserer Kultur," pp. 92–93 in Georg Simmel (ed.), *Das Individuum und die Freiheit. Essais*. Berlin: Wagenbach.

Simmel, Georg ([1890] 1989), "Über sociale Differenzierung," pp. 109–295 in Georg Simmel (ed.), *Aufsätze 1987–1980. Über sociale Differenzierung. Die Probleme der Geschichtsphilosophie (1892)*. Gesamtausgabe 2. Frankfurt am Main: Suhrkamp.

Simmel, Georg ([1908] 1992), *Soziologie. Untersuchungen über die Formen der Vergesellschaftung. Gesamtausgabe Band 11*. Frankfurt am Main: Suhrkamp.

Singelmann, Joachim (1978), *From Agriculture to Services. The Transformation of Industrial Employment*. Beverly Hills, CA: SAGE.

SinghaRoy, Debal K. (2014), *Towards a Knowledge Society: New Identities in Emerging India*. Cambridge: Cambridge University Press.

Sinnreich, Aram (2019), *The Essential Guide to Intellectual Property*. New Haven, CT: Yale University Press.

Sirianni, Carmen (1991), "The self-management of time in postindustrial society," pp. 231–274 in Karl Hinrichs, William Roche and Carmen Sirianni (eds.), *Working Time in Transition. The Political Economy of Working Hours in Industrial Nations*. Philadelphia, PA: Temple University Press.

Skidelsky, Robert (1979), "The decline of Keynesian politics," pp. 55–87 in Colin Crouch (ed.), *State and Economy in Contemporary Capitalism*. London: Croom Helm.

Skidelsky, Robert and Edward Skidelsky (2012), *How Much Is Enough? Money and the Good Life*. New York: Other Press.

Skolnikoff, Eugene B. (1976), "The governability of complexity," pp. 75–88 in Chester L. Cooper (ed.), *Growth in America. Woodrow Wilson International Center for Scholars*. Westport, CT. Westport, Connecticut: Greenwood Press.

Skopek, Nora, Kathrin Kolb, Sandra Buchholz und Hans-Peter Blossfeld (2012), "Einkommensreich- vermögensarm: Die Zusammensetzung von Vermögen und die Bedeutung einzelner Vermögenskomponenten im europäischen Vergleich," *Berliner Journal für Soziologie* 22:163–187.

Smart, Barry (1992), *Modern Conditions, Postmodern Controversies*. London: Routledge.

Smith, Adam (1776), The Wealth of Nations. London; M. Dent.

Smith, Adam (1978), "Early draft of part of the Wealth of Nations," p. 574 in R. L. Meek, D. D. Raphael and P. G. Stein (eds.), *Lectures on Jurisprudence*. Oxford: Oxford University Press.

Smith, Anthony (1986), "Technology, identity, and the information machine," *Daedalus* 115:155–169.

Smith, Roger and Brian Wynne (eds.) (1989), *Expert Evidence: Interpreting Science in the Law*. London: Routledge.

Snow, C. P. (1962), *Science and Government*. New York: Mentor Book.

So, Alvin Y. (1990), *Social Change and Development. Modernization, Dependency, and World-System Theories*. Newbury Park, CA: SAGE.

Soete, Luc (2018), "Destructive creation. Explaining the productivity paradox in the digital age," pp. 29–46 in M. Neufeind, J. O'Reilly, F. Ranft (eds.), *Work in the digital age: Challenges of the fourth industrial revolution*. London: Rowman and Littlefield.

Sohn-Rethel, Alfred (1978), *Intellectual and Manual Labour. A Critique of Epistemology*. Atlantic Highlands, NJ: Humanities Press.

Solga, Heike ([2007] 2011), "Bildungsarmut und Ausbildungslosigkeit in der Bildungs- und Wissensgesellschaft," pp. 4111–448 in Rolf Becker (ed.), *Lehrbuch der Bildungssoziologie*. Wiesbaden: Springer.

Solow, Robert M. (1956), "A contribution to the theory of economic growth," *The Quarterly Journal of Economics* 70:65–94.

Solow, Robert M. (1957), "Technical change and the aggregate production function," *Review of Economics and Statistics* 39:312–320.

Solow, Robert M. (1987), "We'd better watch out. Review of Manufacturing Matters by Stephen S. Cohen and John Zysman," *New York Times Book Review*.

Sombart, Werner (1911), "Discussion," p. 165 in *Verhandlungen des Ersten Deutschen Soziologentages* vom 19–22. Oktober 1910 in Frankfurt am Main. Tübingen: J. C. B. Mohr

Sombart, Werner (1927), *Das Wirtschaftsleben im Zeitalter des Hochkapitalismus*. Band 3: Der moderne Kapitalismus. München: Duncker und Humblot.

Sombart, Werner (1930), "Capitalism," pp. 195–208 in Edwin R. Selig-man and Alvin Johnson (eds.), *Encyclopedia of the Social Sciences*, vol. 3. New York: The Macmillan Company.

Sombart, Werner (1934), *Deutscher Sozialismus*. Berlin: **Buchholz & Weisswange**.

Sorokin, Piritim (1957), *Social and Cultural Dynamics*. New York: American Book Company.
Sorokin, Pitrim and Robert K. Merton (1937), "Social time: A methodological and functional analysis," *American Journal of Sociology* 42:615–629.
Spittler, Gerd (1980), "Abstraktes Wissen als Herrschaftsbasis. Zur Entstehungsgeschichte bürokratischer Herrschaft im Bauerstaat Preussen," *Kölner Zeitschrift für Soziologie und Sozialpsychologie* 32:574–604.
Squicciarini, Mara P. (2014), "Human capital and industrialization: Evidence from the age of enlightenment," NBER Working Paper 20219.
Staley, Richard (2019), "Partisans and the use of knowledge versus science," *Beiträge zur Wissenschaftsgeschichte* 42:220–234.
Starbuck, William H. (1992), "Learning by knowledge-intensive firms," *Journal of Management Studies* 29: 713–740.
Stark, David (1980), "Class struggle and the transformation of the labour process," *Theory and Society* 9:89–130.
Statistics Canada (1986), *The Distribution of Wealth in Canada, 1984*. Ottawa: Statistics Canada.
Stearns, Peter N. (1974), "Comment on Daniel Bells: The coming of post-industrial society," *Transaction* 11:10–22.
Stehr, Nico (1992), *Practical Knowledge*. London: SAGE.
Stehr, Nico (2000), *Knowledge and Economic Conduct: The Foundations of the Modern Economy*. Toronto: University of Toronto Press.
Stehr, Nico (1971), "Statuskonsistenz," *Kölner Zeitschrift für Soziologie und Sozialpsychologie* 23:34–54.
Stehr, Nico (1974), "Die Technik in der öffentlichen Meinung," *Philosophica Naturalis* 15:79–87.
Stehr, Nico (1978), "Man and the environment: A general perspective," *Archives for Philosophy of Law and Social Philosophy* 74:1–17.
Stehr, Nico (1992), *Practical Knowledge: Applying Social Science Knowledge*. London: SAGE.
Stehr, Nico (1994), *Knowledge Societies*. London: SAGE.
Stehr, Nico (2000), *Die Zerbrechlichkeit moderner Gesellschaften. Die Stagnation der Macht und die Chancen des Individuums*. Weilerswist: Velbrück Wissenschaft.
Stehr, Nico (2001), *The Fragility of Modern Societies. Knowledge and Risk in the Information Age*. London: SAGE.
Stehr, Nico (2005), *Knowledge Politics. Governing the Consequences of Science and Technology*. Boulder, CO: Paradigm Publishers.
Stehr, Nico (2009), "Nothing has been decided: The chances and risks of feasible globalization," pp. 334–355 in Samir Dasgupta and Jan Nederveen Pieterse (eds.), *Politics of Globalization*. London: SAGE.
Stehr, Nico (2013), "Mut zur Lücke. Zur Emanzipation des Nichtwissens in der modernen Gesellschaft," *Kursbuch* 173:164–178.
Stehr, Nico (2015a), "Democracy is not an inconvenience," *Nature* 525:449–450.
Stehr, Nico (2015b), "Knowledge society, history of," pp. 105–110 in James D. Wright (editor-in-chief), *International Encyclopedia of the Social & Behavioral Science*. 2nd edition, Volume 13. Oxford: Elsevier.
Stehr, Nico (2015c), *Der zündende Funke. Innovationen fördern als Weg zu sauberer und bezahlbarer Energie für alle*. Wiesbaden: Springer VS.
Stehr, Nico (2015d), *Liberty Is a Daughter of Knowledge*. Cambridge: Cambridge University Press.

Stehr, Nico (2016a), "Exceptional Circumstances. Does Climate Change Trump Democracy?," *Issues in Science and Technology* (Winter):37–44.

Stehr, Nico (2016b), *Information, Power, and Democracy. Liberty Is a Daughter of Knowledge.* Cambridge: Cambridge University Press.

Stehr, Nico (2020), "The atmosphere of democracy: Knowledge and political action," pp. 69–91 in J. Glückler, G. Herrigel and M. Handke (eds.), *Knowledge for Governance.* Knowledge and Space: Vol. 15. Cham: Springer. https://doi.org/10.1007/978-3-030-47150-7_4

Stehr, Nico and Amanda Machin (2020), *Society and Climate.* Singapore: World Scientific Publishers.

Stehr, Nico and Dustin Voss (2020), *Money. A Theory of Modern Society.* New York: Routledge.

Stehr, Nico and Reiner Grundmann (2001), "The authority of complexity," *The British Journal of Sociology* 52:313–332.

Stehr, Nico and Richard V. Ericson (eds.) (1992), *The Culture and Power of Knowledge: Inquiries into Contemporary Societies.* Berlin and New York: de Gruyter.

Stehr, Nico and Volker Meja (1984a), "The development of the sociology of knowledge," pp. 1–18 in Nico Stehr and Volker Meja (eds.), *Society and Knowledge. Contemporary Perspectives on the Sociology of Knowledge.* New Brunswick, NJ: Transaction Books.

Stehr, Nico and Volker Meja (eds.) (1984b), *Society and Knowledge. Contemporary Perspectives on the Sociology of Knowledge.* New Brunswick, NJ: Transaction Books.

Stehr, Nico and Volker Meja (1990), "Relativism and the sociology of knowledge," pp. 285–306 in Volker Meja and Nico Stehr (eds.), *Knowledge and Politics. The Sociology of Knowledge Dispute.* London and New York: Routledge.

Steinbicker, Jochen (2001), "Soziale Ungleichheit in der Informations- und Wissensgesellschaft," *Berliner Journal für Soziologie* 4:441–458.

Steinbicker, Jochen (2011a), *Pfade in die Informationsgesellschaft. Eine historisch-komparative Analyse der Entwicklung zur Informationsgesellschaft in Europa.* Weilerswist: Velbrück Wissenschaft.

Steinbicker, Jochen (2011b), "Peter Drucker: Die Wissensgesellschaft," pp. 20–48 in Jochen Steinbicker (ed.), *Zur Theorie der Informationsgesellschaft.* Wiesbaden: Springer.

Steinmueller, W. Edward (2002), "Knowledge-based economies and information and communication technologies," *International Social Science Journal* 54:141–153.

Stephen R. Stoera, Stephen R. and António M. Magalhães (2004), "Education, knowledge and the network society," *Globalisation, Societies and Education* 2:319–335.

Stewart, Thomas A. (1997), *Intellectual Capital.* The New Wealth of Organizations, New York: Doubleday.

Stich, Stephen P. and Richard E. Nisbett (1984), "Expertise, justification, and the psychology of inductive reasoning," pp. 226–241 in Thomas L. Haskell (ed.), *The Authority of Experts.* Bloomington, IN: Indiana University Press.

Stichweh, Rudolf ([2002] 2004), "Wissensgesellschaft und Wissenschaftssystem," *Swiss Journal of Sociology* 30(2):147–166.

Stichweh, Rudolf (2004a), "Gestaltungsmöglichkeiten des Staates in der Wissensgesellschaft unter Bedingungen globalisierter Funktionssysteme," in *Beitrag zu der Tagung 'Moderner Bundesstaat. Handlungsfähig? Bürgernah Innovativ'?* Berlin: Friedrich-Ebert-Stiftung.

Stichweh, Rudolf (2004b), "Knowledge society and the system of science," *Schweizerische Zeitschrift für Soziologie* 30:147–165.

Stichweh, Rudolf (2007), "Die Universität in der WIssensgesellschaft: Wissensbegriffe und Umweltbeziehungen der modernen Universität," *Vortrag: Ernst & Young. Ausblick am Dreikönigstag 2007*, 5 January 2007, Altes Casino Luzern.

Stigler, George J. (1947), *Trends in Output and Employment*. New York: National Bureau of Economic Research.

Stigler, George J. (1961), "The economics of information," *The Journal of Political Economy* 69:213–225.

Stiglitz, Joseph E. (1999), "Knowledge as a global public good," pp. 308–325 in Inge Kaul, Isabelle Grunberg und Marc A, Stern (Hrsg.), *Global public goods: International cooperation in the 21st century*. New York: Oxford University Press.

Stiglitz, Joseph E. (1999a), "Knowledge as a global public good," pp. 308–325 in Inge Kaul, Isabelle Grunberg and Marc A. Stern (eds.), *Global Public Goods: International Cooperation in the 21st Century*. New York: Oxford University Press.

Stiglitz, Joseph E. (1999b), "On liberty, the right to know, and public discourse: The role of transparency in public life," *Oxford Amnesty Lecture*, Oxford, January 27. http://www1.gsb.columbia.edu/mygsb/faculty/research/pubfiles/1475/Stiglitz_OnLiberty.pdf

Stiglitz, Joseph E. (2002), *Globalisation and Its Discontents*. London: Allen Lane, The Penguin Press.

Stiglitz, Joseph E. (2005), "The ethical economist," *Foreign Affairs* 84:128–134. www.foreignaffairs.com/articles/61208/joseph-e-stiglitz/the-ethical-economist

Stiglitz, Joseph E. (2006), *Making Globalization Work*. London: Penguin Books.

Stiglitz, Joseph E. (2015), "The measurement of wealth. Recessions, sustainability, and innovation," NBER Working Paper 21327.

Stiglitz, Joseph E. (2017), "The revolution of information economics: The past and the present," NBER Working Paper 23780.

Stiglitz, Joseph and Bruce C. Greenwald (2014), *Creating a Learning Society. A New Approach to Growth, Development, and Social Progress*. New York: Columbia University Press.

Stiglitz, Joseph E., A. Sen and J. Fitoussi (2010), *Measuring Our Lives: Why GDP Doesn't Add Up*. New York and London: New Press.

Stinchcombe, Arthur (1968), "The structure of stratification systems," pp. 325–332 in David Sills (ed.), *International Encyclopedia of the Social Sciences*. Volume 15. New York: Crowell Collier and Macmillan.

Stoljarow, Vitali (1963), "Die Entwicklung der Wissenschaft zur unmittelbaren Produktivkraft und die materialistische Geschichtsauffassung," *Deutsche Zeitschrift für Philosophie* 11:826–837.

Storper, Michael and Richard Walker (1983), "The theory of labour and the theory of location," *International Journal of Urban and Regional Research* 7:1–41.

Storper, Michael and Richard Walker (1989), *Capitalist Imperative: Territory Technology and Industries Growth*. Oxford: Basil Blackwell.

Strasser, Hermann (1987), "Diesseits von Stand und Klasse: Prinzipien einer Theorie der sozialen Ungleichheit," pp. 50–92 in Bernard Giessen und Hans Haferkamp (eds.), *Soziologie der sozialen Ungleichheit*. Opladen: Westdeutscher Verlag.

Streckeisen, Peter (2009), "Knowledge society—or contemporary capitalism's fanciest dress," *Analyse & Kritik* 1:181–197.

Stromquist, Nelly P. (2004), "Inequality as a way of life: Education and social class in Latin America," *Pedagogy, Culture and Society* 12(1):95–119.

Sturgis, Patrick, Ian Brunton-Smith and Jonathan Jackson (2021), "Trust in science, social consensus and vaccine confidence," *Nature Human Behaviour* 5:1528–1534.

Sunstein, Cass and Adrian Vermeule (2008), "Conspiracy theories," University of Chicago Public Law & Legal Theory Working Paper No. 199.

Sunstein, Cass and Adrian Vermeule (2020), *Law and Leviathan: Redeeming the Administrative State*. Cambridge, MA: Harvard University Press.

Sunstein, Cass R. (2016), "The most knowledgeable branch," *University of Pennsylvania Law Review* 164:1607–1648.

Suzman, James (2020), *Work. A History of How We Spend Our Time*. London: Bloomsbury.

Swedberg, Richard (1987), "Economic sociology: Past and present," *Current Sociology* 35:1–221.

Swidler, Ann (1986), "Culture in action: symbols and strategies," *American Sociological Review* 51:273–286.

Syverson, Chad (2013), "Will history repeat itself? Comments on 'Is the information technology revolution over?'," *International Productivity Monitor* 25:37–40.

Syverson, Chad (2017), "Challenges to mismeasurement. Explanations for the U.S. productivity slowdown," *Journal of Economic Perspectives* 31:165–186.

Tacik, Pzemyslaw (2018), "Ernst Bloch as a non-simultaneous Jewish Marxist," *Religions* 9:346.

Tambe, Prasanna, Lorin Hitt, Daniel Rock and Erik Brynjolfsson (2020), "Digital Capital and Superstar Firm," NBER Working Paper No. 28285, December. https://www.nber.org/system/files/working_papers/w28285/w28285.pdf

Tawney, Richard H. (1920), *The Acquisitive Society*. New York: Harcourt Brace.

Teece, David J. (1981), "The market for know-how and the efficient international transfer of technology," *Annals of the American Association of Political and Social Science* 458:81–96.

Teece, David J. (1992), "Strategies for capturing the financial benefits from technological innovation," pp. 509–533 in Ralph Landau, Nathan Rosenberg, and David C. Mowery (eds.), *Technology and the Wealth of Nations*. Stanford, CA: Stanford University Press.

Teece, David J. (1998), "Capturing value from knowledge assets: The new economy, markets for know-how, and intangible assets," *California Management Review* 40:55–79.

Teece, David J. (2011), "Human capital, capabilities, and the firm: Literati, numerati, and entrepreneurs in the twenty-first-century enterprise," pp. 528–562 in Alan Burton-Jones and J. C. Spencer (eds.), *The Oxford Handbook of Human Capital*. Oxford: Oxford University Press.

Tenbruck, Friedrich H. (1969), "Regulative Funktionen der Wissenschaft in der pluralistischen Gesellschaft," pp. 61–85 in: Herbert Scholz (ed.), *Die Rolle 82 der Wissenschaft in der modernen Gesellschaft*. Berlin: Duncker & Humblot.

Tenbruck, Friedrich H. (1972), *Zur Kritik der planenden Vernunft*. Freiburg: Karl Alber.

Tenbruck, Friedrich H. (1974), "Max Weber and the sociology of science: A vase reopened," *Zeitschrift für Soziologie* 3:312.

Tenbruck, Friedrich H. (1977), "Genzen der staatlichen Planung," pp. 134–149 in Wilhelm Hennis, Peter Graf Kielmansegg and Ulrich Matz (eds.), *Regierbarkeit. Studien zu ihrer Problematisierung. Band 1*. Stuttgart: Klett-Cotta.

Tenner, Edward (2018), "Who's afraid of the frightful five?," *Hedgehog Review* 20:68–77.

Thrift, Nigel (1999), "The place of complexity," *Theory, Culture & Society* 16:31–70.

Tilly, Charles (1984), *Big Structures, Large Processes, Huge Comparisons*. New York: Russell Sage Foundation.

Tilton, Timothy A. and Daniel Bell (1973), "The next stage of history? A discussion of Daniel Bell's the coming of post-industrial society," *Social Research* 40:728–745.

Tregenna, Fiona (2014), "A new theoretical analysis of deindustrialization," *Cambridge Journal of Economics* 38:1373–1390.

Tinbergen, Jan (1961), "Do communist and free economics show a converging pattern?" *Soviet Studies* 12:333–341.

Touraine, Alain ([1969] 1971), *Post-Industrial Society. Tomorrow's Social History*. New York: Random House.

Touraine, Alain (1977), "Science, intellectuals and politics," pp. 109–130 in Ralf Dahrendorf et al. (eds.), *Scientific-Technological Revolution: Social Aspects*. London: SAGE.

Touraine, Alain (1986), "Krise und Wandel des sozialen Denkens," pp. 15–39 in Johannes Berger (ed.), *Die Moderne. Kontinuitäten und Zäsuren. Sonderband 4. Soziale Welt*. Göttingen: Schwartz & Co.

Touraine, Alain ([1984] 1988), *Return of the Actor. Social Theory in Postindustrial Society*. Minneapolis: University of Minnesota Press.

Touraine, Alan ([2010] 2014), *After the Crisis*. Cambridge: Polity.

Turchin, Peter, Thomas E. Currie, Harvey Whitehouse, Pieter François, Kevin Feeney, Daniel Mullins, Daniel Hoyer et al. (2018), "Quantitative historical analysis uncovers a single dimension of complexity that structures global variation in human social organization." *Proceedings of the National Academy of Sciences* 115, no. 2: E144–E151.

Turkle, Shirly (2005), *The Second Self: Computers and the Human Spirit*. Cambridge, MA: MIT Press.

Ulrich, Peter (1987), *Transformation der ökonomischen Vernunft. Fortschrittsperspektiven der modernen Industriegesellschaft*. Bern und Stuttgart: Paul Haupt.

Unger, Roberto Mangabeira (2019), *The Knowledge Economy*. London: Verso.

United Nations (1991), *Economic Survey of Europe in 1990–1991*. New York: United Nations Publications.

United Nations (1992), *Economic Survey of Europe in 1991–1992*. New York: United Nations Publications.

United Nations Economic Commission for Europe (UNECE) (2016), *Guide on measuring human capital*. www.unece.org/fileadmin/DAM/stats/publications/2016/HumanCapitalGuide.web.pdf

United Nations Educational, Scientific and Cultural Organization (1970), *Statistical Yearbook*. Paris: UNESCO.

United Nations Educational, Scientific and Cultural Organization (1990), *Statistical Yearbook*. Paris: UNESCO.

United Nations Educational, Scientific and Cultural Organization (1991), *Statistical Yearbook*. Paris: UNESCO.

United States National Commission on Technology, Automation and Economic Progress (1966), *Technology and the American Economy*. Washington, DC: United States Government Printing Office.

U.S. Department of Labor (1984), *Technological Change and its Labor Impact in Four Industries*. Washington, DC: U.S. Department of Labor.

Vaitsos, Constantine V. (1989), "Radical technological changes and the new 'order' in the world-economy," *Review* 12:157–189.

Valenza, Robin (2009), "The Economies of Knowledge," pp. 1–36 in Robin Valenza (ed.), *Literature, Language, and the Rise of the Intellectual Disciplines in Britain, 1680–1820*. Cambridge: Cambridge University Press.

Vallas, Steven P., Daniel Lee Kleinman and Dina Biscotti (2011), "Political structures and the making of U.S. biotechnology," pp. 57–76 in Fred Block and Matthew R. Keller (eds.), *State of Innovation: The U.S. Government's Role in Technology Development*. Boulder, CO: Paradigm.

Vats, Anjali (2020), *The Color of Creatorship. Intellectual Property, Race, and the Making of Americans*. Stanford, CA: Stanford University Press.

Veblen, Thorstein (1908), "On the nature of capital: Investment, intangible assets, and the pecuniary magnate," *The Quarterly Journal of Economics* 23:104–136.

Verba, Sudney, Kay Lehman Schlozman and Henry E. Brady (1995), *Voice and Equality. Civic Voluntarism in American Politics*. Cambridge, MA: Harvard University Press.

Vercellone, Carlo (2007), "From formal subsumption to general intellect: Elements for a Marxist reading to the thesis of cognitive capitalism," *Historical Materialism* 15:13–36.

Vidich, Arthur J. and Stanford M. Lyman (1985), *American Sociology. Worldly Rejections of Religion and Their Directions*. New Haven, CT: Yale University Press.

Vogel, Ezra (1980), *Japan as Number One*. New York: Harper.

Vogel, Jacob (2004), "Von der Wissenschafts- zur Wissensgeschichte. Für eine Historisierung der, Wissensgesellschaft,'' *Geschichte und Gesellschaft* 30:639–660.

Walker, Pat (ed.) (1979), *Between Labour and Capital: The Professional-Managerial Class*. Boston, MA: South End Press.

Wang, X. (2012), "When workers do not know: The behavioral effects of minimum wage laws revisited," *Journal of Economic Psychology* 33:951−962. http://dx.doi.org/10.1016/j.joep.2012.05.004

Weber, Max (1922), *Gesammelte Aufsätze zur Wissenschaftslehre*. Tübingen: J.C.B. Mohr (Paul Siebeck).

Weber, Max ([1904] 1922), "Die 'Objektivität' sozialwissenschaftlicher und sozialpolitischer Erkenntnisse," pp. 146–214 in Max Weber (ed.), *Gesammelte Aufsätze zur Wissenschaftslehre*. Tübingen: J.C.B. Mohr (Paul Siebeck).

Weber, Max ([1919] 1948), "Science as a vocation," pp. 129–156 in Hans G. Gerth and C. Wright Mills (eds.), *From Max Weber: Essays in Sociology*. London: Routledge & Kegan Paul.

Weber, Max ([1920] 1948), "The social psychology of world religions," pp. 267–301 in Hans G. Gerth and C. Wright Mills (eds.), *From Max Weber: Essays in Sociology*. London: Routledge & Kegan Paul.

Weber, Max ([1921] 1948), "Politics as a vocation," pp. 77–128 in Hans H. Gerth and C. Wright Mills (eds.), *From Max Weber*. London: Routledge and Kegan Paul.

Weber, Max ([1922] 1948), "Science as a vocation," pp. 129–156 in Hans H. Gerth and C. Wright Mills (eds.), *From Max Weber*. London: Routledge and Kegan Paul.

Weber, Max (1948), *From Max Weber: Essays in Sociology*. London: Routledge & Kegan Paul.

Weber, Max ([1904–5] 1958), *The Protestant Ethic and the Spirit of Capitalism*. New York: Scribner's.

Weber, Max ([1922] 1964), *The Theory of Social and Economic Organization*. Edited with an Introduction by Talcott Parsons. New York: Free Press.

Weber, Max ([1922] 1968), *Economy and Society*. New York: Bedminster Press.

Weber, Max ([1922] 1976), *Wirtschaft und Gesellschaft. 5. bearbeitete Auflage*. Tübingen: J.C.B. Mohr (Paul Siebeck).

Weber, Max ([1920] 1978), *Gesammelte Aufsätze zur Religionssoziologie*. Volume 1. Tübingen: J.C.B. Mohr (Paul Siebeck).

Weber, Max ([1921] 1980), *Gesammelte politische Schriften*. Tübingen: J.C.B. Mohr (Paul Siebeck).

Weber, Max ([1922] 1989), *Science as a Vocation*. Edited by Peter Lassman and Irving Velody. London: Unwin Hyman.

Weber, Max ([1904–5] 1992), *The Protestant Ethic and the Spirit of Capitalism*. London: Routledge.

Webster, Frank (2002), "The information society revisited," pp. 22–33 in Leah A. Lievrouw and Sonia M. Livingstone (eds.), *Handbook of New Media*. London: SAGE.

Weitzman, Martin L. (2009), "On modeling and interpreting the economics of catastrophic climate change," *Review of Economics and Statistics* 91(1):1–19.

Weizsäcker, Carl C. von (1969), *Zur ökonomischen Theorie des technischen Fortschritts*. Göttingen: Vandenhoeck & Ruprecht.

Welsch, Wolfgang (1987), *Unsere Postmoderne Welt*. Weinheim: VCH Verlagsgesellschaft.

White, Stephen K. (1991), *Political Theory and Postmodernism*. Cambridge: Cambridge University Press.

Whitehead, Alfred North (1926), *Science and the Modern World*. Lowell Lectures, 1925. Cambridge: Cambridge University Press.

Whitley, Richard (1988), "The transformation of expertise by new knowledge: Contingencies and limits to skill scientification," *Social Science Information* 27:391–420.

Wiio, Osmo A. (1985), "The information society: Is it really like this?' *Intermedia* 13:12–14.

Wikström, Solveig und Richard Normann (1994), *Knowledge and Value. A New Perspective on Corporate Transformation*. London: Routledge.

Wilensky, Harold L. (1956), *Intellectuals in Labor Unions. Organizational Pressures on Professional Roles*. Glencoe, IL: Free Press.

Wilensky, Harold L. (1964), "The professionalization of everyone," *American Journal of Sociology* 70:137–158.

Wilensky, Harold L. (1971), *Organizational Intelligence. Knowledge and Policy in Government and Industry*. New York: Basic Books.

Williams, Fredrick (1984), *The New Communications*. Belmont, CA: Wadsworth.

Williams, Kate (2018), "Three strategies for attaining legitimacy in policy knowledge: Coherence in identity, process and outcome," *Public Administration* 96:53–69.

Willis, Rebecca (2020), *Too Hot to Handle. The Democratic Challenge of Climate Change*. Bristol: Bristol University Press.

Willke, Helmut (2001), "Die Krisis des Wissens," *Österreichische Zeitschrift für Soziologie* 26:3–26.

Wimmer, Michael (2003), "Ruins of Bildung in a knowledge society: Commenting on the debate about the future of Bildung," *Educational Philosophy and Theory* 35: 167–187.

Winner, Langdon (1980), "Do artefacts have politics?" *Daedalus* 109:121–133.

Winseck, Dwayne (2019), "Internet infrastructure and the persistent myth of U.S. hegemony," pp. 93–120 in Blanye Haggart et al. (Hg.), *Information, Technology and Control in a Changing World*. London: Palgrave.

Wolff, Edward N. (1991), "The distribution of household wealth: Methododological issues, time trends, and cross-sectional comparisons," pp. 92–133 in Lars Osberg (ed.), *Economic Inequality and Poverty. International Perspectives*. Armonk, NY: M.E. Sharpe.

Wolff, Edward N. and William J. Baumol (1989), "Sources of postwar growth of information activity in the United States," pp. 17–46 in Lars Osberg, Edward N. Wolff and William J. Baumol (eds.), *The Information Economy: The Implications of Unbalenced Growth*. Halifax: The Institute for Research on Public Policy.

World Bank (1991), *World Development Report 1991. The Challenge of Development.* New York: Oxford University Press.

World Bank (1992), *World Development Report 1992. Development and the Environment.* New York: Oxford University Press.

World Bank (1999), *Knowledge for Development. World Development Report.* New York: Oxford University Press.

World Bank (2009), *Annual Report.* New York: Oxford University Press.

World Intellectual Property Organization (WIPO) (2020), *World Intellectual Property Report.* Geneva: World Intellectual Property Organization.

Wright, Erik Olin (2019), *How to Be an Anticapitalist in the Twenty First Century.* London: Verso.

Wynne, Brian (1992), "Public understanding of science research: New horizons or hall of mirrors," *Public Understanding of Science* 1:37–43.

Yarney, Gavin (2021), "Rich countries should tithe their vaccines," *Nature* 590:529.

Yarrow, Daniel (2020), "Valuing knowledge: The political economy of human capital accounting," *Review of International Political Economy.* 29:227–254.

Yi, Zeng and James W. Vaupel (1989), "The impact of urbanization and delayed childbearing on population growth in China," *Population and Development Review* 15:425–445.

Young, Allyn (1929), "The sources of wealth: The necessary parts layed by land, capital and labor in the production of wealth," pp. 231–238 in *The Book of Popular Science.*

Zghal, Abdelkader (1973), "The reactivation of tradition in a post-traditional society," *Daedalus* 102:225–237.

Ziemann, Benjamin (2020), "Generationen im 20. und 21. Jahrhundert. Zur Kritik eines problembeladenen Begriffs," *Aus Politik und Zeitgeschichte* 52–53.

Ziewitz, Malte (2016), "Governing algorithms: Myth, mess, and methods," *Science, Technology, & Human Values* 41:3–16.

Zins, Chaim (2007), "Conceptual approaches for defining data, information, and knowledge," *Journal of the American Society for Information and Technology* 58:479–493.

Znaniecki, Florian (1940), *The Social Role of the Man of Knowledge.* New York: Columbia University Press.

Zuboff, Shoshana (1988), *In the Age of the Smart Machine. The Future of Work and Power.* New York: Basic Books.

Zuboff, Shoshana (2015), "Big other: Surveillance capitalism and the prospects of an information civilization," *Journal of Information Technology* 30:75–89.

Zuboff, Shoshana (2019), *The Age of Surveillance Capitalism. The Fight for a Human Future at the New Frontier of Power.* London: Profile Books.

Zuckerman, Harriet (1988), "The sociology of science," pp. 511–574 in Neil J. Smelser (ed.), *Handbook of Sociology.* Newbury Park, CA: SAGE.

zur Nedden, F. (1930), "Technischer Fortschritt und Weltwirtschaftskrise," *Die Hilfe* 36:899–903.

NAME INDEX

The names of editors of anthologies are not listed in the name index.

SUBJECT INDEX

For Product Safety Concerns and Information please contact our EU representative GPSR@taylorandfrancis.com
Taylor & Francis Verlag GmbH, Kaufingerstraße 24, 80331 München, Germany

www.ingramcontent.com/pod-product-compliance
Ingram Content Group UK Ltd.
Pitfield, Milton Keynes, MK11 3LW, UK
UKHW022347190926
475702UK00015B/2143
* 9 7 8 1 0 3 2 2 8 2 9 0 9 *